ROTHMANS RUGBY UNION YEARBOOK 1990-91

Editor: Stephen Jones
Statistician: John Griffiths

ROTHMANS

Queen Anne Press

A QUEEN ANNE PRESS BOOK

© **Rothmans Publications 1990**

First published in Great Britain in 1990 by

Queen Anne Press, a division of
Macdonald & Co (Publishers) Ltd
Orbit House
1 New Fetter Lane
London EC4 1AR

A member of Maxwell Macmillan Pergamon Publishing Corporation

Cover photographs: The International Championship 1990. *Front:* The culmination of the tournament, when Scotland beat England 13-7 at Murrayfield to take the Calcutta Cup, Triple Crown, Championship and Grand Slam. *Back:* The England v Wales match at Twickenham which England won 34-6, their biggest ever score and their highest ever winning margin in the fixture.

Photograph on page 173 by Gary Prior. All other photographs by Colin Elsey/Andrew Cowie of Colorsport.

British Library Cataloguing in Publication Data

Rothmans rugby union yearbook—1990-91
1. Rugby football—Periodicals
796.33'3'05   GV944.8

ISBN 0-356-19162-1

Photoset by Cylinder Typesetting Limited, London

Printed and bound in Great Britain by
BPCC Hazell Books
Aylesbury, Bucks, England
Member of BPCC Ltd

CONTENTS

Scotland have just beaten England for the Grand Slam, the Triple Crown, the Championship and the Calcutta Cup. It was the biggest match British rugby has ever seen and Ian McGeechan and David Sole, coach and captain, begin the celebrations.

EDITORIAL PREFACE

The major innovation this year, following the success of the Rothmans Team of the Decade last time, is that the Player of the Year feature has been expanded. Unashamedly following the tried and trusted example of *Wisden Cricketers' Almanack*, we are proud to institute the Rothmans Five Players of the Year, based on activities in the UK season.

You will find considerable improvements and refinements throughout this edition, and many sections have been expanded. The chief statistical point to note is that the reorganisation of the sections devoted to International Players has now been completed. They now all show each player's caps in chronological rather than alphabetical order for any particular year or tour. For the first time, too, an obituary section is included.

We would like to thank the four Home Unions sincerely for their permission to reproduce all their League fixtures; also the Women's Rugby Union. The major fixtures in the women's game are included for the first time in recognition of the remarkable strides they have made.

As usual, we would like to thank most warmly all our contributors and all the readers who have written in with suggestions and observations. Most of all we would like to record our appreciation of George Abbott, the schools correspondent of this Yearbook since its inception 19 years ago. George, who contributed wonderfully to the *Daily Telegraph* and to *Rugby World* for so many years, steps down after this year. His dedication and professionalism, not to mention his sympathy for the schools game, has undoubtedly played a major part in maintaining interest in the schools sector.

We would also like to thank Chris Rhys for his expert work on the tours section; and Caroline North and Ian Marshall of Queen Anne Press.

PLEASE NOTE: As usual, the statistical sections of the Yearbook go up to 30 April, 1990. Full coverage of all tours in summer 1990 appears in the next issue.

SPECTACULAR ACTION, INFINITE SADNESS

REVIEW OF THE 1989-90 SEASON
The Editor

Every shade of emotion was experienced in the 1989-90 season. It was a spectacular period for the game, especially in Britain. Granted, British teams made barely a dent in the All Blacks on their 1989 tour, but otherwise there were some remarkable incidents and occasions.

For a start the International Championship produced a true Grand Slam shoot-out when both England and Scotland went to Murrayfield with the Grand Slam, Triple Crown and Championship at stake. The match caught the imagination of the public in a wondrous fashion – tickets went for a mere £450 a pair as the day drew close. Scotland won a marvellous victory based on native wit and cunning, and the sport won converts. Scotland, led magnificently and with a fearsome aggression by David Sole, could be proud of themselves. They often struggled during the season but not in the climactic last lap. Ian McGeechan had a marvellous time of it. Along with Roger Uttley he masterminded a British Lions series victory in Australia which some people sniffed at, but which was an outstanding achievement by any yardstick. To come back from a deficit of 0-1 in a three-Test series was praiseworthy in itself. The hard-nosed approach they adopted is essential, and doubly so if the poor overall record of Lions teams is to be improved. Then, pitted against Uttley's England, McGeechan brought his Scotland into the ring in perfect condition for the Grand Slam.

England, devastated, could console themselves with the fact that on every other day bar the big one they were the outstanding team in the event and, conceivably and for a fleeting month, the best in the world. They gave two utterly unforgettable performances in thrashing France and Wales, matches in which Will Carling, their young captain, came through as a player of world class. Crowds throughout English rugby continued to increase at an astonishing rate and there was a wonderful send-off for the season when Bath, by a distance Britain's leading club side, mercilessly and spectacularly took apart the pride of Gloucester in the Pilkington Cup final. Jack Rowell, the Bath coach, chased McGeechan all the way as coach of the year.

For France and especially for Wales, there was bitter disappointment. France often seemed to be a shambles, and in defeat at the hands of Romania in Auch at the end of May, even shambles was hardly the word. Wales were whitewashed for the first time. They have been hammered by losses to rugby league and by internal bickering. The strife continued when coach John Ryan resigned after the Twickenham defeat. Only Neath, who dominated the Welsh club scene, lifted Welsh rugby out of a deep, deep rut. Their all-action style catapulted most of their team into the Welsh squad which toured Namibia. The impetus of the Welsh leagues, which finally begin in September 1990, is sorely needed and, all being well, the Welsh RU, the clubs, the players and the public will soon be scratching their heads and wondering why the devil they took so long to introduce leagues.

Ireland doubtless feel the same. They begin a league structure for 1990-91 and this, together with the arrival of Ciaran Fitzgerald as coach to replace the unsuccessful Jimmy Davidson, should give Irish rugby a new impetus, and also a togetherness. A feature of the Irish set-up of late has been an unprecedented lack of common purpose, and there are even allegations of internal bickering. It has been said so many times, but it bears repeating: European rugby desperately needs a strong, competitive, colourful Ireland. Without them it is only half a game.

England also stood out in official circles. The Rugby Football Union made headlines with their ferocious defence of amateurism. The International Rugby Board, in an agonised debate, have been attempting to tinker with, and ease, the bye-laws. The lead in this has been given by the Southern Hemisphere board members and the majority of observers, whether or not they agreed with it, felt that some changes were inevitable. Indeed, some leeway was produced by the IRB – some loss of earnings remuneration was allowed – although the implacable opposition of the RFU deferred other changes. The RFU's stand is worthy, yet they will inevitably become increasingly isolated and, beyond doubt, mis-understood as being smug and, for want of a better word, rich. That would be unfair. On the other hand, the England players aligned themselves strongly, if not quite as radically, with their Southern Hemisphere brethren. If the RFU do not take note of their own players then they are on dangerous ground.

Thankfully, the shady and disreputable efforts of South Africa to recruit scratch players for dodgy tours eased slightly. Rugby authorities in the country decided to put future tours in abeyance pending an official return. The only matter not in doubt about the whole South African question is that world rugby will be galvanised by their return – but only through the front door, not a furtive catflap entrance.

Still on the non-playing areas there was a striking effort during the season from a referee. Fred Howard of the English panel dismissed players in four major matches, three of them for use of the boot: Kevin Moseley of Wales, Alain Carminati of France and John Gadd of Gloucester. It takes courage to point the finger in these mega-games; to do so three times and unflinchingly was vastly to Mr Howard's credit. That he stood out was thoroughly disappointing, however. Simply, far too many referees have been opting out, failing to dismiss players who deserve it. Mr Howard has given them the lead, and he has been warmly supported. If every referee treats a sending-off offence as just that, we will have a massive rush of dismissals in the short term and afterwards,

7

Jeremy Guscott, whose brilliant skills illuminated the season, in action for the Lions in Australia, where his try in the second Test was a tour highlight.

as the penny drops, hardly any. On the subject of refereeing there was plea from Geoff Cooke, the England team manager. In his end-of-season report he begged, between the lines, for the top referees to take charge of the top games. As he said, rugby is now far too important to impose the principle of 'Buggin's turn' for referees. In general, the leading referees of the four Home Unions could be proud of their contribution to the game.

The global nature of the game – now, at last, benefiting from input from the IRB – continued to delight. The Soviet Union toured England, and by the end of their visit, they found confidence and played superbly against England B. Elsewhere, qualifying competitions for the 1991 World Cup took place. Massive enthusiasm characterised the competitions, and it is imperative that central IRB funding is made available next time round.

We are constantly being reminded of the team ethic in rugby and rightly so. Yet the capacity of individuals to delight is endless. So it was in the case of England captain Carling, of his breathtaking co-centre, Jeremy Guscott; of Paul Ackford and Mike Teague, so brilliant on the Lions tour. Brian Moore, the England hooker, gave the terraces someone to love. Kenny Murphy came through strongly to give Ireland, finally, a true international full-back; Sole was untouchable as Scotland's leader, especially in Europe. There were others outside the international arena whose contributions were beyond praise. Les Cusworth, Leicester's outstanding fly-half, retired at the end of the season, and a game without his quicksilver genius will be less compelling. Floyd Steadman, Saracens' inspiring captain, discarded his playing boots, too, proudly leaving his club near the top of Division 1, in some respects the performance of the decade, considering their limited resources. Simon Halliday, the iron heart of Bath's brilliant form of recent years, decided to give best to a painful ankle and only an unexpected cure will tempt him back. Richard Mogg, the Gloucester warhorse of the centre, passed 500 games but was still well up with the action in a losing cause in the Cup final. David Waters, Newport's indestructible lock, continued to dominate from his station in the middle of the line-out.

Yet the most depressing aspects of the period transcended for depth of feeling anything that failures on the sporting field could ever produce. The Romanian revolution provided the most dramatic television pictures and the most astonishing scenes of rank and file bravery. The aftermath touched rugby in a particular way. Many players, officials and media people had actually experienced life in Ceaucescu's Romania, felt the all-pervading fear and depression and poverty at first hand and marvelled at the ability of the rugby authorities and players to put on a show for visitors, even though Romanians had to report every conversation with a foreigner, and even with the Securitate following every visiting tour.

Several rugby players, including internationals Radu Durbac and Florica Murariu, were killed, Murariu in a tragic accident as he approached a roadblock manned by a nervous young soldier. Rugby responded warmly, especially in England. Several funds were set up and the money rolled in. The culmination was a magnificently supported and often brilliant match between the Four Home Unions (why on earth did officialdom refuse to label the team the British Lions, for such a worthy and even desperate cause?) and a Rest of Europe XV. Romania and also Romanian rugby benefited, and the rest of the world will revel in any resurgence in the country's game. There was a happy portent at the end of the season when Romania won a marvellous victory against France in Auch, even though political discord at home resurfaced later.

There was tragedy at home, too. John Kendall Carpenter, the former England international and president of the RFU in season 1980-81, died suddenly at his home. He had been closely involved with the development of the World Cup as chairman of the organising committee. Raphael Tsagane, the promising Wasps wing, was tragically killed in a car crash which injured three other Wasps players during a short tour in the North of England. To their massive credit, Wasps grieved then dragged themselves back on to the field and won the Courage League Division 1 title two weeks later, dedicating the trophy to their late colleague. Bath's wonderful Cup final victory was a perfect climax to a season of pyrotechnics.

ROTHMANS FIVE PLAYERS OF THE YEAR

We are proud to announce, for the first time, the Rothmans Five Players of the Year, based unashamedly on the famous Wisden Five Cricketers of the Year. The annual selection, made by the *Rothmans Rugby Union Yearbook's* team of contributors, will be based on the previous season in Europe, in the case of this edition season 1989-90, and will include players on all incoming tours during the period. No player can be named more than once. The number of caps given is correct up to 30 April 1990.

PATRICE LAGISQUET

French back play lapsed into mediocrity during the 1989-90 European season, the frequent changes of style and personnel mitigating against traditional brilliance. Yet Patrice Lagisquet was a jewel.

Lagisquet, who has recorded 10.6 in the 100 metres, was always a deadly danger on the left wing and scored two tries of particular significance. The first came when France trailed 9-13 to Australia in the second Test in Lille. They had already lost the first Test in Strasbourg and Jacques Fouroux's experimental team was struggling.

Then, a rare drive by the French back set up, for once, a quick ball. The ball was whipped out to Lagisquet, yet Australia had cover defence in depth. Lagisquet took off. He cut superbly inside Martin and Junee, swerved back to the outside at top pace to outflank Campese, and scored. France were in the lead and they went on to save the series.

The other try killed off Wales in Cardiff at the start of the Championship, and again came when cover defence appeared strong. By a surging change of pace, Lagisquet left Robert Jones and Thorburn for dead. That inspirational try finished the Welsh challenge and, like the vintage score in Lille, bore the hallmark of a gifted, blistering, attacking runner.

Patrice Lagisquet *Born Arcachon, 4 September, 1962; wing; plays for Bayonne; 39 caps for France since first cap against Australia in 1983.*

WILL CARLING

There was a body of opinion prior to the 1990 international season that Will Carling still had to prove himself as an international centre. Carling himself admitted as much, even though he was just beginning his second season as England's captain.

Those doubts were buried in a most conclusive manner. Carling bestrode the international season. He came through as conceivably the leading threequarter in world rugby.

He had a talent to suit every occasion, every match. In tandem with

Patrice Lagisquet   *Steve McDowell*

Will Carling

Jeremy Guscott, he applied the *coup de grâce* to Ireland at Twickenham with some excellent running, even with a classic outside break; he beat Serge Blanco at the end of a brilliant England performance against France in Paris with a check and swerve which left Blanco rooted and almost incredulous as Carling ran on to score.

Carling also had more than a streak of competitiveness, even ruthlessness – his power on the burst and in the tackle visibly upset most of the midfield combinations ranged against him. Even in a losing cause in the Grand Slam match at Murrayfield, Carling had an outstanding game. He also coped well with life as captain, even though his troops were generally of greater seniority and experience. He looked all over a worthy England captain for the World Cup; simply, he made the doubters look foolish.

William David Charles Carling *Born Bradford-on-Avon, Wiltshire, 12 December, 1965; centre; plays for Harlequins; 17 caps for England since first cap against France in 1988.*

STEVE McDOWELL

For many years the athleticism of the All Black forwards has been one of the staples of their success. The fitness and the skills of the New Zealanders are the model for fitness and conditioning regimes in the other countries.

Steve McDowell, New Zealand's loose-head prop, illustrated perfectly during the tour of Ireland and Wales in 1989 that, far from being overhauled, the All Blacks are still racing clean away. McDowell was the tour's most striking figure. Some of his talents, notably his footballing ability, bore comparison with that of a threequarter. The sight of McDowell driving on, ball in hand, deftly catching and passing, was a feature of so many matches on the tour, Tests included. By the end, McDowell was a virtuoso.

There was no loss of effect in the other departments of front row play. The first-string New Zealand front row of Richard Loe, Sean Fitzpatrick and McDowell was the core of the side, the engine powering the trademark rolling mauls. Nor did they budge an inch in the scrums.

And McDowell's ability to add pace to his power, to see his role of a tight forward as merely the prelude to ranging round the field, made him a blueprint for every front row player in the game.

Steven Clark McDowell *Born Rotorua, 27 August, 1961; prop; plays for Bay of Plenty; 24 caps for New Zealand since first cap against Argentina in 1985.*

DAVID SOLE

No one typified the fierce and selfless commitment which brought Scotland their Grand Slam more than David Sole, the captain. Sole cut

David Sole

Paul Ackford

13

an astonishing figure in the Grand Slam match itself. He played with a staggering intensity, he was the very heart of the win, the rock on which England foundered. His familiar white headband bobbed all over the field in the loose and he became only the third Scot ever to lead his country to the Grand Slam.

Sole was an implacable figure throughout the season. In the summer of 1989, he was indestructible on the British Lions loose head in the Test series in Australia. He led the Barbarians in their attempt to unseat the All Blacks at Twickenham; he kept Scotland on course even when their early season form looked doubtful, notably against Ireland in Dublin when their performance gave no hint of what was to come.

It is hard to believe that when he came into the Scottish team in 1986, people doubted if he had the build or the intensity for international rugby – he is small by modern front row standards. England might have concluded, as Sole threw their challenge back in their faces, that it has hardly held him back.

David Michael Barclay Sole *Born Aylesbury, 8 May, 1962; plays for Edinburgh Academicals; prop; 25 caps for Scotland since first cap against France in 1986.*

PAUL ACKFORD

The story of how Paul Ackford took a decade to become an overnight success has been retold frequently in the last two seasons, a period in which Ackford has enjoyed a blazing Indian summer in his career. He played for England B in 1979, but it was only in 1988 that he won his first cap, when the knowledge that he had not done himself justice stirred him mightily.

In Australia with the 1989 Lions, Ackford was still in his first international season, yet he was a key figure. He was a productive source of possession at the front of the line-out, and at the kick-off and drop-out he was seen by the Australian pack as one of the hardest, harshest Lions of all.

He carried on this late and spectacular progress in season 1989-90. Memorably, he brought off an astonishing tackle on Sella, the French centre, when he appeared near the wing during the British Isles match against France in Paris, an event widely replayed on television. He was at the heart of England's challenge during the Championship programme, still almost unerring at the front of the line-out and a massive force in the loose in tandem with his partner, Wade Dooley. Certainly, his form during the last two years would make a case for his selection in any World XV of the era.

Paul John Ackford *Born Hanover, West Germany, 26 February, 1958; lock; plays for Harlequins; 11 caps for England since first cap against Australia in 1988.*

THE REINS OF OPPORTUNITY

With his outstanding technical and physical attributes, Rory Underwood always promised to become England's most successful wing and try-scorer. *Mick Cleary* of the *Observer* **describes his steady advance into the record books after fighting his way out of a mid-career dip.**

The wing has a dream and a nightmare. The dream is of glory – the match-winning try in the corner; hurtling at full stretch, arms extended, body exposed, through the air for the line. The nightmare is of pain and failure. The slightest contact and the wind goes screeching out of the lungs. One nudge and it's over the touch-line to lie, dream shattered, amid the advertising hoardings. When the dream comes off, it is one of the most thrilling sights in rugby and also one of the bravest. That the most spectacular and accomplished movement in the game – a ball zipped along the threequarter line for the fleet-footed wing to set off on his dramatic dash to the corner – should be rewarded with a conversion from the most difficult position is one of the scoring anomalies of the sport. It is the moment the crowd yearns for, the moment that crystallises all the power, beauty and courage that rugby has to offer. One man offers it more regularly than most: Rory Underwood.

Last season he grabbed the reins of opportunity and galloped into history. The first citadel to be rocked was Dan Lambert's 1907 record of five tries in a match. Underwood equalled that one with graceful ease against Fiji in November. The next historical bastion did not get off so lightly. Cyril Lowe's aggregate record of 18 tries for England had stood for 67 years. For a few agonising moments of the England game against Ireland it looked as if it might survive one match longer. Then, five minutes before the end, the ball found its way to Underwood. There was only a half-chance, but no matter, the race was on. The Irish cover swarmed across the field as Underwood blazed onwards. Ten yards from the line, as the defence closed in, Underwood seemed destined to end up in the lower tier of the West Stand. Then he took off: Keith Crossan and Brendan Mullin lunged at him, but too late. Underwood was in at the corner; try number 19 was on the scoreboard and Underwood was in the record books.

That try, like the three that were to follow against France and Wales, was a cameo of self-assurance. Underwood carried conviction in every stride, menace in every thrust for the line. 'Un puncheur', the legendary French centre Jo Maso calls him. 'From the moment he gets the ball, he has only one idea in his head', says Maso, 'and that is to score.'

Yet how different it once was. Underwood, now aged 27, won his first 23 caps for England in solitary confinement, imprisoned within a side that stuttered through each international season. From his cocoon on the wing, Underwood managed only four tries. England whimpered through several years of massive under-achievement while Underwood watched from the wings. 'I was just turning out for England in those days', he recalls. 'It sounds terrible, but although I was very proud to play for England, I just didn't have a massive amount of enthusiasm about the whole set-up. I just drifted along with things and I think it showed in my play. I lacked real drive and purpose.'

Times have changed; England have changed and Underwood has changed. By the time he won his 37th cap in the game against Wales, so breaking David Duckham's record for an English threequarter, he was a player of immense potency and assertiveness. A distant glimpse of the line was all it took for the Underwood muscles to twitch expectantly and for the crowds to strain eagerly forward. Even his defence, which was vulnerable to a hanging kick or to wild passing under pressure, had improved. It was only as recently as 1989 that Underwood sat inconsolable in an England dressing-room after being involved in a gargantuan foul-up which led to Wales's only try and victory at Cardiff Arms Park. (He still can't bring himself to watch the video of that match.) Yet his scything try-saving tackle on Crossan was one of the best tackles of this most recent Championship season.

Underwood has always had ability and physical prowess. Tom McNab, fitness adviser to the England squad and former AAA coach, says of him: 'He has the finest natural physique I've ever come across', and those that McNab has come across include decathlon double

Rory Underwood bears down on the try-line yet again during his brilliant performance against the touring Fijians at Twickenham. Underwood scored five times.

Olympic gold medallist Daley Thompson. McNab reckons that Underwood, given the right conditioning, could dent the Thompson ego in one or two events. Underwood, though, was not born with the Thompson ego, that bloated sense of self-supremacy which is the spur to every great champion. (Some, of course, manage to leave the ego where it belongs – on the track. Others don't.) Not that Underwood has emerged from the shadows of mediocrity by some miracle implant of egomania: he is as modest and self-effacing as he ever was. What he has learned is to react more positively to others around him, to get himself into the game even though the game may be cussedly refusing to come to him and to assess and evaluate his own performances more critically.

The change really came with the arrival of Geoff Cooke and a new England set-up. Underwood responded to the more streamlined, intensive structure. The first warning was posted in 1988 when England thrashed the living daylights out of Ireland. They went into that match, the last of the Five Nations season, without a try to their name. By the end of it they had six, more than they had achieved in four previous Championships. Underwood scored two and his personal roll was on. 'That was the first sign of things to come', says Underwood. 'Gradually we began to play with more confidence and more conviction. There was also far more continuity in selection. Luckily, that continuity included me. I don't train any differently to the way I did: I don't spend hours practising the dive for the corner, but I do approach games, training and international get-togethers in a much more positive frame of mind. If the side plays well – and England, despite the loss to Scotland, are playing well – then the winger tends to play well.'

He has every intention of continuing his shredding of the record books. Not that the books rest well-thumbed on his bedside table: 'Records have never been a motivation', he says. 'Of course I was delighted to break Cyril Lowe's record, but I'm only prospering from the work of others. I thought about a personal milestone only once last season, after the Welsh match, when I scored for the third game running. Perhaps I might get one in every Five Nations match, I thought. We all know what happened next: Scotland, no Grand Slam, no try.'

Underwood is down-to-earth about his achievements. The only time he has his head in the clouds is at work, where he flies Canberras on radar-jamming missions from RAF Wyton in Cambridgeshire. His fascination for flying stemmed from his trips to the family home in Malaysia during holidays from Barnard Castle School in Yorkshire, where he was a contemporary of Rob Andrew. He returned home with tales of ding-dong battles on the rugby fields of Yorkshire, of spectacular surges to the goal-line. His brother, Tony, five years his junior, must have been listening, for within a few years he had embarked on that same glorious route to goal. Tony is now on the verge of full international honours. Of such stuff are Underwood dreams made.

FARR-JONES: A RESERVE MAKES GOOD

Nick Farr-Jones is one of rugby's statesmen – studious and spiky, richly talented and an outstanding captain. *Greg Campbell* **of** *The Australian* **discusses the career of a school reserve who grew to become one of the most influential figures in the world of rugby.**

It seems inconceivable nowadays that Nick Farr-Jones was unable to win selection in his Newington College first XV. Ten years on, Farr-Jones has become Australia's most-capped scrum-half, outdistancing the legendary Ken Catchpole and overtaking the immaculate John Hipwell. And, in the space of three years, Farr-Jones is set to overhaul his first Wallaby captain, Andrew Slack, by leading Australia in most Tests as captain. Considering these feats, and the fact that he is internationally regarded as arguably the world's finest scrum-half, it would be fair to say that Farr-Jones was a late rugby bloomer. But no one could dispute that his entries in the record books are deserved. Just ask long-standing fly-half Michael Lynagh of Farr-Jones' ability as a scrum-half and seek Bob Dwyer's opinion of him as a leader of men, both on and off the field. Both respond most favourably.

Since he was plucked out of Sydney's second division competition – when his club, Sydney University, were fighting to win promotion to the first division – to tour the United Kingdom and Ireland with the Sydney representative team at the end of the 1983 season, Farr-Jones has progressed to experience the heady 1984 Wallaby Grand Slam success and 1986 Bledisloe Cup triumph in New Zealand. There have been the career low points, too, including Australia's 1987 World Cup failure, the series loss to the British Lions in 1989 and the broken jaw suffered when Sydney played the touring Soviet Union in 1990. As a player Farr-Jones delivers a crisp, accurate pass; his ability to expose the short side is well-known; he is a punishing defender and his enthusiasm knows no boundaries. Off the field he is extremely popular, a more than handy golfer and a successful card player. In business, he is a solicitor in Sydney and his all-round intelligence and polite public image see him often in demand for speeches and promotions, for which he gladly offers his services in the true amateur spirit.

During his three years at the helm of the Wallabies, Australia has experienced mixed fortunes. There were record-breaking wins in 1989 over the Lions and France and the David Campese-inspired 1988 tour successes against Scotland at Murrayfield and the Barbarians at Cardiff. Throughout this period, the rugby league vultures have eaten away at the team's prized stock, leaving the national selectors the annual problem of discovering new talents, and asking Dwyer to mould them into top level international players overnight. But now the groundwork seems to have been firmly laid and the results should follow.

Testimony to Australia's ever-changing team is that prop Mark

Hartill was the sole remaining forward from the second and third Tests against the Lions to play in the Tests in France. In addition to these changes, Australia has introduced a more iron-fisted approach to its forwards. 'It was a sign of our immaturity and lack of toughness that we succumbed to some of the tactics the Lions used on us. Had we been experienced we wouldn't have, and we only have ourselves to blame. We let ourselves be flustered', says Farr-Jones. The Lions series, particularly the second Test at Ballymore, still leaves a sour taste in Farr-Jones' mouth. Although he has been the unfortunate victim of some violent rugby, Farr-Jones doesn't believe violence is on the increase at Test match level. 'At Ballymore it was bad – I got whacked. I've forgotten about my broken jaw, and I would have been more upset had I missed some Tests', he explains.

Captaincy is especially dear to Farr-Jones. He never expected to be handed the responsibility but now he relishes the honour. Simon Poidevin, who led the Wallabies in Argentina in 1987, was expected to be reappointed in 1988, but Farr-Jones was nominated when Dwyer succeeded Alan Jones. 'People said in 1985-86 that I'd make a good captain but I never dreamed I'd be appointed. When I was made New South Wales captain in 1987, Jones was up in arms and said that I'd be number 13 on his list. Had his tenure been longer, I would never have got the job', he remarks. In many ways captaincy is natural for Farr-Jones. As a scrum-half, he must be a talker on the field, and as a senior player, he shoulders increased responsibility. 'You have to set an example in every area. You must make sure you don't step out of line, even in little things like dress, the way you conduct yourself and politeness on the field', Farr-Jones says.

Despite the high regard in which he is held both in Australia and abroad, Farr-Jones was criticised by an unnamed Wallaby team-mate in a newspaper article at the beginning of the year. The player shocked all, including fellow players, when he was quoted as saying that Farr-Jones set a bad example on and off the field and was too informal at functions. The comments greatly upset Farr-Jones.

There are some commentators who believe the captaincy has affected his form in recent years. Farr-Jones discounts this: 'A lot of people say my game has changed. If it has, it is because I'm being marked a lot. I still do the things which were so instinctive in 1984-85-86, but I'm being watched much more. When you're a new boy no one is worried about you. They were more worried about the Ellas and Campese'.

Now 28, and having completed his seventh year of international rugby, Farr-Jones has no definite plans for his playing future. He is even unsure about the 1991 World Cup, but there appears little doubt that the Test fires are still burning. 'I won't play the game if I'm not enjoying it. If I wake up one morning and I feel I've had enough and that I would rather be doing something else instead, then I'll pull up stumps', he admits. But there is no doubt that the World Cup is still in

Nick Farr-Jones shows the scars of battle as he whips the ball away to Greg Martin, the full-back, during Australia's defeat at the hands of the British Lions in a stormy second Test in Brisbane.

his sights, particularly after Australia's disappointments in 1987. The next World Cup will, for Farr-Jones, be his first *real* World Cup – last time the Australian squad was based in Sydney and missed the hype and spirit which existed in New Zealand. 'We didn't have any identity like you have when you're on tour. It was as though our normal lives were going on. We missed so many of the World Cup joys', he explains.

In the lead-up to the World Cup, Farr-Jones is adamant the International Rugby Football Board must alter and update the laws of amateurism. After the IRFB rejected the proposed changes in 1990, Farr-Jones was one of many Southern Hemisphere voices who urged individual board member countries to withdraw from the world controlling body. 'Players should be able to receive remuneration for writing books and being involved in promotions. No one gives up their valued time without remuneration. It's going on behind their backs anyway, so why not bring it out into the open? But if there is no progress, the players will contemplate doing their own thing. A rugby circus is not out of the question if it gets the backing', he warns.

In the meantime, Farr-Jones and former Wallaby lock Steve Cutler have co-written a book entitled *Nick and Cuts*, which is mostly a collection of humorous stories gathered during their careers. It is a book that, ten years ago, when he was playing the second fiddle half-back role at school, he would never have envisaged.

TOURS 1989-90
NEW ZEALAND TO CANADA, IRELAND AND WALES

The omens for this tour from the New Zealand angle were excellent. Ireland and Wales were the weakest of the four Home Unions and even the Welsh clubs, who have caused New Zealand teams endless problems in the past, were in a trough. Even before the tour began it was difficult to envisage any of the home teams defeating the tourists and so it turned out. Most of the teams New Zealand met played with great courage – a few, notably Cardiff, Swansea, Neath and Ireland in the Test, managed to stay with the All Blacks for long periods of the match. Yet only in the ferocious encounter with Neath was the final result in any real doubt, and even then the New Zealanders won deservedly.

There was good news all over the park for New Zealand rugby. They founded their effort on an outstanding front row, conceivably the best to tour here. Loe, Fitzpatrick and McDowell had real rugby talents quite apart from their scrummaging power, and McDowell especially had a wonderful tour. Fox, at fly-half, kicked with mechanical accuracy and Gallagher, the full-back later to defect to rugby league, was the real cutting edge in attack, expertly set up by Schuster and Stanley in the midfield. Perhaps the most awesome aspect of the tour was that the visitors could shrug off the loss of injured players.

There was a suspicion throughout that the Kiwis were not over-burdened with depth in the front five and at scrum-half, but their wonderful fitness and endurance and their implacable pride saw them through as one of the most effective teams ever to tour.

THE TOURING PARTY

Captain W T Shelford   **Manager** J A Sturgeon   **Coach** A J Wyllie
Doctor R J Mayhew   **Physiotherapist** D I Abercrombie

FULL-BACKS

J A Gallagher (Wellington)
M J Ridge (Auckland)

THREEQUARTERS

J J Kirwan (Auckland)
V I Tuigamala (Auckland)
T J Wright (Auckland)
C R Innes (Auckland)
B J McCahill (Auckland)
J T Stanley (Auckland)
W K Little (North Harbour)
W J Schuster (Wellington)

HALF-BACKS

G J Fox (Auckland)
F M Botica (North Harbour)
G T M Bachop (Canterbury)
I B Deans (Canterbury)
*J K R Timu (Otago)

FORWARDS

S C McDowell (Bay of Plenty)
G H Purvis (Auckland)
R O Williams (North Harbour)
R W Loe (Waikato)
S B T Fitzpatrick (Auckland)
W D Gatland (Waikato)
G W Whetton (Auckland)
M J Pierce (Wellington)
S R Gordon (Waikato)
I D Jones (North Auckland)
W T Shelford (North Harbour)
M R Brewer (Otago)
A T Earl (Canterbury)
P W Henderson (Otago)
A J Whetton (Auckland)
Z V Brooke (Auckland)
*K J Schuler (Manawatu)

replacement during tour

21

TOUR RECORD

All matches   Played 14   Won 14   Points for 454   Against 122
International matches   Played 2   Won 2   Points for 57   Against 15

SCORING DETAILS

All matches

For: 71T 43C 28PG   454 Pts
Against: 8T   6C 25PG 1DG 122 Pts

International matches

For: 7T   4C   7PG   57 Pts
Against: 5PG   15 Pts

MATCH DETAILS

1989	OPPONENTS	VENUE	RESULT
8 Oct	British Columbia	Vancouver	W 48- 3
14 Oct	Cardiff	Cardiff Arms Park	W 25-15
18 Oct	Pontypool	Pontypool	W 47- 6
21 Oct	Swansea	Swansea	W 37-22
25 Oct	Neath	Neath	W 26-15
28 Oct	Llanelli	Llanelli	W 11- 0
31 Oct	Newport	Newport	W 54- 9
4 Nov	WALES	Cardiff Arms Park	W 34- 9
8 Nov	Leinster	Dublin	W 36- 9
11 Nov	Munster	Cork	W 31- 9
14 Nov	Connacht	Galway	W 40- 6
18 Nov	IRELAND	Lansdowne Road, Dublin	W 23- 6
21 Nov	Ulster	Belfast	W 21– 3
25 Nov	Barbarians	Twickenham	W 21-10

Scorers: 83 – Fox (15PG 19C); 68 – Botica (4T 8PG 14C); 59 – Gallagher (6T 5PG 10C); 32 – Innes (8T); 28 – Brooke (7T); 20 – Wright (5T), Deans (5T); 16 – Bachop (4T), Tuigamala (4T); 12 – Earl, Brewer, Timu (3T each); 8 – McCahill, Loe, Little, Jones (2T each); 4 – Ridge, Kirwan, Schuster, Fitzpatrick, Gatland, G W Whetton, A J Whetton, Pierce, Shelford, Schuler, Stanley (1T each)

Appearances: 10 – McDowell, Earl (inc 2 as replacement), G W Whetton; 9 – Innes (inc 2 as replacement), Wright, Fitzpatrick, Shelford, Little (inc 1 as replacement); 9 – Bachop, Pierce, Gallagher, McCahill (inc 2 as replacement); Brewer (inc 1 as replacement), Brooke (inc 1 as replacement); 7 – Schuster, Fox, Loe, Stanley, Purvis; 6 – Ridge, Botica, Tuigamala, Deans; 5 – Jones, Schuler (inc 1 as replacement), Gatland, Gordon; 4 – Timu, Williams, A J Whetton; 3 – Henderson, Kirwan

MATCH 1   8 October, Vancouver

British Columbia 3 (1PG)   **New Zealand XV 48** (7G 2PG)
British Columbia: S Stewart; T Woods, S Brown, I Stuart, M Wyatt; G Rees (*capt*), C Tynan; E Evans, D Spiers, F Szabo, G Knauer, R van den Brink, R Radu, G Ennis, G McKinnon
Scorer *Penalty Goal:* Wyatt
New Zealand XV: Gallagher; Kirwan, Stanley, McCahill, Tuigamala; Little, Deans; McDowell, Gatland, Purvis, Gordon, G W Whetton (*capt*), Henderson, Earl, Brooke
Scorers *Tries:* Brooke (2), Deans (2), Stanley, Tuigamala, Little
Conversions: Gallagher (7)   *Penalty Goals:* Gallagher (2)
Referee K Morrison (Vancouver Island)

MATCH 2   14 October, Cardiff Arms Park

Cardiff 15 (1G 3PG)   **New Zealand XV 25** (2G 3PG 1T)
Cardiff: M Rayer; C Thomas, M G Ring, G John, S P Ford; D W Evans, A Booth; J Whitefoot, I Watkins, D Young, M Rowley, H Stone, T Crothers (*capt*), M Edwards, R G Collins
Scorers *Try:* Edwards   *Conversion:* Rayer   *Penalty Goals:* Evans (2), Rayer
New Zealand XV: Ridge; Kirwan, Innes, Schuster, Wright; Fox, Bachop; Williams, Fitzpatrick, Loe, Pierce, Jones, A J Whetton, Shelford (*capt*), Brewer
Scorers *Tries:* Loe, A J Whetton, Brewer   *Conversions:* Fox (2)   *Penalty Goals:* Fox (3)
Referee R J Megson (Scotland)

MATCH 3   18 October, Pontypool Park, Pontypool

Pontypool 6 (2PG)   **New Zealand XV 47** (3G 3PG 5T)
Pontypool: G Davies; M Egan, R Bidgood, K Orrell, S White; M Silva,
D Wright; S T Jones, G Jenkins, G Price, D Churchill, K Moseley (*capt*), C Huish,
R Goodey, D Oswald *Replacement* A Carter for Oswald
Scorer *Penalty Goals:* Silva (2)
New Zealand XV: Gallagher; Kirwan, Stanley, Little, Tuigamala; Botica, Bachop;
McDowell, Fitzpatrick, Purvis, Jones, G W Whetton (*capt*), Earl, Brooke, Henderson
Replacement McCahill for Kirwan
Scorers *Tries:* Little, Gallagher, Kirwan, Fitzpatrick, Tuigamala, Bachop, Botica, Jones
Conversions: Gallagher (3) *Penalty Goals:* Gallagher (3)
Referee B Stirling (Ireland)

MATCH 4   21 October, St Helens, Swansea

Swansea 22 (2G 2PG 1T)   **New Zealand XV 37** (5G 1PG 1T)
Swansea: M A Wyatt; M H Titley, K Hopkins, S Parfitt, A Emyr; A Clement,
R N Jones (*capt*); I Buckett, W James, M Morgan, S Williams, P Arnold, I Davies,
S Davies, A Reynolds *Replacement* L Rutherford for Reynolds
Scorers *Tries:* I Davies, Arnold, Hopkins *Conversions:* Wyatt (2) *Penalty Goals:* Wyatt (2)
New Zealand XV: Ridge; Innes, McCahill, Schuster, Wright; Botica, Deans; Williams,
Gatland, Loe, Pierce, Gordon, A J Whetton, Shelford (*capt*), Brewer *Replacements* Little
for Schuster; Earl for Whetton
Scorers *Tries:* Innes (2), Gatland, Brewer (2), Deans *Conversions:* Botica (5)
Penalty Goal: Botica
Referee R Hourquet (France)

MATCH 5   25 October, The Gnoll, Neath

Neath 15 (1G 3PG)   **New Zealand XV 26** (2G 2PG 2T)
Neath: P H Thorburn; C Higgs, C Laity, A G Bateman, A Edmunds; P Williams,
C Bridges (*capt*); B R Williams, K H Phillips (*capt*), J D Pugh, Gareth Llewellyn,
M Whitson, P Pugh, M A Jones, M S Morris
Scorers *Try:* Edmunds *Conversion:* Thorburn *Penalty Goals:* Thorburn (3)
New Zealand XV: Gallagher; Tuigamala, Stanley, Little, Wright; Botica, Bachop;
McDowell, Fitzpatrick, Purvis, Jones, G W Whetton (*capt*), Earl, Brooke, Henderson
Replacements Innes for Tuigamala; Brewer for Henderson
Scorers *Tries:* Gallagher (2), Innes, Brooke *Conversions:* Botica (2)
Penalty Goals: Botica (2)
Referee F A Howard (Lancashire)

MATCH 6   28 October, Stradey Park, Llanelli

Llanelli 0   **New Zealand XV 11** (1PG 2T)
Llanelli: J Bird; S Bowling, N G Davies; S Davies, C Davies, C Stephens, M Griffiths;
A Buchanan, A Lamerton, L Delaney, P S May, P T Davies (*capt*), I Jones, J Williams,
G Jones
New Zealand XV: Ridge; Innes, Stanley, Little, Wright; Fox, Deans; McDowell,
Fitzpatrick, Loe, Pierce, G W Whetton, Earl, Shelford (*capt*), Brewer
Scorers *Tries:* Deans, Earl *Penalty Goal:* Fox
Referee K McCartney (Hawick)

MATCH 7   31 October, Rodney Parade, Newport

Newport 9 (1G 1DG)   **New Zealand XV 54** (7G 3T)
Newport: G Hardacre; D Griffiths, A Evans, L Jones, J Thomas; G Abraham,
N Callard; F Hillman, K Gregory, A Williams, A Perry, D R Waters, G George (*capt*),
I McKim, A Pocock *Replacements* C Scott for Pocock; G Stockwell for Gregory; M Davies
for Hillman

Scorers *Try:* Gregory *Conversion:* Abraham *Dropped Goal:* Abraham
New Zealand XV: Gallagher; Timu, McCahill, Schuster, Wright; Fox, Bachop;
Williams, Gatland, Purvis, Pierce, Gordon, Schuler, Shelford (*capt*), Brooke
Scorers *Tries:* Wright (3), Gallagher (2), Bachop, Timu, Brooke, Schuler, McCahill
Conversions: Fox (7)
Referee O E Doyle (Ireland)

MATCH 8   4 November, Cardiff Arms Park   1st Test

WALES 9 (3PG)   NEW ZEALAND 34 (3G 4PG 1T)

There was never any prospect of a serious challenge by Wales since
their team was still in the throes of rebuilding and the psychological
superiority of the New Zealanders was worth 20 points by itself. There
was even relief in some quarters that this defeat was not still more
embarrassing. Wales certainly put up stiffer resistance than they did on
their ill-starred tour to New Zealand in 1988, and it was a triumph of
sorts that they conceded only four tries.

New Zealand were unstoppable. Their tight forwards kept up a
relentless pressure and they hardly missed Alan Whetton and Michael
Jones, their injured flankers, so well did Earl and Brewer play in their
places. Fox at fly-half led the Welsh defence around by the nose with
inch-perfect kicking and the link between Fox and Bachop, his new
partner, worked splendidly. Wales were desperate for a good start to
bolster morale, but in the first serious New Zealand attack Innes was
driven over by his forwards for a try on his international debut.
Thorburn kicked Wales level with two penalties only for Fox to restore
New Zealand's six-point advantage with two penalties by half-time.

Wales were never again in the contest. Fox added another penalty in
the second half and a beautiful pass by Stanley sent Gallagher away to
make a try for Bachop. Gallagher himself carved out the space for Innes
to score his second try, and a long pass by Stanley made a try for Wright
on the opposite wing.

WALES: P H Thorburn (Neath); M R Hall (Bridgend), D W Evans (Cardiff), M G Ring
(Cardiff), A Emyr (Swansea); A Clement (Swansea), R N Jones (Swansea) (*capt*);
M Griffiths (Bridgend), K H Phillips (Neath), D Young (Cardiff), P T Davies (Llanelli),
G O Llewellyn (Neath), P Pugh (Neath), M A Jones (Neath), G Jones (Llanelli)
Scorer *Penalty Goals:* Thorburn (3)
NEW ZEALAND: Gallagher; Innes, Stanley, Schuster, Wright; Fox, Bachop;
McDowell, Fitzpatrick, Loe, G W Whetton, Pierce, Earl, Shelford (*capt*), Brewer
Scorers *Tries:* Innes (2), Wright, Bachop *Conversions:* Fox (3)
Penalty Goals: Fox (4)
Referee A R MacNeill (Australia)

MATCH 9   8 November, Lansdowne Road, Dublin

Leinster 9 (1G 1PG)   New Zealand XV 36 (4G 3T)

Leinster: F J Dunlea (Lansdowne); J F Sexton (Lansdowne), B J Mullin (London Irish),
P Clinch (Lansdowne) (*capt*), P Purcell (Lansdowne); B A Smith (Oxford U),
L F P Aherne (Lansdowne); N J Popplewell (Greystones), M Kearney (Old Wesley),
D C Fitzgerald (Lansdowne), B Rigney (Greystones), N P T Francis (Blackrock Coll),

P Kenny (Wanderers), K Leahy (Wanderers), A Blair (Old Wesley) *Replacements*
N Farren (Old Wesley) for Dunlea; V J G Cunningham (St Mary's Coll) for Sexton;
C Pim (Old Wesley) for Kenny
Scorers *Try:* Sexton   *Conversion:* Smith   *Penalty Goal:* Smith
New Zealand XV: Ridge; Tuigamala, McCahill, Little, Timu; Botica, Deans;
McDowell, Gatland, Purvis, G W Whetton (*capt*), Jones, Schuler, Brooke, A J Whetton
Replacements Earl for A J Whetton; Innes for Tuigamala
Scorers *Tries:* Timu (2), Brooke, McCahill, G W Whetton, Jones, Innes
Conversions: Botica (4)
Referee G Maurette (France)

MATCH 10   11 November, Musgrave Park, Cork

Munster 9 (3PG)   **New Zealand XV 31** (3G 3PG 1T)
Munster: K Murphy (Cork Const); J Galvin (Old Crescent), M J Kiernan (Dolphin),
C Murphy (Cork Const), P Murray (Shannon); R P Keyes (Cork Const), M T Bradley
(Cork Const); J J Fitzgerald (Young Munster), T J Kingston (Dolphin), T Clohessy
(Young Munster), D G Lenihan (Cork Const), M Galwey (Shannon), P T O'Hara
(Sunday's Well, P C Collins (London Irish) (*capt*), K O'Connell *Replacements* D Larkin
(Garryowen) for Kiernan; P Hogan (Garryowen) for O'Connell
Scorer *Penalty Goals:* Keyes (3)
New Zealand XV: Gallagher; Innes, Stanley, Schuster, Wright; Fox, Bachop; Williams,
Fitzpatrick, Loe, Gordon, Pierce, Brewer, Shelford (*capt*), Brooke *Replacements* Schuler
for Brooke; McCahill for Stanley
Scorers *Tries:* Schuster, Pierce, Innes, Bachop   *Conversions:* Fox (3)
Penalty Goals: Fox (3)
Referee D Leslie (Scotland)

MATCH 11   14 November, Showgrounds, Galway

Connacht 6 (2PG)   **New Zealand XV 40** (1G 2PG 7T)
Connacht: J Staples (London Irish); D Holland (Corinthians), M Feely (Old Belvedere),
M Cosgrave (Wanderers), E Guerin (Galwegians); E Elwood (Galwegians), S O'Beirne
(St Mary's Coll); T P J Clancy (Lansdowne), J O'Riordan (Cork Const), D Henshaw
(Athlone), A Higgins (London Irish), M M F Moylett (Shannon), N McCarthy
(St Mary's Coll) (*capt*), N P Mannion (Corinthians), M Fitzgibbon (Shannon)
Scorer *Penalty Goals:* O'Beirne (2)
New Zealand XV: Ridge; Tuigamala, McCahill, Little, Timu; Botica, Deans;
McDowell, Gatland, Purvis, Jones, G W Whetton, Earl, Shelford (*capt*), Schuler
Scorers *Tries:* Earl (2), Tuigamala, Ridge, Deans, Botica (3)   *Penalty Goals:* Botica (2)
Conversion: Botica
Referee L Peard (Wales)

MATCH 12   18 November, Lansdowne Road, Dublin   2nd Test

IRELAND 6 (2PG)   NEW ZEALAND 23 (1G 3PG 2T)

This was a match played in an atmosphere of some bitterness and the
ill-feeling began even before the whistle. As the All Blacks lined up for
their *haka* the Irish team lined up opposite them and advanced step by
step on the All Blacks as the *haka* progressed. As it ended, the players
were eyeball to eyeball. Some people felt this was a gesture of defiance
by the Irish, others felt that it was a needlessly inflammatory gesture on
the part of Anderson, the Irish captain, and that if the *haka* was to be
used for purposes other than ceremonial it was time to discontinue it.

Unfortunately for Ireland, they could not offer the same sort of bloody-minded commitment in the game itself. They had so little class and composure to call upon and once New Zealand had held off the early barrage it was inevitable that they would win comfortably, even if it was only in the closing stages that the scores began to pile up. Nevertheless, New Zealand were denied tries in the final yard on at least four occasions in the second half.

Aherne, at scrum-half, played valiantly for the Irish in trying to cope with his back-pedalling scrum but Smith, under pressure at fly-half, was not at his best and could not turn any of the pressure towards New Zealand with his kicking. New Zealand led by 13-6 at half-time. Smith managed two penalties for Ireland but Fox, mechanical as ever, put over three for New Zealand. The only try of the half was a splendid one as Gallagher outflanked Ireland at the end of a marvellous All Black back movement. It was not until the last ten minutes that Ireland's brave defence cracked again, letting in Wright and Shelford for tries.

IRELAND: P I Rainey (Ballymena); K J Hooks (Ards), B J Mullin (London Irish), D G Irwin (Instonians), K D Crossan (Instonians); B A Smith (Oxford U), L F P Aherne (Lansdowne); N J Popplewell (Greystones), S J Smith (Ballymena), J J McCoy (Bangor), D G Lenihan (Cork Const), W A Anderson (Dungannon) (*capt*), P M Matthews (Wanderers), N P Mannion (Corinthians), P T O'Hara (Sunday's Well) *Replacements* D C Fitzgerald (Lansdowne) for Popplewell; P P Danaher (Garryowen) for Hooks
Scorer *Penalty Goals:* Smith (2)
NEW ZEALAND: Gallagher; Innes, Stanley, Schuster, Wright; Fox, Bachop; McDowell, Fitzpatrick, Loe, Pierce, G W Whetton, Earl, Shelford (*capt*), Brewer
Scorers *Tries:* Gallagher, Wright, Shelford   *Conversion:* Fox   *Penalty Goals:* Fox (3)
Referee A MacNeill (Australia)

MATCH 13   21 November, Ravenhill, Belfast

Ulster 3 (1PG)   **New Zealand XV 21** (2G 3PG)
Ulster: P I Rainey (Ballymena); S Porter (Malone), D G Irwin (Instonians), J A Hewitt (London Irish), K D Crossan (Instonians); P Russell (Instonians), A Blair (Dungannon); M Reynolds (Malone), S J Smith (Ballymena), J J McCoy (Bangor), W A Anderson (Dungannon) (*capt*), P Johns (Dublin U), W D McBride (Malone), B Robinson (Ballymena), P M Matthews (Wanderers)
Scorer *Penalty Goal:* Russell
New Zealand XV: Ridge; Timu, McCahill, Little, Tuigamala; Botica, Deans; McDowell, Fitzpatrick, Purvis, G W Whetton (*capt*), Gordon, A J Whetton, Brooke, Schuler
Scorers *Tries:* Brooke, Tuigamala   *Conversions:* Botica (2)   *Penalty Goals:* Botica (3)
Referee I R Bullerwell (England)

MATCH 14   25 November, Twickenham

Barbarians 10 (2PG 1T)   **New Zealand XV 21** (3G 1PG)
Barbarians: A G Hastings (London Scottish); T Underwood (Leicester), S Hastings (Watsonians), J C Guscott (Bath), R Underwood (RAF & Leicester); A Clement (Swansea), N C Farr-Jones (Sydney U); D M B Sole (Edinburgh Acads), B C Moore (Nottingham), D Young (Cardiff), W A Dooley (Preston Grasshoppers), P J Ackford (Harlequins), P M Matthews (Wanderers), P T Davies (Llanelli), G W Rees (Nottingham) *Replacement* B J Mullin (London Irish) for Guscott

Scorers *Try:* Matthews *Penalty Goals:* A G Hastings (2)
New Zealand XV: Gallagher; Innes, Schuster, Little, Wright; Fox, Bachop; McDowell, Fitzpatrick, Loe, Pierce, G W Whetton, Earl, Shelford (*capt*), Brewer
Replacement Brooke for Shelford
Scorers *Tries:* Innes, Brooke, Loe *Conversions:* Fox (3) *Penalty Goal:* Fox
Referee C T Norling (Wales)

BRITISH ISLES TO AUSTRALIA 1990

It has been said that the challenge of touring Australia does not compare with visits to New Zealand and South Africa, the two more traditional Lions touring venues. Of this there is no doubt: the 1990 Lions were subjected to nothing like the day-in, day-out pressure that previous teams have experienced in those countries.

For all that, anyone who regards the Australians as a push-over on their own territory was not on this trip. The Lions, battling back heroically from a 1-0 deficit to win the three-Test series, deserve every accolade for a gritty, no-nonsense effort and for restoring some of the balance of world rugby in favour of the Northern Hemisphere. Coach Ian McGeechan, together with Roger Uttley, his assistant, and Finlay Calder, the captain, can take credit for forging a powerful self-belief and team spirit amongst the party. The Lions pack developed well, based partly on the brilliance of Paul Ackford, Dean Richards and Mike Teague, the three England forwards, but chiefly on a hard-nosed attitude shown by the whole bunch. McGeechan stated his one regret after the tour: that he never had time to develop the Lions' back play.

Skipper Calder was never quite at his best as a player, but his motivational powers kept the team on the boil and he came through strongly in the final Test, when he was one of the players of the match in a gripping finale to the tour. The non-Test matches were less taxing than, say, a round of the New Zealand provinces – although it took a late dropped goal by Craig Chalmers to dig the Lions out of the match against New South Wales.

The Tests were all harshly, even bitterly fought. Second Test excesses brought down a savage media campaign on the heads of the Lions, as if they were the only offenders. This served to increase their motivation. All in all, the tour established Australia as a genuine Lions touring venue; it also contributed another proud chapter to British rugby history.

TOUR RECORD
All matches Played 12 Won 11 Lost 1 Points for 360 Against 192
International matches Played 3 Won 2 Lost 1 Points for 50 Against 60
SCORING DETAILS

All matches
For: 50T 26C 27PG 9DG 360 Pts
Against: 18T 12C 30PG 2DG 192 Pts

International matches
For: 3T 1C 10PG 2DG 50 Pts
Against: 6T 6C 7PG 1DG 60 Pts

MATCH DETAILS

1989	OPPONENTS	VENUE	RESULT
10 June	Western Australia	Perth	W 44-0
14 June	Australia B	Melbourne	W 23-18
17 June	Queensland	Brisbane	W 19-15
21 June	Queensland B	Cairns	W 30-6
24 June	New South Wales	Sydney	W 23-21
27 June	New South Wales B	Dubbo	W 39-19
1 July	AUSTRALIA	Sydney	L 12-30
4 July	ACT (Canberra Kookaburras)	Canberra	W 41-25
8 July	AUSTRALIA	Queensland	W 19-12
15 July	AUSTRALIA	Sydney	W 19-18
19 July	NSW Country	Newcastle	W 72-13
23 July	ANZAC XV	Queensland	W 19-15

Scorers: 66 – A G Hastings (2T 1DG 17PG 2C), Dods (1T 8PG 19C); 28 – Mullin (7T), Chalmers (1T 7DG 1PG); 20 – Armstrong (5T); 16 – Andrew (1DG 1PG 5C), Jeffrey (4T), Underwood (4T); 12 – S Hastings (3T), Hall (3T); 8 – Dooley (2T), Devereux (2T), Smith (2T), Evans (2T), Robinson (2T); 4 – White (1T), Moore (1T), Jones (1T), Oti (1T), Norster (1T), Sole (1T), Chilcott (1T), Clement (1T), Guscott (1T); one penalty try
Appearances: 9 – S Hastings (inc 2 as replacement); 8 – Evans (inc 1 as replacement), Underwood (inc 1 as replacement), Ackford, Sole (inc 1 as replacement); 7 – Moore, Young (inc 1 as replacement), Jones, A G Hastings, White, Mullin (inc 1 as replacement), Chalmers (inc 1 as replacement); 6 – Dooley, Robinson, Richards, Griffiths (inc 1 as replacement), Andrew (inc 1 as replacement), Teague, Norster, Hall, Calder, Guscott; 5 – Devereux, Dods, Armstrong, Smith, Chilcott, Jeffrey; 4 – Lenihan; 3 – Oti; 2 – Clement (inc 1 as replacement); 1 – Dean

THE TOURING PARTY

Captain F Calder   **Manager** D C T Rowlands
Coach I R McGeechan   **Assistant Coach** R M Uttley
Hon Medical Officer Dr B Gilfeather   **Physiotherapist** K Murphy

FULL-BACKS

A G Hastings (London Scottish & Scotland)
P W Dods (Gala & Scotland)

THREEQUARTERS

I C Evans (Llanelli & Wales)
R Underwood (Leicester, RAF & England)
C Oti (Wasps & England)
M R Hall (Bridgend & Wales)
S Hastings (Watsonians & Scotland)
J A Devereux (Bridgend & Wales)
B J Mullin (London Irish & Ireland)
J C Guscott (Bath & England)
*****A Clement** (Swansea & Wales)

HALF-BACKS

P M Dean (St Mary's Coll & Ireland)
C M Chalmers (Melrose & Scotland)
R N Jones (Swansea & Wales)
G Armstrong (Jedforest & Scotland)
*****C R Andrew** (Wasps & England)

FORWARDS

D M B Sole (Edinburgh Acads & Scotland)
M Griffiths (Bridgend & Wales)
B C Moore (Nottingham & England)
S J Smith (Ballymena & Ireland)
D Young (Cardiff & Wales)
G J Chilcott (Bath & England)
R L Norster (Cardiff & Wales)
W A Dooley (Preston Grasshoppers & England)
P J Ackford (Harlequins & England)
D G Lenihan (Cork Const & Ireland)
J Jeffrey (Kelso & Scotland)
M C Teague (Gloucester & England)
A Robinson (Bath & England)
F Calder (Stewart's-Melville FP & Scotland)
D B White (Gala, London Scottish & Scotland)
D Richards (Leicester & England)

replacement during tour

MATCH 1   10 June, Perry Lakes Stadium, Perth

Western Australia 0   British Isles 44 (4G 5T)
Western Australia: T Fearn; J Summers, C Stoneman, G Cotter, H Sutherland; G Bermingham, M Ryburn; P Koteka (*capt*), J Kani, T McLennan, P Roberts,

W te Pania, L Tinney, G Mickell, P Richardson *Replacement* G Thompson for Mickell
British Isles: Dods; Evans, Mullin, S Hastings, Underwood; Dean, Jones; Sole, Moore,
Young, Lenihan, Norster, Calder *(capt)*, White, Teague *Replacement* Chalmers for Dean
Scorers *Tries:* Mullin (3), Underwood (2), Evans, White, Moore, S Hastings
Conversions: Dods (4)
Referee P McPhillips (ACT)

MATCH 2   14 June, Olympic Park, Melbourne

Australia B 18 (1G 3T)   **British Isles 23** (1G 3PG 2T)
Australia B (*New South Wales unless stated*): D J Knox; I Siganiyavi (Queensland),
B Girvan (ACT), D J Maguire (Queensland), A S Niuqila; T J Horan, B T Burke *(capt)*;
M N Hartill, T A Lawton (Queensland), E McKenzie, D Frawley, P FitzSimons, B
Nasser (Queensland), S N Tuynman, S R Gourley *Replacement* P Kay for McKenzie
Scorers *Tries:* Knox, Niuqila, Tuynman, penalty try   *Conversion:* Knox
British Isles: A G Hastings; Evans, Devereux, Guscott, Oti; Chalmers, Armstrong;
Griffiths, Smith, Chilcott, Ackford, Dooley, Jeffrey, Richards *(capt)*, Robinson
Scorers *Tries:* Jeffrey (2), Armstrong   *Conversion:* A G Hastings
Penalty Goals: A G Hastings (3)
Referee H van der Westhuizen

MATCH 3   17 June, Ballymore, Brisbane

Queensland 15 (5PG)   **British Isles 19** (3PG 2DG 1T)
Queensland: G J Martin; I Siganiyavi, A Herbert, D J Maguire, P Carozza; M P Lynagh,
P Slattery; C A Lillicrap, M I McBain, D Crowley, W A Campbell *(capt)*, R J McCall,
J S Miller, J M Gardner, S Scott-Young *Replacement* D Williams for Gardner
Scorers *Penalty Goals:* Lynagh (5)
British Isles: A G Hastings; Hall, Devereux, S Hastings, Underwood; Chalmers, Jones;
Sole, Moore, Young, Ackford, Dooley, Teague, Richards, Calder *(capt)* *Replacement*
Mullin for Hall
Scorers *Try:* Jones   *Penalty Goals:* A G Hastings (3)   *Dropped Goals:* Chalmers (2)
Referee A MacNeill (Newcastle)

MATCH 4   21 June, Barlow Park, Cairns

Queensland B 6 (2PG)   **British Isles 30** (4G 2PG)
Queensland B: A King; M Anderson, J Little, T J Horan, B Fielke; M Palm, S Tait;
R Maroney, T A Lawton *(capt)*, M Grank, G Smith, R Korst, I Tabua, T Dodson,
D Wilson
Scorer *Penalty Goals:* Palm (2)
British Isles: Dods; Hall, Mullin, Guscott, Oti; Andrew, Armstrong; Griffiths, Smith,
Chilcott, Lenihan *(capt)*, Dooley, Jeffrey, White, Robinson *Replacement* Evans for Dods
Scorers *Tries:* Oti, Smith, Dooley, Robinson   *Conversions:* Andrew (4)
Penalty Goals: Dods (2)
Referee M Powell (Brisbane)

MATCH 5   24 June, North Sydney Oval, Sydney

New South Wales 21 (1G 5PG)   **British Isles 23** (2PG 3DG 2T)
New South Wales: M Roebuck; A S Niuqila, D K Junee, L F Walker, D I Campese;
K Bray, N C Farr-Jones *(capt)*; M N Hartill, P N Kearns, A Skeggs, S A Cutler,
D Frawley, S R Gourley, S N Tuynman, S P Poidevin
Scorer *Try:* Roebuck   *Conversion:* Roebuck   *Penalty Goals:* Roebuck (5)
British Isles: A G Hastings; Evans, Devereux, Guscott, Oti; Chalmers, Jones; Griffiths,
Moore, Young, Norster, Ackford, Calder *(capt)*, Richards, Teague *Replacements*
Underwood for Oti; S Hastings for Devereux

29

Scorers *Tries:* A G Hastings, Norster   *Penalty Goals:* A G Hastings (2)
Dropped Goals: Chalmers (3)
Referee C Waldron (Queensland)

MATCH 6   27 June, Apex Oval, Dubbo

New South Wales B 19 (1G 3PG 1T)   **British Isles 39** (4G 1PG 3T)
New South Wales B: D J Knox; P Meehan, A Parkes, M Hayes, J Flett; M Patterson,
B T Burke (*capt*); M Murray, E Jones, A Blades, P FitzSimons, J Fewtrell, D Picken,
S T Gavin, D G Carter *Replacements* R Clark for Carter; S Kowalick for Clark
Scorers *Tries:* Burke (2)   *Conversion:* Patterson   *Penalty Goals:* Patterson (3)
British Isles: Dods; Hall, Mullin, S Hastings, Underwood; Andrew, Armstrong; Sole
(*capt*), Smith, Chilcott, Ackford, Dooley, Jeffrey, White, Robinson
Scorers *Tries:* Hall (2), Underwood (2), Armstrong, S Hastings, Sole
Conversions: Dods (4)   *Penalty Goal:* Dods
Referee B Kinsey (New South Wales)

MATCH 7   1 July, Sydney Football Stadium, Sydney   1st Test

AUSTRALIA 30 (4G 1PG 1DG)   **BRITISH ISLES 12** (3PG 1DG)
This was a savage disappointment for the Lions. Even in a four-Test
series few teams have ever come back from a 1-0 deficit: in this three-
Test programme it seemed as if the fate of the tourists was already
sealed after an inexplicably poor performance. Nevertheless, it was a
magnificent day for Australian rugby. The match drew a full and
excited house to the imposing Sydney Football Stadium and the crowd
support, not often a feature of such occasions, was uproarious.

There was an iron will about the Australians, who won a decisive
victory in the important line-outs and who seemed yards faster. Lynagh's
tactical kicking was superlative. The Lions' support play was badly
adrift, and Australia never let their 15-6 half-time lead slip. The Lions
were hit by injury, notably to Teague, who had been so outstanding in
the early part of the tour; and also to Devereux and Scott Hastings, the
centre combination they had hoped to field.

AUSTRALIA: G J Martin (Queensland); A S Niuqila (New South Wales), L F Walker
(New South Wales), D J Maguire (Queensland), D I Campese (New South Wales);
M P Lynagh (Queensland), N C Farr-Jones (New South Wales) (*capt*); C A Lillicrap
(Queensland), T A Lawton (Queensland), D Crowley (Queensland), W A Campbell
(Queensland), S A G Cutler (New South Wales), J S Miller (Queensland), S N Tuynman
(New South Wales), S R Gourley (New South Wales) *Replacements* M N Hartill
(New South Wales) for Lillicrap; M I McBain (Queensland) for Lawton
Scorers *Tries:* Walker, Gourley, Maguire, Martin   *Conversions:* Lynagh (4)
Penalty Goal: Lynagh   *Dropped Goal:* Lynagh
BRITISH ISLES: A G Hastings; Evans, Hall, Mullin, Underwood; Chalmers, Jones;
Sole, Moore, Young, Ackford, Norster, White, Richards, Calder (*capt*)
Scorers *Penalty Goals:* A G Hastings (2), Chalmers   *Dropped Goal:* Chalmers
Referee K Lawrence (New Zealand)

MATCH 8   6 July, Seiffert Oval, Canberra

Australian Capital Territory 25 (2G 3PG 1T)   **British Isles 41** (3G 5PG 2T)
Australian Capital Territory: M Pini; P Alchin, D Starkey, B Girvan (*capt*), C Morton;

G Logan, P Doyle; L Donnellan, J Taylor, G Didier, J Ross, M Sinderberry, F Lopilato, M McInnes, G Bush
Scorers *Tries:* Alchin (2), Doyle   *Conversions:* Pini (2)   *Penalty Goals:* Pini (3)
British Isles: Dods; Hall, Guscott, S Hastings, Underwood; Andrew, Armstrong; Griffiths, Smith, Chilcott, Lenihan, Dooley, Jeffrey, White, Robinson *Replacements* Sole for Robinson; Young for Chilcott
Scorers *Tries:* Dooley, Hall, Armstrong, S Hastings, penalty try
Conversions: Dods (3)   *Penalty Goals:* Dods (5)
Referee B Leask (Queensland)

MATCH 9   8 July, Ballymore, Brisbane   2nd Test

AUSTRALIA 12 (1G 2PG)   **BRITISH ISLES 19** (1G 1DG 2PG 1T)
This was a red-letter day in the Lions' touring history. In a ferocious and often bitter Test they found themselves. They trailed until the closing stages but their authority simply grew and grew throughout the match. Wade Dooley and especially Mike Teague, both of whom missed the first Test, made splendid contributions, but such was the level of performance in the Lions pack that afterwards coach McGeechan flatly refused to single out any player. Jones at scrum-half was the perfect complement – he and Andrew struck up a splendid partnership. On the debit side was the short-tempered nature of proceedings and Young, the Lions prop, was lucky to remain on the field after striking Cutler's head with his boot.

The Lions trailed by 12-9 inside the last five minutes. Lynagh's kicking for Australia was uncannily accurate and when Gavin Hastings dropped another high ball, Martin of Australia swept up to score. Hastings kicked two penalties and Andrew dropped a goal, but two more penalties by Lynagh set up that 12-9 lead. Then, in a glorious and dominant chapter of Lions play based squarely on some deadly box-kicking from Jones, the Lions scored two tries: the first from Hastings after a sweeping movement; then another brilliant effort from Guscott, who chipped deftly between the Australian centres and ran on to score the try which set up a mouth-watering decider in the third Test.

AUSTRALIA: G J Martin (Queensland); I M Williams (New South Wales), L F Walker (New South Wales), D J Maguire (Queensland), D I Campese (New South Wales); M P Lynagh (Queensland), N C Farr-Jones (New South Wales) (*capt*); M N Hartill (New South Wales), T A Lawton (Queensland), D Crowley (Queensland), W A Campbell (Queensland), S A G Cutler (New South Wales), J S Miller (Queensland), S N Tuynman (New South Wales), S R Gourley (New South Wales)
Scorers *Try:* Martin   *Conversion:* Lynagh   *Penalty Goals:* Lynagh (2)
BRITISH ISLES: A G Hastings; Evans, S Hastings, Guscott, Underwood; Andrew, Jones; Sole, Moore, Young, Ackford, Dooley, Teague, Richards, Calder (*capt*)
Scorers *Tries:* A G Hastings, Guscott   *Conversion:* Andrew
Penalty Goals: A G Hastings, Andrew   *Dropped Goal:* Andrew
Referee R Hourquet (France)

MATCH 10   15 July, Sydney Football Stadium   3rd Test

AUSTRALIA 18 (1G 4PG)   **BRITISH ISLES 19** (5PG 1T)
The Lions won their first series for 15 years with their best display of

the tour. In an almost fanatical match their pack controlled most of the play and their right to victory was beyond doubt. Yet because they could not translate their superiority into points on the scoreboard they had to endure all sorts of agonies as Australia pegged back a 19-12 lead to trail by a single point. Yet the Lions' tackling, especially that of captain Calder and of Scott Hastings, cut Australia down and the Lions held on.

The match turned towards the Lions near the start of the second half when Campese tried to run the ball out from his own in-goal after Andrew, another Lions hero, had missed with a drop kick. Campese's action caused as much panic in Australian ranks as it did among the Lions and Martin could not hold a wretched pass that Campese spilled in his direction. Evans came up for the touch-down. Australia had pulled the Lions back to 9-9 with a splendid try by Williams in the first half, but Campese spoiled any hopes of rising Australian morale and the Lions' pressure resumed. Gavin Hastings kicked two more penalties to make it 9-12, and although Lynagh kicked two more of his own to set up a wildly exciting finale, it was the Lions who emerged on their feet.

AUSTRALIA: G J Martin (Queensland); I M Williams (New South Wales), L F Walker (New South Wales), D J Maguire (Queensland), D I Campese (New South Wales); M P Lynagh (Queensland), N C Farr-Jones (New South Wales) (*capt*); M N Hartill (New South Wales), T A Lawton (Queensland), D Crowley (Queensland), W A Campbell (Queensland), S A G Cutler (New South Wales), J S Miller (Queensland), S N Tuynman (New South Wales), S R Gourley (New South Wales)
Scorers *Try:* Williams *Conversion:* Lynagh *Penalty Goals:* Lynagh (4)
BRITISH ISLES: A G Hastings; Evans, Guscott, S Hastings, Underwood; Andrew, Jones; Sole, Moore, Young, Ackford, Norster, Teague, Richards, Calder (*capt*)
Scorers *Try:* Evans *Penalty Goals:* A G Hastings (5)
Referee R Hourquet (France)

MATCH 11   19 July, No 2 Sportsground, Newcastle, New South Wales

New South Wales Country 13 (3PG 1T)   British Isles 72 (8G 6T)
New South Wales Country: M Hamling; D Vignes, A Parkes, F Dazey, I Tonkin; P Tonkin, R Long (*capt*); M Prior, D McCathie, S Lozenkovski, M Stocks, P Challender, B Harris, J Sampson, F Schwenke *Replacement* S McFarlan for Hamling
British Isles: Dods; Hall, Mullin, Devereux, Clement; Chalmers, Armstrong; Griffiths, Smith, Chilcott, Lenihan (*capt*), Norster, Jeffrey, White, Robinson *Replacement* S Hastings for Hall
Scorers *Tries:* Mullin (3), Armstrong (2), Jeffrey (2), Devereux, Chalmers, Chilcott, Robinson, Clement, Dods, Smith *Conversions:* Dods (8)
Referee D Kennedy (New South Wales)

MATCH 12   23 July, Ballymore, Brisbane

ANZAC XV 15 (1G 3PG)   BRITISH ISLES 19 (1G 1PG 2DG 1T)
ANZAC XV (*Australia unless stated*): K J Crowley (Taranaki & New Zealand); I M Williams (New South Wales), D J Maguire (Queensland), F M Botica (North Harbour & New Zealand), D I Campese (New South Wales); M P Lynagh (Queensland), N C Farr-Jones (New South Wales) (*capt*); S C McDowell (Bay of Plenty & New Zealand), M I McBain (Queensland), A J McIntyre (Queensland), W A Campbell (Queensland), S A G Cutler (New South Wales), S P Poidevin (New South Wales), T B Gavin (New South Wales), J S Miller (Queensland)

Scorers *Try:* Williams *Conversion:* Williams *Penalty Goals:* Lynagh (3)
BRITISH ISLES: A G Hastings; Evans, Mullin, Devereux, S Hastings; Chalmers,
Jones; Sole (*capt*), Moore, Young, Norster, Ackford, Robinson, White, Teague
Replacements Andrew for Evans; Clement for Mullin; Griffiths for Young
Scorers *Tries:* Mullin, Devereux *Conversion:* A G Hastings *Penalty Goal:* A G Hastings
Dropped Goals: Chalmers, A G Hastings
Referee K Fitzgerald (ARU)

AUSTRALIA TO FRANCE 1989

Only six players in an Australian side denuded by injury and
unavailability had won more than six caps, and only one of those six,
Mark Hartill, was a forward. This showed the magnitude of the task
facing Australia, albeit in a country where rugby fortunes had waned
of late. Predictably, tour fortunes rose and dipped alarmingly.
Australia lost four of their six provincial matches, this after encouraging
victories in a warm-up visit to Canada where they beat North American
Wolverines and British Columbia.

However, Australia had a decisive and dramatic win the first Test in
Strasbourg, a match which indicated a bright future for many members
of the heroic winning team, notably Horan and Little in the backs.
France responded well to the pressure in the second Test in Lille. They
needed to, because if they had lost that then the dissatisfaction with
coach Jacques Fouroux would certainly have increased. As it was,
Australia could not find the drive and dedication of their first Test win.

The experienced team members, such as Lynagh and Farr-Jones at
half-back, provided the heart of the team, while McCall, for some time
a second string in Wallaby circles, stepped forward into the Test team
with some strong line-out performances. Another significant contribution came from FitzSimons, the lock who has played much of his
club rugby in France.

TOUR RECORD
All matches Played 8 Won 3 Lost 5 Points for 149 Against 140
International matches Played 2 Won 1 Lost 1 Points for 51 Against 40

SCORING DETAILS

All matches						International matches					
For:	17T	9C	20PG	1DG	149 Pts	For:	6T	3C	7PG		51 Pts
Against:	9T	4C	30PG	2DG	140 Pts	Against:	2T	1C	9PG	1DG	40 Pts

MATCH DETAILS

1989	OPPONENTS	VENUE	RESULT
17 Oct	Pyrenees	Toulouse	W 30-22
21 Oct	Languedoc	Béziers	L 10-19
25 Oct	Côte D'Azur	Toulon	W 22-10
28 Oct	Alps	Grenoble	L 7-9
31 Oct	Regional XV	Montferrand	L 10-19
4 Nov	FRANCE	Strasbourg	W 32-15
7 Nov	L'Ile de France	Massy	L 19-21
11 Nov	FRANCE	Lille	L 19-25

Leading points-scorers: Lynagh 62, Palm 19, Horan 16; leading try-scorers: Horan 4, Williams 3.

THE TOURING PARTY

Captain N C Farr-Jones **Manager** A Conway
Coaches R Dwyer, R Templeton

FULL-BACKS
G J Martin (Brisbane U)
M Roebuck (Eastwood)

THREEQUARTERS
D I Campese (Randwick, Sydney)
I M Williams (Eastwood, Sydney)
B Girvan (North Canberra)
A Herbert (Old Boys, Brisbane)
T J Horan (Souths, Brisbane)
D K Junee (Eastwood, Sydney)
J Little (Souths, Brisbane)
D J Maguire (Brothers, Brisbane)

HALF-BACKS
M P Lynagh (Brisbane U)
M Palm (Brisbane U)
P Slattery (Brisbane U)
N C Farr-Jones (Sydney U)

FORWARDS
P N Kearns (Randwick, Sydney)
T A Lawton (Souths, Brisbane)
D Crowley (Souths, Brisbane)
M N Hartill (Gordon, Sydney)
A J Daly (Gordon, Sydney)
E McKenzie (Randwick, Sydney)
D Dix (Sydney U)
P FitzSimons (Sydney U)
R J McCall (Brothers, Brisbane)
M McInnes (Easts, Canberra)
D G Carter (Quirindi, New South Wales)
T Kava (Randwick, Sydney)
B Nasser (Brisbane U)
D Wilson (Eastern Districts, Brisbane)
S Scott-Young (Western Districts, Brisbane)
B T Gavin (Sydney U)

MATCH 1   17 October, Toulouse

Pyrenees 22 (2G 2PG 1T)   **Australian XV 30** (3G 4PG)
Pyrenees: J-L Sadourney (Colomiers); D Berty (Stade Toulousain), E Bonneval (Stade Toulousain), D Charvet (Stade Toulousain), D Dal Pos (Colomiers); T Pebay (Valence D'Agen), F Galthie (Colomiers); J Puginier (Graulhet), R Tremoulet (Graulhet), C Portolan (Stade Toulousain), P Revailler (Graulhet), J-M Cadieu (Stade Toulousain), T Maset (Stade Toulousain) (*capt*), J-C Swiadek (Castres), H Lecomte (Stade Toulousain)
Replacements G Pages (Rodez) for Maset; H Couffignal (Colomiers) for Pebay
Scorers *Tries:* Berty, Sadourney, Pages   *Conversions:* Charvet (2)
Penalty Goals: Charvet (2)
Australian XV: Martin; Williams, Horan, Junee, Campese; Lynagh, Farr-Jones (*capt*); Daly, Kearns, McKenzie, Kava, McCall, Carter, Gavin, Nasser
Scorers *Tries:* Horan (2), Kearns   *Conversions:* Lynagh (3)   *Penalty Goals:* Lynagh (4)
Referee C Debat (Pyrenees)

MATCH 2   21 October, Béziers

Languedoc 19 (5PG 1T)   **Australian XV 10** (1G 1T)
Languedoc: P Bonhoure (Béziers); T Clavieres (Narbonne), R Frentzel (Narbonne), A Hyardet (Béziers), J-P Bullich (Narbonne); D Camberabero (Béziers), H Sanz (Narbonne) (*capt*); J-J Pineda (Narbonne), C Urios (Carcassone), P Gallard (Béziers), G Bourguignon (Narbonne), J-F Gourragne (Béziers), F Vanhems (Montpellier), A Sablayrolles (Narbonne), A Caminati (Béziers)
Scorers *Try:* Urios   *Penalty Goals:* Camberabero (5)
Australian XV: Roebuck; Little, Maguire, Herbert, Girvan; Palm, Slattery; Hartill, Lawton (*capt*), Crowley, FitzSimons, Dix, Wilson, McInnes, Scott-Young *Replacements* Daly for Crowley; Kearns for Lawton
Scorer *Tries:* Wilson, Slattery   *Conversion:* Palm
Referee K Brackston (Wales)

MATCH 3   25 October, Toulon

Côte D'Azur 10 (2PG 1T)   **Australian XV 22** (1G 4PG 1T)
Côte D'Azur (*Toulon unless stated*): J Bianchi; R Juhel (Nice), P Tremouille, R Zago, D Jaubert; B Capitani (Nice), T Ginhac; M Pujolle (Nice), J-F Tordo, J-M Casalini,

34

Y Roux, J-P Alarcon, E Champ (capt), E Melville, A Fabre (Nice) *Replacements*
J Motteroz (Nice) for Melville; E Dasalmartini for Alarcon
Scorers *Try:* Jaubert *Penalty Goals:* Bianchi (2)
Australian XV: Martin; Williams, Little, Horan, Campese; Lynagh, Farr-Jones (capt);
Daly, Kearns, McKenzie, McCall, FitzSimons, Carter, Wilson, Gavin
Scorers *Tries:* Williams, Gavin *Conversion:* Lynagh *Penalty Goals:* Lynagh (4)
Referee J-C Doulcet (Limousin)

MATCH 4   28 October, Grenoble

Alps 9 (2PG 1DG)   **Australian XV 7** (1PG 1T)
Alps (*Grenoble unless stated*): F Velo; S Weller (Battalion de Joinville), A Gely, F Mesnel
(Racing Club de France), J-P Bullich (Narbonne); P Barthelemy (capt), D Mazille;
E Alabarbe (Brive), J-P Cantin, B Lapiate (Valence), A Lorieux (Aix-Les-Bains),
Y Theron (Bourgoin), T' Maset (Stade Toulousain), H Chaffardon, C Monteil
Scorer *Penalty Goals:* Velo (2) *Dropped Goal:* Velo
Australian XV: Martin; Williams, Little, Horan, Junee; Lynagh, Farr-Jones (capt);
Daly, Kearns, McKenzie, FitzSimons, McCall, Carter, Gavin, Nasser *Replacement*
Hartill for McKenzie
Scorers *Try:* Williams *Penalty Goal:* Lynagh
Referee J-C Yché (Bearn)

MATCH 5   31 October, Montferrand

French Selection 19 (5PG 1T)   **Australian XV 10** (1PG 1DG 1T)
French Selection (*Montferrand unless stated*): J-B Lafond (Racing Club de France);
D Faugeron (Brive), A Dicharry, E Nicol, P Saint-André; J-M Lescure (Narbonne),
M Pradier; P Marocco, O Mallaret, F Heyer, J-P Pelloux, D Gaby (capt), X Verdy,
J-M Lhermet, C Deslandes (Racing Club de France)
Scorers *Try:* Verdy *Penalty Goals:* Pradier (5)
Australian XV: Roebuck; Junee, Maguire, Herbert, Girvan; Palm, Slattery; Hartill,
Lawton (capt), Crowley, Kava, Dix, Wilson, McInnes, Scott-Young *Replacement* Gavin
for Kava
Scorers *Try:* Slattery *Penalty Goal:* Palm *Dropped Goal:* Girvan
Referee D Neyrat (Auvergne)

MATCH 6   4 November, Meinau Stadium, Strasbourg   1st Test

FRANCE 15 (4PG 1DG)   AUSTRALIA 32 (2G 4PG 2T)

Australia went into the international as rank outsiders and shorn of
confidence by three defeats in five provincial matches. So the outcome,
Australia's biggest win against France, and by four tries to nil, was as
unexpected as it was substantial.

Australia fielded four new caps: Little at centre, McCall, the veteran
FitzSimons in the second row and the flanker Nasser. Daly, Kearns and
Horan were making only their second appearances, and Little and
Horan were teenagers. But they were skilfully led by the old guard,
especially Farr-Jones, Lynagh, Campese and Williams. The tourists
also cashed in on a dreadful display from the French. The home team
lacked cohesion and a game plan, and their defeat further emphasised
the divisions in French rugby.

France led 12-10 at the interval, courtesy of Camberabero, whose
kicking only papered over the cracks. But Australia picked up the pace
near half-time, and Horan scored a try to add to Lynagh's two penalties.
Shortly after the restart Williams ran in another try. Lynagh converted

and added two more penalties to one from Camberabero. Australia sealed their win with late tries from Campese and Horan. The international was the first to be held in the Meinau Stadium, the home of Strasbourg FC, and was one of the biggest shocks for years.

FRANCE: S Blanco (Biarritz); S Weller (Grenoble), P Sella (Agen), F Mesnel (Racing Club de France), P Lagisquet (Bayonne); D Camberabero (Béziers), P Berbizier (Agen) (*capt*); M Pujolle (Nice), L Armary (Lourdes), L Seigne (Agen), J Condom (Biarritz), G Bourguignon (Narbonne), E Champ (Toulon), L Rodriguez (Dax), M Cecillon (Bourgoin) *Replacements* T Lacroix (Dax) for Camberabero; D Berty (Toulouse) for Blanco

Scorer *Penalty Goals:* Camberabero (4)   *Dropped Goal:* Camberabero

AUSTRALIA: Martin; Williams, Little, Horan, Campese; Lynagh, Farr-Jones (*capt*); Daly, Kearns, Hartill, McCall, FitzSimons, Carter, Gavin, Nasser *Replacement* Junee for Williams

Scorers *Tries:* Horan (2), Williams, Campese   *Conversions:* Lynagh (2)
Penalty Goals: Lynagh (4)
Referee F Burger (South Africa)

MATCH 7   7 November, Massy

L'Ile de France 21 (1G 5PG)   **Australian XV 19** (1G 3PG 1T)

L'Ile de France (*Racing Club de France unless stated*): P Fauthoux (Paris University Club); K Abbou, R Autie, E Blanc, J Ottmann (ASPTT Paris); D Pouyau, J-P Saffore; J-P Benezech, J Castanet (ASPTT Paris), P Couchaux (Paris University Club), M Tchadjian (*capt*), P Serrière, Y Rouquette (Paris University Club), J-P Stolarczyk (Paris University Club), B Dalle *Replacements* P Dubreuille for Benezech; P Roguengo (Paris University Club) for Stolarczyk

Scorers *Try:* Autie   *Conversion:* Pouyau   *Penalty Goals:* Pouyau (5)

Australian XV: Roebuck; Junee, Herbert, Maguire, Girvan; Palm, Slattery; Hartill, Lawton (*capt*), Crowley, Dix, FitzSimons, Wilson, McInnes, Scott-Young *Replacement* Kearns for Lawton

Scorers *Tries:* Junee, Herbert   *Conversion:* Palm   *Penalty Goals:* Palm (3)
Referee P Robin (Perigord)

MATCH 8   11 November, Stade Grimpooris, Lille   2nd Test

FRANCE 25 (1G 5PG 1T)   AUSTRALIA 19 (1G 3PG 1T)

France gained their revenge to level the series 1-1 but the match did not amount to much more than that. France got away with their win thanks first to another superb try from Lagisquet at a crucial time, and secondly to the boot of the new fly-half, Thierry Lacroix, who contributed 17 points on his international debut.

Jacques Fouroux fielded eight players out of their club positions and dropped the old guard, Blanco, Berbizier, Rodriguez and Condom. Both decisions were justified by the result, which was never in any doubt as Australia failed to reproduce the form shown in their Strasbourg win. His most risky decision, to play Sella at full-back, was unhinged as early as the 21st minute when Sella failed to gather a high ball and Kearns punished the error with a try. The half-time score of 13-6 to Australia included three penalties from Lynagh and two from Lacroix.

In the second half, however, Lacroix added another penalty and

Lagisquet bemused four opponents in a brilliant run from halfway for a try converted by Lacroix to put France into the lead after 52 minutes. Lacroix went on to kick two more penalties. The French scoring was completed by a thrilling 80-yard interception try from Andrieu, a try in injury-time from Farr-Jones, converted by Lynagh, serving only to narrow the margin.

FRANCE: P Sella (Agen); S Weller (Grenoble), M Andrieu (Nîmes), F Mesnel (Racing Club de France), P Lagisquet (Bayonne); T Lacroix (Dax), H Sanz (Narbonne) (*capt*); D Bouet (Dax), L Armary (Lourdes), P Ondarts (Biarritz), A Lorieux (Aix-Les-Bains), D Erbani (Agen), E Champ (Toulon), T Devergie (Nîmes), A Carminati (Béziers)
Scorers: *Tries:* Lagisquet, Andrieu   *Conversion:* Lacroix
Penalty Goals: Lacroix (5)
AUSTRALIA: Martin; Williams, Horan, Little, Campese; Lynagh, Farr-Jones (*capt*); Daly, Kearns, Hartill, McCall, FitzSimons, Carter, Gavin, Nasser *Replacement* Junee for Williams
Scorers *Tries:* Kearns, Farr-Jones   *Conversion:* Lynagh   *Penalty Goals:* Lynagh (3)
Referee F Burger (South Africa)

FRANCE TO NEW ZEALAND 1989

Before this tour France had played 14 Test matches in New Zealand and won just one, by 24-19 at Eden Park, Auckland in 1979. This time they did play with real skill and courage in the two-Test series. Yet ultimately it did them no good. They lost both Tests and struggled desperately in the other tour matches.

The low point came when the tourists were beaten by Southland, the humble side in the deep south of the country. Southland, far from being packed with All Blacks, could not even boast a single member of the South Island team. Small wonder that some dissent surfaced. There were widespread rumours that a small faction of players, anxious at the direction taken by Jacques Fouroux, the all-powerful coach, had formed a deputation and demanded changes.

The highlight of the tour came in the first Test, when France launched a storming recovery after trailing 18-0 at half-time. Typically, New Zealand steadied and pulled away once again, but it did save the tour and the marketing prospects of the second Test.

Wellington, who had thrashed Wales in the previous season, were the other provincial team to beat the tourists, yet other games could have been lost. Counties, beaten 67-0 by Waikato just before the tour match, were narrowly held off; Manawatu were beaten only when Lescure scored for France in the last minute of normal time; Bay of Plenty were denied only by a late try from Mesnel. The only comfortable tour victory came over the Seddon Shield combination, which consisted of players from the third division.

TOUR RECORD
All matches   Played 8   Won 4   Lost 4   Points for 180   Against 170
International matches   Played 2   Lost 2   Points for 37   Against 59

SCORING DETAILS

All matches

For: 26T 14C 14PG 2DG
Against: 16T 8C   29PG 1DG

International matches

For: 5T 1C 5PG
Against: 7T 5C 7PG

MATCH DETAILS

1989	OPPONENTS	VENUE	RESULT
7 June	Counties	Pukekohe	W 24-21
10 June	Manawatu	Palmerston North	W 28-23
13 June	Southland	Invercargill	L 7-12
17 June	NEW ZEALAND	Christchurch	L 17-25
21 June	Seddon Shield XV	Blenheim	W 39-13
24 June	Wellington	Wellington	L 23-24
27 June	Bay of Plenty	Rotorua	W 22-18
1 July	NEW ZEALAND	Auckland	L 20-34

Scorers: 38 – Bérot (3T 4C 6PG); 32 – Blanco (2T 3C 6PG); 27 – Lescure (2T 5C 1PG 2DG); 12 – Sanz (3T), Hontas (3T); 8 – Cecillon (2T), Lagisquet (2T), Mesnel (2T), Beraud (2T); 7 – Lafond (2C 1PG); 4 – Sella (1T), Rouge-Thomas (1T), Weller (1T), Chabowski (1T)

THE TOURING PARTY

Captain P Berbizier
Manager/Coach J Fouroux

FULL-BACKS

S Blanco (Biarritz)
J-B Lafond (Racing Club de France)

THREEQUARTERS

S Weller (Grenoble)
P Bérot (Agen)
F Mesnel (Racing Club de France)
P Lagisquet (Bayonne)
P Hontas (Biarritz)
M Andrieu (Nîmes)
P Sella (Agen)
D Charvet (Toulouse)

HALF-BACKS

J-M Lescure (Narbonne)
R Rouge-Thomas (Toulouse)
H Sanz (Narbonne)
P Berbizier (Agen)

FORWARDS

J-P Garuet (Lourdes)
P Ondarts (Biarritz)
H Chabowski (Bourgoin)
D Bouet (Dax)
P Gallard (Béziers)
M Pujolle (Nice)
T Devergie (Nîmes)
J Condom (Biarritz)
P Beraud (Dax)
O Roumat (Dax)
P Benetton (Agen)
A Carminati (Béziers)
M Cecillon (Bourgoin)
D Erbani (Agen)
J-F Tordo (Toulon)
L Rodriguez (Dax)

MATCH 1   7 June, Pukekohe Stadium, Pukekohe

Counties 21 (6PG 1DG)   **France XV 24** (3G 2PG)
Counties: P R Cole; G M Nolan, G Millington, C D Murray, W Tabuarua; S Hollier, G V Thomas; P Curley, J F W Smythe, T A Parsons, J N Coe, D R McDonald, A J Dawson (*capt*), A C Fleming, T H Clarke
Scorer *Penalty Goals:* Hollier (6)   *Dropped Goal:* Hollier
France XV: Blanco; Weller, Sella, Mesnel, Lagisquet; Rouge-Thomas, Berbizier (*capt*); Pujolle, Bouet, Gallard, Erbani, Condom, Carminati, Roumat, Rodriguez *Replacements* Andrieu for Weller; Cecillon for Rodriguez; Ondarts for Gallard
Scorers *Tries:* Sella, Lagisquet (2)   *Conversions:* Blanco (3)   *Penalty Goals:* Blanco (2)
Referee M W Thompson (Auckland)

MATCH 2   10 June, Palmerston Oval, Palmerston North

Manawatu 23 (1G 3PG 2T)   **France XV 28** (2G 3PG 1DG 1T)
Manawatu: P Williams; D A Gosling, G Konia, P J Crosswell, J C Schmidt;

G A Champion, J A Hewitt; G Nesdale, D B Morrison, D A Rowse, A McKenzie, T J McManaway, K J Schuler (*capt*), J A Cruden, B A Whale
Scorers *Tries:* Morrison, Schmidt, Cruden   *Conversion:* Champion
Penalty Goals: Champion (3)
France XV: Bérot; Lafond, Andrieu, Charvet, Hontas; Lescure, Sanz (*capt*); Garuet, Tordo, Chabowski, Roumat, Beraud, Benetton, Carminati, Devergie *Replacements* Cecillon for Devergie; Condom for Benetton
Scorers *Tries:* Lescure (2), Beraud   *Conversions:* Bérot, Lafond
Penalty Goals: Bérot (3)   *Dropped Goal:* Lescure
Referee T R Marshall (Canterbury)

MATCH 3   13 June, Rugby Park, Invercargill

Southland 12 (4PG)   **France XV 7** (1PG 1T)
Southland: G J Crossan; P Johnston, S Bulmer, M D Brown (*capt*), B W Pascoe; S D Culhane, B D Murrell; P J Henderson, B A Youle, R J Palmer, B D McDonald, M J Hewitson, D B Henderson, B K Shepherd, R T Smith
Scorer *Penalty Goals:* Crossan (4)
France XV: Blanco; Bérot, Sella, Andrieu, Lagisquet; Rouge-Thomas, Berbizier (*capt*); Ondarts, Bouet, Pujolle, Roumat, Condom, Erbani, Benetton, Devergie *Replacements* Garuet for Bouet; Cecillon for Roumat
Scorer *Try:* Bérot   *Penalty Goal:* Bérot
Referee L McLachlan (Otago)

MATCH 4   17 June, Lancaster Park, Christchurch   1st Test

NEW ZEALAND 25 (2G 3PG 1T)   **FRANCE 17** (1G 1PG 2T)

New Zealand led 18-0 at half-time, and with memories of the disastrous loss to Southland fresh in the visitors' minds there were massive odds against a French win. However, 13 minutes after the interval, France had clawed their way back to 18-17 thanks to three typical tries. At this stage the French goal-kicker, Bérot, missed two crucial penalties. New Zealand took control again in injury time with a try from Alan Whetton. In the end the match hinged on the kicking – Bérot had two successes from eight attempts, Fox slotted five out of eight.

Traditionally nervous in the opening Test of any series, New Zealand were delighted to commandeer the driving seat so early in this Test. Before half-time, Wright had scored two tries, Fox converting both and landing two penalties.

Within 60 seconds of the second half, Blanco had scored his 28th international try; then Bérot, at last, kicked a penalty and converted Cecillon's try. Blanco promptly finished off another 70-metre move to narrow the margin to one point and excitement mounted. But the final surge from New Zealand brought a further Fox penalty and the clinching try from Whetton after Jones had retrieved a high kick from Fox. Fox again proved to be the match-winner. Gary and Alan Whetton, along with Pierce and Jones, were outstanding in the pack. French pride was partially restored through the brilliant performances of Blanco and Sella.

NEW ZEALAND: J A Gallagher (Wellington); J J Kirwan (Auckland), J T Stanley (Auckland), N J Schuster (Wellington), T J Wright (Auckland); G J Fox (Auckland), I B Deans (Canterbury); S C McDowell (Bay of Plenty), S B T Fitzpatrick (Auckland),

R W Loe (Waikato), A J Whetton (Auckland), M J Pierce (Wellington), M N Jones (Auckland), G W Whetton (Auckland), W T Shelford (North Harbour) (*capt*)
Scorers *Tries:* Wright (2), A Whetton   *Conversions:* Fox (2)   *Penalty Goals:* Fox (3)
FRANCE: Blanco; Bérot, Sella, Mesnel, Lagisquet; Rouge-Thomas, Berbizier (*capt*); Ondarts, Bouet, Garuet, Devergie, Condom, Cecillon, Erbani, Rodriguez *Replacement* Carminati for Rodriguez
Scorers *Tries:* Blanco (2), Cecillon   *Conversion:* Bérot   *Penalty Goal:* Bérot
Referee F A Howard (England)

MATCH 5   21 June, Blenheim

Seddon Shield XV 13 (3PG 1T)   France XV 39 (4G 1DG 3T)
Seddon Shield XV: P G Marfell; K Daly, P Phillips, K G C Boyd, B Baxter; I D Stark, A D Slee; G A Huntley, J J McDonald, P C Nicholson, L R Mason, F W Marfell (*capt*), R G Avery, G Timms, W G Dempster *Replacement* G Elley for Timms
Scorers *Try:* Boyd   *Penalty Goals:* Stark (3)
FRANCE XV: Lafond; Weller, Charvet, Andrieu, Hontas; Lescure, Sanz (*capt*); Pujolle, Chabowski, Gallard, Beraud, Roumat, Tordo, Benetton, Carminati *Replacement* Mesnel for Lafond
Scorers *Tries:* Hontas (3), Chabowski, Beraud, penalty try, Sanz
Conversions: Lescure (4)   *Dropped Goal:* Lescure
Referee D J Bishop (Southland)

MATCH 6   24 June, Athletic Park, Wellington

Wellington 24 (1G 2PG 3T)   France XV 23 (2G 1PG 2T)
Wellington: J A Gallagher; N P Geany, N J Schuster, J Hainsworth, D A Tocker; S Pokere, N A Sorensen (*capt*); B McGratton, D G Fraser, A H Gordon, M H Verhoeven, C D Tregaskis, R E Cheval, M Hudson, I H Adams *Replacement* J Meates for Hudson
Scorers *Tries:* Geany, Tocker (2), Verhoeven   *Conversion:* Gallagher
Penalty Goals: Gallagher (2)
FRANCE XV: Bérot; Andrieu, Mesnel, Charvet, Hontas; Lescure, Sanz (*capt*); Ondarts, Bouet, Garuet, Devergie, Condom, Carminati, Roumat, Cecillon *Replacement* Weller for Hontas
Scorers *Tries:* Bérot (2), Sanz, Weller   *Conversions:* Bérot (2)   *Penalty Goal:* Bérot
Referee K H Lawrence (Bay of Plenty)

MATCH 7   27 June, Rotorua

Bay of Plenty 18 (1G 4PG)   France XV 22 (2G 2PG 1T)
Bay of Plenty: W Jones; P G Woods, D M Shelford, S C Miln, B W Smith; K Irihei, J Tauiwi; W Morehu, J W Ranui (*capt*), A D M McLean, D T Martin, A Connal, R K O'Brien, D J Oswald, S van der Leeden *Replacements* N Haronga for Oswald; R Peacock for van der Leeden
Scorers *Try:* Shelford   *Conversion:* Irihei   *Penalty Goals:* Irihei (4)
FRANCE XV: Lescure; Weller, Lagisquet, Charvet, Lafond; Mesnel, Sanz (*capt*); Pujolle, Chabowski, Gallard, Beraud, Erbani, Benetton, Tordo, Roumat
Scorers *Tries:* Mesnel (2), Sanz   *Conversions:* Lescure, Lafond
Penalty Goals: Lafond, Lescure
Referee I A Blackmore (North Auckland)

MATCH 8   1 July, Eden Park, Auckland   2nd Test

NEW ZEALAND 34 (3G 4PG 1T)   FRANCE 20 (4PG 2T)

In the first Test, France had managed to recover shortly after half-time to within a point of New Zealand. Here, at the same stage, they actually took a one-point lead. The end result, though, was the same as New Zealand recorded their highest number of points in a Test against France since 1906, clinching the series 2-0. Blanco, who had scored two

40

tries in the first Test, was again the dominant figure, but in a different role. His four penalties as replacement kicker for Bérot, plus his hand in a breakaway try by Rouge-Thomas and another by Cecillon, accounted for the French points. By the 58th minute they led 20-19, New Zealand having scored tries through Alan Whetton and Stanley in the first 25 minutes. Fox converted one and kicked three penalties.

Typically, New Zealand dominated the final quarter. Fox regained the lead with a penalty, and both Deans and Fitzpatrick scored tries against a French defence with an ear on the final whistle. Fox added another conversion. The New Zealand front five, as usual, were able to last the pace better in the final quarter.

NEW ZEALAND: J A Gallagher (Wellington); J J Kirwan (Auckland), J T Stanley (Auckland), N J Schuster (Wellington), T J Wright (Auckland); G J Fox (Auckland), I B Deans (Canterbury); S C McDowell (Bay of Plenty), S B T Fitzpatrick (Auckland), R W Loe (Waikato), M J Pierce (Wellington), G W Whetton (Auckland), A J Whetton (Auckland), M N Jones (Auckland), W T Shelford (North Harbour) (*capt*)
Scorers *Tries:* A Whetton, Stanley, Deans, Fitzpatrick *Conversions:* Fox (3)
Penalty Goals: Fox (4)
FRANCE: Blanco, Bérot, Sella, Andrieu, Lagisquet; Rouge-Thomas, Berbizier (*capt*); Ondarts, Bouet, Garuet, Devergie, Condom, Cecillon, Carminati, Rodriguez
Scorers *Tries:* Rouge-Thomas, Cecillon *Penalty Goals:* Blanco (4)
Referee F A Howard (England)

SCOTLAND TO JAPAN 1989

Scotland's 91-8 victory over Kanto in the opening match of their tour to Japan was deceptively easy. The flowing form of that day was later reproduced only in patches – most notably in the first half of the Osaka game against their hosts' national Under-23 team – and in the final match, the Test in Tokyo, the Scots stumbled to defeat. The margin was close enough at 28-24, but Japan had the satisfaction of scoring five tries to one. It was a startling result, and though the Scots toured without their nine Lions they had no excuse in defeat.

Despite their five tries, all excellent in execution, the home team based their win on negative rugby that cannot have helped to better the game in Japan. They set out to kill ball on the ground, and they succeeded only because the Scots could not exact the deserved penalties. Cameron Glasgow missed five kicks at goal before Greig Oliver had to take over. An early cushion of nine or 12 points would have given the Scottish forwards the urge to keep going in Tokyo's heat. Instead, they mainly lagged, although the two flankers, Derek Turnbull and Graham Marshall, could be excused criticism. They at least kept their pace. The Scots found it too much to come back from a deficit of 6-20 at the interval, although Douglas Wyllie's late dropped goal raised hopes in the last few minutes.

Marshall was one of the more notable successes of the venture, playing as open-side flanker in two of his four games, although he had been chosen for the tour as a No 8. Another of the flankers, Adam

41

Buchanan-Smith, enhanced his reputation in spite of being kept out of the Test team by Marshall and Turnbull.

Wilson and Wright, the young Boroughmuir props, emerged from the tour with credit, although only the former played in the Test, keeping his club colleague out of the tight-head berth. Theirs was a healthy rivalry for Scottish rugby. Another of the youngsters, Hawick wing Tony Stanger, who celebrated his 21st birthday on tour, had two good games, one on each wing, and scored three tries. By switching over to the unaccustomed left wing against Kansai he indicated that his future, even in international rugby, need not be confined to one flank.

THE TOURING PARTY

Manager R D S Munro **Coach** J R Dixon
Assistant coach D I Johnston **Captain** A K Brewster

FULL-BACKS

I C Glasgow (Cambridge U)
I J Ramsey (Melrose)

THREEQUARTERS

M D F Duncan (West of Scotland)
A G Stanger (Hawick)
I Tukalo (Selkirk)
B Edwards (Boroughmuir)
S R P Lineen (Boroughmuir)
R R W Maclean (Gloucester)

HALF-BACKS

D S Wyllie (Stewart's-Melville FP)
M Walker (Boroughmuir)
S Jardine (South Glamorgan Institute)
G H Oliver (Hawick)

FORWARDS

A K Brewster (Stewart's-Melville FP)
D F Milne (Heriot's FP)
G D Wilson (Boroughmuir)
P H Wright (Boroughmuir)
I Corcoran (Gala)
J A Hay (Hawick)
D F Cronin (Bath)
C A Gray (Nottingham)
D S Munro (Glasgow High/Kelvinside)
G A E Buchanan-Smith (London Scottish)
D J Turnbull (Hawick)
R I Wainwright (Cambridge U)
G R Marshall (Selkirk)
I A M Paxton (Selkirk)

TOUR RECORD

All matches Played 5 Won 4 Lost 1 Points for 250 Against 73

SCORING DETAILS

All matches

For:	37T	30C	13PG	1DG	250 Pts
Against:	10T	3C	9PG		73 Pts

MATCH DETAILS

1989	OPPONENTS	VENUE	RESULT
14 May	Kanto (East Japan)	Tokyo	W 91-8
17 May	Kyushu	Fukuoka	W 45-0
21 May	Japan Under-23	Osaka	W 51-25
24 May	Kansai (West Japan)	Nagoya	W 39-12
28 May	JAPAN	Tokyo	L 24-28

Scorers: 66 – Glasgow (3T 21C 4PG); 24 – Duncan (6T), Tukalo (6T); 22 – Ramsey (5C 4PG); 17 – Oliver (1C 5PG); 12 – Stanger (3T), Maclean (3T), Gray (3T); 10 – Walker (1T 3C); 8 – Buchanan-Smith (2T), Wainwright (2T); 7 – Wyllie (1T 1DG); 4 – Edwards (1T), Lineen (1T), Brewster (1T), Corcoran (1T), Hay (1T), Paxton (1T), Turnbull (1T)
Appearances: 5 – Maclean (inc 1 as replacement); 4 – Duncan, Tukalo, Lineen, Oliver (inc 1

*as replacement), Brewster, Cronin, Gray, Marshall (inc 1 as replacement), Paxton;
3 – Glasgow, Wyllie, Wilson, Hay, Buchanan-Smith, Turnbull; 2 – Ramsey, Stanger,
Edwards, Walker, Jardine, Wright, Corcoran, Munro, Wainwright; 1 – Milne*

MATCH 1   14 May, Tokyo

Kanto 8 (2T)   **Scotland XV 91** (14G 1PG 1T)
Kanto: *Tries:* K Imaizumi (2)
Scotland XV: Glasgow; Duncan, Edwards, Lineen, Tukalo; Wyllie, Oliver; Brewster
(*capt*), Hay, Wright, Gray, Munro, Marshall, Turnbull, Paxton *Replacement* Maclean
for Duncan
Scorers *Tries:* Tukalo (4), Glasgow (2), Duncan (2), Maclean (2), Edwards, Wyllie,
Brewster, Gray, Paxton   *Conversions:* Glasgow (14)   *Penalty Goal:* Glasgow

MATCH 2   17 May, Fukuoka

Kyushu 0   Scotland XV 45 (5G 1PG 3T)
Scotland XV: Ramsey; Stanger, Maclean, Lineen, Tukalo; Walker, Jardine; Milne,
Corcoran, Wilson, Gray, Cronin, Buchanan-Smith, Wainwright, Paxton (*capt*)
Replacements Oliver for Jardine; Marshall for Wainwright
Scorers *Tries:* Stanger (2), Wainwright (2), Tukalo, Maclean, Walker, Gray
Conversions: Ramsey (3), Walker (2)   *Penalty Goal:* Ramsey

MATCH 3   21 May, Osaka

Japan Under-23 25 (2G 3PG 1T)   **Scotland XV 51** (7G 3PG)
Japan Under-23 *Tries:* H Ouchi (2), S Ochiai   *Conversions:* T Maeda (2)
Penalty Goals: T Maeda (3)
Scotland XV: Glasgow; Duncan, Maclean, Lineen, Tukalo; Wyllie, Oliver; Brewster
(*capt*), Hay, Wright, Gray, Cronin, Buchanan-Smith, Turnbull, Paxton
Scorers *Tries:* Duncan (2), Glasgow, Tukalo, Lineen, Gray, Turnbull
Conversions: Glasgow (7)   *Penalty Goals:* Glasgow (3)

MATCH 4   24 May, Nagoya

Kansai 12 (4PG)   **Scotland XV 39** (3G 3PG 3T)
Kansai: *Penalty Goals:* T Maeda (4)
Scotland XV: Ramsey; Duncan, Edwards, Maclean, Stanger; Walker, Jardine;
Brewster (*capt*), Corcoran, Wilson, Cronin, Munro, Buchanan-Smith, Wainwright,
Marshall
Scorers *Tries:* Duncan (2), Buchanan-Smith (2), Stanger, Corcoran
Conversions: Ramsey (2), Walker   *Penalty Goals:* Ramsey (3)

MATCH 5   28 May, Tokyo

JAPAN 28 (1G 2PG 4T)   **SCOTLAND 24** (1G 5PG 1DG)
JAPAN: T Yamamoto; T Nofomuli, A Kutsuki, S Hirao (*capt*), Y Yoshida; S Aoki,
M Horikoshi; O Ota, T Fujita, S Takara, T Hayashi, A Oyagi, H Kajiwara,
S Nakashima, S Latu
Scorers *Tries:* Yamamoto, Nofomuli, Kutsuki, Yoshida, Hayashi
Conversion: Yamamoto   *Penalty Goals:* Yamamoto (2)
SCOTLAND: Glasgow; Duncan, Maclean, Lineen, Tukalo; Wyllie, Oliver;
Brewster (*capt*), Hay, Wilson, Gray, Cronin, Marshall, Turnbull, Paxton
Scorers *Try:* Hay   *Conversion:* Oliver   *Penalty Goals:* Oliver (5)   *Dropped Goal:* Wyllie
Referee L J Peard (Wales)

FIJI TO FRANCE AND ENGLAND 1989

This was a tour of majestic rugby and occasional abject defeat, of the
highest rugby skills and rank indiscipline. In fact, it was just another

few weeks in the life of rugby in Fiji – whenever did the Fijian touring cocktail not contain the excesses and the excellence?

The tourists were heavily defeated in the Tests against Scotland and England and in the latter match lost discipline and two players to the early bath. Yet in both games, and especially in a wonderful win over a powerful French Barbarians team packed full of leading players, they showed those striking, fleeting skills in all parts of the team. They also came back from a 3-25 deficit to draw with a Côte Basque XV in Bayonne, and outscored England B by four tries to one in a 20-12 victory at Headingley.

THE TOURING PARTY

Captain E Teleni   **Coach** S N Viriviri
Assistant Coach D Robertson   **Manager** S B Seruvakula
Assistant Manager P Waqanicakau

FULL-BACKS	FORWARDS
S **Koroduadua** (Police, Suva)	S **Naiviliwasa** (Police, Suva)
I R **Damu** (Auckland, New Zealand)	I **Torosi** (Army, Suva)
THREEQUARTERS	M **Taga** (QVSOB, Suva)
M **Naituilagilagi** (Army, Suva)	S **Naituku** (Lomaiviti Suva)
L **Eranavula** (Hyatt, Nadroga)	M **Rasari** (Army, Suva)
T **Lovo** (QVSOB, Suva)	I **Savai** (QVSOB, Suva)
T **Vonolagi** (Army, Suva)	T **Wainiqolo** (Baravi, Bua)
J V **Damu** (Auckland, New Zealand)	P **Naruma** (Police, Suva)
I **Waqavatu** (Army, Suva)	M **Qoro** (Nawaka, Nadi)
N **Nadruku** (Hyatt, Nadroga)	A **Dere** (Army, Suva)
HALF-BACKS	M G **Olsson** (PAF, Suva)
	E **Teleni** (Army, Suva)
W **Serevi** (Nasinu, Rewa)	N **Matirawa** (Army, Suva)
M S **Seavula** (Hyatt, Nadroga)	I **Naituku** (Navy, Rewa)
L **Vasuvulagi** (Baravi, Nadroga)	S **Vodo Sadria** (Army, Suva)

TOUR RECORD

All matches   Played 8   Won 3   Drawn 1   Lost 4   Points for 183   Against 215
International matches   Played 2   Lost 2   Points for 40   Against 96

SCORING DETAILS

All matches
For: 28T 16C 12PG 1DG 183Pts
Against: 31T 20C 16PG 1DG 215Pts

International matches
For: 6T 2C 4PG 40Pts
Against: 16T 10C 4PG 96Pts

MATCH DETAILS

1989	OPPONENTS	VENUE	RESULT
11 Oct	French Selection	Nîmes	W 40-26
14 Oct	French Selection	Bergerac	L 15-18
17 Oct	Côte Basque	Bayonne	D 25-25
22 Oct	French Barbarians	Bordeaux	W 32-16
24 Oct	Glasgow	Glasgow	L 11-22
28 Oct	SCOTLAND	Murrayfield	L 17-38
31 Oct	England B	Leeds	W 20-12
4 Nov	ENGLAND	Twickenham	L 23-58

MATCH 1   11 October, Nîmes

French Selection 26 (2G 2PG 2T)   **Fijians 40** (5G 1PG 1DG 1T)
French Selection *Tries:* Piazza, Cecillon, Guirand, Andrieu
Conversions: Vacheron (2)   *Penalty Goals:* Vacheron (2)
Fijian XV *Tries:* Nadruku (2), Savai, Vonolagi, Eranavula, Rasari
Conversions: Serevi (4), Vonolagi   *Penalty Goal:* Vonolagi   *Dropped Goal:* Vonolagi

MATCH 2   14 October, Bergerac

French Selection 18 (6PG)   **Fijians 15** (1G 3PG)
French Selection *Penalty Goals:* Labit (6)
Fijians *Try:* Naituku   *Conversion:* Koroduadua   *Penalty Goals:* Koroduadua (3)

MATCH 3   17 October, Bayonne

Côte Basque 25 (3G 1PG 1T)   **Fijians 25** (2G 3PG 1T)
Côte Basque *Tries:* Ravier, Visensang, Dal Maso, Pucheu   *Conversions:* Lacroix (3)
Penalty Goal: Lacroix
Fijian XV *Tries:* Nadruku, Natuilagilagi, S Naituku   *Conversions:* Koroduadua (2)
Penalty Goals: Koroduadua (3)

MATCH 4   22 October, Bordeaux

French Barbarians 16 (1G 1PG 1DG 1T)   **Fijians 32** (4G 2T)
French Barbarians H P MacNeill (London Irish & Ireland); B Lacombe
(Agen & France), P Sella (Agen & France), D Charvet (Stade Toulousain & France),
E Bonneval (Stade Toulousain & France); H E Botha (Rovigo, Northern Transvaal &
South Africa), P Berbizier (Agen & France) *(capt)*; J-L Tolot (Agen & France),
V Moscato (Bègles-Bordeaux), C Portolan (Stade Toulousain & France), J-M Cadieu
(Stade Toulousain), A Ravier (Bayonne), P J Winterbottom (Harlequins & England),
T Maset (Stade Toulousain), D Erbani (Agen & France) *Replacement* J-M Rancoule
(Stade Toulousain) for Lacombe
Scorers *Tries:* Lacombe, Winterbottom   *Conversion:* Botha   *Penalty Goal:* Botha
Dropped Goal: Botha
Fijian XV: Koroduadua; Erenavula, Naituilagilagi, Nadruku, Waqavatu; Serevi,
Vasuwulagi; S Naituku, Naiviliwasa, Taga, Savai, Rasari, Dere, Teleni *(capt)*, Naruma
Scorers *Tries:* Teleni (2), Serevi, Waqavatu, Savai, Naituilagilagi
Conversions: Koroduadua (3), Serevi
Referee C Norling (Wales)

MATCH 5   25 October, Glasgow

Glasgow 22 (3G 1T)   **Fijian XV 11** (1PG 2T)
Glasgow: D N Barrett (West of Scotland); M D F Duncan (West of Scotland),
I C Jardine (Stirling County), S W McAslan (Glasgow Acads) *(capt)*, D A Stark (Ayr);
G Breckenridge (Glasgow High/Kelvinside), E D McCorkindale
(Glasgow High/Kelvinside); G Graham (Stirling County), K D McKenzie
(Stirling County), G B Robertson (Stirling County), D S Munro
(Glasgow High/Kelvinside), A G J Watt (Glasgow High/Kelvinside), I D Busby
(Glasgow High/Kelvinside), F D Wallace (Glasgow High/Kelvinside), D A McVey (Ayr)
Replacement D R McKee (West of Scotland) for Duncan
Scorers *Tries:* Watt, McKenzie, Stark, Jardine   *Conversions:* Barrett (3)
Fijian XV: I R Damu; Eranavula, Vonolagi, Naituilagilagi, J V Damu; Serevi, Seavula;
Vodo Sadria, Naiviliwasa, S Naituku, Savai, Wainiqolo, Naruma, Qoro, Teleni *(capt)*
Replacements Matirawa for Qoro; Vasuvulagi for J V Damu; Taga for Vodo Sadria
Scorers *Tries:* Seavula, Wainiqolo   *Penalty Goal:* Serevi
Referee S V Griffith (Solihull)

MATCH 6   28 October, Murrayfield   1st Test

SCOTLAND 38 (4G 2PG 2T)   FIJI 17 (3PG 2T)

Scotland, thanks to outstanding individual performances from Gavin Hastings, Sole and Stanger, were able to render the visitors relatively harmless until late on, when they scored two tries. Hastings contributed 18 points, Sole was the outstanding forward while Stanger scored two tries on his debut. Scotland controlled 90 per cent of the match, making tactical adjustments to their game after a poor start. Fiji, by contrast, offered their inventiveness and athleticism, but without the ball they were unwilling to submit to basics. Two forwards, though, were always in the thick of the action – the prop Sairusi Naituku and Rasari, the lock and sevens expert.

SCOTLAND: A G Hastings (London Scottish); A G Stanger (Hawick), S Hastings (Watsonians), S R P Lineen (Boroughmuir), I Tukalo (Selkirk); C M Chalmers (Melrose), G Armstrong (Jedforest); D M B Sole (Edinburgh Acads) (*capt*), K S Milne (Heriot's FP), A P Burnell (London Scottish), C A Gray (Nottingham), D F Cronin (Bath), J Jeffrey (Kelso), G R Marshall (Selkirk); D B White (London Scottish)
Replacement G A E Buchanan-Smith (London Scottish) for Marshall
Scorers *Tries:* Stanger (2), Milne, Gray, A G Hastings, Tukalo
Conversions: A G Hastings (4)   *Penalty Goals:* A G Hastings (2)
FIJI: Koroduadua; Lovo, Eranavula, Nadruku, Waqavatu; Serevi, Vasuwulagi; Taga, Naiviliwasa, S Naituku, Savai, Rasari, Naruma, Dere, Teleni (*capt*)
Scorers *Tries:* Lovo, Rasari   *Penalty Goals:* Koroduadua, Serevi (2)
Referee P Robin (France)

MATCH 7   31 October, Headingley RFC, Leeds

England B 12 (1G 2PG)   **Fijians 20** (2G 2T)
England B: S Pilgrim (Wasps); A Underwood (Leicester), S Irving (Headingley), F Clough (Wasps), E Davis (Harlequins); P Hull (Bristol), C D Morris (Liverpool St Helens); J Leonard (Saracens), K Dunn (Gloucester), J A Probyn (Wasps), S T O'Leary (Wasps), R Kimmins (Orrell), P Tayler (Rosslyn Park), D Thresher (Harlequins), D Pegler (Wasps) (*capt*)
Scorers *Try:* penalty try   *Conversion:* Pilgrim   *Penalty Goals:* Pilgrim (2)
Fijian XV Naituilagilagi; Waqavatu, Lovo, Eranavula, Nadruku; Koroduadua, Seavula; Taga, Naiviliwasa, I Naituku, Savai, Rasari, Dere, Matirawa, Teleni (*capt*)
Scorers *Tries:* Seavula, Eranavula, Nadruku, Waqavatu   *Conversions:* Koroduadua (2)
Referee R Clark (Scotland)

MATCH 8   4 November, Twickenham   2nd Test

ENGLAND 58 (6G 2PG 4T)   FIJI 23 (2G 1PG 2T)

Although 14 tries were scored the game suffered from an unpleasant undercurrent which culminated in two sendings-off in the second half. Referee Brian Stirling was forced to dismiss Fijian threequarters Tevita Vonolagi and Noa Nadruku for reckless tackles in spite of repeated warnings.

On the credit side, Rory Underwood's five tries equalled the English record set by Daniel Lambert in 1907, and in this his 34th international, the Leicester wing equalled Cyril Lowe's England record of 18 tries. He made Vonolagi's life a misery. The basis of the England win was the control of the forwards, which allowed Hill and Andrew the time to dictate tactics behind the scrum. The first ten minutes of each half were crucial – Underwood scored his first two tries in the opening salvo, and after the break a collection of tries from Skinner, Bailey, Linnett and Underwood again consigned the tourists to rare but spectacular counter-attacks.

ENGLAND: S D Hodgkinson (Nottingham); R Underwood (RAF & Leicester), J C Guscott (Bath), W D C Carling (Harlequins) (*capt*), M D Bailey (Wasps); C R Andrew (Wasps), R J Hill (Bath); M S Linnett (Moseley), B C Moore (Nottingham), A R Mullins (Harlequins), W A Dooley (Preston Grasshoppers), P J Ackford (Harlequins), M G Skinner (Harlequins), P J Winterbottom (Harlequins), D W Egerton (Bath)
Replacements G W Rees (Nottingham) for Winterbottom; S J Halliday (Bath) for Bailey
Scorers *Tries:* Underwood (5), Skinner, Bailey, Linnett, Ackford, Guscott
Conversions: Hodgkinson (5), Andrew   *Penalty Goals:* Hodgkinson (2)
FIJI: Naituilagilagi; Lovo, Eranavula, Nadruku, Vonolagi; Koroduadua, Vasuwulagi; Taga, Naiviliwasa, S Naituku, Savai, Rasari, Matirawa, Dere, Teleni (*capt*)
Scorers *Tries:* Eranavula, Teleni, Rasari, Savai   *Conversions:* Koroduadua (2)
Penalty Goal: Koroduadua
Referee B W Stirling (Ireland)

SOVIET UNION TO ENGLAND 1989

Despite the encouraging form shown lately in the FIRA Championship – in which they have finished runners-up to France – and in recent wins against Italy and Romania, the Soviet Union failed to win any of their matches in a five-game tour just before Christmas 1989. Yet there were signs towards the end of their visit that lessons had been digested. Many of their faults lay in naïveté, which was mainly due to their lack of contact with the rest of the rugby-playing world. Fitness and enthusiasm abounded however, and although their points total was 54 to 94 against, there was only a 10-8 deficit in tries scored.

The Soviets provided several players of genuine quality. The form of Mironov and Tikhonov gained them selection for the Barbarians Easter tour and for the European XV which played the Four Home Unions at Twickenham in April to raise funds for Romania. Malchanov and Bakuradze in the front row were unusually quick about the field, and full-back Dzagnidze impressed. Segeev was an excellent lock. The tourists needed more rugby acumen, and that may arrive with greater exposure to the world scene. Nonetheless, they thrilled the capacity crowd at Northampton in the tour climax against England B. Suddenly, there was a much-needed injection of confidence and pace and the Soviets, adrift at half-time, went on to score two excellent tries.

TOUR RECORD
Played 5   Won 0   Drew 1   Points for 54   Against 94

SCORING DETAILS
All matches
For: 8T 5C 4PG 54 Pts
Against: 10T 9C 11PG 1DG 94 Pts

MATCH DETAILS

1989	OPPONENTS	VENUE	RESULT
9 Dec	Cornwall	Redruth	D 12-12
13 Dec	Combined Services	Aldershot	L 3-18
16 Dec	England Students	Stourbridge	L 15-16
20 Dec	North Division	Aspatria	L 14-30
23 Dec	England B	Northampton	L 10-18

Points scorers: 18 – Dzagnidze; 12 – Tikhonov, Mironov; 4 – Plotnikov, Malchanov, Zuev

THE TOURING PARTY
Captain I Mironov   **Manager** G A Mironov   **Assistant manager** V Grachev
Coaches D Kavtalashvilli, V Masivra

FULL-BACKS	FORWARDS
N Dzagnidze (AIA Kutaisi)	S Molchanov (Slava Moscow)

THREEQUARTERS
I Kuperman (ATS Krasnoiarsk)
M Parshin (Slava Moscow)
I Necheaev (Gagarin Academy)
E Zuev (AIA Kutaisi)
V Kanna (Aviator Kiev)
V Varapaev (Gagarin Academy)

FORWARDS
S Molchanov (Slava Moscow)
R Malakov (Lokomotiv Moscow)
I Khokhlovskairvlin (SKA Alma Ata)
A Mishakov (Fini Moscow)
S Sergeev (Fini Moscow)
R Khairulin (Gagarin Academy)
A Sokolov (Lokomotiv Moscow)
N Plotnikov (Lokomotiv Moscow)
V Negodin (ATS Krasnoiarsk)
E Koroliov (Aviator Kiev)
Z Bakuradze (Almavili Tbilisi)
A Malinin (ATS Krasnoiarsk)
A Tikhonov (Gagarin Academy)

HALF-BACKS
I Mironov (Gagarin Academy)
M Lozabezidze (AIA Kutaisi)
I Frantzuzov (Gagarin Academy)

MATCH 1   9 December, Redruth
Cornwall 12 (3PG 1DG)   **Soviet Union 12** (1G 2PG)
Cornwall: *Penalty Goals:* Chapman (2), Rule   *Dropped Goal:* Chapman
Soviet Union: *Try:* Tikhonov   *Conversion:* Mironov   *Penalty Goals:* Mironov (2)

MATCH 2   13 December, Aldershot
Combined Services 18 (2G 2PG)   **Soviet Union 3** (1PG)
Combined Services: *Tries:* Graham, penalty try   *Conversions:* Hull (2)
Penalty Goals: Hull (2)
Soviet Union: *Penalty Goal:* Dzagnidze

MATCH 3   16 December, Stourbridge
England Students 16 (1G 2PG 1T)   **Soviet Union 15** (2G 1PG)
England Students *Tries:* De Glanville, Moon   *Conversion:* Strett
Penalty Goals: Strett (2)
Soviet Union: *Tries:* Plotnikov, Tikhonov   *Conversions:* Dzagnidze

MATCH 4   20 December, Aspatria
North Division 30 (4G 2PG)   **Soviet Union 14** (1G 2T)
North Division *Tries:* Heslop (2), Hunter, Kimmins   *Conversions:* Strett (4)
Penalty Goals: Strett (2)
Soviet Union *Tries:* Dzagnidze, Mironov   *Conversion:* Dzagnidze (2)

MATCH 5   23 December, Northampton

England B 18 (2G 2PG)   **Soviet Union 10** (1G 1T)
England B: S Langford (Orrell); F Packman (Northampton), F Clough (Wasps),
J R D Buckton (Saracens), E Davis (Harlequins); D Pears (Harlequins), S M Bates
(Wasps); M S Linnett (Moseley), J Olver (Harlequins), A R Mullins (Harlequins),
D Baldwin (Sale), J Etheridge (Gloucester), M G Skinner (Harlequins), M C Teague
(Gloucester), D Pegler (Wasps) (*capt*)
Scorers *Tries:* Clough (2)   *Conversions:* Pears (2)   *Penalty Goals:* Pears (2)
Soviet Union: Dzagnidze; Zuev, Parshin, Necheaev, Kuperman; Mironov (*capt*),
Frantzuzov; Bakuradze, Malakov, Molchanov, Sergeev, Plotnikov, Sokolov, Negolin,
Tikhonov
Scorers *Tries:* Molchanov, Zuev   *Conversion:* Dzagnidze
Referee D Leslie (Scotland)

WALES B TO CANADA 1989

Graham Clutton *Western Mail*

This tour was given B status even though the Welsh party took a strong
squad. Apart from a few unavailabilities and the absence of those
Welshmen picked for the 1989 Lions party, it was a powerful selection.

Although coach John Ryan later resigned after poor results in the
1990 Championship this was a reasonably successful tour, the only
blemish on the record being a 21-21 draw against British Columbia, by a
league the strongest province in Canada. Yet again, refereeing inter-
pretations were found to differ and there was a sour note when Mark
Jones, the Wales B No 8, was sent off in the 'test' against Rugby
Canada.

THE TOURING PARTY

Captain P H Thorburn   **Manager** D M Lloyd
Coach J Ryan   **Assistant Coach** S Addicot

FULL-BACK	FORWARDS
P H Thorburn (Neath)	**R L Evans** (Llanelli)
THREEQUARTERS	**L Delaney** (Llanelli)
S P Ford (Cardiff)	**I J Watkins** (Ebbw Vale)
D B Griffiths (Newport)	**S T Jones** (Pontypool)
A Emyr (Swansea)	**P John** (Pontypridd)
D W Evans (Cardiff)	**A J Sutton** (Newbridge)
M G Ring (Cardiff)	**G O Llewellyn** (Neath)
C J Jones (Pontypridd)	**I W Jones** (Llanelli)
C Laity (Neath)	**H Williams-Jones** (South Wales Police)
HALF-BACKS	**D J Bryant** (Pontypridd)
C J Stephens (Llanelli)	**D Hopkins** (Pontypridd)
P D Turner (Newbridge)	**M A Jones** (Neath)
C Bridges (Neath)	**M Budd** (Bridgend)
K Ellis (Bridgend)	**J D M Wakeford** (South Wales Police)

TOUR RECORD

All matches Played 6 Won 5 Drawn 1 Points for 245 Against 76
International match Played 1 Won 1 Points for 31 Against 29

SCORING DETAILS

All matches

For: 45T 16C 11PG   245 Pts
Against: 12T 5C 5PG 1DG 76 Pts

International match

For: 5T 4C 1PG 31 Pts
Against: 5T 3C 1DG 29 Pts

MATCH DETAILS

1989	OPPONENTS	VENUE	RESULT
24 May	Nova Scotia President's XV	Halifax	W 70-3
27 May	Ontario	Toronto	W 23-10
31 May	Saskatchewan	Regina	W 47-0
3 June	RUGBY CANADA	Edmonton	W 31-29
6 June	Alberta	Calgary	W 53-13
9 June	British Columbia	Vancouver	D 21-21

Leading points-scorers: 60 – Thorburn (2T 14C 8PG); 48 – Ford (12T); 32 – A Emyr (8T). Bryant, M Jones, Ring and Laity all scored three tries while Ford scored seven in the match against Saskatchewan.

MATCH 1 24 May, The Commons, Halifax

Nova Scotia President's XV 3 (1PG) **Wales B 70** (5G 10T)
Nova Scotia *Penalty Goal:* Starkey
Wales B *Tries:* Ford (3), M A Jones (3), Ring (2), Emyr (2), Stephens, Bridges, Budd, Thorburn, penalty try *Conversions:* Stephens, Thorburn (4)

MATCH 2 27 May, Etobicoke Centennial Stadium, Toronto

Ontario 10 (2PG 1T) **Wales B 23** (1G 3PG 2T)
Ontario *Try:* Stea *Penalty Goals:* D Lougheed (2)
Wales B *Tries:* Emyr (2), Bryant *Conversion:* Turner *Penalty Goals:* Turner (3)

MATCH 3 31 May, Regina

Saskatchewan XV 0 Wales B 47 (1PG 11T)
Wales B *Tries:* Ford (7), Emyr, Ellis, Laity, D Evans *Penalty Goal:* Thorburn

MATCH 4 3 June, Ellerslie Park, Edmonton

RUGBY CANADA 29 (3G 1DG 2T) **WALES B 31** (4G 1PG 1T)
RUGBY CANADA *(British Columbia unless stated):* S Stewart; P Palmer, S Brown, D Speranza, S Gray; G Rees, C Tynan; E Evans, D Spiers, P Szabo, A Charron (Ontario), N Hadley, G Mackinnon, R Radu *(capt)*, G Ennis *Replacements* M Tuppa for Mackinnon; B Ross for Speranza
Scorers *Tries:* Szabo (2), Spiers, Mackinnon, Tynan *Conversions:* Rees (3)
Dropped Goal: Rees
WALES B: Thorburn *(capt)*; Ford, C J Jones, D W Evans, Emyr; Stephens, Bridges; S T Jones, Watkins, Delaney, Wakeford, Llewellyn, Budd, M A Jones, Bryant
Scorers *Tries:* Stephens, Ford, Emyr, Thorburn, C J Jones *Conversions:* Thorburn (4)
Penalty Goal: Thorburn
Referee D Reordon (USA)

MATCH 5 6 June, Ontario RFC, Calgary

Alberta 13 (1G 1PG 1T) **Wales B 53** (5G 1PG 5T)
Alberta *Tries:* Patel, Coote *Conversion:* Loshuk *Penalty Goal:* Loshuk

Wales B *Tries:* Ellis (3), Laity (2), Emyr (2), Bryant (2), Ring   *Conversions:* Thorburn (5)
Penalty Goal: Thorburn

MATCH 6   9 June, Brockton Oval, Vancouver

British Columbia 21 (1G 1PG 3T)   **Wales B 21** (1G 5PG)
British Columbia *Tries:* McKay, Tuppa, Evans, Wannamaker   *Conversion:* Graf
Penalty Goal: Rees
Wales B *Try:* Ford   *Conversion:* Thorburn   *Penalty Goals:* Thorburn (5)

OTHER TOURS

Argentina to New Zealand 1989
2 Jul: North Auckland 16, Argentinian XV 22 (Whangerei) **5 Jul:** King Country 4,
Argentinian XV 9 (Taupo) **8 Jul:** Auckland 61, Argentinian XV 6 (Auckland) **11 Jul:**
Wairarapa Bush 4, Argentinian XV 22 (Masterton) **15 Jul:** NEW ZEALAND 60,
ARGENTINA 9 (first Test, Dunedin) **19 Jul:** Hanan Shield XV 6, Argentinian XV 17
(Timaru) **22 Jul:** Canterbury 33, Argentinian XV 16 (Canterbury) **25 Jul:** Waikato 30,
Argentinian XV 12 (Hamilton) **29 Jul:** (second Test, Wellington) NEW ZEALAND 49,
ARGENTINA 12

Western Samoa to Europe 1989
27 Sept: North-West Germany 0, Western Samoan XV 118 **30 Sept:** WEST GERMANY
9, WESTERN SAMOA 54 **3 Oct:** Belgium B 12, Western Samoan XV 38 **7 Oct:**
BELGIUM 8, WESTERN SAMOA 37 **11 Oct:** Romania B 15, Western Samoan XV 19
14 Oct: ROMANIA 32, WESTERN SAMOA 24 **25 Oct:** French Selection 48, Western
Samoan XV 20 **28 Oct:** French Selection 16, Western Samoan XV 15 **1 Nov:** French
Police 25, Western Samoan XV 35 **4 Nov:** Oxford University 19, Western Samoan XV 22
8 Nov: West Hartlepool 0, Western Samoan XV 10 **11 Nov:** Cambridge University 13,
Western Samoan XV 33

First National Bank (World XV) to South Africa 1989
19 Aug: Natal 20, FNB XV 33 (Durban) **22 Aug:** President's XV 36, FNB XV 13 (Port
Elizabeth) **26 Aug:** (first Test, Cape Town) SOUTH AFRICA 20, FNB 19 **29 Aug:**
Northern Transvaal 19, FNB XV 32 (Pretoria) **1 Sept:** (second Test, Johannesburg)
SOUTH AFRICA 22, FNB XV 16

Ireland to North America 1989
30 Aug: British Columbia 18, Ireland XV 21 (Vancouver) **2 Sept:** CANADA 21,
IRELAND XV 24 (Victoria) **6 Sept:** Mid-West (USA) 6, Ireland XV 58 (Chicago)
9 Sept: USA Eagles 7, Ireland XV 32 (New York)

SCOTLAND'S BARRIER TO ENGLAND GRAND SLAM GLORY

The International Championship 1990

By any standards it was a remarkable Championship season and one which ended in high drama. When Scotland and England met at Murrayfield the only tangible trophy – the Calcutta Cup – was at stake, but so were all the other titles: Grand Slam, Triple Crown and the Championship title itself. It was a match that caught the attention of the sporting world – the demand for tickets was incredible and the game was beamed live to many countries. The build-up was given even more spice by the fact that England's season to date had seen three memorable performances, and expectations were at an all-time high. If anything was to fire Scotland it was the arrival of a lauded, confident England side. As it turned out a stern, compelling match was well won by Scotland, whose combination of pragmatism and heroism was unstoppable on the day and for whom David Sole, the captain, played brilliantly.

It was Scotland's second Grand Slam inside six seasons but only their third ever. They were by no means in vintage form in their three previous games, which brought sketchy victories over Ireland and Wales and a more confident one over France. Yet saving the best till last they came through, and their back row of Calder, White and Jeffrey together with the competitiveness of Armstrong gave the side a sound heart. It was also a considerable triumph for Ian McGeechan, the coach. His expert guidance had seen off Australia on the Lions tour; now he completed a superb double with the Grand Slam.

Naturally, to miss out after such a dedicated and successful, even brilliant, campaign was a devastating experience for England. Their preparations were painstaking and interminable. For all their final failure, no one could deny that their victories over France in Paris and Wales at Twickenham, coming within a fortnight of each other, represented the high point of the Northern Hemisphere rugby season. In both these games there was forward play of high order; almost every forward was prominent in the loose play, running and handling happily. England also possessed the best line-out of the Championship. On that sound platform, England's backs produced some pyrotechnics – Underwood, Guscott and especially Carling often played with breathtaking brilliance and the revival of the Andrew/Hill partnership at half-back after an unpromising start some time ago was a resounding success.

The only check on praise for Scotland and England must be the almost complete lack of quality among the other three teams. It was another painful season for Wales, as severe administrative problems kicked off the season in the aftermath of the rebel tour. They lost at home to France when a win was desperately needed, they were thrashed by England at Twickenham and subsided to both Scotland and Ireland for their first-ever whitewash in the Championship. John Ryan, the coach, resigned after the Twickenham debacle, but the attempts of his successor, Ron Waldron, to bring in some fire and pace to the side only succeeded in reducing the power. Only Robert Jones and David Evans, the half-backs, and Phil Davies in the pack could really be exempted from criticism. It was the worst Welsh season imaginable.

Ireland limped on and saved themselves from a whitewash by beating Wales on the last day of Championship action. Yet it was still a sorry season, with the side unsettled in personnel and attitudes. Jim Davidson, the coach, duly left at the end of the season. No such luck for France. Jacques Fouroux remained their guiding influence even though a growing number of people in the country believe that his incoherent selection policy and his failure to bring feuding parties together for the national good should have heralded a change long ago. Yet after a season in which even France's class players played badly and in which France were crushed by Scotland and England, the Fouroux ship sailed on.

The final table was:

	P	W	D	L	F	A	Pts
Scotland	4	4	0	0	60	26	8
England	4	3	0	1	90	26	6
France	4	2	0	2	61	78	4
Ireland	4	1	0	3	36	75	2
Wales	4	0	0	4	42	84	0

A rare moment of sheer delight for Wales as Arthur Emyr, the scorer, and David Evans celebrate the try of the international season after a sweeping movement in the Cardiff match against Scotland.

20 January, Twickenham
ENGLAND 23 (2G 1PG 2T)   IRELAND 0

(The Save & Prosper International)

There were just a few signs of restlessness on the pitch and in the stands as England stuttered until late on in the match. They were up against one of the least formidable Irish teams in memory, but for a long time there was a lack of direction and finishing power. By the end, with three splendid England tries in the last eight minutes, all that was forgotten, and rightly so. When England found their feet they were irresistible, Carling and Guscott in the centre and Underwood on the wing showing electric form, and they were beautifully served by Hill at scrum-half, returning to the Championship to bring sorely needed craft and a snappy service from the base of the scrum. When Underwood stole into the corner for a typical try in the second half he became his country's leading try-scorer with 19. The old record of 18 by Cyril Lowe, set in 1913-23, was finally erased from the books.

Ireland were hampered by indecision at half-back where Russell, the new fly-half, was nervous and prone to error. They did win some possession, notably through Francis in the line-out, but overall they were hardly a threat. They had no scoring power to call on and anything less than a large English margin would have been a grave disappointment for the English.

The only England try-scorer in the first half was Probyn, backing up faithfully and seizing a loose ball to score. Yet the final burst brought some thrilling rugby. Egerton, replacing the injured Dean Richards at No 8, plunged over from short range after a series of England attacks in which they ran a succession of penalties. As Ireland were forced on to the back foot there was an extra yard of space for Carling and Guscott and they cashed in. Guscott carved out the space for Underwood's try with a break and superb high pass to his right, and Underwood's traditional strength as a finisher held off the cover in a thrilling chase. Shortly afterwards, a memorable run by Carling sent Guscott on the way to another try and England's Championship season was well and truly launched.

ENGLAND: S D Hodgkinson (Nottingham); R Underwood (RAF & Leicester), W D C Carling (Harlequins) *(capt)*, J C Guscott (Bath), M D Bailey (Wasps); C R Andrew (Wasps), R J Hill (Bath); P A G Rendall (Wasps), B C Moore (Nottingham), J A Probyn (Wasps), P J Ackford (Harlequins), W A Dooley (Preston Grasshoppers), M G Skinner (Harlequins), D W Egerton (Bath), P J Winterbottom (Harlequins)
Scorers *Tries:* Underwood, Probyn, Carling, Guscott   *Conversions:* Hodgkinson (2) *Penalty Goal:* Hodgkinson
IRELAND: K Murphy (Constitution); M J Kiernan (Dolphin), B J Mullin (Blackrock Coll), D G Irwin (Instonians), K D Crossan (Instonians); P Russell (Instonians), L F P Aherne (Lansdowne); D C Fitzgerald (Lansdowne), S J Smith (Ballymena), G Halpin (Wanderers), N P T Francis (Blackrock Coll), W A Anderson (Dungannon) *(capt)*, P M Matthews (Wanderers), N P Mannion (Corinthians), P T J O'Hara (Sunday's Well) *Replacement* J P MacDonald (Malone) for Smith
Referee P Robin (France)

20 January, Cardiff Arms Park
WALES 19 (4PG 1DG 1T)   **FRANCE 29** (3G 1PG 2T)

(Sponsored by UDT)

At the end of the first quarter Wales were level and beginning to find their feet. The forwards, especially, were gaining the upper hand and confidence began to flow. Then, a moment of madness on the part of Moseley, the Welsh lock, probably cost Wales the game. He was clearly seen, by referee Howard and most of the crowd, to stamp on Andrieu, the French back. He was sent off, and after that Wales struggled desperately. In some ways it was an encouraging Welsh performance, because they never caved in and the French were certain of their victory only when Rodriguez, taking advantage of a tiring two-man Welsh back row, scored a try from a five-yard scrum. Until then, there was splendid resistance from Thorburn, Evans and especially from skipper Robert Jones, and some storming forward play from Phil Davies. However, it was hardly a classy international and the French backs had an extra yard of pace.

Wales conceded an early try to Lafond, the French full-back deputising for the injured Blanco. There was a memorable Welsh try later in the first half when Robert Jones chipped cleverly down the right wing and Titley burst on to the ball to score. Yet there was no escape and no denying France. Camberabero scored early in the second half and both Sella and Lagisquet scored striking tries. Sella followed a high kick, snatched it almost out of the grasp of Thorburn as it came down and scored near the posts; later, Lagisquet scored a marvellous individual try when a chance of pace and a sprint to the corner found the Welsh defence completely outflanked and outpaced. Rodriguez made his charge to seal the game and all Wales could offer in the second half was a dropped goal and a penalty goal.

In retrospect the Moseley incident was even more crucial than it seemed at the time. The new-look Welsh team, with coach John Ryan still trying to establish himself, needed to buy time in order to find itself. This defeat put them under pressure and that pressure told at all points as the season wore on.

WALES: P H Thorburn (Neath); M H Titley (Swansea), M G Ring (Cardiff), M Hall (Cardiff), A Emyr (Swansea); D W Evans (Cardiff), R N Jones (Swansea) *(capt)*;
M Griffiths (Cardiff), K H Phillips (Neath), D Young (Cardiff), K Moseley (Pontypool), A G Allen (Newbridge), P T Davies (Llanelli), M A Jones (Neath), G Jones (Llanelli)
Replacement H Williams-Jones (South Wales Police) for Young
Scorers *Try:* Titley   *Penalty Goals:* Thorburn (4)   *Dropped Goal:* Evans
FRANCE: J-B Lafond (Racing Club de France); M Andrieu (Nîmes), P Sella (Agen), D Charvet (Toulouse), P Lagisquet (Bayonne); D Camberabero (Béziers), P Berbizier (Agen) *(capt)*; P Ondarts (Biarritz), L Armary (Lourdes), J-P Garuet (Lourdes), T Devergie (Nîmes), D Erbani (Agen), O Roumat (Dax), L Rodriguez (Dax) *(capt)*, E Champ (Toulon)
Scorers *Tries:* Lafond, Sella, Camberabero, Lagisquet, Rodriguez
Conversions: Camberabero (3)   *Penalty Goal:* Camberabero
Referee F Howard (England)

3 February, Parc des Princes
FRANCE 7 (1PG 1T)   ENGLAND 26 (1G 4PG 2T)

This was one of the greatest England performances in memory. Even allowing for the fact that France were directionless and muddled it was an outstanding win. To play in the Parc des Princes is always an ordeal, but such was England's dominance, not to mention the loud support of their travelling supporters, that they could easily have been playing at Twickenham. England's pack were on top in every phase, Moore standing out as hooker and pack leader and Dooley and Ackford dominant in the line-out. Above all, England played with supreme discipline and confidence and there was barely a single sustained period of French pressure in the whole match.

Another key to England's victory was the goal-kicking of Hodgkinson. It was a wicked day for kickers – a gale-force wind swirled all round the bowl of the stadium – yet Hodgkinson was able to give England an early 9-0 lead with three beautifully-struck kicks. This was vital in settling England and sapping French morale. Remarkably, England led 13-0 at half-time. Andrew dodged back towards the blindside after a line-out and chipped beautifully down to the French left-hand corner. Underwood, following up at pace, was able to shepherd the ball over the line for a classic try of its kind. Early in the second half it was all over. Charvet, the French centre, making a rare appearance, tried to chip over the top of the England midfield. But the ball cannoned off Carling, the England captain. Guscott was on to the ball in a flash, hacked it on, picked up a handy bounce and scored.

There was a French comeback of sorts when Charvet managed a penalty and Lagisquet, one of very few Frenchmen to find his true form, scored a try down the French left. However, a storming England attack, which as usual involved some strong running by the forwards, made some space for Andrew. He veered back towards the right, picked himself up after being tripped by a French forward and fed Carling. England's captain checked slightly, then left Blanco for dead with an outside break and a try.

FRANCE: S Blanco (Biarritz); M Andrieu (Nîmes), P Sella (Agen), D Charvet (Toulouse), P Lagisquet (Bayonne); F Mesnel (Racing Club de France), P Berbizier (Agen) (*capt*); P Ondarts (Biarritz), L Armary (Lourdes), J-P Garuet (Lourdes), T Devergie (Nîmes), D Erbani (Agen), O Roumat (Dax), L Rodriguez (Dax) (*capt*), E Champ (Toulon)
Replacement P Marocco (Montferrand) for Armary
Scorers *Try:* Lagisquet   *Penalty Goal:* Charvet
ENGLAND: S D Hodgkinson (Nottingham); R Underwood (RAF & Leicester), W D C Carling (Harlequins) (*capt*), J Guscott (Bath), M D Bailey (Wasps); C R Andrew (Wasps), R J Hill (Bath); P A G Rendall (Wasps), B C Moore (Nottingham), J A Probyn (Wasps), P J Ackford (Harlequins), W A Dooley (Preston Grasshoppers), M G Skinner (Harlequins), M C Teague (Gloucester), P J Winterbottom (Harlequins)
Scorers *Tries:* Underwood, Guscott, Carling   *Conversion:* Hodgkinson
Penalty Goals: Hodgkinson (4)
Referee O E Doyle (Ireland)

3 February, Lansdowne Road
IRELAND 10 (2PG 1T)   **SCOTLAND 13** (1G 1PG 1T)

(Sponsored by Digital)

There was no hint at this early stage of the Championship that Scotland would go on to win the Grand Slam. They trailed for much of the match, and although they probably deserved their win, it was a poor performance in a nervous, halting game. The Irish forwards put in a storming effort but only up to a point. They could not sustain the drive until the end and gave Scotland breathing-space to strike back in the final quarter.

There was a welcome return to form for Matthews on the Irish flank and some teasing garryowens from Smith at fly-half. Smith often tested Gavin Hastings at full-back and Hastings had a poor day with his kicking, too. He was replaced as kicker by Chalmers and, in fact, lost his position for the rest of the season. Scotland's most impressive feature was their refusal to panic – that and the excellent performance of Derek White, the No 8. White had not enjoyed a successful Lions tour, but in Dublin he was back at his best, scoring both Scotland's tries. Chalmers at fly-half managed to keep his head under pressure and his partner, Armstrong, had a courageous match inside him.

Ireland were clear by half-time. Kiernan kicked a goal and John Fitzgerald, the Irish loose head, forced his way over for a try from a line-out. At this stage, there was every reason for Irish optimism: their back row held the edge over their more illustrious opposite numbers, and O'Hara was particularly impressive on the openside. However, the Scottish tight forwards finally began to assert themselves and to win some possession from the line-out. An incisive run by Lineen, who burst through close to the forwards to link up with Jeffrey, set up White's first try. Chalmers converted and confidence visibly began to seep back. Kiernan kicked his second penalty, but the closing stages of the match belonged to Scotland. Chalmers reduced the deficit to one point with a penalty, then White broke powerfully from a scrum for a solo try to win the match. White's pace from a standing start took him clear of the Irish back row and Scotland were on their way.

IRELAND: K Murphy (Constitution); M J Kiernan (Dolphin), B J Mullin (Blackrock Coll), D G Irwin (Instonians), K D Crossan (Instonians); B A Smith (Oxford U), L F P Aherne (Lansdowne); J J Fitzgerald (Young Munster), J P McDonald (Malone), D C Fitzgerald (Lansdowne), W A Anderson (Dungannon) *(capt)*, D G Lenihan (Cork Const) *(capt)*, P M Matthews (Wanderers), N P Mannion (Corinthians), P T J O'Hara (Sunday's Well)
Scorers *Try:* J J Fitzgerald   *Penalty Goals:* Kiernan (2)
SCOTLAND: A G Hastings (London Scottish); A G Stanger (Hawick), S Hastings (Watsonians), S R P Lineen (Boroughmuir), I Tukalo (Selkirk); C M Chalmers (Melrose), G Armstrong (Jedforest); D M B Sole (Edinburgh Acads) *(capt)*, K S Milne (Heriot's FP), A P Burnell (London Scottish), C A Gray (Nottingham), D F Cronin (Bath), J Jeffrey (Kelso), D B White (London Scottish), F Calder (Stewart's-Melville FP)
Scorers *Tries:* White (2)   *Conversion:* Chalmers   *Penalty Goal:* Chalmers

17 February, Twickenham
ENGLAND 34 (3G 4PG 1T) WALES 6 (1G)

(The British Gas Challenge)

England have been tortured by Wales throughout recent history but aspects of this marvellous English win almost made England followers believe that it was worth the wait. England simply swept Wales away in every department. They were mighty ball-winners and they finished Wales off with real wit and pace – and that pace did not come only from the backs. England's pack charged around the field, inter-passing at speed as a tribute to their dedication to fitness and footballing. It was a stunning sight and Rendall, Moore and Winterbottom certainly showed up as well as the deadly Underwood and Carling. Behind them, Hodgkinson had another splendid match, untroubled in defence and calm and collected as he put over the vital early goals. He rounded off his day with an imperious touch-line goal against the wind.

The Welsh side simply could not handle it. They were impossibly young and willowy in key positions and their fitness standards were vastly inferior to those of the opposition. David Evans and Robert Jones beavered manfully to make the most of a slow trickle of possession and only the superb Phil Davies in the Welsh pack really caused England problems.

England opened at roughly a point a minute, Hodgkinson putting over two penalties and Carling taking advantage of poor Welsh tackling for a try in the corner. There was another hint of Wales' defensive frailty when Underwood scored later in the half, but the Welsh were rapidly caving in against the onslaught. England added two more striking tries in the second half, Underwood running 80 yards for his second after an interception, and some brilliant work by Underwood, Winterbottom and Moore carved a foot of space for Hill to cross in the left-hand corner. Hodgkinson added two conversions and two more penalties, and only a late and brave try by Phil Davies interrupted the flow of the game. John Ryan, the Welsh coach, resigned in the days after the game after a melancholy period in charge, more than anything else a victim of circumstances.

ENGLAND: S D Hodgkinson (Nottingham); S J Halliday (Bath), W D C Carling (Harlequins) *(capt)*, J C Guscott (Bath), R Underwood (RAF & Leicester); C R Andrew (Wasps), R J Hill (Bath); P A G Rendall (Wasps), B C Moore (Nottingham), J A Probyn (Wasps), P J Ackford (Harlequins), W A Dooley (Preston Grasshoppers), M G Skinner (Harlequins), M C Teague (Gloucester), P J Winterbottom (Harlequins)
Scorers *Tries:* Carling, Underwood (2), Hill *Conversions:* Hodgkinson (3)
Penalty Goals: Hodgkinson (4)
WALES: P H Thorburn (Neath); M H Titley (Swansea), M G Ring (Cardiff), M R Hall (Cardiff), A Emyr (Swansea); D W Evans (Cardiff), R N Jones (Swansea) *(capt)*; M Griffiths (Cardiff), K H Phillips (Neath), L Delaney (Llanelli), G O Llewellyn (Neath), A G Allen (Newbridge), P T Davies (Llanelli), M A Jones (Neath), R G Collins (Cardiff)
Scorers *Try:* Davies *Conversion:* Thorburn
Referee D Leslie (Scotland)

17 February, Murrayfield
SCOTLAND 21 (2G 3PG)   FRANCE 0

(The Royal Bank Match)

This was another low point for France, who appeared dishevelled and even lacking in heart as Scotland powered away to win. There was nothing irresistible about the Scottish effort but the Scots' togetherness, their pace on to the ball and their ability to take chances took them to a comfortable victory. It was not an outstanding game and was ruined by windy conditions, yet it was a deeply satisfying afternoon for the Scots, the day when they first sensed the chance of later glories. Nor were France helped by indiscipline – Fred Howard, the referee, was forced to dismiss a player for the second international in succession when he saw Carminati of France stamping on Jeffrey of Scotland. France had held Scotland to a 3-0 lead at half-time, even though the French were playing into a strong wind before the break. But Carminati's banishment – he later left the sport for rugby league in France – finished their chances. Even Blanco and Rodriguez, the two outstanding Frenchmen of recent years, seemed sadly out of form and Scotland cruised away in the second half.

For Scotland, there was good work from both locks, Cronin and Gray, in the loose but the two outstanding figures of the match were Sole and Jeffrey, who were on storming form in the loose. Some of Sole's driving recalled the best that any All Black forward could produce. Gavin Hastings was back to his best form at full-back, even though his goal-kicking remained shaky; but he made a striking contrast to the fumblings of Blanco at the other end as he dealt expertly with the few French attacks. Chalmers stretched Scotland's half-time lead after Carminati's footwork had conceded a penalty. Calder scored the first try of the match when he followed up a kick and chase for a try which Chalmers converted. Later, Tukalo managed to hold off Hontas, his opposite number, to carve out a try for himself down the left, and again Chalmers kicked the goal. He had succeeded Gavin Hastings as first-choice goal-kicker and retained the responsibility for the rest of the season.

SCOTLAND: A G Hastings (London Scottish); A G Stanger (Hawick), S Hastings (Watsonians), S R P Lineen (Boroughmuir), I Tukalo (Selkirk); C M Chalmers (Melrose), G Armstrong (Jedforest); D M B Sole (Edinburgh Acads) *(capt)*, K S Milne (Heriot's FP), A P Burnell (London Scottish), C A Gray (Nottingham), D F Cronin (Bath), J Jeffrey (Kelso), D B White (London Scottish), F Calder (Stewart's-Melville FP)
Scorers *Tries:* Calder, Tukalo   *Conversions:* Chalmers (2)   *Penalty Goals:* Chalmers (2), A G Hastings
FRANCE: S Blanco (Biarritz); P Hontas (Biarritz), P Sella (Agen), F Mesnel (Racing Club de France), P Lagisquet (Bayonne); D Camberabero (Béziers), H Sanz (Narbonne); M Pujolle (Nice), L Armary (Lourdes), P Ondarts (Biarritz), T Devergie (Nîmes), O Roumat (Dax), A Carminati (Béziers), L Rodriguez (Dax) *(capt)*, J-M Lhermet (Montferrand)
Referee F Howard (England)

John Jeffrey of Scotland achieves lift-off as the forwards contest possession after a drop-out in the Wales-Scotland match at Cardiff.

3 March, Cardiff Arms Park
WALES 9 (1G 1PG)   SCOTLAND 13 (3PG 1T)

(The British Coal Match)

This was the first Welsh team prepared by Ron Waldron, who succeeded to the coach's post – one of the hottest seats in British sport – when John Ryan resigned following the defeat by England. Waldron set out his stall by drafting in seven Neath players, including an all-action but smallish front row in Brian Williams, Phillips and Pugh. As expected, there was more devil about the Welsh effort, but they lacked the bulk and power to put Scotland off their game. It was not a high-class match, and the tension and weight of expectation weighed heavily on both sides.

In fact, Wales had more of the game and could easily have won had they taken their chances. They battered away at the Scottish line during two extended periods of pressure in the second half but they lacked variation, and eventually Scotland worked out the head-down charges of the Welsh pack and held them off. Wales based their efforts on adrenalin when a cool head in midfield might have demanded more use of the backs.

The Scots lacked imagination and penetration in midfield and leaned heavily on their superior back row and the pace of Calder and Jeffrey. They took the lead with a try in the first half from Cronin. Armstrong, the Scottish scrum-half, burst down the touch-line at the front of a line-out, linked with Sole and Jeffrey, and Cronin crashed over. Scotland were leading by 10-3 at half-time, Chalmers kicking two penalties for Scotland to one by Thorburn for Wales. Scotland were never in control of affairs in the second half and were in danger after Wales scored a brilliant try. Robert Jones and Hall made the initial break with a sharp scissors move and Hall and Collins took the ball back to the left against the grain of the Scottish defence. Collins and Bateman put Emyr over near the opposite corner for what was probably the try of the international season. However, Wales did not trust their backs too frequently and a penalty by Chalmers kept Scotland in front.

WALES: P H Thorburn (Neath); M R Hall (Cardiff), M G Ring (Cardiff), A G Bateman (Neath), A Emyr (Swansea); D W Evans (Cardiff), R N Jones (Swansea) *(capt)*; B R Williams (Neath), K H Phillips (Neath), J D Pugh (Neath), Gareth Llewellyn (Neath), P T Davies (Llanelli), M A Perego (Llanelli), M A Jones (Neath), R G Collins (Cardiff) *Replacement* A Clement (Swansea) for Evans
Scorers *Try:* Emyr   *Conversion:* Thorburn   *Penalty Goal:* Thorburn
SCOTLAND: A G Hastings (London Scottish); A G Stanger (Hawick), S Hastings (Watsonians), S R P Lineen (Boroughmuir), I Tukalo (Selkirk); C M Chalmers (Melrose), G Armstrong (Jedforest); D M B Sole (Edinburgh Acads) *(capt)*, K S Milne (Heriot's FP), A P Burnell (London Scottish), C A Gray (Nottingham), D F Cronin (Bath), J Jeffrey (Kelso), D B White (London Scottish), F Calder (Stewart's-Melville FP)
Scorers *Try:* Cronin   *Penalty Goals:* Chalmers (3)
Referee R Hourquet (France)

3 March, Parc des Princes
FRANCE 31 (2G 5PG 1T) IRELAND 12 (4PG)

The omens for Ireland were drastically unpromising. In the event there were some happy surprises because their pack fought valiantly and gained parity throughout much of the match. In truth, however, France did not have to play particularly well to win easily. This match, according to cynics, was for the title of the second division and its many limitations were cruelly exposed, especially in Ireland's lack of imagination and scoring power and France's lack of real, sustained authority.

France, to be fair, were disrupted by injury. They lost Lhermet, their promising new flanker, in the first quarter after he had made a striking opening to his international career. They also lost Serge Blanco with a torn calf muscle. Melville, a South African, arrived as replacement for Lhermet, grist to the mill of those who claim that the rules of qualification are far too loose. The backbone of the French effort was the goal-kicking and all-round expertise of Didier Camberabero at fly-half. Camberabero has always struggled for a regular place in Jacques Fouroux's plans but he gave an assured performance. He kicked five penalties and two conversions. He also sliced open the Irish defence with a classic and sustained diagonal break and made the space for Mesnel to score on the end of an inside pass. In the second half, Mesnel sealed the day with a try after a solo run. Lagisquet, the French left wing who was one of the most dangerous runners of the whole international season, cruised in for a try early in the last quarter.

All of Ireland's points came from Kiernan. His four penalty goals – two in each half – just about sustained some Irish momentum, and they also took Kiernan past Andy Irvine's record for most points by an individual in the Championship. Kiernan's total after the match was 281. There was no real sign of an Irish scoring machine to add to Kiernan's kicks. Lenihan, Francis and O'Hara competed splendidly but Smith at fly-half, for all his efforts, could not coax a return from those outside him, especially in the absence of Mullin from the centre.

FRANCE: S Blanco (Biarritz); P Hontas (Biarritz), P Sella (Agen), F Mesnel (Racing Club de France), P Lagisquet (Bayonne); D Camberabero (Béziers), H Sanz (Narbonne); M Pujolle (Nice), L Armary (Lourdes), P Ondarts (Biarritz), J Condom (Biarritz), T Devergie (Nîmes), O Roumat (Dax), L Rodriguez (Dax) (*capt*), J-M Lhermet (Montferrand) *Replacements* E Melville (Toulon) for Lhermet; M Andrieu (Nîmes) for Blanco
Scorers *Tries:* Mesnel (2), Lagisquet *Conversions:* Camberabero (2)
Penalty Goals: Camberabero (5)
IRELAND: K Murphy (Constitution); K J Hooks (Ards), M J Kiernan (Dolphin), P P A Danaher (Garryowen), K D Crossan (Instonians); B A Smith (Oxford U), L F P Aherne (Lansdowne); J J Fitzgerald (Young Munster), T J Kingston (Dolphin), D C Fitzgerald (Lansdowne), N P T Francis (Blackrock Coll), D G Lenihan (Cork Const) (*capt*), W D McBride (Malone), N P Mannion (Corinthians), P T J O'Hara (Sunday's Well)
Scorer *Penalty Goals:* Kiernan (4)
Referee K McCartney (Scotland)

17 March, Murrayfield
SCOTLAND 13 (3PG 1T)   **ENGLAND 7** (1PG 1T)

(The Royal Bank Match)

This was probably the most eagerly-awaited match in the history of the International Championship as all the trophies – mythical or otherwise – were at stake. Appropriately, the atmosphere at Murrayfield was explosive and the game lived up to the occasion. Scotland triumphantly carried off the spoils with a magnificent performance, full of bite and devil and sheer good sense. They were supported uproariously from the terraces. Against this onslaught England played by no means badly, but they were drained of their earlier pomp.

The Scottish heroes, if it is fair to single out anyone, were David Sole, the captain, and Finlay Calder. Sole set a stirring, implacable example and Calder managed to cut off many England movements at source. The tackling of the Scottish back row and midfield confounded English attempts to establish continuity, and one splendid tackle by Scott Hastings on Rory Underwood when it seemed as if the Englishman was through was typical of the play.

England never imposed themselves, and the expected line-out domination did not materialise. They also ran some kickable penalties, raising questions as to who was wielding authority on the pitch. It was a grave disappointment, even a savage one, after the previous events of the season. A lack of discipline from England allowed Craig Chalmers to kick Scotland into a 6-0 lead inside the first ten minutes but then a splendid England move, launched by Teague, Hill and Carling and ending with Guscott dummying his way over, brought England back to 6-4, and this playing against the wind. A third penalty by Chalmers made it 9-4 at half-time, but Scotland struck a hammer blow early in the second half when Stanger ran on to a clever chip ahead by Gavin Hastings to score. A penalty by Hodgkinson was England's only reply, and all they had to show for some heart-stopping late efforts to regain the Championship for which they seemed destined but which the raging Scots certainly deserved. It was only the third Scottish Grand Slam in history, following those of 1925 and 1984.

SCOTLAND: A G Hastings (London Scottish); A G Stanger (Hawick), S Hastings (Watsonians), S R P Lineen (Boroughmuir), I Tukalo (Selkirk); C M Chalmers (Melrose), G Armstrong (Jedforest); D M B Sole (Edinburgh Acads) *(capt)*, K S Milne (Heriot's FP), A P Burnell (London Scottish), C A Gray (Nottingham), D F Cronin (Bath), J Jeffrey (Kelso), D B White (London Scottish), F Calder (Stewart's-Melville FP) *Replacement* D J Turnbull (Hawick) for White
Scorers *Try:* Stanger   *Penalty Goals:* Chalmers (3)
ENGLAND: S D Hodgkinson (Nottingham); S J Halliday (Bath), W D C Carling (Harlequins) *(capt)*, J C Guscott (Bath), R Underwood (RAF & Leicester); C R Andrew (Wasps), R J Hill (Bath); P A G Rendall (Bath), B C Moore (Nottingham), J A Probyn (Wasps), P J Ackford (Harlequins), W A Dooley (Preston Grasshoppers), M G Skinner (Harlequins), M C Teague (Gloucester), P J Winterbottom (Harlequins)
Scorers *Try:* Guscott   *Penalty Goal:* Hodgkinson
Referee D J Bishop (New Zealand)

24 March, Lansdowne Road
IRELAND 14 (1G 2T)   WALES 8 (2T)

(Sponsored by Digital)

This match came just a week after the Grand Slam summit and it paled by comparison. It was a stuttering, mistake-ridden match and the defeat of Wales represented the first whitewash of their history. They probably deserved better in this match, but the weaknesses throughout the team promised nothing in the way of long-term revival.

At least Ireland rescued something from a forgettable season with a victory based on a passionate forward display. Lenihan added to his string of powerful displays and Pat O'Hara in the back row was a considerable force. Throughout the season, he played with the sort of authority Ireland have lacked in the back row and he made up in some measure for the absence through illness of Phil Matthews. Outside there was precious little inspiration. Ken Murphy at full-back continued his advance and was unlucky not to score a try. He was cut down by a desperate ankle-tap after bursting through almost to the line.

It was another difficult day for Ron Waldron, the Welsh coach, and for his Neath-based team. For all their efforts, Brian Williams and Kevin Phillips did not wield the power and authority in the scrum to complement their efforts in the loose and Gareth Llewellyn had a largely unsuccessful day in the line-out. Mark Jones and Andy Allen did their best to motivate the Welsh forward effort but real passion, confidence and endurance, once again, were absent.

Ireland served notice that they intended to avoid the whitewash when a storming drive led by Francis drew in the Welsh defence. Smith was able to score at the posts when the ball was released. McBride scored at the back of an Irish push-over attempt later in the first half and Wales, for some reason spurning kicks at goal, turned to play downwind trailing 10-0. They gave themselves every chance when powerful running by Morris, Collins and Robert Jones set up a splendid try for debutant Ford, but a try by Kingston, who was drafted in just before the kick-off, sealed Ireland's win and a late try by Llewellyn was a single, small consolation.

IRELAND: K Murphy (Constitution); K J Hooks (Ards), M J Kiernan (Dolphin), B J Mullin (Blackrock Coll), K D Crossan (Instonians); B A Smith (Oxford U), M T Bradley (Constitution); J J Fitzgerald (Young Munster), T J Kingston (Dolphin), D C Fitzgerald (Lansdowne), N P T Francis (Blackrock Coll), D G Lenihan (Cork Const) *(capt)*, W D McBride (Malone), N P Mannion (Corinthians), P T J O'Hara (Sunday's Well)
Scorers *Tries:* Smith, McBride, Kingston   *Conversion:* Kiernan
WALES: P H Thorburn (Neath); S P Ford (Cardiff), M G Ring (Cardiff), A G Bateman (Neath), A Emyr (Swansea); D W Evans (Cardiff), R N Jones (Swansea) *(capt)*; B R Williams (Neath), K H Phillips (Neath), H Williams–Jones (South Wales Police), G O Llewellyn (Neath), A G Allen (Newbridge), M S Morris (Neath), M A Jones (Neath), R G Collins (Cardiff) *Replacements* A Clement (Swansea) for Thorburn; A Edmunds (Neath) for Evans
Scorers *Tries:* Ford, Llewellyn
Referee D J Bishop (New Zealand)

RESULTS OF INTERNATIONAL MATCHES *(up to 30 April 1990)*

Years for Five Nations' matches are for the second half of the season: eg 1972 means season 1971-72. Years for matches against touring teams from the Southern Hemisphere refer to the actual year of the match.

Points-scoring was first introduced in 1886, when an International Board was formed by Scotland, Ireland and Wales. Points-values varied between countries until 1890, when England agreed to join the Board, and uniform values were adopted. The table below shows points-values from the 1890-91 season onwards.

Northern Hemisphere seasons	Try	Conversion	Penalty goal	Dropped goal	Goal from mark
1890-91	1	2	2	3	3
1891-92 to 1892-93	2	3	3	4	4
1893-94 to 1904-05	3	2	3	4	4
1905-06 to 1947-48	3	2	3	4	3
1948-49 to 1970-71	3	2	3	3	3
1971-72 onwards	4	2	3	3	3*

★The goal from mark ceased to exist when free kick clause was introduced, 1977-78. WC indicates a fixture played during the Rugby World Cup.

ENGLAND v SCOTLAND
Played 106   England won 50, Scotland won 39, Drawn 17

1871 Raeburn Place (Edinburgh) **Scotland** 1G 1T to 1T	1886 Raeburn Place **Drawn** no score
1872 The Oval (London) **England** 1G 1DG 2T to 1DG	1887 Manchester **Drawn** 1T each
1873 Glasgow **Drawn** no score	1888 No Match
	1889 No Match
1874 The Oval **England** 1DG to 1T	1890 Raeburn Place **England** 1G 1T to 0
1875 Raeburn Place **Drawn** no score	1891 Richmond (London) **Scotland** 2G 1DG (9) to 1G (3)
1876 The Oval **England** 1G 1T to 0	1892 Raeburn Place **England** 1G (5) to 0
1877 Raeburn Place **Scotland** 1DG to 0	1893 Leeds **Scotland** 2DG (8) to 0
1878 The Oval **Drawn** no score	1894 Raeburn Place **Scotland** 2T (6) to 0
1879 Raeburn Place **Drawn** Scotland 1DG England 1G	1895 Richmond **Scotland** 1PG 1T (6) to 1PG (3)
1880 Manchester **England** 2G 3T to 1G	1896 Glasgow **Scotland** 1G 2T (11) to 0
1881 Raeburn Place **Drawn** Scotland 1G 1T England 1DG 1T	1897 Manchester **England** 1G 1DG 1T (12) to 1T (3)
1882 Manchester **Scotland** 2T to 0	1898 Powderhall (Edinburgh) **Drawn** 1T (3) each
1883 Raeburn Place **England** 2T to 1T	1899 Blackheath **Scotland** 1G (5) to 0
1884 Blackheath (London) **England** 1G to 1T	1900 Inverleith (Edinburgh) **Drawn** no score
1885 No Match	

ROTHMANS RUGBY UNION YEARBOOK 1990-91

1901 Blackheath
Scotland 3G 1T (18) to 1T (3)

1902 Inverleith
England 2T (6) to 1T (3)

1903 Richmond
Scotland 1DG 2T (10) to 2T (6)

1904 Inverleith
Scotland 2T (6) to 1T (3)

1905 Richmond
Scotland 1G 1T (8) to 0

1906 Inverleith
England 3T (9) to 1T (3)

1907 Blackheath
Scotland 1G 1T (8) to 1T (3)

1908 Inverleith
Scotland 1G 2DG 1T (16) to 2 G (10)

1909 Richmond
Scotland 3G 1T (18) to 1G 1T (8)

1910 Inverleith
England 1G 3T (14) to 1G (5)

1911 Twickenham
England 2G 1T (13) to 1G 1T (8)

1912 Inverleith
Scotland 1G 1T (8) to 1T (3)

1913 Twickenham
England 1T (3) to 0

1914 Inverleith
England 2G 2T (16) to 1G 1DG 2T (15)

1920 Twickenham
England 2G 1T (13) to 1DG (4)

1921 Inverleith
England 3G 1T (18) to 0

1922 Twickenham
England 1G 2T (11) to 1G (5)

1923 Inverleith
England 1G 1T (8) to 2T (6)

1924 Twickenham
England 3G 1DG (19) to 0

1925 Murrayfield
Scotland 2G 1DG (14)
to 1G 1PG 1T (11)

1926 Twickenham
Scotland 2G 1DG 1T (17) to 3T (9)

1927 Murrayfield
Scotland 1G 1DG 4T (21)
to 2G 1PG (13)

1928 Twickenham
England 2T (6) to 0

1929 Murrayfield
Scotland 4T (12) to 2T (6)

1930 Twickenham
Drawn no score

1931 Murrayfield
Scotland 5G 1T (28) to 2G 1PG 2T (19)

1932 Twickenham
England 2G 2T (16) to 1T (3)

1933 Murrayfield
Scotland 1T (3) to 0

1934 Twickenham
England 2T (6) to 1T (3)

1935 Murrayfield
Scotland 2G (10) to 1DG 1T (7)

1936 Twickenham
England 3T (9) to 1G 1PG (8)

1937 Murrayfield
England 2T (6) to 1PG (3)

1938 Twickenham
Scotland 2PG 5T (21)
to 3PG 1DG 1T (16)

1939 Murrayfield
England 3PG (9) to 2T (6)

1947 Twickenham
England 4G 1DG (24) to 1G (5)

1948 Murrayfield
Scotland 2T (6) to 1PG (3)

1949 Twickenham
England 2G 3T (19) to 1PG (3)

1950 Murrayfield
Scotland 2G 1T (13) to 1G 1PG 1T (11)

1951 Twickenham
England 1G (5) to 1T (3)

1952 Murrayfield
England 2G 1DG 2T (19) to 1T (3)

1953 Twickenham
England 4G 2T (26) to 1G 1T (8)

1954 Murrayfield
England 2G 1T (13) to 1T (3)

1955 Twickenham
England 1PG 2T (9) to 1PG 1T (6)

1956 Murrayfield
England 1G 2PG (11) to 1PG 1T (6)

1957 Twickenham
England 2G 1PG 1T (16) to 1PG (3)

1958 Murrayfield
Drawn 1PG (3) each

1959 Twickenham
Drawn 1PG (3) each

1960 Murrayfield
England 3G 1PG 1DG (21)
to 3PG 1T (12)

1961 Twickenham
England 1PG 1T (6) to 0

1962 Murrayfield
Drawn 1PG (3) each

1963 Twickenham
England 2G (10) to 1G 1DG (8)

1964 Murrayfield
Scotland 3G (15) to 1PG 1T (6)

1965 Twickenham
Drawn England 1T (3) Scotland 1DG (3)

1966 Murrayfield
Scotland 1PG 1T (6) to 1DG (3)

66

1967 Twickenham
England 3G 2PG 1DG 1T (27)
to 1G 2PG 1T (14)

1968 Murrayfield
England 1G 1PG (8) to 1PG 1DG (6)

1969 Twickenham
England 1G 1T (8) to 1PG (3)

1970 Murrayfield
Scotland 1G 2PG 1T (14) to 1G (5)

1971 Twickenham
Scotland 2G 1DG 1T (16) to 3PG 2T (15)

★1971 Murrayfield
Scotland 4G 1PG 1T (26) to 1PG 1DG (6)
★ *Special Centenary match – non-championship*

1972 Murrayfield
Scotland 4PG 1DG 2T (23) to 3PG (9)

1973 Twickenham
England 2G 2T (20) to 1G 1PG 1T (13)

1974 Murrayfield
Scotland 1G 2PG 1T (16)
to 1PG 1DG 2T (14)

1975 Twickenham
England 1PG 1T (7) to 2PG (6)

1976 Murrayfield
Scotland 2G 2PG 1T (22)
to 1G 2PG (12)

1977 Twickenham
England 2G 2PG 2T (26) to 2PG (6)

1978 Murrayfield
England 2G 1PG (15) to 0

1979 Twickenham
Drawn 1PG 1T (7) each

1980 Murrayfield
England 2G 2PG 3T (30)
to 2G 2PG (18)

1981 Twickenham
England 1G 3PG 2T (23)
to 1G 1PG 2T (17)

1982 Murrayfield
Drawn Scotland 2PG 1DG (9)
England 3PG (9)

1983 Twickenham
Scotland 1G 3PG 1DG 1T (22)
to 3PG 1DG (12)

1984 Murrayfield
Scotland 2G 2PG (18) to 2PG (6)

1985 Twickenham
England 2PG 1T (10) to 1PG 1T (7)

1986 Murrayfield
Scotland 3G 5PG (33) to 2PG (6)

1987 Twickenham
England 2G★ 3PG (21) to 1G 2PG (12)
★includes one penalty try

1988 Murrayfield
England 2PG 1DG (9) to 2PG (6)

1989 Twickenham
Drawn England 4PG (12)
Scotland 1G 2PG (12)

1990 Murrayfield
Scotland 3PG 1T (13) to 1PG 1T (7)

ENGLAND v IRELAND
Played 103   England won 59, Ireland won 36, Drawn 8

1875 The Oval (London)
England 1G 1DG 1T to 0

1876 Dublin
England 1G 1T to 0

1877 The Oval
England 2G 2T to 0

1878 Dublin
England 2G 1T to 0

1879 The Oval
England 2G 1DG 2T to 0

1880 Dublin
England 1G 1T to 1T

1881 Manchester
England 2G 2T to 0

1882 Dublin
Drawn 2T each

1883 Manchester
England 1G 3T to 1T

1884 Dublin
England 1G to 0

1885 Manchester
England 2T to 1T

1886 Dublin
England 1T to 0

1887 Dublin
Ireland 2G to 0

1888 No Match

1889 No Match

1890 Blackheath (London)
England 3T to 0

1891 Dublin
England 2G 3T (9) to 0

1892 Manchester
England 1G 1T (7) to 0

1893 Dublin
England 2T (4) to 0

1894 Blackheath
Ireland 1DG 1T (7) to 1G (5)

1895 Dublin
England 2T (6) to 1T (3)

1896 Leeds
Ireland 2G (10) to 1DG (4)

1897 Dublin
Ireland 1GM 3T (13) to 2PG 1T (9)

1898 Richmond (London)
Ireland 1PG 2T (9) to 1PG 1T (6)

1899 Dublin
Ireland 1PG 1T (6) to 0

1900 Richmond
England 1G 1DG 2T (15) to 1DG (4)

1901 Dublin
Ireland 2G (10) to 1PG 1T (6)

1902 Leicester
England 2T (6) to 1T (3)

1903 Dublin
Ireland 1PG 1T (6) to 0

1904 Blackheath
England 2G 3T (19) to 0

1905 Cork
Ireland 1G 4T (17) to 1T (3)

1906 Leicester
Ireland 2G 2T (16) to 2T (6)

1907 Dublin
Ireland 1G 1GM 3T (17) to 1PG 2T (9)

1908 Richmond
England 2G 1T (13) to 1PG (3)

1909 Dublin
England 1G 2T (11) to 1G (5)

1910 Twickenham
Drawn no score

1911 Dublin
Ireland 1T (3) to 0

1912 Twickenham
England 5T (15) to 0

1913 Dublin
England 1PG 4T (15) to 1DG (4)

1914 Twickenham
England 1G 4T (17) to 1G 1DG 1T (12)

1920 Dublin
England 1G 3T (14) to 1G 1PG 1T (11)

1921 Twickenham
England 1G 1DG 2T (15) to 0

1922 Dublin
England 4T (12) to 1T (3)

1923 Leicester
England 2G 1DG 3T (23) to 1G (5)

1924 Belfast
England 1G 3T (14) to 1T (3)

1925 Twickenham
Drawn 2T (6) each

1926 Dublin
Ireland 2G 1PG 2T (19) to 3G (15)

1927 Twickenham
England 1G 1T (8) to 1PG 1T (6)

1928 Dublin
England 1DG 1T (7) to 2T (6)

1929 Twickenham
Ireland 2T (6) to 1G (5)

1930 Dublin
Ireland 1DG (4) to 1T (3)

1931 Twickenham
Ireland 1PG 1T (6) to 1G (5)

1932 Dublin
England 1G 2PG (11) to 1G 1PG (8)

1933 Twickenham
England 1G 4T (17) to 1PG 1T (6)

1934 Dublin
England 2G 1T (13) to 1T (3)

1935 Twickenham
England 1G 3PG (14) to 1T (3)

1936 Dublin
Ireland 2T (6) to 1T (3)

1937 Twickenham
England 1PG 2T (9) to 1G 1T (8)

1938 Dublin
England 6G 1PG 1T (36) to 1G 3T (14)

1939 Twickenham
Ireland 1G (5) to 0

1947 Dublin
Ireland 2G 1PG 3T (22) to 0

1948 Twickenham
Ireland 1G 2T (11) to 2G (10)

1949 Dublin
Ireland 1G 2PG 1T (14) to 1G (5)

1950 Twickenham
England 1T (3) to 0

1951 Dublin
Ireland 1PG (3) to 0

1952 Twickenham
England 1T (3) to 0

1953 Dublin
Drawn 2PG 1T (9) each

1954 Twickenham
England 1G 1PG 2T (14) to 1PG (3)

1955 Dublin
Drawn Ireland 1PG 1T (6)
England 2T (6)

1956 Twickenham
England 1G 3PG 2T (20) to 0

1957 Dublin
England 1PG 1T (6) to 0

1958 Twickenham
England 1PG 1T (6) to 0

1959 Dublin
England 1PG (3) to 0

1960 Twickenham
England 1G 1DG (8) to 1G (5)

1961 Dublin
Ireland 1G 2PG (11) to 1G 1T (8)

1962 Twickenham
England 2G 1PG 1T (16) to 0

1963 Dublin
Drawn no score

1964 Twickenham
Ireland 3G 1T (18) to 1G (5)

1965 Dublin
Ireland 1G (5) to 0

1966 Twickenham
Drawn 1PG 1T (6) each

1967 Dublin
England 1G 1PG (8) to 1PG (3)

1968 Twickenham
Drawn England 2PG 1DG (9)
Ireland 3PG (9)

1969 Dublin
Ireland 1G 2PG 1DG 1T (17)
to 4PG 1T (15)

1970 Twickenham
England 2DG 1T (9) to 1PG (3)

1971 Dublin
England 3PG (9) to 2T (6)

1972 Twickenham
Ireland 1PG 1DG 1T (16)
to 1G 2PG (12)

1973 Dublin
Ireland 2G 1PG 1DG (18) to 1G 1PG (9)

1974 Twickenham
Ireland 2G 1PG 1DG 2T (26)
to 1G 5PG (21)

1975 Dublin
Ireland 2G (12) to 1G 1DG (9)

1976 Twickenham
Ireland 2PG 1DG 1T (13) to 4PG (12)

1977 Dublin
England 1T (4) to 0

1978 Twickenham
England 2G 1PG (15) to 2PG 1DG (9)

1979 Dublin
Ireland 1G 1PG 1DG (12) to 1PG 1T (7)

1980 Twickenham
England 3G 2PG (24) to 3PG (9)

1981 Dublin
England 1G 1T (10) to 2 DG (6)

1982 Twickenham
Ireland 1G 2PG 1T (16) to 1G 3PG (15)

1983 Dublin
Ireland 1G 5PG 1T (25) to 5PG (15)

1984 Twickenham
England 3PG 1DG (12) to 3PG (9)

1985 Dublin
Ireland 2PG 1DG 1T (13) to 2PG 1T (10)

1986 Twickenham
England * 3G 1PG 1T (25)
to 1G 2PG 2T (20)
includes one penalty try

1987 Dublin
Ireland 1G 1PG 2T (17) to 0

1988 Twickenham
England 4G 1PG 2T (35) to 1DG (3)

*1988 Dublin
England 2G 3PG (21) to 1G 1T (10)
Non-championship match

1989 Dublin
England 1G 2PG 1T (16) to 1PG (3)

1990 Twickenham
England 2G 1PG 2T (23) to 0

ENGLAND v WALES
Played 96   England won 37, Wales won 47, Drawn 12

1881 Blackheath (London)
England 7G 1DG 6T to 0

1882 No Match

1883 Swansea
England 2G 4T to 0

1884 Leeds
England 1G 2T to 1G

1885 Swansea
England 1G 4T to 1G 1T

1886 Blackheath
England 1GM 2T to 1G

1887 Llanelli
Drawn no score

1888 No Match

1889 No Match

1890 Dewsbury
Wales 1T to 0

1891 Newport
England 2G 1T (7) to 1G (3)

1892 Blackheath
England 3G 1T (17) to 0

1893 Cardiff
Wales 1G 1PG 2T (12) to 1G 3T (11)

1894 Birkenhead
England 4G 1GM (24) to 1T (3)

1895 Swansea
England 1G 3T (14) to 2T (6)

1896 Blackheath
England 2G 5T (25) to 0

1897 Newport
Wales 1G 2T (11) to 0

1898 Blackheath
England 1G 3T (14) to 1DG 1T (7)

1899 Swansea
Wales 4G 2T (26) to 1T (3)

1900 Gloucester
Wales 2G 1PG (13) to 1T (3)

1901 Cardiff
Wales 2G 1T (13) to 0

1902 Blackheath
Wales 1PG 2T (9) to 1G 1T (8)

1903 Swansea
Wales 3G 2T (21) to 1G (5)

1904 Leicester
Drawn England 1G 1PG 2T (14)
Wales 2G 1GM (14)

1905 Cardiff
Wales 2G 5T (25) to 0

1906 Richmond (London)
Wales 2G 2T (16) to 1T (3)

1907 Swansea
Wales 2G 4T (22) to 0

1908 Bristol
Wales 3G 1PG 1DG 2T (28)
to 3G 1T (18)

1909 Cardiff
Wales 1G 1T (8) to 0

1910 Twickenham
England 1G 1PG 1T (11) to 2T (6)

1911 Swansea
Wales 1PG 4T (15) to 1G 2T (11)

1912 Twickenham
England 1G 1T (8) to 0

1913 Cardiff
England 1G 1DG 1T (12) to 0

1914 Twickenham
England 2G (10) to 1G 1DG (9)

1920 Swansea
Wales 1G 1PG 2DG 1T (19) to 1G (5)

1921 Twickenham
England 1G 1DG 3T (18) to 1T (3)

1922 Cardiff
Wales 2G 6T (28) to 2T (6)

1923 Twickenham
England 1DG 1T (7) to 1T (3)

1924 Swansea
England 1G 4T (17) to 3T (9)

1925 Twickenham
England 1PG 3T (12) to 2T (6)

1926 Cardiff
Drawn 1T (3) each

1927 Twickenham
England 1G 1PG 1GM (11)
to 1PG 2T (9)

1928 Swansea
England 2G (10) to 1G 1T (8)

1929 Twickenham
England 1G 1T (8) to 1T (3)

1930 Cardiff
England 1G 1PG 1T (11) to 1T (3)

1931 Twickenham
Drawn England 1G 2PG (11)
Wales 1G 1GM 1T (11)

1932 Swansea
Wales 1G 1PG 1DG (12) to 1G (5)

1933 Twickenham
Wales 1DG 1T (7) to 1T (3)

1934 Cardiff
England 3T (9) to 0

1935 Twickenham
Drawn England 1PG (3) Wales 1T (3)

1936 Swansea
Drawn no score

1937 Twickenham
England 1DG (4) to 1T (3)

1938 Cardiff
Wales 1G 2PG 1T (14) to 1G 1T (8)

1939 Twickenham
England 1T (3) to 0

1947 Cardiff
England 1G 1DG (9) to 2T (6)

1948 Twickenham
Drawn England 1PG (3) Wales 1T (3)

1949 Cardiff
Wales 3T (9) to 1DG (3)

1950 Twickenham
Wales 1G 1PG 1T (11) to 1G (5)

1951 Swansea
Wales 4G 1T (23) to 1G (5)

1952 Twickenham
Wales 1G 1T (8) to 2T (6)

1953 Cardiff
England 1G 1PG (8) to 1PG (3)

1954 Twickenham
England 3T (9) to 1PG 1T (6)

1955 Cardiff
Wales 1PG (3) to 0

1956 Twickenham
Wales 1G 1T (8) to 1PG (3)

1957 Cardiff
England 1PG (3) to 0

1958 Twickenham
Drawn England 1T (3) Wales 1PG (3)

1959 Cardiff
Wales 1G (5) to 0

1960 Twickenham
England 1G 2PG 1T (14) to 2PG (6)

1961 Cardiff
Wales 2T (6) to 1T (3)

1962 Twickenham
Drawn no score

1963 Cardiff
England 2G 1DG (13) to 1PG 1T (6)

1964 Twickenham
Drawn 2T (6) each

1965 Cardiff
Wales 1G 1DG 2T (14) to 1PG (3)

1966 Twickenham
Wales 1G 2PG (11) to 1PG 1T (6)

1967 Cardiff
Wales 5G 2PG 1DG (34) to 4PG 3T (21)

1968 Twickenham
Drawn England 1G 1PG 1T (11)
Wales 1G 1DG 1T (11)

1969 Cardiff
Wales 3G 2PG 1DG 2T (30) to 3PG (9)

1970 Twickenham
Wales 1G 1DG 3T (17) to 2G 1PG (13)

1971 Cardiff
Wales 2G 1PG 2DG 1T (22)
to 1PG 1T (6)

1972 Twickenham
Wales 1G 2PG (12) to 1PG (3)

1973 Cardiff
Wales 1G 1PG 4T (25) to 2PG 1DG (9)

1974 Twickenham
England 1G 2PG 1T (16)
to 1G 2PG (12)

1975 Cardiff
Wales 1G 2PG 2T (20) to 1T (4)

1976 Twickenham
Wales 3G 1PG (21) to 3PG (9)

1977 Cardiff
Wales 2PG 2T (14) to 3PG (9)

1978 Twickenham
Wales 3PG (9) to 2PG (6)

1979 Cardiff
Wales 2G 1DG 3T (27) to 1PG (3)

1980 Twickenham
England 3PG (9) to 2T (8)

1981 Cardiff
Wales 1G 4PG 1DG (21) to 5PG 1T (19)

1982 Twickenham
England 3PG 2T (17) to 1DG 1T (7)

1983 Cardiff
Drawn 2PG 1DG 1T (13) each

1984 Twickenham
Wales 1G 4PG 2DG (24) to 5PG (15)

1985 Cardiff
Wales 2G 3PG 1DG (24)
to 1G 2PG 1DG (15)

1986 Twickenham
England 6PG 1DG (21)
to 1G 3PG 1DG (18)

1987 Cardiff
Wales 5PG 1T (19) to 4PG (12)

1987 Brisbane *WC*
Wales 2G 1T (16) to 1PG (3)

1988 Twickenham
Wales 1DG 2T (11) to 1PG (3)

1989 Cardiff
Wales 1G 2PG (12) to 2PG 1DG (9)

1990 Twickenham
England 3G 4PG 1T (34) to 1G (6)

ENGLAND v FRANCE
Played 65   England won 34, France won 24, Drawn 7

1906 Paris
England 4G 5T (35) to 1G 1T (8)

1907 Richmond (London)
England 5G 1DG 4T (41)
to 2G 1PG (13)

1908 Paris
England 2G 3T (19) to 0

1909 Leicester
England 2G 4T (22) to 0

1910 Paris
England 1G 2T (11) to 1T (3)

1911 Twickenham
England 5G 2PG 2T (37) to 0

1912 Paris
England 1G 1DG 3T (18) to 1G 1T (8)

1913 Twickenham
England 1G 5T (20) to 0

1914 Paris
England 6G 3T (39) to 2G 1T (13)

1920 Twickenham
England 1G 1PG (8) to 1T (3)

1921 Paris
England 2G (10) to 2PG (6)

1922 Twickenham
Drawn England 1G 2PG (11)
France 1G 2T (11)

1923 Paris
England 1G 1DG 1T (12) to 1PG (3)

1924 Twickenham
England 2G 3T (19) to 1DG 1T (7)

1925 Paris
England 2G 1GM (13) to 1G 2T (11)

1926 Twickenham
England 1G 2T (11) to 0

1927 Paris
France 1T (3) to 0

1928 Twickenham
England 3G 1T (18) to 1G 1T (8)

1929 Paris
England 2G 2T (16) to 2T (6)

1930 Twickenham
England 1G 2T (11) to 1G (5)

1931 Paris
France 2DG 2T (14) to 2G 1T (13)

1947 Twickenham
England 2T (6) to 1PG (3)

1948 Paris
France 1G 1DG 2T (15) to 0

1949 Twickenham
England 1G 1DG (8) to 1DG (3)

1950 Paris
France 2T (6) to 1T (3)

1951 Twickenham
France 1G 1DG 1T (11) to 1T (3)

1952 Paris
England 2PG (6) to 1T (3)

1953 Twickenham
England 1G 2T (11) to 0

1954 Paris
France 1G 1DG 1T (11) to 1T (3)

1955 Twickenham
France 2G 2DG (16) to 2PG 1T (9)

1956 Paris
France 1G 2PG 1T (14) to 2PG 1T (9)

1957 Twickenham
England 3T (9) to 1G (5)

1958 Paris
England 1G 1PG 2T (14) to 0

1959 Twickenham
Drawn 1PG (3) each

1960 Paris
Drawn France 1PG (3) England 1T (3)

1961 Twickenham
Drawn 1G (5) each

1962 Paris
France 2G 1T (13) to 0

1963 Twickenham
England 2PG (6) to 1G (5)

1964 Paris
England 1PG 1T (6) to 1T (3)

1965 Twickenham
England 2PG 1T (9) to 1PG 1T (6)

1966 Paris
France 2G 1T (13) to 0

1967 Twickenham
France 2G 1PG 1DG (16)
to 3PG 1DG (12)

1968 Paris
France 1G 1PG 2DG (14)
to 2PG 1DG (9)

1969 Twickenham
England 2G 3PG 1T (22)
to 1G 1DG (8)

1970 Paris
France 4G 1PG 2DG 2T (35)
to 2G 1PG (13)

1971 Twickenham
Drawn England 1G 3PG (14)
France 1G 1PG 1DG 1T (14)

1972 Paris
France 5G 1PG 1T (37) to 1G 2PG (12)

1973 Twickenham
England 2PG 2T (14) to 1G (6)

1974 Paris
Drawn 1G 1PG 1DG (12) each

1975 Twickenham
France 4G 1PG (27) to 4PG 2T (20)

1976 Paris
France 3G 3T (30) to 1G 1PG (9)

1977 Twickenham
France 1T (4) to 1PG (3)

1978 Paris
France 2G 1PG (15) to 2DG (6)

1979 Twickenham
England 1PG 1T (7) to 1G (6)

1980 Paris
England 1PG 2DG 2T (17)
to 1G 1PG 1T (13)

1981 Twickenham
France 1G 2DG 1T (16) to 4 PG (12)

1982 Paris
England 2G 5PG (27) to
1G 2PG 1DG (15)

1983 Twickenham
France 2G 1PG 1T (19)
to 4PG 1DG (15)

1984 Paris
France 3G 1PG 1DG 2T (32)
to 2G 2PG (18)

1985 Twickenham
Drawn England 2PG 1DG (9)
France 3DG (9)

1986 Paris
France* 2G 3PG 2T (29)
to 2PG 1T (10)
* *includes one penalty try*

1987 Twickenham
France 1G 1PG 2DG 1T (19)
to 4PG 1DG (15)

1988 Paris
France 2PG 1T (10) to 2PG 1DG (9)

1989 Twickenham
England 1PG 2T (11) to 0

1990 Paris
England 1G 4PG 2T (26) to 1PG 1T (7)

ENGLAND v NEW ZEALAND
Played 15   England won 3, New Zealand won 12, Drawn 0

1905 Crystal Palace (London)
New Zealand 5T (15) to 0

1925 Twickenham
New Zealand 1G 1PG 3T (17)
to 1G 1PG 1T (11)

1936 Twickenham
England 1DG 3T (13) to 0

1954 Twickenham
New Zealand 1G (5) to 0

1963 *1* Auckland
New Zealand 3G 1PG 1DG (21)
to 1G 2PG (11)

2 Christchurch
New Zealand 1GM 2T (9)
to 1PG 1T (6)
New Zealand won series 2-0

1964 Twickenham
New Zealand 1G 2PG 1T (14) to 0

1967 Twickenham
New Zealand 4G 1T (23)
to 1G 1PG 1T (11)

1973 Twickenham
New Zealand 1G 1DG (9) to 0

1973 Auckland
England 2G 1T (16) to 1G 1T (10)

1978 Twickenham
New Zealand 1G 2PG 1T (16)
to 1PG 1DG (6)

1979 Twickenham
New Zealand 2PG 1T (10) to 3PG (9)

1983 Twickenham
England 1G 3PG (15) to 1G 1PG (9)

1985 *1* Christchurch
New Zealand 6PG (18) to 1G 1PG 1T (13)

2 Wellington
New Zealand 3G 3PG 1DG 3T (42)
to 2G 1DG (15)
New Zealand won series 2-0

ENGLAND v SOUTH AFRICA
Played 9   England won 2, South Africa won 6, Drawn 1

1906 Crystal Palace (London)
Drawn 1T (3) each

1913 Twickenham
South Africa 2PG 1T (9) to 1T (3)

1932 Twickenham
South Africa 1DG 1T (7) to 0

1952 Twickenham
South Africa 1G 1PG (8) to 1T (3)

1961 Twickenham
South Africa 1G (5) to 0

1969 Twickenham
England 1G 1PG 1T (11) to 1G 1PG (8)

1972 Johannesburg
England 1G 4PG (18) to 3PG (9)

1984 *1* Port Elizabeth
South Africa 3G 5PG (33)
to 4PG 1DG (15)

2 Johannesburg
South Africa 4G 1PG 2T (35) to 3PG (9)
South Africa won series 2-0

ENGLAND v AUSTRALIA
Played 16   England won 6, Australia won 10, Drawn 0

1909 Blackheath (London)
Australia 3T (9) to 1T (3)

1928 Twickenham
England 3G 1T (18) to 1G 2T (11)

1948 Twickenham
Australia 1G 2T (11) to 0

1958 Twickenham
England 1PG 2T (9) to 1PG 1DG (6)

1963 Sydney
Australia 3G 1T (18) to 3T (9)

1967 Twickenham
Australia 1G 2PG 3DG 1T (23)
to 1G 2PG (11)

1973 Twickenham
England 1G 2PG 2T (20) to 1PG (3)

1975 *1* Sydney
Australia 2PG 2DG 1T (16)
to 1G 1PG (9)

2 Brisbane
Australia 2G 2PG 3T (30)
to 2G 3PG (21)
Australia won series 2-0

1976 Twickenham
England 1G 3PG 2T (23) to 2PG (6)

1982 Twickenham
England 1G 3PG (15) to 1PG 2T (11)

1984 Twickenham
Australia 2G 1PG 1T (19) to 1PG (3)

1987 Sydney *WC*
Australia 1G 3PG 1T (19) to 1G (6)

1988 *1* Brisbane
Australia 6PG 1T (22) to 1G 2PG 1T (16)

2 Sydney
Australia 3G 2PG 1T (28) to 2T (8)
Australia won series 2-0

1988 Twickenham
England 3G 2PG 1T (28) to
2G 1PG 1T (19)

SCOTLAND v IRELAND
Played 101   Scotland won 51, Ireland won 45, Drawn 4, Abandoned 1

1877 Belfast
Scotland 4G 2DG 2T to 0

1878 No Match

1879 Belfast
Scotland 1G 1DG 1T to 0

1880 Glasgow
Scotland 1G 2DG 2T to 0

1881 Belfast
Ireland 1DG to 1T

1882 Glasgow
Scotland 2T to 0

1883 Belfast
Scotland 1G 1T to 0

1884 Raeburn Place (Edinburgh)
Scotland 2G 2T to 1T

1885 Belfast
Abandoned Ireland 0 Scotland 1T

1885 Raeburn Place
Scotland 1G 2T to 0

1886 Raeburn Place
Scotland 3G 1DG 2T to 0

1887 Belfast
Scotland 1G 1GM 2T to 0

1888 Raeburn Place
Scotland 1G to 0

1889 Belfast
Scotland 1DG to 0

1890 Raeburn Place
Scotland 1DG 1T to 0

1891 Belfast
Scotland 3G 1DG 2T (14) to 0

1892 Raeburn Place
Scotland 1T (2) to 0

1893 Belfast
Drawn no score

1894 Dublin
Ireland 1G (5) to 0

1895 Raeburn Place
Scotland 2T (6) to 0

1896 Dublin
Drawn no score

1897 Powderhall (Edinburgh)
Scotland 1G 1PG (8) to 1T (3)

1898 Belfast
Scotland 1G 1T (8) to 0

1899 Inverleith (Edinburgh)
Ireland 3T (9) to 1PG (3)

1900 Dublin
Drawn no score

1901 Inverleith
Scotland 3T (9) to 1G (5)

1902 Belfast
Ireland 1G (5) to 0

1903 Inverleith
Scotland 1T (3) to 0

1904 Dublin
Scotland 2G 3T (19) to 1T (3)

1905 Inverleith
Ireland 1G 2T (11) to 1G (5)

1906 Dublin
Scotland 2G 1GM (13) to 2T (6)

1907 Inverleith
Scotland 3G (15) to 1PG (3)

1908 Dublin
Ireland 2G 2T (16) to 1G 1PG 1T (11)

1909 Inverleith
Scotland 3T (9) to 1PG (3)

1910 Belfast
Scotland 1G 3T (14) to 0

1911 Inverleith
Ireland 2G 2T (16) to 1DG 2T (10)

1912 Dublin
Ireland 1PG 1DG 1T (10) to 1G 1T (8)

1913 Inverleith
Scotland 4G 3T (29) to 2G 1DG (14)

1914 Dublin
Ireland 2T (6) to 0

1920 Inverleith
Scotland 2G 1PG 2T (19) to 0

1921 Dublin
Ireland 3T (9) to 1G 1T (8)

1922 Inverleith
Scotland 2T (6) to 1T (3)

1923 Dublin
Scotland 2G 1T (13) to 1T (3)

1924 Inverleith
Scotland 2G 1T (13) to 1G 1T (8)

1925 Dublin
Scotland 2G 1DG (14) to 1G 1PG (8)

1926 Murrayfield
Ireland 1T (3) to 0

1927 Dublin
Ireland 2T (6) to 0

1928 Murrayfield
Ireland 2G 1T (13) to 1G (5)

1929 Dublin
Scotland 2G 2T (16) to 1DG 1T (7)

1930 Murrayfield
Ireland 1G 3T (14) to 1G 2T (11)

1931 Dublin
Ireland 1G 1T (8) to 1G (5)

1932 Murrayfield
Ireland 4G (20) to 1G 1T (8)

1933 Dublin
Scotland 2DG (8) to 2T (6)

1934 Murrayfield
Scotland 2G 1PG 1T (16) to 3T (9)

1935 Dublin
Ireland 4T (12) to 1G (5)

1936 Murrayfield
Ireland 1DG 2T (10) to 1DG (4)

1937 Dublin
Ireland 1G 2T (11) to 1DG (4)

1938 Murrayfield
Scotland 2G 1PG 1DG 2T (23)
to 1G 3T (14)

1939 Dublin
Ireland 1PG 1GM 2T (12) to 1T (3)

1947 Murrayfield
Ireland 1T (3) to 0

1948 Dublin
Ireland 2T (6) to 0

1949 Murrayfield
Ireland 2G 1PG (13) to 1PG (3)

1950 Dublin
Ireland 3G 2PG (21) to 0

1951 Murrayfield
Ireland 1DG 1T (6) to 1G (5)

1952 Dublin
Ireland 1PG 3T (12) to 1G 1PG (8)

1953 Murrayfield
Ireland 4G 2T (26) to 1G 1PG (8)

1954 Belfast
Ireland 2T (6) to 0

1955 Murrayfield
Scotland 2PG 1DG 1T (12) to 1PG (3)

1956 Dublin
Ireland 1G 3T (14) to 2G (10)

1957 Murrayfield
Ireland 1G (5) to 1PG (3)

1958 Dublin
Ireland 2PG 2T (12) to 2T (6)

1959 Murrayfield
Ireland 1G 1PG (8) to 1PG (3)

1960 Dublin
Scotland 1DG 1T (6) to 1G (5)

1961 Murrayfield
Scotland 2G 1PG 1T (16) to 1G 1T (8)

1962 Dublin
Scotland 1G 2PG 1DG 2T (20)
to 1PG 1T (6)

1963 Murrayfield
Scotland 1PG (3) to 0

1964 Dublin
Scotland 2PG (6) to 1PG (3)

1965 Murrayfield
Ireland 2G 1DG 1T (16) to 1PG 1DG (6)

1966 Dublin
Scotland 1G 2T (11) to 1PG (3)

1967 Murrayfield
Ireland 1G (5) to 1PG (3)

1968 Dublin
Ireland 1G 1PG 2T (14) to 2PG (6)

1969 Murrayfield
Ireland 2G 2T (16) to 0

1970 Dublin
Ireland 2G 2T (16) to 1G 1DG 1T (11)

1971 Murrayfield
Ireland 1G 2PG 2T (17) to 1G (5)

1972 No Match

1973 Murrayfield
Scotland 2PG 3DG 1T (19)
to 2PG 2T (14)

1974 Dublin
Ireland 1G 1PG (9) to 2PG (6)

1975 Murrayfield
Scotland 2PG 2DG 2T (20)
to 1G 1PG 1T (13)

1976 Dublin
Scotland 4PG 1DG (15) to 2PG (6)

1977 Murrayfield
Scotland 2PG 1DG 3T (21)
to 1G 3PG 1DG (18)

1978 Dublin
Ireland 1G 2PG (12) to 3PG (9)

1979 Murrayfield
Drawn 1PG 2T (11) each

1980 Dublin
Ireland 1G 3PG 1DG 1T (22)
to 2G 1PG (15)

1981 Murrayfield
Scotland 1PG 1DG 1T (10)
to 1G 1PG (9)

1982 Dublin
Ireland 6PG 1DG (21) to 1G 2PG (12)

1983 Murrayfield
Ireland 1G 3PG (15)
to 2PG 1DG 1T (13)

1984 Dublin
Scotland *3G 2PG 2T (32) to 1G 1PG (9)
includes one penalty try

1985 Murrayfield
Ireland 2G 1PG 1DG (18)
to 4PG 1DG (15)

1986 Dublin
Scotland 2PG 1T (10) to 1G 1PG (9)

1987 Murrayfield
Scotland 1G 2DG 1T (16)
to 1G 1PG 1DG (12)

1988 Dublin
Ireland 2G 1PG 1DG 1T (22)
to 2G 2PG (18)

1989 Murrayfield
Scotland 4G 3PG 1T (37) to 3G 1PG (21)

1990 Dublin
Scotland 1G 1PG 1T (13) to 2PG 1T (10)

75

SCOTLAND v WALES
Played 94   Scotland won 40, Wales won 52, Drawn 2

1883 Raeburn Place (Edinburgh)
Scotland 3G to 1G

1884 Newport
Scotland 1DG 1T to 0

1885 Glasgow
Drawn no score

1886 Cardiff
Scotland 2G 1T to 0

1887 Raeburn Place
Scotland 4G 8T to 0

1888 Newport
Wales 1T to 0

1889 Raeburn Place
Scotland 2T to 0

1890 Cardiff
Scotland 1G 2T to 1T

1891 Raeburn Place
Scotland 1G 2DG 6T (15) to 0

1892 Swansea
Scotland 1G 1T (7) to 1T (2)

1893 Raeburn Place
Wales 1PG 3T (9) to 0

1894 Newport
Wales 1DG 1T (7) to 0

1895 Raeburn Place
Scotland 1G (5) to 1GM (4)

1896 Cardiff
Wales 2T (6) to 0

1897 No Match

1898 No Match

1899 Inverleith (Edinburgh)
Scotland 1GM 2DG 3T (21) to 2G (10)

1900 Swansea
Wales 4T (12) to 1T (3)

1901 Inverleith
Scotland 3G 1T (18) to 1G 1T (8)

1902 Cardiff
Wales 1G 3T (14) to 1G (5)

1903 Inverleith
Scotland 1PG 1T (6) to 0

1904 Swansea
Wales 3G 1PG 1T (21) to 1T (3)

1905 Inverleith
Wales 2T (6) to 1T (3)

1906 Cardiff
Wales 3T (9) to 1PG (3)

1907 Inverleith
Scotland 2T (6) to 1PG (3)

1908 Swansea
Wales 2T (6) to 1G (5)

1909 Inverleith
Wales 1G (5) to 1PG (3)

1910 Cardiff
Wales 1G 3T (14) to 0

1911 Inverleith
Wales 2G 1DG 6T (32)
to 1DG 2T (10)

1912 Swansea
Wales 2G 2DG 1T (21) to 2T (6)

1913 Inverleith
Wales 1G 1T (8) to 0

1914 Cardiff
Wales 2G 1PG 2DG 1T (24) to 1G (5)

1920 Inverleith
Scotland 2PG 1T (9) to 1G (5)

1921 Swansea
Scotland 1G 1PG 2T (14) to 2DG (8)

1922 Inverleith
Drawn Scotland 1PG 2T (9)
Wales 1G 1DG (9)

1923 Cardiff
Scotland 1G 2T (11) to 1G 1PG (8)

1924 Inverleith
Scotland 4G 1PG 4T (35) to 2G (10)

1925 Swansea
Scotland 1G 1DG 5T (24)
to 1G 1PG 2T (14)

1926 Murrayfield
Scotland 1G 1PG (8) to 1G (5)

1927 Cardiff
Scotland 1G (5) to 0

1928 Murrayfield
Wales 2G 1T (13) to 0

1929 Swansea
Wales 1G 3T (14) to 1PG 1DG (7)

1930 Murrayfield
Scotland 1G 1DG 1T (12)
to 1G 1DG (9)

1931 Cardiff
Wales 2G 1T (13) to 1G 1T (8)

1932 Murrayfield
Wales 1PG 1T (6) to 0

1933 Swansea
Scotland 1G 1PG 1T (11) to 1T (3)

1934 Murrayfield
Wales 2G 1T (13) to 1PG 1T (6)

1935 Cardiff
Wales 1DG 2T (10) to 2T (6)

1936 Murrayfield
Wales 2G 1T (13) to 1T (3)

1937 Swansea
Scotland 2G 1T (13) to 2T (6)

1938 Murrayfield
Scotland 1G 1PG (8) to 2T (6)

1939 Cardiff
Wales 1G 1PG 1T (11) to 1PG (3)

1947 Murrayfield
Wales 2G 1PG 3T (22) to 1G 1PG (8)

1948 Cardiff
Wales 1G 1PG 2T (14) to 0

1949 Murrayfield
Scotland 2T (6) to 1G (5)

1950 Swansea
Wales 1PG 1DG 2T (12) to 0

1951 Murrayfield
Scotland 2G 1PG 1DG 1T (19) to 0

1952 Cardiff
Wales 1G 2PG (11) to 0

1953 Murrayfield
Wales 1PG 3T (12) to 0

1954 Swansea
Wales 1PG 4T (15) to 1T (3)

1955 Murrayfield
Scotland 1G 1PG 1DG 1T (14)
to 1G 1T (8)

1956 Cardiff
Wales 3T (9) to 1PG (3)

1957 Murrayfield
Scotland 1PG 1DG 1T (9)
to 1PG 1T (6)

1958 Cardiff
Wales 1G 1T (8) to 1PG (3)

1959 Murrayfield
Scotland 1PG 1T (6) to 1G (5)

1960 Cardiff
Wales 1G 1PG (8) to 0

1961 Murrayfield
Scotland 1T (3) to 0

1962 Cardiff
Scotland 1G 1T (8) to 1DG (3)

1963 Murrayfield
Wales 1PG 1DG (6) to 0

1964 Cardiff
Wales 1G 1PG 1T (11) to 1T (3)

1965 Murrayfield
Wales 1G 2PG 1T (14) to 2PG 2DG (12)

1966 Cardiff
Wales 1G 1T (8) to 1PG (3)

1967 Murrayfield
Scotland 1G 1DG 1T (11) to 1G (5)

1968 Cardiff
Wales 1G (5) to 0

1969 Murrayfield
Wales 1G 2PG 2T (17) to 1PG (3)

1970 Cardiff
Wales 3G 1T (18) to 1PG 1DG 1T (9)

1971 Murrayfield
Wales 2G 1PG 2T (19) to 4PG 2T (18)

1972 Cardiff
Wales 3G 3PG 2T (35) to 1G 2PG (12)

1973 Murrayfield
Scotland 1G 1T (10) to 3PG (9)

1974 Cardiff
Wales 1G (6) to 0

1975 Murrayfield
Scotland 3PG 1DG (12) to 2PG 1T (10)

1976 Cardiff
Wales 2G 3PG 1DG 1T (28) to 1G (6)

1977 Murrayfield
Wales 2G 2PG (18) to 1G 1DG (9)

1978 Cardiff
Wales 1PG 1DG 4T (22) to 2PG 2T (14)

1979 Murrayfield
Wales 1G 3PG 1T (19) to 3PG 1T (13)

1980 Cardiff
Wales 1G 1PG 2T (17) to 1G (6)

1981 Murrayfield
Scotland *2G 1PG (15) to 2PG (6)
*includes one penalty try

1982 Cardiff
Scotland 4G 2DG 1T (34)
to 1G 4PG (18)

1983 Murrayfield
Wales 1G 3PG 1T (19) to 1G 3PG (15)

1984 Cardiff
Scotland 2G 1PG (15) to 1G 1PG (9)

1985 Murrayfield
Wales 1G 4PG 1DG 1T (25) to 2G 1PG 2DG (21)

1986 Cardiff
Wales 5PG 1DG 1T (22) to 1PG 3T (15)

1987 Murrayfield
Scotland 2G 2PG 1DG (21)
to 1G 2PG 1DG (15)

1988 Cardiff
Wales 2G 1PG 2DG 1T (25)
to 4PG 2T (20)

1989 Murrayfield
Scotland 1G 2PG 1DG 2T (23)
to 1PG 1T (7)

1990 Cardiff
Scotland 3PG 1T (13) to 1G 1PG (9)

SCOTLAND v FRANCE

Played 61   Scotland won 29, France won 29, Drawn 3

1910 Inverleith (Edinburgh)
Scotland 3G 4T (27) to 0

1911 Paris
France 2G 2T (16) to 1G 1DG 2T (15)

1912 Inverleith
Scotland 5G 1PG 1T (31) to 1T (3)

1913 Paris
Scotland 3G 2T (21) to 1T (3)

1914 No Match

1920 Paris
Scotland 1G (5) to 0

1921 Inverleith
France 1T (3) to 0

1922 Paris
Drawn 1T (3) each

1923 Inverleith
Scotland 2G 2T (16) to 1GM (3)

1924 Paris
France 4T (12) to 1PG 1DG 1T (10)

1925 Inverleith
Scotland 2G 5T (25) to 1DG (4)

1926 Paris
Scotland 1G 1PG 4T (20) to 1PG 1T (6)

1927 Murrayfield
Scotland 4G 1PG (23) to 2T (6)

1928 Paris
Scotland 5T (15) to 2T (6)

1929 Murrayfield
Scotland 1PG 1T (6) to 1T (3)

1930 Paris
France 1DG 1T (7) to 1T (3)

1931 Murrayfield
Scotland 2PG (6) to 1DG (4)

1947 Paris
France 1G 1T (8) to 1PG (3)

1948 Murrayfield
Scotland 2PG 1T (9) to 1G 1PG (8)

1949 Paris
Scotland 1G 1T (8) to 0

1950 Murrayfield
Scotland 1G 1T (8) to 1G (5)

1951 Paris
France 1G 2PG 1T (14) to 2PG 2T (12)

1952 Murrayfield
France 2G 1PG (13) to 1G 2PG (11)

1953 Paris
France 1G 1PG 1DG (11) to 1G (5)

1954 Murrayfield
France 1T (3) to 0

1955 Paris
France 1PG 4T (15) to 0

1956 Murrayfield
Scotland 2PG 2T (12) to 0

1957 Paris
Scotland 1PG 1DG (6) to 0

1958 Murrayfield
Scotland 1G 1PG 1T (11) to 2PG 1T (9)

1959 Paris
France 2DG 1T (9) to 0

1960 Murrayfield
France 2G 1T (13) to 1G 1PG 1T (11)

1961 Paris
France 1G 1PG 1DG (11) to 0

1962 Murrayfield
France 1G 2PG (11) to 1PG (3)

1963 Paris
Scotland 1G 1PG 1DG (11)
to 1PG 1DG (6)

1964 Murrayfield
Scotland 2G (10) to 0

1965 Paris
France 2G 2T (16) to 1G 1T (8)

1966 Murrayfield
Drawn Scotland 1T (3) France 1PG (3)

1967 Paris
Scotland 2PG 1DG (9) to 1G 1T (8)

1968 Murrayfield
France 1G 1T (8) to 1PG 1T (6)

1969 Paris
Scotland 1PG 1T (6) to 1PG (3)

1970 Murrayfield
France 1G 1DG 1T (11) to 2PG 1T (9)

1971 Paris
France 2G 1PG (13) to 1G 1PG (8)

1972 Murrayfield
Scotland 1G 1PG 1DG 2T (20)
to 1G 1PG (9)

1973 Paris
France 3PG 1DG 1T (16)
to 2PG 1DG 1T (13)

1974 Murrayfield
Scotland 1G 3PG 1T (19) to 1PG 1DG (6)

1975 Paris
France 1PG 1DG 1T (10) to 3PG (9)

1976 Murrayfield
France 3PG 1T (13) to 1PG 1DG (6)

1977 Paris
France 2G 1PG 2T (23) to 1PG (3)

1978 Murrayfield
France 1G 3PG 1T (19)
to 1G 1PG 1DG 1T (16)

1979 Paris
France 2PG 1DG 3T (21)
to 1G 1PG 2T (17)

1980 Murrayfield
Scotland 2G 2PG 1T (22)
to 1PG 1DG 2T (14)

1981 Paris
France 1G 2PG 1T (16)
to 1G 1PG (9)

1982 Murrayfield
Scotland 3PG 1DG 1T (16)
to 1PG 1T (7)

1983 Paris
France 1G 3PG 1T (19)
to 1G 1PG 2DG (15)

1984 Murrayfield
Scotland 1G 5PG (21)
to 1G 1PG 1DG (12)

1985 Paris
France 1PG 2T (11) to 1PG (3)

1986 Murrayfield
Scotland 6PG (18) to 2PG 1DG 2T (17)

1987 Paris
France 3PG 1DG 4T (28)
to 1G 4PG 1T (22)

1987 Christchurch *WC*
Drawn Scotland 4PG 2T (20)
France 1G 2PG 2T (20)

1988 Murrayfield
Scotland 4PG 1DG 2T (23)
to 1G 1PG 1DG (12)

1989 Paris
France 2G 1PG 1T (19)
to 1PG (3)

1990 Murrayfield
Scotland 2G 3PG (21) to 0

SCOTLAND v NEW ZEALAND

Played 13   Scotland won 0, New Zealand won 11, Drawn 2

1905 Inverleith (Edinburgh)
New Zealand 4T (12) to 1DG 1T (7)

1935 Murrayfield
New Zealand 3G 1T (18) to 1G 1T (8)

1954 Murrayfield
New Zealand 1PG (3) to 0

1964 Murrayfield
Drawn no score

1967 Murrayfield
New Zealand 1G 2PG 1T (14)
to 1DG (3)

1972 Murrayfield
New Zealand 1G 2T (14) to 2PG 1DG (9)

1975 Auckland
New Zealand 4G (24) to 0

1978 Murrayfield
New Zealand 2G 2PG (18)
to 1G 1DG (9)

1979 Murrayfield
New Zealand 2G 2T (20) to 2PG (6)

1981 *1* Dunedin
New Zealand 1PG 2T (11) to 1T (4)

2 Auckland
New Zealand 6G 1T (40) to 1G 2PG
1DG (15)
New Zealand won series 2-0

1983 Murrayfield
Drawn Scotland 5PG 2DG 1T (25)
New Zealand 2G 3PG 1T (25)

1987 Christchurch *WC*
New Zealand 2G 6PG (30) to 1PG (3)

SCOTLAND v SOUTH AFRICA

Played 8   Scotland won 3, South Africa won 5, Drawn 0

1906 Glasgow
Scotland 2T (6) to 0

1912 Inverleith
South Africa 2G 2T (16) to 0

1932 Murrayfield
South Africa 2T (6) to 1T (3)

1951 Murrayfield
South Africa 7G 1DG 2T (44) to 0

1960 Port Elizabeth
South Africa 3G 1T (18) to 2G (10)

1961 Murrayfield
South Africa 2PG 2T (12) to 1G (5)

1965 Murrayfield
Scotland 1G 1DG (8) to 1G (5)

1969 Murrayfield
Scotland 1PG 1T (6) to 1PG (3)

SCOTLAND v AUSTRALIA

Played 12   Scotland won 7, Australia won 5, Drawn 0

1927 Murrayfield
Scotland 2G (10) to 1G 1T (8)

1947 Murrayfield
Australia 2G 2T (16) to 1PG 1DG (7)

1958 Murrayfield
Scotland 2PG 2T (12) to 1G 1T (8)

1966 Murrayfield
Scotland 1G 1PG 1T (11) to 1G (5)

1968 Murrayfield
Scotland 2PG 1T (9) to 1PG (3)

1970 Sydney
Australia 1G 1PG 5T (23) to 1PG (3)

1975 Murrayfield
Scotland 1G 1T (10) to 1PG (3)

1981 Murrayfield
Scotland 1G 5PG 1DG (24)
to 1PG 3T (15)

1982 *1* Brisbane
Scotland 1G 1PG 1DG (12) to 1PG 1T (7)

    2 Sydney
Australia 3G 5PG (33) to 3PG (9)
*Series drawn 1-1

1984 Murrayfield
Australia 3G 5PG 1T (37) to 4PG (12)

1988 Murrayfield
Australia 3G 2PG 2T (32)
to 1G 1PG 1T (13)

IRELAND v WALES
Played 93   Ireland won 32, Wales won 56, Drawn 5

1882 Dublin
Wales 2G 2T to 0

1883 No Match

1884 Cardiff
Wales 1DG 2T to 0

1885 No Match

1886 No Match

1887 Birkenhead
Wales 1DG 1T to 3T

1888 Dublin
Ireland 1G 1DG 1T to 0

1889 Swansea
Ireland 2T to 0

1890 Dublin
Drawn 1G each

1891 Llanelli
Wales 1G 1DG (6) to 1DG 1T (4)

1892 Dublin
Ireland 1G 2T (9) to 0

1893 Llanelli
Wales 1T (2) to 0

1894 Belfast
Ireland 1PG (3) to 0

1895 Cardiff
Wales 1G (5) to 1T (3)

1896 Dublin
Ireland 1G 1T (8) to 1DG (4)

1897 No Match

1898 Limerick
Wales 1G 1PG 1T (11) to 1PG (3)

1899 Cardiff
Ireland 1T (3) to 0

1900 Belfast
Wales 1T (3) to 0

1901 Swansea
Wales 2G (10) to 3T (9)

1902 Dublin
Wales 1G 1DG 2T (15) to 0

1903 Cardiff
Wales 6T (18) to 0

1904 Belfast
Ireland 1G 3T (14) to 4T (12)

1905 Swansea
Wales 2G (10) to 1T (3)

1906 Belfast
Ireland 1G 2T (11) to 2T (6)

1907 Cardiff
Wales 2G 1PG 1DG 4T (29) to 0

1908 Belfast
Wales 1G 2T (11) to 1G (5)

1909 Swansea
Wales 3G 1T (18) to 1G (5)

1910 Dublin
Wales 1DG 5T (19) to 1T (3)

1911 Cardiff
Wales 2G 1PG 1T (16) to 0

1912 Belfast
Ireland 1G 1DG 1T (12) to 1G (5)

1913 Swansea
Wales 2G 1PG 1T (16) to 2G 1PG (13)

1914 Belfast
Wales 1G 2T (11) to 1T (3)

1920 Cardiff
Wales 3G 1DG 3T (28) to 1DG (4)

1921 Belfast
Wales 1PG 1T (6) to 0

1922 Swansea
Wales 1G 2T (11) to 1G (5)

1923 Dublin
Ireland 1G (5) to 1DG (4)

1924 Cardiff
Ireland 2G 1T (13) to 1DG 2T (10)

1925 Belfast
Ireland 2G 1PG 2T (19) to 1T (3)

1926 Swansea
Wales 1G 2T (11) to 1G 1PG (8)

1927 Dublin
Ireland 2G 1PG 2T (19) to 1G 1DG (9)

1928 Cardiff
Ireland 2G 1T (13) to 2G (10)

1929 Belfast
Drawn 1G (5) each

1930 Swansea
Wales 1PG 3T (12) to 1PG 1DG (7)

1931 Belfast
Wales 1G 1DG 2T (15) to 1T (3)

1932 Cardiff
Ireland 4T (12) to 1DG 2T (10)

1933 Belfast
Ireland 1PG 1DG 1T (10) to 1G (5)

1934 Swansea
Wales 2G 1T (13) to 0

1935 Belfast
Ireland 2PG 1T (9) to 1PG (3)

1936 Cardiff
Wales 1PG (3) to 0

1937 Belfast
Ireland 1G (5) to 1PG (3)

1938 Swansea
Wales 1G 1PG 1T (11) to 1G (5)

1939 Belfast
Wales 1DG 1T (7) to 0

1947 Swansea
Wales 1PG 1T (6) to 0

1948 Belfast
Ireland 2T (6) to 1T (3)

1949 Swansea
Ireland 1G (5) to 0

1950 Belfast
Wales 2T (6) to 1PG (3)

1951 Cardiff
Drawn Wales 1PG (3) to Ireland 1T (3)

1952 Dublin
Wales 1G 1PG 2T (14) to 1PG (3)

1953 Swansea
Wales 1G (5) to 1T (3)

1954 Dublin
Wales 3PG 1DG (12) to 2PG 1T (9)

1955 Cardiff
Wales 3G 1PG 1T (21) to 1PG (3)

1956 Dublin
Ireland 1G 1PG 1DG (11) to 1PG (3)

1957 Cardiff
Wales 2PG (6) to 1G (5)

1958 Dublin
Wales 3T (9) to 1PG 1T (6)

1959 Cardiff
Wales 1G 1T (8) to 1PG 1T (6)

1960 Dublin
Wales 2G (10) to 2PG 1T (9)

1961 Cardiff
Wales 2PG 1T (9) to 0

1962 Dublin
Drawn Ireland 1DG (3) Wales 1PG (3)

1963 Cardiff
Ireland 1G 2PG 1DG (14)
to 1DG 1T (6)

1964 Dublin
Wales 3G (15) to 2PG (6)

1965 Cardiff
Wales 1G 1PG 1DG 1T (14)
to 1G 1PG (8)

1966 Dublin
Ireland 1PG 1DG 1T (9) to 1PG 1T (6)

1967 Cardiff
Ireland 1T (3) to 0

1968 Dublin
Ireland 1PG 1DG 1T (9) to 1PG 1DG (6)

1969 Cardiff
Wales 3G 1PG 1DG 1T (24)
to 1G 2PG (11)

1970 Dublin
Ireland 1G 1PG 1DG 1T (14) to 0

1971 Cardiff
Wales 1G 2PG 1DG 3T (23) to 3PG (9)

1972 No Match

1973 Cardiff
Wales 1G 2PG 1T (16) to 1G 2PG (12)

1974 Dublin
Drawn Ireland 3PG (9)
Wales 1G 1PG (9)

1975 Cardiff
Wales 3G 2PG 2T (32) to 1T (4)

1976 Dublin
Wales 3G 4PG 1T (34) to 3PG (9)

1977 Cardiff
Wales 2G 2PG 1DG 1T (25) to 3PG (9)

1978 Dublin
Wales 4PG 2T (20) to 3PG 1DG 1T (16)

1979 Cardiff
Wales 2G 4PG (24) to 2G 3PG (21)

1980 Dublin
Ireland 3G 1PG (21) to 1PG 1T (7)

1981 Cardiff
Wales 2PG 1DG (9) to 2T (8)

1982 Dublin
Ireland 1G 2PG 2T (20)
to 1G 1PG 1DG (12)

1983 Cardiff
Wales 1G 3PG 2T (23) to 3PG (9)

1984 Dublin
Wales 1G 4PG (18) to 3PG (9)

1985 Cardiff
Ireland 2G 3PG (21) to 1G 1DG (9)

1986 Dublin
Wales 1G 3PG 1T (19) to 1G 2PG (12)

1987 Cardiff
Ireland 2G 1PG (15) to 1PG 2T (11)

1987 Wellington *WC*
Wales 1PG 2DG 1T (13) to 2PG (6)

1988 Dublin
Wales 1G 1PG 1DG (12) to 1G 1PG (9)

1989 Cardiff
Ireland 1G 3PG 1T (19) to 3PG 1T (13)

1990 Dublin
Ireland 1G 2T (14) to 2T (8)

IRELAND v FRANCE
Played 63   Ireland won 25, France won 33, Drawn 5

1909 Dublin
Ireland 2G 1PG 2T (19) to 1G 1T (8)

1910 Paris
Ireland 1G 1T (8) to 1T (3)

1911 Cork
Ireland 3G 1DG 2T (25) to 1G (5)

1912 Paris
Ireland 1G 2T (11) to 2T (6)

1913 Cork
Ireland 3G 3T (24) to 0

1914 Paris
Ireland 1G 1T (8) to 2T (6)

1920 Dublin
France 5T (15) to 1DG 1T (7)

1921 Paris
France 4G (20) to 2G (10)

1922 Dublin
Ireland 1G 1PG (8) to 1T (3)

1923 Paris
France 1G 3T (14) to 1G 1T (8)

1924 Dublin
Ireland 2T (6) to 0

1925 Paris
Ireland 1PG 2T (9) to 1T (3)

1926 Belfast
Ireland 1G 1PG 1T (11) to 0

1927 Paris
Ireland 1G 1PG (8) to 1T (3)

1928 Belfast
Ireland 4T (12) to 1G 1T (8)

1929 Paris
Ireland 2T (6) to 0

1930 Belfast
France 1G (5) to 0

1931 Paris
France 1T (3) to 0

1947 Dublin
France 4T (12) to 1G 1PG (8)

1948 Paris
Ireland 2G 1T (13) to 2T (6)

1949 Dublin
France 2G 2PG (16) to 3PG (9)

1950 Paris
Drawn France 1DG (3) Ireland 1PG (3)

1951 Dublin
Ireland 1PG 2T (9) to 1G 1T (8)

1952 Paris
Ireland 1G 1PG 1T (11) to 1G 1PG (8)

1953 Belfast
Ireland 2G 2T (16) to 1DG (3)

1954 Paris
France 1G 1T (8) to 0

1955 Dublin
France 1G (5) to 1PG (3)

1956 Paris
France 1G 2DG 1T (14) to 1G 1PG (8)

1957 Dublin
Ireland 1G 1PG 1T (11) to 2PG (6)

1958 Paris
France 1G 1PG 1DG (11) to 2PG (6)

1959 Dublin
Ireland 1PG 1DG 1T (9) to 1G (5)

1960 Paris
France 1G 3DG 3T (23) to 2T (6)

1961 Dublin
France 2PG 2DG 1T (15) to 1PG (3)

1962 Paris
France 1G 2T (11) to 0

1963 Dublin
France 3G 2DG 1T (24) to 1G (5)

1964 Paris
France 3G 1DG 3T (27) to 1DG 1T (6)

1965 Dublin
Drawn 1T (3) each

1966 Paris
France 1G 1PG 1T (11) to 1PG 1DG (6)

1967 Dublin
France 1G 2DG (11) to 1PG 1T (6)

1968 Paris
France 2G 1PG 1DG (16) to 2PG (6)

1969 Dublin
Ireland 1G 3PG 1DG (17) to 2PG 1T (9)

1970 Paris
France 1G 1DG (8) to 0

1971 Dublin
Drawn Ireland 2PG 1T (9)
France 2PG 1DG (9)

1972 Paris
Ireland 2PG 2T (14) to 1G 1PG (9)

*1972 Dublin
Ireland 3G 2PG (24) to 1G 2T (14)
* *Non-championship match*

1973 Dublin
Ireland 2PG (6) to 1T (4)

1974 Paris
France 1G 1PG (9) to 2PG (6)

1975 Dublin
Ireland 2G 1PG 2DG 1T (25)
to 1PG 1DG (6)

1976 Paris
France 2G 2PG 2T (26) to 1PG (3)

1977 Dublin
France 1G 3PG (15) to 2PG (6)

1978 Paris
France 2PG 1T (10) to 3PG (9)

1979 Dublin
Drawn Ireland 3PG (9)
France 1G 1PG (9)

1980 Paris
France 1G 2PG 1DG 1T (19)
to 1G 3PG 1DG (18)

1981 Dublin
France 3PG 2DG 1T (19)
to 3PG 1T (13)

1982 Paris
France 1G 4PG 1T (22) to 3PG (9)

1983 Dublin
Ireland 1G 4PG 1T (22)
to 1G 2PG 1T (16)

1984 Paris
France 1G 4PG 1DG 1T (25) to 4PG (12)

1985 Dublin
Drawn Ireland 5PG (15)
France 2G 1PG (15)

1986 Paris
France 1G 4PG 1DG 2T (29) to 3PG (9)

1987 Dublin
France 1G 3PG 1T (19)
to 1G 1PG 1T (13)

1988 Paris
France 1G 1PG 4T (25) to 2PG (6)

1989 Dublin
France 2G 2PG 2T (26) to 1G 5PG (21)

1990 Paris
France 2G 5PG 1T (31) to 4PG (12)

IRELAND v NEW ZEALAND
Played 10   Ireland won 0, New Zealand won 9, Drawn 1

1905 Dublin
New Zealand 3G (15) to 0

1924 Dublin
New Zealand 1PG 1T (6) to 0

1935 Dublin
New Zealand 1G 2PG 2T (17)
to 2PG 1T (9)

1954 Dublin
New Zealand 1G 1PG 1DG 1T (14)
to 1PG (3)

1963 Dublin
New Zealand 1PG 1T (6) to 1G (5)

1973 Dublin
Drawn Ireland 2PG 1T (10)
New Zealand 1G 1T (10)

1974 Dublin
New Zealand 1G 3PG (15) to 2PG (6)

1976 Wellington
New Zealand 1PG 2T (11) to 1PG (3)

1978 Dublin
New Zealand 2DG 1T (10) to 2PG (6)

1989 Dublin
New Zealand 1G 3PG 2T (23) to 2PG (6)

IRELAND v SOUTH AFRICA
Played 10   Ireland won 1, South Africa won 8, Drawn 1

1906 Belfast
South Africa 1PG 4T (15)
to 1PG 3T (12)

1912 Dublin
South Africa 4G 6T (38) to 0

1931 Dublin
South Africa 1G 1T (8) to 1PG (3)

1951 Dublin
South Africa 1G 1DG 3T (17) to 1G (5)

1960 Dublin
South Africa 1G 1T (8) to 1PG (3)

1961 Cape Town
South Africa 3G 1PG 2T (24)
to 1G 1PG (8)

1965 Dublin
Ireland 2PG 1T (9) to 1PG 1T (6)

1970 Dublin
Drawn 1G 1PG (8) each

1981 *1* Cape Town
South Africa 1G 3PG 2T (23)
to 2G 1PG (15)

2 Durban
South Africa 1PG 3DG (12)
to 2PG 1T (10)
South Africa won series 2-0

IRELAND v AUSTRALIA
Played 12   Ireland won 6, Australia won 6, Drawn 0

1927 Dublin
Australia 1G (5) to 1PG (3)

1947 Dublin
Australia 2G 2T (16) to 1PG (3)

1958 Dublin
Ireland 1PG 2T (9) to 2T (6)

1967 Dublin
Ireland 1PG 2DG 2T (15) to 1G 1DG (8)

1967 Sydney **Ireland** 1G 1DG 1T (11) to 1G (5)	*2* Sydney **Ireland** 1PG 2DG (9) to 1PG (3) *Ireland won series 2-0*
1968 Dublin **Ireland** 2G (10) to 1T (3)	1981 Dublin **Australia** 3PG 1DG 1T (16) to 4PG (12)
1976 Dublin **Australia** 1G 2PG 2T (20) to 2PG 1T (10)	1984 Dublin **Australia** 1PG 3DG 1T (16) to 3PG (9)
1979 *1* Brisbane **Ireland** 2G 4PG 1DG (27) to 1G 2PG (12)	1987 Sydney *WC* **Australia** 4G 3PG (33) to 2G 1PG (15)

WALES v FRANCE

Played 63   Wales won 36, France won 24, Drawn 3

1908 Cardiff **Wales** 3G 1PG 6T (36) to 1DG (4)	1948 Swansea **France** 1G 2T (11) to 1PG (3)
1909 Paris **Wales** 7G 4T (47) to 1G (5)	1949 Paris **France** 1G (5) to 1T (3)
1910 Swansea **Wales** 8G 1PG 2T (49) to 1G 2PG 1T (14)	1950 Cardiff **Wales** 3G 1PG 1T (21) to 0
1911 Paris **Wales** 3G (15) to 0	1951 Paris **France** 1G 1PG (8) to 1T (3)
1912 Newport **Wales** 1G 3T (14) to 1G 1T (8)	1952 Swansea **Wales** 2PG 1DG (9) to 1G (5)
1913 Paris **Wales** 1G 2T (11) to 1G 1T (8)	1953 Paris **Wales** 2T (6) to 1PG (3)
1914 Swansea **Wales** 5G 2T (31) to 0	1954 Cardiff **Wales** 2G 3PG (19) to 2G 1PG (13)
1920 Paris **Wales** 2T (6) to 1G (5)	1955 Paris **Wales** 2G 2PG (16) to 1G 1PG 1DG (11)
1921 Cardiff **Wales** 2PG 2T (12) to 1DG (4)	1956 Cardiff **Wales** 1G (5) to 1T (3)
1922 Paris **Wales** 1G 2T (11) to 1T (3)	1957 Paris **Wales** 2G 1PG 2T (19) to 2G 1T (13)
1923 Swansea **Wales** 2G 1PG 1T (16) to 1G 1T (8)	1958 Cardiff **France** 2G 2DG (16) to 1PG 1T (6)
1924 Paris **Wales** 1DG 2T (10) to 2T (6)	1959 Paris **France** 1G 1PG 1T (11) to 1PG (3)
1925 Cardiff **Wales** 1G 2T (11) to 1G (5)	1960 Cardiff **France** 2G 2T (16) to 1G 1PG (8)
1926 Paris **Wales** 1DG 1T (7) to 1G (5)	1961 Paris **France** 1G 1T (8) to 2T (6)
1927 Swansea **Wales** 2G 5T (25) to 1DG 1T (7)	1962 Cardiff **Wales** 1PG (3) to 0
1928 Paris **France** 1G 1T (8) to 1T (3)	1963 Paris **France** 1G (5) to 1PG (3)
1929 Cardiff **Wales** 1G 1T (8) to 1T (3)	1964 Cardiff **Drawn** 1G 2PG (11) each
1930 Paris **Wales** 2DG 1T (11) to 0	1965 Paris **France** 2G 1PG 1DG 2T (22) to 2G 1T (13)
1931 Swansea **Wales** 5G 1DG 2T (35) to 1T (3)	1966 Cardiff **Wales** 2PG 1T (9) to 1G 1T (8)
1947 Paris **Wales** 1PG (3) to 0	1967 Paris **France** 1G 1PG 2DG 2T (20) to 1G 2PG 1DG (14)

1968 Cardiff
France 1G 1PG 1DG 1T (14)
to 2PG 1T (9)

1969 Paris
Drawn France 1G 1PG (8)
Wales 1G 1T (8)

1970 Cardiff
Wales 1G 2PG (11) to 2T (6)

1971 Paris
Wales 1PG 2T (9) to 1G (5)

1972 Cardiff
Wales 4PG 2T (20) to 2PG (6)

1973 Paris
France 3PG 1DG (12) to 1DG (3)

1974 Cardiff
Drawn 3PG 1DG 1T (16) each

1975 Paris
Wales 1G 1PG 4T (25) to 2PG 1T (10)

1976 Cardiff
Wales 5PG 1T (19) to 1G 1PG 1T (13)

1977 Paris
France 1G 2PG 1T (16) to 3PG (9)

1978 Cardiff
Wales 1G 2DG 1T (16) to 1DG 1T (7)

1979 Paris
France 2PG 2T (14) to 3PG 1T (13)

1980 Cardiff
Wales 1G 3T (18) to 1G 1DG (9)

1981 Paris
France 5PG 1T (19) to 1G 3PG (15)

1982 Cardiff
Wales 6PG 1T (22) to 1G 2PG (12)

1983 Paris
France 3PG 1DG 1T (16) to 1G 1PG (9)

1984 Cardiff
France 1G 4PG 1DG (21)
to 1G 2PG 1T (16)

1985 Paris
France 2PG 2T (14) to 1PG (3)

1986 Cardiff
France 2G 1DG 2T (23) to 5PG (15)

1987 Paris
France 1G 2PG 1T (16) to 3PG (9)

1988 Cardiff
France 2PG 1T (10) to 1G 1PG (9)

1989 Paris
France 3G 2PG 1DG 1T (31) to 4PG (12)

1990 Cardiff
France 3G 1PG 2T (29)
to 4PG 1DG 1T (19)

WALES v NEW ZEALAND
Played 15   Wales won 3, New Zealand won 12, Drawn 0

1905 Cardiff
Wales 1T (3) to 0

1924 Swansea
New Zealand 2G 1PG 2T (19) to 0

1935 Cardiff
Wales 2G 1T (13) to 1G 1DG 1T (12)

1953 Cardiff
Wales 2G 1PG (13) to 1G 1PG (8)

1963 Cardiff
New Zealand 1PG 1DG (6) to 0

1967 Cardiff
New Zealand 2G 1PG (13)
to 1PG 1DG (6)

1969 *1* Christchurch
New Zealand 2G 1PG 2T (19) to 0

  2 Auckland
New Zealand 3G 5PG 1DG (33)
to 2PG 2T (12)
New Zealand won series 2-0

1972 Cardiff
New Zealand 5PG 1T (19)
to 4PG 1T (16)

1978 Cardiff
New Zealand 3PG 1T (13) to 4PG (12)

1980 Cardiff
New Zealand 2G 1PG 2T (23)
to 1PG (3)

1987 Brisbane *WC*
New Zealand 7G 1PG 1T (49) to 1G (6)

1988 *1* Christchurch
New Zealand 6G 4T (52) to 1PG (3)

  2 Auckland
New Zealand 8G 2PG (54) to 1G 1PG (9)
New Zealand won series 2-0

1989 Cardiff
New Zealand 3G 4PG 1T (34) to 3PG (9)

WALES v SOUTH AFRICA
Played 7   Wales won 0, South Africa won 6, Drawn 1

1906 Swansea
South Africa 1G 2T (11) to 0

1912 Cardiff
South Africa 1PG (3) to 0

1931 Swansea
South Africa 1G 1T (8) to 1T (3)

1951 Cardiff
South Africa 1DG 1T (6) to 1T (3)

1960 Cardiff
South Africa 1PG (3) to 0

1964 Durban
South Africa 3G 2PG 1DG (24) to
1PG (3)

1970 Cardiff
Drawn 1PG 1T (6) each

WALES v AUSTRALIA
Played 13   Wales won 8, Australia won 5, Drawn 0

1908 Cardiff
Wales 1PG 2T (9) to 2T (6)

1927 Cardiff
Australia 3G 1T (18) to 1G 1T (8)

1947 Cardiff
Wales 2PG (6) to 0

1958 Cardiff
Wales 1PG 1DG 1T (9) to 1T (3)

1966 Cardiff
Australia 1G 1PG 1DG 1T (14)
to 1G 1PG 1T (11)

1969 Sydney
Wales 2G 2PG 1T (19) to 2G 2PG (16)

1973 Cardiff
Wales 4PG 3T (24) to 0

1975 Cardiff
Wales 3G 1PG 1DG 1T (28) to 1PG (3)

1978 *1* Brisbane
Australia 1G 4PG (18) to 2T (8)

   2 Sydney
Australia 3PG 2DG 1T (19)
to 2PG 1DG 2T (17)
Australia won series 2-0

1981 Cardiff
Wales 1G 3PG 1DG (18)
to 1G 1PG 1T (13)

1984 Cardiff
Australia 3G 2PG 1T (28) to 1G 1PG (9)

1987 Rotorua *WC*
Wales 2G 2PG 1T (22)
to 2G 2PG 1DG (21)

FRANCE v NEW ZEALAND
Played 26   France won 5, New Zealand won 21, Drawn 0

1906 Paris
New Zealand 4G 6T (38) to 1G 1T (8)

1925 Toulouse
New Zealand 3G 5T (30) to 2T (6)

1954 Paris
France 1T (3) to 0

1961 *1* Auckland
New Zealand 2G 1DG (13) to 2DG (6)

   2 Wellington
New Zealand 1G (5) to 1T (3)

   3 Christchurch
New Zealand 4G 3PG 1T (32) to 1T (3)
New Zealand won series 3-0

1964 Paris
New Zealand 1PG 1DG 2T (12)
to 1PG (3)

1967 Paris
New Zealand 3G 1PG 1T (21)
to 3PG 1DG 1T (15)

1968 *1* Christchurch
New Zealand 3PG 1T (12)
to 2PG 1DG (9)

   2 Wellington
New Zealand 3PG (9) to 1PG (3)

   3 Auckland
New Zealand 2G 2PG 1DG (19)
to 1DG 3T (12)
New Zealand won series 3-0

1973 Paris
France 1G 1PG 1T (13) to 2PG (6)

1977 *1* Toulouse
France 1G 3PG 1DG (18)
to 2PG 1DG 1T (13)

   2 Paris
New Zealand 1G 2PG 1DG (15)
to 1PG (3)
Series drawn 1-1

1979 *1* Christchurch
New Zealand 1G 3PG 2T (23)
to 1G 1DG (9)

   2 Auckland
France 1G 1PG 1DG 3T (24)
to 1G 3PG 1T (19)
Series drawn 1-1

1981 *1* Toulouse
New Zealand 2PG 1DG 1T (13)
to 2PG 1DG (9)

2 Paris
New Zealand *2G 2PG (18) to 2PG (6)
*indicates a penalty try
New Zealand won series 2-0

1984 *1* Christchurch
New Zealand 2PG 1T (10) to 1G 1DG (9)

2 Auckland
New Zealand 2G 5PG 1T (31)
to 2PG 3T (18)
New Zealand won series 2-0

1986 Christchurch
New Zealand 1G 1PG 3DG (18)
to 3DG (9)

1986 *1* Toulouse
New Zealand 3PG 2DG 1T (19)
to 1PG 1T (7)

2 Nantes
France 1G 2PG 1T (16) to 1PG (3)

1987 Auckland *WC*
New Zealand 1G 4PG 1DG 2T (29)
to 1G 1PG (9)

1989 *1* Christchurch
New Zealand 2G 3PG 1T (25)
to 1G 1PG 2T (17)

2 Auckland
New Zealand 3G 4PG 1T (34)
to 4PG 2T (20)
New Zealand won series 2-0

FRANCE v SOUTH AFRICA
Played 19   France won 3, South Africa won 12, Drawn 4

1913 Bordeaux
South Africa 4G 1PG 5T (38) to 1G (5)

1952 Paris
South Africa 2G 1PG 4T (25)
to 1DG (3)

1958 *1* Cape Town
Drawn South Africa 1T (3)
France 1DG (3)

2 Johannesburg
France 1PG 2DG (9) to 1G (5)
France won series 1-0, with 1 draw

1961 Paris
Drawn no score

1964 Springs (SA)
France 1G 1PG (8) to 1PG 1T (6)

1967 *1* Durban
South Africa 4G 1PG 1T (26) to 1T (3)

2 Bloemfontein
South Africa 2G 1PG 1T (16) to 1PG (3)

3 Johannesburg
France 2G 1PG 2DG (19)
to 1G 2PG 1T (14)

4 Cape Town
Drawn South Africa 1PG 1DG (6)
France 1PG 1T (6)
South Africa won series 2-1, with 1 draw

1968 *1* Bordeaux
South Africa 4PG (12) to 3T (9)

2 Paris
South Africa 2G 1PG 1T (16)
to 1G 2DG (11)
South Africa won series 2-0

1971 *1* Bloemfontein
South Africa 2G 3PG 1DG (22)
to 2PG 1T (9)

2 Durban
Drawn 1G 1DG (8) each
South Africa won series 1-0, with 1 draw

1974 *1* Toulouse
South Africa 3PG 1T (13) to 1T (4)

2 Paris
South Africa 2PG 1T (10) to 2T (8)
South Africa won series 2-0

1975 *1* Bloemfontein
South Africa 3G 4PG 2T (38)
to 3G 1PG 1T (25)

2 Pretoria
South Africa 2G 7PG (33)
to 1G 3PG 1DG (18)
South Africa won series 2-0

1980 Pretoria
South Africa 4G 3PG 1T (37)
to 1G 3PG (15)

FRANCE v AUSTRALIA
Played 20   France won 11, Australia won 7, Drawn 2

1928 Paris
Australia 1G 2T (11) to 1G 1T (8)

1948 Paris
France 2G 1T (13) to 2PG (6)

1958 Paris
France 2G 2DG 1T (19) to 0

1961 Sydney
France 2DG 3T (15) to 1G 1PG (8)

1967 Paris
France 1G 4PG 1DG (20)
to 1G 1PG 1DG 1T (14)

1968 Sydney
Australia 1G 1PG 1DG (11) to 2G (10)

1971 *1* Toulouse
Australia 1G 1PG 1T (13) to 1PG 2T (11)

    2 Paris
France 1G 4PG (18) to 3PG (9)
Series drawn 1-1

1972 *1* Sydney
Drawn Australia 2PG 2T (14)
France 1G 2T (14)

    2 Brisbane
France 2G 1T (16) to 5PG (15)
France won series 1-0, with 1 draw

1976 *1* Bordeaux
France 3G (18) to 4PG 1DG (15)

    2 Paris
France 2G 1PG 1DG 4T (34) to 2PG (6)
France won series 2-0

1981 *1* Brisbane
Australia 1G 1PG 2T (17)
to 1G 2PG 1DG (15)

    2 Sydney
Australia 2G 4PG (24) to 2DG 2T (14)
Australia won series 2-0

1983 *1* Clermont-Ferrand
Drawn France 3PG 2DG (15)
Australia 1G 1PG 2DG (15)

    2 Paris
France 1G 3PG (15) to 1PG 1DG (6)
France won series 1-0, with 1 draw

1986 Sydney
Australia 1G 6PG 1DG (27) to 1G 2T (14)

1987 Sydney *WC*
France 4G 2PG (30) to 2G 3PG 1DG (24)

1989 *1* Strasbourg
Australia 2G 4PG 2T (32)
to 4PG 1DG (15)

    2 Lille
France 1G 5PG 1T (25)
to 1G 3PG 1T (19)
Series drawn 1-1

NEW ZEALAND v SOUTH AFRICA

Played 37   New Zealand won 15, South Africa won 20, Drawn 2

1921 *1* Dunedin
New Zealand 2G 1T (13) to 1G (5)

    2 Auckland
South Africa 1G 1DG (9) to 1G (5)

    3 Wellington
Drawn no score
Series drawn 1-1, with 1 draw

1928 *1* Durban
South Africa 2PG 2DG 1T (17) to 0

    2 Johannesburg
New Zealand 1PG 1DG (7)
to 1PG 1GM (6)

    3 Port Elizabeth
South Africa 1G 2T (11) to 2T (6)

    4 Cape Town
New Zealand 2PG 1DG 1T (13)
to 1G (5)
Series drawn 2-2

1937 *1* Wellington
New Zealand 2PG 1DG 1T (13)
to 1DG 1T (7)

    2 Christchurch
South Africa 2G 1PG (13) to 2T (6)

    3 Auckland
South Africa 1G 4T (17) to 2PG (6)
South Africa won series 2-1

1949 *1* Cape Town
South Africa 5PG (15)
to 1G 1PG 1DG (11)

    2 Johannesburg
South Africa 1PG 1DG 2T (12)
to 1PG 1DG (6)

    3 Durban
South Africa 3PG (9) to 1T (3)

    4 Port Elizabeth
South Africa 1G 1PG 1DG (11)
to 1G 1T (8)
South Africa won series 4-0

1956 *1* Dunedin
New Zealand 2G (10) to 1PG 1T (6)

    2 Wellington
South Africa 1G 1T (8) to 1T (3)

    3 Christchurch
New Zealand 1G 2PG 2T (17)
to 2G (10)

    4 Auckland
New Zealand 1G 2PG (11) to 1G (5)
New Zealand won series 3-1

1960 *1* Johannesburg
South Africa 2G 1PG (13) to 0

    2 Cape Town
New Zealand 1G 1PG 1DG (11)
to 1T (3)

    3 Bloemfontein
Drawn 1G 2PG (11) each

    4 Port Elizabeth
South Africa 1G 1PG (8) to 1PG (3)
South Africa won series 2-1, with 1 draw

1965 *1* Wellington
New Zealand 2T (6) to 1DG (3)

    2 Dunedin
New Zealand 2G 1T (13) to 0

    3 Christchurch
South Africa 2G 1PG 2T (19)
to 2G 1PG 1T (16)

4 Auckland
New Zealand 1G 1DG 4T (20) to 1PG (3)
New Zealand won series 3-1

1970 *1* Pretoria
South Africa 1G 2PG 1DG 1T (17) to 1PG 1T (6)

2 Cape Town
New Zealand 1PG 2T (9) to 1G 1PG (8)

3 Port Elizabeth
South Africa 1G 2PG 1T (14) to 1PG (3)

4 Johannesburg
South Africa 1G 4PG 1T (20) to 1G 4PG (17)
South Africa won series 3-1

1976 *1* Durban
South Africa 1G 1PG 1DG 1T (16) to 1PG 1T (7)

2 Bloemfontein
New Zealand 1G 2PG 1DG (15) to 3PG (9)

3 Cape Town
South Africa 1G 2PG 1DG (15) to 2PG 1T (10)

4 Johannesburg
South Africa 1G 2PG 1DG (15) to 1PG 1DG 2T (14)
South Africa won series 3-1

1981 *1* Christchurch
New Zealand 1G 2T (14) to 1G 1DG (9)

2 Wellington
South Africa 1G 5PG 1DG (24) to 4PG (12)

3 Auckland
New Zealand 1G 4PG 1DG 1T (25) to 2G 2PG 1T (22)
New Zealand won series 2-1

NEW ZEALAND v AUSTRALIA
Played 87   New Zealand won 61, Australia won 21, Drawn 5

1903 Sydney
New Zealand 1G 1PG 2GM 2T (22) to 1PG (3)

1905 Dunedin
New Zealand 1G 3T (14) to 1T (3)

1907 *1* Sydney
New Zealand 4G 2T (26) to 1PG 1GM (6)

2 Brisbane
New Zealand 1G 3T (14) to 1G (5)

3 Sydney
Drawn 1G (5) each
New Zealand won series 2-0, with 1 draw

1910 *1* Sydney
New Zealand 2T (6) to 0

2 Sydney
Australia 1G 2T (11) to 0

3 Sydney
New Zealand 2G 6T (28) to 2G 1PG (13)
New Zealand won series 2-1

1913 *1* Wellington
New Zealand 3G 5T (30) to 1G (5)

2 Dunedin
New Zealand 3G 1DG 2T (25) to 2G 1T (13)

3 Christchurch
Australia 2G 2T (16) to 1G (5)
New Zealand won series 2-1

1914 *1* Sydney
New Zealand 1G (5) to 0

2 Brisbane
New Zealand 1G 4T (17) to 0

3 Sydney
New Zealand 2G 4T (22) to 1DG 1T (7)
New Zealand won series 3-0

1929 *1* Sydney
Australia 2PG 1T (9) to 1G 1PG (8)

2 Brisbane
Australia 1G 2PG 2T (17) to 1PG 2T (9)

3 Sydney
Australia 3PG 2T (15) to 2G 1T (13)
Australia won series 3-0

1931 Auckland
New Zealand 1G 4PG 1T (20) to 2G 1T (13)

1932 *1* Sydney
Australia 2G 2PG 2T (22) to 2G 1DG 1T (17)

2 Brisbane
New Zealand 1G 1PG 1DG 3T (21) to 1T (3)

3 Sydney
New Zealand 3G 2T (21) to 2G 1T (13)
New Zealand won series 2-1

1934 *1* Sydney
Australia 2G 3PG 2T (25) to 1G 2T (11)

2 Sydney
Drawn 1T (3) each
Australia won series 1-0, with 1 draw

1936 *1* Wellington
New Zealand 1G 2T (11) to 1PG 1T (6)

2 Dunedin
New Zealand 4G 1PG 5T (38) to 2G 1PG (13)
New Zealand won series 2-0

1938 *1* Sydney
New Zealand 3G 2PG 1T (24) to 3PG (9)

2 Brisbane
New Zealand 2G 1DG 2T (20) to 1G 1PG 2T (14)

3 Sydney
New Zealand 1G 2PG 1T (14)
to 1PG 1T (6)
New Zealand won series 3-0

1946 *1* Dunedin
New Zealand 5G 2T (31) to 1G 1T (8)

2 Auckland
New Zealand 1G 3PG (14) to 2G (10)
New Zealand won series 2-0

1947 *1* Brisbane
New Zealand *2G 1T (13) to 1G (5)
*includes one penalty try

2 Sydney
New Zealand 3G 4PG (27)
to 1G 3PG (14)
New Zealand won series 2-0

1949 *1* Wellington
Australia 1G 2T (11) to 1PG 1T (6)

2 Auckland
Australia 2G 1PG 1T (16)
to 1PG 1DG 1T (9)
Australia won series 2-0

1951 *1* Sydney
New Zealand 1G 1PG (8) to 0

2 Sydney
New Zealand 1G 1DG 3T (17)
to 1G 1PG 1T (11)

3 Brisbane
New Zealand 2G 2T (16) to 2PG (6)
New Zealand won series 3-0

1952 *1* Christchurch
Australia 1G 1DG 2T (14) to 1PG 2T (9)

2 Wellington
New Zealand 2PG 1DG 2T (15)
to 1G 1PG (8)
Series drawn 1-1

1955 *1* Wellington
New Zealand 2G 1PG 1T (16)
to 1G 1PG (8)

2 Dunedin
New Zealand 1G 1DG (8) to 0

3 Auckland
Australia 1G 1T (8) to 1T (3)
New Zealand won series 2-1

1957 *1* Sydney
New Zealand 2G 3PG 2T (25)
to 1G 2PG (11)

2 Brisbane
New Zealand 2G 1DG 1GM 2T (22)
to 2PG 1T (9)
New Zealand won series 2-0

1958 *1* Wellington
New Zealand 2G 5T (25) to 1T (3)

2 Christchurch
Australia 1PG 1T (6) to 1T (3)

3 Auckland
New Zealand 1G 4PG (17)
to 1G 1PG (8)
New Zealand won series 2-1

1962 *1* Brisbane
New Zealand 1G 1PG 1DG 3T (20)
to 2PG (6)

2 Sydney
New Zealand 1G 2PG 1T (14) to 1G (5)
New Zealand won series 2-0

1962 *1* Wellington
Drawn New Zealand 2PG 1T (9)
Australia 3PG (9)

2 Dunedin
New Zealand 1PG (3) to 0

3 Auckland
New Zealand 2G 1DG 1T (16)
to 1G 1PG (8)
New Zealand won series 2-0, with 1 draw

1964 *1* Dunedin
New Zealand 1G 2PG 1DG (14)
to 2PG 1T (9)

2 Christchurch
New Zealand 3G 1T (18) to 1T (3)

3 Wellington
Australia 1G 3PG 1DG 1T (20) to 1G (5)
New Zealand won series 2-1

1967 Wellington
New Zealand 4G 2PG 1DG (29)
to 1PG 2T (9)

1968 *1* Sydney
New Zealand 3G 1PG 3T (27)
to 1G 2PG (11)

2 Brisbane
New Zealand *2G 2PG 1T (19)
to 5PG 1T (18)
*includes one penalty try
New Zealand won series 2-0

1972 *1* Wellington
New Zealand 3G 1DG 2T (29)
to 2PG (6)

2 Christchurch
New Zealand 2G 2PG 3T (30)
to 1G 1DG 2T (17)

3 Auckland
New Zealand 4G 2PG 2T (38)
to 1PG (3)
New Zealand won series 3-0

1974 *1* Sydney
New Zealand 1PG 2T (11) to 1G (6)

2 Brisbane
Drawn 1G 2PG 1T (16) each

3 Sydney
New Zealand 2G 1T (16) to 2PG (6)
New Zealand won series 2-0, with 1 draw

1978 *1* Wellington
New Zealand 3PG 1T (13)
to 1G 2PG (12)

2 Christchurch
New Zealand 2G 1PG 1DG 1T (22) to 1PG 1DG (6)

3 Auckland
Australia 2G 1PG 1DG 3T (30) to 1G 2PG 1T (16)
New Zealand won series 2-1

1979 Sydney
Australia 3PG 1DG (12) to 1PG 1DG (6)

1980 *1* Sydney
Australia 1G 1DG 1T (13) to 3PG (9)

2 Brisbane
New Zealand 1G 2PG (12) to 1G 1PG (9)

3 Sydney
Australia 2G 1PG 1DG 2T (26) to 2PG 1T (10)
Australia won series 2-1

1982 *1* Christchurch
New Zealand 2G 1PG 2T (23) to 1G 2PG 1T (16)

2 Wellington
Australia 1G 3PG 1T (19) to 1G 2PG 1T (16)

3 Auckland
New Zealand 2G 5PG 2DG (33) to 1G 3PG 1DG (18)
New Zealand won series 2-1

1983 Sydney
New Zealand 1G 4PG (18) to 2T (8)

1984 *1* Sydney
Australia 1G 1PG 1DG 1T (16) to 2PG 1DG (9)

2 Brisbane
New Zealand 5PG 1T (19) to 1G 3PG (15)

3 Sydney
New Zealand 1G 5PG 1T (25) to 1G 6PG (24)
New Zealand won series 2-1

1985 Auckland
New Zealand 2PG 1T (10) to 1G 1PG (9)

1986 *1* Wellington
Australia 1G 1PG 1T (13) to 1G 2PG (12)

2 Dunedin
New Zealand 2PG 1DG 1T (13) to 3PG 1DG (12)

3 Auckland
Australia 1G 4PG 1T (22) to 3PG (9)
Australia won series 2-1

1987 Sydney
New Zealand 1G 3PG 1DG 3T (30) to 3PG 1DG 1T (16)

1988 *1* Sydney
New Zealand 3G 2PG 2T (32) to 1PG 1T (7)

2 Brisbane
Drawn Australia 1G 3PG 1T (19)
New Zealand 2G 1PG 1T (19)

3 Sydney
New Zealand 3G 4PG (30) to 1G 1PG (9)
New Zealand won series 2-0, with 1 draw

1989 Auckland
New Zealand 2G 4PG (24) to 1G 2PG (12)

SOUTH AFRICA v AUSTRALIA
Played 28   South Africa won 21, Australia won 7, Drawn 0

1933 *1* Cape Town
South Africa 1G 1PG 3T (17) to 1PG (3)

2 Durban
Australia 3G 1PG 1T (21) to 1PG 1T (6)

3 Johannesburg
South Africa 1G 1DG 1T (12) to 1T (3)

4 Port Elizabeth
South Africa 1G 1PG 1T (11) to 0

5 Bloemfontein
Australia 1G 1DG 2T (15) to 1DG (4)
South Africa won series 3-2

1937 *1* Sydney
South Africa 1PG 2T (9) to 1G (5)

2 Sydney
South Africa 4G 2T (26) to 1G 2PG 2T (17)
South Africa won series 2-0

1953 *1* Johannesburg
South Africa 2G 2PG 3T (25) to 1PG (3)

2 Cape Town
Australia 3G 1T (18) to 1G 3T (14)

3 Durban
South Africa 3G 1T (18) to 1G 1PG (8)

4 Port Elizabeth
South Africa 2G 2PG 2DG (22) to 2PG 1T (9)
South Africa won series 3-1

1956 *1* Sydney
South Africa 1PG 2T (9) to 0

2 Brisbane
South Africa 1DG 2T (9) to 0
South Africa won series 2-0

1961 *1* Johannesburg
South Africa 2G 6T (28) to 1PG (3)

2 Port Elizabeth
South Africa 1G 3PG 1DG 2T (23) to 1G 2PG (11)
South Africa won series 2-0

1963 *1* Pretoria
South Africa 1G 2PG 1T (14) to 1T (3)

2 Cape Town
Australia 1PG 1DG 1T (9) to 1G (5)

3 Johannesburg
Australia 1G 1PG 1DG (11) to 3PG (9)

4 Port Elizabeth
South Africa 2G 3PG 1T (22)
to 1PG 1DG (6)
Series drawn 2-2

1965 *1* Sydney
Australia 4PG 2T (18) to 1G 1PG 1T (11)

2 Brisbane
Australia 4PG (12) to 1G 1T (8)
Australia won series 2-0

1969 *1* Johannesburg
South Africa 3G 3PG 2T (30)
to 1G 2PG (11)

2 Durban
South Africa 2G 1PG 1T (16) to 3PG (9)

3 Cape Town
South Africa 1G 1PG 1T (11) to 1PG (3)

4 Bloemfontein
South Africa 2G 2PG 1T (19)
to 1G 1PG (8)
South Africa won series 4-0

1971 *1* Sydney
South Africa 2G 1PG 1DG 1T (19)
to 1G 2PG (11)

2 Brisbane
South Africa 1G 1PG 2T (14)
to 1PG 1DG (6)

3 Sydney
South Africa 3G 1PG (18) to 1PG 1T (6)
South Africa won series 3-0

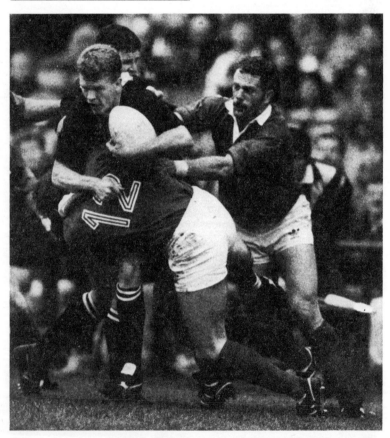

Ireland v New Zealand, 1989. Ireland's David Irwin (No 12) halts John Gallagher's progress, supported by Phil Matthews.

WORLD CUP WINNERS
New Zealand Once 1987

GRAND SLAM WINNERS
Wales 8 times: 1908, 1909, 1911, 1950, 1952, 1971, 1976, 1978.
England 8 times: 1913, 1914, 1921, 1923, 1924, 1928, 1957, 1980.
France 4 times: 1968, 1977, 1981, 1987.   Scotland 3 times: 1925, 1984, 1990.
Ireland once: 1948.

TRIPLE CROWN WINNERS
Wales 17 times: 1893, 1900, 1902, 1905, 1908, 1909, 1911, 1950, 1952, 1965, 1969, 1971, 1976, 1977, 1978, 1979, 1988.   England 15 times: 1883, 1884, 1892, 1913, 1914, 1921, 1923, 1924, 1928, 1934, 1937, 1954, 1957, 1960, 1980.   Scotland 10 times: 1891, 1895, 1901, 1903, 1907, 1925, 1933, 1938, 1984, 1990.   Ireland 6 times: 1894, 1899, 1948, 1949, 1982, 1985.

INTERNATIONAL CHAMPIONSHIP WINNERS

Year	Winner	Year	Winner	Year	Winner	Year	Winner
1883	England	1910	England	1938	Scotland	1967	France
1884	England	1911	Wales	1939	{ England, Wales, Ireland	1968	France
1885*	——	1912	{ England, Ireland			1969	Wales
1886	{ England, Scotland	1913	England	1947	{ Wales, England	1970	{ France, Wales
1887	Scotland	1914	England			1971	Wales
1888*	——			1948	Ireland	1972*	——
1889*	——	1920	{ England, Scotland, Wales	1949	Ireland	1973	Quintuple tie
1890	{ England, Scotland	1921	England	1950	Wales		
1891	Scotland	1922	Wales	1951	Ireland	1974	Ireland
1892	England	1923	England	1952	Wales	1975	Wales
1893	Wales	1924	England	1953	England	1976	Wales
1894	Ireland	1925	Scotland	1954	{ England, France, Wales	1977	France
1895	Scotland	1926	{ Scotland, Ireland			1978	Wales
1896	Ireland			1955	{ France, Wales	1979	Wales
1897*	——	1927	{ Scotland, Ireland	1956	Wales	1980	England
1898*	——			1957	England	1981	France
1899	Ireland	1928	England	1958	England	1982	Ireland
1900	Wales	1929	Scotland	1959	France	1983	{ France, Ireland
1901	Scotland	1930	England	1960	{ France, England		
1902	Wales	1931	Wales	1961	France	1984	Scotland
1903	Scotland	1932	{ England, Wales, Ireland	1962	France	1985	Ireland
1904	Scotland			1963	England	1986	{ France, Scotland
1905	Wales	1933	Scotland	1964	{ Scotland, Wales		
1906	{ Ireland, Wales	1934	England			1987	France
1907	Scotland	1935	Ireland	1965	Wales	1988	{ Wales, France
1908	Wales	1936	Wales	1966	Wales	1989	France
1909	Wales	1937	England			1990	Scotland

Matches not completed, for various reasons

Wales have won the title outright most times, 21; England have won it 18 times, Scotland 13, Ireland 10, and France 9.

OTHER INTERNATIONAL MATCHES 1989-90

BLEDISLOE CUP 1989

5 August 1989, Eden Park, Auckland
NEW ZEALAND 24 (2G 4PG)   AUSTRALIA 12 (1G 2PG)

NEW ZEALAND: J A Gallagher (Wellington); J J Kirwan (Auckland), J T Stanley (Auckland), N J Schuster (Wellington), T J Wright (Auckland); G J Fox (Auckland), I B Deans (Canterbury); S C McDowell (Bay of Plenty), S B T Fitzpatrick (Auckland), R W Loe (Waikato), G W Whetton (Auckland), M J Pierce (Wellington), A J Whetton (Auckland), W T Shelford (North Harbour) (*capt*), M R Brewer (Otago)
Scorers *Tries:* Gallagher, Loe *Conversions:* Fox (2) *Penalty Goals:* Fox (4)
AUSTRALIA: G J Martin (Queensland); I Williams (New South Wales), T J Horan (Queensland), L F Walker (New South Wales), D I Campese (New South Wales); M P Lynagh (Queensland), N C Farr-Jones (*capt*); A J McIntyre (Queensland), P N Kearns (New South Wales), A J Daly (New South Wales), S A G Cutler (New South Wales), W A Campbell (Queensland), J S Miller (Queensland), S P Poidevin (New South Wales), S N Tuynman (New South Wales) *Replacement* B T Gavin (New South Wales) for Campbell
Scorers *Try:* Campese *Conversion:* Lynagh *Penalty Goals:* Lynagh (2)
Referee S R Hilditch (Ireland)

23 September 1989, Varsity Stadium, Toronto
CANADA 21 (1G 5PG)   USA 3 (1PG)

CANADA (*all British Colombia*): S Stewart; T Woods, S Brown, I Stuart, M Wyatt; G Rees, J Graf; P Szabo, D Spiers, E Evans, J Robertson, N Hadley, R Radu, G McKinnon, G Ennis (*capt*)
Scorers *Try:* Brown *Conversion:* Wyatt *Penalty Goals:* Wyatt (5)
USA: A Montgomery (Mystic River); B Williams (Los Angeles), K Higgins (OMBAC), C O'Brien (Old Blues, California), G Hein (OMBAC); M Caulder (Old White), M Saunders (OMBAC) (*capt*); C Lippert (OMBAC), P Johnston (Louisville), F Paoli (Denver Barbarians), M Siano (Philadelphia Whitemarsh), K Swords (Beacon Hill), R Isaac (Denver Barbarians), B Vizard (OMBAC), G Lambert (Life Chiropractic Coll)
Scorer *Penalty Goal:* O'Brien
Referee R C Quittenton (England)

4 October 1989, Parc des Princes, Paris
(*French Revolution Bicentennial match*)
FRANCE 27 (3G 3PG)   BRITISH LIONS XV 29 (1G 4PG 1DG 2T)

FRANCE: S Blanco (Biarritz); B Lacombe (Agen), P Sella (Agen), M Andrieu (Nîmes), P Lagisquet (Bayonne); D Camberabero (Béziers), P Berbizier (Agen) (*capt*); M Pujolle (Nice), D Bouet (Dax), L Seigne (Agen), G Bourguignon (Narbonne), T Devergie (Nîmes), P Benetton (Agen), L Rodriguez (Dax), O Roumat (Dax) *Replacement* H Chabowski (Nîmes) for Pujolle
Scorers *Tries:* Blanco, Benetton, Camberabero *Conversions:* Camberabero (3)
Penalty Goals: Camberabero (3)

BRITISH LIONS XV: A G Hastings (Scotland); S Hastings (Scotland), B J Mullin (Ireland), J C Guscott (England), R Underwood (England); C R Andrew (England) (*capt*), R Jones (Wales); M Griffiths (Wales), S J Smith (Ireland), J A Probyn (England), P J Ackford (England), D F Cronin (Scotland), R A Robinson (England), D W Egerton (England), P M Matthews (Ireland)
Scorers *Tries:* Andrew, A G Hastings (2)   *Conversion:* A G Hastings
Penalty Goals: A G Hastings (4)   *Dropped Goal:* Andrew
Referee J B Anderson (Scotland)

9 December 1989, Murrayfield
SCOTLAND 32 (3G 2PG 2T)   ROMANIA 0

SCOTLAND: A G Hastings (London Scottish); A G Stanger (Hawick), S Hastings (Watsonians), S R P Lineen (Boroughmuir), W L Renwick (London Scottish); D S Wyllie (Stewart's-Melville FP), G Armstrong (Jedforest); D M B Sole (Edinburgh Acads) (*capt*), K S Milne (Heriot's FP), A P Burnell (London Scottish), D F Cronin (Bath), C A Gray (Nottingham), F Calder (Stewart's-Melville FP), D B White (London Scottish), J Jeffrey (Kelso)
Scorers *Tries:* Stanger (3), White, Sole   *Conversions:* A G Hastings (3)
Penalty Goals: A G Hastings (2)
ROMANIA: M Toader; S Chirila, A Lungu, G Sava, B Serban; G Ignat, D Neaga; G Leonte, G Ion, G Dumitrescu, S Ciorescu, C Raducanu, O Sugar, H Dumitras (*capt*), I Doja *Replacement* M Motoc for Sugar
Referee S R Hilditch (Ireland)

22 April 1990, Twickenham
FOUR HOME UNIONS 43 (6G 1PG 1T)
REST OF EUROPE 18 (1G 3T)
(Rugby for Romania fund-raising match)

FOUR HOME UNIONS: A G Hastings (Scotland); A G Stanger (Scotland), W D C Carling (England), J C Guscott (England), R Underwood (England); C R Andrew (England), R J Hill (England); D M B Sole (Scotland) (*capt*), B C Moore (England), M Griffiths (Wales), D F Cronin (Scotland), N P T Francis (Ireland), J Jeffrey (Scotland), N P Mannion (Ireland), P J Winterbottom (England) *Replacements* C M Chalmers (Scotland) for Carling; D J Turnbull (Scotland) for Mannion
Scorers *Tries:* Carling (2), Cronin, Jeffrey, Guscott, Andrew, Hastings
Conversions: Hastings (6)   *Penalty Goal:* Hastings
REST OF EUROPE: M Toader (Romania); M Dancla (Tarbes), J-C Langlade (Hyeres), N Fulina (Romania), P Lagisquet (France); B Capitani (Nice), A Hueber (Lourdes); M Pujolle (France), P Dintrans (France) (*capt*), G Rossi (Italy), M Cecillon (France), S Ciorescu (Romania), H Dumitras (Romania), A Tikhonov (Soviet Union), T Janecek (France) *Replacements* I Mironov (Soviet Union) for Dancla; P Capdeville (Tarbes) for Rossi; K Tapper (Sweden) for Tikhonov; F Gaetaniello (Italy) for Lagisquet
Scorers *Tries:* Fulina, Mironov, Tikhonov, Langlade   *Conversion:* Toader
Referee F Howard (England)

1 May 1990, Battaglini Stadium, Rovigo
ITALY XV 15 (1G 3PG)   ENGLAND XV 33 (4G 2PG 1DG)

ITALY XV: L Troiani; E Venturi, J Morelli, S Barba, M Cuttita; M Bonomi, F Pietrosanti; G Grespan, C Pratichetti, A Piazza, R Saetti, R Favaro, P Pedroni, C Covi (*capt*), P Reale *Replacements* G Pivetta for Pratichetti; L Francescato for Pietrosanti; D Tebaldi for Bonomi

Scorers *Try:* Cuttita   *Conversion:* Troiani   *Penalty Goals:* Troiani (3)
ENGLAND XV: S D Hodgkinson (Nottingham); N Heslop (Orrell), W D C Carling
(Harlequins) (*capt*), J R D Buckton (Saracens), C Oti (Wasps); C R Andrew (Wasps),
S M Bates (Wasps); M S Linnett (Moseley), B C Moore (Nottingham), J A Probyn (Wasps),
R Kimmins (Orrell), W A Dooley (Preston Grasshoppers), N Back (Nottingham),
D A Cusani (Orrell), J Wells (Leicester) *Replacements* J Olver (Harlequins) for Moore;
J F Clough (Wasps) for Carling
Scorers *Tries:* Oti, Buckton, Back, Andrew   *Conversions:* Hodgkinson (4)
Penalty Goals: Hodgkinson (2)   *Dropped Goal:* Andrew
Referee P Frantschi (France)

24 May 1990, Stade Patrice Brocas, Auch
FRANCE 6 (2PG)   ROMANIA 12 (3PG 1DG)

FRANCE: S Blanco; P Hontas, J-C Langlade, P Saint-André, D Camberabero;
J-P Lescarboura, H Sanz; M Pujolle, P Dintrans (*capt*), P Gallard, G Bourguignon,
J Condom, O Roumat, T Devergie, T Janecek *Replacement* P Ondarts for Gallard
Scorer *Penalty Goals:* Lescarboura (2)
ROMANIA: H Dumitru; M Toader, A Lungu, N Fulina, S Chirila; G Ignat, D Neaga;
G Leonte, G Ion, G Dumitrescu, S Ciorescu, C Colocariu, G Dinu, H Dumitras (*capt*),
A Radulescu
Scorer *Penalty Goals:* Ignat (3)   *Dropped Goal:* Ignat
Referee I Bullerwell (England)

*John Wells prepares to sweep up a line-out ball won by Wade Dooley during the England XV's
victory over an Italian XV in Rovigo.*

B INTERNATIONALS 1989-90

12 November 1989, La Teste
France B 28 (3G 1PG 1DG 1T)   Wales B 15 (4PG 1DG)

France B: J-B Lafond; E Fachan, A Hyardet, E Bonneval, E Berty; P Rouge-Thomas, A Hueber (*capt*); G Lascube, J Tordo, P Gallard, O Roumat, F Ado, J-M Lhermet, A Chaffardon, D Monteil *Replacements* D Cortolos for Monteil; P Alabarde for Gallard
Scorers *Tries:* Chaffardon, Rouge-Thomas, Lafond, Berty
Conversions: Lafond (3)   *Penalty Goal:* Lafond   *Dropped Goal:* Rouge-Thomas
Wales B: M Rayer (Cardiff); A Harries (Newbridge), A Davies (Cambridge U & Neath), A Bateman (Neath), A Edmunds (Neath); C Stephens (Llanelli), A Booth (Neath); J Rowlands (Newbridge), P John (Pontpridd), H Williams-Jones (South Wales Police), A Allen (Newbridge), J Wakeford (South Wales Police), M Budd (Bridgend), M Edwards (Cardiff), D Bryant (Bridgend) (*capt*) *Replacement* S Lewis (Pontypridd) for Stephens
Scorers *Penalty Goals:* Davies (4)   *Dropped Goal:* Stephens
Referee R Clark (Scotland)

9 December 1989, Murrayfield
Scotland B 22 (1G 1PG 3DG 1T)   Ireland B 22 (1G 4PG 1T)

Scotland B: D N Barrett (West of Scotland); A Moore (Edinburgh Acads), B Edwards (Boroughmuir), I C Jardine (Stirling County), S T G Porter (Malone); D K Shiel (Jedforest), D Bryson (Gala); G Graham (Stirling County), K D McKenzie (Stirling County), G D Wilson (Boroughmuir), J F Richardson (Edinburgh Acads), G W Weir (Melrose), A J Macklin (London Scottish) (*capt*), J D Busby (Glasgow High/Kelvinside), D E W Leckie (Edinburgh Acads)
Scorers *Tries:* Moore, Busby   *Conversion:* Shiel   *Penalty Goal:* Barrett
Dropped Goals: Shiel (3)
Ireland B: K Murphy (Constitution); J E Staples (London Irish), J A Hewitt (London Irish), P D Clinch (Lansdowne), P V Murray (Shannon); P Russell (Instonians), A C Rolland (Blackrock College); B M McKibbin (Instonians), J P McDonald (Malone), P M Clohessy (Young Munster), B J Rigney (Greystones), M J Galwey (Shannon), P C Collins (London Irish) (*capt*), P Kenny (Wanderers), B F Robinson (Ballymena) *Replacement* P S Johns (Dublin U) for Galwey
Scorers *Tries:* Murray, Collins   *Conversion:* Russell   *Penalty Goals:* Russell (4)
Referee R Yeman (Wales)

21 January 1990, Stade Charles Mathon, Oyonnax
France B 31 (2G 5PG 1T)   Scotland B 9 (3PG)

France B: J Bianchi (Toulon); D Berty (Toulouse), P Tremouille (Toulon), B Labat (Tarbes), P Hontas (Biarritz); J-M Lescure (Narbonne), S Milhas (Auch); P Capdevielle (Tarbes), D Minaro (Béziers), F Heyer (Montferrand), H Miorin (Toulouse), J-M Cadieu (Toulouse), J-M Lhermet (Montferrand), E Melville (Toulon), A Cigagna (Toulouse) (*capt*) *Replacements* M Tachdjian (Racing Club de France) for Melville; R Tremoulet (Graulhet) for Minaro
Scorers *Tries:* Bianchi, Lhermet, Berty   *Conversions:* Bianchi (2)
Penalty Goals: Bianchi (5)
Scotland B: D N Barrett (West of Scotland); A Moore (Edinburgh Acads), P F Rouse (Dundee HSFP), B Edwards (Boroughmuir), S T G Porter (Malone); G M Breckenridge (Glasgow High/Kelvinside), D Bryson (Gala); G Graham (Stirling County), I Corcoran (Gala), G D Wilson (Boroughmuir), J F Richardson (Edinburgh Acads), D S Munro (Glasgow High/Kelvinside), A J Macklin (London Scottish) (*capt*), J D Busby (Glasgow High/Kelvinside), A E D MacDonald (Cambridge U)

Scorer *Penalty Goals:* Barrett (3)
Referee G Simmonds (Wales)

4 February 1990, Jean Rouin Stadium, Paris
France B 15 (1G 3PG)   England B 15 (5PG)

France B: F Velo; B Lacombe, E Bonneval, B Labat, P Hontas; P Rouge-Thomas,
J Milhas; P Capdevielle, D Bouet, F Heyer, J-M Cadieu, H Miorin, T Maset, A Cigagna,
J-M Lhermet *Replacement* J-C Lescure for Rouge-Thomas
Scorers *Try:* Lhermet   *Conversion:* Velo   *Penalty Goals:* Velo (3)
England B: A J Buzza (Cambridge U); J Fallon (Richmond), B Barley (Wakefield),
J Buckton (Saracens), N Heslop (Orrell); D Pears (Harlequins), D Morris (Liverpool St
Helens); J Leonard (Saracens), N Hitchen (Orrell), A Mullins (Harlequins), D Baldwin
(Sale), S O'Leary (Wasps), P Tayler (Rosslyn Park), T Rodber (Northampton),
D Pegler (Wasps) *(capt)*
Scorer *Penalty Goals:* Pears (5)
Referee B Smith (Ireland)

*Milhas, the French scrum-half, gets the ball away in the France B-England B match at the
Jean Bouin Stadium, Paris. Winds of almost hurricane force made the game a lottery and the
draw was an apt result.*

NATIONAL TRIAL MATCHES 1989-90

SCOTLAND

6 January 1990, Murrayfield
Blues 45 (2G 2PG 1DG 6T)   Reds 4 (1T)

Blues: A G Hastings (London Scottish); A G Stanger (Hawick), S Hastings (Watsonians), S R P Lineen (Boroughmuir), W L Renwick (London Scottish); D S Wyllie (Stewart's-Melville FP), G H Oliver (Hawick); D M B Sole (Edinburgh Acads) *(capt)*, K S Milne (Heriot's FP), A P Burnell (London Scottish), C A Gray (Nottingham), D F Cronin (Bath), D J Turnbull (Hawick), G A E Buchanan-Smith (London Scottish), G R Marshall (London Scottish) *Replacement* A J Macklin (London Scottish) for Marshall
Scorers *Tries:* S Hastings (2), A G Hastings, Oliver, Gray, Marshall, Buchanan-Smith, Macklin   *Conversions:* A G Hastings (2)   *Penalty Goals:* A G Hastings (2)
Dropped Goal: Wyllie
Reds: P W Dods (Gala); A Moore (Edinburgh Acads), P F Rouse (Dundee HSFP), I C Jardine (Stirling County), I Tukalo (Selkirk); I C Glasgow (Heriot's FP), S Jardine (South Glam Inst); G Graham (Stirling County), J Allan (Edinburgh Acads), I G Milne (Heriot's FP), J F Richardson (Edinburgh Acads), A E D MacDonald (Cambridge U), J Jeffrey (Kelso), F Calder (Stewart's-Melville FP) *(capt)*, C D Hogg (Melrose)
Replacement B Edwards (Boroughmuir) for Rouse
Scorer *Try:* Moore
Referee J B Anderson (Currie)

Finlay Calder, beavering away in the losing cause of the junior side in the Scottish trial, tackles Greig Oliver in possession after the senior side, the Blues, won a scrum.

FIRA CHAMPIONSHIP 1989-90

Chris Rhys

For the first time there was a three-way tie after the 1989-90 FIRA Championship, which was temporarily reduced again to a one-year championship because of World Cup preliminaries in 1990 and finals in 1991. France, Romania and the Soviet Union all recorded three wins from their four games, with Italy and Poland losing all their matches against the top three nations.

France seemed to have sewn up the championship until they came a cropper against Romania at Auch. A historic first win on French soil was achieved thanks to the boot of Ignat, who kicked three penalties and a dropped goal to two penalties from Lescarboura. Romania had made remarkable progress out of the ruins of their much-chronicled political traumas, and their sole defeat had come at the start of the season at Baia Mare against the Soviet Union. The Soviets scored tries through Parshin and Tikhonov, Dzagnidze taking the tally to 21 with a conversion, a dropped goal and two penalties. Dumitras scored the lone Romanian try with Toader (2) and Domocos adding penalties.

The Soviet Union suffered their loss in Moscow when the French beat them 22-14. France were 16-0 up at half-time but lost the try count 3-2 as Tikhonov (2) and Vorapiev answered earlier French efforts from Penaud and Bianchi.

Italy left Poland in the relegation place with a 34-3 win spearheaded by two of their five tries scored by Marcello Cuttita. Italian defeats were 12-15 by the Soviet Union – the Soviets' fifth successive win in a row against Italy – the usual loss to France, this time by 22-12 and two tries to nil, and 16-9 to Romania, where Ion's try four minutes from the end, added to Ignat's four penalties, offset three penalties from Troiani. Poland may seem a surprise packet in Group A over countries such as Spain and Holland, but 14 of their side play club rugby in the French championship. They promised much, but achieved nothing after conceding 30 points to Italy, France and the Soviet Union. That Romania failed to add substantially to the collection can be attributed to the fact that their 25-19 win over Poland was achieved on the same day as their 'senior' side was on duty against Italy.

RESULTS

1989	*Venue*				
5 Oct	Baia Mare	Romania	13	Soviet Union	21
5 Nov	Moscow	Soviet Union	15	Italy	12
1990					
18 Feb	Albi	France	22	Italy	12
8 Apr	Napoli	Italy	34	Poland	3
14 Apr	Bucharest	Romania	25	Poland	19

14 Apr	Frascati	Italy	9	Romania	16
18 May	Le Creusot	France	32	Poland	9
20 May	Moscow	Soviet Union	14	France	22
24 May	Auch	France	6	Romania	12
27 May	Warsaw	Poland	12	Soviet Union	31

FINAL TABLE

	P	W	D	L	F	A	Pts
France	4	3	0	1	82	47	10
Soviet Union	4	3	0	1	81	59	10
Romania	4	3	0	1	66	55	10
Italy	4	1	0	3	67	56	6
Poland	4	0	0	4	43	122	4

GROUP B1 RESULTS

1989	*Venue*				
10 Feb	Menzel	Tunisia	12	Morocco	12*
10 Mar	Casablanca	Morocco	20	Belgium	6
24 Mar	Porto	Portugal	12	Tunisia	6
7 Apr	Brussels	Belgium	P	Tunisia	P
5 May	Waterloo	Belgium	12	Portugal	24
10 May	Harare	Tunisia	12	Morocco	9*
26 May	Lisbon	Portugal	12	Tunisia	6

* The countries agreed that their World Cup qualifying match would count as the first game had finished as a draw.

GROUP B1 FINAL TABLE

	P	W	D	L	F	A	Pts
Portugal	3	3	0	0	52	28	9
Morocco	3	1	0	2	39	35	5
Tunisia	2	1	0	1	18	21	4
Belgium	2	0	0	2	18	44	2

GROUP B2 RESULTS

1989	*Venue*				
17 Sept	Heidelberg	West Germany	6	Holland	12*
29 Oct	Madrid	Spain	29	Holland	15*
1990					
4 Mar	Hilversum	Holland	45	Bulgaria	10
18 Mar	Brno	Czechoslovakia	6	Holland	29
22 Apr	Sofia	Bulgaria	12	West Germany	40
29 Apr	Prague	Czechoslovakia	22	Spain	22
5 May	Hanover	West Germany	32	Czechoslovakia	7
20 May	Madrid	Spain	w/o	Bulgaria	
3 June	Sofia	Bulgaria	P	Czechoslovakia	P

* also World Cup qualifiers

GROUP B2 FINAL TABLE

	P	W	D	L	F	A	Pts
Spain	4	3	1	0	60	45	11
Holland	4	3	0	1	101	41	10
West Germany	4	2	0	2	86	60	8
Czechoslovakia	3	0	1	2	35	83	6
Bulgaria	3	0	0	3	22	85	3

GROUP C RESULTS
1990

29 Apr	Andorra	Andorra	26	Luxembourg	6
13 May	Luxembourg	Luxembourg	6	Yugoslavia	28
20 May	Split	Yugoslavia	3	Andorra	9

GROUP C FINAL TABLE

	P	W	D	L	F	A	Pts
Andorra	2	2	0	0	35	9	6
Yugoslavia	2	1	0	1	31	15	4
Luxembourg	2	0	0	2	12	54	2

In the FIRA Championship, three points are awarded for a win, two points for a draw and one point for a loss.

Season	Winners	Runners-Up	Third
1973-74	**France**	Romania	Spain
1974-75	**Romania**	France	Italy
1975-76	**France**	Italy	Romania
1976-77	**Romania**	France	Italy
1977-78	**France**	Romania	Spain
1978-79	**France**	Romania	Soviet Union
1979-80	**France**	Romania	Italy
1980-81	**Romania**	France	Soviet Union
1981-82	**France**	Italy	Romania
1982-83	**Romania**	Italy	Soviet Union
1983-84	**France**	Romania	Italy
1984-85	**France**	Romania	Soviet Union
1985-86	**France**	Soviet Union	Italy
1986-87	**France**	Soviet Union	Romania
1987-88	**France**	Soviet Union	Romania
1988-89	**France**	Soviet Union	Romania
1989-90	{ **France** **Romania** **Soviet Union**		

OTHER INTERNATIONAL TOURNAMENTS 1989-90

SOUTH PACIFIC CHAMPIONSHIP 1990

Auckland predictably retained the South Pacific Championship with a 100 per cent record, Queensland finishing runners-up and New South Wales third. Fiji, together with Canterbury and Wellington, managed just one victory. The 'decider' was Auckland's 55-13 win against New South Wales, in which they scored nine tries to two. Queensland, who had beaten Auckland 16-11 last season, were unable to close the gap but this was still the most successful season yet for Australian sides.

	Auckland	Can'bury	Fiji	NSW	Q'land	Wel'ton
Auckland	–	36-12	21-8	55-13	27-12	49-9
Canterbury	12-36	–	7-20	21-23	16-31	30-21
Fiji	8-21	20-7	–	16-19	12-21	10-34
New South Wales	13-55	23-21	19-16	–	3-12	25-20
Queensland	12-27	31-16	21-12	12-3	–	59-10
Wellington	9-49	21-30	34-10	20-25	10-59	–

FINAL TABLE

	P	W	D	L	F	A	Pts
Auckland	5	5	0	0	188	54	20
Queensland	5	4	0	1	135	68	16
New South Wales	5	3	0	2	83	124	12
Canterbury	5	1	0	4	86	131	5
Fiji	5	1	0	4	66	102	5
Wellington	5	1	0	4	94	173	5

WORLD CUP 1991: QUALIFYING MATCHES

AFRICAN ZONE (5-12 May 1990, Zimbabwe)
Zimbabwe 22, Ivory Coast 9; Tunisia 16, Morocco 12; Zimbabwe 16, Morocco 0; Tunisia 12, Ivory Coast 7; Morocco 11, Ivory Coast 4; Zimbabwe 24, Tunisia 13
Qualifier (to Pool 2 of tournament proper): **Zimbabwe**

ASIAN/PACIFIC ZONE (8-15 April 1990, Hong Kong)
Korea 7, Western Samoa 74; Tonga 16, Japan 28; Tonga 3, Western Samoa 12; Japan 26, Korea 10; Tonga 45, Korea 22, Japan 11, Western Samoa 37
Qualifiers (to Pool 3 of tournament proper): **Western Samoa** (to Pool 2 of tournament proper): **Japan**

AMERICAN ZONE (first-named team played at home)
Canada 21, USA 3; Argentina 23, USA 6; Canada 15, Argentina 6; USA 6, Argentina 13; USA 14, Canada 12; Argentina 15, Canada 19
Qualifiers (to pool 4 of tournament proper): **Canada** (to pool 3 of tournament proper): **Argentina** (to pool 1 of tournament proper): **USA**

EUROPEAN ZONE
Tournament A
Pre-qualifying tournament A was to produce one team to go through to join Spain, Belgium and Poland in pre-qualifying group B in Madrid, 29 October 1989.
Section A (knock-out basis): Czechoslovakia 23, Yugoslavia 6 (prelim match); Czechoslovakia 13, Portugal 15; West Germany 6, Netherlands 12; Portugal 3, Netherlands 32

Section A winners: **Netherlands**

Section B (league basis, played in Tours, France, May 1989

Final Table:	P	W	L	D	F	A	Pts
Sweden	3	3	0	0	98	25	9
Denmark	3	2	1	0	42	57	7
Switzerland	3	0	3	0	49	74	5
Israel	3	0	3	0	31	64	3

Section B Winners: **Sweden**

Play-off: (15 October, Copenhagen): Netherlands 24, Sweden 3

Tournament winner: **Netherlands**

Tournament B (Madrid, 29 October - 5 November)
Pre-qualifying tournament B was to produce two teams to go through to join Italy and Romania in European Zone preliminary round, to be played in Italy in October 1990.
Poland 25, Belgium 23; Spain 29, Netherlands 15; Belgium 12, Netherlands 32; Spain 23, Poland 9; Spain 58, Belgium 6; Netherlands 33, Poland 27

Finishing order: Spain 9 pts; Netherlands 7 pts; Poland 5 pts; Belgium 3 pts

Qualifiers: **Spain, Netherlands**

Matches remaining: **EUROPEAN PRELIMINARY ROUND** (Italy, October 1990, to produce two teams for tournament proper): Italy, Romania, Spain, Netherlands

FANTASTIC FIJIAN TRIUMPH
The 1990 Cathay Pacific – Hong Kong Bank Sevens

David Lawrenson   *Rugby News*

The news that the IRB were to sanction a world sevens competition to be held every four years from 1993 was received with some apprehension by the colony, which for years has seen its own sevens as the world's premier event. They needn't worry – such is the standing of the tournament that Hong Kong is by far and away the best rugby event in the world. The Hong Kong RU has achieved this by superb organisation and innovation. The 1990 tournament was no exception, with West Germany and the Soviet Bears making their debuts. This year also marked the first break in the ranks of the elite Five Nations when Wales became the first Home Union to send a national team. The Scottish representatives were the Borderers, while the Barbarians boasted an all-English line-up. The British representatives, looking like teams which had been thrown together for the event, progressed to the quarter-finals of the Cup without really setting the stadium alight. The Borderers boasted Chalmers, Armstrong, Jeffrey and Stanger, fresh from their Grand Slam triumph, and they naturally seemed a little more at home in a game which the Scots invented, accounting for Sri Lanka 24-0 and Japan 30-0. The Barbarians, who included Andrew, Carling, Moore, Guscott, Winterbottom and Skinner, overcame a spirited West German side 24-0 in their first game and went on to beat Canada 26-6. All the seeded teams made it through to the quarter-finals of the Cup competition on the second day, New Zealand and Fiji looking ominously strong.

The Bowl and Plate events threw up several intriguing contests on the Sunday. The West Germans survived a stiff test by Papua New Guinea in the quarter-final of the Bowl before eventually winning 16-8. They went on to take the trophy with a 38-12 victory over Thailand in the final. The Plate competition saw some keenly contested matches before Hong Kong thrashed Japan in the final. In their Cup quarter-final against New Zealand the Scottish Borderers struck first with a try by Hogg. But their joy was short-lived as New Zealand muscled their way to a 20-12 victory. The Barbarians didn't have matters all their own way against Western Samoa, who scored first, but the Englishmen rallied and their 18-10 win put them on course for a semi-final meeting with New Zealand. Fiji brushed aside the challenge of Tonga by 28-12, then it was left to Wales to spring the biggest surprise of the tournament by seeing off Australia. Emyr, the big Swansea wing, powered in for a hat-trick, giving his side a richly deserved 16-10 victory. The Barbarians went down 24-6 in their eagerly-awaited semi-final match against the All Blacks, succumbing to errors under pressure. Wales were so injury-hit by the time they faced Fiji in their semi-final that they had to call on Scots John Jeffrey and Eric Paxton as replacements. Indeed, Jeffrey got into the action after only two minutes when he replaced Aled Williams. Wales took the lead with a try, inevitably from Emyr, which Bridges converted, but the Fijians soon slipped into overdrive, running in six tries in their 34-6 win.

So the capacity crowd in Government Stadium got the final they wanted, the popular Fijians against the team everyone loves to hate, New Zealand. After five minutes Fiji were 10-0 down, but there is always hope when there is an inspirational player like Serevi around. Nadruku narrowed the gap with a try which Serevi converted just before half-time, but after the interval New Zealand piled on the pressure in the hope of forcing their opponents into errors. The tactic was succeeding as the Fijians desperately looked for a way of breaking out of their own 22 – but then they found it, and in startling fashion. A frantic passing movement began near the right touch-line, and by the time the ball came to Serevi in the middle he could only help it on its way with his fingertips. The pass was falling low to Nadruku when suddenly instinct took over and he flicked the ball through his legs to Cama, waiting on the left wing. The big threequarter had all the room he needed and sprinted 70 yards to score under the posts. It was a breathtaking piece of rugby which visibly shook the opposition. Immediately the All Blacks looked mortal. Rasari made the most of it with two tries, the second of which ended the match at 22-10 as the crowd invaded the pitch.

Pool A: New Zealand 42, Arabian Gulf 0; South Korea 22, Arabian Gulf 6; New Zealand 38, South Korea 4 **Pool B:** Scottish Borderers 24, Sri Lanka 0; Japan 20, Sri Lanka 12; Scottish Borderers 30, Japan 0 **Pool C:** Western Samoa 14, Papua New Guinea 4; Tunisia 18, Papua New Guinea 6; Western Samoa 28, Tunisia 8 **Pool D:** Barbarians 24, West Germany 0; Canada 18, West Germany 4; Barbarians 26, Canada 6 **Pool E:** Fiji 34, Thailand 0; Thailand 12, American Eagles 18; Fiji 28, American Eagles 6 **Pool F:** Tonga 16, Kwang-Hua Taipei 4; Kwang-Hua Taipei 6, Soviet Bears 22; Tonga 18, Soviet Bears 16 **Pool G:** Wales 44, Singapore 0; Hong Kong 38, Singapore 0; Wales 6, Hong Kong 4 **Pool H:** Australia 48, Malaysia 0; Malaysia 0, Netherlands 18; Australia 42, Netherlands 0

Cup: Quarter-finals: New Zealand 20, Scottish Borderers 12; Western Samoa 10, Barbarians 18; Fiji 28, Tonga 12; Wales 16, Australia 10 **Semi-finals:** New Zealand 24, Barbarians 6; Fiji 34, Wales 6 **Final:** New Zealand 10, Fiji 22

Plate: Quarter-finals: Korea 12, Japan 18; Tunisia 16, Canada 8; American Eagles 30, Soviet Bears 4; Hong Kong 22, Netherlands 6 **Semi-finals:** Japan 18, Tunisia 6; American Eagles 6, Hong Kong 16 **Final:** Japan 12, Hong Kong 33

Bowl: Quarter-finals: Arabian Gulf 24, Sri Lanka 0; Papua New Guinea 8, West Germany 16; Thailand 13, Kwang-Hua Taipei 8; Singapore 6, Malaysia 12 **Semi-finals:** Arabian Gulf 4, West Germany 20; Thailand 10, Malaysia 4 **Final:** West Germany 28, Thailand 12

ENGLAND SHORT OF THE SUMMIT

THE 1989-90 SEASON IN ENGLAND

David Hands *The Times*

'When people look back to 1990 they will remember it for Scotland's Grand Slam, not for the team that came second'. David Sole's judgment in the immediate aftermath of the Calcutta Cup match at Murrayfield was starkly honest, yet the Scottish captain did insufficient justice to the team that did come second that day – England. While many prizes rested on the outcome of 80 minutes in Edinburgh, the international and domestic season contained much that was memorable for the English players and public and it would be totally wrong to conclude that because the Grand Slam and International Championship were not won the season was a failure. The England management would certainly subscribe to that view: they have always stressed that their long-term ambition is success in the World Cup of 1991, when they will be pitted against New Zealand, the world champions, in the opening game. Thus 1989-90 was no more than a stepping-stone.

There was progress on many fronts, although not all the game's adherents considered the financial implications of various decisions taken during the season as progressive – the trend, for example, towards paid club officials which saw Gosforth, Leicester and Bristol advertising for directors of coaching. The relaxation by the International Rugby Football Board of the amateur regulations relating to compensation for time away from work preparing for internationals was stoutly opposed by the RFU and, although they were overruled on that issue, they forced a rethink on the regulations relating to communication for reward. It was a season in which England's international players organised meetings with Dudley Wood, the RFU secretary, so that the game's administrators could be as informed as possible of the views of the players. It was a season in which more sponsors than ever poured more money than ever into English rugby, sustaining the unfashionable County Championship and presenting a new competition for junior clubs, the Provincial Insurance Cup.

Twickenham took on a new appearance with the development of the new, three-tier North Stand, due for completion in November 1990. This is only the first of a three-part project which will see the East and West Stands follow suit. From such intense activity it would be easy to conclude that rugby union in England is riding the crest of a wave. In one sense it is, aided considerably by the achievements of the national side, but the game is still coming to terms with the competitive demands of the 1990s, which have been largely imposed by rising standards elsewhere in the world. It is still building a structure for the development of the game among children to compensate for the reduction in

The England team which beat Wales at Twickenham. L-R, back row: K McCartney (touch-judge), D Leslie (referee), F J Clough (replacement), D W Egerton (replacement), W A Dooley, M G Skinner, P J Ackford, M C Teague, P J Winterbottom, J A Probyn, P A G Rendall, C R Andrew, M D Bailey (replacement), M Linnett (replacement), J B Anderson (touch-judge); front row: S Bates (replacement), R J Hill, S D Hodgkinson, B C Moore, W D C Carling (capt), R Underwood, J C Guscott, S J Halliday, J Olver (replacement)

schools rugby; still agonising about what constitutes an amateur player yet constantly demanding more time and more commitment in terms of preparation for club, divisional and international rugby.

At the latter level England's was a distinguished season which started with a glut of points against Fiji and ended heartbreakingly short of the first Grand Slam since 1980. The same nucleus of players remained from the previous season, many of them the better for the 1989 British Lions tour to Australia – none more so than Rob Andrew, England's fly-half. Andrew returned home assured at last of the abilities that had shone so precociously when he was a student in 1982 but had provided only fitful illumination subsequently. He benefited considerably from the return to the fold of Richard Hill. Hill, first capped in 1984, captained England in 1987 but was dropped at the end of that season after the undisciplined Wales-England match. The Bath scrum-half achieved international status through his capacity for sheer hard work and that quality has never since deserted him, even at difficult times.

England's finest hour for many a year came when they beat France 26-7 in Paris. It was a brilliant performance in all respects, and Simon Hodgkinson was outstanding, kicking goals with all the aplomb of a seasoned international (it was, in fact, his fourth cap). The record 34-6 defeat of a poor Welsh XV which followed gave England and Scotland all to play for the following month: Grand Slam, Triple Crown, Championship, Calcutta Cup, the lot. Sadly, England fell at the final hurdle. Away from home they failed to adapt to the opposition and the referee and reverted slightly to type.

Another team to stare success in the eye only to drop their gaze were Gloucester, that perennial bench-mark in English rugby. In March they led the Courage Clubs Championship with one match remaining and had reached the Pilkington Cup final; but when both competitions were over they were left with nothing. The defeat of Gloucester by Nottingham in their final game left Wasps London's first League winners, somewhat to their surprise, but the Cup final represented Gloucester's nadir: Bath, still the best club in England even though they had lost their grip on the League, ran up a record score of 48-6 and realised a potential which, at present, can only be aimed at, not matched, by any other side in the country.

Perhaps the surprise package of the season were Saracens, promoted to the First Division with Bedford after the 1988-89 campaign. While Bedford sank without trace, Saracens' admirable organisation saw them through to third place in the League. However, they lost Tony Russ, their coach, to Leicester, where he becomes director of coaching this season, and Floyd Steadman, their scrum-half and captain. Steadman retired at the end of the season, as did the popular Les Cusworth, the former England fly-half who captained Leicester in the absence all season of the injured Dean Richards, and whose on-field attitude should serve as a model for all aspiring players.

ENGLISH INTERNATIONAL PLAYERS
(up to 30 April 1990)

ABBREVIATIONS

A – Australia; *Arg* – Argentina; *F* — France; *Fj*– Fiji; *I* – Ireland; *J* – Japan; *M* – Maoris; *NZ* – New Zealand; *R* – Romania; *S* – Scotland; *SA* – South Africa; *US* – United States; *W* – Wales; (C) – Centenary match v Scotland at Murrayfield, 1971 (non-championship); *P* – England v President's Overseas XV at Twickenham in RFU's Centenary season, 1970-71; (R) – Replacement. Entries in square brackets [ ] indicate appearances in the World Cup.

Note: Years given for Five Nations' matches are for second half of season; eg 1972 means season 1971-72. Years for all other matches refer to the actual year of the match. When a series has taken place, figures have been used to denote the particular matches in which players have featured. Thus 1984 *SA* 2 indicates that a player appeared in the second Test of the series.

Aarvold, C D (Cambridge U, W Hartlepool, Headingley, Blackheath) 1928 *A, W, I, F, S*, 1929 *W, I, F*, 1931 *W, S, F*, 1932 *SA, W, I, S*, 1933 *W*
Ackford, P J (Harlequins) 1988 *A*, 1989 *S, I, F, W, R, Fj*, 1990 *I, F, W, S*
Adams, A A (London Hospital) 1910 *F*
Adams, F R (Richmond) 1875 *I, S*, 1876 *S*, 1877 *I*, 1878 *S*, 1879 *S, I*
Adey, G J (Leicester) 1976 *I, F*
Adkins, S J (Coventry) 1950 *I, F, S*, 1953 *W, I, F, S*
Agar, A E (Harlequins) 1952 *SA, W, S, I, F*, 1953 *W, I*
Alcock, A (Guy's Hospital) 1906 *SA*
Alderson, F H R (Hartlepool R) 1891 *W, I, S*, 1892 *W, S*, 1893 *W*
Alexander, H (Richmond) 1900 *I, S*, 1901 *W, I, S*, 1902 *W, I*
Alexander, W (Northern) 1927 *F*
Allison, D F (Coventry) 1956 *W, I, S, F*, 1957 *W*, 1958 *W, S*
Allport, A (Blackheath) 1892 *W*, 1893 *I*, 1894 *W, I, S*
Anderson, S (Rockcliff) 1899 *I*
Anderson, W F (Orrell) 1973 *NZ* 1
Anderton, C (Manchester FW) 1889 *M*
Andrew, C R (Cambridge U, Nottingham, Wasps) 1985 *R, F, S, I, W*, 1986 *W, S, I, F*, 1987 *I, F, W*, [*J*(R), *US*], 1988 *S, I* 1,2, *A*1,2, *Fj, A*, 1989 *S, I, F, W, R, Fj*, 1990 *I, F, W, S*
Archer, H (Bridgwater A) 1909 *W, F, I*
Armstrong, R (Northern) 1925 *W*
Arthur, T G (Wasps) 1966 *W, I*
Ashby, R C (Wasps) 1966 *I, F*, 1967 *A*
Ashcroft, A (Waterloo) 1956 *W, I, S, F*, 1957 *W, I, F, S*, 1958 *W, A, I, F, S*, 1959 *I, F, S*
Ashcroft, A H (Birkenhead Park) 1909 *A*
Ashford, W (Richmond) 1897 *W, I*, 1898 *S, W*
Ashworth, A (Oldham) 1892 *I*
Askew, J G (Cambridge U) 1930 *W, I, F*
Aslett, A R (Richmond) 1926 *W, I, F, S*, 1929 *S, F*
Assinder, E W (O Edwardians) 1909 *A, W*
Aston, R L (Blackheath) 1890 *S, I*
Auty, J R (Headingley) 1935 *S*

Bailey, M D (Cambridge U, Wasps) 1984 *SA* 1,2, 1987 [*US*], 1989 *Fj*, 1990 *I, F, S* (R)
Bainbridge, S (Gosforth, Fylde) 1982 *F, W*, 1983 *F, W, S, I, NZ*, 1984 *S, I, F, W*, 1985 *NZ* 1,2, 1987 *F, W, S*, [*J, US*]
Baker, D G S (OMTs) 1955 *W, I, F, S*
Baker, E M (Moseley) 1895 *W, I, S*, 1896 *W, I, S*, 1897 *W*
Baker, H C (Clifton) 1887 *W*
Bance, J F (Bedford) 1954 *S*
Barley, B (Wakefield) 1984 *I, F, W, A*, 1988 *A*1,2, *Fj*
Barnes, S (Bristol, Bath) 1984 *A*, 1985 *R* (R), *NZ* 1,2, 1986 *S* (R), *F* (R), 1987 *I* (R), 1988 *Fj*
Barr, R J (Leicester) 1932 *SA, W, I*
Barrett, E I M (Lennox) 1903 *S*
Barrington, T J M (Bristol) 1931 *W, I*
Barrington-Ward, L E (Edinburgh U) 1910 *W, I, F, S*
Barron, J H (Bingley) 1896 *S*, 1897 *W, I*
Bartlett, J T (Waterloo) 1951 *W*
Bartlett, R M (Harlequins) 1957 *W, I, F, S*, 1958 *I, F, S*

Barton, J (Coventry) 1967 *I, F, W*, 1972 *F*
Batchelor, T B (Oxford U) 1907 *F*
Bates, S M (Wasps) 1989 *R*
Bateson, A H (Otley) 1930 *W, I, F, S*
Bateson, H D (Liverpool) 1879 *I*
Batson, T (Blackheath) 1872 *S*, 1874 *S*, 1875 *I*
Batten, J M (Cambridge U) 1874 *S*
Baume, J L (Northern) 1950 *S*
Baxter, J (Birkenhead Park) 1900 *W, I, S*
Bazley, R C (Waterloo) 1952 *I, F*, 1953 *W, I, F, S*, 1955 *W, I, F, S*
Beaumont, W B (Fylde) 1975 *I, A* 1(R),2, 1976 *A, W, S, I, F*, 1977 *S, I, F, W*, 1978 *F, W, S, I, NZ*, 1979 *S, I, F, W, NZ*, 1980 *I, F, W, S*, 1981 *W, S, I, F, Arg* 1,2, 1982 *A, S*
Bedford, H (Morley) 1889 *M*, 1890 *S, I*
Bedford, L L (Headingley) 1931 *W, I*
Beer, I D S (Harlequins) 1955 *F, S*
Beese, M C (Liverpool) 1972 *W, I, F*
Bell, F J (Northern) 1900 *W*
Bell, H (New Brighton) 1884 *I*
Bell, J L (Darlington) 1878 *I*
Bell, P J (Blackheath) 1968 *W, I, F, S*
Bell, R W (Northern) 1900 *W, I, S*
Bendon, G J (Wasps) 1959 *W, I, F, S*
Bennett, N O (St Mary's Hospital, Waterloo) 1947 *W, S, F*, 1948 *A, W, I, S*
Bennett, W N (Bedford, London Welsh) 1975 *S, A* 1, 1976 *S* (R), 1979 *S, I, F, W*
Bennetts, B B (Penzance) 1909 *A, W*
Bentley, J (Sale) 1988 *I* 2, *A* 1
Bentley, J E (Gipsies) 1871 *S*, 1872 *S*
Berridge, M J (Northampton) 1949 *W, I*
Berry, H (Gloucester) 1910 *W, I, F, S*
Berry, J (Tyldesley) 1891 *W, I, S*
Berry, J T W (Leicester) 1939 *W, I, S*
Beswick, E (Swinton) 1882 *I, S*
Biggs, J M (UCH) 1878 *S*, 1879 *I*
Birkett, J G G (Harlequins) 1906 *S, F, SA*, 1907 *F, W, S*, 1908 *F, W, I, S*, 1910 *W, I, S*, 1911 *W, F, I, S*, 1912 *W, I, S, F*
Birkett, L (Clapham R) 1875 *S*, 1877 *I, S*
Birkett, R H (Clapham R) 1871 *S*, 1875 *S*, 1876 *S*, 1877 *I*
Bishop, C C (Blackheath) 1927 *F*
Black, B H (Blackheath) 1930 *W, I, F, S*, 1931 *W, I, S, F*, 1932 *S*, 1933 *W*
Blacklock, J H (Aspatria) 1898 *I*, 1899 *I*
Blakeway, P J (Gloucester) 1980 *I, F, W, S*, 1981 *W, S, I, F*, 1982 *I, F, W*, 1984 *I, F, W, SA* 1, 1985 *R, F, S, I*
Blakiston, A F (Northampton) 1920 *S*, 1921 *W, I, S, F*, 1922 *W, F*, 1923 *S, F*, 1924 *W, I, F, S*, 1925 *NZ, W, I, S, F*
Blatherwick, T (Manchester) 1878 *I*
Body, J A (Gipsies) 1872 *S*, 1873 *S*
Bolton, C A (United Services) 1909 *F*
Bolton, R (Harlequins) 1933 *W*, 1936 *S*, 1937 *S*, 1938 *W, I*
Bolton, W N (Blackheath) 1882 *I, S*, 1883 *W, I, S*, 1884 *W, I, S*, 1885 *I*, 1887 *I, S*
Bonaventura, M S (Blackheath) 1931 *W*
Bond, A M (Sale) 1978 *NZ*, 1979 *S, I, NZ*, 1980 *I*, 1982 *I*

Bonham-Carter, E (Oxford U) 1891 *S*
Bonsor, F (Bradford) 1886 *W, I, S,* 1887 *W, S,* 1889 *M*
Boobbyer, B (Rosslyn Park) 1950 *W, I, F, S,* 1951 *W, F,* 1952 *S, I, F*
Booth, L A (Headingley) 1933 *W, I, S,* 1934 *S,* 1935 *W, I, S*
Botting, I J (Oxford U) 1950 *W, I*
Boughton, H J (Gloucester) 1935 *W, I, S*
Boyle, C W (Oxford U) 1873 *S*
Boyle, S B (Gloucester) 1983 *W, S, I*
Boylen, F (Hartlepool R) 1908 *F, W, I, S*
Bradby, M S (United Services) 1922 *I, F*
Bradley, R (W Hartlepool) 1903 *W*
Bradshaw, H (Bramley) 1892 *S,* 1893 *W, I, S,* 1894 *W, I, S*
Brain, S E (Coventry) 1984 *SA* 2, *A* (R), 1985 *R, F, S, I, W, NZ* 1,2, 1986 *W, S, I, F*
Braithwaite, J (Leicester) 1905 *NZ*
Braithwaite-Exley, B (Headingley) 1949 *W*
Brettargh, A T (Liverpool OB) 1900 *W,* 1903 *I, S,* 1904 *W, I, S,* 1905 *I, S*
Brewer, J (Gipsies) 1876 *I*
Briggs, A (Bradford) 1892 *W, I, S*
Brinn, A (Gloucester) 1972 *W, I, S*
Broadley, T (Bingley) 1893 *W, S,* 1894 *W, I, S,* 1896 *S*
Bromet, W E (Richmond) 1891 *W, I,* 1892 *W, I, S,* 1893 *W, I, S,* 1895 *W, I, S,* 1896 *I*
Brook, P W P (Harlequins) 1930 *S,* 1931 *F,* 1936 *S*
Brooke, T J (Richmond) 1968 *F, S*
Brooks, F G (Bedford) 1906 *SA*
Brooks, M J (Oxford U) 1874 *S*
Brophy, T J (Liverpool) 1964 *I, F, S,* 1965 *W, I,* 1966 *W, I, F*
Brough, J W (Silloth) 1925 *NZ, W*
Brougham, H (Harlequins) 1912 *W, I, S, F*
Brown, A A (Exeter) 1938 *S*
Brown, L G (Oxford U, Blackheath) 1911 *W, F, I, S,* 1913 *SA, W, F, I, S,* 1914 *W, I, S, F,* 1921 *W, I, S, F,* 1922 *W*
Brown, T W (Bristol) 1928 *S,* 1929 *W, I, S, F,* 1932 *S,* 1933 *W, I, S*
Brunton, J (N Durham) 1914 *W, I, S*
Brutton, E B (Cambridge U) 1886 *S*
Bryden, C C (Clapham R) 1876 *I,* 1877 *S*
Bryden, H A (Clapham R) 1874 *S*
Buckingham, R A (Leicester) 1927 *F*
Bucknall, A L (Richmond) 1969 *SA,* 1970 *I, W, S, F,* 1971 *W, I, F, S* (2[1C])
Buckton, J R D (Saracens) 1988 *A* (R)
Budd, A (Blackheath) 1878 *I,* 1879 *S, I,* 1881 *W, S*
Budworth, R T D (Blackheath) 1890 *W,* 1891 *W, S*
Bull, A G (Northampton) 1914 *W*
Bullough, E (Wigan) 1892 *W, I, S*
Bulpitt, M P (Blackheath) 1970 *S*
Bulteel, A J (Manchester) 1876 *I*
Bunting, W L (Moseley) 1897 *I, S,* 1898 *I, S, W,* 1899 *S,* 1900 *S,* 1901 *I, S*
Burland, D W (Bristol) 1931 *W, I, F,* 1932 *I, S,* 1933 *W, I, S*
Burns, B H (Blackheath) 1871 *S*
Burton, G W (Blackheath) 1879 *S, I,* 1880 *S,* 1881 *I, W, S*
Burton, H C (Richmond) 1926 *W*
Burton, M A (Gloucester) 1972 *W, I, F, S, SA,* 1974 *F, W,* 1975 *S, A* 1,2, 1976 *A, W, S, I, F,* 1978 *F, W*
Bush, J A (Clifton) 1872 *S,* 1873 *S,* 1875 *S,* 1876 *I, S*
Butcher, C J S (Harlequins) 1984 *SA* 1,2, *A*
Butcher, W V (Streatham) 1903 *S,* 1904 *W, I, S,* 1905 *W, I, S*
Butler, A G (Harlequins) 1937 *W, I*
Butler, P E (Gloucester) 1975 *A* 1, 1976 *F*
Butterfield, J (Northampton) 1953 *F, S,* 1954 *W, NZ, I, S, F,* 1955 *W, I, F, S,* 1956 *W, I, S, F,* 1957 *W, I, F, S,* 1958 *W, A, I, F, S,* 1959 *W, I, F, S*
Byrne, F A (Moseley) 1897 *W*
Byrne, J F (Moseley) 1894 *W, I, S,* 1895 *I, S,* 1896 *I,* 1897 *W, I, S,* 1898 *I, S, W,* 1899 *I*

Cain, J J (Waterloo) 1950 *W*
Campbell, D A (Cambridge U) 1937 *W, I*
Candler, P L (St Bart's Hospital) 1935 *W,* 1936 *NZ, W, I, S,* 1937 *W, I, S,* 1938 *W, S*
Cannell, L B (Oxford U, St Mary's Hospital) 1948 *F,*

1949 *W, I, F, S,* 1950 *W, I, F, S,* 1952 *SA, W,* 1953 *W, I, F,* 1956 *I, S, F,* 1957 *W, I*
Caplan, D W N (Headingley) 1978 *S, I*
Cardus, R M (Roundhay) 1979 *F, W*
Carey, G M (Blackheath) 1895 *W, I, S,* 1896 *W, I*
Carleton, J (Orrell) 1979 *NZ,* 1980 *I, F, W, S,* 1981 *W, S, I, F, Arg* 1,2, 1982 *A, S, I, F, W,* 1983 *F, W, S, I, NZ,* 1984 *S, I, F, W, A*
Carling, W D C (Durham U, Harlequins) 1988 *F, W, S, I* 1,2, *A2, Fj, A,* 1989 *S, I, F, W, Fj,* 1990 *I, F, W, S*
Carpenter, A D (Gloucester) 1932 *SA*
Carr, R S L (Manchester) 1939 *W, I, S*
Cartwright, V H (Nottingham) 1903 *W, I, S,* 1904 *W, S,* 1905 *W, I, S, NZ,* 1906 *W, I, S, F, SA*
Catcheside, H C (Percy Park) 1924 *W, I, F, S,* 1926 *W, I,* 1927 *I, S*
Cattell, R H B (Blackheath) 1895 *W, I, S,* 1896 *W, I, S,* 1900 *W*
Cave, J W (Richmond) 1889 *M*
Cave, W T C (Blackheath) 1905 *W*
Challis, R (Bristol) 1957 *I, F, S*
Chambers, E L (Bedford) 1908 *F,* 1910 *W, I*
Chantrill, B S (Bristol) 1924 *W, I, F, S*
Chapman, C E (Cambridge U) 1884 *W*
Chapman, F E (Hartlepool) 1910 *W, I, F, S,* 1912 *W,* 1914 *W, I*
Cheesman, W I (OMTs) 1913 *SA, W, F, I*
Cheston, E C (Richmond) 1873 *S,* 1874 *S,* 1875 *I, S,* 1876 *S*
Chilcott, G J (Bath) 1984 *A,* 1986 *I, F,* 1987 *F* (R), *W,* [*J, US, W*(R)], 1988 *I* 2(R), *Fj,* 1989 *I* (R), *F, W, R*
Christopherson, P (Blackheath) 1891 *W, S*
Clark, C W H (Liverpool) 1876 *I*
Clarke, A J (Coventry) 1935 *W, I, S,* 1936 *NZ, W, I*
Clarke, S J S (Cambridge U, Blackheath) 1963 *W, I, F, S, NZ* 1,2, *A,* 1964 *NZ, W, I,* 1965 *I, F, S*
Clayton, J H (Liverpool) 1871 *S*
Clements, J W (O Cranleighans) 1959 *I, F, S*
Cleveland, C R (Blackheath) 1887 *W, S*
Clibborn, W G (Richmond) 1886 *W, I, S,* 1887 *W, I, S*
Clough, F J (Cambridge U, Orrell) 1986 *I, F,* 1987 [*J*(R), *US*]
Coates, C H (Yorkshire W) 1880 *S,* 1881 *S,* 1882 *S*
Coates, V H M (Bath) 1913 *SA, W, F, I, S*
Cobby, W (Hull) 1900 *W*
Cockerham, A (Bradford Olicana) 1900 *W*
Colclough, M J (Angoulême, Wasps, Swansea) 1978 *S, I,* 1979 *NZ,* 1980 *F, W, S,* 1981 *W, S, I, F,* 1982 *A, S, I, F, W,* 1983 *F, NZ,* 1984 *S, I, F, W,* 1986 *W, S, I, F*
Coley, E (Northampton) 1929 *F,* 1932 *W*
Collins, P J (Camborne S of M) 1952 *S, I, F*
Collins, W E (O Cheltonians) 1874 *S,* 1875 *I, S,* 1876 *I, S*
Considine, S G U (Bath) 1925 *F*
Conway, G S (Cambridge U, Rugby, Manchester) 1920 *F, I, S,* 1921 *F,* 1922 *W, I, F, S,* 1923 *W, I, S,* 1924 *W, I, F, S,* 1925 *NZ,* 1927 *W*
Cook, J G (Bedford) 1937 *S*
Cook, P W (Richmond) 1965 *I, F*
Cooke, D A (Harlequins) 1976 *W, S, I, F*
Cooke, D H (Harlequins) 1981 *W, S, I, F,* 1984 *I,* 1985 *R, F, S, I, W, NZ* 1,2
Cooke, P (Richmond) 1939 *W, I*
Coop, T (Leigh) 1892 *S*
Cooper, J G (Moseley) 1909 *A, W*
Cooper, M J (Moseley) 1973 *F, S, NZ* 2 (R), 1975 *F, W,* 1976 *A, W,* 1977 *S, I, F, W*
Coopper, S F (Blackheath) 1900 *W,* 1902 *W, I,* 1905 *W, I, S,* 1907 *W*
Corbett, L J (Bristol) 1921 *F,* 1923 *W, I,* 1924 *W, I, F, S,* 1925 *NZ, W, I, S, F,* 1927 *W, I, S, F*
Corless, B J (Coventry, Moseley) 1976 *A, I* (R), 1977 *S, I, F, W,* 1978 *F, W, S, I*
Cotton, F E (Loughborough Colls, Coventry, Sale) 1971 *S* (2[1C]), *P,* 1973 *W, I, F, S, NZ* 2, *A,* 1974 *S, I,* 1975 *I, F, W,* 1976 *A, W, S, I, F,* 1977 *S, I, F, W,* 1978 *S, I,* 1979 *NZ,* 1980 *I, F, W, S,* 1981 *W*
Coulman, M J (Moseley) 1967 *A, I, F, S, W,* 1968 *W, I, F, S*
Coulson, T J (Coventry) 1927 *W,* 1928 *A, W*
Court, E D (Blackheath) 1885 *W*
Coverdale, H (Blackheath) 1910 *F,* 1912 *I, F,* 1920 *W*
Cove-Smith, R (OMTs) 1921 *S, F,* 1922 *I, F, S,* 1923 *W, I, S, F,* 1924 *W, I, S, F,* 1925 *NZ, W, I, S, F,* 1927

111

Freeman, H (Marlborough N) 1872 S, 1873 S, 1874 S
French, R J (St Helens) 1961 W, I, F, S
Fry, H A (Liverpool) 1934 W, I, S
Fry, T W (Queen's House) 1880 I, S, 1881 W
Fuller, H G (Bath) 1882 I, S, 1883 W, I, S, 1884 W

Gadney, B C (Leicester, Headingley) 1932 I, S, 1933 I,
S, 1934 W, I, S, 1935 S, 1936 NZ, W, I, S, 1937 S, 1938
W
Gamlin, H T (Blackheath) 1899 W, S, 1900 W, I, S,
1901 S, 1902 W, I, S, 1903 W, I, S, 1904 W, I, S
Gardner, E R (Devonport Services) 1921 W, I, S, 1922
W, I, F, 1923 W, I, S, F
Gardner, H P (Richmond) 1878 I
Garnett, H W T (Bradford) 1877 S
Gavins, M N (Leicester) 1961 W
Gay, D J (Bath) 1968 W, I, F, S
Gent, D R (Gloucester) 1905 NZ, 1906 W, I, 1910 W, I
Genth, J S M (Manchester) 1874 S, 1875 S
George, J T (Falmouth) 1947 S, F, 1949 I
Gerrard, R A (Bath) 1932 SA, W, I, S, 1933 W, I, S,
1934 W, I, S, 1936 NZ, W, I, S
Gibbs, G A (Bristol) 1947 F, 1948 I
Gibbs, J C (Harlequins) 1925 NZ, W, 1926 F, 1927 W,
I, S, F
Gibbs, N (Harlequins) 1954 S, F
Giblin, L F (Blackheath) 1896 W, I, 1897 S
Gibson, A S (Manchester) 1871 S
Gibson, C O P (Northern) 1901 W
Gibson, G R (Northern) 1899 W, 1901 S
Gibson, T A (Northern) 1905 W, S
Gilbert, F G (Devonport Services) 1923 W, I
Gilbert, R (Devonport A) 1908 W, I, S
Giles, J L (Coventry) 1935 W, I, 1937 W, I, 1938 I, S
Gittings, W J (Coventry) 1967 NZ
Glover, P B (Bath) 1967 A, 1971 F, P
Godfray, R E (Richmond) 1905 NZ
Godwin, H O (Coventry) 1959 F, S, 1963 S, NZ 1,2, A,
1964 NZ, I, F, S, 1967 NZ
Gordon-Smith, G W (Blackheath) 1900 W, I, S
Gotley, A L H (Oxford U) 1910 F, S, 1911 W, F, I, S
Graham, D (Aspatria) 1901 W
Graham, H J (Wimbledon H) 1875 I, S, 1876 I, S
Graham, J D G (Wimbledon H) 1876 I
Gray, A (Otley) 1947 W, I, S
Green, J (Skipton) 1905 I, 1906 S, F, SA, 1907 F, W,
I, S
Green, J F (West Kent) 1871 S
Greenwell, J H (Rockcliff) 1893 W, I
Greenwood, J E (Cambridge U, Leicester) 1912 F,
1913 SA, W, F, I, S, 1914 W, S, F, 1920 W, F, I, S
Greenwood, J R H (Waterloo) 1966 I, F, S, 1967 A,
1969 I
Greg, W (Manchester) 1876 I, S
Gregory, G G (Bristol) 1931 I, S, F, 1932 SA, W, I, S,
1933 W, I, S, 1934 W, I, S
Gregory, J A (Blackheath) 1949 W
Grylls, W M (Redruth) 1905 I
Guest, R H (Waterloo) 1939 W, I, S, 1947 W, I, S, F,
1948 A, W, I, S, 1949 F, S
Guillemard, A G (West Kent) 1871 S, 1872 S
Gummer, C H A (Plymouth A) 1929 F
Gunner, C R (Marlborough N) 1876 I
Gurdon, C (Richmond) 1880 I, S, 1881 I, W, S, 1882 I,
S, 1883 S, 1884 W, S, 1885 I, 1886 W, I, S
Gurdon, E T (Richmond) 1878 S, 1879 I, 1880 S, 1881
I, W, S, 1882 S, 1883 W, I, S, 1884 W, I, S, 1885 W, I,
1886 S
Guscott, J C (Bath) 1989 R, Fj, 1990 I, F, W, S

Haigh, L (Manchester) 1910 W, I, S, 1911 W, F, I, S
Hale, P M (Moseley) 1969 SA, 1970 I, W
Hall, C (Gloucester) 1901 I, S
Hall, J (N Durham) 1894 W, I, S
Hall, J P (Bath) 1984 S (R), I, F, SA 1,2, A, 1985 R, F,
S, I, W, NZ 1,2, 1986 W, S, 1987 I, F, W, S
Hall, N M (Richmond) 1947 W, I, S, F, 1949 W, I,
1952 SA, W, S, I, F, 1953 W, I, F, S, 1955 W, I
Halliday, S J (Bath) 1986 W, S, 1987 S, 1988 S, I 1,2, A
1, A, 1989 S, I, F, W, R, Fj (R), 1990 W, S
Hamersley, A St G (Marlborough N) 1871 S, 1872 S,
1873 S, 1874 S
Hamilton-Hill, E A (Harlequins) 1936 NZ, W, I

Hamilton-Wickes, R H (Cambridge U) 1924 I, 1925
NZ, W, I, S, F, 1926 W, I, S, 1927 W
Hammett, E D G (Newport) 1920 W, F, S, 1921 W, I,
S, F, 1922 W
Hammond, C E L (Harlequins) 1905 S, NZ, 1906 W, I,
S, F, 1908 W, I
Hancock, A W (Northampton) 1965 F, S, 1966 F
Hancock, G E (Birkenhead Park) 1939 W, I, S
Hancock, J H (Newport) 1955 W, I
Hancock, P F (Blackheath) 1886 W, I, 1890 W
Hancock, P S (Richmond) 1904 W, I, S
Handford, F G (Manchester) 1909 W, F, I, S
Hands, R H M (Blackheath) 1910 F, S
Hanley, J (Plymouth A) 1927 W, S, F, 1928 W, I, F, S
Hannaford, R C (Bristol) 1971 W, I, F
Hanvey, A J (Aspatria) 1926 W, I, F, S
Harding, E H (Devonport Services) 1931 I
Harding, R M (Bristol) 1985 R, F, S, 1987 S, [A, J,
W], 1988 I 1(R),2, A 1,2, Fj
Harding, V S J (Saracens) 1961 F, S, 1962 W, I, F, S
Hardwick, P F (Percy Park) 1902 I, S, 1903 W, I, S,
1904 W, I, S
Hardy, E M P (Blackheath) 1951 I, F, S
Hare, W H (Nottingham, Leicester) 1974 W, 1978 F,
NZ, 1979 NZ, 1980 I, F, W, S, 1981 W, S, Arg 1,2,
1982 F, W, 1983 F, W, S, NZ, 1984 S, I, F, W, SA
1,2,
Harper, C H (Exeter) 1899 W
Harriman, A T (Harlequins) 1988 A
Harris, S W (Blackheath) 1920 I, S
Harris, T W (Northampton) 1929 S, 1932 I
Harrison, A C (Hartlepool R) 1931 I, S
Harrison, A L (United Services, RN) 1914 I, F
Harrison, G (Hull) 1877 I, S, 1879 S, I, 1880 S, 1885
W, I
Harrison, H C (United Services, RN) 1909 S, 1914 I,
S, F
Harrison, M E (Wakefield) 1985 NZ 1,2, 1986 S, I, F,
1987 I, F, W, S, [A, J, US, W], 1988 F, W
Hartley, B C (Blackheath) 1901 S, 1902 S
Haslett, L W (Birkenhead Park) 1926 I, F
Hastings, G W D (Gloucester) 1955 W, I, F, S, 1957
W, I, F, S, 1958 W, A, I, F, S
Havelock, H (Hartlepool R) 1908 F, W, I
Hawcridge, J J (Bradford) 1885 W, I
Hayward, L W (Cheltenham) 1910 I
Hazell, D St G (Leicester) 1955 W, I, F, S
Hearn, R D (Bedford) 1966 F, S, 1967 I, F, S, W
Heath, A H (Oxford U) 1876 S
Heaton, J (Waterloo) 1935 W, I, S, 1939 W, I, S, 1947
I, S, F
Henderson, A P (Edinburgh Wands) 1947 W, I, S, F,
1948 I, S, F, 1949 W, I
Henderson, R S F (Blackheath) 1883 W, S, 1884 W, S,
1885 W
Heppell, W G (Devonport A) 1903 I
Herbert, A J (Wasps) 1958 F, S, 1959 W, I, F, S
Hesford, R (Bristol) 1981 S (R), 1982 A, S, F (R), 1983
F (R), 1985 R, F, S, I, W
Hetherington, J G G (Northampton) 1958 A, I, 1959
W, I, F, S
Hewitt, E N (Coventry) 1951 W, I, F
Hewitt, W W (Queen's House) 1881 I, W, S, 1882 I
Hickson, J L (Bradford) 1887 W, I, S, 1890 W, S, I
Higgins, R (Liverpool) 1954 W, NZ, I, S, 1955 W, I,
F, S, 1957 W, I, F, S, 1959 W
Hignell, A J (Cambridge U, Bristol) 1975 A 2, 1976 A,
W, S, I, 1977 S, I, F, W, 1978 W, 1979 S, I, F, W
Hill, B A (Blackheath) 1903 I, S, 1904 W, I, 1905 W,
NZ, 1906 SA, 1907 F, W
Hill, R J (Bath) 1984 SA 1,2, 1985 I (R), NZ 2 (R), 1986
F (R), 1987 I, F, W, [US], 1989 Fj, 1990 I, F, W, S
Hillard, R J (Oxford U) 1925 NZ
Hiller, R (Harlequins) 1968 W, I, F, S, 1969 I, F, S,
W, SA, 1970 I, W, S, 1971 I, F, S (2[1C]), P, 1972 W, I
Hind, A E (Leicester) 1905 NZ, 1906 W
Hind, G R (Blackheath) 1910 S, 1911 I
Hobbs, R F A (Blackheath) 1899 S, 1903 W
Hobbs, R G S (Richmond) 1932 SA, W, I, S
Hodges, H A (Nottingham) 1906 W, I
Hodgkinson, S D (Nottingham) 1989 R, Fj, 1990 I, F,
W, S
Hodgson, J Mc D (Northern) 1932 SA, W, I, S, 1934

113

W, I, 1936 *I*
Hodgson, S A M (Durham City) 1960 *W, I, F, S,* 1961
SA, W, 1962 *W, I, F, S,* 1964 *W*
Hofmeyr, M B (Oxford U) 1950 *W, F, S*
Hogarth, T B (Hartlepool R) 1906 *F*
Holford, G (Gloucester) 1920 *W, F*
Holland, D (Devonport A) 1912 *W, I, S*
Holliday, T E (Aspatria) 1923 *S, F,* 1925 *I, S, F,* 1926
F, S
Holmes, C B (Manchester) 1947 *S,* 1948 *I, F*
Holmes, E (Manningham) 1890 *S, I*
Holmes, W A (Nuneaton) 1950 *W, I, F, S,* 1951 *W, I,
F, S,* 1952 *SA, S, I, F,* 1953 *W, I, F, S*
Holmes, W B (Cambridge U) 1949 *W, I, F, S*
Hook, W G (Gloucester) 1951 *S,* 1952 *SA, W*
Hooper, C A (Middlesex W) 1894 *W, I, S*
Hopley, F J V (Blackheath) 1907 *F, W,* 1908 *I*
Hordern, P C (Gloucester) 1931 *I, S, F,* 1934 *W*
Horley, C H (Swinton) 1885 *I*
Hornby, A N (Manchester) 1877 *I, S,* 1878 *S, I,* 1880 *I,*
1881 *I, S,* 1882 *I, S*
Horrocks-Taylor, J P (Cambridge U, Leicester,
Middlesbrough) 1958 *W, A,* 1961 *S,* 1962 *S,* 1963 *NZ*
1,2, *A,* 1964 *NZ, W*
Horsfall, E L (Harlequins) 1949 *W*
Horton, A L (Blackheath) 1965 *W, I, F, S,* 1966 *F, S,*
1967 *NZ*
Horton, J P (Bath) 1978 *W, S, I, NZ,* 1980 *I, F, W, S,*
1981 *W,* 1983 *S, I,* 1984 *SA* 1,2
Horton, N E (Moseley, Toulouse) 1969 *I, F, S, W,*
1971 *I, F, S,* 1974 *S,* 1975 *W,* 1977 *S, I, F, W,* 1978 *F,
W,* 1979 *S, I, F, W,* 1980 *I*
Hosen, R W (Bristol, Northampton) 1963 *NZ* 1,2, *A,*
1964 *F, S,* 1967 *A, I, F, S, W*
Hosking, G R d'A (Devonport Services) 1949 *W, I, F,
S,* 1950 *W*
Houghton, S (Runcorn) 1892 *I,* 1896 *W*
Howard, P D (O Millhillians) 1930 *W, I, F, S,* 1931 *W,
I, S, F*
Hubbard, G C (Blackheath) 1892 *W, I*
Hubbard, J C (Harlequins) 1930 *S*
Hudson, A (Gloucester) 1906 *W, I, F,* 1908 *F, W, I, S,*
1910 *F*
Hughes, G E (Barrow) 1896 *S*
Hulme, F C (Birkenhead Park) 1903 *W, I,* 1905 *W, I*
Hunt, J T (Manchester) 1882 *I, S,* 1884 *W*
Hunt, R (Manchester) 1880 *I,* 1881 *W, S,* 1882 *I*
Hunt, W H (Manchester) 1876 *S,* 1877 *I, S,* 1878 *I*
Huntsman, R P (Headingley) 1985 *NZ* 1,2
Hurst, A C B (Wasps) 1962 *S*
Huskisson, T F (OMTs) 1937 *W, I, S,* 1938 *W, I,* 1939
W, I, S
Hutchinson, F (Headingley) 1909 *F, I, S*
Hutchinson, J E (Durham City) 1906 *I*
Hutchinson, W C (RIE Coll) 1876 *S,* 1877 *I*
Hutchinson, W H H (Hull) 1875 *I,* 1876 *I*
Huth, H (Huddersfield) 1879 *S*
Hyde, J P (Northampton) 1950 *F, S*
Hynes, W B (United Services, RN) 1912 *F*

Ibbitson, E D (Headingley) 1909 *W, F, I, S*
Imrie, H M (Durham City) 1906 *NZ,* 1907 *I*
Inglis, R E (Blackheath) 1886 *W, I, S*
Irvin, S H (Devonport A) 1905 *W*
Isherwood, F W (Ravenscourt Park) 1872 *S*

Jackett, E J (Leicester, Falmouth) 1905 *NZ,* 1906 *W, I,
S, F, SA,* 1907 *W, I, S,* 1909 *W, F, I, S*
Jackson, A H (Blackheath) 1878 *I,* 1880 *I*
Jackson, B S (Broughton Park) 1970 *S* (R), *F*
Jackson, P B (Coventry) 1956 *W, I, F,* 1957 *W, I, F, S,*
1958 *W, A, F, S,* 1959 *W, I, F, S,* 1961 *S,* 1963 *W, I, F,
S*
Jackson, W J (Halifax) 1894 *S*
Jacob, F (Cambridge U) 1897 *W, I, S,* 1898 *I, S, W,*
1899 *W, I*
Jacob, H P (Blackheath) 1924 *W, I, F, S,* 1930 *F*
Jacob, P G (Blackheath) 1898 *I*
Jacobs, C R (Northampton) 1956 *W, I, S, F,* 1957 *W,
I, F, S,* 1958 *W, A, I, F, S,* 1960 *W, I, F, S,* 1961 *SA,
W, I, F, S,* 1963 *NZ* 1,2, *A,* 1964 *W, I, F, S*
Jago, R A (Devonport A) 1906 *W, I, SA,* 1907 *W, I*
Janion, J P A G (Bedford) 1971 *W, I, F, S* (2[1C]), *P,*

1972 *W, S, SA,* 1973 *A,* 1975 *A* 1,2
Jarman, J W (Bristol) 1900 *W*
Jeavons, N C (Moseley) 1981 *S, I, F, Arg* 1,2, 1982 *A,
S, I, F, W,* 1983 *F, W, S, I*
Jeeps, R E G (Northampton) 1956 *W,* 1957 *W, I, F, S,*
1958 *W, A, I, F, S,* 1959 *I,* 1960 *W, I, F, S,* 1961 *SA,
W, I, F, S,* 1962 *W, I, F, S*
Jeffery, G L (Blackheath) 1886 *W, I, S,* 1887 *W, I, S*
Jennins, C R (Waterloo) 1967 *A, I, F*
Jewitt, J (Hartlepool R) 1902 *W*
Johns, W A (Gloucester) 1909 *W, F, I, S,* 1910 *W, I, F*
Johnston, W R (Bristol) 1910 *W, I, S,* 1912 *W, I, S, F,*
1913 *SA, W, F, I, S,* 1914 *W, I, S, F*
Jones, F P (N Brighton) 1893 *S*
Jones, H A (Barnstaple) 1950 *W, I, F*
Jorden, A M (Cambridge U, Blackheath, Bedford) 1970
F, 1973 *I, F, S,* 1974 *F,* 1975 *W, S*
Jowett, D (Heckmondwike) 1889 *M,* 1890 *S, I,* 1891
W, I, S
Judd, P E (Coventry) 1962 *W, I, F, S,* 1963 *S, NZ* 1,2,
A, 1964 *NZ,* 1965 *I, F, S,* 1966 *W, I, F, S,* 1967 *A, I,
F, S, W, NZ*

Kayll, H E (Sunderland) 1878 *S*
Keeling, J H (Guy's Hospital) 1948 *A, W*
Keen, B W (Newcastle U) 1968 *W, I, F, S*
Keeton, G H (Leicester) 1904 *W, I, S*
Kelly, G A (Bedford) 1947 *W, I, S,* 1948 *W*
Kelly, T S (London Devonians) 1906 *W, I, S, F, SA,*
1907 *F, W, I, S,* 1908 *F, I, S*
Kemble, A T (Liverpool) 1885 *W, I,* 1887 *I*
Kemp, D T (Blackheath) 1935 *W*
Kemp, T A (Richmond) 1937 *W, I,* 1939 *S,* 1948 *A, W*
Kendall, P D (Birkenhead Park) 1901 *S,* 1902 *W,* 1903
S
Kendall-Carpenter, J MacG K (Oxford U, Bath) 1949
I, F, S, 1950 *W, I, F, S,* 1951 *I, F, S,* 1952 *SA, W, S, I,
F,* 1953 *W, I, F, S,* 1954 *W, NZ, I, F*
Kendrew, D A (Leicester) 1930 *W, I,* 1933 *I, S,* 1934
S, 1935 *W, I,* 1936 *W, I*
Kennedy, R D (Camborne S of M) 1949 *I, F, S*
Kent, C P (Rosslyn Park) 1977 *S, I, F, W,* 1978 *F* (R)
Kent, T (Salford) 1891 *W, I, S,* 1892 *W, I, S*
Kershaw, C A (United Services, RN) 1920 *W, F, I, S,*
1921 *W, I, S, F,* 1922 *W, I, S, F,* 1923 *W, I, S, F*
Kewley, E (Liverpool) 1874 *S,* 1875 *S,* 1876 *I, S,* 1877
I, S, 1878 *S*
Kewney, A L (Leicester) 1906 *W, I, S, F,* 1909 *A, W,
F, I, S,* 1911 *W, F, I, S,* 1912 *I, S,* 1913 *SA*
Key, A (O Cranleighans) 1930 *I,* 1933 *W*
Keyworth, M (Swansea) 1976 *A, W, S, I*
Kilner, B (Wakefield T) 1880 *I*
Kindersley, R S (Exeter) 1883 *W,* 1884 *S,* 1885 *W*
King, I (Harrogate) 1954 *W, NZ, I*
King, J A (Headingley) 1911 *W, F, I, S,* 1912 *W, I, S,*
1913 *SA, W, F, I, S*
King, Q E M A (Army) 1921 *S*
Kingston, P (Gloucester) 1975 *A* 1,2, 1979 *I, F, W*
Kitching, A E (Blackheath) 1913 *I*
Kittermaster, H J (Harlequins) 1925 *NZ, W, I,* 1926
W, I, F, S
Knight, F (Plymouth) 1909 *A*
Knight, P M (Bristol) 1972 *F, S, SA*
Knowles, E (Millom) 1896 *S,* 1897 *S*
Knowles, T C (Birkenhead Park) 1931 *S*
Krige, J A (Guy's Hospital) 1920 *W*

Labuschagne, N A (Harlequins, Guy's Hospital) 1953
W, 1955 *W, I, F, S*
Lagden, R O (Richmond) 1911 *S*
Laird, H C C (Harlequins) 1927 *W, I, S,* 1928 *A, W, I,
F, S,* 1929 *W, I*
Lambert, D (Harlequins) 1907 *F,* 1908 *F, W, S,* 1911
W, F, I
Lampkowski, M S (Headingley) 1976 *A, W, S, I*
Lapage, W N (United Services, RN) 1908 *F, W, I, S*
Larter, P J (Northampton, RAF) 1967 *A, NZ,* 1968 *W,
I, F, S,* 1969 *I, F, S, W, SA,* 1970 *I, W, F, S,* 1971 *W,
I, F, S* (2[1C]), *P,* 1972 *SA,* 1973 *NZ* 1, *W*
Law, A F (Richmond) 1877 *S*
Law, D E (Birkenhead Park) 1927 *I*
Lawrence, Hon H A (Richmond) 1873 *S,* 1874 *S,* 1875
I, S

114

Lawrie, P W (Leicester) 1910 *S*, 1911 *S*
Lawson, R G (Workington) 1925 *I*
Lawson, T M (Workington) 1928 *A, W*
Leadbetter, M M (Broughton Park) 1970 *F*
Leadbetter, V H (Edinburgh Wands) 1954 *S, F*
Leake, W R M (Harlequins) 1891 *W, I, S*
Leather, G (Liverpool) 1907 *I*
Lee, F H (Marlborough N) 1876 *S*, 1877 *I*
Lee, H (Blackheath) 1907 *F*
Le Fleming, J (Blackheath) 1887 *W*
Leslie-Jones, F A (Richmond) 1895 *W, I*
Lewis, A O (Bath) 1952 *SA, W, S, I, F*, 1953 *W, I, F, S*, 1954 *F*
Leyland, R (Waterloo) 1935 *W, I, S*
Linnett, M S (Moseley) 1989 *Fj*
Livesay, R O'H (Blackheath) 1898 *W*, 1899 *W*
Lloyd, R H (Harlequins) 1967 *NZ*, 1968 *W, I, F, S*
Locke, H M (Birkenhead Park) 1923 *S, F*, 1924 *W, F, S*, 1925 *W, I, S, F*, 1927 *W, I, S*
Lockwood, R E (Heckmondwike) 1887 *W, I, S*, 1889 *M*, 1891 *W, I, S*, 1892 *W, I, S*, 1893 *W, I*, 1894 *W, I*
Login, S H M (RN Coll) 1876 *I*
Lohden, F C (Blackheath) 1893 *W*
Longland, R J (Northampton) 1932 *S*, 1933 *W, S*, 1934 *W, I, S*, 1935 *W, I, S*, 1936 *NZ, W, I, S*, 1937 *W, I, S*, 1938 *W, I, S*
Lowe, C N (Cambridge U, Blackheath) 1913 *SA, W, F, I, S*, 1914 *W, I, S, F*, 1920 *W, F, I, S*, 1921 *W, I, S, F*, 1922 *W, I, F, S*, 1923 *W, I, S, F*
Lowrie, F (Wakefield T) 1889 *M*, 1890 *W*
Lowry, W M (Birkenhead Park) 1920 *F*
Lozowski R A P (Wasps) 1984 *A*
Luddington, W G E (Devonport Services) 1923 *W, I, S, F*, 1924 *W, I, F, S*, 1925 *W, I, S, F*, 1926 *W*
Luscombe, F (Gipsies) 1872 *S*, 1873 *S*, 1875 *I, S*, 1876 *I, S*
Luscombe, J H (Gipsies) 1871 *S*
Luxmoore, A F C C (Richmond) 1900 *S*, 1901 *W*
Luya, H F (Waterloo, Headingley) 1948 *W, I, S, F*, 1949 *W*
Lyon, A (Liverpool) 1871 *S*
Lyon, G H d'O (United Services, RN) 1908 *S*, 1909 *A*

McCanlis, M A (Gloucester) 1931 *W, I*
McFadyean, C W (Moseley) 1966 *I, F, S*, 1967 *A, I, F, S, W, NZ*, 1968 *W, I*
MacIlwaine, A H (United Services, Hull & E Riding) 1912 *W, I, S, F*, 1920 *I*
Mackie, O G (Wakefield T, Cambridge U) 1897 *S*, 1898 *I*
Mackinlay, J E H (St George's Hospital) 1872 *S*, 1873 *S*, 1875 *I*
MacLaren, W (Manchester) 1871 *S*
MacLennan, R R F (OMTs) 1925 *I, S, F*
McLeod, N F (RIE Coll) 1879 *S, I*
Madge, R J P (Exeter) 1948 *A, W, I, S*
Malir, F W S (Otley) 1930 *W, I, S*
Mangles, R H (Richmond) 1897 *W, I*
Manley, D C (Exeter) 1963 *W, I, F, S*
Mann, W E (United Services, Army) 1911 *W, F, I*
Mantell, N D (Rosslyn Park) 1975 *A 1*
Markendale, E T (Manchester R) 1880 *I*
Marques, R W D (Cambridge U, Harlequins) 1956 *W, I, S, F*, 1957 *W, I, F, S*, 1958 *W, A, I, F, S*, 1959 *W, I, F, S*, 1960 *W, I, F, S*, 1961 *SA, W*
Marquis, J C (Birkenhead Park) 1900 *I, S*
Marriott, C J B (Blackheath) 1884 *W, I, S*, 1886 *W, I, S*, 1887 *I*
Marriott, E E (Manchester) 1876 *I*
Marriott, V R (Harlequins) 1963 *NZ 1,2, A*, 1964 *NZ*
Marsden, G H (Morley) 1900 *W, I, S*
Marsh, H (RIE Coll) 1873 *S*
Marsh, J (Swinton) 1892 *I*
Marshall, H (Blackheath) 1893 *W*
Marshall, M W (Blackheath) 1873 *S*, 1874 *S*, 1875 *I, S*, 1876 *I, S*, 1877 *I, S*, 1878 *S, I*
Marshall, R M (Oxford U) 1938 *I, S*, 1939 *W, I, S*
Martin, C R (Bath) 1985 *F, S, I, W*
Martin, N O (Harlequins) 1972 *F* (R)
Martindale, S A (Kendal) 1929 *F*
Massey, E J (Leicester) 1925 *W, I, S*
Mathias, J L (Bristol) 1905 *W, I, S, NZ*
Matters, J C (RNE Coll) 1899 *S*

Matthews, J R C (Harlequins) 1949 *F, S*, 1950 *I, F, S*, 1952 *SA, W, S, I, F*
Maud, P (Blackheath) 1893 *W, I*
Maxwell, A W (New Brighton, Headingley) 1975 *A 1*, 1976 *A, W, S, I, F*, 1978 *F*
Maxwell-Hyslop, J E (Oxford U) 1922 *I, F, S*
Maynard, A F (Cambridge U) 1914 *W, I, S*
Meikle, G W C (Waterloo) 1934 *W, I, S*
Meikle, S S C (Waterloo) 1929 *S*
Mellish, F W (Blackheath) 1920 *W, F, I, S*, 1921 *W, I*
Melville, N D (Wasps) 1984 *A*, 1985 *I, W, NZ 1,2*, 1986 *W, S, I, F*, 1988 *F, W, S, I 1*
Merriam, L P B (Blackheath) 1920 *W, F*
Michell, A T (Oxford U) 1875 *I, S*, 1876 *I*
Middleton, B B (Birkenhead Park) 1882 *I*, 1883 *I*
Middleton, J A (Richmond) 1922 *S*
Miles, J H (Leicester) 1903 *W*
Millett, H (Richmond) 1920 *F*
Mills, F W (Marlborough N) 1872 *S*, 1873 *S*
Mills, S G F (Gloucester) 1981 *Arg 1,2*, 1983 *W*, 1984 *SA 1, A*
Mills, W A (Devonport A) 1906 *W, I, S, F, SA*, 1907 *F, W, I, S*, 1908 *F, W*
Milman, D L K (Bedford) 1937 *W*, 1938 *W, I, S*
Milton, C H (Camborne S of M) 1906 *I*
Milton, J G (Camborne S of M) 1904 *W, I, S*, 1905 *S*, 1907 *I*
Milton, W H (Marlborough N) 1874 *S*, 1875 *I*
Mitchell, F (Blackheath) 1895 *W, I, S*, 1896 *W, I, S*
Mitchell, W G (Richmond) 1890 *W, S, I*, 1891 *W, I, S*, 1893 *S*
Mobbs, E R (Northampton) 1909 *A, W, F, I, S*, 1910 *I, F*
Moberly, W O (Ravenscourt Park) 1872 *S*
Moore, B C (Nottingham) 1987 *S, [A, J, W]*, 1988 *F, W, S, I 1 2, A 1,2, Fj, A*, 1989 *S, I, F, W, R, Fj*, 1990 *I, F, W, S*
Moore, E J (Blackheath) 1883 *I, S*
Moore, N J N H (Bristol) 1904 *W, I, S*
Moore, P B C (Blackheath) 1951 *W*
Moore, W K T (Leicester) 1947 *W, I*, 1949 *F, S*, 1950 *I, F, S*
Mordell, R J (Rosslyn Park) 1978 *W*
Morfitt, S (W Hartlepool) 1894 *W, I, S*, 1896 *W, I, S*
Morgan, J R (Hawick) 1920 *W*
Morgan, W G D (Medicals, Newcastle) 1960 *W, I, F, S*, 1961 *SA, W, I, F, S*
Morley, A J (Bristol) 1972 *SA*, 1973 *NZ 1, W, I*, 1975 *S, A 1,2*
Morris, A D W (United Services, RN) 1909 *W, W, F*
Morris, C D (Liverpool St Helens) 1988 *A*, 1989 *S, I, F, W*
Morrison, P H (Cambridge U) 1890 *W, S, I*, 1891 *I*
Morse, S (Marlborough N) 1873 *S*, 1874 *S*, 1875 *S*
Mortimer, W (Marlborough N) 1899 *W*
Morton, H J S (Blackheath) 1909 *I, S*, 1910 *W, I*
Moss, F (Broughton) 1885 *W, I*, 1886 *W*
Mullins, A R (Harlequins) 1989 *Fj*
Mycock, J (Sale) 1947 *W, I, S, F*, 1948 *A*
Myers, E (Bradford) 1920 *I, S*, 1921 *W, I*, 1922 *W, I, F, S*, 1923 *W, I, S, F*, 1924 *W, I, S, F*, 1925 *S, F*
Myers, H (Keighley) 1898 *I*

Nanson, W M B (Carlisle) 1907 *F, W*
Nash, E H (Richmond) 1875 *I*
Neale, B A (Rosslyn Park) 1951 *I, F, S*
Neale, M E (Blackheath) 1912 *F*
Neame, S (O Cheltonians) 1879 *S, I*, 1880 *I, S*
Neary, A (Broughton Park) 1971 *W, I, F, S (2[1C]), P*, 1972 *W, I, F, S, SA*, 1973 *NZ 1, W, I, F, S, NZ 2, A*, 1974 *S, I, F, W*, 1975 *I, F, W, S, A 1*, 1976 *A, W, S, I, F*, 1977 *I*, 1978 *F* (R), 1979 *S, I, F, W, NZ*, 1980 *I, F, W, S*
Nelmes, B G (Cardiff) 1975 *A 1,2*, 1978 *W, S, I, NZ*
Newbold, C J (Blackheath) 1904 *W, I, S*, 1905 *W, I, S*
Newman, S C (Oxford U) 1947 *F*, 1948 *A, W*
Newton, A W (Blackheath) 1907 *S*
Newton, P A (Blackheath) 1882 *S*
Newton-Thompson, J O (Oxford U) 1947 *S, F*
Nichol, W (Brighouse R) 1892 *W, S*
Nicholas, P L (Exeter) 1902 *W*
Nicholson, B E (Harlequins) 1938 *W, I*
Nicholson, E S (Leicester) 1935 *W, I, S*, 1936 *NZ, W*

Nicholson, E T (Birkenhead Park) 1900 *W, I*
Nicholson, T (Rockcliff) 1893 *I*
Ninnes, B F (Coventry) 1971 *W*
Norman, D J (Leicester) 1932 *SA, W*
North, E H G (Blackheath) 1891 *W, I, S*
Northmore, S (Millom) 1897 *I*
Novak, M J (Harlequins) 1970 *W, S, F*
Novis, A L (Blackheath) 1929 *S, F,* 1930 *W, I, F,* 1933 *I, S*

Oakeley, F E (United Services, RN) 1913 *S,* 1914 *I, S, F*
Oakes, R F (Hartlepool R) 1897 *W, I, S,* 1898 *I, S, W,* 1899 *W, S*
Oakley, L F L (Bedford) 1951 *W*
Obolensky, A (Oxford U) 1936 *NZ, W, I, S*
Old, A G B (Middlesbrough, Leicester, Sheffield) 1972 *W, I, F, S, SA,* 1973 *NZ 2, A,* 1974 *S, I, F, W,* 1975 *I, A* 2, 1976 *S, I,* 1978 *F*
Oldham, W L (Coventry) 1908 *S,* 1909 *A*
O'Neill, A (Teignmouth, Torquay A) 1901 *W, I, S*
Openshaw, W E (Manchester) 1879 *I*
Orwin, J (Gloucester, RAF, Bedford) 1985 *R, F, S, I, W, NZ* 1,2, 1988 *F, W, S, I* 1,2, *A* 1,2
Osborne, R R (Manchester) 1871 *S*
Osborne, S H (Oxford U) 1905 *S*
Oti, C (Cambridge U, Nottingham, Wasps) 1988 *S, I* 1, 1989 *S, I, F, W, R*
Oughtred, B (Hartlepool R) 1901 *S,* 1902 *W, I, S,* 1903 *W, I*
Owen, J E (Coventry) 1963 *W, I, F, S, A,* 1964 *NZ,* 1965 *W, I, F, S,* 1966 *I, F, S,* 1967 *NZ*
Owen-Smith, H G O (St Mary's Hospital) 1934 *W, I, S,* 1936 *NZ, W, I, S,* 1937 *W, I, S*

Page, J J (Bedford, Northampton) 1971 *W, I, F, S,* 1975 *S*
Pallant, J N (Notts) 1967 *I, F, S*
Palmer, A C (London Hospital) 1909 *I, S*
Palmer, F H (Richmond) 1905 *W*
Palmer, G V (Richmond) 1928 *I, F, S*
Palmer, J A (Bath) 1984 *SA* 1,2, 1986 *I* (R)
Pargetter, T A (Coventry) 1962 *S,* 1963 *F, NZ* 1
Parker, G W (Gloucester) 1938 *I, S*
Parker, Hon S (Liverpool) 1874 *S,* 1875 *S*
Parsons, E I (RAF) 1939 *S*
Parsons, M J (Northampton) 1968 *W, I, F, S*
Patterson, W M (Sale) 1961 *SA, S*
Pattisson, R M (Blackheath) 1883 *I, S*
Paul, J E (RIE Coll) 1875 *S*
Payne, A T (Bristol) 1935 *I, S*
Payne, C M (Harlequins) 1964 *I, F, S,* 1965 *I, F, S,* 1966 *W, I, F, S*
Payne, J H (Broughton) 1882 *S,* 1883 *W, I, S,* 1884 *I,* 1885 *W, I*
Pearce, G S (Northampton) 1979 *S, I, F, W,* 1981 *Arg* 1,2, 1982 *A, S,* 1983 *F, W, S, I, NZ,* 1984 *S, SA* 2, *A,* 1985 *R, F, S, I, W, NZ* 1,2, 1986 *W, S, I, F,* 1987 *I, F, W, S, [A, US, W],* 1988 *Fj*
Pearson, A W (Blackheath) 1875 *I, S,* 1876 *I, S,* 1877 *S,* 1878 *S, I*
Peart, T G A H (Hartlepool R) 1964 *F, S*
Pease, F E (Hartlepool R) 1887 *I*
Penny, S H (Leicester) 1909 *A*
Penny, W J (United Hospitals) 1878 *I,* 1879 *S, I*
Percival, L J (Rugby) 1891 *I,* 1892 *I,* 1893 *S*
Periton, H G (Waterloo) 1925 *W,* 1926 *W, I, F, S,* 1927 *W, I, S, F,* 1928 *A, I, F, S,* 1929 *W, I, S, F,* 1930 *W, I, F, S*
Perrott, E S (O Cheltonians) 1875 *I*
Perry, D G (Bedford) 1963 *F, S, NZ* 1,2, *A,* 1964 *NZ, W, I,* 1965 *W, I, F, S,* 1966 *W, I, F*
Perry, S V (Cambridge U, Waterloo) 1947 *W, I,* 1948 *A, W, I, S, F*
Peters, J (Plymouth) 1906 *S, F,* 1907 *I, S,* 1908 *W*
Phillips, C (Birkenhead Park) 1880 *S,* 1881 *I, S*
Phillips, M S (Fylde) 1958 *A, I, F, S,* 1959 *W, I, F, S,* 1960 *W, I, F, S,* 1961 *W,* 1963 *W, I, F, S, NZ* 1,2, *A,* 1964 *NZ, W, I, F, S*
Pickering, A S (Harrogate) 1907 *I*
Pickering, R D A (Bradford) 1967 *I, F, S, W,* 1968 *F, S*
Pickles, R C W (Bristol) 1922 *I, S*
Pierce, R (Liverpool) 1898 *I,* 1903 *S*

Pilkington, W N (Cambridge U) 1898 *S*
Pillman, C H (Blackheath) 1910 *W, I, F, S,* 1911 *W, F, I, S,* 1912 *W, F,* 1913 *SA, W, F, I, S,* 1914 *W, I, S*
Pillman, R L (Blackheath) 1914 *F*
Pinch, J (Lancaster) 1896 *W, I,* 1897 *S*
Pinching, W W (Guy's Hospital) 1872 *S*
Pitman, I J (Oxford U) 1922 *S*
Plummer, K C (Bristol) 1969 *W,* 1976 *S, I, F*
Poole, F O (Oxford U) 1895 *W, I, S*
Poole, R W (Hartlepool R) 1896 *S*
Pope, E B (Blackheath) 1931 *W, S, F*
Portus, G V (Blackheath) 1908 *F, I*
Poulton, R W (later **Poulton Palmer**) (Oxford U, Harlequins, Liverpool) 1909 *F, I, S,* 1910 *W,* 1911 *S,* 1912 *W, I, S,* 1913 *SA, W, F, I, S,* 1914 *W, I, S, F*
Powell, D L (Northampton) 1966 *W, I,* 1969 *I, F, S, W,* 1971 *W, I, F, S* (2[1C])
Pratten, W E (Blackheath) 1927 *S, F*
Preece, I (Coventry) 1948 *I, S, F,* 1949 *F, S,* 1950 *W, I, F, S,* 1951 *W, I, F*
Preece, P S (Coventry) 1972 *SA,* 1973 *NZ* 1, *W, I, F, S, NZ* 2, 1975 *I, F, W, A* 2, 1976 *W* (R)
Preedy, M (Gloucester) 1984 *SA* 1
Prentice, F D (Leicester) 1928 *I, F, S*
Prescott, R E (Harlequins) 1937 *W, I,* 1938 *I,* 1939 *W, I, S*
Preston, N J (Richmond) 1979 *NZ,* 1980 *I, F*
Price, H L (Harlequins) 1922 *I, S,* 1923 *W, I*
Price, J (Coventry) 1961 *I*
Price, P L A (RIE Coll) 1877 *I, S,* 1878 *S*
Price, T W (Cheltenham) 1948 *S, F,* 1949 *W, I, F, S*
Probyn, J A (Wasps) 1988 *F, W, S, I* 1,2, *A* 1,2, *A,* 1989 *S, I, R* (R), 1990 *I, F, W, S*
Prout, D H (Northampton) 1968 *W, I*
Pullin, J V (Bristol) 1966 *W,* 1968 *W, I, F, S,* 1969 *I, F, S, W, SA,* 1970 *I, W, S, F,* 1971 *W, I, F, S* (2[1C]), *P,* 1972 *W, I, F, S, SA,* 1973 *NZ* 1, *W, I, F, S, NZ* 2, *A,* 1974 *S, I, F, W,* 1975 *I, W* (R), *S, A,* 1,2, 1976 *F*
Purdy, S J (Rugby) 1962 *S*
Pyke, J (St Helens Recreation) 1892 *W*
Pym, J A (Blackheath) 1912 *W, I, S, F*

Quinn, J P (New Brighton) 1954 *W, NZ, I, S, F*

Rafter, M (Bristol) 1977 *S, F, W,* 1978 *F, W, S, I, NZ,* 1979 *S, I, F, W, NZ,* 1980 *W* (R), 1981 *W, Arg* 1,2
Ralston, C W (Richmond) 1971 *S* (C), *P,* 1972 *W, I, F, S, SA,* 1973 *NZ* 1, *W, I, F, S, NZ* 2, *A,* 1974 *S, I, F, W,* 1975 *I, F, W, S*
Ramsden, H E (Bingley) 1898 *W, S*
Ranson, J M (Rosslyn Park) 1963 *NZ* 1,2, *A,* 1964 *W, I, F, S*
Raphael, J E (OMTs) 1902 *W, I, S,* 1905 *W, S, NZ,* 1906 *W, S, F*
Ravenscroft, J (Birkenhead Park) 1881 *I*
Rawlinson, W C W (Blackheath) 1876 *S*
Redfern, S (Leicester) 1984 *I* (R)
Redman, N C (Bath) 1984 *A,* 1986 *S* (R), 1987 *I, S, [A, J, W],* 1988 *Fj*
Redmond, G F (Cambridge U) 1970 *F*
Redwood, B W (Bristol) 1968 *W, I*
Rees, G W (Nottingham) 1984 *SA* 2 (R), *A,* 1986 *I, F,* 1987 *F, W, S, [A, J, US, W],* 1988 *S*(R), *I* 1,2, *A* 1,2, *Fj,* 1989 *W* (R), *R* (R), *Fj* (R)
Reeve, J S R (Harlequins) 1929 *F,* 1930 *W, I, F, S,* 1931 *W, I, S*
Regan, M (Liverpool) 1953 *W, I, F, S,* 1954 *W, NZ, I, S, F,* 1956 *I, S, F*
Rendall, P A G (Wasps) 1984 *W, SA* 2, 1986 *W, S,* 1987 *I, F, S, [A, J, W],* 1988 *F, W, S, I* 1,2, *A* 1,2, *A,* 1989 *S, I, F, W, R,* 1990 *I, F, W, S*
Rew, H (Blackheath) 1929 *S, F,* 1930 *F, S,* 1931 *W, S, F,* 1934 *W, I, S*
Reynolds, F J (O Cranleighans) 1937 *S,* 1938 *I, S*
Reynolds, S (Richmond) 1900 *W, I, S,* 1901 *I*
Rhodes, J (Castleford) 1896 *W, I, S*
Richards, D (Leicester) 1986 *I, F,* 1987 *S, [A, J, US, W],* 1988 *F, W, S, I* 1, *A* 1,2, *Fj, A,* 1989 *S, I, F, W, R*
Richards, E E (Plymouth A) 1929 *S, F*
Richards, J (Bradford) 1891 *W, I, S*
Richards, S B (Richmond) 1965 *W, I, F, S,* 1967 *A, I, F, S, W*
Richardson, J V (Birkenhead Park) 1928 *A, W, I, F, S*

Richardson, W R (Manchester) 1881 *I*
Rickards, C H (Gipsies) 1873 *S*
Rimmer, G (Waterloo) 1949 *W, I*, 1950 *W*, 1951 *W, I, F*, 1952 *SA, W*, 1954 *W, NZ, I, S*
Rimmer, L I (Bath) 1961 *SA, W, I, F, S*
Ripley, A G (Rosslyn Park) 1972 *W, I, F, S, SA*, 1973 *NZ 1, W, I, F, S, NZ 2, A*, 1974 *S, I, F, W*, 1975 *I, F, S, A* 1,2, 1976 *A, W, S*
Risman, A B W (Loughborough Colls) 1959 *W, I, F, S*, 1961 *SA, W, I, F*
Ritson, J A S (Northern) 1910 *F, S*, 1912 *F*, 1913 *SA, W, F, I, S*
Rittson-Thomas, G C (Oxford U) 1951 *W, I, F*
Robbins, G L (Coventry) 1986 *W, S*
Robbins, P G D (Oxford U, Moseley, Coventry) 1956 *W, I, S, F*, 1957 *W, I, F, S*, 1958 *W, A, I, S*, 1960 *W, I, F, S*, 1961 *SA, W*, 1962 *S*
Roberts, A D (Northern) 1911 *W, F, I, S*, 1912 *I, S, F*, 1914 *I*
Roberts, E W (RNE Coll) 1901 *W, I*, 1905 *NZ*, 1906 *W, I*, 1907 *S*
Roberts, G D (Harlequins) 1907 *S*, 1908 *F, W*
Roberts, J (Sale) 1960 *W, I, F, S*, 1961 *SA, W, I, F, S*, 1962 *W, I, F, S*, 1963 *W, I, F, S*, 1964 *NZ*
Roberts, R S (Coventry) 1932 *I*
Roberts, S (Swinton) 1887 *W, I*
Roberts, V G (Penryn, Harlequins) 1947 *F*, 1949 *W, I, F, S*, 1950 *I, F, S*, 1951 *W, I, F, S*, 1956 *W, I, S, F*
Robertshaw, A R (Bradford) 1886 *W, I, S*, 1887 *W, S*
Robinson, A (Blackheath) 1889 *M*, 1890 *W, S, I*
Robinson, E F (Coventry) 1954 *S*, 1961 *I, F, S*
Robinson, G C (Percy Park) 1897 *I, S*, 1898 *I*, 1899 *W*, 1900 *I, S*, 1901 *I, S*
Robinson, J J (Headingley) 1893 *S*, 1902 *W, I, S*
Robinson, R A (Bath) 1988 *A* 2, *Fj, A*, 1989 *S, I, F, W*
Robson, A (Northern) 1924 *W, I, F, S*, 1926 *W*
Robson, M (Oxford U) 1930 *W, I, F, S*
Rogers, D P (Bedford) 1961 *I. F, S*, 1962 *W, I, F*, 1963 *W, I, F, S, NZ* 1,2, *A*, 1964 *NZ, W, I, F, S*, 1965 *W, I, F, S*, 1966 *W, I, F, S*, 1967 *A, S, W, NZ*, 1969 *I, F, S, W*
Rogers, J H (Moseley) 1890 *W, S, I*, 1891 *S*
Rogers, W L Y (Blackheath) 1905 *W, I*
Rollitt, D M (Bristol) 1967 *I, F, S, W*, 1969 *I, F, S, W*, 1975 *S, A* 1,2
Roncoroni, A D S (West Herts, Richmond) 1933 *W, I, S*
Rose, W M H (Cambridge U, Coventry, Harlequins) 1981 *I, F*, 1982 *A, S, I*, 1987 *I, F, W, S*, [A]
Rossborough, P A (Coventry) 1971 *W*, 1973 *NZ* 2, *A*, 1974 *S, I*, 1975 *I, F*
Rosser, D W A (Wasps) 1965 *W, I, F, S*, 1966 *W*
Rotherham, Alan (Richmond) 1883 *W, S*, 1884 *W, S*, 1885 *W, I*, 1886 *W, I, S*, 1887 *W, I, S*
Rotherham, Arthur (Richmond) 1898 *S, W*, 1899 *W, I, S*
Roughley, D (Liverpool) 1973 *A*, 1974 *S, I*
Rowell, R E (Leicester) 1964 *W*, 1965 *W*
Rowley, A J (Coventry) 1932 *SA*
Rowley, H C (Manchester) 1879 *S, I*, 1880 *I, S*, 1881 *I, W, S*, 1882 *I, S*
Royds, P M R (Blackheath) 1898 *S, W*, 1899 *W*
Royle, A V (Broughton R) 1889 *M*
Rudd, E L (Liverpool) 1965 *W, I, S*, 1966 *W, I, S*
Russell, R F (Leicester) 1905 *NZ*
Rutherford, D (Percy Park, Gloucester) 1960 *W, I, F, S*, 1961 *SA*, 1965 *W, I, F, S*, 1966 *W, I, F, S*, 1967 *NZ*
Ryalls H J (N Brighton) 1885 *W, I*
Ryan, P H (Richmond) 1955 *W, I*

Sadler, E H (Army) 1933 *I, S*
Sagar, J W (Cambridge U) 1901 *W, I*
Salmon, J L B (Harlequins) 1985 *NZ* 1,2, 1986 *W, S*, 1987 *I, F, W, S*, [A, J, US, W]
Sample, C H (Cambridge U) 1884 *I*, 1885 *I*, 1886 *S*
Sanders, D L (Harlequins) 1954 *W, NZ, I, S, F*, 1956 *W, I, S, F*
Sanders, F W (Plymouth A) 1923 *I, S, F*
Sandford, J R P (Marlborough N) 1906 *I*
Sangwin, R D (Hull and E Riding) 1964 *NZ, W*
Sargent, G A F (Gloucester) 1981 *I* (R)
Savage, K F (Northampton) 1966 *W, I, F, S*, 1967 *A, I, F, S, W, NZ*, 1968 *W, F, S*

Sawyer, C M (Broughton) 1880 *S*, 1881 *I*
Saxby, L E (Gloucester) 1932 *SA, W*
Schofield, J W (Manchester) 1880 *I*
Scholfield, J A (Preston Grasshoppers) 1911 *W*
Schwarz, R O (Richmond) 1899 *S*, 1901 *W, I*
Scorfield, E S (Percy Park) 1910 *F*
Scott, C T (Blackheath) 1900 *W, I*, 1901 *I, W*
Scott, E K (St Mary's Hospital, Redruth) 1947 *W*, 1948 *A, W, I, S*
Scott, F S (Bristol) 1907 *W*
Scott, H (Manchester) 1955 *F*
Scott, J P (Rosslyn Park, Cardiff) 1978 *F, W, S, I, NZ*, 1979 *S* (R), *I, F, W, NZ*, 1980 *I, F, W, S*, 1981 *W, S, I, F, Arg* 1,2, 1982 *I, F*, 1983 *F, W, S, I, NZ*, 1984 *S, I, F, W, SA* 1,2
Scott, J S M (Oxford U) 1958 *F*
Scott, M T (Cambridge U) 1887 *I*, 1890 *S, I*
Scott, W M (Cambridge U) 1889 *M*
Seddon, R L (Broughton R) 1887 *W, I, S*
Sellar, K A (United Services, RN) 1927 *W, I, S*, 1928 *A, W, I, F*
Sever, H S (Sale) 1936 *NZ, W, I, S*, 1937 *W, I, S*, 1938 *W, I, S*
Shackleton, I R (Cambridge U) 1969 *SA*, 1970 *I, W, S*
Sharp, R A W (Oxford U, Wasps, Redruth) 1960 *W, I, F, S*, 1961 *I, F*, 1962 *W, I, F*, 1963 *W, I, F, S*, 1967 *A*
Shaw, C H (Moseley) 1906 *S, SA*, 1907 *F, W, I, S*
Shaw, F (Cleckheaton) 1898 *I*
Shaw, J F (RNE Coll) 1898 *S, W*
Sheppard, A (Bristol) 1981 *W* (R), 1985 *W*
Sherrard, C W (Blackheath) 1871 *S*, 1872 *S*
Sherriff, G A (Saracens) 1966 *S*, 1967 *A, NZ*
Shewring, H E (Bristol) 1905 *I, NZ*, 1906 *W, S, F, SA*, 1907 *F, W, I, S*
Shooter, J H (Morley) 1899 *I, S*, 1900 *I, S*
Shuttleworth, D W (Headingley) 1951 *S*, 1953 *F*
Sibree, H J H (Harlequins) 1908 *F*, 1909 *I, S*
Silk, N (Harlequins) 1965 *W, I, F, S*
Simms, K G (Cambridge U, Liverpool, Wasps) 1985 *R, F, S, I, W*, 1986 *I, F*, 1987 *I, F, W*, [A, J, W], 1988 *F, W*
Simpson, C P (Harlequins) 1965 *W*
Simpson, P D (Bath) 1983 *NZ*, 1984 *S*, 1987 *I*
Simpson, T (Rockcliff) 1902 *S*, 1903 *W, I, S*, 1904 *I, S*, 1905 *I, S*, 1906 *S, SA*, 1909 *W*
Skinner, M G (Harlequins) 1988 *F, W, S, I* 1,2, 1989 *Fj*, 1990 *I, F, W, S*
Sladen, G M (United Services, RN) 1929 *W, I, S*
Slemen, M A C (Liverpool) 1976 *I, F*, 1977 *S, I, F, W*, 1978 *F, W, S, I, NZ*, 1979 *S, I, F, W, NZ*, 1980 *I, F, W, S*, 1981 *W, S, I, F*, 1982 *A, S, I, F, W*, 1983 *NZ*, 1984 *S*
Slocock, L A N (Liverpool) 1907 *F, W, I, S*, 1908 *F, W, I, S*
Slow, C F (Leicester) 1934 *S*
Small, H D (Oxford U) 1950 *W, I, F, S*
Smallwood, A M (Leicester) 1920 *F, I*, 1921 *W, I, S, F*, 1922 *I, S*, 1923 *W, I, S, F*, 1925 *I, S*
Smart, C E (Newport) 1979 *W, NZ*, 1981 *S, I, F, Arg* 1,2, 1982 *A, S, I, F, W*, 1983 *F, W, S, I*
Smart, S E J (Gloucester) 1913 *SA, W, F, I, S*, 1914 *W, I, S, F*, 1920 *W, I, S*
Smeddle, R W (Cambridge U) 1929 *W, I, S*, 1931 *F*
Smith, C C (Gloucester) 1901 *W*
Smith, D F (Richmond) 1910 *W, I*
Smith, J V (Cambridge U, Rosslyn Park) 1950 *W, I, F, S*
Smith, K (Roundhay) 1974 *F, W*, 1975 *W, S*
Smith, M J K (Oxford U) 1956 *W*
Smith, S J (Sale) 1973 *I, F, S, A*, 1974 *I, F*, 1975 *W* (R), 1976 *F*, 1977 *F* (R), 1979 *NZ*, 1980 *I, F, W, S*, 1981 *W, S, I, F, Arg* 1,2, 1982 *A, S, I, F, W*, 1983 *F, W, S*
Smith, S R (Richmond) 1959 *W, F, S*, 1964 *F, S*
Smith, S T (Wasps) 1985 *R, F, S, I, W, NZ* 1,2, 1986 *W, S*
Smith, T A (Northampton) 1951 *W*
Soane, F (Bath) 1893 *S*, 1894 *W, I, S*
Sobey, W H (O Millhillians) 1930 *W, F, S*, 1932 *SA, W*
Solomon, B (Redruth) 1910 *W*
Sparks, R H W (Plymouth A) 1928 *I, F, S*, 1929 *W, I, S*, 1931 *I, S, F*

117

Speed, H (Castleford) 1894 *W, I, S*, 1896 *S*
Spence, F W (Birkenhead Park) 1890 *I*
Spencer, J (Harlequins) 1966 *W*
Spencer, J S (Cambridge U, Headingley) 1969 *I, F, S, W, SA*, 1970 *I, W, S, F*, 1971 *W, I, S* (2[1C]), *P*
Spong, R S (O Millhillians) 1929 *F*, 1930 *W, I, F, S*, 1931 *F*, 1932 *SA, W*
Spooner, R H (Liverpool) 1903 *W*
Springman, H H (Liverpool) 1879 *S*, 1887 *S*
Spurling, A (Blackheath) 1882 *I*
Spurling, N (Blackheath) 1886 *I, S*, 1887 *W*
Squires, P J (Harrogate) 1973 *F, S, NZ* 2, *A*, 1974 *S, I, F, W*, 1975 *I, F, W, S, A* 1,2, 1976 *A, W*, 1977 *S, I, F, W*, 1978 *F, W, S, I, NZ*, 1979 *S, I, F, W*
Stafford, R C (Bedford) 1912 *W, I, S, F*
Stafford, W F H (RE) 1874 *S*
Stanbury, E (Plymouth A) 1926 *W, I, S*, 1927 *W, I, S, F*, 1928 *A, W, I, F, S*, 1929 *W, I, S, F*
Standing, G (Blackheath) 1883 *W, I*
Stanger-Leathes, C F (Northern) 1905 *I*
Stark, K J (O Alleynians) 1927 *W, I, S, F*, 1928 *A, W, I, F, S*
Starks, A (Castleford) 1896 *W, I*
Starmer-Smith, N C (Harlequins) 1969 *SA*, 1970 *I, W, S, F*, 1971 *S* (C), *F*
Start, S P (United Services, RN) 1907 *S*
Steeds, J H (Saracens) 1949 *F, S*, 1950 *I, F, S*
Steele-Bodger, M R (Cambridge U) 1947 *W, I, S, F*, 1948 *A, W, I, S, F*
Steinthal, F E (Ilkley) 1913 *W, F*
Stevens, C B (Penzance-Newlyn, Harlequins) 1969 *SA*, 1970 *I, W, S*, 1971 *P*, 1972 *W, I, F, S, SA*, 1973 *NZ* 1, *W, I, F, S, NZ* 2, *A*, 1974 *S, I, F, W*, 1975 *I, F, W, S*
Still, E R (Oxford U, Ravenscourt P) 1873 *S*
Stirling, R V (Leicester, RAF, Wasps) 1951 *W, I, F, S*, 1952 *SA, W, S, I, F*, 1953 *W, I, F, S*, 1954 *W, NZ, I, S, F*
Stoddart, A E (Blackheath) 1885 *W, I*, 1886 *W, I, S*, 1889 *M*, 1890 *W, I*, 1893 *W, S*
Stoddart, W B (Liverpool) 1897 *W, I, S*
Stokes, F (Blackheath) 1871 *S*, 1872 *S*, 1873 *S*
Stokes, L (Blackheath) 1875 *I*, 1876 *S*, 1877 *I, S*, 1878 *S*, 1879 *S, I*, 1880 *I, S*, 1881 *I, W, S*
Stone, F le S (Blackheath) 1914 *F*
Stoop, A D (Harlequins) 1905 *S*, 1906 *S, F, SA*, 1907 *F, W*, 1910 *W, I, S*, 1911 *W, F, I, S*, 1912 *W, S*
Stoop, F M (Harlequins) 1910 *S*, 1911 *F, I*, 1913 *SA*
Stout, F M (Richmond) 1897 *W, I*, 1898 *I, S, W*, 1899 *I, S*, 1903 *S*, 1904 *W, I, S*, 1905 *W, I, S*
Stout, P W (Richmond) 1898 *S, W*, 1899 *W, I, S*
Stringer, N C (Wasps) 1982 *A* (R), 1983 *NZ* (R), 1984 *SA* 1 (R), *A*, 1985 *R*
Strong, E L (Oxford U) 1884 *W, I, S*
Summerscales, G E (Durham City) 1906 *NZ*
Sutcliffe, J W (Heckmondwike) 1889 *M*
Swarbrick, D W (Oxford U) 1947 *W, I, F*, 1948 *A, W*, 1949 *I*
Swayne, D H (Oxford U) 1931 *W*
Swayne, J W R (Bridgwater) 1929 *W*
Swift, A H (Swansea) 1981 *Arg* 1,2, 1983 *F, W, S*, 1984 *SA* 2
Syddall, J P (Waterloo) 1982 *I*, 1984 *A*
Sykes, A R V (Blackheath) 1914 *F*
Sykes, F D (Northampton) 1955 *F, S*, 1963 *NZ* 2, *A*
Sykes, P W (Wasps) 1948 *F*, 1952 *S, I, F*, 1953 *W, I, F*
Syrett, R E (Wasps) 1958 *W, A, I, F*, 1960 *W, I, F, S*, 1962 *W, I, F*

Tallent, J A (Cambridge U, Blackheath) 1931 *S, F*, 1932 *SA, W*, 1935 *I*
Tanner, C C (Cambridge U, Gloucester) 1930 *S*, 1932 *SA, W, I, S*
Tarr, F N (Leicester) 1909 *A, W, F*, 1913 *S*
Tatham, W M (Oxford U) 1882 *S*, 1883 *W, I, S*, 1884 *W, I, S*
Taylor, A S (Blackheath) 1883 *W, I*, 1886 *W, I*
Taylor, E W (Rockcliff) 1892 *I*, 1893 *I*, 1894 *W, I, S*, 1895 *W, I, S*, 1896 *W, I*, 1897 *W, I, S*, 1899 *I*
Taylor, F (Leicester) 1920 *F, I*
Taylor, F M (Leicester) 1914 *W*
Taylor, H H (Blackheath) 1879 *S*, 1880 *S*, 1881 *I, W*, 1882 *S*
Taylor, J T (W Hartlepool) 1897 *I*, 1899 *I*, 1900 *I*, 1901 *W, I*, 1902 *W, I, S*, 1903 *W, I*, 1905 *S*
Taylor, P J (Northampton) 1955 *W, I*, 1962 *W, I, F, S*
Taylor, R B (Northampton) 1966 *W*, 1967 *I, F, S, W, NZ*, 1969 *F, S, W, SA*, 1970 *I, W, S, F*, 1971 *S* (2[1C])
Taylor, W J (Blackheath) 1928 *A, W, I, F, S*
Teague, M C (Gloucester) 1985 *F* (R), *NZ* 1,2, 1989 *S, I, F, W, R*, 1990 *F, W, S*
Teden, D E (Richmond) 1939 *W, I, S*
Teggin, A (Broughton R) 1884 *I*, 1885 *W*, 1886 *I, S*, 1887 *I, S*
Tetley, T S (Bradford) 1876 *S*
Thomas, C (Barnstaple) 1895 *W, I, S*, 1899 *I*
Thompson, P H (Headingley, Waterloo) 1956 *W, I, S, F*, 1957 *W, I, F, S*, 1958 *W, A, I, F, S*, 1959 *W, I, F, S*
Thomson, G T (Halifax) 1878 *S*, 1882 *I, S*, 1883 *W, I, S*, 1884 *I, S*, 1885 *I*
Thomson, W B (Blackheath) 1892 *W*, 1895 *W, I, S*
Thorne, J D (Bristol) 1963 *W, I, F*
Tindall, V R (Liverpool U) 1951 *W, I, F, S*
Tobin, F (Liverpool) 1871 *S*
Todd, A F (Blackheath) 1900 *I, S*
Todd, R (Manchester) 1877 *S*
Toft, H B (Waterloo) 1936 *S*, 1937 *W, I, S*, 1938 *W, I, S*, 1939 *W, I, S*
Toothill, J T (Bradford) 1890 *S, I*, 1891 *W, I*, 1892 *W, I, S*, 1893 *W, I, S*, 1894 *W, I*
Tosswill, L R (Exeter) 1902 *W, I, S*
Touzel, C J C (Liverpool) 1877 *I, S*
Towell, A C (Bedford) 1948 *F*, 1951 *S*
Travers, B H (Harlequins) 1947 *W, I*, 1948 *A, W*, 1949 *F, S*
Treadwell, W T (Wasps) 1966 *I, F, S*
Trick, D M (Bath) 1983 *I*, 1984 *SA* 1
Tristram, H B (Oxford U) 1883 *S*, 1884 *W, S*, 1885 *W*, 1887 *S*
Troop, C L (Aldershot S) 1933 *I, S*
Tucker, J S (Bristol) 1922 *W*, 1925 *NZ, W, I, S, F*, 1926 *W, I, F, S*, 1927 *W, I, S, F*, 1928 *A, W, I, F, S*, 1929 *W, I, F*, 1930 *W, I, F, S*, 1931 *W*
Tucker, W E (Blackheath) 1894 *W, I*, 1895 *W, I, S*
Tucker, W E (Blackheath) 1926 *I*, 1930 *W, I*
Turner, D P (Richmond) 1871 *S*, 1872 *S*, 1873 *S*, 1874 *S*, 1875 *I, S*
Turner, E B (St George's Hospital) 1876 *I*, 1877 *I*, 1878 *I*
Turner, G R (St George's Hospital) 1876 *S*
Turner, H J C (Manchester) 1871 *S*
Turner, M F (Blackheath) 1948 *S, F*
Turquand-Young, D (Richmond) 1928 *A, W*, 1929 *I, S, F*
Twynam, H T (Richmond) 1879 *I*, 1880 *I*, 1881 *W*, 1882 *I*, 1883 *I*, 1884 *W, I, S*

Underwood, A M (Exeter) 1962 *W, I, F, S*, 1964 *I*
Underwood, R (Leicester, RAF) 1984 *I, F, W, A*, 1985 *R, F, S, I, W*, 1986 *W, I, F*, 1987 *I, F, W, S*, [*A, J, W*], 1988 *F, W, S, I* 1,2, *A* 1,2, *Fj, A*, 1989 *S, I, F, W, R, Fj*, 1990 *I, F, W, S*
Unwin, E J (Rosslyn Park, Army) 1937 *S*, 1938 *W, I, S*
Unwin, G T (Blackheath) 1898 *S*
Uren, R (Waterloo) 1948 *I, S, F*, 1950 *I*
Uttley, R M (Gosforth) 1973 *I, F, S, NZ* 2, *A*, 1974 *I, F, W*, 1975 *F, W, S, A* 1,2, 1977 *S, I, F, W*, 1978 *NZ*, 1979 *S*, 1980 *I, F, W, S*

Valentine, J (Swinton) 1890 *W*, 1896 *W, I, S*
Vanderspar, C H R (Richmond) 1873 *S*
Van Ryneveld, C B (Oxford U) 1949 *W, I, F, S*
Varley, H (Liversedge) 1892 *S*
Vassall, H (Blackheath) 1881 *W, S*, 1882 *I, S*, 1883 *W*
Vassall, H H (Blackheath) 1908 *I*
Vaughan, D B (Headingley) 1948 *A, W, I, S*, 1949 *I, F, S*, 1950 *W*
Vaughan-Jones, A (Army) 1932 *I, S*, 1933 *W*
Verelst, C L (Liverpool) 1876 *I*, 1878 *I*
Vernon, G F (Blackheath) 1878 *S, I*, 1880 *I, S*, 1881 *I*
Vickery, G (Aberavon) 1905 *I*
Vivyan, E J (Devonport A) 1901 *W*, 1904 *W, I, S*
Voyce, A T (Gloucester) 1920 *I, S*, 1921 *W, I, S, F*, 1922 *W, I, F, S*, 1923 *W, I, S, F*, 1924 *W, I, F, S*, 1925 *NZ, W, I, S, F*, 1926 *W, I, F, S*

Wackett, J A S (Rosslyn Park) 1959 *W, I*

Wade, C G (Richmond) 1883 *W, I, S,* 1884 *W, S,* 1885 *W,* 1886 *W, I*
Wade, M R (Cambridge U) 1962 *W, I, F*
Wakefield, W W (Harlequins) 1920 *W, F, I, S,* 1921 *W, I, S, F,* 1922 *W, I, F, S,* 1923 *W, I, S, F,* 1924 *W, I, F, S,* 1925 *NZ, W, I, S, F,* 1926 *W, I, F, S,* 1927 *S, F*
Walker, G A (Blackheath) 1939 *W, I*
Walker, H W (Coventry) 1947 *W, I, S, F,* 1948 *A, W, I, S, F*
Walker, R (Manchester) 1874 *S,* 1875 *I,* 1876 *S,* 1879 *S,* 1880 *S*
Wallens, J N S (Waterloo) 1927 *F*
Walton, E J (Castleford) 1901 *W, I,* 1902 *I, S*
Walton, W (Castleford) 1894 *S*
Ward, G (Leicester) 1913 *W, F, S,* 1914 *W, I, S*
Ward, H (Bradford) 1895 *W*
Ward, J I (Richmond) 1881 *I,* 1882 *I*
Ward, J W (Castleford) 1896 *W, I, S*
Wardlow, C S (Northampton) 1969 *SA* (R), 1971 *W, I, F, S* (2[1C])
Warfield, P J (Rosslyn Park, Durham U) 1973 *NZ* 1, *W, I,* 1975 *I, F, S*
Warr, A L (Oxford U) 1934 *W, I*
Watkins, J A (Gloucester) 1972 *SA,* 1973 *NZ* 1, *W, NZ* 2, *A,* 1975 *F, W*
Watkins, J K (United Services, RN) 1939 *W, I, S*
Watson, F B (United Services, RN) 1908 *S,* 1909 *S*
Watson, J H D (Blackheath) 1914 *W, S, F*
Watt, D E J (Bristol) 1967 *I, F, S, W*
Webb, C S H (Devonport Services, RN) 1932 *SA, W, I, S,* 1933 *W, I, S,* 1935 *S,* 1936 *NZ, W, I, S*
Webb, J M (Bristol) 1987 [*A(R), J, US, W*], 1988 *F, W, S, I* 1,2, *A* 1,2, *A,* 1989 *S, I, F, W*
Webb, J W G (Northampton) 1926 *F, S,* 1929 *S*
Webb, R E (Coventry) 1967 *S, W, NZ,* 1968 *I, F, S,* 1969 *I, F, S, W,* 1972 *I, F*
Webb, St L H (Bedford) 1959 *W, I, F, S*
Webster, J G (Moseley) 1972 *W, I, SA,* 1973 *NZ* 1, *W, NZ* 2, 1974 *S, W,* 1975 *I, F, W*
Wedge, T G (St Ives) 1907 *F,* 1909 *W*
Weighill, R H G (RAF, Harlequins) 1947 *S, F,* 1948 *S, F*
Wells, C M (Cambridge U, Harlequins) 1893 *S,* 1894 *W, S,* 1896 *S,* 1897 *W, S*
West, B R (Loughborough Colls, Northampton) 1968 *W, I, F, S,* 1969 *SA,* 1970 *I, W, S*
Weston, H T F (Northampton) 1901 *S*
Weston, L E (W of Scotland) 1972 *F, S*
Weston, M P (Richmond, Durham City) 1960 *W, I, F, S,* 1961 *SA, W, I, F, S,* 1962 *W, I, F,* 1963 *W, I, F, S, NZ* 1,2, *A,* 1964 *NZ, W, I, F, S,* 1965 *F, S,* 1966 *S,* 1968 *F, S*
Weston, W H (Northampton) 1933 *I, S,* 1934 *I, S,* 1935 *W, I, S* 1936 *NZ, W, S,* 1937 *W, I, S,* 1938 *W, I, S*
Wheatley, A A (Coventry) 1937 *W, I, S,* 1938 *W, S*
Wheatley, H F (Coventry) 1936 *I,* 1937 *S,* 1938 *W, S,* 1939 *W, I, S*
Wheeler, P J (Leicester) 1975 *F, W,* 1976 *A, W, S, I,* 1977 *S, I, F, W,* 1978 *F, W, S, I, NZ,* 1979 *S, I, F, W, NZ,* 1980 *I, F, W, S,* 1981 *W, S, I, F,* 1982 *A, S, I, F, W,* 1983 *F, S, I, NZ,* 1984 *S, I, F, W*
White, C (Gosforth) 1983 *NZ,* 1984 *S, I, F*
White, D F (Northampton) 1947 *W, I, S,* 1948 *I, F,* 1951 *S,* 1952 *SA, W, S, I, F,* 1953 *W, I, S*
Whiteley, E C P (O Alleynians) 1931 *S, F*
Whiteley, W (Bramley) 1896 *W*
Whitley, H (Northern) 1929 *W*
Wightman, B J (Moseley, Coventry) 1959 *W,* 1963 *W, I, NZ* 2, *A*
Wigglesworth, H J (Thornes) 1884 *I*
Wilkins, D T (United Services, RN, Roundhay) 1951 *W, I, F, S,* 1952 *SA, W, S, I, F,* 1953 *W, I, F, S*
Wilkinson, E (Bradford) 1886 *W, I, S,* 1887 *W, S*
Wilkinson, H (Halifax) 1929 *W, I, S,* 1930 *F*
Wilkinson, H J (Halifax) 1889 *M*
Wilkinson, P (Law Club) 1872 *S*
Wilkinson, R M (Bedford) 1975 *A* 2, 1976 *A, W, S, I, F*
Willcocks, T J (Plymouth) 1902 *W*
Willcox, J G (Oxford U, Harlequins) 1961 *I, F, S,* 1962

W, I, F, S, 1963 *W, I, F, S,* 1964 *NZ, W, I, F, S*
William-Powlett, P B R W (United Services, RN) 1922 *S*

Williams, C G (Gloucester, RAF) 1976 *F*
Williams, C S (Manchester) 1910 *F*
Williams, J E (O Millhillians and Sale) 1954 *F,* 1955 *W, I, F, S,* 1956 *I, S, F,* 1965 *W*
Williams, J M (Penzance-Newlyn) 1951 *I, S*
Williams, P N (Orrell) 1987 *S,* [*A, J, W*]
Williams, S G (Devonport A) 1902 *W, I, S,* 1903 *I, S,* 1907 *I, S*
Williams, S H (Newport) 1911 *W, F, I, S*
Williamson, R H (Oxford U) 1908 *W, I, S,* 1909 *A, F*
Wilson, A J (Camborne S of M) 1909 *I*
Wilson, C E (Blackheath) 1898 *I*
Wilson, C P (Cambridge U, Marlborough N) 1881 *W*
Wilson, D S (Met Police, Harlequins) 1953 *F,* 1954 *W, NZ, I, S, F,* 1955 *F, S*
Wilson, G S (Tyldesley) 1929 *W, I*
Wilson, K J (Gloucester) 1963 *F*
Wilson, R P (Liverpool OB) 1891 *W, I, S*
Wilson, W C (Richmond) 1907 *I, S*
Winn, C E (Rosslyn Park) 1952 *SA, W, S, I, F,* 1954 *W, S, F*
Winterbottom, P J (Headingley, Harlequins) 1982 *A, S, I, F, W,* 1983 *F, W, S, I, NZ,* 1984 *S, F, W, SA* 1,2, 1986 *W, S, I, F,* 1987 *I, F, W,* [*A, J, US, W*], 1988 *F, W, S,* 1989 *R, Fj,* 1990 *I, F, W, S*
Wintle, T C (Northampton) 1966 *S,* 1969 *I, F, S, W*
Wodehouse, N A (United Services, RN) 1910 *W,* 1911 *W, F, I, S,* 1912 *W, I, S, F,* 1913 *SA, W, F, I, S*
Wood, A (Halifax) 1884 *I*
Wood, A E (Gloucester, Cheltenham) 1908 *F, W, I*
Wood, G W (Leicester) 1914 *W*
Wood, R (Liversedge) 1894 *I*
Wood, R D (Liverpool OB) 1901 *I,* 1903 *W, I*
Woodgate, E E (Paignton) 1952 *W*
Woodhead, E (Huddersfield) 1880 *I*
Woodruff, C G (Harlequins) 1951 *W, I, F, S*
Woods, S M J (Cambridge U, Wellington) 1890 *W, S, I,* 1891 *W, I, S,* 1892 *I, S,* 1893 *W, I,* 1895 *W, I, S*
Woods, T (Bridgwater) 1908 *S*
Woods, T (United Services, RN) 1920 *S,* 1921 *W, I, S, F*
Woodward, C R (Leicester) 1980 *I* (R), *F, W, S,* 1981 *W, S, I, F, Arg* 1,2, 1982 *A, S, I, F, W,* 1983 *I, NZ,* 1984 *S, I, F, W*
Woodward, J E (Wasps) 1952 *SA, W, S,* 1953 *W, I, F, S,* 1954 *W, NZ, I, S, F,* 1955 *W, I,* 1956 *S*
Wooldridge, C S (Oxford U, Blackheath) 1883 *W, I, S,* 1884 *W, I, S,* 1885 *I*
Wordsworth, A J (Cambridge U) 1975 *A* 1 (R)
Worton, J R B (Harlequins, Army) 1926 *W,* 1927 *W*
Wrench, D F B (Harlequins) 1964 *F, S*
Wright, C C G (Cambridge U, Blackheath) 1909 *I, S*
Wright, F T (Edinburgh Acady, Manchester) 1881 *S*
Wright, I D (Northampton) 1971 *W, I, F, S,* (R)
Wright, J C (Met Police) 1934 *W*
Wright, J F (Bradford) 1890 *W*
Wright, T P (Blackheath) 1960 *W, I, F, S,* 1961 *SA, W, I, F, S,* 1962 *W, I, F, S*
Wright, W H G (Plymouth) 1920 *W, F*
Wyatt, D M (Bedford) 1976 *S* (R)

Yarranton, P G (RAF, Wasps) 1954 *W, NZ, I,* 1955 *F, S*
Yiend, W (Hartlepool R, Gloucester) 1889 *M,* 1892 *W, I, S,* 1893 *I, S*
Young, A T (Cambridge U, Blackheath, Army) 1924 *W, I, F, S,* 1925 *NZ, F,* 1926 *I, F, S,* 1927 *I, S, F,* 1928 *A, W, I, F, S,* 1929 *I*
Young, J R C (Oxford U, Harlequins) 1958 *I,* 1960 *W, I, F, S,* 1961 *SA, W, I, F*
Young, M (Gosforth) 1977 *S, I, F, W,* 1978 *F, W, S, I, NZ,* 1979 *S*
Young, P D (Dublin Wands) 1954 *W, NZ, I, S, F,* 1955 *W, I, F, S*
Youngs, N G (Leicester) 1983 *I, NZ,* 1984 *S, I, F, W*

ENGLISH INTERNATIONAL RECORDS

Both team and individual records are for official England international matches up to 30 April 1990.

TEAM RECORDS

Highest score
60 v Japan (60-7) 1987 Sydney
v individual countries
19 v Argentina (19-19) 1981 Buenos Aires
28 v Australia (28-19) 1988 Twickenham
58 v Fiji (58-23) 1989 Twickenham
41 v France (41-13) 1907 Richmond
36 v Ireland (36-14) 1938 Dublin
60 v Japan (60-7) 1987 Sydney
16 v N Zealand (16-10) 1973 Auckland
58 v Romania (58-3) 1989 Bucharest
30 v Scotland (30-18) 1980 Murrayfield
18 v S Africa (18-9) 1972 Johannesburg
34 v United States (34-6) 1987 Sydney
34 v Wales (34-6) 1990 Twickenham

Biggest winning points margin
55 v Romania (58-3) 1989 Bucharest
v individual countries
6 v Argentina (12-6) 1981 Buenos Aires
17 v Australia ⎰ (20-3) 1973 Twickenham
            ⎱ (23-6) 1976 Twickenham
35 v Fiji (58-23) 1989 Twickenham
37 v France (37-0) 1911 Twickenham
32 v Ireland (35-3) 1988 Twickenham
53 v Japan (60-7) 1987 Sydney
13 v N Zealand (13-0) 1936 Twickenham
55 v Romania (58-3) 1989 Bucharest
20 v Scotland (26-6) 1977 Twickenham
 9 v S Africa (18-9) 1972 Johannesburg
28 v United States (34-6) 1987 Sydney
28 v Wales (34-6) 1990 Twickenham

Highest score by opposing team
42 N Zealand (15-42) 1985 Wellington
by individual countries
19 Argentina (19-19) 1981 Buenos Aires
30 Australia (21-30) 1975 Brisbane
23 Fiji (58-23) 1989 Twickenham
37 France (12-37) 1972 Colombes
26 Ireland (21-26) 1974 Twickenham
 7 Japan (60-7) 1987 Sydney
42 N Zealand (15-42) 1985 Wellington
15 Romania (22-15) 1985 Twickenham
33 Scotland (6-33) 1986 Murrayfield
35 S Africa (9-35) 1984 Johannesburg

 6 United States (34-6) 1987 Sydney
34 Wales (21-34) 1967 Cardiff

Biggest losing points margin
27 v N Zealand (15-42) 1985 Wellington
27 v Scotland (6-33) 1986 Murrayfield
v individual countries
20 v Australia (8-28) 1988 Sydney
25 v France (12-37) 1972 Colombes
22 v Ireland (0-22) 1947 Dublin
27 v N Zealand (15-42) 1985 Wellington
27 v Scotland (6-33) 1986 Murrayfield
26 v S Africa (9-35) 1984 Johannesburg
25 v Wales (0-25) 1905 Cardiff
No defeats v Argentina, Fiji, Japan, Romania or United States

---

Most tries by England in an international
13 v Wales 1881 Blackheath

Most tries against England in an international
8 by Wales (6-28) 1922 Cardiff

Most points by England in International Championship in a season – 90
in season 1989-90

Most tries by England in International Championship in a season – 20
in season 1913-14

INDIVIDUAL RECORDS

Most capped player
A Neary   43   1971-80
in individual positions
Full-back
W H Hare   25   1974-84

Wing
R Underwood   38   1984-90
Centre
P W Dodge   32[1]   1978-85
Fly-half
C R Andrew   30(31)[2]   1985-90
Scrum-half
S J Smith   28   1973-83
Prop
G S Pearce   35   1979-88
Hooker
J V Pullin   42   1966-76
Lock
W B Beaumont   34   1975-82
W A Dooley   34   1985-90
Flanker
A Neary   43   1971-80
No 8
J P Scott   31(34)[3]   1978-84

[1]*David Duckham, 36 caps, played 14 times at centre and 22 times on the wing*
[2]*Andrew has also played once as a full-back*
[3]*Scott also played three times as a lock*

Longest international career
J Heaton 13 seasons 1935-47

Most internationals as captain
W B Beaumont 21 1978-82

Most points in internationals – 240
W H Hare (25 matches) 1974-84

Most points in International Championship in a season – 44
W H Hare (4 matches) 1983-84

Most points in an international – 22
D Lambert v France 1911 Twickenham

Most tries in internationals – 22
R Underwood (38 matches) 1984-90

Most tries in International Championship in a season – 8
C N Lowe (4 matches) 1913-14

Most tries in an international – 5
D Lambert v France 1907 Richmond
R Underwood v Fiji 1989 Twickenham

Most conversions in internationals – 19
S D Hodgkinson (6 matches) 1989-90

Most conversions in International Championship in a season – 7
G S Conway (4 matches) 1923-24

Most conversions in an international – 8
S D Hodgkinson v Romania 1989 Bucharest

Most dropped goals in internationals – 9
C R Andrew (31 matches) 1985-90

Most penalty goals in internationals – 67
W H Hare (25 matches) 1974-84

Most penalty goals in International Championship in a season – 14
W H Hare (4 matches) 1982-83

Most points on overseas tour – 48
W N Bennett (4 matches) Australia 1975
W H Hare scored 79 points on the N American tour of 1982, but this was not a major tour

Most points in a tour match – 36
W N Bennett v Western Australia 1975
   Perth

Most tries in a tour match – 4
A J Morley v Western Australia 1975
   Perth
P S Preece v New South Wales 1975
   Sydney
R E Webb scored 4 tries v Canada in 1967, and J Carleton scored 4 against Mid-West at Cleveland in 1982, but these were not on major tours

TOSHIBA
DIVISIONAL CHAMPIONSHIP 1989

Michael Austin

In the fifth season of the revived Championship London retained the title in the final series of matches, which at least brought a competition with limited spectator appeal to a natural climax. London beat the North, the champions in 1986 and 1987, by 18-12 at Otley. They had trailed 12-9, but with three minutes remaining and the scores level, Ben Clarke, the Saracens No 8 in his first season at senior club level, burst over for the try which sealed the Championship. A draw would have been enough for London to take the title on superior points difference. Clarke epitomised the alternative value of the competition, especially in a season when the national team had a potentially settled look. It was not so much the performance of the England probables in the Championship that was meaningful as the qualities of the chasing pack of international hopefuls.

Thus the competition, played on three consecutive Saturdays in December, assisted with the eventual selection of the England team that gained an honourable draw with France in the B international seven weeks later. Jim Fallon, the Richmond and South & South-West wing, who was the Championship's joint leading try-scorer with four, along with Clarke, was among those to emerge. Others included David Pears, the North outside-half, Tim Rodber, the Midlands No 8, and David Baldwin, the Sale lock forward, who made an immediate impression after being brought into the North side against the Midlands the evening before the match. The North had been unlucky to lose Pears with 'flu before the decisive game against London, and then Dewi Morris, his England B half-back partner, within ten minutes of the match after he was accidentally kicked on the head.

London, expertly coached by Dick Best, were far more convincing than they had looked against the South-West in the previous game. Their hallmarks were dominant forwards, the peerless line-out jumping of Paul Ackford, the control of Rob Andrew at outside-half and the calm authority of Steve Pilgrim, the full-back. The match against the South-West had yielded 33 penalties and free kicks from a French referee, a problem aggravated by the language barrier. But ultimately, London's eloquent play beat a depleted South-West team.

Throughout the Championship the South-West were without Stuart Barnes, John Hall and Gareth Chilcott, who had opted out, and David Egerton, Andy Robinson and Jeremy Guscott were also absent at times. The perennial problem of integrating Bath, Bristol and Gloucester players prevailed.

Although the North maintained their unbeaten record in fixtures against the South-West, they lost Tony Underwood, younger brother of Rory, with a broken jaw after 15 minutes. He was absent for three months and would otherwise have challenged for what was effectively a vacancy on England's left wing.

Alan Davies, the Midlands' coach for five seasons, including their title-winning year of 1985, said on the eve of the competition that he would resign at the end of the season to concentrate on his club duties with Nottingham. The gap will be difficult to fill. The Midlands were deprived by injury of Brian Moore, Dean Richards and Paul Dodge and these absences, together with the unavailability of Les Cusworth throughout the Championship were fully reflected in their poor performances. Their midfield back play was abject and they scored only

Jeff Probyn, London's tight-head prop, hands off possession to Craig Luxton, his scrum-half, during London's win over the South-West at Imber Court.

two tries in three games. Simon Hodgkinson kicked 29 of their 40 points, two fewer than Andrew, the competition's leading scorer.

Final Table	P	W	D	L	F	A	Pts
London	3	3	0	0	66	30	6
North	3	2	0	1	50	42	4
South & South-West	3	1	0	2	61	74	2
Midlands	3	0	0	3	40	71	0

2 December, Coventry RFC

Midlands Division 6 (2PG)   **London Division 20** (1G 2PG 2T)
Midlands Division (*Nottingham unless stated*): S D Hodgkinson (*capt*); B J Evans (Leicester), I Bates (Leicester), G H Hartley, F Packman (Northampton); A J Sutton, B Gabriel; M Linnett (Moseley), T Thacker (Leicester), G S Pearce (Northampton), D Hindmarch, M Bayfield (Bedford), J Wells (Leicester), T Rodber (Northampton & Army), G W Rees
Scorer *Penalty Goals:* Hodgkinson (2)
London Division (*Wasps unless stated*): S Pilgrim; A T Harriman (Harlequins), F J Clough, W D C Carling (Harlequins), E Davis (Harlequins); C R Andrew, S M Bates; P A G Rendall, J Olver (Harlequins), J A Probyn, P J Ackford (Harlequins), N Edwards (Harlequins), M G Skinner (Harlequins), B Clarke (Saracens), D Pegler (*capt*)
Scorers *Tries:* Clarke (2), Carling   *Conversion:* Andrew   *Penalty Goals:* Pilgrim, Andrew
Referee C J High (Manchester Society)

2 December, Bristol RFC

South & South-West Division 15 (2G 1PG)   **Northern Division 21** (2G 2PG 1DG)
South & South-West Division (*Bath unless stated*): J M Webb (Bristol); J Fallon (Richmond), A Adebayo, S J Halliday (*capt*), P Blackett; M Hamlin (Gloucester), R J Hill; A Sharp (Bristol), K Dunn (Gloucester), R Pascall (Gloucester), J Etheridge (Gloucester), J Morrison, M C Teague (Gloucester), D Sims (Gloucester), R A Robinson
Scorers *Tries:* Fallon, Halliday   *Conversions:* Webb (2)   *Penalty Goal:* Webb
Northern Division (*Orrell unless stated*): S Langford; A Underwood (Leicester), G Childs (Northern), B Barley (Wakefield), R Underwood (Leicester & RAF); D Pears (Harlequins), C D Morris (Liverpool St Helens); M Whitcombe (Sale), N Hitchen, D Southern (*capt*), R Kimmins, W A Dooley (Preston Grasshoppers), S Hodgson (Sale), C Cusani, P Manley *Replacement* S B Burnhill (Sale) for T Underwood
Scorers *Tries:* R Underwood, Burnhill   *Conversions:* Pears (2)   *Penalty Goals:* Pears (2)   *Dropped Goal:* Pears
Referee B Stirling (Ireland)

9 December, Imber Court, Met Police RFC

London Division 28 (2G 4PG 1T)   **South & South-West Division 12** (1G 2PG)
London Division (*Wasps unless stated*): S Pilgrim; S T Smith, F J Clough, W D C Carling (Harlequins), E Davis (Harlequins); C R Andrew, S M Bates; J Leonard (Saracens), C J Olver (Harlequins), J A Probyn, N Edwards (Harlequins), P J Ackford (Harlequins), M G Skinner (Harlequins), B Clarke (Saracens), D Pegler (*capt*) *Replacements* J Buckton (Saracens) for Pilgrim; C Luxton (Harlequins) for Bates
Scorers *Tries:* Pegler, Pilgrim, Clarke   *Conversions:* Andrew (2)   *Penalty Goals:* Andrew (4)
South & South-West Division (*Gloucester unless stated*): J M Webb (Bristol); J Fallon (Richmond), A Adebayo (Bath), S J Halliday (Bath) (*capt*), S Walklin (Plymouth Albion); M Livesey (Richmond), R J Hill (Bath); A Sharp (Bristol), K Dunn, R Pascall, N C Redman (Bath), J Etheridge, M C Teague, D Sims, I Smith
Scorers *Try:* Fallon   *Conversion:* Livesey   *Penalty Goals:* Livesey (2)
Referee F Casteret (France)

9 December, Moseley RFC

Midlands Division 9 (3PG)   **Northern Division 17** (1G 1PG 2T)
Midlands Division (*Leicester unless stated*): S D Hodgkinson (Nottingham) (*capt*);
B J Evans, T Buttimore, I Bates, F Packman (Northampton); A J Sutton (Nottingham),
B Gabriel (Nottingham); M Linnett (Moseley), T Thacker, G S Pearce (Northampton),
D Hindmarch (Nottingham), M Bayfield (Bedford), J Wells, T Rodber (Northampton &
Army), G W Rees (Nottingham)
Scorer *Penalty Goals:* Hodgkinson (3)
Northern Division (*Orrell unless stated*): S Langford; N Heslop, G Childs (Northern),
B Barley (Wakefield), R Underwood (Leicester & RAF); D Pears (Harlequins),
C D Morris (Liverpool St Helens); M Whitcombe (Sale), N Hitchen, D Southern (*capt*),
D Baldwin (Sale), D A Cusani, S Hodgson (Sale), C Cusani, P Buckton (Liverpool St
Helens)
Scorers *Tries:* Underwood, Heslop, Morris   *Conversion:* Pears   *Penalty Goal:* Pears
Referee E Morrison (Bristol)

16 December, Otley RFC

Northern Division 12 (1G 1PG 1DG)   **London Division 18** (2G 1PG 1DG)
Northern Division (*Orrell unless stated*): S Langford; N Heslop, G Childs (Northern),
B Barley (Wakefield), R Underwood (Leicester & RAF); J Stabler (West Hartlepool),
C D Morris (Liverpool St Helens); M Whitcombe (Sale), N Hitchen, D Southern (*capt*),
W A Dooley (Preston Grasshoppers), R Kimmins, S Hodgson (Sale), C Cusani,
P J Winterbottom (Harlequins) *Replacement* N Summers (Headingley) for Morris
Scorers *Try:* Kimmins   *Conversion:* Stabler   *Penalty Goal:* Stabler   *Dropped Goal:*
Stabler
London Division (*Wasps unless stated*): S Pilgrim; S T Smith, F J Clough, W D C Carling
(Harlequins), E Davis (Harlequins); C R Andrew, C Luxton (Harlequins);
P A G Rendall, C J Olver (Harlequins), J A Probyn, N Edwards (Harlequins), S O'Leary,
M G Skinner (Harlequins), B Clarke (Saracens), D Pegler (*capt*)
Scorers *Tries:* Davis, Clarke   *Conversions:* Andrew (2)   *Penalty Goal:* Andrew
Dropped Goal: Andrew
Referee J B Anderson (Scotland)

16 December, Bath RFC

South & South-West Division 34 (5G 1T)   **Midlands Division 25** (1G 4PG 1DG 1T)
South & South-West Division (*Bath unless stated*): J Callard; A W Swift, S J Halliday
(*capt*), J C Guscott, J Fallon (Richmond); M Hamlin (Gloucester), R J Hill; A Sharp
(Bristol), K Dunn (Gloucester), R Pascall (Gloucester), N C Redman, J Etheridge
(Gloucester), A Dun (Bristol), D Sims (Gloucester), R A Robinson *Replacement* P Jones
(Gloucester) for Sharp
Scorers *Tries:* Fallon (2), Sims, Hill, Swift, penalty try   *Conversions:* Callard (5)
Midlands Division (*Nottingham unless stated*): S D Hodgkinson (*capt*); B Evans
(Leicester), T Buttimore (Leicester), I Bates (Leicester), F Packman (Northampton);
A J Sutton, B Gabriel; M Linnett (Moseley), T Thacker (Leicester), G S Pearce
(Northampton), D Hindmarch, S Lloyd (Moseley), J Wells (Leicester), T Rodber
(Northampton & Army), G W Rees
Scorers *Tries:* Rodber, Packman   *Conversion:* Hodgkinson   *Penalty Goals:*
Hodgkinson (4)   *Dropped Goal:* Buttimore
Referee F A Howard (Liverpool Society)

125

PILKINGTON CUP 1989-90
RFU Club Competition

Michael Austin

5 May, Twickenham
Bath 48 (5G 2PG 3T)   **Gloucester 6** (1G)

An elixir mixed by coach Jack Rowell confirmed that Bath remain the golden champions with the biggest winning margin in any final in the history of the competition. Bath's demolition of Gloucester was comprehensive as temperatures rose into the 80s, and that the match was sadly one-sided was universally acknowledged. Keith Richardson, the Gloucester coach, said that his side were hit by as good a performance as they are ever likely to see. He added that he could not have imagined any club team playing better than Bath on the day. There could be no greater praise.

Bath were magnificent as they made their sixth final appearance in the past seven years, and they have yet to lose. The dismissal after 57 minutes of Gadd, the Gloucester flanker, by Fred Howard for stamping on Egerton compounded the problems of a side already trailing 28-6. Gadd was suspended for 90 days by the Gloucester Disciplinary Committee after becoming the third player to be sent off in a final. He followed Nigel Horton, the Moseley and England lock, ordered off for punching against Gloucester in 1972, and Bob Mordell, the Rosslyn Park flanker, banished during the game against Gosforth in 1976. These matters scarcely concerned Bath, who mixed back and forward play so successfully that Rowell, the former Gosforth coach not noted for ecstatic remarks, asserted that this was the best Bath team ever.

A capacity crowd of 52,000 fell 7,300 short of the world record attendance for a club match, which was set in the previous final, only because of the rebuilding of the North Stand, but magic was in the air for those present. An astonishing half-time lead of 25 points made almost every senior club around the country feel grateful they were not in Gloucester's boots during the second half, which was televised live for the first time. The game was without malice and Bath thrived on team skills with a still unavoidable emphasis on individuals, notably Redman, whose collection of the kick-off was impeccable and whose play around the field supplemented the back row. Tries abounded – not least the 80-yard runaway interception just before half-time by Swift – turning later events into the formality that Gloucester's modest form leading up to the match had suggested. Gloucester survived happily in the scrums, took the line-outs 19-13, but were simply run off their feet. Errors enveloped them, missed touch-kicks punished them and poor tactics compounded the difficulties.

Bath led by 9 points in the first quarter after Withey swept away from

Tony Swift, the Bath wing, has run the length of the field and, tiring only slightly, prepares to touch down yet another wonderful Bath try in the final against Gloucester.

a line-out and raced 60 metres for a try, having fended off three tackles. This was the thin end of the wedge for Gloucester. Dunn responded with a try from a maul but Gloucester, overrun by Bath's scalding pace, were also outstripped in speed of thought. There was to be no escape from the 42-point thrashing which eclipsed the record 20-point win in a final achieved by Coventry in 1974 over London Scottish, in the days of David Duckham. Halliday, the England centre, playing his last game before retirement, converted the final try to crown the rhapsody of power which only the fine tuning of Bath could achieve.

Bath: J Callard; A H Swift, S J Halliday, J C Guscott, A Adebayo; S Barnes (*capt*), R J Hill; V E Ubogu, R G R Dawe, G J Chilcott, N C Redman, D F Cronin, R A Robinson, D W Egerton, K Withey *Replacement* S Knight for Hill
Scorers *Tries:* Swift (2), Withey, Guscott, Callard, Dawe, Redman, Ubogu
Conversions: Barnes (4), Halliday   *Penalty Goals:* Barnes (2)
Gloucester: T Smith; D Morgan, D Caskie, R Mogg, J Breeze; M Hamlin (*capt*), M Hannaford; M Preedy, K Dunn, R Pascall, N Scrivens, J Brain, J Gadd, M C Teague I Smith
Scorers *Try:* Dunn   *Conversion:* T Smith
Referee F A Howard (Liverpool Society)

Home advantage proved no help once again in the semi-finals as Bath and Gloucester brought the number of successful away teams at that stage to a staggering 27 – there have been only 11 home semi-final winners in the competition's 19-year history. The march of Bath into the final proved far more predictable than that of Gloucester, who travelled in every round, but victories at Nottingham and Northampton extended Gloucester's remarkable unbeaten record in the Cup against Midlands clubs for 15 seasons.

Bath's straightforward win over Moseley, the only club to beat them in eight years and 30 matches in the competition, yielded a place in the final after 16 points in the last ten minutes had brushed aside Richmond 35-3. Their other conquests were Headingley, who had reached the fourth round with their first wins after qualifying nine times, and Harlequins, who had the misfortune to be drawn at the Recreation Ground in the previous round.

Gloucester beat a resurgent Northampton side in the semi-finals after winning with surprising ease by 26-16 at Nottingham, where they later suffered a defeat which cost them the Courage League title. A try by Mogg and Tim Smith's conversion brought Gloucester a last-minute win over Wasps in a third round which paired six first division clubs.

Wasps' defeat continued their uncanny run of near misses. In the previous four years they had been beaten in two finals, knocked out after extra time of a semi-final and then narrowly eliminated in a quarter-final at Leicester. Gloucester's travels even took them to an athletics stadium, at Gateshead, borrowed for the day by Gosforth, a shadow of the side which won the competition 13 years earlier.

Coventry, another club with a glorious past in the competition, lost in the second round for the second successive season, this time to Liverpool St Helens. More recent finalists took an undignified tumble, London Welsh suffering a 43-3 home defeat, comprehensively their biggest in the competition, at the hands of Leicester. Northampton reached their first semi-final, 12 years after their previous appearance in the last eight, by producing one of the surprise results of the season when outplaying Leicester 23-7. Steele, the fly-half, scored 19 points. The competition provided good therapy for Moseley, who cast aside their poor League performances and beat Saracens, then Bristol by 15-13 in the quarter-finals. James, their wing, executed a match-saving tackle in the last minute on Knibbs, the Bristol centre.

Orrell and Nottingham remain enigmas, falling just short of joining the hardy perennials – Bath, Gloucester, Harlequins, Wasps, Bristol and Leicester – at the top of the Cup rankings. In recent times, the draw has been persistently unkind to Orrell, who lost 12-6 at Nottingham and took welcome disciplinary action when imposing a club suspension on Charles Cusani, who committed a late and high tackle on Hodgkinson, the Nottingham and England full-back.

Earlier rounds brought distinction for Berry Hill, who eliminated London Scottish 15-12 by the margin of four penalty goals and a dropped goal by Hoare to three Scottish tries. Hastings, the Scotland full-back, missed seven place kicks as Berry Hill, a village club from the Forest of Dean, relived the glamour of knocking out London Welsh in both the two previous seasons. Other meritorious performances were given by Worthing, who held Metropolitan Police to 14-10, and Drybrook in their 15-9 defeat by London Welsh at the Old Deer Park. Wakefield showed their under-rated skills by beating Waterloo.

The competition included 14 newcomers, who increased the total participants to 197 in 19 seasons and the second of Pilkington's initial three-year sponsorship agreement. They were Barnstaple, Crediton, Drybrook, Kersal, Mansfield, Mid-Cheshire College, Northern, Old Colfeians, Old Leamingtonians, Old Yardleians, Otley, Rotherham, Stafford and Swanage & Wareham.

RESULTS

First Round

Askeans 10, Redruth 18; Barking 16, Old Alleynians 12 (aet); Barnstaple 10, Reading 6; Broughton Park 15, Aspatria 18; Cheshunt 0, London Scottish 27; Drybrook 19, Old Colfeians 10; Dudley Kingswinford 13, Vipers 11; Ealing 10, Metropolitan Police 14; Exeter 12, High Wycombe 7; Fylde 27, Kersal 12; Harrogate 54, Peterborough 7; Hartlepool Rovers 29, Old Yardleians 3; Havant 14, Southend 6; Lydney 10, Berry Hill 13; Lymm 9, Wakefield 18; Mansfield 0, Otley 29; Mid-Cheshire College 20, Crediton 0; Northern 31, Roundhay 16; North Walsham 15, Swanage & Wareham 3; Nuneaton 31,

Stockwood Park 4; Old Leamingtonians 10, Newark 20; Oxford 11, Combe Down 17; Ruislip 6, Worthing 16; *Sheffield 13, Rotherham 13; Sidcup 3, London Welsh 29; Stafford 9, Vale of Lune 25; Streatham-Croydon 22, Taunton 9; West Hartlepool 30, Bedworth 7

Rotherham won on 'away team' rule after extra time

Second Round
Barking 3, Rugby 38; Barnstaple 7, Richmond 22; Berry Hill 15, London Scottish 12; Blackheath 17, Havant 0; Combe Down 0, Gosforth 26; Exeter 44, Streatham-Croydon 7; Harrogate 21, Aspatria 13; Hartlepool Rovers 9, West Hartlepool 15; Headingley 15, Otley 9; Liverpool St Helens 17, Coventry 6; London Irish 13, Plymouth Albion 17; London Welsh 15; Drybrook 9; Mid-Cheshire College 10, Nuneaton 16; Newark 12, Fylde 28; Northampton 25, Northern 4; Redruth 0, North Walsham 22; Sale 43, Rotherham 10; Vale of Lune 24, Dudley Kingswinford 12; Wakefield 19, Waterloo 3; Worthing 10, Metropolitan Police 14

Third Round
Bath 9, Harlequins 0; Bedford 7, Richmond 12; Bristol 29, Liverpool St Helens 0; Fylde 15, Gosforth 17; Harrogate 3, West Hartlepool 12; Headingley 12, North Walsham 0; London Welsh 3, Headingley 43; Metropolitan Police 4, Northampton 16; Moseley 28, Berry Hill 11; Nuneaton 7, Saracens 16; Plymouth Albion 0; Orrell 7; Rosslyn Park 9, Nottingham 30; Sale 26, Blackheath 16; Vale of Lune 13, Exeter 18; Wakefield 16, Rugby 9; Wasps 19, Gloucester 23

Fourth Round
Bath 25, Headingley 3; Bristol 26, Exeter 3; Gosforth 15, Gloucester 26; Leicester 43, West Hartlepool 15; Moseley 10, Saracens 6; Northampton 22, Wakefield 10; Nottingham 12, Orrell 6; Richmond 14, Sale 12

Quarter-finals
Moseley 15, Bristol 13; Northampton 23, Leicester 7; Nottingham 16, Gloucester 26; Richmond 3, Bath 35

Semi-finals
Moseley 7, Bath 21; Northampton 12, Gloucester 17

Previous finals (*all at Twickenham*)
1972 Gloucester 17 Moseley 6
1973 Coventry 27 Bristol 15
1974 Coventry 26 London Scottish 6
1975 Bedford 28 Rosslyn Park 12
1976 Gosforth 23 Rosslyn Park 14
1977 Gosforth 27 Waterloo 11
1978 Gloucester 6 Leicester 3
1979 Leicester 15 Moseley 12
1980 Leicester 21 London Irish 9
1981 Leicester 22 Gosforth 15
1982 Gloucester 12 Moseley 12
     (Title shared)
1983 Bristol 28 Leicester 22
1984 Bath 10 Bristol 9
1985 Bath 24 London Welsh 15
1986 Bath 25 Wasps 17
1987 Bath 19 Wasps 12
1988 Harlequins 28 Bristol 22
1989 Bath 10 Leicester 6

COUNTY CUP WINNERS 1989-90

Berkshire	**Reading**
Buckinghamshire	**High Wycombe**
Cheshire	**Winnington Park**
Cornwall	**Camborne**
Cumbria	**Aspatria**
Dorset/Wilts	**Salisbury**
Devon	**Exeter**
Durham	**Hartlepool Rovers**
Eastern Counties	**Sudbury**
East Midlands	**Kettering**
Gloucestershire	**Lydney**
Hampshire	**Basingstoke**
Hertfordshire	**Tabard**
Kent	**Gravesend**
Lancashire	**Liverpool St Helens**
Leicestershire	**Syston**
Middlesex	**Ealing**
North Midlands	**Hereford**
Northumberland	**Gosforth**
Notts, Lincs & Derbys	**Newark**
Oxfordshire	**Banbury**
Somerset	**Midsomer Norton**
Staffordshire	**Lichfield**
Surrey	**Sutton & Epsom**
Sussex	**Lewes**
Warwickshire	**Bedworth**
Yorkshire	**Wakefield**

WASPS' LATE RUN FOR THE TITLE

THE COURAGE LEAGUES 1989-90

Wasps climbed to the top of Division 1 only on the last afternoon of League action and they did so partly by default – Gloucester needed to win at Nottingham to clinch their first title, and it seemed as if half of Gloucester city was in the Midlands to cheer them on. But they crashed to an inspired Nottingham and Wasps, defeating Saracens at Sudbury, heard to their delight that they were champions. It was a rich moment for Rob Andrew and his men as they were presented with the trophy – albeit a replica – live on television.

Bath made some unaccountable slips in the programme. They were to prove themselves England's outstanding club in the Pilkington final but missed the chance of retaining their title by losing at Nottingham and at Saracens. At the other end of the table, Bedford endured a miserable season and sank into Division 2.

A revitalised Nottingham once again drew large crowds to Franklins Gardens. They were promoted along with Liverpool St Helens. It is vital that Northampton, the old Midland giants, continue to prosper and perhaps even more important that Liverpool should maintain their new-found status. The North desperately needs at least one other established top flight club alongside the splendid Orrell outfit.

Gosforth escaped relegation to Division 3 because there was none. The size of national divisions is increased for 1990-91, so Gosforth remained in Division 2. There was no such good fortune for London Welsh, who won some fine victories during the season but not in the league programme. They slip out of the national set-up altogether.

Overall, it was another thrilling League season and ample reward for the generous sponsorship of Courage. Nothing could be a better tribute to the success of the league system in England than the fact that Leagues begin in Wales and Ireland in 1990-91.

NATIONAL DIVISION

National 1

	P	W	D	L	F	A	Pts
Wasps	11	9	0	2	250	106	18
Gloucester	11	8	1	2	214	139	17
Bath	11	8	0	3	258	104	16
Saracens	11	7	1	3	168	167	15
Leicester	11	6	0	5	248	184	12
Nottingham	11	6	0	5	187	148	12
Harlequins	11	6	0	5	218	180	12
Orrell	11	5	0	6	221	132	10
Bristol	11	4	0	7	136	144	8
Rosslyn Park	11	4	0	7	164	243	8
Moseley	11	2	0	9	138	258	4
Bedford	11	0	0	11	70	467	0

National 2

	P	W	D	L	F	A	Pts
Northampton	11	9	1	1	192	135	19
L'pool St Helens	11	8	2	1	154	106	18
Richmond	11	7	1	3	282	135	15
Coventry	11	6	1	4	206	185	13
London Irish	11	6	0	5	228	247	12
Rugby	11	5	0	6	238	172	10
Plymouth Albion	11	5	0	6	206	164	10
Headingley	11	5	0	6	161	226	10
Sale	11	4	0	7	153	182	8
Blackheath	11	3	2	6	141	205	8
Waterloo	11	3	0	8	147	193	6
Gosforth	11	1	1	9	108	266	3

no relegation

National 3

	P	W	D	L	F	A	Pts
London Scottish	11	11	0	0	258	92	22
Wakefield	11	7	1	3	210	126	15
West Hartlepool	11	5	2	4	175	110	12
Sheffield	11	6	0	5	176	174	12
Askeans	11	6	0	5	170	235	12
Exeter	11	5	1	5	149	153	11
Rounday	11	5	0	6	156	166	10
Fylde	11	5	0	6	169	222	10
Vale of Lune	11	4	0	7	154	219	8
Nuneaton	11	4	0	7	127	196	8
Lydney	11	3	0	8	153	166	6
London Welsh	11	3	0	8	141	179	6

Area North

	P	W	D	L	F	A	Pts
Broughton Pk	10	8	0	2	246	111	16
Morley	10	8	0	2	169	115	16
Stourbridge	10	7	0	3	146	133	14
Durham City	10	6	0	4	195	169	12
Kendal	10	6	0	4	130	136	12
Preston G'h	10	5	0	5	122	109	10
Lichfield	10	5	0	5	110	121	10
Northern	10	4	0	6	139	144	8
Winnington Pk	10	4	0	6	142	152	8
Walsall	10	2	0	8	143	183	4
Stoke	10	0	0	10	88	257	0

No relegation

Area South

	P	W	D	L	F	A	Pts
Met Police	10	9	0	1	255	74	18
Clifton	10	8	1	1	240	122	17
Redruth	10	7	0	3	151	84	14
Camborne	10	6	1	3	164	113	13
Havant	10	5	1	4	132	126	11
Sudbury	10	5	0	5	162	138	10
Southend	10	4	2	4	124	125	10
Basingstoke	10	3	1	6	138	144	7
Cheltenham	10	2	0	8	107	201	4
Maidstone	10	2	0	8	64	237	4
Salisbury	10	1	0	9	74	247	2

LONDON ZONE

London 1

	P	W	D	L	F	A	Pts
North Walsham	10	9	0	1	231	94	18
Ealing	10	9	0	1	230	95	18
Cheshunt	10	7	2	1	155	80	16
Sutton & Epsom	10	5	0	5	127	140	10
Sidcup	10	4	1	5	131	126	9
O Alleynians	10	4	1	5	157	168	9
Ruislip	10	4	0	6	117	116	8
Streatham/Croy	10	3	1	6	88	202	7
Lewes	10	3	0	7	98	150	6
O Gaytonians	10	2	1	7	133	180	5
US Portsmouth	10	2	0	8	91	207	4

London 2 North

	P	W	D	L	F	A	Pts
Thurrock	10	9	1	0	318	58	19
Eton Manor	10	9	1	0	187	76	19
Woodford	10	6	1	3	153	163	13
Barking	10	5	1	4	141	151	11
Finchley	10	5	0	5	140	147	10
Bishop's Stort	10	4	2	4	114	144	10
Norwich	10	4	1	5	163	145	9
O Albanians	10	3	1	6	119	138	7
Ipswich	10	3	1	6	101	146	7
O Merchant Tay	10	1	1	8	70	196	3
Grasshoppers	10	1	0	9	83	225	2

London 2 South

	P	W	D	L	F	A	Pts
O Mid-Whitgift	10	10	0	0	182	53	20
Camberley	10	9	0	1	180	75	18
Gravesend	10	7	0	3	179	107	14
Tunbridge Wells	10	7	0	3	189	133	14
Guildford & God	10	6	0	4	163	88	12
O Colfeians	10	4	0	6	120	142	8
O Brockleians	10	4	0	6	132	180	8
Esher	10	3	0	7	84	107	6
Worthing	10	3	0	7	116	175	6
Dartfordians	10	1	0	9	77	165	2
Alton	10	1	0	9	87	284	2

London 3 North-East

	P	W	D	L	F	A	Pts
Chingford	10	10	0	0	160	50	20
Harlow	10	9	0	1	258	83	18
Romf'd & Gidea P	10	8	0	2	186	86	16
Westcliff	10	6	0	4	116	151	12
Colchester	10	5	0	5	215	154	10
Brentwood	10	5	0	5	157	160	10
Cambridge	10	4	0	6	132	100	8
West Norfolk	10	4	0	6	115	192	8
Cantabrigians	10	1	1	8	111	173	3
Saffron Walden	10	1	1	8	79	275	3
Met Pol, Chigwell	10	1	0	9	61	166	2

London 3 North-West

	P	W	D	L	F	A	Pts
Tabard	10	10	0	0	264	75	20

	P	W	D	L	F	A	Pts
Fullerians	10	7	1	2	184	106	15
Hertford	10	6	1	3	163	115	13
Upper Clapton	10	6	0	4	180	125	12
Welwyn	10	5	2	3	142	122	12
Mill Hill	10	5	1	4	183	133	11
St Mary's H	10	4	0	6	108	160	8
Hemel Hempst'd	10	2	3	5	135	152	7
Kingsburians	10	3	1	6	122	213	7
Bacavians	10	2	1	7	121	238	5
Twickenham	10	0	0	10	100	263	0

London 3 South-East

	P	W	D	L	F	A	Pts
Westcombe Pk	10	9	1	0	227	89	19
O Juddian	10	8	1	1	248	110	17
Charlton Pk	10	6	0	4	142	99	12
Horsham	10	5	1	4	110	103	11
O Beccehamians	10	5	0	5	105	102	10
Crawley	10	4	1	5	143	122	9
Beckenham	10	4	0	6	155	168	8
Gillingham Anch	10	4	0	6	135	164	8
Hove	10	4	0	6	139	216	8
Bognor	10	3	0	7	105	194	6
East Grinstead	10	1	0	9	69	211	2

London 3 South-West

	P	W	D	L	F	A	Pts
Dorking	10	9	0	1	233	74	18
Purley	10	9	0	1	190	128	18
O Reigatian	10	7	0	3	130	72	14
O Walcountians	10	6	0	4	162	99	12
KCS OB	10	5	0	5	153	102	10
Portsmouth	10	5	0	5	143	145	10
Guy's Hospital	10	4	1	5	131	172	9
O Emanuel	10	4	0	6	107	176	8
O Whitgiftians	10	2	0	8	92	148	4
O Guildfordians	10	2	0	8	104	180	4
Southampton	10	1	1	8	54	203	3

Eastern Counties 1

	P	W	D	L	F	A	Pts
Canvey Island	10	8	0	2	377	98	16
O Edwardians	10	7	1	2	178	85	15
Rochford	10	7	0	3	244	124	14
Shelford	10	7	0	3	240	120	14
Crusaders	10	7	0	3	112	113	14
Braintree	10	5	0	5	122	169	10
Ely	10	4	1	5	137	161	9
Basildon	10	4	0	6	182	145	8
Bury St Edmunds	10	4	0	6	119	170	8
Redbridge	10	1	0	9	72	303	2
Ipswich YMCA	10	0	0	10	63	358	0

Eastern Counties 2

	P	W	D	L	F	A	Pts
Chelmsford	10	9	0	1	166	64	18
Woodbridge	10	8	0	2	202	95	16
Campion	10	8	0	2	206	100	16
Lowestoft & Yar	10	7	0	3	132	72	14
Maldon	10	5	0	5	138	123	10
Upminster	10	4	0	6	125	138	8
Sth Woodham Fer	10	4	0	6	93	143	8
East London	10	4	0	6	56	146	8
Port of London	10	3	0	7	149	138	6
Diss	10	3	0	7	61	175	6
Wanstead	10	0	0	10	41	175	0

Eastern Counties 3

	P	W	D	L	F	A	Pts
Bancroft	10	10	0	0	240	48	20
Holt	10	7	1	2	178	87	15
Wymondham	10	6	2	2	157	87	14
Ilford Wands	10	6	1	3	165	72	13
Beccles	10	4	2	4	126	146	10
Harwich & Dov	10	4	2	4	98	123	10
Newmarket	10	4	0	6	125	113	8
O Brentwoods	10	4	0	6	137	206	8
O Bealonians	10	3	1	6	89	128	7
Laken'm Hewett	10	2	1	7	92	173	5
Thetford	10	0	0	10	40	264	0

Eastern Counties 4

	P	W	D	L	F	A	Pts
London Hosp	9	8	0	1	258	71	16
O Palmerians	9	8	0	1	144	45	16
Clacton	9	6	0	3	173	129	12
Loughton	9	5	0	4	164	93	10
Felixstowe	9	5	0	4	125	66	10
Fakenham	9	4	0	5	123	123	8
Stowmarket	9	3	1	5	113	129	7
Southwold	9	3	0	6	82	126	6
Mayfield OB	9	1	0	8	44	334	2
Wisbech *	9	1	1	7	59	169	1

* 2 points deducted for failure to pay fine

Eastern Counties 5

	P	W	D	L	F	A	Pts
Haverhill	9	8	0	1	204	67	16
Thames Sports	9	8	0	1	125	19	16
Dereham	9	7	0	2	203	70	14
Ongar	9	6	0	3	192	70	12
Billericay	9	6	0	3	141	95	12
Swaffham	9	3	0	6	88	141	6
Norwich Union	9	3	0	6	72	137	6
March	9	2	0	7	83	161	4
Thurston	9	2	0	7	101	183	4

| Chigwell | 9 | 0 | 0 | 9 | 15 | 281 | 0 |

Eastern Counties 6

	P	W	D	L	F	A	Pts
O Cooperians	9	8	0	1	410	44	16
Essex Police	9	8	0	1	251	89	16

Hadleigh	9	7	0	2	233	52	14
Broadland	9	6	0	3	224	152	12
Brightlingsea	9	5	0	4	154	114	10
Burnham	9	4	0	5	104	118	8
Witham	9	4	0	5	84	147	8
Sawston	9	2	0	7	108	155	4
Orwell	9	1	0	8	18	440	2
Mistley	9	0	0	9	45	320	0

Hampshire 1

	P	W	D	L	F	A	Pts
Eastleigh	10	9	1	0	236	80	19

Millbrook	10	7	0	3	184	117	14
Winchester	10	6	1	3	148	119	13
Jersey	10	6	0	4	111	82	12
Sandown & Sh	10	6	0	4	101	117	12
Esso	10	5	0	5	138	100	10
Petersfield	10	5	0	5	135	124	10
Gosport	10	5	0	5	130	131	10
Guernsey	10	2	0	8	98	186	4

| Andover | 10 | 2 | 0 | 8 | 80 | 172 | 4 |
| Fareham | 10 | 1 | 0 | 9 | 63 | 196 | 2 |

Hampshire 2

	P	W	D	L	F	A	Pts
Isle of Wight	12	12	0	0	256	71	24
Farnborough	12	10	0	2	296	100	20

Tottonians	12	9	1	2	299	57	19
NewMilton	12	8	1	3	168	108	17
Trojans**	12	8	1	3	151	119	15
Jersey UB	12	6	0	6	107	142	12
Romsey	12	5	1	6	217	122	11
Nomads	12	5	0	7	107	147	10
Ventnor	12	4	1	7	136	178	9
Overton	12	4	1	7	120	165	9
Ellingham	12	2	0	10	113	226	4
Fordingbridge	12	1	0	11	79	401	2
Waterlooville*	12	1	0	11	58	271	0

* 2 points deducted for failure to pay fine
** 2 points deducted for ineligible player

Hertfordshire 1

	P	W	D	L	F	A	Pts
Letchworth	7	6	0	1	175	48	12

O Elizabethans	7	6	0	1	118	42	12
O Verulamians	7	4	1	2	101	37	9
Stevenage	7	4	0	3	80	55	8
Barnet	7	3	0	4	65	100	6
Hitchin	7	2	1	4	42	84	5

| Harpenden | 7 | 0 | 2 | 5 | 42 | 139 | 2 |
| Tring | 7 | 1 | 0 | 6 | 27 | 145 | 2 |

Hertfordshire 2

	P	W	D	L	F	A	Pts
Royston	8	7	0	1	126	86	14
Datchworth	8	6	1	1	112	61	13
St Albans	8	2	1	5	46	66	5
Watford	8	2	1	5	89	113	5
OAshmoleans	8	1	1	6	54	101	3

Kent 1

	P	W	D	L	F	A	Pts
Park House	10	7	1	2	130	76	15

Medway	10	7	0	3	175	86	14
Snowdown CW	10	7	0	3	170	107	14
Betteshanger	10	6	0	4	163	162	12
Sevenoaks	10	5	1	4	131	103	11
Erith	10	5	0	5	112	114	10
Thanet Wands	10	5	0	5	117	154	10
O Dunstonians	10	3	2	5	126	105	8
Bromley	10	4	0	6	148	128	8
Dover	10	3	0	7	54	154	6

| Canterbury | 10 | 1 | 0 | 9 | 74 | 211 | 2 |

Kent 2

	P	W	D	L	F	A	Pts
Sittingbourne	10	8	0	2	171	66	16
Met Pol, Hayes	10	6	1	3	173	94	13

Folkestone	10	6	1	3	145	95	13
Tonbridge	10	6	0	4	169	99	12
O Elthamians	10	6	0	4	108	116	12
O Shootershill	10	4	3	3	122	87	11
Linton	10	4	0	6	122	151	8
Ashford	10	4	0	6	91	155	8
Nat West Bank	10	3	1	6	116	170	7
New Ash Green	10	3	0	7	79	126	6

| Midland Bank | 10 | 2 | 0 | 8 | 85 | 222 | 4 |

Kent 3

	P	W	D	L	F	A	Pts
Sheppey	10	9	0	1	160	75	18
Cranbrook	10	8	0	2	166	83	16

Lloyds Bank	10	7	0	3	186	138	14
Vigo*	10	6	0	4	123	65	10
Greenwich	10	5	0	5	126	89	10
Deal	10	5	0	5	141	134	10
Citizens	10	4	0	6	87	112	8
O Olavians	10	4	0	6	100	177	8
O Williamsonians	10	3	0	7	100	147	6
O Gravesendians	10	3	0	7	106	176	6

| Darenth Valley | 10 | 1 | 0 | 9 | 55 | 154 | 2 |

* 2 points deducted for failure to pay fine

Kent 4

	P	W	D	L	F	A	Pts
Orpington	10	8	1	1	244	79	17
STC Footscray	10	8	1	1	134	43	17
Bexley	10	8	0	2	156	32	16
Whitstable	10	8	0	2	155	47	16
East Peckham	10	5	0	5	111	107	10
Centurians*	9	3	1	5	31	198	7
Edenbridge	10	3	0	7	56	98	6
Westerham	10	3	0	7	73	168	6
U of Kent	10	2	0	8	88	108	4
Thames Poly*	9	2	0	7	58	126	4
Lordswood**	10	2	1	7	75	175	3

* *match postponed and not required to be replayed*
** *2 points deducted for failure to pay fine*

Middlesex 1

	P	W	D	L	F	A	Pts
Uxbridge	10	9	0	1	141	89	18
London NZ	10	7	0	3	295	106	14
Staines	10	7	0	3	189	82	14
Sudbury Court	10	6	0	4	134	147	12
Harrow	10	5	0	5	103	100	10
Hendon	10	5	0	5	89	158	10
Lensbury	10	4	0	6	122	132	8
O Meadonians	10	4	0	6	111	127	8
Centaurs	10	3	0	7	113	184	6
Hampstead	10	3	0	7	91	185	6
O Millhillians	10	2	0	8	103	181	4

Middlesex 2

	P	W	D	L	F	A	Pts
Hackney	10	9	1	0	211	89	19
O Abbotstonians	10	6	1	3	139	115	13
O Grammarians	10	6	1	3	97	81	13
Haringey	10	6	0	4	197	95	12
Orleans FP	10	6	0	4	111	113	12
O Haberdashers	10	4	1	5	105	98	9
O Paulines	10	4	1	5	112	171	9
St Bart's H	10	3	1	6	109	148	7
Civil Service	10	2	2	6	101	132	6
Osterley	10	2	1	7	76	138	5
Barclays Bank	10	2	1	7	85	163	5

Middlesex 3

	P	W	D	L	F	A	Pts
Bank of Eng	10	8	1	1	214	129	17
Hamm'th & Ful	10	7	1	2	184	93	15
Antlers	10	7	1	2	167	87	15
Wembley	10	6	0	4	179	147	12
O Tottonians	10	5	0	5	154	138	10
Richmd Thames	10	5	0	5	161	183	10
O Isleworthians	10	4	1	5	126	128	9
Quintin	10	4	0	6	145	155	8
O Hamptonians	10	3	0	7	106	141	6
Meadhurst	10	3	0	7	119	257	6
London Cornish	10	1	0	9	72	169	2

Middlesex 4

	P	W	D	L	F	A	Pts
Enfield Ignat	10	9	0	1	232	54	18
Roxeth Man OB	10	8	0	2	166	47	16
UCS OB	10	8	0	2	173	83	16
HAC	10	5	1	4	194	114	11
Pinner & Gramm	10	5	0	5	91	107	10
Northolt	10	4	1	5	63	108	9
Belsize Pk	10	4	1	5	122	169	9
Feltham*	10	4	1	5	112	107	7
London French	10	3	0	7	105	187	6
Royal Free Hosp	10	2	0	8	70	277	4
O Actonians	10	1	0	9	81	156	2

* *2 points deducted for failure to pay fine*

Middlesex 5

	P	W	D	L	F	A	Pts
St Nicholas OB	7	7	0	0	181	45	14
Hayes	7	4	0	3	107	56	8
Brunel U	7	4	0	3	116	75	8
Middlesex H	7	3	1	3	78	95	7
GWR*	7	4	0	3	127	138	6
British Airways	7	3	0	4	78	102	6
ST & C	7	2	1	4	31	45	5
Kodak	7	0	0	7	48	210	0

* *2 points deducted for failure to pay fine*

Surrey 1

	P	W	D	L	F	A	Pts
O Blues	10	9	0	1	278	81	18
O Wimbledonians	10	8	1	1	163	98	17
Warlingham	10	8	0	2	155	80	16
Merton	10	7	0	3	127	80	14
Harrodians	10	6	0	4	134	149	12
Cranleigh	10	5	0	5	127	107	10
John Fisher OB	10	4	0	6	125	104	8
O Rutlishians	10	3	1	6	119	147	7
Effingham	10	2	0	8	65	202	4
O Tiffinians	10	2	0	8	62	203	4
O Cranleighans	10	0	0	10	83	187	0

Surrey 2

	P	W	D	L	F	A	Pts
Wimbledon	10	9	0	1	331	56	18
Raynes Pk Hosp	10	9	0	1	179	54	18
Char X/West*	10	7	1	2	182	108	13
Mitcham	10	5	0	5	104	124	10
Cobham	10	3	2	5	94	145	8
Wandsworthians	10	4	0	6	96	166	8
O Haileyburians	10	4	0	6	104	178	8
U Vandals	10	3	1	6	95	119	7
Law Society	10	3	1	6	82	137	7
O Johnians	10	3	1	6	76	163	7
Bec OB	10	2	0	8	79	172	4

* *2 points deducted for breach of regulations*

135

Surrey 3

	P	W	D	L	F	A	Pts
Shirley Wands	10	9	0	1	193	67	18
Farnham	10	7	2	1	128	75	16
Kingston	10	7	0	3	151	134	14
O Pelhamrians	10	6	0	4	179	86	12
Chobham	10	5	1	4	161	114	11
O Reedonians	10	5	1	4	174	134	11
Battersea Irons	10	5	0	5	175	136	10
Old Freemans	10	4	0	6	124	147	8
O Suttonians	10	3	0	7	73	160	6
Chipstead	10	1	0	9	79	193	2
KCH	10	1	0	9	85	276	2

Surrey 4

	P	W	D	L	F	A	Pts
O Bevonians	10	9	1	0	209	42	19
Reigate & Red	10	8	2	0	241	70	18
O Caterhamians	10	8	1	1	224	70	17
BBC	10	6	0	4	136	80	12
Surrey U*	10	6	0	4	178	113	8
O Croydonians	10	4	0	6	145	158	8
L Fire Brigade	10	4	0	6	100	174	8
Surrey Police	10	3	0	7	87	127	6
R Holloway Coll	10	3	0	7	79	191	6
Old Epsomians	10	1	0	9	76	191	2
Shene Old Grams	10	1	0	9	78	337	2

* 4 points deducted for failure to pay fines

Surrey 5

	P	W	D	L	F	A	Pts
Gibraltar Engs	6	6	0	0	193	13	12
Racal Decca	6	4	0	2	51	28	8
Economicals	6	4	0	2	78	149	8
Oxted	6	2	1	3	72	77	5
Haslemere	6	2	1	3	52	79	5
Woking	6	1	0	5	45	84	2
Lightwater*	6	1	0	5	45	106	0

* 4 points deducted for failure to pay fine

Sussex 1

	P	W	D	L	F	A	Pts
Chichester	10	10	0	0	211	59	20
Haywards Heath	10	7	1	2	137	77	15
Brighton	10	7	1	2	136	94	15
Eastbourne	10	7	0	3	134	46	14
Heathfield	10	6	1	3	167	132	13
Seaford	10	4	1	5	113	144	9
Uckfield	10	4	0	6	83	118	8
Burgess Hill	10	4	0	6	103	149	8
Sussex Pol	10	2	1	7	76	121	5
St Francis	10	1	0	9	102	201	2
Crowborough	10	0	1	9	53	174	1

Sussex 2

	P	W	D	L	F	A	Pts
Hastings & Bex	8	8	0	0	323	69	16
O Brightonians	8	7	0	1	204	76	14
Pulborough	8	6	0	2	164	98	12
RMP Chichester	8	5	0	3	95	167	10
Hellingly	8	4	0	4	137	94	8
Plumpton	8	2	0	6	102	154	4
Midhurst	8	2	0	6	72	167	4
Brighton Poly*	8	2	0	6	88	137	2
Sussex U*	8	0	0	8	31	254	−2

* 2 points deducted for breach of Rule 6

Sussex 3

	P	W	D	L	F	A	Pts
Ditchling	5	5	0	0	88	25	10
W Sussex Ins HE	5	3	1	1	83	38	7
Sunallon	5	3	0	2	69	41	6
BA Wingspan	5	2	0	3	37	43	4
Newick	5	1	1	3	43	64	3
Arun	5	0	0	5	16	125	0

NORTH ZONE

North 1

	P	W	D	L	F	A	Pts
Otley	10	9	0	1	141	77	18
Harrogate	10	8	0	2	188	82	16
Bradford & Bing	10	8	0	2	156	100	16
Aspatria	10	6	2	2	162	119	14
Middlesbrough	10	6	0	4	133	105	12
Wigton	10	4	1	5	114	120	9
Hartlepool R	10	4	0	6	152	144	8
Halifax	10	4	0	6	104	151	8
Hull Ionians	10	2	0	8	110	198	4
Tynedale	10	1	1	8	125	145	3
Birkenhead Pk	10	1	0	9	77	221	2

North 2

	P	W	D	L	F	A	Pts
Rotherham	10	9	0	1	214	134	18
Widnes	10	7	0	3	186	115	14
Wigan	10	7	0	3	174	106	14
Huddersfield	10	7	0	3	125	104	14
Wharfedale	10	5	1	4	158	136	11
Alnwick	10	5	0	5	145	132	10
Sandal	10	4	1	5	151	112	9
Lymm	10	4	0	6	130	158	8
West Park	10	3	0	7	133	185	6
Carlisle	10	2	1	7	102	242	5
New Brighton	10	0	1	9	93	187	1

North-West 1

	P	W	D	L	F	A	Pts
Sandbach	10	9	0	1	229	64	18
Egremont	10	8	0	2	192	86	16
Davenport	10	7	1	2	155	93	15
Wirral	10	7	1	2	129	110	15
Cockermouth	10	6	1	3	127	127	13
Macclesfield	10	3	1	6	119	139	7
Mid-Cheshire	10	3	1	6	93	131	7
Caldy	10	3	1	6	101	222	7
Sedgley Park	10	2	0	8	91	132	4
Rochdale	10	2	0	8	97	153	4
Chester	10	2	0	8	106	182	4

North-West 2

	P	W	D	L	F	A	Pts
Manchester	10	8	1	1	212	62	17
Netherhall	10	7	0	3	131	69	14
Warrington	10	7	0	3	161	115	14
O Aldwinians	10	7	0	3	139	100	14
Penrith	10	5	2	3	143	108	12
Wilmslow	10	5	1	4	157	103	11
Workington	10	4	0	6	119	118	8
Blackburn	10	4	0	6	122	173	8
Mersey Pol	10	3	0	7	98	122	6
Southport	10	2	0	8	47	262	4
Moresby	10	1	0	9	60	157	2

NW East 1

	P	W	D	L	F	A	Pts
O Salians	10	9	0	1	248	52	18
Kersal	10	9	0	1	232	59	18
Metrovick	10	8	0	2	177	81	16
Littleborough	10	6	1	3	154	64	13
Broughton	10	6	0	4	208	99	12
Tyldesley	10	5	0	5	117	89	10
Crewe & Nant	10	4	1	5	139	116	9
Old Bedians	10	3	0	7	110	192	6
Gtr Mcr Fire S	10	3	0	7	74	183	6
Toc H	10	1	0	9	58	309	2
Colne & Nelson	10	0	0	10	65	338	0

NW East 2

	P	W	D	L	F	A	Pts
Ashton-U-Lyne	10	8	0	2	160	65	16
Man YMCA	10	7	1	2	179	82	15
Calder Vale	10	7	0	3	166	76	14
Chorley	10	7	0	3	132	91	14
Bury	10	6	1	3	177	88	13
Bolton	10	6	0	4	105	94	12
Congleton	10	5	0	5	139	84	10
Dukinfield	10	5	0	5	110	105	10
Marple	10	2	0	8	77	140	4
N Manchester	10	0	1	9	64	248	1
Agecroft	10	0	1	9	65	301	1

NW East 3

	P	W	D	L	F	A	Pts
Wigan Tech	6	5	0	1	151	70	10
Lostock	6	5	0	1	107	49	10
Holmes Chapel	6	3	0	3	72	55	6
Bowden	6	3	0	3	57	63	6
Shell Carr	6	3	0	3	54	98	6
Atherton	6	1	0	5	44	89	2
Oldham College	6	1	0	5	36	97	2

NW East North

	P	W	D	L	F	A	Pts
Ashton on M	10	9	1	0	261	63	19
DLS Salford	10	8	2	0	213	106	18
Kirkby Lonsdale	10	7	0	3	140	147	14
Windermere	10	6	1	3	174	94	13
Burnage	10	6	0	4	84	78	12
Vickers	10	5	0	5	119	153	10
Oldham	10	4	0	6	105	138	8
Furness	10	3	0	7	113	110	6
Eccles	10	3	0	7	74	166	6
Heaton Moor	10	2	0	8	101	172	4
Fleetwood	10	0	0	10	61	218	0

NW North 1

	P	W	D	L	F	A	Pts
Keswick	9	8	0	1	217	63	16
Rossendale	9	7	1	1	188	47	15
Thornton Cleves	9	6	1	2	141	101	13
St Benedicts	9	5	0	4	148	96	10
Whitehaven	9	5	0	4	116	127	10
Upper Eden	9	4	0	5	114	127	8
Carnforth	9	4	0	5	125	161	8
Blackpool	9	2	0	7	104	163	4
Millom	9	2	0	7	61	144	4
British Steel	9	1	0	8	54	239	2

NW North 2

	P	W	D	L	F	A	Pts
Silloth	2	2	0	0	45	17	4
Creighton	3	1	0	2	50	24	2
Smith Bros	1	1	0	0	3	0	2
Clitheroe	2	1	0	1	12	52	2
Ambleside	2	0	0	2	19	36	0

NW West 1

	P	W	D	L	F	A	Pts
St Edwards OB	10	10	0	0	237	80	20
Oldershaw	10	8	0	2	201	104	16
Newton-Le-Ws	10	7	1	2	139	122	15
S Liverpool	10	5	1	4	139	97	11
Liverpool Collt	10	5	0	5	124	110	10
Ormskirk	10	4	1	5	141	138	9
Douglas (IoM)	10	4	1	5	143	196	9
Ruskin Park	10	4	0	6	119	110	8
Leigh	10	3	0	7	71	182	6
O Instonians	10	2	0	8	87	211	4
O Parkonians	10	1	0	9	91	142	2

NW West 2

	P	W	D	L	F	A	Pts
Vulcan	10	8	0	2	260	125	16
Hoylake	10	8	0	2	147	57	16
Port Sunlight	10	7	1	2	160	89	15
Sefton	10	7	0	3	115	88	14
O Anselmians	10	6	1	3	159	117	13
O Rockferrians	10	5	0	5	175	196	10
Aspull	10	4	0	6	147	151	8
Shell Stanlow	10	4	0	6	77	126	8
Eagle	10	3	0	7	130	160	6
Hightown	10	1	0	9	71	169	2
Birchfield	10	1	0	9	71	234	2

NW West 3

	P	W	D	L	F	A	Pts
Vagabonds	8	7	1	0	146	56	15
Wallasey	8	7	0	1	113	50	14
Mossley Hill	8	6	0	2	151	56	12
St Marys OB	8	5	0	3	206	58	10
Helsby	8	4	0	4	127	101	8
Moore	8	1	2	5	71	115	4
Halton	8	2	0	6	61	159	4
Lucas	8	1	1	6	51	183	3
Burtonwood	8	1	0	7	42	190	2

Yorkshire 1

	P	W	D	L	F	A	Pts
West P Bramhope	10	9	0	1	217	63	18
Driffield	10	8	1	1	149	93	17
Bridlington	10	7	1	2	151	84	15
Doncaster	10	5	0	5	131	93	10
Cleckheaton	10	3	3	4	108	121	9
Barnsley	10	3	2	5	101	122	8
N Ribblesdale	10	2	4	4	125	161	8
Castleford	10	3	2	5	94	143	8
Hemsworth	10	2	3	5	83	148	7
Pocklington	10	2	2	6	112	134	6
Hudd'field YMCA	10	2	0	8	88	197	4

Yorkshire 2

	P	W	D	L	F	A	Pts
Malton & Norton	10	7	0	3	212	91	14
York RI	10	6	2	2	154	82	14
O Otliensians	10	6	0	4	117	94	12
Goole	10	5	1	4	125	105	11
Yarnbury	10	5	0	5	119	101	10
Wheatley Hills	10	5	0	5	150	159	10
Ilkley	10	4	2	4	128	145	10
Moortown	10	5	0	5	104	128	10
Wath	10	4	1	5	129	102	9
Scarborough	10	4	0	6	75	139	8
Sheff Tigers	10	1	0	9	64	231	2

Yorkshire 3

	P	W	D	L	F	A	Pts
Leodiensians	10	9	1	0	247	49	19
Knottingley	10	9	1	0	230	55	19
Wibsey	10	5	1	4	109	126	11
O Modernians	10	5	0	5	166	95	10
Hessle	10	4	2	4	140	136	10
West Leeds	10	4	1	5	117	126	9
Rodillians	10	4	1	5	138	181	9
Marist	10	3	1	6	139	187	7
Airebronians	10	3	0	7	96	216	6
Leeds CSSA	10	2	1	7	84	188	5
Baildon	10	2	1	7	69	176	5

Yorkshire 4

	P	W	D	L	F	A	Pts
Bradford Salem	10	10	0	0	272	56	20
Sheffield Oaks	10	9	0	1	215	93	18
Northallerton	10	8	0	2	279	66	16
Dinnington	10	6	0	4	234	92	12
Halifax Vandals	10	6	0	4	207	138	12
O Rishworthians	10	4	1	5	113	128	9
Heath	10	3	1	6	100	211	7
Yorkshire CW	10	3	0	7	116	161	6
Hullensians	10	2	1	7	67	129	5
Leeds YMCA	10	2	1	7	85	209	5
Phoenix Park	10	0	0	10	33	438	0

Yorkshire 5

	P	W	D	L	F	A	Pts
Wetherby	10	9	0	1	219	79	18
Ossett	10	9	0	1	213	75	18
Skipton	10	8	0	2	175	79	16
Burley	10	8	0	2	129	68	16

	P	W	D	L	F	A	Pts
Danum Phoenix	10	4	0	6	128	138	8
DLS Sheff	10	4	0	6	113	124	8
Leeds Corinths	10	3	1	6	90	129	7
Withernsea	10	3	0	7	58	147	6
Yorkshire Main	10	2	1	7	89	143	5
BP Chemicals	10	2	0	8	92	172	4
Rowntrees	10	2	0	8	79	231	4

Yorkshire 6

	P	W	D	L	F	A	Pts
Castle Coll	8	7	0	1	213	42	14
Knaresborough	8	7	0	1	106	43	14
Hull & ER	8	6	1	1	181	81	13
Adwick-le-St	8	4	0	4	107	123	8
Mosborough	8	3	1	4	82	86	7
Hornsea	8	3	0	5	114	105	6
Stockbridge	8	2	0	6	52	202	4
Maltby OB	8	1	1	6	83	146	3
Armthorpe Mark	8	1	1	6	56	166	3

Durham/Northumberland 1

	P	W	D	L	F	A	Pts
Ashington	10	8	1	1	247	69	17
Horden	10	6	2	2	228	81	14
Darlington	10	6	1	3	141	140	13
Seghill	10	6	1	3	148	176	13
Whitby	10	6	0	4	131	128	12
Redcar	10	5	0	5	170	120	10
Sunderland	10	5	0	5	127	106	10
Acklam	10	5	0	5	128	150	10
Mowden Pk	10	3	1	6	121	173	7
Hartlepool	10	1	0	9	65	178	2
Ponteland	10	1	0	9	81	266	2

Durham/Northumberland 2

	P	W	D	L	F	A	Pts
Bishop Auckland	10	9	0	1	204	78	18
Darlington RA	10	8	0	2	133	66	16
Winlaton Vulcs	10	8	0	2	146	88	16
Seaham	10	7	0	3	194	116	14
Medicals	10	4	1	5	140	152	9
Billingham	10	4	0	6	120	124	8
Percy Pk	10	4	0	6	102	159	8
Consett	10	3	1	6	176	126	7
North Durham	10	3	0	7	74	150	6
Wallsend	10	3	0	7	77	173	6
North Shields	10	1	0	9	81	215	2

Durham/Northumberland 3

	P	W	D	L	F	A	Pts
Barnard Castle	10	8	0	2	192	114	16
Seaton Carew	10	8	0	2	139	134	16
Chester-Le-St	10	7	0	3	168	94	14
Wensleydale	10	7	0	3	179	108	14
Houghton	10	6	0	4	124	133	12
Guisborough	10	5	0	5	148	140	10
S Tyneside Coll	10	4	0	6	145	156	8
H'pool TDSOB	10	4	0	6	101	113	8
H'pool BBOB	10	3	0	7	171	189	6
Wearside	10	3	0	7	105	149	6
Prudhoe	10	0	0	10	86	228	0

Durham/Northumberland 4

	P	W	D	L	F	A	Pts
Newton Aycliffe	6	6	0	0	140	32	12
Durham CS	6	5	0	1	73	33	10
Sedgefield	6	3	1	2	123	63	7
Richmondshire	6	3	1	2	118	72	7
Jarrovians	6	2	0	4	66	87	4
Hartlepool Ath	6	1	0	5	74	115	2
Shildon	6	0	0	6	17	209	0

North-East 1

	P	W	D	L	F	A	Pts
Stockton	10	9	1	0	263	106	19
Gateshead Fell	10	7	1	2	154	131	15
York	10	7	0	3	187	110	14
Keighley	10	6	0	4	108	114	12
O Brodleians	10	5	1	4	164	134	11
O Crossleyans	10	4	0	6	162	131	8
Morpeth	10	4	0	6	114	146	8
Thornensians	10	4	0	6	77	128	8
Novocastrians	10	3	0	7	118	183	6
Blaydon	10	3	0	7	86	170	6
Selby	10	1	1	8	114	194	3

North-East 2

	P	W	D	L	F	A	Pts
Bramley	10	10	0	0	218	70	20
Roundhegians	10	8	0	2	177	71	16
Westoe	10	7	0	3	144	97	14
Beverley	10	6	0	4	113	84	12
Pontefract	10	5	0	5	119	135	10
Ripon	10	4	0	6	111	103	8
Blyth	10	4	0	6	106	142	8
O Hymerians	10	4	0	6	127	183	8
Newcastle U	10	4	0	6	100	185	8
Rockcliff	10	2	0	8	95	151	4
Ryton	10	1	0	9	111	200	2

MIDLANDS ZONE
Midlands 1

	P	W	D	L	F	A	Pts
Hereford	10	9	0	1	245	112	18
B'ham & S'hull	10	8	0	2	140	85	16
Newark	10	7	1	2	208	155	15
Derby	10	6	0	4	144	130	12
Barker's Butts	10	5	0	5	162	153	10
Sutton Cold	10	5	0	5	137	167	10
Leighton Buzz	10	4	0	6	141	152	8
Mansfield	10	4	0	6	100	169	8
Stockwood Pk	10	3	0	7	105	129	6
Westleigh	10	3	0	7	112	162	6
Paviors	10	0	1	9	84	164	1

Midlands 2 East

	P	W	D	L	F	A	Pts
Towcestrians	10	10	0	0	174	52	20
Vipers	10	9	0	1	172	64	18
Matlock	10	7	0	3	171	94	14
Moderns	10	6	0	4	121	108	12
Peterborough	10	5	0	5	145	127	10
Syston	10	4	0	6	116	102	8
Stewarts & Llds	10	4	0	6	98	106	8
Scunthorpe	10	4	0	6	85	113	8
Kettering	10	3	0	7	104	159	6
Lincoln	10	3	0	7	98	169	6
Stoneygate	10	0	0	10	66	256	0

Midlands 2 West

	P	W	D	L	F	A	Pts
Camp Hill	10	8	0	2	189	81	16
Wolverhampton	10	7	2	1	172	67	16
Bedworth	10	7	1	2	174	94	15
Bromsgrove	10	6	2	2	107	59	14
Keresley	10	6	2	2	135	97	14
Stafford	10	4	1	5	103	127	9
O Yardleians	10	3	2	5	109	128	8
Burton	10	3	1	6	152	115	7
Dudley Kings	10	2	1	7	64	173	5
Newbold	10	2	0	8	80	152	4
Dixonians	10	1	0	9	73	265	2

East Midlands/Leicestershire

	P	W	D	L	F	A	Pts
Biggleswade	10	10	0	0	199	67	20
Wellingborough	10	8	0	2	176	90	16
Belgrave	10	6	1	3	158	127	13
Luton	10	6	1	3	130	106	13
Bedford Ath	10	6	0	4	117	79	12
N'pton Trinity	10	5	0	5	103	114	10

Long Buckby	10	4	0	6	104	117	8
Aylestone St J	10	3	0	7	81	178	6
Lutterworth	10	2	1	7	107	152	5
Oadby Wyggs	10	2	0	8	122	216	4
Hinckley	10	1	1	8	123	174	3

Staffs/Warwicks

	P	W	D	L	F	A	Pts
Leamington	10	9	0	1	215	67	18
Willenhall	10	9	0	1	173	69	18
Tamworth	10	6	0	4	149	93	12
Leek	10	5	0	5	139	118	10
O Leamington	10	5	0	5	121	111	10
Newcastle	10	5	0	5	107	108	10
Stratford on A	10	5	0	5	119	135	10
Old Longtonians	10	5	0	5	138	160	10
Coventry Welsh	10	4	0	6	139	136	8
Nuneaton OE	10	2	0	8	107	174	4
Handsworth	10	0	0	10	46	282	0

East Midlands 1

	P	W	D	L	F	A	Pts
Ampthill	10	9	0	1	175	88	18
Northampton MO	10	8	0	2	158	95	16
Brackley	10	7	0	3	215	95	14
N'pton BBOB	10	7	0	3	143	73	14
Northampton OS	10	5	0	5	194	126	10
Huntingdon	10	5	0	5	107	103	10
Rushden & H	10	5	0	5	114	151	10
O Northamptons	10	4	0	6	98	150	8
Daventry	10	3	0	7	101	155	6
Well'boro OG	10	2	0	8	83	169	4
Corby	10	0	0	10	69	252	0

East Midlands 2

	P	W	D	L	F	A	Pts
St Neots	10	10	0	0	179	71	20
Bedford Queens	10	9	0	1	216	71	18
N'pton Casuals	10	7	1	2	159	77	15
Dunstablians	10	7	0	3	184	97	14
Bedford Swifts	10	5	0	5	130	100	10
Oundle	10	3	1	6	143	186	7
Westwood	10	3	0	7	119	182	6
Vauxhall Motors	10	3	0	7	92	196	6
St Ives	10	2	1	7	101	133	5
Colworth House	10	2	1	7	87	234	5
Deepings	10	2	0	8	99	162	4

East Midlands 3

	P	W	D	L	F	A	Pts
Bugbrooke	10	9	0	1	278	41	18

Beds Pol	10	9	0	1	160	57	18
O Welling	10	5	0	5	153	139	10
Cutler Hammer	10	4	0	6	103	132	8
Potton	10	2	0	8	53	225	4
N'pton Heathens	10	1	0	9	70	223	2

Leicestershire 1

	P	W	D	L	F	A	Pts
Coalville	10	10	0	0	228	39	20
O Bosworth	10	9	0	1	217	92	18
Market Bosworth	10	8	0	2	145	94	16
South Leicester	10	7	0	3	173	115	14
Wigston	10	4	1	5	147	157	9
Birstall Comm	10	3	1	6	113	138	7
Loughborough	10	3	0	7	109	121	6
Kibworth	10	3	0	7	111	150	6
Melton Mowbray	10	3	0	7	68	137	6
O Newtonians	10	3	0	7	89	169	6
West Leicester	10	1	0	9	62	250	2

Leicestershire 2

	P	W	D	L	F	A	Pts
O Ashbeians	9	9	0	0	284	75	18
New Parks OB	9	8	0	1	229	60	16
Aylestonians	9	6	1	2	206	97	13
Anstey	9	6	0	3	221	44	12
Oakham	9	5	1	3	232	100	11
Shepsted	9	3	0	6	83	141	6
Burbage*	8	2	0	6	82	143	6
Braunstone Town	9	2	0	7	70	167	4
South Wigston*	8	2	0	6	60	255	4
Aylestone Ath	9	0	0	9	32	417	0

* Match not played – points awarded to Burbage

Notts, Lincs & Derbys 1

	P	W	D	L	F	A	Pts
Chesterfield	10	10	0	0	194	41	20
Amber Valley	10	8	0	2	179	57	16
Worksop	10	7	0	3	119	100	14
Southwell	10	6	0	4	152	82	12
Spalding	10	6	0	4	149	134	12
Mellish	10	4	1	5	94	121	9
Sleaford	10	3	1	6	92	138	7
Stamford	10	3	0	7	90	164	6
East Retford	10	2	1	7	103	148	5
Kesteven	10	2	1	7	89	172	5
West Bridgford	10	2	0	8	63	167	4

Notts, Lincs & Derbys 2

	P	W	D	L	F	A	Pts
Glossop	10	8	1	1	171	69	17
Nott'm Casuals	10	7	1	2	153	80	15
Nottinghamians	10	7	1	2	153	80	15
Market Rasen	10	5	1	4	174	102	11
All Spartans	10	5	1	4	136	87	11
Dronfield	9	4	0	5	94	83	8
Grimsby	9	4	0	5	92	105	8
Long Eaton	10	4	0	6	114	178	8
Keyworth	10	3	0	7	68	144	6
Nott'm Constab	10	3	0	7	85	186	6
Ilkeston	10	2	1	7	51	167	5

Notts, Lincs & Derbys 3

	P	W	D	L	F	A	Pts
Belper	10	9	0	1	141	40	18
Melbourne	10	7	1	2	194	69	15
Rolls Royce	10	7	0	3	114	89	14
Ashbourne	10	6	1	3	195	63	13
Boston	10	6	0	4	130	72	12
Cleethorpes	10	6	0	4	127	161	12
Barton & Dist	10	4	1	5	91	150	9
Ashfield	10	2	3	5	112	111	7
Boots Ath	10	2	1	7	78	136	5
North Kesteven	10	1	1	8	83	183	3
Skegness	10	1	0	9	60	251	2

Notts, Lincs & Derbys 4 East

	P	W	D	L	F	A	Pts
Bingham	7	6	1	0	202	16	13
Gainsborough	7	5	1	1	138	16	11
Meden Vale	7	4	2	1	144	30	10
Bourne	7	4	0	3	90	81	8
Ollerton	7	4	0	3	77	94	8
Harworth Coll	7	1	0	6	69	152	2
Yarborough Bees	7	1	0	6	40	212	2
Horncastle	7	1	0	6	70	229	2

Notts, Lincs & Derbys 4 West

	P	W	D	L	F	A	Pts
East Leake	7	6	0	1	125	61	12
Tupton	7	6	0	1	90	53	12
Hope Valley	7	5	0	2	127	59	10
Bakewell	6	3	0	3	138	46	6
Buxton	6	3	0	3	59	59	6
Rainworth	7	2	0	5	37	192	4
Leesbrook Ast	6	1	0	5	20	28	2
Bolsover	6	0	0	6	43	141	0

North Midlands 1

	P	W	D	L	F	A	Pts
Worcester	10	8	0	2	237	72	16
Whitchurch	10	8	0	2	176	124	16
Aston O Edwards	10	7	0	3	163	139	14
Ludlow	10	6	0	4	147	97	12

141

Kings Norton	10	5	1	4	131	106	11
Luctonians	10	4	0	6	109	123	8
Evesham	10	4	0	6	112	170	8
Bridgnorth	10	3	2	5	95	153	8
Shrewsbury	10	3	0	7	135	169	6
Kidderminster	10	3	0	7	138	215	6
Newport	10	2	1	7	81	156	5

North Midlands 2

	P	W	D	L	F	A	Pts
Veseyans	10	9	1	0	180	95	19
Woodrush	10	8	0	2	192	66	16
O Halesonians	10	8	0	2	202	106	16
West Mid Pol	10	5	0	5	204	140	10
Selly Oak	10	5	0	5	153	149	10
Telford	10	5	0	5	167	186	10
Droitwich	10	5	0	5	130	149	10
Erdington	10	3	0	7	103	160	6
Pershore	10	2	1	7	107	183	5
Malvern	10	2	0	8	123	181	4
Five Ways OE	10	2	0	8	100	246	4

North Midlands 3

	P	W	D	L	F	A	Pts
O Griffinians	10	8	0	2	184	104	16
Redditch	10	7	0	3	187	105	14
Old Centrals*	9	7	0	2	135	99	14
B'ham City Offs*	9	6	1	2	124	82	13
Tenbury	10	6	0	4	143	120	12
Birchfield	10	5	0	5	138	140	10
Warley	10	4	2	4	130	145	10
B'ham Welsh	10	3	1	6	95	136	7
Edwardians	10	3	0	7	100	168	6
Bournville	10	2	0	8	90	116	4
O Saltleians	10	1	0	9	45	156	2

* Match declared void

North Midlands 4

	P	W	D	L	F	A	Pts
Ross-on-Wye	12	12	0	0	298	67	24
Bromyard	12	9	1	2	167	90	19
Kynoch	12	9	0	3	179	81	18
Market Dray	12	7	1	4	206	101	15
Upton-U-Severn	12	6	2	4	119	126	14
Ledbury*	11	6	1	4	119	74	13
Yardley & Dist	12	4	2	6	119	111	10
Bewdley & Stour*	11	5	0	6	109	155	10
Witton*	10	4	0	6	65	143	8
Oswestry*	11	3	1	7	108	163	7
Birmingham CS*	11	2	1	8	55	191	5
O Moseleians	12	2	0	10	65	143	4
Thimblemill	12	1	1	10	64	226	3

* Matches not played declared void

Staffordshire 1

	P	W	D	L	F	A	Pts
Uttoxeter	6	5	1	0	119	46	11
Eccleshall	6	4	0	2	105	64	8
Burntwood	6	4	0	2	110	95	8
GEC	6	3	0	3	106	75	6
Rugeley	6	2	1	3	106	75	5
Trentham	6	1	0	5	61	105	2
Wedensbury	6	1	0	5	26	171	2

Staffordshire 2

	P	W	D	L	F	A	Pts
Rubery Owen	8	6	1	1	123	57	13
Linley	8	4	3	1	90	59	11
Wulfrun	8	5	0	3	88	75	10
Wheaton Aston	8	4	2	2	85	78	10
Michelin	8	3	2	3	81	81	8
Cannock	8	3	1	4	115	87	7
Sankey Vending	8	3	1	4	76	92	7
Cheadle	8	2	1	5	60	128	5
O Oaks	8	0	1	7	41	102	1

Warwickshire 1

	P	W	D	L	F	A	Pts
Broadstreet	10	9	0	1	261	74	18
Trinity Guild	10	9	0	1	168	120	18
Coventry Sar	10	5	1	4	111	92	11
Kenilworth	10	5	0	5	147	111	10
Spartans	10	4	2	4	93	161	10
Southam	10	4	1	5	106	125	9
Dunlop	10	4	0	6	124	88	8
Stoke OB	10	4	0	6	100	125	8
O Wheatlyans	10	4	0	6	95	160	8
O Coventrians	10	3	1	6	74	151	7
Manor Pk	10	1	1	8	95	167	3

Warwickshire 2

	P	W	D	L	F	A	Pts
GEC Coventry	9	9	0	0	275	39	18
O Laurentians	9	5	1	3	153	95	11
Rugby St Ands	9	5	1	3	118	122	11
Atherstone	9	5	0	4	141	88	10
Harbury	9	5	0	4	127	150	10
Coventrians	9	4	0	5	101	152	8
Earlsdon	8	3	0	5	94	99	6
Silhillians	9	3	0	6	70	125	6
O Warwickians	7	2	0	5	57	149	4
Berkswell & Bal	8	1	0	7	62	179	2

Warwickshire 3

	P	W	D	L	F	A	Pts
Rugby Welsh	9	7	1	1	185	73	15

Claverdon	9	6	1	2	138	82	13

Shipston-on-St	9	6	1	2	116	75	13
Pinley	9	5	1	3	116	79	11
Alcester	9	5	0	4	123	118	10
Warwick	9	3	3	3	107	96	9
Standard	9	4	0	5	123	108	8
Coventry PO	9	3	1	5	76	128	7
Shottery	9	1	0	8	73	127	2
Coventry Tech	9	1	0	8	39	210	2

SOUTH & SOUTH-WEST ZONE

South-West 1

	P	W	D	L	F	A	Pts
Maidenhead	10	8	0	2	251	132	16
Weston-s-Mare	10	8	0	2	186	133	16

Berry Hill	10	7	0	3	211	121	14
Brixham	10	7	0	3	132	105	14
High Wycombe	10	5	0	5	187	129	10
Matson	10	5	0	5	123	101	10
St Ives	10	5	0	5	151	154	10
Taunton	10	4	0	6	175	198	8
Reading	10	3	0	7	128	207	6
Stroud	10	2	0	8	88	272	4

Oxford	10	1	0	9	103	183	2

South-West 2

	P	W	D	L	F	A	Pts
Gordon League	10	10	0	0	236	86	20
Torquay	10	7	1	2	187	109	15

Redingensians	10	5	1	4	118	154	11
Cinderford	10	5	0	5	154	123	10
Barnstaple	10	5	0	5	120	104	10
Abbey	10	5	0	5	130	133	10
Banbury	10	4	1	5	106	165	9
Henley	10	4	0	6	132	189	8
Newbury	10	3	0	7	125	149	6
Bournemouth	10	3	0	7	111	171	6

Bridgwater	10	2	1	7	122	158	5

Western Counties

	P	W	D	L	F	A	Pts
Penryn	10	8	1	1	150	80	17

Avonmouth	10	8	0	2	162	96	16
Okehampton	10	7	0	3	152	58	14
Launceston	10	5	1	4	125	98	11
O Culverhays	10	5	1	4	155	130	11
Newquay Hornets	10	5	0	5	99	113	10
Clevedon	10	3	2	5	106	135	8
Truro	10	4	0	6	103	138	8
Tiverton	10	3	0	7	139	173	6

Cirencester	10	2	1	7	70	201	5
Dev & Corn Pol	10	2	0	8	123	162	4

Southern Counties

	P	W	D	L	F	A	Pts
Marlow	10	8	1	1	163	61	17

Swanage & War'm	10	8	0	2	230	72	16
Slough	10	8	0	2	171	85	16
Aylesbury	10	8	0	2	138	100	16
Wimborne	10	4	2	4	97	133	10
Bracknell	10	4	0	6	153	147	8
Chiltern	10	4	0	6	132	130	8
Swindon	10	4	0	6	127	167	8
Windsor	10	3	0	7	128	229	6
Bletchley	10	2	0	8	87	202	4

Oxford OB	10	0	1	9	88	188	1

Cornwall & Devon

	P	W	D	L	F	A	Pts
Penzance & N'lyn	10	9	0	1	256	96	18

Sidmouth	10	9	0	1	165	73	18
Devonport Servs	10	7	0	3	223	117	14
Plymouth CS	10	7	0	3	181	125	14
Crediton	10	5	1	4	184	139	11
Teignmouth	10	4	2	4	128	138	10
Bideford	10	4	0	6	163	123	8
Exeter Saracens	10	3	0	7	61	110	6
Illogan Pk	10	3	0	7	91	193	6

Falmouth	10	2	1	7	109	176	5
Wadebridge Cams	10	0	0	10	29	300	0

Cornwall 1

	P	W	D	L	F	A	Pts
Hayle	10	9	0	1	171	76	18

Liskeard/Looe	10	7	1	2	163	124	15
St Austell	10	6	2	2	110	76	14
Saltash	10	6	0	4	184	122	12
Stithians	10	5	1	4	93	92	11
Bodmin	10	4	2	4	112	104	10
Veor	10	5	0	5	119	116	10
Bude	10	3	1	6	116	117	7

Redruth Albany	10	2	1	7	112	157	5
Helston	10	2	1	7	91	141	5
St Just	10	0	3	7	80	226	3

Cornwall 2

	P	W	D	L	F	A	Pts
St Agnes	5	4	0	1	103	29	8
Roseland	5	4	0	1	66	37	8

St Day	5	4	0	1	43	18	8
Lankelly	5	2	0	3	59	70	6
Camborne SoM	5	1	0	4	39	108	2

| Redruth GSOB | 5 | 0 | 0 | 5 | 38 | 86 | 0 |

RAF St Mawgan withdrew. Their results and the walkovers awarded to Camborne and Redruth are void.

Devon 1

	P	W	D	L	F	A	Pts
Exmouth	10	10	0	0	252	70	20
Cullompton	10	8	0	2	209	104	16
South Molton	10	6	2	2	233	85	14
Ivybridge	10	5	1	4	180	123	11
Paignton	10	5	0	5	158	149	10
Topsham	10	5	0	5	130	217	10
Totnes	10	4	1	5	119	176	9
Newton Abbot	10	4	0	6	108	112	8
Old Technicians	10	4	0	6	68	118	8
Plymouth Argaum	10	1	2	7	87	179	4
Prince Rock	10	0	0	10	65	276	0

Devon 2A

	P	W	D	L	F	A	Pts
Jesters	9	9	0	0	164	35	18
OPO	9	8	0	1	140	59	16
OPM	9	7	0	2	150	72	14
Plymstock	9	6	0	3	128	101	12
DHSOB	9	4	0	5	123	117	8
Plympton	9	3	1	5	63	106	7
Victoria	9	2	1	6	58	86	5
St Columba	9	2	1	6	70	129	5
Plymouth YMCA	9	1	1	7	106	184	3
Tamar Saracens	9	1	0	8	28	141	2

Devon 2B

	P	W	D	L	F	A	Pts
Ilfracombe	7	5	1	1	145	46	11
Dartmouth	7	5	1	1	100	39	11
Kingsbridge	7	5	1	1	95	55	11
Withycombe	7	4	1	2	92	37	9
Honiton	7	3	0	4	89	89	6
Tavistock	7	3	0	4	53	108	6
North Tawton	7	1	0	6	36	120	2
Salcombe	7	0	0	7	59	175	0

Gloucestershire/Somerset

	P	W	D	L	F	A	Pts
Combe Down	9	8	0	1	223	80	16
Midsomer Norton	9	6	0	3	159	154	12
Spartans	9	5	0	4	133	111	10
Frome	8	5	0	3	119	100	10
Whitehall	9	4	0	5	107	93	8
Keynsham	9	4	0	5	146	139	8
Cleve	9	3	0	6	113	122	6
Coney Hill	8	3	0	5	104	158	6

| Drybrook | 9 | 3 | 0 | 6 | 130 | 194 | 6 |
| O Redcliffians | 9 | 3 | 0 | 6 | 119 | 202 | 6 |

Avon & Somerset Constabulary withdrew. Their results are void.

Gloucestershire 1

	P	W	D	L	F	A	Pts
Dings Crusaders	10	9	0	1	190	103	18
Gloucester OB	10	8	0	2	262	80	16
Cheltenham N	10	7	0	3	216	102	14
St Mary's OB	10	7	0	3	163	111	14
Saintbridge FP	10	5	1	4	146	151	11
Longlevens	10	5	1	4	95	126	11
O Patesians	10	4	0	6	140	173	8
North Bristol	10	3	1	6	127	172	7
Bream	10	2	1	7	112	215	5
Widden OB	10	1	2	7	85	182	4
Tredworth	10	1	0	9	86	207	2

Gloucestershire 2

	P	W	D	L	F	A	Pts
Brockworth	10	8	1	1	222	99	17
Ashley Down	10	8	0	2	169	58	16
Thornbury	10	8	0	2	213	129	16
Frampton Cott	10	6	0	4	140	91	12
O Cryptians	10	5	0	5	137	125	10
Cheltenham Sar	10	5	0	5	120	121	10
Cotham Park	10	4	1	5	148	179	9
Barton Hill	10	4	0	6	124	140	8
Bristol Sar	10	3	0	7	81	170	6
O Colstonians	10	3	0	7	77	178	6
O Bristolians	10	0	0	10	99	240	0

Gloucestershire 3

	P	W	D	L	F	A	Pts
Hucclecote	10	10	0	0	275	86	20
Chipping Sod	10	8	0	2	231	85	16
Cheltenham CS	10	6	0	4	152	123	12
Bristol Tele	9	5	1	3	133	79	11
Painswick	10	5	0	5	162	103	10
Dursley	10	5	0	5	156	159	10
Kingswood	10	5	0	5	123	173	10
O Elizabethans	10	4	1	5	140	153	9
Caincross	10	4	0	6	130	151	8
Smiths Indust	10	1	0	9	101	232	2
Tewkesbury	9	0	0	9	54	313	0

Gloucestershire 4A

	P	W	D	L	F	A	Pts
Old Richians	6	6	0	0	130	13	12

Chosen Hill	6	5	0	1	107	42	10
All Blues	6	4	0	2	101	44	8
Minchinhampton	6	3	0	3	82	70	6
Gloucester CS	6	2	0	4	72	109	4
Dowty	6	1	0	5	38	171	2
Newent	6	0	0	6	37	118	0

Gloucestershire 4B

	P	W	D	L	F	A	Pts
Bishopston	6	6	0	0	95	32	12
Bristol Aero	6	4	0	2	127	50	8
Southmead	6	4	0	2	116	58	8
Broadplain	6	4	0	2	102	77	8
Aretians	6	2	0	4	122	88	4
Tetbury	6	1	0	5	93	103	2
O Cothamians	6	0	0	6	28	275	0

Somerset 1

	P	W	D	L	F	A	Pts
Oldfield OB	10	9	1	0	214	97	19
Walcot OB	10	8	0	2	217	137	16
O Sulians	10	6	1	3	132	110	13
St Bern OB	10	6	0	4	140	90	12
Hornets	10	5	1	4	115	128	11
Bristol Harl	10	5	0	5	140	105	10
Yeovil	10	3	2	5	126	137	8
Yatton	10	4	0	6	115	129	8
Minehead	10	4	0	6	132	168	8
Gordano	10	1	1	8	100	192	3
Avonvale	10	1	0	9	72	210	2

Somerset 2

	P	W	D	L	F	A	Pts
Wiveliscombe	11	10	0	1	263	50	20
Imperial	11	8	0	3	143	85	16
Winscombe	11	6	1	4	128	130	13
Wells	11	6	0	5	126	115	12
Avon	11	6	0	5	138	154	12
Tor	11	6	0	5	101	133	12
Stothert & Pitt	11	5	1	5	92	92	11
Burnham-on-Sea	11	5	0	6	133	132	10
North Petherton	11	5	0	6	139	144	10
Crewkerne	11	4	0	7	166	157	8
Bath OE	11	2	0	9	73	183	4
St Brendans	11	2	0	9	62	189	4

Somerset 3A

	P	W	D	L	F	A	Pts
Blagdon	6	6	0	0	236	12	12
Backwell	6	5	0	1	176	63	10
O Ashtonians	6	4	0	2	100	121	8
Cheddar Valley	6	3	0	3	69	124	6

Bath Civil Serv	6	2	0	4	72	143	4
Chew Valley	6	1	0	5	45	133	2
South-West Gas	6	0	0	6	48	150	0

Somerset 3B

	P	W	D	L	F	A	Pts
Wellington	6	6	0	0	208	16	12
Chard	6	5	0	1	297	35	10
Westland	6	3	1	2	120	86	7
Aller	6	3	0	3	86	101	6
Morganians	6	2	1	3	81	140	5
Castle Cary	6	1	0	5	31	278	2
Wincanton	6	0	0	6	37	204	0

Berks, Dorset & Wilts 1

	P	W	D	L	F	A	Pts
Sherborne	10	10	0	0	355	59	20
Corsham	10	9	0	1	184	109	18
Dorchester	10	7	1	2	272	74	15
Weymouth	10	6	0	4	122	160	12
Chippenham	10	5	1	4	141	114	11
Devizes	10	5	1	4	126	123	11
Wootton Bassett	10	4	1	5	133	121	9
North Dorset	10	2	1	7	125	255	5
Puddletown	9	2	0	7	87	160	4
Aldermaston	10	1	1	8	76	166	3
REME Arborfield	9	0	0	9	36	316	0

Devizes were awarded 2 League points after REME failed to honour their fixture

Berks, Dorset & Wilts 2

	P	W	D	L	F	A	Pts
Melksham	10	9	1	0	251	53	19
Lytchet Minst	10	7	1	2	241	75	15
Trowbridge	10	7	0	3	152	124	14
Bradford-on-A	10	6	2	2	105	88	14
Swindon Coll	10	6	1	3	145	80	13
Marlborough	10	5	2	3	168	124	12
Westbury	10	4	0	6	156	102	8
Hungerford	10	3	0	7	102	203	6
Oakmedians	10	2	1	7	63	234	5
Supermarine	10	2	0	8	84	177	4
Poole	10	0	0	10	80	287	0

Berks, Dorset & Wilts 3E

	P	W	D	L	F	A	Pts
Minety	6	5	1	0	118	37	11
Tadley	6	4	1	1	77	40	9
Calne	6	3	1	2	76	70	7
Berkshire SH	6	3	0	3	85	66	6
Thatcham	6	2	2	2	69	85	6
Amesbury	6	1	1	4	50	84	3
Colerne	6	0	0	6	53	146	0

Berks, Dorset & Wilts 3W

	P	W	D	L	F	A	Pts
Dorset Inst	5	4	1	0	118	58	9
Warminster	5	3	0	2	85	54	6
Bridport	5	3	0	2	79	50	6
Blandford	5	2	1	2	71	56	5
Portcastrians	5	1	0	4	38	102	2
Plessey	5	1	0	4	47	118	2

Bucks & Oxon 1

	P	W	D	L	F	A	Pts
Grove	10	9	0	1	183	70	18
Littlemore	10	5	2	3	218	108	12
Olney	10	6	0	4	202	122	12
Chinnor	10	5	2	3	136	125	12
Pennanians	10	5	1	4	145	154	11
Milton Keynes	10	5	0	5	131	211	10
Beaconsfield	10	4	1	5	163	159	9

Drifters	10	4	1	5	98	161	9
Oxford Marathon	10	4	0	6	109	153	8
Bicester	10	1	3	6	106	163	5
Cholsey	10	2	0	8	106	171	4

Bucks & Oxon 2

	P	W	D	L	F	A	Pts
Wheatley	9	9	0	0	216	32	18
Didcot	9	7	0	2	235	78	14
Witney	9	6	1	2	192	68	13
Abingdon	9	5	2	2	171	60	12
Phoenix	9	5	1	3	155	97	11
Buckingham	9	4	1	4	148	133	9
Chesham	9	3	0	6	96	159	6
Gosford AB	9	2	1	6	91	188	5
Harwell	9	1	0	8	33	290	2
Chipping Norton	9	0	0	9	60	292	0

TOSHIBA COUNTY CHAMPIONSHIP 1989-90

7 April, Twickenham
Lancashire 32 (3G 2T 2PG)   **Middlesex 9** (1G 1PG)

Chris Jones   *The Standard*

This was the last time the Toshiba name would be attached to the competition and it proved that without Cornwall in the final you cannot expect a big crowd for county rugby's showpiece. Last season's final, between Cornwall and Durham, attracted a crowd of nearly 30,000. This time, only around 7,000 fans made their way to Twickenham and spread themselves either side of halfway. They witnessed the Dewi Morris hat-trick show as the England scrum-half was given a dream ride by a Lancashire pack made up of seven Orrell men, plus Sean Gallagher of Waterloo.

Middlesex reached Twickenham courtesy of the try rule after drawing 15-15 against Cornwall in Redruth, enabling Floyd Steadman, their captain, to mark his final county season in style. Unfortunately, Middlesex did not possess the forward strength to seriously threaten Lancashire and were unable to provide Steadman with a winning finale. The Middlesex game plan consisted of running whatever ball their pack could steal from the Orrell – sorry, Lancashire – men.

The game's pattern was set as early as the eighth minute when a Lancashire scrum on the Middlesex line ended with Morris darting over for the opening try. Robinson kicked a penalty for Middlesex only for Strett to reply with two for a Lancashire side which boasted ex-England captain Bill Beaumont as their chairman of selectors. This was Beaumont's first chance to savour rugby life again as he was formerly a 'banned' man. He had been reinstated as an amateur by the International Board and sat in the committee box instead of his normal place in the television commentary position.

Beaumont's men were only a point ahead at half-time, thanks to a high tackle on Robinson which earned a penalty try and gave Robinson a simple conversion. This situation did not last for long, and Morris and Brendan Hanavan went over for two tries each in a one-sided second half to clinch the trophy.

The county competition gained ADT security systems as a new sponsor, but also relinquished its independence to share the divisional competition dates in December 1990. Both will run at the same time, confirming the official downgrading of county rugby.

Many people with the interests of the competition itself at heart may have been dismayed at Cornwall's demise because their magnificent supporters had galvanised the whole affair when they descended on

147

Dewi Morris, Welsh-born but hero of Lancashire, twists over the line to score in the final despite the efforts of Adrian Thompson of Middlesex.

Twickenham for the previous final. As soon as Cornwall were knocked out the hopes for another bumper Twickenham crowd quickly receded. However, Middlesex were worthy semi-final winners in one sense – they adopted a bold approach and ran the ball straight back at Cornwall. They came through by scoring three tries to one in the drawn match, helped by notable performances from Thompson, the fly-half, and All Black prop Williams, who was having a season with London Welsh.

In the other semi-final at Orrell, the Coventry-based Warwickshire pack were outplayed by the Orrell-based Lancashire men. Lancashire were without Morris at scrum-half, but O'Toole was an able replacement and the perfect complement to his dynamic forwards. Hanavan and Heslop were dangerous on the wing and Hanavan's two tries, together with a penalty try and another by Manley, the outstanding Orrell flanker, kept Lancashire away and clear.

TEAMS IN THE FINAL

Lancashire (*Orrell unless stated*): S Langford; N Heslop, B Wellens (Liverpool St Helens), M Fielden (Fylde), B Hanavan (Fylde); M Strett, D Morris (Liverpool St Helens); M Hynes, N Hitchen, S Southern (*capt*), R Kimmins, D Cusani, S Gallagher (Waterloo), C Cusani, P Manley

Scorers *Tries:* Morris (3), Hanavan (2)   *Conversions:* Strett (2), Langford
Penalty Goals: Strett (2)
Middlesex: S Robinson (Saracens); M Wedderburn (Harlequins), G Leleu (London
Welsh), R A P Lozowski (Wasps), S Smith (Wasps); A Thompson (Harlequins),
F Steadman (Saracens) *(capt)*; G Holmes (Wasps), J McFarland (Saracens), P Curtis
(Harlequins), J Fowler (Richmond), S Dear (Rosslyn Park), C Sheasby (Harlequins),
L Adamson (Saracens), M Rigby (Wasps) *Replacement* M Hobley (Coventry) for Curtis
Scorers *Tries* penalty try   *Conversion:* Robinson   *Penalty Goal:* Robinson
Referee I Bullerwell (East Midlands)

TEAMS IN THE SEMI-FINALS

3 March, Redruth RFC
Cornwall 15 (1G 3PG)   **Middlesex 15** (1PG 3T)

Cornwall: C Alcock (Camborne & RN) *(capt)*; B Trevaskis (Bath), A Mead (Devon &
Cornwall Police), S Rogers (Camborne), D Weeks (Camborne); G Champion (Devon &
Cornwall Police), D Rule (Camborne); J May (Redruth), R G R Dawe (Bath), R Keast
(Redruth), M Haag (Bath), A Reed (Plymouth Albion), J Polglase (Camborne),
G Williams (Redruth), A Bick (Lydney)
Scorers *Try:* Haag   *Conversion:* Champion   *Penalty Goals:* Champion (3)
Middlesex: S Robinson (Saracens); M Wedderburn (Harlequins), A Thompson
(Harlequins), R A P Lozowski (Wasps), S Smith (Wasps); M Fletcher (Harlequins),
F Steadman (Saracens) *(capt)*; G Holmes (Wasps), J McFarland (Saracens), R Williams
(London Welsh), L Adamson (Saracens), S Dear (Rosslyn Park), P Lindley (Saracens),
C Sheasby (Harlequins), M Rigby (Wasps)
Scorers *Tries:* Lozowski, Wedderburn, Rigby   *Penalty Goal:* Fletcher
Referee E Morrison (Bristol)

3 March, Orrell RFC
Lancashire 26 (2G 2PG 2T)   **Warwickshire 14** (2PG 2T)

Lancashire *(Orrell unless stated)*: S Langford; B Hanavan (Fylde), B Wellens (Liverpool
St Helens), M Fielden (Fylde), N Heslop; M Strett, C O'Toole; M Hynes, N Hitchen,
S Southern *(capt)*, R Kimmins, D Cusani, S Gallagher (Waterloo), C Cusani, P Manley
Scorers *Tries:* penalty try, Hanavan (2), Manley   *Conversions:* Langford, Strett
Penalty Goals: Strett (2)
Warwickshire: *(Coventry unless stated)*: S Hall (Barker's Butts) *(capt)*; K Shaw (Barker's
Butts), R Massey (Nuneaton), A Warwood (Leicester), A Parton (Loughborough U);
G Mitchell, S Thomas; G Tregilgas, A Farrington, D Garforth (Nuneaton), P Bowman
(Rugby), S Smith, R Travers, G Robbins, P Thomas
Scorers *Tries:* Parton, Travers   *Penalty Goals:* S Thomas (2)
Referee A Spreadbury (Somerset)

DIVISIONAL ROUNDS

Northern Division

Cheshire	6	Cumbria	26
Northumberland	9	Lancashire	0
Yorkshire	29	Durham	16
Durham	9	Northumberland	9
Lancashire	49	Cumbria	0
Yorkshire	40	Cheshire	3

Cheshire	6	Northumberland	19
Durham	6	Lancashire	14
Yorkshire	25	Cumbria	19
Cheshire	7	Lancashire	47
Cumbria	32	Durham	21
Northumberland	10	Yorkshire	16
Cumbria	12	Northumberland	33
Durham	27	Cheshire	18
Lancashire	29	Yorkshire	13

	P	W	D	L	F	A	Pts
Lancashire	5	4	0	1	139	35	8
Yorkshire	5	4	0	1	123	77	8
Northumberland	5	3	1	1	80	43	7
Cumbria	5	2	0	3	89	134	4
Durham	5	1	1	3	79	102	3
Cheshire	5	0	0	5	40	159	0

Midlands Division (Group A)

Staffordshire	18	Leicestershire	9
Leicestershire	26	North Midlands	28
North Midlands	9	Staffordshire	12

	P	W	D	L	F	A	Pts
Staffordshire	2	2	0	0	30	18	4
North Midlands	2	1	0	1	37	38	2
Leicestershire	2	0	0	2	35	46	0

Midlands Division (Group B)

Notts, Lincs & Derbys	15	Warwickshire	13
Warwickshire	21	East Midlands	11
East Midlands	7	Notts, Lincs & Derbys	10

	P	W	D	L	F	A	Pts
Notts, Lincs & Derbys	2	2	0	0	25	20	4
Warwickshire	2	1	0	1	34	26	2
East Midlands	2	0	0	2	18	31	0

Play-off Matches

Semi-finals:

| Notts, Lincs & Derbys | 7 | North Midlands | 29 |
| Staffordshire | 19 | Warwickshire | 23 |

Divisional Final:

| North Midlands | 12 | Warwickshire | 29 |

London Division (Group A)

Middlesex	17	Hertfordshire	0
Hertfordshire	21	Middlesex	22
Kent	9	Hertfordshire	9

	P	W	D	L	F	A	Pts
Middlesex	2	2	0	0	39	21	4
Hertfordshire	2	0	1	1	30	31	1
Kent	2	0	1	1	9	26	1

London Division (Group B)

Surrey	7	Eastern Counties	19
Hampshire	13	Eastern Counties	4
Sussex	12	Surrey	28
Surrey	3	Hampshire	14
Eastern Counties	30	Sussex	6
Sussex	4	Hampshire	21

	P	W	D	L	F	A	Pts
Hampshire	3	3	0	0	48	11	6
Eastern Counties	3	2	0	1	53	26	4
Surrey	3	1	0	2	38	45	2
Sussex	3	0	0	3	22	79	0

Play-off:

| Middlesex | 16 | Hampshire | 13 |

South-Western Division
Division 1

Cornwall	6	Berkshire	6
Gloucestershire	22	Dorset & Wilts	8
Berkshire	14	Gloucestershire	9
Cornwall	53	Dorset & Wilts	6
Dorset & Wilts	18	Berkshire	15
Gloucestershire	22	Cornwall	47

	P	W	D	L	F	A	Pts
Cornwall	3	2	1	0	106	34	5
Berkshire	3	1	1	1	35	33	3
Gloucestershire	3	1	0	2	53	69	2
Dorset & Wilts	3	1	0	2	32	90	2

Division 2

Oxfordshire	7	Devon	18
Somerset	28	Buckinghamshire	14
Buckinghamshire	23	Oxfordshire	6
Devon	19	Somerset	10
Devon	10	Buckinghamshire	3
Oxfordshire	7	Somerset	16

	P	W	D	L	F	A	Pts
Devon	3	3	0	0	47	20	6
Somerset	3	2	0	1	54	40	4
Buckinghamshire	3	1	0	2	40	44	2
Oxfordshire	3	0	0	3	20	57	0

ENGLISH COUNTY CHAMPIONS 1889-1990

FIRST SYSTEM

1889 **Yorkshire**, undefeated, declared champions by RU (scored 18G 17T to 1G 3T)

1890 **Yorkshire**, undefeated, declared champions (scored 10G 16T to 2G 4T)

SECOND SYSTEM

1891	**Lancashire** champions.	Group Winners — Yorkshire, Surrey, Gloucestershire.
1892	**Yorkshire** champions.	Group winners — Lancashire, Kent, Midlands.
1893	**Yorkshire** champions.	Group Winners — Cumberland, Devon, Middlesex.
1894	**Yorkshire** champions.	Group Winners — Lancashire, Gloucestershire, Midlands.
1895	**Yorkshire** champions.	Group Winners — Cumberland, Devon, Midlands.

THIRD SYSTEM

	Champions	*Runners-up*	*Played at*
1896	**Yorkshire**	Surrey	Richmond
1897	**Kent**	Cumberland	Carlisle
1898	**Northumberland**	Midlands	Coventry
1899	**Devon**	Northumberland	Newcastle
1900	**Durham**	Devon	Exeter
1901	**Devon**	Durham	W Hartlepool
1902	**Durham**	Gloucestershire	Gloucester
1903	**Durham**	Kent	W Hartlepool
1904	**Kent**	Durham	Blackheath (2nd meeting)
1905	**Durham**	Middlesex	W Hartlepool
1906	**Devon**	Durham	Exeter
1907	**Devon** and **Durham** joint champions after drawn games at W Hartlepool and Exeter		
1908	**Cornwall**	Durham	Redruth
1909	**Durham**	Cornwall	W Hartlepool
1910	**Gloucestershire**	Yorkshire	Gloucester
1911	**Devon**	Yorkshire	Headingley
1912	**Devon**	Northumberland	Devonport
1913	**Gloucestershire**	Cumberland	Carlisle
1914	**Midlands**	Durham	Leicester
1920	**Gloucestershire**	Yorkshire	Bradford

FOURTH SYSTEM

	Champions	*Runners-up*	*Played at*
1921	**Gloucestershire (31)**	Leicestershire (4)	Gloucester
1922	**Gloucestershire (19)**	N Midlands (0)	Birmingham
1923	**Somerset (8)**	Leicester (6)	Bridgwater
1924	**Cumberland (14)**	Kent (3)	Carlisle
1925	**Leicestershire (14)**	Gloucestershire (6)	Bristol
1926	**Yorkshire (15)**	Hampshire (14)	Bradford
1927	**Kent (22)**	Leicestershire (12)	Blackheath
1928	**Yorkshire (12)**	Cornwall (8)	Bradford
1929	***Middlesex (9)**	Lancashire (8)	Blundellsands
1930	**Gloucestershire (13)**	Lancashire (7)	Blundellsands
1931	**Gloucestershire (10)**	Warwickshire (9)	Gloucester
1932	**Gloucestershire (9)**	Durham (3)	Blaydon
1933	**Hampshire (18)**	Lancashire (7)	Boscombe
1934	**E Midlands (10)**	Gloucestershire (0)	Northampton
1935	**Lancashire (14)**	Somerset (0)	Bath

1936	Hampshire (13)	Northumberland (6)	Gosforth
1937	Gloucestershire (5)	E Midlands (0)	Bristol
1938	Lancashire (24)	Surrey (12)	Blundellsands
1939	Warwickshire (8)	Somerset (3)	Weston
1947	†Lancashire (14)	Gloucestershire (3)	Gloucester
1948	Lancashire (5)	E Counties (0)	Cambridge
1949	Lancashire (9)	Gloucestershire (3)	Blundellsands
1950	Cheshire (5)	E Midlands (0)	Birkenhead Park
1951	E Midlands (10)	Middlesex (0)	Northampton
1952	Middlesex (9)	Lancashire (6)	Twickenham
1953	Yorkshire (11)	E Midlands (3)	Bradford
1954	Middlesex (24)	Lancashire (6)	Blundellsands
1955	Lancashire (14)	Middlesex (8)	Twickenham
1956	Middlesex (13)	Devon (9)	Twickenham
1957	Devon (12)	Yorkshire (3)	Plymouth
1958	Warwickshire (16)	Cornwall (8)	Coventry
1959	Warwickshire (14)	Gloucestershire (9)	Bristol
1960	Warwickshire (9)	Surrey (6)	Coventry
1961	oCheshire (5)	Devon (3)	Birkenhead Park
1962	Warwickshire (11)	Hampshire (6)	Twickenham
1963	Warwickshire (13)	Yorkshire (10)	Coventry
1964	Warwickshire (8)	Lancashire (6)	Coventry
1965	Warwickshire (15)	Durham (9)	Hartlepool
1966	Middlesex (6)	Lancashire (0)	Blundellsands
1967	*Surrey and Durham		
1968	Middlesex (9)	Warwickshire (6)	Twickenham
1969	Lancashire (11)	Cornwall (9)	Redruth
1970	Staffordshire (11)	Gloucestershire (9)	Burton-on-Trent
1971	Surrey (14)	Gloucestershire (3)	Gloucester
1972	Gloucestershire (11)	Warwickshire (6)	Coventry
1973	Lancashire (17)	Gloucestershire (12)	Bristol
1974	Gloucestershire (22)	Lancashire (12)	Blundellsands
1975	Gloucestershire (13)	E Counties (9)	Gloucester
1976	Gloucester (24)	Middlesex (9)	Richmond
1977	Lancashire (17)	Middlesex (6)	Blundellsands
1978	N Midlands (10)	Gloucestershire (7)	Moseley
1979	Middlesex (19)	Northumberland (6)	Twickenham
1980	Lancashire (21)	Gloucestershire (15)	Vale of Lune
1981	Northumberland (15)	Gloucestershire (6)	Gloucester
1982	Lancashire (7)	North Midlands (3)	Moseley

FIFTH SYSTEM

	Champions	Runners-up	Played at
1983	Gloucestershire (19)	Yorkshire (7)	Bristol
1984	Gloucestershire (36)	Somerset (18)	Twickenham
1985	Middlesex (12)	Notts, Lincs and Derbys (9)	Twickenham

SIXTH SYSTEM

1986	Warwickshire (16)	Kent (6)	Twickenham
1987	Yorkshire (22)	Middlesex (11)	Twickenham
1988	Lancashire (23)	Warwickshire (18)	Twickenham
1989	Durham (13)	Cornwall (9)	Twickenham
1990	Lancashire (32)	Middlesex (9)	Twickenham

*After a draw at Twickenham.   †After a draw, 8-8, at Blundellsands.   oAfter a draw 0-0, at Plymouth.
**Surrey and Durham drew 14 each at Twickenham and no score at Hartlepool and thus became joint champions. Gloucestershire have won the title 15 times, Lancashire 14, Yorkshire 12, Warwickshire 9, Middlesex 8, Durham 8 (twice jointly), Devon 7 (once jointly), Kent 3 times, Hampshire, East Midlands, Cheshire and Northumberland twice each, Surrey twice (once jointly), and Cornwall, Midlands (3rd System), Somerset, Cumberland, Leicestershire, Staffordshire and North Midlands once each.*

THE BARBARIANS 1989-90

Geoffrey Windsor-Lewis

The Barbarians played their first match on 27 December 1890 against Hartlepool Rovers, and they played Cardiff for the first time at Easter 1891. From the first match the club has always maintained the belief held by Percy Carpmael, the founder, that rugby should be played as an attacking game. Season 1990-91 will celebrated as the club's centenary and the old principles will be firmly adhered to. It promises to be the most exciting season in the history of the club.

The celebrations begin with two mouth-watering games – the Barbarians play England at Twickenham on 29 September and a week later meet Wales at the National Stadium. The matches will be as important to the home sides as they are to the Barbarians. There will be a return to Cardiff in November for the Barbarians match against Argentina, who will also be touring in England, Scotland and Ireland. Scotland join the celebrations in September 1991 when the Barbarians visit Murrayfield. Ireland's turn comes soon after with a short tour to the country, during which the club will meet Cork Constitution and Old Wesley, two teams also celebrating centenaries.

The keynote event off the field is the Centenary Dinner, to be held in London on the night prior to the England match. All old Barbarians will be invited for what will be a massive reunion. The old Barbarians will find a departure from tradition – the centenary year sees the start of a sponsorship agreement between the club and Scottish Amicable. Initially, the agreement will run for three years and provides a marvellous opportunity for both parties. The club president, Mickey Steele-Bodger, who played a major role in negotiations, was recently made a CBE for services to rugby.

The centrepiece of the 99th season was the match against the touring All Blacks and, appropriately, Twickenham was packed for the occasion. The 10-21 defeat did not represent the efforts of the Barbarians, because they trailed by only two points with five minutes remaining. However, the superior team-work of the touring side saw them through and maintained their unblemished record for the tour. Yet, for the first time, the All Blacks were matched at forward – Paul Ackford, Wade Dooley, Phil Matthews and David Sole, the captain, played superbly. It was Matthews who gave his side the lead, charging round the front of the line-out to score after Ackford had won the ball. David Young was hauled down inches short soon afterwards, just when a second try seemed certain. It was 10-6 to the Barbarians at half-time. In the second half the All Blacks scored three tries, all from scrums close to the Barbarians line. Craig Innes, bursting in from the blind-side wing, scored one try and set up another for Richard Loe, the prop. Zinzan Brooke was the other try-scorer.

Gavin Hastings of the Barbarians and Craig Innes of New Zealand contest the ball in the final match of the New Zealand tour when the Barbarians, until a typical New Zealand last-quarter charge, were well in the running.

The October trip to Newport, which began the season, brought a comfortable win for a strong Barbarian team. There were seven tries, six of them converted by Craig Chalmers, the Scottish fly-half. Jeremy Guscott initiated some superb attacking movements against a brave and competitive home team.

The Barbarians were on the receiving end of some brilliant attacking when they met Leicester at Welford Road amid the traditional electric atmosphere and sell-out crowd. The Tigers' forwards were inspired and Barry Evans and Rory Underwood were at their most sharp on the Leicester wings. It was 22-0 to Leicester by half-time, and although the final score was a slightly more respectable 32-16 there was to be no comeback for the Barbarians. It was Les Cusworth's last appearance in the fixture. Cusworth, a loyal Barbarian, has done so much to raise the pulse of the annual Christmas holiday fixture. He is warmly remembered by the Barbarians, especially for the try he scored to clinch the Hong Kong Sevens title for the Barbarians in 1980.

It was Cusworth who pulled the Barbarians round when they trailed 4-18 to an inspired East Midlands team in the Mobbs Memorial match at Northampton before a capacity crowd. Cusworth's half-time talk had the desired effect. He demanded that every ball should be run and the Barbarians scored four tries in the first eight minutes of the second half. Some sharp play at scrum-half from Floyd Steadman helped to carve out the gaps and in the end, a 40-18 win banished memories of the half-time deficit. Irish full-back Kenny Murphy followed his grand-

155

father and father into Barbarian colours, an achievement which gave the club great delight.

More history was made for the Easter visit to South Wales in that two Soviets, Igor Mironov and Alexander Tikhonov, were chosen. Mironov, the Soviet captain and centre and Tikhonov, the big forward, were popular members of the party. Cardiff defeated the Barbarians while the tourists managed to repeat their 1989 victory over Swansea at St Helens. The Barbarians led Cardiff at half-time and it was only towards the end, when Stone of Cardiff scored an interception try from a desperate Barbarian attack, that Cardiff could be sure of victory. At Swansea, the Barbarians held off a powerful Swansea rally for a well-deserved victory.

The Barbarians were delighted to be able to accept an invitation to the Hong Kong Sevens, a remarkable tournament which continues to grow in appeal to players and spectators every year. The problem for the teams from the United Kingdom is that the International Championship finishes only a short time before, preventing any worthwhile practice. The Barbarians improved with every game, beating West Germany and Canada in their pool and overcoming Western Samoa in the quarter-final. In the semi-final they met New Zealand. They were unlucky to be only level at half-time and in the second half the power of the All Blacks told. So the New Zealanders went through to the final, only to be defeated by the inspired Fijians. This final will never be forgotten by those present: it produced rugby of the highest standard. The awesome physical presence of the Fijians, allied to brilliance in attack and speed into the tackle, earned them the title.

RESULTS 1989-90

Played 6   Won 3   Lost 3   Points for 143   (15G 3PG 11T)   **Points against 125** (14G 6PG 1DG 5T)
1989

10 Oct	**Beat Newport** at Rodney Parade, Newport 40 (6G 1T) to 13 (1G 1PG 1T)
25 Nov	**Lost to New Zealand** at Twickenham 10 (2PG 1T) to 21 (3G 1PG)
27 Dec	**Lost to Leicester** at Welford Road 16 (2G 1T) to 32 (3G 2PG 2T)
1990	
7 Mar	**Beat East Midlands** at Franklin Gardens 40 (4G 4T) to 18 (3G)
14 Apr	**Lost to Cardiff** at Cardiff Arms Park 13 (1G 1PG 1T) to 22 (2G 1PG 1DG 1T)
16 Apr	**Beat Swansea** at St Helens, Swansea 24 (2G 3T) to 19 (2G 1PG 1T)

31 Mar-1 Apr   **Cathay Pacific-Hong Kong Bank Invitation Sevens**
Pool D: Barbarians 24, West Germany 0; Barbarians 26, Canada 6
Quarter-final: Barbarians 18, Western Samoa 10
Semi-final: Barbarians 6, New Zealand 24

PLAYERS 1989-90

Abbreviations *N* – Newport; *NZ* – New Zealand; *L* – Leicester; *EM* – East Midlands;
HK – Hong Kong Sevens; *SW1* – Cardiff; *SW2* – Swansea; (R) – Replacement; * – New
Barbarian

Full-backs: P W Dods (Gala & Scotland) [*N*]; A G Hastings (London Scottish &
Scotland) [*NZ*]; J M Webb (Bristol & England) [*L*]; * K J Murphy (Cork Const &
Ireland) [*EM, SW1, SW2 on wing*]; * I Mironov (Gagarin Academy & Soviet Union)
[*SW1, SW2 at centre*]

Threequarters: M R Hall (Bridgend & Wales) [*N*]; B J Mullin (London Irish & Ireland)
[*N, NZ*(R)]; J C Guscott (Bath & England) [*N, NZ, HK*]; W L Renwick (London
Scottish) [*N*]; R Underwood (RAF, Leicester & England) [*NZ*]; S Hastings (Watsonians
& Scotland) [*NZ*]; * T Underwood (Leicester) [*NZ, EM*]; D I Campese (Milan &
Australia) [*L*]; S J Halliday (Bath & England) [*L*]; W D C Carling (Harlequins &
England) [*L, HK*]; S T Smith (Wasps & England) [*L*]; S T Hackney (Nottingham) [*EM,
SW2*]; * S Davies (Llanelli) [*EM*]; * S A Parfitt (Swansea) [*EM, SW1*]; B J Evans
(Leicester) [*HK, SW1*]; * E Davis (Harlequins) [*SW1*]; R A Bidgood (Pontypool)
[*SW2*]; * R A P Lozowski (Wasps & England) [*SW2*]

Half-backs: C M Chalmers (Melrose & Scotland) [*N, NZ*]; * G Armstrong (Jedforest &
Scotland) [*N*]; * N C Farr-Jones (New South Wales & Australia) [*NZ*]; * A Davies
(Cambridge University) [*L*]; C R Andrew (Wasps & England) [*HK*]; L F P Aherne
(Lansdowne & Ireland) [*L*]; L Cusworth (Leicester & England) [*EM*]; * F A Steadman
(Saracens) [*EM*]; * A Thompson (Harlequins) [*SW1, SW2*]; S M Bates (Wasps) [*SW1*];
R H Q B Moon (Rosslyn Park) [*HK*]; * C Bridges (Neath) [*SW1*(R), SW2]

Forwards: N Popplewell (Greystones) [*N*]; P John (Pontypridd) [*N*]; D C Fitzgerald
(Lansdowne & Ireland) [*N*]; N G B Edwards (Harlequins) [*N, EM*]; * J Morrison (Bath)
[*N*]; D F Pickering (Neath & Wales) [*N*]; O Williams (Bridgend) [*N*]; G J Roberts
(Llanelli & Wales) [*N*]; D M B Sole (Edinburgh Acads & Scotland) [*NZ*]; B C Moore
(Nottingham & England) [*NZ, HK*]; D Young (Cardiff & Wales) [*NZ*]; P J Ackford
(Harlequins & England) [*NZ*]; W A Dooley (Preston Grasshoppers & England) [*NZ*];
P M Matthews (Dublin Wanderers & Ireland) [*NZ*]; P T Davies (Llanelli & Wales)
[*NZ*]; G W Rees (Nottingham & England) [*NZ*]; * A Mullins (Harlequins) [*L*]; J Olver
(Harlequins) [*L*]; * M Linnett (Moseley & England) [*L*]; R Kimmins (Orrell) [*L, SW1*];
* Gareth Llewellyn (Neath & Wales) [*L*]; G Jones (Llanelli & Wales) [*L*]; N P Mannion
(Corinthians & Ireland) [*L*]; R A Robinson (Bath & England) [*L*]; M Howe (Bedford)
[*L*(R)]; M Griffiths (Cardiff & Wales) [*EM*]; * K Gregory (Newport) [*EM*];
* A P Burnell (London Scottish & Scotland) [*EM, SW2*]; * N Francis (Blackrock
College & Ireland) [*EM, SW2*]; * G George (Newport) [*EM*]; * S Povoas (Leicester)
[*EM*]; * I R Smith (Leicester) [*EM*]; * H Roberts (Richmond) [*EM*(R), SW1, SW2];
* C M A Sheasby (Harlequins) [*HK*]; M G Skinner (Harlequins & England) [*HK, SW1,
SW2*(R)]; P J Winterbottom (Harlequins & England) [*HK*]; J A Probyn (Wasps &
England) [*SW1*]; * W James (Swansea) [*SW1*(R)]; * B R Williams (Neath & Wales)
[*SW1, SW2*]; * A Tikhonov (Gagarin Academy & Soviet Union) [*SW1, SW2*];
M C Teague (Gloucester & England) [*SW1*]; * D J Pegler (Wasps) [*SW1*]; * A Allen
(Newbridge & Wales) [*SW2*]; * D S Munro (Glasgow High/Kelvinside) [*SW2*];
* K P Rafferty (Heriot's FP) [*SW2*]; * S D Holmes (Cambridge University) [*SW1*]

HOMESPUN CAMBRIDGE TRIUMPHANT
THE VARSITY MATCH 1989
(for the Bowring Bowl)

12 December, Twickenham
Cambridge University 22 (2G 2PG 1T)
Oxford University 13 (1G 1PG 1T)

There was some disquiet among neutrals and even some old Oxford blues at the cosmopolitan nature of the Oxford side. The criticisms were refuted by Brian Smith, Oxford's Australian captain who plays for Ireland. For whatever reasons, however, Oxford simply did not blend on the day; they were unsure of themselves and made many errors. Cambridge, more homespun in the make-up of their side and more calculating and organised, came through strongly to win. They gave a powerful performance in the first half and led by 15-0; they held on in the second half after Oxford came storming back to 15-13. Buzza, at full-back, gave a commanding display and his leadership ushered Cambridge on their way, although they owed their win in good part to the unwitting charity of the opposition.

The Oxford pack played powerfully after a slow start but outside the Dark Blues struggled and Kent Bray, the full-back, had an eminently forgettable day as lack of match fitness obscured his talents. Furthermore, much of the Oxford strategy was based on Smith himself, and under the pressure of the occasion he was not at his considerable best.

Graham Davies, the Cambridge left wing, opened the scoring with a try converted by Adrian, his brother; Simms, in the Cambridge centre, sprinted off for a try, seizing the ball after an ambitious miss-move in the Oxford midfield had gone disastrously wrong. Adrian Davies converted for the 15-0 lead as Oxford floundered. Yet they dragged themselves back with a try by Hein, the American wing, on the stroke of half-time; then another storming Oxford movement launched Hein over for his second after the break. Smith kicked a splendid goal and added a penalty, and even though Adrian Davies kicked his second penalty to take the score to 18-13 Oxford continued to hammer away, with Egan in the back row particularly prominent.

Yet Jones, the Oxford prop, conceded a needless penalty near the Cambridge line. Cambridge lifted the siege, and at the other end a mistake by Bray let Adrian Davies in for the clinching try. It sealed a match which provided real spectacle for another huge attendance, even though hair-raising mistakes played a large part in the entertainment.

Cambridge University: A J Buzza (Redruth CS & Hughes Hall) *(capt)*; D S Bell (Edinburgh Academy & Clare), N J Simms (West Park & Robinson), P G Reed (Oundle & Magdalene), G Davies (Pencoed CS & Magdalene); A Davies (Pencoed CS & Robinson),

Graham Davies of Cambridge turns for home and an early try in the Varsity match.

A H Booth (Bishop Gore & Hughes Hall); J Foster (Magdalen Coll S & Robinson),
J Ashworth (George Fox, Lancaster & Homerton), S A Wordley (Queen Mary's CS,
Walsall & Downing), A Macdonald (Gordonstoun & Hughes Hall), J J O'Callaghan
(Gonzaga Coll & Sidney Sussex), R J Pool-Jones (King's, Macclesfield & Magdalene),
J B Wilby (QEGS Wakefield & St Edmund's), S D Holmes (Cockermouth GS &
St Edmund's)
Scorers *Tries:* G Davies, A Davies, Simms *Conversions:* A Davies (2)
Penalty Goals: A Davies (2)
Oxford University: K A Bray (Rockhampton GS, Queensland & Mansfield); G M Hein
(Tait HS, USA & St Anne's), D M Curtis (Falcon Coll, Zimbabwe & St Anne's),
J R Elliott (Ampleforth Coll & St Anne's), D J Cook (St John's, Leatherhead & Christ
Church); B A Smith (Brisbane State & St Anne's) *(capt),* S Taylor (Whitgift & University);
A M Jones (Brisbane State & St Anne's), E R Norwitz (SA Collegiate & University),
D W James (Highland HS, USA & St Anne's), T Coker (St Paul's, Brisbane & Lady
Margaret Hall), J C Fewtrell (Knox GS, Sydney & St Anne's), R Horrocks-Taylor
(Bradford GS & St Peter's), W M van der Merwe (Grey Coll, Bloemfontein & St Anne's),
M S Egan (Terenure Coll, Dublin & St Anne's)
Scorers *Tries:* Hein (2) *Conversion:* Smith *Penalty Goal:* Smith
Referee C Norling (Welsh RU)

7 December, Iffley Road
Oxford University Greyhounds 7 (1PG 1T)
Cambridge University LX Club 18 (2G 1PG 1DG)

Oxford University Greyhounds: M Oliver (Ruskin); S Okoli (Worcester), G Atchison (Balliol), I Richards (Wadham),
J Watson (St John's); E C Egan (Jesus) *(capt),* G Fell (Balliol); A Orr (Balliol), M R Humphreys (Brasenose), S Whiteside
(Queen's), D Wood (St Catherine's), J Murphy-O'Connor (Greyfriars), L Jones (St Edmund Hall), M Reader (University),
M Merrick (Christ Church) *Replacements* N Fitzwater (Keble) for Oliver; N George (Exeter) for Okoli; G Stevens
(Greyfriars) for Atchison
Scorers *Try:* Watson *Penalty Goal:* Oliver
Cambridge University LX Club: A J Tunningley (Downing); R Given (Jesus), D Wooler (St Catharine's), D Mallalieu
(Hughes Hall), D Macrae (St Catharine's); D Shufflebotham (Magdalene), S James (Hughes Hall); J Tarrant
(St Edmund's), L M Mair (Gonville & Caius), D Meirion-Jones (Magdalene), C Thomas (Hughes Hall), A Robertson
(Magdalene) *(capt),* R Jenkins (Downing), N Allen (St John's), P Davis (Churchill)
Scorers *Tries:* Shufflebotham, Macrae *Conversions:* Mallalieu (2) *Penalty Goal:* Mallalieu
Dropped Goal: Shufflebotham
Referee G Norris (Gloucester)

13 December, Stoop Memorial Ground
Oxford University Under-21 3 (1DG)
Cambridge University Under-21 16 (2G 1T)

Oxford University Under-21: W Fitzwater (Keble); S Okoli (Worcester), N George (Exeter), G Atchison (Balliol),
R Sennitt (St Edmund Hall); E C Egan (Jesus) *(capt),* G D Stevens (Greyfriars); D Thomson (Oriel), M R Humphreys
(Brasenose), S Whiteside (Queen's), J Murphy-O'Connor (Greyfriars), O Davies (Pembroke), L Jones (St Edmund Hall),
A J Boag (St Edmund Hall), M Merrick (Christ Church) *Replacement* J Cale (Balliol) for Okoli
Scorer *Dropped Goal:* Egan
Cambridge University Under-21: S Burns (Magdalene); R Given (Jesus), S Brammar (Emmanuel), D Macrae
(St Catharine's), L Medlock (Robinson); S Johnson (Magdalene), R Heap (Magdalene) *(capt);* R Brown (Pembroke),
A Kennedy (Pembroke), M Chapple (Trinity), M Duthie (Queens), B Gibson (Churchill), P Davis (Churchill), N Allen
(St John's), R Jenkins (Downing) *Replacements* M Jordan (Robinson) for Macrae; M Horn (Trinity Hall) for Kennedy
Scorers *Tries:* Gibson (2), Given *Conversions:* Johnson (2)
Referee E Morrison (Bristol)

Cambridge University 22, M R Steele-Bodger's XV 14; Oxford University 18, Major R V Stanley's XV 33

VARSITY MATCH RESULTS

108 Matches played   Oxford 46 wins   Cambridge 49 wins   13 Draws

*Match played at Oxford 1871-72; Cambridge 1872-73; The Oval 1873-74 to 1879-80; Blackheath 1880-81 to 1886-87; Queen's Club 1887-88 to 1920-21; then Twickenham.   *At this date no match could be won unless a goal was scored.*

1871-72	Oxford	1G 1T to 0
1872-73	Cambridge	1G 2T to 0
1873-74	Drawn	1T each
1874-75*	Drawn	Oxford 2T to 0
1875-76	Oxford	1T to 0
1876-77	Cambridge	1G 2T to 0
1877-78	Oxford	2T to 0
1878-79	Drawn	No score
1879-80	Cambridge	1G 1DG to 1DG
1880-81	Drawn	1T each
1881-82	Oxford	2G 1T to 1G
1882-83	Oxford	1T to 0
1883-84	Oxford	3G 4T to 1G
1884-85	Oxford	3G 1T to 1T
1885-86	Cambridge	2T to 0
1886-87	Cambridge	3T to 0
1887-88	Cambridge	1DG 2T to 0
1888-89	Cambridge	1G 1T to 0
1889-90	Oxford	1G 1T to 0
1890-91	Drawn	1G each
1891-92	Cambridge	2T to 0
1892-93	Drawn	No score
1893-94	Oxford	1T to 0
1894-95	Drawn	1G each
1895-96	Cambridge	1G to 0
1896-97	Oxford	1G 1DG to 1G 1T
1897-98	Oxford	2T to 0
1898-99	Cambridge	1G 2T to 0
1899-1900	Cambridge	2G 4T to 0
1900-01	Oxford	2G to 1G 1T
1901-02	Oxford	1G 1T to 0
1902-03	Drawn	1G 1T each
1903-04	Oxford	3G 1T to 2G 1T
1904-05	Cambridge	3G to 2G
1905-06	Cambridge	3G (15) to 2G 1T (13)
1906-07	Oxford	4T (12) to 1G 1T (8)
1907-08	Oxford	1G 4T (17) to 0
1908-09	Oxford	1G (5) each
1909-10	Oxford	4G 5T (35) to 1T (3)
1910-11	Oxford	4G 1T (23) to 3G 1T (18)
1911-12	Oxford	2G 3T (19) to 0
1912-13	Cambridge	2G (10) to 1T (3)
1913-14	Cambridge	1DG 3T (13) to 1T (3)
1914-18	*No matches*	
1919-20	Cambridge	1PG 1DG (7) to 1G (5)
1920-21	Oxford	1G 4T (17) to 1G 3T (14)
1921-22	Oxford	1G 2T (11) to 1G (5)
1922-23	Cambridge	3G 2T (21) to 1G 1T (8)
1923-24	Oxford	3G 2T (21) to 1G 1PG 2T (14)
1924-25	Oxford	1G 2T (11) to 2T (6)
1925-26	Cambridge	3G 6T (33) to 1T (3)
1926-27	Cambridge	3G 5T (30) to 1G (5)
1927-28	Cambridge	2G 2PG 2T (22) to 1G 3T (14)
1928-29	Cambridge	1G 3T (14) to 1PG 1DG 1T (10)
1929-30	Oxford	1G 1DG (9) to 0
1930-31	Drawn	Oxford 1PG (3) Cambridge 1T (3)
1931-32	Oxford	1DG 2T (10) to 1T (3)
1932-33	Oxford	1G 1T (8) to 1T (3)
1933-34	Oxford	1G (5) to 1T (3)
1934-35	Cambridge	2G 1PG 1DG 4T (29) to 1DG (4)
1935-36	Drawn	No score
1936-37	Cambridge	2T (6) to 1G (5)
1937-38	Oxford	1G 4T (17) to 1DG (4)
1938-39	Cambridge	1G 1PG (8) to 2PG (6)
1939-45	*War-time series*	
1945-46	Cambridge	1G 2T (11) to 1G 1PG (8)
1946-47	Oxford	1G 1DG 2T (15) to 1G (5)
1947-48	Cambridge	2PG (6) to 0
1948-49	Oxford	1G 1DG 2T (14) to 1G 1PG (8)
1949-50	Oxford	1T (3) to 0
1950-51	Oxford	1G 1PG (8) to 0
1951-52	Oxford	2G 1T (13) to 0
1952-53	Cambridge	1PG 1T (6) to 1G (5)
1953-54	Drawn	Oxford 1PG 1T (6) Cambridge 2PG (6)
1954-55	Cambridge	1PG (3) to 0
1955-56	Oxford	1PG 2T (9) to 1G (5)
1956-57	Cambridge	1G 1PG 1DG 1T (14) to 2PG 1T (9)
1957-58	Oxford	1T (3) to 0
1958-59	Cambridge	1G 1PG 3T (17) to 1PG 1T (6)
1959-60	Oxford	3PG (9) to 1PG (3)
1960-61	Cambridge	2G 1T (13) to 0
1961-62	Cambridge	1DG 2T (9) to 1DG (3)
1962-63	Cambridge	1G 1PG 1DG 1T (14) to 1G 1PG 1DG (11)
1963-64	Cambridge	2G 1PG 2T (19) to 1G 1PG 1DG (11)
1964-65	Oxford	2G 1PG 2T (19) to 1PG 1GM (6)
1965-66	Drawn	1G each
1966-67	Oxford	1G 1T (8) to 1DG 1T (6)
1967-68	Cambridge	1T 1PG (6) to 0
1968-69	Cambridge	1T 1PG 1DG (9) to 2T (6)
1969-70	Oxford	3PG (9) to 2PG (6)
1970-71	Oxford	1G 1DG 2T (14) to 1PG (3)
1971-72	Oxford	3PG 3T (21) to 1PG (3)
1972-73	Cambridge	1G 1PG 1DG 1T (16) to 2PG (6)
1973-74	Cambridge	1PG 1DG 2T (14) to 1G 2PG (12)
1974-75	Cambridge	1G 2PG 1T (16) to 5PG (15)
1975-76	Cambridge	2G 5PG 1DG 1T (34) to 3PG 1DG (12)
1976-77	Cambridge	1G 3PG (15) to 0
1977-78	Oxford	4PG 1T (16) to 2PG 1T (10)
1978-79	Cambridge	2G 3PG 1T (25) to 1PG 1T (7)
1979-80	Oxford	2PG 1DG (9) to 1PG (3)
1980-81	Cambridge	3PG 1T (13) to 3PG (9)
1981-82	Cambridge	3PG (9) to 2PG (6)
1982-83	Cambridge	3PG 1DG 2T (20) to 1G 1PG 1T (13)
1983-84	Cambridge	4PG 2T (20) to 3PG (9)
1984-85	Cambridge	4G 2T (32) to 1PG 1T (7)
1985-86	Oxford	1PG 1T (7) to 2PG (6)
1986-87	Oxford	3PG 2DG (15) to 1PG 1DG 1T (10)
1987-88	Cambridge	1DG 3T (15) to 2PG 1T (10)
1988-89	Oxford	2G 1DG 3T (27) to 1DG 1T (7)
1989-90	Cambridge	2G 2PG 1T (22) to 1G 1PG 1T (13)

THE WAR-TIME MATCHES

1939-40	Oxford	1G 1DG 2T (15) to 1T (3) (at Cambridge)		Cambridge	1G 3T (14) to 2G 1T (13) (at Oxford)
1940-41	Cambridge	1G 2T (11) to 1G 1DG (9) (at Oxford)		Cambridge	2G 2T (16) to 1T (3) (at Cambridge)
	Cambridge	2G 1T (13) to 0 (at Cambridge)	1943-44	Cambridge	2G 1T (13) to 1DG (4) (at Cambridge)
1941-42	Cambridge	1PG 2T (9) to 1PG 1T (6) (at Cambridge)		Oxford	2T (6) to 1G (5) (at Oxford)
	Cambridge	1G 2PG 2T (17) 1G 1T (8) (at Oxford)	1944-45	Drawn	1T (3) each (at Oxford)
1942-43	Cambridge	1G 1DG (9) to 0 (at Oxford)		Cambridge	2G 2T (16) to DG (4) (at Cambridge)

OXFORD and CAMBRIDGE BLUES 1872-1989

(Each year indicates a separate appearance, and refers to the first half of the season. Thus 1879 refers to the match played in the 1879-80 season). (R) indicates an appearance as a Replacement.

OXFORD

Abbott, J S	1954-55
Abell, G E B	1923-24-25-26
Adamson, J A	1928-29-31
Adcock, J R L	1961
Aitken, G G	1922-24
Aldridge, J E	1888
Alexander, H	1897-98
Alexander, P C	1930
Allaway, R C P	1953-54-55
Allen, C P	1881-82-83
Allen, T	1909
Allen, W C	1910
Allison, M G	1955
Almond, R G P	1937
Ashby, C J	1973
Asher, A G G	1881-82-83-84
Asquith, P R	1974
Atkinson, C C	1876
Back, A	1878
Badenoch, D F	1971
Baden-Powell, F S	1873
Baggaley, J C	1953-54
Bain, D McL	1910-11-12-13
Bainbrigge, J H	1874-76-77
Baird, J S	1966-67
Baiss, R S H	1894-95
Baker, C D	1891-93
Baker, D G S	1951-52
Baker, E M	1893-94-95-96
Baker, P	1980 (R)
Baker, R T	1968
Balfour, E R	1893-94-95
Bannerman, J MacD	1927-28
Barker, A C	1966-67
Barnes, S	1981-82-83
Barr, D C A	1980
Barry, C E	1897-98-99
Barry, D M	1968-69-70
Barwick, W M	1880-81
Bass, R G	1961
Batchelor, T B	1906
Bateson, H D	1874-75-77
Baxter, T J	1958-59
Beamish, S H	1971
Beare, A	1982
Bedford, T P	1965-66-67
Behn, A R	1968-69
Bell, D L	1970
Benson, E T	1928
Bentley, P J	1960
Berkeley, W V	1924-25-26
Berry, C W	1883-84
Bettington, R H B	1920-22
Bevan, J H	1946
Bibby, A J	1980-81
Binham, P A	1971
Birrell, H B	1953
Black, B H	1929
Blair, A S	1884
Blencowe, L C	1907-08
Bloxham, C T	1934-35-36-37
Blyth, P H	1885-86
Bolton, W H	1873-74-75
Bonham-Carter, E	1890-91
Boobbyer, B	1949-50-51
Booker, J L	1880
Booth, J L	1956
Bos, F H ten	1958-59-60
Boswell, J D	1885-86-87
Botfield, A S G	1871
Botting, I J	1949-50
Bourdillon, H	1873-74-75
Bourns, C	1903
Bowers, J B	1932-34

Boyce, A W	1952-53
Boyd, A de H	1924
Boyd, E F	1912
Boyle, D S	1967-68-69
Brace, D O	1955-56
Bradby, G F	1882-85
Bradford, C C	1887
Branfoot, E P	1878-79
Bray, C N	1979
Bray, K A	1989
Bremridge, H	1876-77
Brett, J A	1935-36-37
Brett, P V	1978
Brewer, R J	1965
Brewer, T J	1951
Bridge, D J W	1946-47-48
Brierley, H	1871
Britton, R B	1963-64
Bromet, W E	1889
Brooks, A W	1980-81-82
Brooks, M J	1873
Brooks, W	1872
Broster, L R	1912
Broughton, R C	1965
Brown, L G	1910-11-12
Brown, M E O	1988
Brunskill, R F	1873-74
Bryan, T A	1975-76-77
Bryer, L W	1953
Buchanan, F G	1909-10
Bucknall, A L	1965-66
Budge, K J	1977-78-79
Budworth, R T D	1887-88-89
Bullard, G L	1950-51
Bullock, H	1910-11
Bulpett, C W L	1871
Burnet, P J	1960
Burrow, K C	1933
Burse, R M	1974
Bush, A	1934
Bussell, J G	1903-04
Butcher, W M	1954
Butler, F E R	1959-60
Button, E L	1936
Byers, R M	1926
Caccia, H A	1926
Cadell, P R	1890
Cairns, A G	1899-1900-01
Calcraft, W J	1986-87
Cameron, A J	1988
Campbell, E	1919-20-21
Campbell, W	1987
Cannell, L B	1948-49-50
Cardale, C F	1929-30
Carey, G M	1891-92-94
Carey, W J	1894-95-96-97
Carlyon, H B	1871
Carroll, B M	1970-71
Carroll, P R	1968-69-70
Carter, C R	1885
Cartwright, V H	1901-02-03-04
Cass, T	1961
Castens, H H	1886-87
Cattell, R H B	1893
Cave, H W	1881
Cawkwell, G L	1946-47
Chadwick, A J	1898-99
Chambers, J C	1921
Champain, F H B	1897-98-99
Champneys, F W	1874-75-76
Charles, A E S	1932
Cheesman, W I	1910-11
Cheyne, H	1903-04
Chislett, J	1986-87

Cholmondeley, F G	1871-73
Christopherson, P	1886-87-88
Clark, R B	1978-79
Clarke, E J D	1973
Clarke, I A	1913
Clauss, P R	1889-90-91
Clements, B S	1975
Cleveland, C R	1885-86
Cochran, P C	1889-91
Cohen B A	1884
Coker, J B H	1965
Coker, T	1988-89
Cole, B W	1945
Coleman, D J	1982-83
Coles, D G G	1937-38
Coles, P	1884-85-86
Coles, S C	1954-56-57
Collingwood, J A	1961-62
Colville, A H	1892-93
Conway-Rees, J	1891-92-93
Cook, D J	1988 (R)-89
Cooke, J L	1968-69
Cooke, P	1936-37
Cooke, W R	1976
Cookson, G H F	1891-92
Cooper, A H	1951
Cooper, M McG	1934-35-36
Cooper, R A	1937
Cooper, R M	1946
Cornish, W H	1876
Couper, T	1899-1900
Court, E D	1882-83
Cousins, F C	1885-86
Coutts, I D F	1951
Coventry, R G T	1889-90-91
Cowen, T J	1938
Cowlishaw, F I	1890-91
Cox, G V	1878
Cozens-Hardy, B	1904-05-06
Crabbie, J E	1898-99-1900-01
Craig, F J R	1963-64-65
Crane, C M	1985-86-87
Cranmer, P	1933-34
Crawfurd, J W F A	1900
Creese, N A H	1951
Cridlan, A G	1928-29-30
Croker, J R	1966-67
Crole, G B	1913-19
Cronje, S N	1907-08
Crosse, C W	1874
Crowe, P J	1981-82-83
Crump, L M	1896
Cuff, T W	1945
Cunningham, G	1907-08-09
Currie, J D	1954-55-56-57
Curry, J A H	1961
Curtis, A B	1949
Curtis, D M	1989
Dalby, C	1923
Davey, P	1967
Davey, R A E	1972
David, A M	1921-22
Davies, D B	1905-06-07
Davies, D E	1951
Davies, D M	1958-59-60
Davies, J A B	1920
Davies, L L J	1927
Davies, N	1969
Davies, R H	1955-56-57
Davies S J T	1972-73
Davies, W G	1977
Davis, R A	1974-75
Davis, T M E	1978-79-80
Dawkins, P M	1959-60-61

Rosier, J R H	1983	Stobie, A M	1945	Waldock, H F	1919-20
Ross, W S	1980	Stobie, W D K	1947	Waldron, O C	1965-67
Rotherham, A	1882-83-84	Stone, T	1897	Walford, M M	1935-36-37
Roughead, W N	1924-25-26	Stoneman, B M	1962	Walker, A	1880
Rousseau, W P	1929	Stoop, A D	1902-03-04	Walker, J C	1955
Row, A W L	1921	Strand-Jones, J	1899-1900-01	Walker, J G	1879-80-81
Rowley, J V D'A	1929	Stratton, J W	1897	Walker, M	1950-51
Rucker, R W	1874-76	Strong, E L	1881-83	Wall, T W	1875-76-77
Rudd, E L	1963-64	Strong, W I N	1924-25	Wallace, A C	1922-23-24-25
Russell, H	1872-73-74-75	Stuart-Watson, J L	1935	Walton, E J	1900-01
Russell, J H	1929	Summerskill, W H J	1945	Ward, J M	1972
Russell-Roberts, F D	1931	Surtees, E A	1885	Ware, M A	1961-62
Rydon, R A	1985-86	Sutherland, I W	1938	Warr, A L	1933-34
		Sutherland, J G B	1885	Waterman, J S	1974
Sachs, D M	1962	Sutton, M A	1945-46	Wates, C S	1961
Sampson, D H	1945	Swan, M W	1957	Watkins, L	1879
Sampson, H F	1910-11	Swanston, J F A	1897-98-99-1900	Watkinson, A F	1977-78
Sanctuary, C F S	1879-80	Swanzy, A J	1901-02	Watson, P W	1954-55
Sandford, J R P	1902-03	Swarbrick, D W	1946-47-48	Watt, K A	1976
Saunders, C J	1951	Swayne, D H	1930-31	Watts, I H	1937-38
Sawtell, P R	1972	Sweatman, E A	1927	Watts, L D	1957-58
Sayer, J	1871			Webster, J G M	1980-81
Sayer, J B	1887	Taberer, H M	1892	Webster, J P	1982-83
Scholefield, B G	1920-21	Tahany, M P	1945	Welsh, A R	1984
Scott, J S M	1957-58	Tanner, T L	1931	Wensley, S C	1988
Searle, J P	1981-82	Tarr, F N	1907-08-09	Wesche, V V G	1924
Seccombe, L S	1925	Tatham, W M	1881-82-83	Weston, B A G	1957
Selby, E	1891	Taylor, E G	1926-27-28	Weston, J W	1871
Sexton, C M	1976	Taylor, J A	1974	White, G L	1976-77
Seymour, T M	1971-73	Taylor, S C	1989	White, N T	1905-06
Shacksnovis, A	1922-23	Terry, H F	1900-01	Whyte, A G D	1963
Sharp, H S	1910-11	Theron, T P	1923	Whyte, D J	1963
Sharp, R A W	1959-60-61	Thomas, A C	1979	Wilcock, R M	1962
Sharp, R G	1919	Thomas, T R	1938	Wilcock, S H	1957-58-59
Shaw, C	1974-75	Thomas, W E	1911-12	Wilkinson, J V S	1904
Shearman, M	1878-79	Thomas, W L	1893-94	Wilkinson, W E	1891
Sheffield, R W	1873-74	Thomson, B E	1951-52	Willcox, J G	1959-60-61-62
Sheil, A G R	1958	Thomson, C	1896	Williams, A D	1988
Shillito, G V	1930	Thomson, F W	1912-13	Williams, C D	1945
Sidgwick, A	1872	Thomson, J B	1983	Williams, I M	1988
Siepmann, C A	1921	Thomson, W J	1895-96	Williams, J R	1969
Silk, N	1961-62-63	Thorburn, C W	1964	Williams, S R	1988 (R)
Sim, A C	1876	Thorniley-Walker, M J	1967	Williamson, A C	1913
Simmie, M S	1965-66	Tongue, P K	1975	Williamson, R H	1906-07-08
Simonet, P M	1984	Torry, P J	1968-69	Willis, D C	1975-76-77
Simpson, E P	1887	Travers, B H	1946-47	Willis, T G	1985-86-88
Simpson, H B	1920	Tristram, H B	1882-83-84	Wilson, C T M	1948
Skipper, D J	1952	Troup, D S	1928	Wilson, D B	1874
Slater, N T	1960	Tudor, H A	1878-79-80-81	Wilson, G A	1946-48
Sloan, T	1908	Turcan, H H	1928	Wilson, J	1967-68
Sloane, A D	1902	Turner, A B	1884	Wilson, J H G	1888-89-90
Small, H D	1949-50	Turner, F H	1908-09-10	Wilson, N G C	1967
Smith, A R	1894-95-96-97			Wilson, R W	1956
Smith, B A	1988-89			Wilson, S	1963-64
Smith, I S	1923	Ubogu, V E	1987	Wilson, S E	1890
Smith, J A	1892-93	Unwin, G T	1894-95-96	Wilson, W G	1887
Smith, M J K	1954-55			Wimperis, E J	1951
Southee, E A	1913	Valentine, A C	1923-24-25	Winn, C E	1950
Speed, R R	1967-68-69	Van Der Merwe, W M	1989	Winn, R R	1953
Spence, K M	1951-52	Van Der Riet, E F	1920-21	Witney, N K J	1970-71
Spencer, B L	1960	Van Ryneveld, A J	1946-47-48	Wix, R S	1904-05-06-07
Spragg, F F	1926	Van Ryneveld, C B	1947-48-49	Wood, A E	1904
Springman, P	1877-78	Vassall, H	1879-80-81-82	Wood, D E	1952-53
Squire, W H S	1882-83-84	Vassall, H H	1906-07-08	Wood, G F	1919
Stafford, P M W	1961-62	Vecqueray, A H	1877-78	Woodhead, P G	1974
Stagg, P K	1961-62	Vecqueray, G C	1873	Woodrow, D K	1978-79-80
Starmer-Smith, N C	1965-66	Vessey, S J R	1984-85-86-87-88	Wooldridge, C S	1882
Steel, J J	1953	Vidal, R W S	1872	Wordsworth, C R	1922-23-24
Steinthal, F E	1906	Vincent, A N	1948-49	Wordsworth, C W	1902
Stevens, D T	1959			Wordsworth, J R	1885
Stewart, A	1947-48	Wade, C G	1882-83-84	Wray, M O	1933-34
Stewart, W B	1892	Waide, S L	1932	Wyatt, D M	1981
Steyn, S S L	1911-12	Wake, H B L	1922	Wydell, H A	1951
Stileman, W M C	1988	Wakefield, W H	1891-92	Wynter, E C C	1947
Still, E R	1871-73	Wakelin, W S	1964		
		Waldock, F A	1919	Young, J R C	1957-58

CAMBRIDGE

Aarvold, C D 1925-26-27-28
Ackford, P J 1979
Adams, G C A 1929
Adams, H F S 1884-85
Agnew, C M 1875-76
Agnew, G W 1871-72-73
Agnew, W L 1876-77-78
Albright, G S 1877
Alderson, F H R 1887-88
Alexander, E P 1884-85-86
Alexander, J W 1905-06
Allan, C J 1962
Allan, J L F 1956
Allchurch, T J 1980-81
Allen, A D 1925-26-27
Allen, D B 1975
Allen, J 1875-76
Anderson, W T 1931-32
Andrew, C R 1982-83-84
Anthony, A J 1967
Archer, G M D 1950-51
Arthur, T G 1962
Ashcroft, A H 1908-09
Ashford, C L 1929
Ashworth, J 1988-89
Askew, J G 1929-30-31
Asquith, J P K 1953
Aston, R L 1889-90
Atkinson, M L 1908-09
Attfield, S J W 1982-84

Back, F F 1871-72
Bailey, G H 1931
Bailey, M D 1982-83-84-85
Bailey, R C 1982-83
Balding, I A 1961
Balfour, A 1896-97
Bance, J F 1945
Barker, R E 1966
Barlow, C S 1923-24-25-26
Barlow, R M M 1925
Barrow, C 1950
Barter, A F 1954-55-56
Bartlett, R M 1951
Bateman-Champain, P J C 1937
Batten, J M 1871-72-73-74
Batty, P A 1919-20
Baxter, R 1871-72-73
Baxter, W H B 1912-13
Bealey, R J 1874
Beard, P L 1987
Bearne, K R F 1957-58-59
Beazley, T A G 1971
Bedell-Sivright, D R
1899-1900-01-02
Bedell-Sivright, J V
1900-01-02-03
Beer, I D S 1952-53-54
Bell, D S 1989
Bell, R W 1897-98-99
Bell, S P 1894-95-96
Bennett, G M 1897-98
Bennett, N J 1981
Benthall, E C 1912
Beringer, F R 1951-52
Beringer, G G 1975-76
Berman, J V 1966
Berry, S P 1971
Bevan, G A J 1951
Bevan, J A 1877-80
Bevan, W 1887
Biddell, C W 1980-81
Biggar, M A 1971
Bird, D R J 1958-59
Birdwood, C R B 1932
Bishop, C C 1925
Black, M A 1897-98
Blair, P C B 1910-11-12-13
Blake, W H 1875
Boggon, R P 1956

Bole, E 1945-46-47
Bonham-Carter, J 1873
Booth, A H 1989
Bordass, J H 1923-24
Borthwick, T J L 1985
Boughton-Leigh, C E W 1878
Boulding, P V 1975-76
Bowcott, H M 1927-28
Bowcott, J E 1933
Bowen, R W 1968
Bowhill, J W 1888-89
Bowman, J H 1933-34
Boyd, C W 1909
Boyd-Moss, R J 1980-81-82
Brandram, R A 1896
Brash, J C 1959-60-61
Brathwaite, G A 1934
Breakey, J N F 1974-75(R)-77
Bree-Frink, F C 1888-89-90
Briggs, P D 1962
Bromet, E 1887-88
Brook, P W P 1928-29-30-31
Brookstein, R 1969
Brooman, R J 1977-78
Browell, H H 1877-78
Brown, A C 1920-21
Brown, S L 1975-76
Browning, O C 1934
Bruce Lockhart, J H 1910
Bruce Lockhart, L 1945-46
Bruce Lockhart, R B 1937-38
Brutton, E B 1883-85-86
Bryant, S S 1988
Bryce, R D H 1965
Bull, H A 1874-75
Bunting, W L 1894-95
Burt-Marshall, J 1905
Burton, B C 1882-83
Bush, J D 1983
Bussey, W M 1960-61-62
Butler, E T 1976-77-78
Buzza, A J 1988-89

Cake, J J 1988
Campbell, D A 1936
Campbell, H H 1946
Campbell, J A 1897-98-99
Campbell, J D 1927
Campbell, J W 1973-74
Campbell, R C C 1907
Candler, P L 1934
Cangley, B T G 1946
Carey, G V 1907-08
Carpmael, W P 1885
Carris, H E 1929
Carter, C P 1965
Cave, J W 1887-88
Cave, W T C 1902-03-04
Chadwick, W O 1936-37-38
Chalmers, P S 1979
Chambers, E L 1904
Chapman, C E 1881-84
Chapman, E S 1879-80
Chapman, G M 1907-08-09
Chapman, J M 1873
Chilcott, E W 1883
Child, H H 1875-76
Clarke, B D F 1978
Clarke, S J S 1962-63
Clayton, H R 1876-77-78
Clayton, J R W 1971
Clements, J W 1953-54-55
Clifford, P H 1876-77-78
Clough, F J 1984-85-86-87
Coates, C H 1877-78-79
Coates, V H M 1907
Cobby, W 1900
Cock, T A 1899
Cocks, F W 1935
Coghlan, G B 1926-27-28

Cohen, A S 1922
Colbourne, G L 1883
Coley, M 1964
Collett, G F 1898
Collier, R B 1960-61
Collin, T 1871
Collins, W O H 1931
Collis, W R F 1919-20
Collison, L H 1930
Combe, P H 1984-85
Considine, W C D 1919
Conway, G S 1919-20-21
Cook, D D B 1920-21
Cook, S 1920-21
Cooke, S J 1981
Cooper, H S 1881
Cooper, P T 1927-28
Cope, W 1891
Corry, T M 1966
Cosh, N J 1966
Covell, G A B 1949
Cove-Smith, R 1919-20-21
Cox, F L 1879
Craig, H J 1891
Craigmile, H W C 1920
Crichton-Miller, D 1928
Crothers, G 1977(R)
Crow, W A M 1961-62
Cullen, J C 1980-81-82
Cumberlege, B S 1910-11-12-13
Cumberlege, R F 1897
Cumming, D C 1922-23-24
Currie, W C 1905
Cushing, A 1986

Dalgleish, K J 1951-52-53
Dalton, E R 1872-73-74
Dalton, W L T 1875-76
Daniell, J 1898-99-1900
Darby, A J L 1896-97-98
Darch, W J 1875
David, P W 1983
Davies, A 1988-89
Davies, G 1988-89
Davies, G 1948-49-50
Davies, G H 1980-81
Davies, H J 1958
Davies, J C 1949
Davies, J S 1977
Davies, P M 1952-53-54
Davies, T G R 1968-69-70
Davies, W G 1946-47
Deakin, J E 1871
Delafield, G E 1932
De Nobriga, A P 1948
De Villiers, D I 1913
Devitt, Sir T G 1923-24-25
Dewhurst, J H 1885-86
Dick, R C S 1933
Dickins, J P 1972-73
Dickson, J W 1881
Dinwiddy, H P 1934-35
Dixon, A M 1928
Dixon, C 1894
Dods, M 1938
Doherty, H D 1950
Doherty, W D 1913
Don Wauchope, A R 1880-81
Dorward, A F 1947-48-49
Douglas, E A 1882-83-84
Douglas, R N 1891
Douty, P S 1924
Dovey, B A 1960
Downes, K D 1936-37-38
Downey, W J 1954-55-56-57
Doyle, M G 1965
Drake-Lee, N J 1961-62-63
Drake, T R 1965
Druce, W G 1893-94
Drummond, N W 1971

Name	Year	Name	Year	Name	Year
Scott, J M	1927	Tait, J G	1880-82	Waller, G S	1932
Scott, M T	1885-86-87	Talbot, S C	1900	Wallis, H T	1895-96
Scott, R R F	1957	Tallent, J A	1929-30-31	Ward, R O C	1903
Scott, W B	1923-24	Tanner, C C	1930	Ware, C H	1882
Scott, W M	1888	Tarsh, D N	1955	Warfield, P J	1974
Scoular, J G	1905-06	Taylor, A S	1879-80-81	Warlow, S	1972-74
Seddon, E R H	1921	Taylor, D G	1982	Waters, F H	1927-28-29
Shackleton, I R	1968-69-70	Taylor, H B J	1894-96	Waters, J B	1902-03-04
Shaw, P A V	1977	Taylor, W J	1926	Watherston, J G	1931
Shepherd, J K	1950	Templer, J L	1881-82	Watson, C F K	1919-20
Sherrard, P	1938	Thomas, B E	1960-61-62	Watt, J R	1970
Shipsides, J	1970	Thomas, D R	1972-73-74	Webb, G K M	1964-65
Shirer, J A	1885	Thomas, H W	1912	Webster, A P	1971
Silk, D R W	1953-54	Thomas, J	1945	Wells, C M	1891-92
Sim, R G	1966-67	Thomas, M D C	1986-87	Wells, T U	1951
Simms, K G	1983-84-85	Thomas, N B	1966	Wetson, M T	1958-59-60
Simms, N J	1989	Thomas, R C C	1949	Wheeler, P J F	1951-52-53
Simpson, C P	1890	Thomas, T J	1895-96	White, J B	1922
Simpson, F W	1930-31	Thomas, W H	1886-87	White, W N	1947
Sisson, J P	1871	Thompson, M J M	1950	Whiteway, S E A	1893
Skinner, R C O	1970-71	Thompson, R	1890	Wiggins, C E M	1928
Slater, K J P	1964	Thompson, R V	1948-49	Wiggins, C M	1964
Smallwood, A M	1919	Thorman, W H	1890	Wilby, J B	1989
Smeddle, R W	1928-29-30-31	Thorne, C	1911	Wilkinson, R M	1971-72-73
Smith, A F	1873-74	Thornton, J F	1976-78-79	Will, J G	1911-12-13
Smith, A R	1954-55-56-57	Threlfall, R	1881-83	Williams, A G	1926-27
Smith, H K P	1920	Timmons, F J	1983	Williams, C C U	1950
Smith, H Y L	1878-79-80-81	Todd, A F	1893-94-95	Williams, C H	1930
Smith, J	1889	Todd, T	1888	Williams, C R	1971-72-73
Smith, J J E	1926	Topping, N P	1986-87	Williams, D B	1973
Smith, J M	1972	Touzel, C J C	1874-75-76	Williams, E J H	1946
Smith, J V	1948-49-50	Tredwell, J R	1968	Williams, H A	1876
Smith, K P	1919	Trethewy, A	1888	Williams, J M	1949
Smith, M A	1966-67	Trubshaw, A R	1919	Williams, L T	1874-75
Smith, P K	1970	Tucker, W E	1892-93-94	Williams, N E	1950
Smith, S R	1958-59	Tucker, W E	1922-23-24-25	Williams, P T	1888-89
Smith, S T	1982-83	Tudsbery, F C T	1907-08	Williamson, I S	1972
Sobey, W H	1925-26	Tunningley, A J	1988 (R)	Williamson, P R	1984
Spencer, J S	1967-68-69	Turnbull, B R	1924-25	Willis, H	1949-50-51
Spicer, N	1901-02	Turner, J A	1956	Wilson, A H	1911-12-13
Spray, K A N	1946-47	Turner, J M P C	1985	Wilson, C P	1877-78-79-80
Sprot, A	1871	Turner, M F	1946	Wilton, C W	1936
Stauton, H	1891	Tyler, R H	1978-79-80	Winthrop, W Y	1871
Stead, R J	1977			Wintle, T C	1960-61
Steeds, J H	1938	Umbers, R H	1954	Withyman, T A	1985-86
Steel, D Q	1877	Ure, C McG	1911	Wood, G E	1974-75-76
Steele, H K	1970			Wood, G E C	1919
Steele, J T	1879-80	Valentine, G E	1930	Woodall, B J C	1951
Steele-Bodger, M R	1945-46	Van Schalkwijk, J	1906	Woodroffe, O P	1952
Stevenson, H J	1977(R)-79	Vaughan, G P	1949	Woods, S M J	1888-89-90
Stevenson, L E	1884-85	Vaux, J G	1957	Wooler, W	1933-34-35
Steward, R	1875-76	Vickerstaff, M	1988	Wordley, S A	1988-89
Stewart, A A	1975-76	Vincent, C A	1913	Wordsworth, A J	1973-75
Stewart, J R	1935	Vivian, J M	1976	Wotherspoon, W	1888-89
Stileman, W M C	1985	Vyvyan, C B	1987-88	Wrench, D F B	1960
Stokes, R R	1921			Wright, C C G	1907-08
Stone, R J	1901	Wace, H	1873-74	Wrigley, P T	1877-78-79-80
Storey, E	1878-79-80	Waddell, G H	1958-60-61	Wyles, K T	1985-86
Storey, L H T	1909	Wade, M R	1958-59-60-61	Wynne, E H	1887
Storey, T W P	1889-90-91-92	Wainwright, J F	1956		
Stothard, N A	1979	Wainwright, M A	1980		
Style, H B	1921	Wainwright, R I	1986-87-88	Yetts, R M	1879-80-81
Surtees, A A	1886	Wakefield, W W	1921-22	Young, A B S	1919-20
Sutherland, J F	1908	Walker, A W	1929-30	Young, A T	1922-23-24
Sutton, A J	1987-88	Walker, D R	1980-81	Young, J S	1935
Swanson, J C	1938	Walker, E E	1899-1900	Young, J V	1906
Swayne, F G	1884-85-86	Walker, R M	1963	Young, P D	1949
Symington, A W	1911-12-13	Walkey, J R	1902	Young, S K	1974
Synge, J S	1927	Wallace, W M	1912-13	Young, W B	1935-36-37

VARSITY MATCH REFEREES

(From 1881, when referees first officiated at the match. Prior to this date, the match was controlled by a pair of umpires elected by the Universities.) Each year indicates a separate appearance, and refers to the first half of the season. Thus 1881 refers to the match played in the 1881-82 season.

Name	Year	Name	Year	Name	Year
Allan, M A	1933-34	Burnett, D I H	1980-82	Currey, F I	1885
Ashmore, H L	1891-92-93-95-96	Burrell, R P	1963	Dallas, J D	1910-12
Bean, A S	1948-49	Clark, K H	1973	D'Arcy, D P	1968
Bolton, W N	1882	Cooper, Dr P F	1951-53	David, I	1954-55
Boundy, L M	1958	Crawford, S H	1920	Evans, G	1907

Findlay, J C	1904-08	Jones, T	1950	Sanson, N R	1976
Freethy, A E	1923-25-27-29-31-32	Lamb, Air Cdre G C	1970	Sturrock, J C	1921
Gadney, C H	1935-36-37-38-45-47	Lambert, N H	1946	Taylor, H H	1881
Gillespie, J I	1905	Lawrence, Capt H D	1894	Titcombe, M H	1969
Harnett, G H		Lewis, R	1971	Trigg, J A F	1983
.	1897-98-99-1900-01-02	Marsh, F W	1906	Vile, T H	1922-24-26-28
Hill, G R	1883-84-86-87-88-89-90	Murdoch, W C W	1952	Walters, D G	
Hosie, A M	1979	Norling, C	1977-78-81-88-89		1957-60-61-62-64-65-66
Howard, F A	1986	Pattinson, K A	1974	Welsby, A	1975
Jeffares, R W	1930	Potter-Irwin, F C	1909-11-13-19	Williams, R C	1959
John, K S	1956-67	Prideaux, L	1984	Williams, T	1903
Johnson, R F	1972	Quittenton, R C	1985-87		

Troy Coker, the Australian vice-captain of Oxford, in trouble from Cambridge forwards during the 1989 Varsity Match at Twickenham.

COMMERCIAL UNION UAU CHAMPIONSHIP 1989-90

14 March, Twickenham
Loughborough University 25 (2G 3PG 1T)
Swansea University 16 (1G 2PG 1T)

Although the trophy bore a new name, the same hands kept a grip on it as Loughborough beat off Swansea's spirited challenge in the third successive final between the two teams. The match did not reach great heights, but it was always interesting.

Swansea, who marked the occasion by introducing a new strip, were the more positive and attacking force throughout the match. Loughborough, playing their part in this role reversal, depended considerably on tactical kicking from their fly-half, Frost. On a fine spring day, Swansea's strategy could have worked, but their enthusiasm kindled too many mistakes and the first-half scoring was restricted to five penalties. Loughborough's Frost shaded Powell by the odd penalty as the teams turned around at 9-6 at half-time.

The larger Loughborough pack managed to assert its authority, especially in the line-outs, and although Swansea pressed strongly at the beginning of the second half, Johnson of Loughborough consolidated their lead after Spiller had opened up the Welsh defence with a shrewd chip. Swansea fought back and reduced the arrears with a try by Adebayo. Currie pushed Loughborough further ahead with a try which was converted by Frost, and again Swansea, still feeding their three-quarters at every opportunity, reduced the deficit. This time, Ball made a strong run from midfield to score and Powell added the conversion.

Swansea spent a period camped outside the Loughborough line, but could not make the breakthrough. Finally, in the dying seconds of the match, they launched their last attack, only for Spiller to intercept deep in his own half. The ball was swiftly transferred to Parton, who ran some 70 metres down the right touch-line to seal Loughborough's victory.

Loughborough Students: A Parton; D Currie, D Spiller, J Bancroft, S Johnson; R Frost, P Miles; G Baldwin, J Hudson, G Wareham, G Sweetman, D Jones, J Hastings, G Taylor (*capt*), E Peters
Scorers: *Tries:* Johnson, Currie, Parton   *Conversions:* Frost (2)   *Penalty Goals:* Frost (3)
Swansea University: R Jones; J Devonald, J Ball, P Flood, A Adebayo; J Powell, A Moore; D Francis (*capt*), R Tandy, I Buckett, N Bissett, J Lewis, A Heywood, M Bennett, M Langley
Scorers: *Tries:* Adebayo, Ball   *Conversion:* Powell   *Penalty Goals:* Powell (2)
Referee I Bullerwell (East Midlands)
Loughborough have won the title 23 times, Durham 8, Liverpool and Swansea 7, Bristol 5, Manchester 4, Cardiff 3, Bangor and UWIST 2, Aberystwyth, Birmingham, Leeds and Newcastle once each.

Loughborough's victory extended their record number of Championship wins, but they were fortunate to make their familiar way to Twickenham. Indeed, many thought that the best team in the competition did not reach the final. Cardiff, strengthened by an academic merger of the old University College and UWIST, had beaten Swansea in the Welsh group and then steamrollered their way to the semi-finals. At that point, they were literally seconds away from a notable win when they conceded an unnecessary penalty, allowing Loughborough to level the scores, and then conceded a further penalty in extra time.

Representative matches: English Universities 18, Irish Universities 34 (Sunbury); English Universities 13, Welsh Universities 7 (Richmond); Irish Universities 25, Welsh Universities 4 (Dublin); Scottish Universities 8, English Universities 30 (Edinburgh); Welsh Universities 37, Scottish Universities 16; Irish Universities 25, Welsh Universities 4; British Polytechnics 27, UAU 4 (Morley); Welsh Students 9, French Students 18; English Students 37, Welsh Students 3; English Students 32, French Students 4; French Students 12, Scottish Students 6; English Colleges 42, Welsh Colleges 7; British Polytechnics 6, Public School Wanderers 46

DIVISIONAL RESULTS
Eastern Division
NORTH-EAST GROUP

	P	W	D	L	F	A	Pts
Newcastle	3	3	0	0	87	29	6
Durham	3	2	0	1	67	27	4
Hull	3	1	0	2	28	65	2
Leeds	3	0	0	3	18	79	0

EAST MIDLANDS GROUP

	P	W	D	L	F	A	Pts
Loughbor'h	3	3	0	0	108	11	6
Nottingham	3	2	0	1	39	44	4
Sheffield	3	1	0	2	41	46	2
Bradford	3	0	0	3	24	111	0

Winners in each Group proceed to Challenge Round. Runners-up and winners of Divisional play-off matches proceed to Preliminary Round.

Divisional Play-off matches: Sheffield 20, Leeds 3; Hull 12, Bradford 0

Western Division
NORTH-WEST GROUP

	P	W	D	L	F	A	Pts
Manchester	4	3	1	0	105	17	7
UMIST	4	3	1	0	65	28	7
Liverpool	4	2	0	2	52	63	4
Lancaster	4	1	0	3	26	90	2
Salford	4	0	0	4	37	87	0

WEST MIDLANDS GROUP

	P	W	D	L	F	A	Pts
Birmingham	4	4	0	0	117	16	8
Warwick	4	3	0	1	49	25	6
Leicester	4	2	0	2	66	80	4
Keele	4	1	0	3	46	81	2
Aston	4	0	0	4	16	92	0

Winners in each Group proceed to Challenge Round. Runners-up and third-placed teams proceed to Preliminary Round.

Southern Division
NORTH-THAMES GROUP

	P	W	D	L	F	A	Pts
Brunel	5	5	0	0	83	28	10
Essex	5	4	0	1	51	58	8
East Anglia	5	3	0	2	95	42	6
UC London	5	2	0	3	61	69	4
City	5	1	0	4	72	77	2
Buckingham	5	0	0	5	13	101	0

SOUTH THAMES GROUP

	P	W	D	L	F	A	Pts
Imperial Coll	5	5	0	0	173	17	10
Sussex	5	4	0	1	113	86	8
Surrey	5	3	0	2	81	65	6
LSE	5	2	0	3	64	189	2
RHBNC	5	1	0	4	57	65	2
Kent	5	0	0	5	44	133	0

Eric Peters, the Loughborough No 8, negotiates a double-tackle, including headlock, and prepares to pass to his support in the final at Twickenham.

SOUTH-WEST GROUP

	P	W	D	L	F	A	Pts
Exeter	4	3	1	0	131	51	7
Bristol	4	2	1	1	60	45	5
Bath	4	2	0	2	89	69	4
Southampton	4	2	0	2	51	83	4
Reading	4	0	0	4	26	109	0

Welsh Division

	P	W	D	L	F	A	Pts
Cardiff	4	4	0	0	84	22	8
Swansea	4	3	0	1	106	13	4*
Aberystwyth	4	2	0	2	50	134	4
Bangor	4	1	0	3	24	45	2
Medicals	4	0	0	4	38	88	0

Winners proceed to Challenge Round. Runners-up and third-placed teams proceed to Preliminary Round. * 2 points deducted

Preliminary Round: UMIST 9, Sheffield 13; Nottingham 6, Hull 0; Durham 49, Liverpool 8; Essex 3, Bath 27; Swansea 73, Leicester 0; Warwick 10, Aberystwyth 13; Bristol 46, Surrey 3; Sussex 19, East Anglia 13

Challenge Round: Exeter 12, Nottingham 6; Loughborough 24, Sheffield 0; Cardiff 45, Bath 3; Manchester 6, Durham 21; Imperial College 12, Swansea 31; Brunel 17, Aberystwyth 12; Newcastle 42, Sussex 3; Birmingham 6, Bristol 10

Quarter-finals: Essex 14, Loughborough 39; Cardiff 36, Durham 3; Brunel 3, Swansea 53; Newcastle 11, Bristol 21

Semi-finals: Loughborough 13, Cardiff 10 (Stourbridge RFC); Swansea 28, Bristol 6 (University College, Cardiff)

BRITISH POLYTECHNICS CUP 1990

14 March 1990, Sutton Coldfield RFC
South-West Polytechnic 6 (1G)
Sheffield Polytechnic 15 (1G 3PG)

Neither team had won the Cup before and this was hardly a spectacular final. Nevertheless, after the excesses of finals day in the previous season, when there was trouble on the pitch and in the crowd, this contest restored the good name of rugby in the Polys sector. There was only one serious incident, when the referee warned Saverimutto of Sheffield and Skrimshire of South-West after an altercation.

Sheffield put their greater experience to good use and their half-backs, Saverimutto and Gregory, exerted control behind the superior pack. South-West, formerly known as Plymouth Poly, have rarely emerged from even the group matches in previous years, so their achievement in reaching the final at all was praiseworthy. South-West had beaten Bristol and Wales, traditionally the two strongest teams in the sector, during the season.

Sheffield were 12-0 in the lead in the first quarter. Vanham, their wing, raced 70 yards after a South-West movement broke down. Gregory kicked the conversion and also scored two penalty goals. At this stage, a big score was on the cards. But South-West came back well, and restricted Sheffield to a single score in the rest of the match, when Gregory kicked his third penalty. Bryan, the South-West scrum-half, scored a try in the last act of the match to bring about a respectable result.

Sheffield Polytechnic: M Leopard; M Wildgoose, M Old, D Hill, N Vanham; G Gregory, C Saverimutto; R Moss, B Ludlum, D Fitzgerald, G Davies, W Davison, M Yeoman, M Winefield, M Mills
Scorers *Try:* Vanham   *Conversion:* Gregory   *Penalty Goals:* Gregory (3)
South-West Polytechnic: J Shervington; A Barlow, A Tanner, C Gunning, P Arista; A Jackman, G Bryan; J Holland, A Cuthbert, A Gwinnell, J Skrimshire, H Housen, A Duggan, A Rowbotham, J Newall *Replacement* M Pearcy for Skrimshire
Scorers *Try:* Vanham   *Conversion:* Gregory
Referee A John (North Midlands)

First round proper: Leeds 22, Nottingham 6; Liverpool w/o Leicester; South-West w/o Middlesex; South Bank 29, Thames 9; City of London 14, Portsmouth 9; Oxford 10, Bristol 15; Coventry 22, Staffordshire 3; Sheffield 16, Newcastle 6
Quarter-finals: Leeds 15, Liverpool 3; South-West 11, South Bank 7; City of London 13, Bristol 27; Coventry 4, Sheffield 7
Semi-finals: Leeds 9, South-West 10; Bristol 12, Sheffield 19ⁱ
Second XVs final: Nottingham II 16, Staffordshire II 9
Third XVs final: Staffordshire III 3, Sheffield III 9
First XVs plate final: Wales 16, Lancashire 19
Second XVs plate final: Newcastle 26, Birmingham 11
Wales Poly (formerly Glamorgan) have won the title 9 times; Kingston 3 times; Bristol, Liverpool and Leeds twice each; Manchester, Middlesex and Coventry (formerly Lanchester) and Sheffield once each.

HOSPITALS' CHALLENGE CUP 1990

Rupert Cherry

7 March, Old Deer Park
St Mary's Hospital 9 (2PG 1DG)
The London Hospital 6 (2PG)

St Mary's achieved their 29th victory in the Hospitals' Cup, only one behind Guy's record – but only just. Their defeat of The London in the final again was a close-run event. In spite of a small collection of international and first-class players, Mary's were never in complete command of the competition. They scored far fewer points than usual and right through to the end the final could have gone either way.

This naturally made some excitement for the large crowd, but they could hardly admire the general standard of play. As ever the tackling was quick, sound and hard, but the passing was wild. Both sides created chances to score tries only to fling them away by throwing the ball at the next man's head or feet, and sometimes even to the opposition. The London must regret one particularly clumsy pass when they had an overlap. So the match had to be decided by goal-kicking, and here too there were faults on each side. McLaren missed a comparatively easy kick from 30 yards in the first minutes and later Martin, The London's place-kicker, did exactly the same thing. However, Mary's exerted pressure through the strong driving of their pack while The London found their best method of attack was to bombard the Mary's full-back with high up-and-unders. The best that came from both these tactics was the chance of a kick at a penalty goal, and while McLaren and Martin each kicked two, the former's neat dropped goal after a fine forward surge led by O'Leary proved to be the winning score. Martin's two long-range efforts in the last few minutes might have made some people catch their breath, but they failed to find the target.

St Mary's: A Field; R Wintle, D Gillan (*capt*), K G Simms, J Walters; D McLaren, I O'Connor; D Vaughan, L O'Hara, A Ellery, P Tooze-Hobson, S O'Leary, J Hartley, S Kelly, P Mitchell
Scorer *Penalty Goals:* McLaren (2)   *Dropped Goal:* McLaren
The London: P Isaac; N Payne, P Merrifield, R McCarthy, I Hamilton; H Thomas, C Jones; R Baker, C Mann, S Curry (*capt*), P Barnes, A Cruickshank, A Martin, P Moore, W McAllister
Scorer *Penalty Goals:* Martin (2)
Referee D Taylor (London Society)

First Round: Barts 9, Kings College Hospital 6; Guy's 39, St George's 17
Second Round: Guy's 10, St Mary's 19; St Thomas's 0, Charing Cross/Westminster 24; The London 4, Barts 0; Royal Free 9, UCH/Middlesex 11
Semi-finals: Charing Cross/Westminster 6, St Mary's 10; The London 16, UCH/Middlesex 6

Guy's have won the Cup 30 times, St Mary's 29, St Thomas's 17, The London 11, St Bartholomew's 9, St George's and Westminster 3 times each, and Middlesex once.

THE INTER-SERVICES TOURNAMENT 1990

Rupert Cherry

The Army maintained their position at the head of the three armed services by winning the championship for the third year in succession, although not as impressively as they had done in previous years. They beat the Royal Navy and the RAF simply by taking the chances that came their way, scoring seven tries in the two matches, only one of which could be said to have been carefully designed. It was scored by 'Chalky' Atkins, the Army's wing, in the last few minutes of the game against the RAF. Atkins had been moved from the left to the right wing for this match so that his hard tackling might check the RAF's greatest asset, Rory Underwood.

As it turned out the RAF forwards won very little of the ball against the heavy Army pack, and Underwood was, as so often, starved of passes. Atkins, then, had little to do, but he got a scoring chance when Steve Commander made a clever switch of attack, and Atkins had the line at his mercy. That was not enough for him: although the Army scarcely needed the extra points for a conversion – they led by 23-10 at the time – he insisted on dodging past three or four opponents behind their goal-line to touch down behind the posts. After that he was content to be beaten by Underwood, who ran in a classic try from halfway in the last minute, which mattered not at all.

The Navy had probably the best of the three packs of forwards, but although their captain, Chris Alcock, led the side for the sixth time and made his usual exciting excursions into attack, they could not put together many concerted movements behind the scrum.

This was the fifth time that the Army had won the championship three years running.

10 March, Twickenham
Royal Navy 7 (1PG 1T)   **Army 16** (2G 1T)
for the Willis Faber Trophy

Royal Navy: Lt C Alcock (HMS Seahawk) (*capt*); Lt M Speakman (HMS Broadsword), LWEM(R) D Oakley (HMS Collingwood), POMEA A Kellett (HMS Brilliant), Lt S D Phillips (DNR London); Sub Lt B Nicholas (RAE Farnborough), ! .PT I Torpey (HMS Newcastle); POWtr J M Hirst (HMS Nelson), L/Sea (S)(SM) R Joy (HMS Dolphin), Cpl I Bevan (CTC RM), Cpl S Trench (40 Cdo RM), Mne R W Armstrong (CTC RM), LPT I Russell (HMS Raleigh), Cpl J Bryant (40 Cdo RM), Sgt M Reece (DNR London) *Replacements* 2nd Lt M Tanner (Leicester U) for Trench; POPT S Jones (HMS Drake) for Russell
Scorers *Try:* Alcock   *Penalty Goal:* Kellett
Army: Lt R Preston (DWR); L/Cpl S Bartliff (R Sigs), Sgt C Spowart (APTC), Lt S Hopkin (KOBR), Sgt E Atkins (R Sigs); 2nd Lt M Walker (RAMC),

2nd Lt B Taylor (DWR); Sgt D Coghlan (RHA), Lt J Caskey (R Irish), 2nd Lt A Ellery (RAMC), Major B McCall (REME) (*capt*), Lt R Castleton (ACC), L/Cpl K Ferdinand (REME), L/Cpl R Nelson (RE), 2nd Lt T Rodber (Grn Howards)
Scorers *Tries:* Hopkin (2), Spowart   *Conversions:* Walker, Spowart
Referee E Morrison (Gloucester Society)

24 March, Twickenham
Royal Navy 14 (1G 2T)   **RAF 22** (2G 2PG 1T)
for the Windsor Life Trophy

Royal Navy: Lt C Alcock (HMS Seahawk) (*capt*); Lt M Speakman (HMS Broadsword), LWEM(R) D Oakley (HMS Collingwood), LPT R Packer (HMS Collingwood), Lt S Phillips (DNR London); POMEA A Kellett (HMS Brilliant), LPT I Torpey (HMS Newcastle); POWtr J M Hirst (HMS Nelson), L/Sea (S)(SM) R Joy (HMS Dolphin), Cpl I Bevan (CTC RM), 2nd Lt M Tanner (Leicester U), Mne R W Armstrong (CTC RM), LPT I Russell (HMS Raleigh), Sgt M Reece (MoD DNR London), Cpl J Bryant (40 Cdo RM) *Replacements* Lt M Deller (HMS Seahawk) for Alcock; Lt M Hawden (HMS Ark Royal) for Speakman
Scorers *Tries:* Russell (2), Torpey   *Conversion:* Kellett
RAF: Cpl N Raikes (Lyneham); SAC S K Crossland (Finningley), Flt Lt I Goslin (Henlow), SAC R Smith (West Drayton), Flt Lt R Underwood (Wyton); Cpl P Hull (Locking), Sgt S Worrall (Finningley) (*capt*); Jnr Tech D Breed (St Athan), Flt Lt R L Miller (Chivenor), Flt Lt N Carter (Marham), Sgt B Richardson (Pitreavie Castle), F/O R Burn (Cranwell), Cpl C D Morgan (Newton), F/O C Natapu (Cranwell), F/O F Clifford (Rheindahlen)
Scorers *Tries:* Crossland (2), Underwood   *Conversions:* Raikes (2)
Penalty Goals: Raikes (2)
Referee D W Matthews (Liverpool Society)

31 March, Twickenham
Army 32 (2G 3PG 1DG 2T)   **RAF 14** (2PG 2T)
for the Windsor Life Challenge Cup

Army: Lt R Preston (DWR); L/Cpl S Bartliff (R Sigs), Sgt C Spowart (APTC), Lt S Hopkin (KOBR), Sgt E Atkins (R Sigs); Sgt S Commander (RHA), 2nd Lt B Taylor (DWR); Cpl G Graham (Argyll & Sutherland Highlanders), Lt J Caskey (R Irish), 2nd Lt A Ellery (RAMC), Major B McCall (REME) (*capt*), Lt R Castleton (ACC), L/Cpl K Ferdinand (REME), L/Cpl R Nelson (RE), 2nd Lt T Rodber (Grn Howards) *Replacements* Lt J Layard (RA) for Bartliff; Lt G Knight (DWR) for Rodber
Scorers *Tries:* Bartliff (2), Rodber, Atkins   *Conversions:* Spowart (2)
Penalty Goals: Spowart (3)   *Dropped Goal:* Commander
RAF: Cpl N Raikes (Lyneham); SAC S K Crossland (Finningley), Flt Lt I Goslin (Henlow), SAC R Smith (West Drayton), Flt Lt R Underwood (Wyton); Cpl P Hull (Locking), Sgt S Worrall (Finningley) (*capt*); Jnr Tech D Breed (St Athan), Flt Lt R L Miller (Chivenor), Flt Lt N Carter (Marham), Sgt B Richardson (Pitreavie Castle), F/O R Burn (Cranwell), Cpl C D Morgan (Newton), F/O C Natapu (Cranwell), F/O F Clifford (Rheindahlen) *Replacements* Cpl S Lazenby (Brize Norton) for Raikes; Cpl S Roke (St Athan) for Hull
Scorers *Tries:* Clifford, Underwood   *Penalty Goals:* Raikes (2)
Referee S W Piercy (Yorkshire Society)

Inter-Services Under-21 Tournament
Army 12, Royal Navy 12; Army 18, RAF 6; RAF 11, Royal Navy 30 *Winners:* Army
Inter-Services Colts (Under-19) Championship
Army 16, Royal Navy 10; Army 21, RAF 6; RAF 12, Royal Navy 4 *Winners:* Army

Inter-Services Tournament Champions

The Army have won the Tournament outright 28 times, the Royal Navy 16 times, and the RAF 11 times.

1920 **Navy**	1948 Triple Tie	1969 **Army**
1921 **Navy**	1949 { **Army** / **RAF** }	1970 **Navy**
1922 **Navy**		1971 **RAF**
1923 **RAF**	1950 **Army**	1972 **Army**
1924 Triple Tie	1951 **Navy**	1973 **Navy**
1925 { **Army** / **RAF** }	1952 **Army**	1974 **Navy**
	1953 **Army**	1975 Triple Tie
1926 **Army**	1954 Triple Tie	1976 **Army**
1927 **Navy**	1955 **RAF**	1977 **Navy**
1928 **Army**	1956 Triple Tie	1978 Triple Tie
1929 **Army**	1957 **Army**	1979 **RAF**
1930 **Army**	1958 **RAF**	1980 **Army**
1931 **Navy**	1959 **RAF**	1981 **Navy**
1932 **Army**	1960 **Army**	1982 **RAF**
1933 **Army**	1961 **Navy**	1983 **Army**
1934 **Army**	1962 **RAF**	1984 Triple Tie
1935 Triple Tie	1963 **Army**	1985 **RAF**
1936 **Army**	1964 **Army**	1986 **RAF**
1937 **Army**	1965 **Army**	1987 **Navy**
1938 **Navy**	1966 **Navy**	1988 **Army**
1939 **Navy**	1967 **Army**	1989 **Army**
1946 **Army**	1968 **Army**	1990 **Army**
1947 **RAF**		

Royal Navy v Army Royal Navy have won 31, Army 39, and 3 matches have been drawn
Royal Navy v RAF Royal Navy have won 36, RAF 25, and 4 matches have been drawn
Army v RAF Army have won 38, RAF 19, and 8 matches have been drawn

THE MIDDLESEX SEVENS 1990
(*Sponsored by Save & Prosper*)

Rupert Cherry

Harlequins' domination of the Middlesex Sevens continued in 1990. They set records by winning for the fifth year in succession, and for the 13th time. They played rather better than they had done in previous years: their support for each other, the ingenious ways in which their pattern of passing created openings and their very sound tackling presented the 53,000 crowd with a fine example of the art of sevens.

Again they met Rosslyn Park in the final and beat them by an even more handsome margin than in 1989. Park, with four former Harlequins in their side, were perhaps rather fortunate to reach the final. They did so because of a controversial try scored by Richard Moon against Bath in the semi-final. Moon and Stuart Barnes raced for the ball as it rolled over the Bath line. It certainly looked on the television replay as if Barnes had made the touch-down, but the referee, who of course could not see the replay, awarded a try to Moon.

In the other semi-final, Harlequins overcame a fast and agile Loughborough Students side simply because of their greater expertise. This was a fine performance by the Quins, for the Students had made themselves quite a reputation for fighting back. They had overcome Wasps in extra time by 20-16, having been 0-16 down, and had turned a 0-10 deficit against Saracens into a 14-10 victory.

The final, as is often the case, was not so exciting, but it was distinguished by a remarkable failure of Will Carling, the England captain, to score for Harlequins after crossing the Rosslyn Park line. He was literally held up right off the ground by Alex Woodhouse who, with Simon Hunter, forced him over the dead-ball line. Carling made up for his error with two tries afterwards, and a magnificent 70-yard run by Everton Davis and another long sprint by Stuart Thresher put the Harlequins well on top.

RESULTS

Sixth Round: Rosslyn Park I 26, London Welsh 6; London Scottish 6, Harlequins II 16; Blackheath I 10, Rosslyn Park II 20; Blackheath II 6, Bath 24; Swansea 10, Saracens 20; Loughborough Students 20, Wasps 16; Richmond I 10, West London Institute 24; Richmond II 4, Harlequins I 22
Seventh Round: Rosslyn Park I 18, Harlequins II 13; Rosslyn Park II 12, Bath 22; Saracens 10, Loughborough Students 14; West London Institute 6, Harlequins I 34
Semi-finals: Rosslyn Park I 10, Bath 6; Loughborough Students 10, Harlequins I 20
Final: Rosslyn Park I 10, Harlequins I 26

Teams in Final

Rosslyn Park: K Wyles, S Hunter, N Chesworth; R H Q B Moon; T Hyde; A Woodhouse, A Dent
Scorers *Tries:* Moon, Chesworth　*Conversion:* Woodhouse

Will Carling about to score for Harlequins in the final while a former Harlequin, Simon Hunter, chases hopefully in the cause of Rosslyn Park.

Harlequins: E Davis, W D C Carling, A Thompson; R Glenister; S Thresher;
P J Winterbottom, C Luxton
Scorers *Tries:* Carling (2), Davis, Thompson, Thresher   *Conversions:* Thresher (3)
Referee R C Rees (London)

WINNERS

1926	Harlequins
1927	Harlequins
1928	Harlequins
1929	Harlequins
1930	London Welsh
1931	London Welsh
1932	Blackheath
1933	Harlequins
1934	Barbarians
1935	Harlequins
1936	Sale
1937	London Scottish
1938	Metropolitan Police
1939	Cardiff
1940	St Mary's Hospital
1941	Cambridge University
1942	St Mary's Hospital
1943	St Mary's Hospital
1944	St Mary's Hospital
1945	Notts
1946	St Mary's Hospital
1947	Rosslyn Park
1948	Wasps
1949	Heriot's FP
1950	Rosslyn Park
1951	Richmond II
1952	Wasps
1953	Richmond
1954	Rosslyn Park
1955	Richmond
1956	London Welsh
1957	St Luke's College
1958	Blackheath
1959	Loughborough Colleges
1960	London Scottish
1961	London Scottish
1962	London Scottish
1963	London Scottish
1964	Loughborough Colleges
1965	London Scottish
1966	Loughborough Colleges
1967	Harlequins
1968	London Welsh
1969	St Luke's College
1970	Loughborough Colleges
1971	London Welsh
1972	London Welsh
1973	London Welsh
1974	Richmond
1975	Richmond
1976	Loughborough Colleges
1977	Richmond
1978	Harlequins
1979	Richmond
1980	Richmond
1981	Rosslyn Park
1982	Stewart's-Melville FP
1983	Richmond
1984	London Welsh
1985	Wasps
1986	Harlequins
1987	Harlequins
1988	Harlequins
1989	Harlequins
1990	Harlequins

*Harlequins have won the title 13 times, Richmond 9 (including one by their second VII),
London Welsh 8, London Scottish 6, St Mary's Hospital and Loughborough Colleges 5 each,
Rosslyn Park 4, Wasps 3, Blackheath and St Luke's College (now Exeter University) twice,
Barbarians, Sale, Met Police, Cardiff, Cambridge University, Notts (now Nottingham),
Heriot's FP and Stewart's-Melville FP once each*

PROMISING WALES LOSE DIRECTION

SCHOOLS RUGBY 1989-90

George Abbott

It was important for the *Wales* (Senior Group) to lay a solid foundation of success in the 1989-90 season, for in August 1990 they were to face the challenging test of a tour in New Zealand, their first major venture overseas since they visited Zimbabwe in 1985. They started satisfactorily in January with a 15-0 victory over a lighter *Scotland* (18 Group) side, which had previously lost 21-8 to France after holding their formidable opponents up to half-time. Then, after defeating the Welsh Youth XV 11-4, they were out-played in the set pieces by a strong English pack, and although a late Welsh rally narrowed the margin from 14-0 to 14-6 *England* were good value for their victory. *Wales* then suffered two narrow defeats by Ireland and France, while *England* also lost twice, to Ireland 15-6 and France 20-9. For the last match they were considerably weakened by a stomach bug, which affected as many as seven of the squad to a greater or lesser degree.

The honours therefore went to *Ireland* and *France*, both of whom won all three matches. For *Ireland*, who owed their success mainly to the fine all-round work of a dominant pack, it was the highly-prized Triple Crown. *France* have never played Ireland at 18 Group level, but they came through triumphantly against the other three countries, although they were considered a little fortunate in beating Wales 4-3 and England's gallant effort against them undoubtedly lost something through their gastric problems. *Scotland* had no success, but with possession limited to scraps their backs showed some touches of real class and as a unit were probably at least as strong as any of their rivals.

At the lower age level *England* (16 Group) played three international matches against Continental opposition, beating Italy 18-6, Portugal 23-14 and Spain 35-3. The *Welsh Schools* (Intermediate Group), whose age limit is a year lower than England's, continued their run of success against Scotland and Italy by winning 22-0 and 25-8 respectively. They also played a B international against Italy B, winning 12-0.

A season without defeat is a highly valued event at any level, and among the better-known names in England only four achieved such a record in 1989-90. They were *Oundle*, *Bloxham* and *St Dunstan's*, who finish their first XV fixtures before Christmas, and *Mount St Mary's*, who play a few more matches in the Spring Term.

Oundle richly deserved top ranking. With a talented group of players competing for first-team places, they won all 12 games and scored 387 points to 51 in a series of high-quality performances. *Bloxham* survived several close calls, finishing the term with a record of 12 wins and two draws to improve on their excellent figures of 1988, when they won 12 and lost two games. *St Dunstan's* drew as many as five of their 16 fixtures, but enjoyed their first unbeaten season since 1971, aided by the fact that they were able to field a settled team, using only 18 players. Victories over Stonyhurst and Ampleforth in September got the gifted *Mount St Mary's* team off to a fine start and they went on to gain 15 successes in all before drawing their final fixture with Bradford GS, when they were weakened by the calls of representative matches.

Among those schools which did not quite gain the distinction of going through the season undefeated there were several who had much of which they could be proud. *Campion* (Hornchurch), playing open rugby of high class, won 20 matches and scored nearly 700 points, though at the end they suffered an unexpected setback against Reigate GS. That result showed *Cowley* (St Helens) in a very favourable light, for on their biennial visit to Surrey they recorded a clear-cut victory over Reigate, finishing with most impressive figures (W19, L1) and scoring 690 points to 112. Out of 133 tries, 65 were scored by the wings.

The *RGS, High Wycombe* played rugby of a high standard, with 100 tries coming from the threequarters. They lost their opening fixture to Berkhamsted, but won the remaining 22 and then went on tour to Ireland, where they won two games and lost one. In the strong south-eastern circuit there was little to choose between Epsom, St Paul's and Wellington (Berkshire). *St Paul's,* fielding a team of balanced strength, defeated the other two, but lost twice when depleted by injuries. *Epsom* and *Wellington,* who do not meet, both lost to St Paul's alone and both won their other 11 school matches.

Queen Elizabeth's Hospital (Bristol) were fortunate in having to make very few changes throughout the season and gained a good supply of ball from the set pieces. They won 15 of their 16 games, losing only to Llandovery (15-10). *King's, Taunton,* another sound team, suffered only one defeat (albeit a heavy one, to an exceptional Blackrock XV in Dublin). *Millfield* had the distinction of a victory over Blackrock and they enjoyed a great deal of success with 11 wins in all, though they lost by narrow margins to Llandovery and King's, Taunton.

Cheltenham enjoyed a highly satisfactory term. Their ten victims included Downside, Rugby, Marlborough and Sherborne and their two defeats, by *Clifton* (who staged a welcome revival) and Radley, were by very narrow margins. *Downside's* lively, enterprising team won their last nine matches after losing two and drawing one of the first four, and then added three victories on tour in Hong Kong. *Canford* had a good season at several levels, with the first XV winning nine out of 12 games and the second and Under-15 teams both losing only once. *Sherborne,* short of experienced players, had one of their less distinguished campaigns with only five successes in 12 fixtures. Competent rugby, with kicking kept to a minimum, brought *King's,*

Bruton their best results for some years (W10, L3). Sound teamwork proved highly effective for *Clayesmore*, who won 13 of their 15 matches, scoring 51 tries. *Truro* again led the field in their area, winning the Cornwall Schools Cup and finishing the term with an overall record of W12, D2, L2.

It was a difficult term for *Rugby* (W6, L8), but they produced a great performance, their best by a long way, against the all-conquering Oundle XV, whom they led 9-8 with only three minutes remaining before finally going down 9-14. *Bromsgrove* had a good season with nine wins and a draw in 14 games, ending with a victory over King Edward's, Birmingham in the 158th fixture between the two schools. *Solihull* enjoyed their best record for years with 16 successes and only two losses.

In the north the *Ampleforth* XV, if not of vintage quality, was still capable of most attractive football (W11, D1, L2). Their defeats were against Mount St Mary's and *Pocklington*, who rated the 18-10 victory over Ampleforth as their best effort of a season in which they won 15 out of 20 matches, with a good young pack and a gifted pair of half-backs as their main assets. *Silcoates* had a pleasing record (W17, L4), highlighted by successes against three of their strongest rivals, Bradford, Leeds and Wakefield Grammar Schools. *Sedbergh's* figures (W6, D1, L4) were not particularly distinguished – they are judged by high standards – but their strong forwards gave a good account of themselves. The high point of the season was the centenary match with Loretto, which Sedbergh won 20-15.

A lively *Stonyhurst* side with strong backs gave some outstanding displays, winning 14 and drawing one out of 18 fixtures. They were at their best in a 32-3 victory over *Arnold* (Blackpool), whose big, strong pack contributed much to their successes (W13, L5). The most notable of those results came in a tight contest with Cowley, when Arnold hung on to win 13-12 and inflicted on Cowley their only defeat. *Kirkham GS* suffered severely from injuries early in the season, when three of their four losses occurred. Of their later fixtures they lost only one, to Stonyhurst, while registering 16 wins and two draws. A run of nine victories in October and November was the peak of the season for *King's, Macclesfield* (W15, D1, L5). *St Bees* came through a series of tight matches with satisfactory results (W8, L4). *Durham* started their season enterprisingly with an international tournament including teams from France, Portugal, Scotland and Wales, as well as Peterhouse from Zimbabwe, the winners. Well equipped with pace, Durham went on to win 12 of their 16 school matches, although they lost heavily to Ampleforth.

The *Bedford* XV, built around 13 members of the squad that had toured New Zealand and Fiji in the summer, were outplayed by the redoubtable Oundle team and also lost to St Paul's in a revived fixture, but won more school matches (ten) than ever before. *Radley* had nine victories and three defeats; their form was variable, but at times (notably against Rugby, whom they defeated 32-0) they played rugby of a very high standard. *Eton*, where rugby is growing in popularity, enjoyed one of their best seasons, finishing with seven wins in a row and winning eight in all out of 11 games in a strengthened fixture list.

In East Anglia *Bishop's Stortford* (W10, D2, L2) did well, as did *The Perse*, whose 11 victories, set against two defeats, included a narrow win against their local rivals, The Leys. Starting without a single old colour, *The Oratory* had much work to do, but the team developed so well that nine wins were achieved and only two games were lost. The defeats came from Eton and the useful *Shiplake* XV, whose 13 successes from 15 fixtures were highly commendable.

Caterham's style of running rugby produced 57 tries, more than half of them by the wings, in 15 games, of which they won 11. Although small, *Eastbourne* possessed ample pace; sharpened by a tour of Australia in August, they finished with figures of W11, D1, L3. The fortunes of *Sevenoaks* changed dramatically in October. Before half-term they won only two out of six fixtures, but the forwards made marked improvements and they used their strong-running backs well later on to gain seven wins in a row.

No school in Scotland established a supremacy to compare with that of Merchiston Castle in 1988-89. *Merchiston* themselves finished with good but not outstanding figures (W16, L4) and the best record was that of *George Watson's*, who won 21 games and lost only two, spreading the ball wide and scoring many tries on the wings. The *Edinburgh Academy* (W14, D2, L2) were generally in control through the strength of their pack, while *Loretto*, young and light, worked hard to achieve 11 victories in 15 matches. *Stewart's-Melville*, with strong backs and improving forwards, won 17, drew one and lost five; and *St Aloysius* retained the Scottish Schools Cup, winning 18 matches in all and losing three.

In Northern Ireland *Methodist College, Belfast* were again unbeaten by any of their local rivals. They retained the Ulster Schools Cup with a 15-0 victory over *Campbell College*, who were equally worthy finalists, since like MCB they had not lost to another school in the province.

A revival of interest among the state schools in Wales was helped greatly by the inauguration of the Welsh Schools Cup, played initially in leagues, with the league leaders going through to the knock-out stages after Christmas. *Neath College*, among the favourites from the start, fulfilled expectations by beating *Nantyglo* 42-21 in the final. *Gowerton* (Swansea) maintained their high traditions with very fluent back play and were unbeaten until they went down narrowly to the powerful *Pontypool College* XV in the Cup in February. Among the independent schools *Christ, Brecon* and *Llandovery* possessed their usual share of talented players, but *Monmouth* had one of their less noteworthy seasons.

Millfield featured prominently, as often before, in the seven-a-side tournaments in March. Their successes included the highly-rated Surrey and Oxfordshire events, but in the most prestigious of all, the National Schools Open run by Rosslyn Park, they were eliminated in the quarter-finals by *Neath College*, who went on to win the competition by beating *Llandovery* 16-14 and then *Mount St Mary's* 12-8 in two closely-contested games. *Ampleforth*, who had won both the Open and the Festival (for schools playing rugby for one term only) in 1989, opted to compete in the Open, since a new regulation barred them from entering both events, and reached the last eight, losing 12-6 Mount St Mary's. The Festival produced a big surprise, with *Caterham*, who had barely scraped through the first day as distinctly fortunate group winners, improving all the time to defeat *Tonbridge* 24-4 in the semi-final and *Sevenoaks* 20-12 in the final.

The following players took part in the 18 Group international matches. (Countries played against are shown in square brackets.)
Abbreviations: *E* – England, *F* – France, *I* – Ireland, *J* – Japan, *S* – Scotland, *W* – Wales, (R) – Replacement.

ENGLAND
Full-back: M S Mapletoft (Lawrence Sheriff, Rugby) [*W, S, I, F*]
Threequarters: J C Belton (Durham) [*W, S, I*]; M Dawson (Mount St Mary's) [*I*(R), *F*]; S J Thompson (Warwick) [*W, S, I, F*]; P E McCarthy (Mount St Mary's) [*W, S, I, F*]; R A Davies (Poynton County HS) [*W, S, I, F*]
Half-backs: D Edwards (Pocklington) [*W, S, I, F*]; K P P Bracken (Stonyhurst) [*W, S, I, F*]
Forwards: D E Crompton (Exeter College) [*W, S, I, F*]; M P Regan (St Brendan's) [*W, S, I, F*]; D M Richards (Shiplake) [*W, S, I*]; J P Cooke (Marple Hall) [*S*(R), *F*]; M L Wright (Sharnbrook Upper, Beds) [*W, S, I, F*]; J B Daniell (Eton) [*W, S, I, F*]; D Wyer-Roberts (Bedford) [*I*(R)]; R B Cable (Vyners, Ickenham) [*W, S, I*]; D A Williams (Queen's, Taunton) [*I*(R), *F*]; J P Griffiths (Crossley Heath, Halifax) [*W, S, I, F*]; E D Rollitt (St Paul's) [*W, S, I, F*]
Bracken was captain in all four matches

IRELAND
Full-back: R Garvey (De La Salle, Churchtown) [*W, S, E*]
Threequarters: D O'Dowd (Rockwell) [*W, S, E*]; R Hunter (Methodist College, Belfast) [*W, S, E*]; B Cotter (St Mary's, Rathmines) [*W, S*]; R Casey (Christian Brothers, Cork) [*E*]; G Collins (Methodist College, Belfast) [*W, S, E*]
Half-backs: D Humphreys (Ballymena Academy) [*W, S, E*]; F Downes (Crescent, Limerick) [*W, S, E*]
Forwards: P Parker (Royal Belfast Academical Institution) [*W, S, E*]; I Blake (Terenure) [*W, S*]; G Purdy (Regent House) [*W*(R), *E*]; P Wallace (Crescent, Limerick) [*W, S, E*]; N Nolan (Cistercian College, Roscrea) [*W, S, E*]; R Wilson (Royal Belfast Academical Institution) [*W, S, E*]; L Toland (St Clement's, Limerick) [*W, S, E*]; A Deyermond (Methodist College, Belfast) [*W, S, E*]; F Butler (Blackrock) [*W, S, E*]; F Fitzgerald (Rockwell) [*W*(R)]
Humphreys was captain in all three matches

SCOTLAND

Full-back: M M Thomson (Stewart's-Melville) [*F, W, J, E, I*]
Threequarters: J W K Anderson (Merchiston Castle) [*F, W, J, E, I*]; P L Crawford
(Morrison's Academy) [*F*]; B R Eriksson (Merchiston Castle) [*W, J, E, I*]; K R Milligan
(Stewart's-Melville) [*F, W, J, E, I*]; M J A Craig (St Aloysius) [*F, W, J, E*]; S Tait
(Kelso HS) [*J*(R), *E*(R)]; N Penny (Stewart's-Melville) [*I*]
Half-backs: G P J Townsend (Galashiels Academy) [*F, W, J, E, I*]; S E Gilliland
(North Berwick HS) [*F, W, J, E, I*]
Forwards: R K Hastings (Kelvinside Academy) [*F, W, I*]; T J Smith (Rannoch) [*J, E*];
M H Rutherford (Merchiston Castle) [*F, W, J, E, I*]; A S Mason (Glasgow Academy) [*F*];
J K McKechnie (Dundee HS) [*W, J, E, I*]; D R M Hathway (George Watson's) [*F, W, J, I*];
P E Darroch (St Aloysius) [*J*(R), *E*]; M B Rudkin (George Watson's) [*F, W, J, E, I*];
R P Lockhart (George Heriot's) [*F, W, J, E, I*]; A H Gray (Galashiels Academy) [*F*(R)];
A B Millar (Berwickshire HS) [*F, W*]; M G Browne (Stranraer Academy) [*J, E, I*];
M McNeill (Ross HS) [*F, W, J, E, I*]
Milligan was captain in all five matches

WALES

Full-backs: R Fowler (Hartridge HS) [*S, I, F*]; P Armstrong (St Cyres) [*E*]
Threequarters: M Liddiatt (St Cyres) [*S*]; P Wintle (Cynffig) [*E, I, F*]; A Palfrey (St Cyres)
[*S, E, I, F*]; M Wintle (Cynffig) [*S, E, I, F*]; J Lewis (Llandovery) [*S, E, F*(R)]; J Hopkins
(Maesydderwen) [*I, F*]
Half-backs: Dean Morgan (Neath College) [*S, E*]; P Williams (Neath College) [*I, F*];
H Harris (Glantaf) [*S, E, I, F*]
Forwards: S Price (Tonyrefail) [*S, E, I, F*]; J Evans (Neath College) [*S, E, I, F*]; R Thomas
(Amman Valley) [*S, E, I, F*]; L Harvey (Maesteg) [*S, F*]; M Glover (Neath College) [*E, I*];
P Hewitt (Pontypool College) [*E*(R), *F*(R)]; C Langley (St Cyres) [*S, E, I, F*]; D Cooper
(Nantyglo) [*S, E, I, F*]; David Morgan (Bishop Gore) [*S, E, I, F*]; S Quinnell
(Graig, Llanelli) [*S, E, I, F*]
Evans was captain in all four matches

MATCH DETAILS (18 Group)

23 December, Myreside, Edinburgh

SCOTLAND 8 (2T)   **FRANCE 21** (3PG 3T)
SCOTLAND *Tries:* Gilliland, Thomson
FRANCE *Tries:* Juzon, Brunel, Cazeaux   *Penalty Goals:* Hueber (3)
Referee I M Bullerwell (England)

6 January, Bridgend

WALES 15 (1PG 3T)   **SCOTLAND 0**
WALES *Tries:* Langley, Quinnell, Palfrey   *Penalty Goal:* Dean Morgan
Referee T Spreadbury (England)

31 March, Hartlepool

ENGLAND 14 (1PG 1DG 2T)   **WALES 6** (1G)
ENGLAND *Tries:* Rollitt, Mapletoft   *Penalty Goal:* McCarthy   *Dropped Goal:* McCarthy
WALES *Try:* Quinnell   *Conversion:* Dean Morgan
Referee R Clark (Scotland)

31 March, Murrayfield

SCOTLAND 19 (2G 1PG 1T)   **JAPAN 31** (2G 1PG 4T)
SCOTLAND *Tries:* Browne, Craig, Rudkin   *Conversions:* Thomson (2)
Penalty Goal: Thomson
JAPAN *Tries:* Arei (2), Nakata, Fukatsu (2), Yoshida   *Conversions:* Owashi (2)
Penalty Goal: Owashi
Referee C J High (England)

4 April, Murrayfield

SCOTLAND 6 (1G)   **ENGLAND 32** (2G 5T)
SCOTLAND *Try:* Eriksson   *Conversion:* Tait
ENGLAND *Tries:* McCarthy, Mapletoft, Belton (2), Rollitt, Bracken, Cable
Conversions: McCarthy, Mapletoft
Referee M C Debat (France)

6 April, Ravenhill, Belfast

IRELAND 12 (4PG)   **WALES 10** (2PG 1T)
IRELAND *Penalty Goals:* Humphreys (4)
WALES *Try:* Evans   *Penalty Goals:* Hopkins (2)
Referee D Leslie (Scotland)

14 April, Lansdowne Road, Dublin

IRELAND 14 (1G 2T)   **SCOTLAND 10** (1G 1T)
IRELAND *Tries:* Butler (2), O'Dowd   *Conversion:* Garvey
SCOTLAND *Tries:* Thomson, Milligan   *Conversion:* Townsend
Referee E F Morrison (England)

18 April, Oxford

ENGLAND 6 (1G)   **IRELAND 15** (1G 3PG)
ENGLAND *Try:* Edwards   *Conversion:* McCarthy
IRELAND *Try:* Parker   *Conversion:* Garvey   *Penalty Goals:* Garvey, Humphreys (2)
Referee C Norling (Wales)

18 April, Aberaman

WALES 3 (1PG)   **FRANCE 4** (1T)
WALES *Penalty Goal:* Hopkins
FRANCE *Try:* Labeyrie
Referee K McCartney (Scotland)

21 April, Carmaux

FRANCE 20 (1G 2PG 2T)   **ENGLAND 9** (1G 1PG)
FRANCE *Tries:* Moni, Susbielles, Cazeaux   *Conversion:* Deauze   *Penalty Goals:* Hueber (2)
ENGLAND *Try:* Davies   *Conversion:* Thompson   *Penalty Goal:* Thompson
Referee M Roelands (Belgium)

ENGLAND'S FINEST PERFORMANCE

COLTS AND YOUTH 1989-90

Michael Stevenson

In April England Colts entertained France at Harrogate, in what is usually their toughest fixture. That they won and won so decisively (24-11) and with such élan was noteworthy; it was also highly significant because it was the first time that they had ever beaten France since the inception of the fixture in 1977. Several of the press thought that it was one of the best, if not the best game we had seen all season. It was a major improvement on the England performance against Wales at Wrexham earlier in April, when Wales won a mistake-ridden game.

Sadly, the contest was everything that the French game was not: it was scrappy, negative and markedly lacking in skill. Wales appeared to possess talent, although they shut the game up tight as a tick in the second half, ignoring even the obvious talent of their fly-half, Neil Jenkins, and relying on considerable forward dominance and the annihilation of a makeshift England front row for their victory. The England squad met at Ilkley and, behind closed doors, the lessons of the two defeats were spelled out by coach Graham Smith: 'We decided that we must take chances and keep the ball in our hands. We hoped to exert pressure in the scrums and to use all our options at line-outs, scrums and penalties. Running at them out of defence and punishing errors, especially with penalties, was discussed as well as confidence in each other's abilities and pride in the team'.

The ambitious mixture worked, and against France, England were totally transformed from the shambles at Wrexham. Serge Blanco had played in the first England v France fixture and he would have appreciated the best English back play, although France were most impressive, especially in the centre, where Gratien and Balard were outstanding. England's win, based on forward domination, and especially on the work of the back row of Rennell, Bannon and Wilkins, was all the more admirable as they avoided the narrow, constricted tactics that had characterised their performance at Wrexham.

Despite the understandable euphoria over the French match, the past season may be seen primarily as the one in which Colts' rugby arrived, especially as far as England was concerned. Mike Glogg, chairman of the England Colts selectors, was invited, along with Graham Smith, to meet Don Rutherford, Geoff Cooke, Roger Uttley, Will Carling, John Elliott and others at Twickenham: 'We were asked to report on the players we had seen coming through and whether we had any outstanding potential. Uttley and Cooke spelled out the features of English rugby that needed improving and the sort of priorities that we all should possess'. This significant meeting showed that the RFU is now viewing the role of the national colts as a vital one.

Mike Glogg reports: 'In the process of scouring the country for Colts talent, I have learned a great deal about the state of the game at school and youth level. We have talent galore – the Daily Mail Cup final for 15-year-olds at Twickenham and the excellent showing of the 16 Group under Mike Williams are proof enough of this – but I am equally certain that there is a desperate lack of good coaching and development at the next stage. The England Schools 18 Group is increasingly in danger of catering only for a select band of independent schools; also the Colts operate effectively in only a handful of clubs and counties such as Lancashire and Yorkshire. Much more must be done to encourage excellence, otherwise we shall continue to offer only mediocrity to gifted players who deserve much more. I think the RFU has to take the lead. It cannot just continue to preside over organisational drift'.

As for Wales Youth, following a convincing victory over Welsh Students and a narrow win (13-11) against Italian Youth, they suffered a set-back when they met Welsh Schools at Stradey Park, Llanelli in February. Wales Youth led 4-3 at the interval and both sides mounted some fine movements, especially in counter-attack, without being able to translate them into points. Two tries for the Schools by their talented centre, Wintle, settled the result (4-11) but the match generally was a great success.

A visit to Stade Lombard, Cavaillon for a demanding meeting with French Juniors followed. Wales suffered a crucial set-back when their skilled and capable fly-half, Neil Jenkins, was struck down with food poisoning. Darran Edwards, a utility back, replaced him and Wales started well, scoring a try in the first five minutes and leading 10-7 at the interval. Gradually, however, extreme heat and a hard, poorly-grassed playing surface, plus the discrepancy in weight between the sides, took their toll. France finished as decisive winners by 28-13.

Scotland, like Wales, run a two-tier system, and at Under-18 level have played nine games without defeat. Most gratifying was their victory over the Japanese tourists – the visitors' only defeat in six matches. The Colts' (Under-19s) one match was played at Millbrae, Ayr, against England, and resulted in victory for the visitors by 17-9. In the 'Roses' County Championship final Yorkshire, whose rugged pack controlled the one-sided encounter, beat Lancashire by 34-3 and by six tries to nil. The National Westminster Bank announced that their sponsorship at Colts level would continue for another three years at least. They will be making £25,000 available each year.

The improved co-operation between different levels of Youth rugby was illustrated by the invitation extended by the Under-21s to former Colts to join their squad. The six invited players were Jon Wray, Alistair Saverimutto and Steve Ojomoh from Bath, Niall Griffiths from Leicester, Neil Matthews of Gloucester and Rory Jenkins of Brixham.

The following players took part in the Colts/Youth international matches. Countries played against are shown in square brackets.
Abbreviations: E – England, F – France, It – Italy, J – Japan, N – Netherlands, S – Scotland, W – Wales, (R) – Replacement

ENGLAND
Full-backs: T Allison (Bishop's Stortford) [F, It, S, W], A Sales (Morley) [S(R)]
Threequarters: J Bonney (Southend) [F, It, S, W], C Emmerson (Halifax) [F, It, S, W], P Ingram (Northampton) [F, It, S, W], A McAdam (Barker's Butts) [F, It, S, W]
Half-backs: D Willett (Exeter University) [F, S, W], A Sales (Morley) [It], S Douglas (Gosforth) [F, It, S, W], B Short (Harlequins) [W(R)]
Forwards: B Fennell (Rosslyn Park) [F, It, S], P Delaney (Wasps) [It, W], P Simmonds (Bedford) [F, S], G Rowntree (Leicester) [F, It, S, W], P Winter (Blaydon) [W], R Bramley (Wakefield) [F, It, S, W], S Fletcher (West Park) [It], R Baxter (Exeter) [F, S, W], M Rennell (Abbey) [F, It, S, W], L Bannon (Rosslyn Park) [F, It, S], C Wilkins (Wasps) [F, It, S, W], D Blyth (Waterloo) [W]
Richard Bramley was captain in all four matches

SCOTLAND
UNDER-18
Full-backs: K Logan (Stirling County) [J, N]
Threequarters: S S Littlewood (Boroughmuir) [J, N], I A McLeod (Corstorphine) [N], D C Bain (Melrose) [J], D R Hamilton (Dunfermline) [J, N], P J Stanger (Hawick) [J], J McKinney (Dyce) [N], W M Tonkin (Currie) [N(R)]
Half-backs: M McKenzie (Stirling County) [J, N], G G Burns (Stewart's-Melville FP) [J, N]
Forwards: S McDonald (Kelso Harlequins) [J, N], K R Allan (Melrose) [J, N], R B McNulty (Trinity Academicals) [J, N], K Scott (Hawick Harlequins) [N(R)], D G Burns (Biggar) [J, N], S J Campbell (West of Scotland) [J, N], A G Ness (Glasgow High/Kelvinside) [J, N], D Nichol (Selkirk Youth) [N(R)], A J Graham (Dundee HSFP) [J, N], D K Forster (Jed Thistle) [J, N]
Ness was captain in both games

UNDER-19 *(Against England)*
Full-back: A M Fraser (Edinburgh Academicals)
Threequarters: S S Littlewood (Boroughmuir), R J S Shepherd (Edinburgh Academicals), C N White (Watsonians), M P Craig (Edinburgh Wanderers)
Half-backs: B Duncan (West of Scotland), A D Nicol (Heriot's FP)
Forwards: A N Pringle (Musselburgh), L B A Thomson (Selkirk), F M Graham (Boroughmuir), A J Kittle (Ross High), S J Campbell (West of Scotland), C J Pow (Musselburgh), S Lindsay (Stirling County) (R), J M Clinkenbeard (Currie), D W A Gilchrist (Gala), E A Murchison (Loughborough Students), G McGill (Dundee HSFP) (R)
Nicol was captain

WALES
Full-backs: J Westwood (Abercarn) [E, F, It]
Threequarters: P Jones (Pencoed) [F, It], G Matthews (Tondu) [E], S Gibbs (Pencoed) [E, F, It], R Brown (Crumlin) [E, F, It], G Thomas (Blackwood) [E, F, It]
Half-backs: N Jenkins (Pontypridd) [E, It], D Edwards (Seven Sisters) [F]; P Young (Oakdale) [E, F, It]
Forwards: P Harriman (Trefil) [It], D Thomas (Pontypool) [E, F], G Davies (Llantrisant) [E, F, It], H Daniels (Llanelli) [F(R)], K Allen (New Dock Stars) [E, F, It], D Higgins (Cardiff) [E, F], A Gwilym (Tonyrefail) [E, F], C Goodwin (Mold) [E, F, It], D Senger (Llanelli) [It], I Callaghan (Neath Colts) [E, It], R Nixon (Waunarlwydd) [F], F Jones (Tylorstown) [E, F, It], P Jones (Bridgend Athletic) [It]
Scott Gibbs was captain in all three matches

MATCH DETAILS 1989-90

10 February, South Wales Police Ground, Bridgend

Wales Youth 13 (1G 1PG 1T) **Italian Youth 11** (1PG 2T)
Wales *Tries:* Jenkins, Davies *Conversion:* Jenkins *Penalty Goal:* Jenkins
Italy *Tries:* Amore, Birteg *Penalty Goal:* Dolfin
Referee R J Megson (Scotland)

4 March, Stade Lombard, Cavaillon

France Youth 28 (3G 1PG 1DG 1T) **Welsh Youth 13** (1G 1PG 1T)
France *Tries:* Urcelay (3), Faure *Conversions:* Viars (3) *Penalty Goal:* Viars
Dropped Goal: Faure
Wales *Tries:* Higgins, Goodwin *Conversion:* Edwards *Penalty Goal:* Edwards
Referee W W Calder (Scotland)

17 March, Segni

Italian Youth 17 (1G 1PG 2T) **England Colts 15** (1G 3PG)
Italy *Tries:* Soncini (2), Signore *Conversion:* Calenne *Penalty Goal:* Calenne
England *Try:* McAdam *Conversion:* Allison *Penalty Goals:* Allison (3)
Referee D Neyrat (France)

1 April, Hilversum

Netherlands Under-19 0 **Scotland Under-18 32** (1G 2PG 5T)
Scotland *Tries:* Logan, Littlewood, McKinney, Tonkin, McKenzie, Burns
Conversion: McKenzie *Penalty Goals:* McKenzie (2)

7 April, Murrayfield

Scotland Under-18 28 (3G 2PG 1T) **Japan Schools 23** (2G 1PG 2T)
Scotland *Tries:* Logan, McKenzie, Ness, Graham *Conversions:* Bain (3)
Penalty Goals: Bain (2)
Japan *Tries:* Motoki, Masuho, Fukatsu, Matsumoto *Conversions:* Owashi (2)
Penalty Goal: Owashi
Referee R S Clark (Scotland)

7 April, Wrexham

Welsh Youth 12 (3PG 1DG) **England Colts 6** (2PG)
Wales *Penalty Goals:* Jenkins (3) *Dropped Goal:* Jenkins
England *Penalty Goals:* Allison (2)
Referee G Black (Ireland)

21 April, Harrogate

England Colts 24 (2G 4PG) **France Youth 11** (1PG 2T)
England *Tries:* Douglas, Willett *Conversions:* Allison (2) *Penalty Goals:* Allison (4)
France *Tries:* Viars, Balard *Penalty Goal:* Rolland
Referee D Leslie (Scotland)

28 April, Millbrae, Ayr

Scotland Under-19 9 (1G 1PG) **England Colts 17** (1G 1PG 2T)
Scotland *Try:* Craig *Conversion:* Duncan *Penalty Goal:* Shepherd
England *Tries:* Bonney, McAdam, Willett *Conversion:* Willett *Penalty Goal:* Allison
Referee D Henderson (Ulster)

SCOTLAND'S SWEETEST SLAM

THE 1989-90 SEASON IN SCOTLAND

Bill McMurtrie *Glasgow Herald*

Whatever their sport, Scots enjoy victory all the more when they defeat England. The 1989-90 Grand Slam was thus the sweeter, not only because it was settled in the Murrayfield match in which all was at stake – Calcutta Cup, Triple Crown, International Championship, Grand Slam – but also because it was unexpected. Each Scottish win could be savoured on its own. Yet the manner of victory on every occasion was not enough to bloat the Scots with too much confidence. Scotland struggled to find their game in beating Ireland 13-10 at Lansdowne Road; the surge for 21-0 against France flowed most strongly after Alain Carminati had been sent off; and not even overwhelming scrummaging could induce a wider margin than 13-9 against Wales at Cardiff Arms Park. Suddenly Scotland were on the verge of the ultimate for the second time in six years. In the two weeks after Cardiff emotions swelled to unprecedented heights. For the first time two of the home countries were to meet in a winner-take-all contest.

Going into the deciding match, coach Ian McGeechan had the psychologically difficult task of tuning the Scottish players to a perfectly-balanced key. The tight wins away from home helped to keep heads level, yet even against an English team averaging more than 27 points a game the Scots had unbending belief in themselves. Not even in 1984 had Murrayfield generated such an atmosphere as that which greeted the English and Scottish teams. Instead of running on to the pitch David Sole and his team walked, steely-eyed. The ploy, Sole's idea, was as much of a challenge as any *haka*. For 80 minutes the commitment on both sides was unrelenting. The Scottish forwards, though, often had an extra nudge. Theirs, it seemed, was the greater thirst for victory, and out of their reserves they drew what had been subdued in successive wins against Ireland, France, and Wales. Tony Stanger's timely try immediately after the interval, added to the penalty goal that Craig Chalmers kicked just before half-time, stretched Scotland's 6-4 lead by seven valuable points.

Afterwards, Geoff Cooke, England's team manager, allocated those scores their perspective. He would have settled for a two-point deficit at half-time, even 4-9, but it was a killer to fall nine points in arrears just when England ought to have been looking to exploit the wind which, though blustery and gusting, was in their favour in the second half. Sole confirmed later that the match was faster and more intense than any he had ever experienced.

So ended an international season in which Scotland won all six of their matches, recording victories against Fiji and Romania at Murrayfield as well as the clean sweep in the Championship. Not since 1924-25 (also a Grand Slam year) and the next had Scotland won six in a row. Fiji and Romania were beaten by 38-17 and 32-0 respectively, but no one could delude himself that those matches were anything but warm-ups for the Championship. The drawing together of the team was valuable in carrying the Scots through an uneasy Dublin game, when they came from behind with two tries by Derek White. It was a rare away win for the Scots, and Sole summed it up by pointing out that he had had to wait until his 22nd cap before playing for Scotland in an international win outside Murrayfield. To win in Dublin while not playing well was a sign of a potentially good team, and the pieces fitted more easily into place against France, especially after Fred Howard had dismissed Carminati for stamping on John Jeffrey's face.

Cardiff was always going to be difficult. Scotland had won there only three times since the war, and Wales became even more of an unknown quantity when Ron Waldron, succeeding John Ryan as coach, brought his Neath style and personnel with him. The new-look Welsh, though beaten, gave Scotland what Sole reckoned was as hard a game as he has known at Cardiff. What followed was the match of the century, at least in British rugby. Once it was over the Scots' initial relief soon swelled into unbridled joy.

Sole took over as Scotland's captain when Finlay Calder missed the game against Fiji. Calder, who had commanded Scotland in the 1989 Championship and captained the Lions in Australia, resumed at wing forward against Romania, but he was content to follow another's lead. The transition was smooth and easy. Consistency in selection helped. For each of the Championship matches the Scots fielded the same XV: the only change was enforced when Derek Turnbull took over from the injured White late in the first half of the Grand Slam decider.

At lower levels Scotland did not meet with such success. The B international XV drew 22-22 with Ireland at Murrayfield in a curtain-raiser to the Romanian match and lost to France by 9-31 at Oyonnax. The Under-21 team suffered their fourth successive defeat by Wales, this time by 10-24 at Ayr, and on the same day the Under-19 side lost by 9-17 against England. The Under-18 international XV were more successful, beating the Netherlands and Japan Schools. It was the Japanese boys' only defeat in six matches in Scotland.

Glasgow upset the old order in the McEwan's District Championship, winning the title outright for the first time since 1974. A draw with Edinburgh, champions for the three previous seasons, was followed by successive wins against the North and Midlands, the South and the Anglo-Scots. The base for success was laid in a September tour to Ireland with a 21-6 win over Connacht and an 18-18 draw with Munster and, following up, Glasgow beat the Fijian tourists by 22-11.

Before the Championship decider at Burnbrae the Anglo-Scots had won all three games, and with only added time remaining in the final match it seemed that the exiles had taken the title for the first time. The scores were level at 15-15, and the Anglo-Scots had the better overall try count, the Championship's tie-breaker. A belated penalty goal by David Barrett, his sixth in the match, won the game and the title for Glasgow. Barrett scored 50 points in the Championship and 79 in all of Glasgow's seven matches, both records for the district. Two players from Glasgow clubs scored more than 300 points in the season. Calum MacDonald had 312 (281 for Stirling County) and Robbie Stewart 306 (all for Kilmarnock), while Graeme Stirling was the leading try-scorer with 27, all but one for Edinburgh Wanderers.

The South retained the Under-21 district title and deposed Glasgow as Under-18 champions. Club trophies also went to the Borders. Melrose, winning the title for the first time, followed Kelso as McEwan's National League Champions, and Gala Wanderers beat Ayr in the SRU/Digital Youth Leagues final. Kelso won their own sevens in the autumn and the Jedforest tournament in the spring. Jed also won two sevens, taking the Hawick and Langholm trophies, but the Borders' other major prizes went to outsiders – Orrell at Selkirk, the Saltires (the Scottish invitation club drawing their seven from south of the border) at Gala, and Randwick at Melrose. The Sydney club, the first Southern Hemisphere visitors to the prestigious Melrose tournament, left their mark with a display of all-round competence that provided David Campese with ample opportunity to shine.

In the McEwan's National League confidence in youth paid off for Melrose, who won the Championship for the first time in the competition's 17 years. As a measure of ability and potential, four of their youngsters were chosen in Scotland's squad for the tour to New Zealand. Craig Redpath, 'Doddie' Weir and Graham Shiel, none more than 20, were included for the tour along with Craig Chalmers, Scotland's 21-year-old fly-half.

Jim Telfer and Keith Robertson were the father figures behind the success. Telfer coached the team to his own high requirements, and the 40-times capped Robertson, playing into retirement, was captain, although he missed much of the first half of the season through injury. Melrose lost only one McEwan's League match, their only defeat of the season, surprisingly at the Greenyards. Their conquerors were Ayr, who were to be relegated along with West of Scotland. Andy Purves and Keith Sudlow scored tries for Melrose, but two penalty goals by Robbie Kemp and a dropped goal by Bevan Martin, Ayr's New Zealand fly-half, procured a 9-8 win for the visitors.

That result left the competition neatly poised over the mid-winter break, and going into the full round of League matches the Championship was still open. Heriot's, celebrating their centenary, and Jedforest were also in contention. Melrose beat Jed 14-3 at the Greenyards with tries by Craig Redpath and Leroux van Niekerk, and less than four miles away, Gala defeated Heriot's 19-14.

The Scottish team which beat England at Murrayfield. L-R, back row: A C Redpath, A K Brewster, D J Turnbull, D S Wyllie, J Allan, G H Oliver (all replacements), middle row: L J Peard (touch-judge), S R P Lineen, A C Stanger, J Jeffrey, C A Gray, D F Cronin, D B White, A P Burnell, K S Milne, W D Bevan (touch-judge), D J Bishop (referee); front row: G Armstrong, I Tukalo, F Calder, D M B Sole (capt), S Hastings, C M Chalmers, A G Hastings.

A draw with Kelso at Poynder Park was the only other hiccup in the Melrose season, and they finished a point clear of both Heriot's and Jed, the Edinburgh club taking second place on points difference. Heriot's were running well before they slipped to defeats by Stirling County and Melrose on successive Saturdays and Jed led the table by one point from Melrose after the autumn stage. On the resumption Heriot's' 23-3 home win over Jed kept the excitement boiling.

Edinburgh Academicals were fourth, but pride of place among the also-rans must surely go to Stirling County, who finished fifth in their first season in Division 1. They were almost unbeatable at home, conquering Stewart's-Melville, Hawick, Kelso, Heriot's and Boroughmuir at Bridgehaugh before Jed halted their run with a 7-3 win. Kelso, winners of the title for the previous two seasons, and Hawick, ten times champions, both lost their first four League matches and finished in the lower half of the table, although latterly neither was under threat of relegation. West dropped to Division 2 for the first time and Currie, runners-up to Edinburgh Wanderers in Division 2, will make their debut in the top flight in 1990-91.

McEWAN'S NATIONAL LEAGUE

Division 1	P	W	D	L	F	A	Pts
Melrose	12	10	1	1	247	107	21
Heriot's FP	13	10	0	3	276	132	20
Jedforest	13	10	0	3	203	149	20
Edinburgh Acs	13	9	0	4	212	145	18
Stirling County	13	7	1	5	207	216	15
Boroughmuir	13	7	0	6	246	150	14
Glasgow H/K	13	6	1	6	181	195	13
Gala	13	5	2	6	187	223	12
Hawick	13	5	1	7	187	173	11
Selkirk	13	5	0	8	235	256	10
Kelso	13	4	1	8	195	221	9
Stewart's-Mel	12	4	1	7	140	225	9
Ayr	13	3	0	10	139	281	6
W of Scotland	13	1	0	12	126	308	2

Previous champions: Hawick 10 times, 1973-74 to 1977-78, 1981-82, 1983-84 to 1986-87; Gala 3 times, 1979-80, 1980-81, 1982-83; Kelso twice, 1987-88 to 1988-89; Heriot's 1978-79

Division 2	P	W	D	L	F	A	Pts
Edinburgh W	13	12	0	1	332	147	24
Currie	13	10	1	2	299	177	21
Kilmarnock	13	7	2	4	213	158	16
Preston Lodge	13	7	1	5	209	177	15
Hillhead-Jord	13	7	1	5	140	213	15
Musselburgh	13	6	2	5	189	162	14
Corstorphine	13	6	1	6	225	194	13
Glasgow Acs	13	5	1	7	225	230	11

Watsonians	13	4	2	7	187	218	10
Langholm	13	5	0	8	192	226	10
Dunfermline	13	5	0	8	161	219	10
Kirkcaldy	13	4	1	8	163	181	9
Dalziel HSFP	13	4	0	9	203	256	8
Gordonians	13	3	0	10	114	294	6

Division 3	P	W	D	L	F	A	Pts
Dundee HSFP	13	12	1	0	446	100	25
Royal High	13	10	1	2	286	130	21
Wigtownshire	13	10	0	3	217	159	20
Clarkston	12	8	1	3	157	178	17
Portobello FP	13	6	1	6	155	168	13
Biggar	12	6	0	6	127	155	12
Howe of Fife	13	5	0	8	215	185	10
Grangemouth	12	5	0	7	151	195	10
Highland	13	5	0	8	111	212	10
Aberdeen GSFP	12	5	0	7	125	235	10
Trinity Acs	13	4	1	8	182	220	9
Haddington	13	4	0	9	148	200	8
East Kilbride	13	3	2	8	147	202	8
Morgan FP	13	2	1	10	113	241	5

Division 4	P	W	D	L	F	A	Pts
Perthshire	13	11	0	2	289	90	22
Peebles	13	10	0	3	311	99	20
Cartha QP	13	9	0	4	175	131	18
Leith Acs	13	9	0	4	181	176	18
St Boswells	13	8	0	5	219	145	16
Dumfries	12	8	0	4	204	152	16
Linlithgow	13	7	0	6	128	135	14

Hutchesons'	13	5	1	7	189	189	11
Cambuslang	11	5	0	6	97	147	10
Edinburgh U	12	5	0	7	133	226	10
Penicuik	12	4	0	8	91	187	8
Greenock W	13	3	1	9	129	220	7
Paisley	12	2	0	10	137	240	4
Alloa	13	1	0	12	95	241	2

Division 5	P	W	D	L	F	A	Pts
Lismore	13	11	0	2	260	83	22
Waysiders	13	11	0	2	230	101	22
Hillfoots	13	10	1	2	213	65	21
Ardrossan Acs	13	10	0	3	191	83	20
Madras Coll FP	13	9	1	3	196	171	19
Aberdeenshire	13	6	1	6	134	174	13
Dunbar	12	6	0	6	170	95	12
Murrayfield	12	6	0	6	139	167	12
Glenrothes	13	4	0	9	117	140	8
Livingston	11	4	0	7	116	164	8
Moray	13	3	1	9	135	233	7
Broughton FP	13	3	0	10	109	201	6
Lenzie	13	2	2	9	80	193	6
Aberdeen U	13	1	0	12	97	317	2

Division 6	P	W	D	L	F	A	Pts
North Berwick	13	12	0	1	205	85	24
Stewartry	13	11	1	1	194	134	23
St Andrews U	13	10	1	2	307	120	21
Cumbernauld	13	10	0	3	234	110	20
Harris Ac FP	12	6	0	6	132	157	12
Earlston	13	5	1	7	195	162	11
Clydebank	13	5	1	7	176	148	11
Montrose	12	5	1	6	138	168	11
Drumpellier	12	5	0	7	100	141	10
Carnoustie FP	13	5	0	8	164	208	10
Marr	13	5	0	8	105	150	10
Walkerburn	13	3	2	8	131	196	8
Panmure	13	2	0	11	123	275	4
Old Aloysians	12	1	1	10	103	253	3

Division 7	P	W	D	L	F	A	Pts
Lasswade	13	11	1	1	200	93	23
Falkirk	13	11	0	2	378	75	22

Forrester FP	13	11	0	2	237	106	22
Duns	13	9	0	4	189	116	18
Rosyth & Dist	13	9	0	4	186	121	18
Irvine	12	6	0	6	222	119	12
Garioch	12	6	0	6	136	158	12
Cumnock	13	6	0	7	143	165	12
Garnock	13	6	0	7	151	185	12
Ross High	13	5	1	7	185	192	11
Birkmyre	13	3	0	10	110	269	6
Strathmore	13	3	0	10	88	271	6
Stobswell FP	13	2	0	11	115	305	4
Dalkeith	13	1	0	12	83	248	2

District League Champions (*promoted to Division 7*):
East: Holy Cross
Midlands: RAF Kinloss
West: Whitecraigs

SCOTCH BEEF BORDER LEAGUE

	P	W	D	L	F	A	Pts
Melrose	12	11	1	0	260	88	23
Jedforest	11	8	0	3	197	150	16
Hawick	12	6	1	5	151	122	13
Gala	12	5	1	6	177	167	11
Selkirk	12	4	1	7	200	201	9
Kelso	12	3	2	7	174	195	8
Langholm	11	1	0	10	64	300	2

McEWAN'S DISTRICT CHAMPIONSHIP

	P	W	D	L	F	A	Pts
Glasgow	4	3	1	0	78	54	7
Anglo-Scots	4	3	0	1	58	51	6
Edinburgh	4	2	1	1	93	65	5
South	4	1	0	3	60	84	2
North & Midlands	4	0	0	4	47	82	0

Edinburgh won the McEwan's tankards for scoring most tries, 13. Glasgow had 8, the Anglo-Scots 7, North & Midlands 6 and the South 5.

McEWAN'S DISTRICT CHAMPIONSHIP 1989-90

25 November, New Anniesland, Glasgow
Glasgow 19 (1G 3PG 1T)   **Edinburgh 19** (1G 3PG 1T)

Glasgow: D N Barrett (West of Scotland); M D F Duncan (West of Scotland), I C Jardine (Stirling County), D R McKee (West of Scotland), D A Stark (Ayr); G M Breckenridge (Glasgow High/Kelvinside), E D McCorkindale (Glasgow High/Kelvinside); G Graham (Stirling County), K D McKenzie (Stirling County), G B Robertson (Stirling County), A G J Watt (Glasgow High/Kelvinside), J S Hamilton (Stirling County), D A McVey (Ayr), J D Busby (Glasgow High/Kelvinside), F D Wallace (Glasgow High/Kelvinside) (*capt*)
Scorers *Tries:* Breckenridge, McKenzie   *Conversion:* Barrett   *Penalty Goals:* Barrett (3)

Edinburgh: S B Douglas (Boroughmuir); P D Steven (Heriot's FP), D J Stoddart (Heriot's FP), S R P Lineen (Boroughmuir), M R DeBusk (Boroughmuir); D S Wyllie (Stewart's-Melville FP), J E Dun (Edinburgh Acads); A K Brewster (Stewart's-Melville FP) *(capt)*, K S Milne (Heriot's FP), G D Wilson (Boroughmuir), J D Price (Boroughmuir), J F Richardson (Edinburgh Acads), K P Rafferty (Heriot's FP), F Calder (Stewart's-Melville FP), S J Reid (Boroughmuir)
Scorers *Tries:* Calder (2)   *Conversion:* Steven   *Penalty Goals:* Steven (3)
Referee K W McCartney (Hawick)

25 November, Netherdale, Galashiels
South 23 (1G 2PG 1DG 2T)   **North & Midlands 6** (2PG)

South: P W Dods (Gala); H G Hogg (Jedforest), A G Stanger (Hawick), A J Douglas (Jedforest), G R T Baird (Kelso); D K Shiel (Jedforest), G H Oliver (Hawick); N A McIlroy (Jedforest), I Corcoran (Gala), K S Sudlow (Melrose), R S Graham (Hawick), G W Weir (Melrose), D J Turnbull (Hawick), G R Marshall (Selkirk), J Jeffrey (Kelso) *(capt)*
Scorers *Tries:* Hogg, Baird, Oliver   *Conversion:* Dods   *Penalty Goals:* Dods (2)   *Dropped Goal:* Shiel
North & Midlands: H A Murray (Heriot's FP); D J McLaughlin (Boroughmuir), P F Rouse (Dundee HSFP), B Edwards (Boroughmuir), C J Macartney (Boroughmuir); C D Evans (Aberdeen GSFP), M J de G Allingham (Heriot's FP); A D G McKenzie (Highland), M W Scott (Dunfermline), J L Scobbie (Stirling County), B H Bell (Highland) *(capt)*, I A M Paxton (Selkirk), D M McIvor (Edinburgh Acads), B Ireland (Stirling County), D E W Leckie (Edinburgh Acads)
Scorers *Penalty Goals:* Rouse, Macartney
Referee M S Clayton (Whitecraigs)

2 December, Imber Court, East Moseley
Anglo-Scots 16 (1G 2PG 1T)   **South 15** (1G 1PG 2DG)

Anglo-Scots: A G Hastings (London Scottish) *(capt)*; N J Grecian (London Scottish), A M Warwood (Leicester), D W Caskie (Gloucester), W L Renwick (London Scottish); R I Cramb (London Scottish), S Jardine (South Glam Inst); D J D Butcher (London Scottish), B W Gilchrist (London Scottish), A P Burnell (London Scottish), C A Gray (Nottingham), D F Cronin (Bath), A J Macklin (London Scottish), G A E Buchanan-Smith (London Scottish), D B White (London Scottish)
Scorers *Tries:* Hastings, Cronin   *Conversion:* Grecian   *Penalty Goals:* Hastings, Grecian
South: P W Dods (Gala); A G Stanger (Hawick), H G Hogg (Jedforest), A J Douglas (Jedforest), G R T Baird (Kelso); D K Shiel (Jedforest), G Armstrong (Jedforest); N A McIlroy (Jedforest), I Corcoran (Gala), K S Sudlow (Melrose), R S Graham (Hawick), G W Weir (Melrose), D J Turnbull (Hawick), J Jeffrey (Kelso) *(capt)*, C D Hogg (Melrose)
Scorers *Try:* Douglas   *Conversion:* Dods   *Penalty Goal:* Dods   *Dropped Goals:* Shiel (2)
Referee J M Fleming (Boroughmuir)

2 December, Goldenacre, Edinburgh
Edinburgh 25 (3PG 4T)   **North & Midlands 22** (2G 2PG 1T)

Edinburgh: S B Douglas (Boroughmuir); P D Steven (Heriot's FP), S Hastings (Watsonians), S R P Lineen (Boroughmuir), M R DeBusk (Boroughmuir); D S Wyllie (Stewart's-Melville FP), J E Dun (Edinburgh Acads); D M B Sole (Edinburgh Acads), K S Milne (Heriot's FP), G D Wilson (Boroughmuir), J D Price (Boroughmuir), J F Richardson (Edinburgh Acads), K P Rafferty (Heriot's FP), F Calder (Stewart's-Melville FP) *(capt)*, S J Reid (Boroughmuir)
Scorers *Tries:* Steven, Hastings, Wyllie, Sole   *Penalty Goals:* Steven (3)
North & Midlands: H A Murray (Heriot's FP); D J McLaughlin (Boroughmuir), P F Rouse (Dundee HSFP), B Edwards (Boroughmuir), C J Macartney (Boroughmuir); C D Evans (Aberdeen GSFP), M J de G Allingham (Heriot's FP); I J Michie (Dunfermline), M W Scott (Dunfermline), J L Scobbie (Stirling County), B H Bell (Highland) *(capt)*, I A M Paxton (Selkirk), H J Edwards (Boroughmuir), B Ireland (Stirling County), D E W Leckie (Edinburgh Acads)
Scorers *Tries:* McLaughlin, Allingham, Ireland   *Conversions:* Macartney (2)   *Penalty Goals:* Macartney (2)
Referee W W Calder (Selkirk)

16 December, Grange Road, Cambridge
Anglo-Scots 12 (1G 2PG)   **Edinburgh 9** (1G 1PG)

Anglo-Scots: J C W Beazley (London Scottish); N J Grecian (London Scottish), A M Warwood (Leicester), D W Caskie (Gloucester), W L Renwick (London Scottish); R I Cramb (London Scottish), S Jardine (South Glam Inst); D J D Butcher (London Scottish), B W Gilchrist (London Scottish), A P Burnell (London Scottish), C A Gray (Nottingham), D F Cronin (Bath), A J Macklin (London Scottish) *(capt)*, G A E Buchanan-Smith (London Scottish), D B White (London Scottish)
Scorer *Try:* Grecian   *Conversion:* Grecian   *Penalty Goal:* Grecian
Edinburgh: I C Glasgow (Heriot's FP); P D Steven (Heriot's FP), D J Stoddart (Heriot's FP), S R P Lineen (Boroughmuir), A Moore (Edinburgh Acads); D S Wyllie (Stewart's-Melville FP), M S Robertson (Boroughmuir); A K Brewster (Stewart's-Melville FP), K S Milne (Heriot's FP), I G Milne (Heriot's FP), J D Price (Boroughmuir), J F Richardson (Edinburgh Acads) *(capt)*, F Calder (Stewart's-Melville FP), M Steele (Watsonians), S J Reid (Boroughmuir)
Scorers *Try:* Steven   *Conversion:* Glasgow   *Penalty Goal:* Glasgow
Referee A P Thompson (London)

16 December, Hawkhill, Leith
North & Midlands 10 (1G 1T)   **Glasgow 19** (2G 1PG 1T)

North & Midlands: H A Murray (Heriot's FP); D J McLaughlin (Boroughmuir), P F Rouse (Dundee HSFP), B Edwards (Boroughmuir), C J Macartney (Boroughmuir); C D Evans (Aberdeen GSFP), M J de G Allingham

(Heriot's FP); A D G McKenzie (Highland), M W Scott (Dunfermline), J L Scobbie (Stirling County), B H Bell (Highland), I A M Paxton (Selkirk) (*capt*), H J Edwards (Boroughmuir), B Ireland (Stirling County), D E W Leckie (Edinburgh Acads)
Scorers *Tries:* Allingham, Bell *Conversion:* Macartney
Glasgow: D N Barrett (West of Scotland); D A Stark (Ayr), I C Jardine (Stirling County), D R McKee (West of Scotland), P P Manning (Ayr); G M Breckenridge (Glasgow High/Kelvinside), E D McCorkindale (Glasgow High/Kelvinside); G Graham (Stirling County), K D McKenzie (Stirling County), G B Robertson (Stirling County), A G J Watt (Glasgow High/Kelvinside), D A Jackson (Hillhead-Jordanhill), D A McVey (Ayr), J D Busby (Glasgow High/Kelvinside), F D Wallace (Glasgow High/Kelvinside) (*capt*)
Scorers *Tries:* Barrett, Stark, Manning *Conversions:* Barrett (2) *Penalty Goal:* Barrett
Referee R J Megson (Edinburgh Wanderers)

23 December, McKane Park, Dunfermline
North & Midlands 9 (1G 1PG) **Anglo-Scots 15** (1PG 3T)

North & Midlands: H A Murray (Heriot's FP); D J McLaughlin (Boroughmuir), P F Rouse (Dundee HSFP), B Edwards (Boroughmuir) (*capt*), C J Macartney (Boroughmuir); A H Robertson (Kirkcaldy), M J de G Allingham (Heriot's FP); I J Michie (Dunfermline), M W Scott (Dunfermline), J L Scobbie (Stirling County), G McKenzie (Dunfermline), D McNaughton (Dundee HSFP), D M McIvor (Edinburgh Acads), B Ireland (Stirling County), D E W Leckie (Edinburgh Acads)
Scorers *Try:* Murray *Conversion:* Macartney *Penalty Goal:* Macartney
Anglo-Scots: A G Hastings (London Scottish) (*capt*); N J Grecian (London Scottish), A M Warwood (Leicester), D W Caskie (Gloucester), W L Renwick (London Scottish); R I Cramb (London Scottish), S Jardine (South Glam Inst); D J D Butcher (London Scottish), B W Gilchrist (London Scottish), I Corcoran (Gala), C A Gray (Nottingham), D F Cronin (Bath), A J Macklin (London Scottish), G A E Buchanan-Smith (London Scottish), D B White (London Scottish) *Replacement* L M Mair (Cambridge U) for Macklin
Scorers *Tries:* Caskie (2), Gilchrist *Penalty Goal:* Hastings
Referee J M Fleming (Boroughmuir)

23 December, The Greenyards, Melrose
South 10 (2PG 1T) **Glasgow 22** (2G 2PG 1T)

South: P W Dods (Gala); A G Stanger (Hawick), H G Hogg (Jedforest), A J Douglas (Jedforest), G R T Baird (Kelso); D K Shiel (Jedforest), G Armstrong (Jedforest); N A McIlroy (Jedforest), I Corcoran (Gala), K S Sudlow (Melrose), R S Graham (Hawick), G W Weir (Melrose), G R Marshall (Selkirk), J Jeffrey (Kelso) (*capt*), C D Hogg (Melrose)
Scorers *Try:* Baird *Penalty Goals:* Dods (2)
Glasgow: D N Barrett (West of Scotland); D A Stark (Ayr), I C Jardine (Stirling County), D R McKee (West of Scotland), P P Manning (Ayr); G M Breckenridge (Glasgow High/Kelvinside), E D McCorkindale (Glasgow High/Kelvinside); G Graham (Stirling County), K D McKenzie (Stirling County), G B Robertson (Stirling County), A G J Watt (Glasgow High/Kelvinside), D A Jackson (Hillhead-Jordanhill), D A McVey (Ayr), J D Busby (Glasgow High/Kelvinside), F D Wallace (Glasgow High/Kelvinside) (*capt*)
Scorers *Tries:* Stark, Manning, Watt *Conversions:* Barrett (2) *Penalty Goals:* Barrett (2)
Referee R S Clark (Stewart's-Melville FP)

30 December, Myreside, Edinburgh
Edinburgh 40 (5G 2PG 1T) **South 12** (4PG)

Edinburgh: I C Glasgow (Heriot's FP); P D Steven (Heriot's FP), S Hastings (Watsonians), S R P Lineen (Boroughmuir), A Moore (Edinburgh Acads); D S Wyllie (Stewart's-Melville FP), M S Robertson (Boroughmuir); D M B Sole (Edinburgh Acads), K S Milne (Heriot's FP), I G Milne (Heriot's FP) (*capt*), J D Price (Boroughmuir), J F Richardson (Edinburgh Acads), F Calder (Stewart's-Melville FP), G J Drummond (Boroughmuir), S J Reid (Boroughmuir)
Scorers *Tries:* Hastings (3), Wyllie, Richardson, penalty try *Conversions:* Steven (5) *Penalty Goals:* Steven (2)
South: P W Dods (Gala); A G Stanger (Hawick), A C Redpath (Melrose), A G Shiel (Melrose), G R T Baird (Kelso); D K Shiel (Jedforest), G Armstrong (Jedforest); N A McIlroy (Jedforest), I Corcoran (Gala), K S Sudlow (Melrose), R S Graham (Hawick), G W Weir (Melrose), A Redpath (Melrose), J Jeffrey (Kelso) (*capt*), C D Hogg (Melrose)
Replacements J A Hay (Hawick) for Graham; G H Oliver (Hawick) for Armstrong
Scorer *Penalty Goals:* Dods (4)
Referee E F Morrison (Bristol)

30 December, Burnbrae, Milngavie
Glasgow 18 (6PG) **Anglo-Scots 15** (1G 1PG 2DG)

Glasgow: D N Barrett (West of Scotland); D A Stark (Ayr), I C Jardine (Stirling County), D R McKee (West of Scotland), P P Manning (Ayr); G M Breckenridge (Glasgow High/Kelvinside), E D McCorkindale (Glasgow High/Kelvinside); G Graham (Stirling County), K D McKenzie (Stirling County), G B Robertson (Stirling County), A G J Watt (Glasgow High/Kelvinside), D A Jackson (Hillhead-Jordanhill), D A McVey (Ayr), J D Busby (Glasgow High/Kelvinside), F D Wallace (Glasgow High/Kelvinside) (*capt*)
Scorer *Penalty Goals:* Barrett (6)
Anglo-Scots: A G Hastings (London Scottish) (*capt*); N J Grecian (London Scottish), A M Warwood (Leicester), D W Caskie (Gloucester), W L Renwick (London Scottish); R I Cramb (London Scottish), S Jardine (South Glam Inst); D J D Butcher (London Scottish), B W Gilchrist (London Scottish), A P Burnell (London Scottish), C A Gray (Nottingham), D F Cronin (Bath), A J Macklin (London Scottish), G A E Buchanan-Smith (London Scottish), D B White (London Scottish) *Replacement* L M Mair (Cambridge U) for Cronin
Scorers *Try:* Grecian *Conversion:* Grecian *Penalty Goal:* Grecian *Dropped Goals:* Cramb (2)
Referee K D Harrower (Forrester FP)

SCOTTISH INTERNATIONAL PLAYERS
(up to 30 April 1990)

ABBREVIATIONS

A – Australia; E – England; F – France; Fj - Fiji; I – Ireland; NZ – New Zealand; R – Romania; SA – South Africa; W – Wales; Z – Zimbabwe; (C) – Centenary match v England at Murrayfield, 1971 (non-championship); P – Scotland v President's Overseas XV at Murrayfield in SRU's Centenary season, 1972-73; (R) Replacement. Entries in square brackets [ ] indicate appearances in the World Cup.

Note: Years given for Five Nations' matches are for second half of season; eg 1972 means season 1971-72. Years for all other matches refer to the actual year of the match. When a series has taken place, figures have been used to denote the particular matches in which players have featured. Thus 1981 NZ 1, 2 indicates that a player appeared in the first and second Tests of the series. The abandoned game with Ireland at Belfast in 1885 is now included as a cap-match.

Abercrombie, C H (United Services) 1910 *I, E*, 1911 *F, W*, 1913 *F, W*

Abercrombie, J G (Edinburgh U) 1949 *F, W, I*, 1950 *F, W, I, E*

Agnew, W C C (Stewart's Coll FP) 1930 *W, I*

Ainslie, R (Edinburgh Inst FP) 1879 *I, E*, 1880 *I, E*, 1881 *E*, 1882 *I, E*

Ainslie, T (Edinburgh Inst FP) 1881 *E*, 1882 *I, E*, 1883 *W, I, E*, 1884 *W, I, E*, 1885 *W, I1,2*

Aitchison, G R (Edinburgh Wands) 1883 *I*

Aitchison, T G (Gala) 1929 *W, I, E*

Aitken, A I (Edinburgh Inst FP) 1889 *I*

Aitken, G G (Oxford U) 1924 *W, I, E*, 1925 *F, W, I, E*, 1929 *F*

Aitken, J (Gala) 1977 *E, I, F*, 1981 *F, W, E, I, NZ1,2, R, A*, 1982 *E, I, F, W*, 1983 *F, W, E, NZ*, 1984 *W, E, I, F, R*

Aitken, R (London Scottish) 1947 *W*

Allan, B (Glasgow Acads) 1881 *I*

Allan, J L (Melrose) 1952 *F, W, I*, 1953 *W*

Allan, J L F (Cambridge U) 1957 *I, E*

Allan, J W (Melrose) 1927 *F*, 1928 *I*, 1929 *F, W, I, E*, 1930 *F, E*, 1931 *F, W, I, E*, 1932 *SA, W, I*, 1934 *I, E*

Allan, R C (Hutchesons' GSFP) 1969 *I*

Allardice, W D (Aberdeen GSFP) 1948 *A, F, W, I*, 1949 *F, W, I, E*

Allen, H W (Glasgow Acads) 1873 *E*

Anderson, A H (Glasgow Acads) 1894 *I*

Anderson, D G (London Scottish) 1889 *I*, 1890 *W, I, E*, 1891 *W, E*, 1892 *W, E*

Anderson, E (Stewart's Coll FP) 1947 *I, E*

Anderson, J W (W of Scotland) 1872 *E*

Anderson, T (Merchiston) 1882 *I*

Angus, A W (Watsonians) 1909 *W*, 1910 *F, W, E*, 1911 *W, I*, 1912 *F, W, I, E, SA*, 1913 *F, W*, 1914 *E*, 1920 *F, W, I, E*

Anton, P A (St Andrew's U) 1873 *E*

Armstrong, G (Jedforest) 1988 *A*, 1989 *W, E, I, F, Fj, R*, 1990 *I, F, W, E*

Arneil, R J (Edinburgh Acads, Leicester and Northampton) 1968 *I, E, A*, 1969 *F, W, I, E, SA*, 1970 *F, W, I, E, A*, 1971 *F, W, I, E (2[1C])*, 1972 *F, W, E, NZ*

Arthur, A (Glasgow Acads) 1875 *E*, 1876 *E*

Arthur, J W (Glasgow Acads) 1871 *E*, 1872 *E*

Asher, A G G (Oxford U) 1882 *I*, 1884 *W, I, E*, 1885 *W*, 1886 *I, E*

Auld, W (W of Scotland) 1889 *W*, 1890 *W*

Auldjo, L J (Abertay) 1878 *E*

Bain, D McL (Oxford U) 1911 *E*, 1912 *F, W, E, SA*, 1913 *F, W, I, E*, 1914 *W, I*

Baird, G R T (Kelso) 1981 *A*, 1982 *E, I, F, W, A* 1,2, 1983 *I, F, W, E, NZ*, 1984 *W, E, I, F, A*, 1985 *I, W, E*, 1986 *F, W, E, I, R*, 1987 *E*, 1988 *I*

Balfour, A (Watsonians) 1896 *W, I, E*, 1897 *E*

Balfour, L M (Edinburgh Acads) 1872 *E*

Bannerman, E M (Edinburgh Acads) 1872 *E*, 1873 *E*

Bannerman, J M (Glasgow HSFP) 1921 *F, W, I, E*, 1922 *F, W, I, E*, 1923 *F, W, I, E*, 1924 *F, W, I, E*, 1925 *F, W, I, E*, 1926 *F, W, I, E*, 1927 *F, W, I, E, A*, 1928 *F, W, I, E*, 1929 *F, W, I, E*

Barnes, I A (Hawick) 1972 *W*, 1974 *F* (R), 1975 *E* (R), *NZ*, 1977 *I, F, W*

Barrie, R W (Hawick) 1936 *E*

Bearne, K R F (Cambridge U, London Scottish) 1960 *F, W*

Beattie, J A (Hawick) 1929 *F, W*, 1930 *W*, 1931 *F, W, I, E*, 1932 *SA, W, I, E*, 1933 *W, E, I*, 1934 *I, E*, 1935 *W, I, E, NZ*, 1936 *W, I, E*

Beattie, J R (Glasgow Acads) 1980 *I, F, W, E*, 1981 *F, W, E, I*, 1983 *F, W, E, NZ*, 1984 *E* (R), *R, A*, 1985 *I*, 1986 *F, W, E, I, R*, 1987 *I, F, W, E*

Bedell-Sivright, D R (Cambridge U, Edinburgh U) 1900 *W*, 1901 *W, I, E*, 1902 *W, I, E*, 1903 *W, I*, 1904 *W, I, E*, 1905 *NZ*, 1906 *W, I, E, SA*, 1907 *W, I, E*, 1908 *W, I*

Bedell-Sivright, J V (Cambridge U) 1902 *W*

Begbie, T A (Edinburgh Wands) 1881 *I, E*

Bell, D L (Watsonians) 1975 *I, F, W, E*

Bell, J A (Clydesdale) 1901 *W, I, E*, 1902 *W, I, E*

Bell, L H I (Edinburgh Acads) 1900 *E*, 1904 *W, I*

Berkeley, W V (Oxford U) 1926 *F*, 1929 *F, W, I*

Berry, C W (Fettesian-Lorettonians) 1884 *I, E*, 1885 *W, I*1, 1887 *I, W, E*, 1888 *W, I*

Bertram, D M (Watsonians) 1922 *F, W, I, E*, 1923 *F, W, I, E*, 1924 *W, I, E*

Biggar, A G (London Scottish) 1969 *SA*, 1970 *F, I, E, A*, 1971 *F, W, I, E (2[1C])*, 1972 *F, W*

Biggar, M A (London Scottish) 1975 *I, F, W, E*, 1976 *W, E, I*, 1977 *I, F, W*, 1978 *I, F, W, E, NZ*, 1979 *W, E, I, F, NZ*, 1980 *I, F, W, E*

Birkett, G A (Harlequins, London Scottish) 1975 *NZ*

Bishop, J M (Glasgow Acads) 1893 *I*

Bisset, A A (RIE Coll) 1904 *W*

Black, A W (Edinburgh U) 1947 *F, W*, 1948 *E*, 1950 *W, I, E*

Black, W P (Glasgow HSFP) 1948 *F, W, I, E*, 1951 *E*

Blackadder, W F (W of Scotland) 1938 *E*

Blaikie, C F (Heriot's FP) 1963 *I, E*, 1966 *E*, 1968 *A*, 1969 *F, W, I, E*

Blair, P C B (Cambridge U) 1912 *SA*, 1913 *F, W, I, E*

Bolton, W H (W of Scotland) 1876 *E*

Borthwick, J B (Stewart's Coll FP) 1938 *W, I*

Bos, F H ten (Oxford U, London Scottish) 1959 *E*, 1960 *F, W, SA*, 1961 *F, SA, W, I, E*, 1962 *F, W, I, E*, 1963 *F, W, I, E*

Boswell, J D (W of Scotland) 1889 *W, I*, 1890 *W, I, E*, 1891 *W, I, E*, 1892 *W, I, E*, 1893 *I, E*, 1894 *I, E*

Bowie, T C (Watsonians) 1913 *I, E*, 1914 *I, E*

Boyd, G M (Glasgow HSFP) 1926 *E*

Boyd, J L (United Services) 1912 *E, SA*

Boyle, A C W (London Scottish) 1963 *F, W, I*

Boyle, A H W (St Thomas's Hospital, London Scottish) 1966 *A*, 1967 *F, NZ*, 1968 *F, W, I*

Brash, J C (Cambridge U) 1961 *E*

Breakey, R W (Gosforth) 1978 *E*

Brewis, N T (Edinburgh Inst FP) 1876 *E*, 1878 *E*, 1879 *I, E*, 1880 *I, E*

Brewster, A K (Stewart's-Melville FP) 1977 *E*, 1980 *I, F*, 1986 *I, R*

Brown, A H (Heriot's FP) 1928 *E*, 1929 *F, W*

Brown, A R (Gala) 1971 *E* (2[1C]), 1972 *F, W, E*

Brown, C H C (Dunfermline) 1929 *E*

Brown, D I (Cambridge U) 1933 *W, E, I*

201

Brown, G L (W of Scotland) 1969 *SA*, 1970 *F, W,* (R), *I, E, A,* 1971 *F, W, I, E* (2[1C]), 1972 *F, W, E, NZ,* 1973 *E* (R), *P,* 1974 *W, E, I, F,* 1975 *I, F, W, E, A,* 1976 *F, W, E, I*
Brown, J A (Glasgow Acads) 1908 *W, I*
Brown, J B (Glasgow Acads) 1879 *I, E,* 1880 *I, E,* 1881 *I, E,* 1882 *I, E,* 1883 *W, I, E,* 1884 *W, I, E,* 1885 *I* 1,2, 1886 *W, I, E*
Brown, P C (W of Scotland, Gala) 1964 *F, NZ, W, I, E,* 1965 *I, E, SA,* 1966 *A,* 1969 *I, E,* 1970 *W, E,* 1971 *F, W, I, E* (2[1C]), 1972 *F, W, E, NZ,* 1973 *F, W, I, E, P*
Brown, T G (Heriot's FP) 1929 *W*
Brown, W D (Glasgow Acads) 1871 *E,* 1872 *E,* 1873 *E,* 1874 *E,* 1875 *E*
Brown, W S (Edinburgh Inst FP) 1880 *I, E,* 1882 *I, E,* 1883 *W, E*
Browning, A (Glasgow HSFP) 1920 *I,* 1922 *F, W, I,* 1923 *W, I, E*
Bruce, C R (Glasgow Acads) 1947 *F, W, I, E,* 1949 *F, W, I, E*
Bruce, N S (Blackheath, Army and London Scottish) 1958 *F, A, I, E,* 1959 *F, W, I, E,* 1960 *F, W, I, E, SA,* 1961 *F, SA, W, I, E,* 1962 *F, W, I, E,* 1963 *F, W, I, E,* 1964 *F, NZ, W, I, E*
Bruce, R M (ordonians) 1947 *A,* 1948 *F, W, I*
Bruce-Lockhart, J H (London Scottish) 1913 *W,* 1920 *E*
Bruce-Lockhart, L (London Scottish) 1948 *E,* 1950 *F, W,* 1953 *I, E*
Bruce-Lockhart, R B (Cambridge U and London Scottish) 1937 *I,* 1939 *I, E*
Bryce, C C (Glasgow Acads) 1873 *E,* 1874 *E*
Bryce, R D H (W of Scotland) 1973 *I* (R)
Bryce, W E (Selkirk) 1922 *W, I, E,* 1923 *F, W, I, E,* 1924 *F, W, I, E*
Brydon, W R C (Heriot's FP) 1939 *W*
Buchanan, A (Royal HSFP) 1871 *E*
Buchanan, F G (Kelvinside Acads and Oxford U) 1910 *E,* 1911 *F, W*
Buchanan, J C R (Stewart's Coll FP) 1921 *W, I, E,* 1922 *W, I, E,* 1923 *F, W, I, E,* 1924 *F, W, I, E,* 1925 *F, I*
Buchanan-Smith, G A E (London Scottish) 1989 *Fj* (R)
Bucher, A M (Edinburgh Acads) 1897 *E*
Budge, G M (Edinburgh Wands) 1950 *F, W, I, E*
Bullmore, H H (Edinburgh U) 1902 *I*
Burnell, A P (London Scottish) 1989 *E, I, F, Fj, R,* 1990 *I, F, W, E*
Burnet, P J (London Scottish and Edinburgh Acads) 1960 *SA*
Burnet, W (Hawick) 1912 *E*
Burnet, W A (W of Scotland) 1934 *W,* 1935 *W, I, E, NZ,* 1936 *W, I, E*
Burnett, J N (Heriot's FP) 1980 *I, F, W, E*
Burrell, G (Gala) 1950 *F, W, I,* 1951 *SA*

Cairns, A G (Watsonians) 1903 *W, I, E,* 1904 *W, I, E,* 1905 *W, I, E,* 1906 *W, I, E*
Calder, F (Stewart's-Melville FP) 1986 *F, W, E, I, R,* 1987 *I, F, W, E,* [*F, Z, R, NZ*], 1988 *I, F, W, E,* 1989 *W, E, I, F, R,* 1990 *I, F, W, E*
Calder, J H (Stewart's-Melville FP) 1981 *F, W, E, I, NZ* 1,2, *R, A,* 1982 *E, I, F, W, A* 1,2, 1983 *I, F, W, E, NZ,* 1984 *W, E, I, F, A,* 1985 *I, F, W*
Callander, G J (Kelso) 1984 *R,* 1988 *I, F, W, E, A*
Cameron, A (Glasgow HSFP) 1948 *W,* 1950 *I, E,* 1951 *F, W, I, E, SA,* 1953 *I, E,* 1955 *F, W, I, E,* 1956 *F, W, I*
Cameron, A D (Hillhead HSFP) 1951 *F,* 1954 *F, W*
Cameron, A W (Watsonians) 1887 *W,* 1893 *W,* 1894 *I*
Cameron, D (Glasgow HSFP) 1953 *I, E,* 1954 *F, NZ, I, E*
Cameron, N W (Glasgow U) 1952 *E,* 1953 *F, W*
Campbell, A J (Hawick) 1984 *I, F, R,* 1985 *I, F, W, E,* 1986 *F, W, E, I, R,* 1988 *F, W, A*
Campbell, G T (London Scottish) 1892 *W, I, E,* 1893 *I, E,* 1894 *W, I, E,* 1895 *W, I, E,* 1896 *W, I, E,* 1897 *I,* 1899 *I,* 1900 *E*
Campbell, H H (Cambridge U, London Scottish) 1947 *I, E,* 1948 *I, E*
Campbell, J A (W of Scotland) 1878 *E,* 1879 *I, E,* 1881 *I, E*
Campbell, J A (Cambridge U) 1900 *I*

Campbell, N M (London Scottish) 1956 *F, W*
Campbell-Lamerton, J R E (London Scottish) 1986 *F,* 1987 [*Z, R*(R)]
Campbell-Lamerton, M J (Halifax, Army, London Scottish) 1961 *F, SA, W, I,* 1962 *F, W, I, E,* 1963 *F, W, I, E,* 1964 *I, E,* 1965 *F, W, I, E, SA,* 1966 *F, W, I, E*
Carmichael, A B (W of Scotland) 1967 *I, NZ,* 1968 *F, W, I, E, A,* 1969 *F, W, I, E, SA,* 1970 *F, W, I, E, A,* 1971 *F, W, I, E* (2[1C]), 1972 *F, W, E, NZ,* 1973 *F, W, I, E, P,* 1974 *W, E, I, F,* 1975 *I, F, W, E, NZ, A,* 1976 *F, W, E, I,* 1977 *E, I* (R), *F, W,* 1978 *I*
Carmichael, J H (Watsonians) 1921 *F, W, I*
Carrick, J S (Glasgow Acads) 1876 *E,* 1877 *E*
Cassels, D Y (W of Scotland) 1880 *E,* 1881 *I,* 1882 *I, E,* 1883 *W, I, E*
Cathcart, C W (Edinburgh U) 1872 *E,* 1873 *E,* 1876 *E*
Cawkwell, G L (Oxford U) 1947 *F*
Chalmers, C M (Melrose) 1989 *W, E, I, F, Fj,* 1990 *I, F, W, E*
Chalmers, T (Glasgow Acads) 1871 *E,* 1872 *E,* 1873 *E,* 1874 *E,* 1875 *E,* 1876 *E*
Chambers, H F T (Edinburgh U) 1888 *W, I,* 1889 *W, I*
Charters, R G (Hawick) 1955 *W, I, E*
Chisholm, D H (Melrose) 1964 *I, E,* 1965 *E, SA,* 1966 *F, I, E, A,* 1967 *F, W, NZ,* 1968 *F, W, I*
Chisholm, R W T (Melrose) 1955 *I, E,* 1956 *F, W, I, E,* 1958 *F, W, A, I,* 1960 *SA*
Church, W C (Glasgow Acads) 1906 *W*
Clark, R L (Edinburgh Wands, Royal Navy) 1972 *F, W, E, NZ,* 1973 *F, W, I, E, P*
Clauss, P R A (Oxford U) 1891 *W, I, E,* 1892 *W, E,* 1895 *I*
Clay, A T (Edinburgh Acads) 1886 *W, I, E,* 1887 *I, W, E,* 1888 *W*
Clunies-Ross, A (St Andrews U) 1871 *E*
Coltman, S (Hawick) 1948 *I,* 1949 *F, W, I, E*
Colvile, A G (Merchistonians, Blackheath) 1871 *E,* 1872 *E*
Connell, G C (Trinity Acads and London Scottish) 1968 *E, A,* 1969 *F, E,* 1970 *F*
Cooper, M McG (Oxford U) 1936 *W, I*
Cordial, I F (Edinburgh Wands) 1952 *F, W, I, E*
Cotter, J L (Hillhead HSFP) 1934 *I, E*
Cottington, G S (Kelso) 1934 *I, E,* 1935 *W, I,* 1936 *E*
Coughtrie, S (Edinburgh Acads) 1959 *F, W, I, E,* 1962 *W, I, E,* 1963 *F, W, I, E*
Couper, J H (W of Scotland) 1896 *W, I,* 1899 *I*
Coutts, F H (Melrose, Army) 1947 *W, I, E*
Coutts, I D F (Old Alleynians) 1951 *F,* 1952 *E*
Cowan, R C (Selkirk) 1961 *F,* 1962 *F, W, I, E*
Cowie, W L K (Edinburgh Wands) 1953 *E*
Cownie, W B (Watsonians) 1893 *W, I, E,* 1894 *W, I, E,* 1895 *W, I, E*
Crabbie, G E (Edinburgh Acads) 1904 *W*
Crabbie, J E (Edinburgh Acads, Oxford U) 1900 *W,* 1902 *I,* 1903 *W, I,* 1904 *E,* 1905 *W*
Craig, J B (Heriot's FP) 1939 *W*
Cramb, R I (Harlequins) 1987 [*R*(R)], 1988 *I, F, A*
Cranston, A G (Hawick) 1976 *W, E, I,* 1977 *E, W,* 1978 *F* (R), *W, E, NZ,* 1981 *NZ* 1,2
Crawford, J A (Army, London Scottish) 1934 *I*
Crawford, W H (United Services, RN) 1938 *W, I, E,* 1939 *W, E*
Crichton-Miller, D (Gloucester) 1931 *W, I, E*
Crole, G B (Oxford U) 1920 *F, W, I, E*
Cronin, D F (Bath) 1988 *I, F, W, E, A,* 1989 *W, E, I, F, Fj, R,* 1990 *I, F, W, E*
Cross, M (Merchistonians) 1875 *E,* 1876 *E,* 1877 *I, E,* 1878 *E,* 1879 *I, E,* 1880 *I, E*
Cross, W (Merchistonians) 1871 *E,* 1872 *E*
Cumming, R S (Aberdeen U) 1921 *F, W*
Cunningham, G (Oxford U) 1908 *W, I,* 1909 *W, E,* 1910 *F, I, E,* 1911 *E*
Cunningham, R F (Gala) 1978 *NZ,* 1979 *W, E*
Currie, L R (Dunfermline) 1947 *A,* 1948 *F, W, I,* 1949 *F, W, I, E*
Cuthbertson, W (Kilmarnock, Harlequins) 1980 *I,* 1981 *W, E, I, NZ* 1,2, *R, A,* 1982 *E, I, F, W, A* 1,2, 1983 *I, F, W, NZ,* 1984 *W, E, A*

Dalgleish, A (Gala) 1890 *W, E,* 1891 *W, I,* 1892 *W,* 1893 *W,* 1894 *W, I*
Dalgleish, K J (Edinburgh Wands, Cambridge U) 1951

I, E, 1953 *F, W*
Dallas, J D (Watsonians) 1903 *E*
Davidson, J A (London Scottish, Edinburgh Wands) 1959 *E*, 1960 *I, E*
Davidson, J N G (Edinburgh U) 1952 *F, W, I, E*, 1953 *F, W*, 1954 *E*
Davidson, J P (RIE Coll) 1873 *E*, 1874 *E*
Davidson, R S (Royal HSFP) 1893 *E*
Davies, D S (Hawick) 1922 *F, W, I, E*, 1923 *F, W, I, E*, 1924 *F, E*, 1925 *W, I, E*, 1926 *F, W, I, E*, 1927 *F, W, I*
Dawson, J C (Glasgow Acads) 1947 *A*, 1948 *F, W*, 1949 *F, W, I*, 1950 *F, W, I, E*, 1951 *F, W, I, E, SA*, 1952 *F, W, I, E*, 1953 *E*
Deans, C T (Hawick) 1978 *F, W, E, NZ*, 1979 *W, E, I, F, NZ*, 1980 *I, F*, 1981 *F, W, E, I, NZ* 1,2, *R, A*, 1982 *E, I, F, W, A* 1,2, 1983 *I, F, W, E, NZ*, 1984 *W, E, I, F, A*, 1985 *I, F, W, E*, 1986 *F, W, E, I, R*, 1987 *I, F, W, E, [F, Z, R, NZ]*
Deans, D T (Hawick) 1968 *E*
Deas, D W (Heriot's FP) 1947 *F, W*
Dick, L G (Loughborough Colls, Jordanhill, Swansea) 1972 *W* (R), *E*, 1974 *W, E, I, F*, 1975 *I, F, W, E, NZ, A*, 1976 *F*, 1977 *E*
Dick, R C S (Cambridge U, Guy's Hospital) 1934 *W, I, E*, 1935 *W, I, E, NZ*, 1936 *W, I, E*, 1937 *W*, 1938 *W, I, E*
Dickson, G (Gala) 1978 *NZ*, 1979 *W, E, I, F, NZ*, 1980 *W*, 1981 *F*, 1982 *W* (R)
Dickson, M R (Edinburgh U) 1905 *I*
Dickson, W M (Blackheath, Oxford U) 1912 *F, W, E, SA*, 1913 *F, W, I*
Dobson, J (Glasgow Acads) 1911 *E*, 1912 *F, W, I, E, SA*
Dobson, J D (Glasgow Acads) 1910 *I*
Dobson, W G (Heriot's FP) 1922 *W, I, E*
Docherty, J T (Glasgow HSFP) 1955 *F, W*, 1956 *E*, 1958 *F, W, A, I, E*
Dods, F P (Edinburgh Acads) 1901 *I*
Dods, J H (Edinburgh Acads) 1895 *W, I, E*, 1896 *W, I, E*, 1897 *I, E*
Dods, P W (Gala) 1983 *I, F, W, E, NZ*, 1984 *W, E, I, F, R, A*, 1985 *I, F, W, E*, 1989 *W, E, I, F*
Donald, D G (Oxford U) 1914 *W, I*
Donald, R L H (Glasgow HSFP) 1921 *W, I, E*
Donaldson, W P (Oxford U, W of Scotland) 1893 *I*, 1894 *I*, 1895 *E*, 1896 *I, E*, 1899 *I*
Don-Wauchope, A R (Fettesian-Lorettonians) 1881 *E*, 1882 *E*, 1883 *W*, 1884 *W, I, E*, 1885 *W, I* 1,2, 1886 *W, I, E*, 1888 *I*
Don-Wauchope, P H (Fettesian-Lorettonians) 1885 *I* 1,2, 1886 *W*, 1887 *I, W, E*
Dorward, A F (Cambridge U, Gala) 1950 *F*, 1951 *SA*, 1952 *F, I, E*, 1953 *F, W, E*, 1955 *F*, 1956 *I, E*, 1957 *F, W, I, E*
Dorward, T F (Gala) 1938 *W, I, E*, 1939 *I, E*
Douglas, G (Jedforest) 1921 *W*
Douglas, J (Stewart's Coll FP) 1961 *F, SA, W, I, E*, 1962 *F, W, I, E*, 1963 *F, W, E*
Douty, P S (London Scottish) 1927 *A*, 1928 *F, W*
Drew, D (Glasgow Acads) 1871 *E*, 1876 *E*
Druitt, W A H (London Scottish) 1936 *W, I, E*
Drummond, A H (Kelvinside Acads) 1938 *W, I*
Drummond, C W (Melrose) 1947 *F, W, I, E*, 1948 *F, I, E*, 1950 *F, W, I, E*
Drybrough, A S (Edinburgh Wands, Merchistonians) 1902 *I*, 1903 *I*
Dryden, R H (Watsonians) 1937 *E*
Drysdale, D (Heriot's FP) 1923 *F, W, I, E*, 1924 *F, W, I, E*, 1925 *F, W, I, E*, 1926 *F, W, I, E*, 1927 *F, W, I, E, A*, 1928 *F, W, I, E*, 1929 *F*
Duff, P L (Glasgow Acads) 1936 *W, I*, 1938 *W, I, E*, 1939 *W*
Duffy, H (Jedforest) 1955 *F*
Duke, A (Royal HSFP) 1888 *W, I*, 1889 *W, I*, 1890 *W, I*, *E*
Duncan, A W (Edinburgh U) 1901 *W, I, E*, 1902 *W, I, E*
Duncan, D D (Oxford U) 1920 *F, W, I, E*
Duncan, M D F (W of Scotland) 1986 *F, W, E, R*, 1987 *I, F, W, E, [F, Z, R, NZ]*, 1988 *I, F, W, E, A*, 1989 *W*
Duncan, M M (Fettesian-Lorettonians) 1888 *W*
Dunlop, J W (W of Scotland) 1875 *E*
Dunlop, Q (W of Scotland) 1971 *E* (2[1C])
Dykes, A S (Glasgow Acads) 1932 *E*

Dykes, J C (Glasgow Acads) 1922 *F, E*, 1924 *I*, 1925 *F, W, I*, 1926 *F, W, I, E*, 1927 *F, W, I, E, A*, 1928 *F, I*, 1929 *F, W, I*
Dykes, J M (Clydesdale, Glasgow HSFP) 1898 *I, E*, 1899 *W, E*, 1900 *W, I*, 1901 *W, I, E*, 1902 *E*

Edwards, D B (Heriot's FP) 1960 *I, E, SA*
Elgie, M K (London Scottish) 1954 *NZ, I, E, W*, 1955 *F, W, I, E*
Elliot, C (Langholm) 1958 *E*, 1959 *F*, 1960 *F*, 1963 *E*, 1964 *F, NZ, W, I, E*, 1965 *F, W, I*
Elliot, M (Hawick) 1895 *W*, 1896 *E*, 1897 *I, E*, 1898 *I, E*
Elliot, T (Gala) 1905 *E*
Elliot, T (Gala) 1955 *W, I, E*, 1956 *F, W, I, E*, 1957 *F, W, I, E*, 1958 *W, A, I*
Elliot, T G (Langholm) 1968 *W, A*, 1969 *F, W*, 1970 *E*
Elliot, W I D (Edinburgh Acads) 1947 *F, W, E, A*, 1948 *F, W, I, E*, 1949 *F, W, I, E*, 1950 *F, W, I, E*, 1951 *F, W, I, E, SA*, 1952 *F, W, I, E*, 1954 *NZ, I, E, W*
Emslie, W D (Royal HSFP) 1930 *F*, 1932 *I*
Evans, H L (Edinburgh U) 1885 *I* 1,2
Ewart, E N (Glasgow Acads) 1879 *E*, 1880 *I, E*

Fahmy, Dr E C (Abertillery) 1920 *F, W, I, E*
Fasson, F H (London Scottish, Edinburgh Wands) 1900 *W*, 1901 *W, I*, 1902 *W, E*
Fell, A N (Edinburgh U) 1901 *W, I, E*, 1902 *W, E*, 1903 *W, E*
Ferguson, J H (Gala) 1928 *W*
Ferguson, W G (Royal HSFP) 1927 *A*, 1928 *F, W, I, E*
Fergusson, E A J (Oxford U) 1954 *F, NZ, I, E, W*
Finlay, A B (Edinburgh Acads) 1875 *E*
Finlay, J F (Edinburgh Acads) 1871 *E*, 1872 *E*, 1874 *E*, 1875 *E*
Finlay, N J (Edinburgh Acads) 1875 *E*, 1876 *E*, 1878 *E*, 1879 *I, E*, 1880 *I, E*, 1881 *I, E*
Finlay, R (Watsonians) 1948 *E*
Fisher, A T (Waterloo, Watsonians) 1947 *I, E*
Fisher, C D (Waterloo) 1975 *NZ, A*, 1976 *W, E, I*
Fisher, D (W of Scotland) 1893 *I*
Fisher, J P (Royal HSFP, London Scottish) 1963 *E*, 1964 *F, NZ, W, I, E*, 1965 *F, W, I, E, SA*, 1966 *F, W, I, E, A*, 1967 *F, W, I, E, NZ*, 1968 *F, W, I, E*
Fleming, C J N (Edinburgh Wands) 1896 *I, E*, 1897 *I*
Fleming, G R (Glasgow Acads) 1875 *E*, 1876 *E*
Fletcher, H N (Edinburgh U) 1904 *E*, 1905 *W*
Flett, A B (Edinburgh U) 1901 *W, I, E*, 1902 *W, I*
Forbes, J L (Watsonians) 1905 *W*, 1906 *I, E*
Ford, D St C (United Services, RN) 1930 *I, E*, 1931 *E*, 1932 *W, I*
Ford, J R (Gala) 1893 *I*
Forrest, J E (Glasgow Acads) 1932 *SA*, 1935 *E, NZ*
Forrest, J G S (Cambridge U) 1938 *W, I, E*
Forrest, W T (Hawick) 1903 *W, I, E*, 1904 *W, I, E*, 1905 *W, I*
Forsayth, H H (Oxford U) 1921 *F, W, I, E*, 1922 *W, I, E*
Forsyth, I W (Stewart's Coll FP) 1972 *NZ*, 1973 *F, W, I, E, P*
Forsyth, J (Edinburgh U) 1871 *E*
Foster, R A (Hawick) 1930 *W*, 1932 *SA, I, E*
Fox, J (Gala) 1952 *F, W, I, E*
Frame, J N M (Edinburgh U, Gala) 1967 *NZ*, 1968 *F, W, I, E*, 1969 *W, I, E, SA*, 1970 *F, W, I, E, A*, 1971 *F, W, I, E* (2[1C]), 1972 *F, W, E*, 1973 *P* (R)
France, C (Kelvinside Acads) 1903 *I*
Fraser, C F P (Glasgow U) 1888 *W*, 1889 *W*
Fraser, J W (Edinburgh Inst FP) 1881 *E*
Fraser, R (Cambridge U) 1911 *F, W, I, E*
French, J (Glasgow Acads) 1886 *W*, 1887 *I, W, E*
Frew, A (Edinburgh U) 1901 *W, I, E*
Frew, G M (Glasgow HSFP) 1906 *SA*, 1907 *W, I, E*, 1908 *W, I, E*, 1909 *W, I, E*, 1910 *F, W, I*, 1911 *I, E*
Friebe, J P (Glasgow HSFP) 1952 *E*
Fulton, A K (Edinburgh U, Dollar Acads) 1952 *F*, 1954 *F*
Fyfe, K C (Cambridge U, Sale, London Scottish) 1933 *W, E*, 1934 *E*, 1935 *W, I, E, NZ*, 1936 *W, E*, 1939 *I*

Gallie, G H (Edinburgh Acads) 1939 *W*
Gallie, R A (Glasgow Acads) 1920 *F, W, I, E*, 1921 *F, W, I, E*

203

Gammell, W B B (Edinburgh Wands) 1977 *I, F, W,* 1978 *W, E*
Geddes, I C (London Scottish) 1906 *SA,* 1907 *W, I, E,* 1908 *W, E*
Geddes, K I (London Scottish) 1947 *F, W, I, E*
Gedge, H T S (Oxford U, London Scottish, Edinburgh Wands) 1894 *W, I, E,* 1896 *E,* 1899 *W, E*
Gedge, P M S (Edinburgh Wands) 1933 *I*
Gemmill, R (Glasgow HSFP) 1950 *F, W, I, E,* 1951 *F, W, I*
Gibson, W R (Royal HSFP) 1891 *I, E,* 1892 *W, I, E,* 1893 *W, I, E,* 1894 *W, I, E,* 1895 *W, I, E*
Gilbert-Smith, D S (London Scottish) 1952 *E*
Gilchrist, J (Glasgow Acads) 1925 *F*
Gill, A D (Gala) 1973 *P,* 1974 *W, E, I, F*
Gillespie, J I (Edinburgh Acads) 1899 *E,* 1900 *W, E,* 1901 *W, I, E,* 1902 *W, I,* 1904 *I, E*
Gillies, A C (Watsonians) 1924 *W, I, E,* 1925 *F, W, E,* 1926 *F, W,* 1927 *F, W, I, E*
Gilray, C M (Oxford U, London Scottish) 1908 *E,* 1909 *W, E,* 1912 *I*
Glasgow, R J C (Dunfermline) 1962 *F, W, I, E,* 1963 *I, E,* 1964 *I, E,* 1965 *W, I*
Glen, W S (Edinburgh Wands) 1955 *W*
Gloag, L G (Cambridge U) 1949 *F, W, I, E*
Goodfellow, J (Langholm) 1928 *W, I, E*
Goodhue, F W J (London Scottish) 1890 *W, I, E,* 1891 *W, I, E,* 1892 *W, I, E*
Gordon, R (Edinburgh Wands) 1951 *W,* 1952 *F, W, I, E,* 1953 *W*
Gordon, R E (Royal Artillery) 1913 *F, W, I*
Gordon, R J (London Scottish) 1982 *A 1,2*
Gore, A C (London Scottish) 1882 *I*
Gossman, B M (W of Scotland) 1980 *W,* 1983 *F, W*
Gossman, J S (W of Scotland) 1980 *E (R)*
Gowans, J J (Cambridge U, London Scottish) 1893 *W,* 1894 *W, E,* 1895 *W, I, E,* 1896 *I, E*
Gowland, G C (London Scottish) 1908 *W,* 1909 *W, E,* 1910 *F, W, I, E*
Gracie, A L (Harlequins) 1921 *F, W, I, E,* 1922 *F, W, I, E,* 1923 *F, W, I, E,* 1924 *F*
Graham, I N (Edinburgh Acads) 1939 *I, E*
Graham, J (Kelso) 1926 *I, E,* 1927 *F, W, I, E, A,* 1928 *F, W, I, E,* 1930 *I, E,* 1932 *SA, W*
Graham, J H S (Edinburgh Acads) 1876 *E,* 1877 *I, E,* 1878 *E,* 1879 *I, E,* 1880 *I, E,* 1881 *I, E*
Grant, D (Hawick) 1965 *F, E, SA,* 1966 *F, W, I, E, A,* 1967 *F, W, I, E, NZ,* 1968 *F*
Grant, D M (East Midlands) 1911 *W, I*
Grant, M L (Harlequins) 1955 *F,* 1956 *F, W,* 1957 *F*
Grant, T O (Hawick) 1960 *I, E, SA,* 1964 *F, NZ, W*
Grant, W St C (Craigmount) 1873 *E,* 1874 *E*
Gray, C A (Nottingham) 1989 *W, E, I, F, Fj, R,* 1990 *I, F, W, E*
Gray, D (W of Scotland) 1978 *E,* 1979 *I, F, NZ,* 1980 *I, F, W, E,* 1981 *F*
Gray, G L (Gala) 1935 *NZ,* 1937 *W, I, E*
Gray, T (Northampton, Heriot's FP) 1950 *E,* 1951 *F, E,* 1930 *E*
Greenlees, H D (Leicester) 1927 *A,* 1928 *F, W,* 1929 *I, E,* 1930 *E*
Greenlees, J R C (Cambridge U, Kelvinside Acads) 1900 *I,* 1902 *W, I, E,* 1903 *W, I, E*
Greenwood, J T (Dunfermline and Perthshire Acads) 1952 *F,* 1955 *F, W, I, E,* 1956 *F, W, I, E,* 1957 *F, W, E,* 1958 *F, W, A, I, E,* 1959 *F, W, I*
Greig, A (Glasgow HSFP) 1911 *I*
Greig, L L (Glasgow Acads, United Services) 1905 *NZ,* 1906 *SA,* 1907 *W,* 1908 *W, I*
Greig, R C (Glasgow Acads) 1893 *W,* 1897 *I*
Grieve, C F (Oxford U) 1935 *W,* 1936 *E*
Grieve, R M (Kelso) 1935 *W, I, E, NZ,* 1936 *W, I, E*
Gunn, A W (Royal HSFP) 1912 *F, W, I, SA,* 1913 *F*

Hamilton, A S (Headingley) 1914 *W,* 1920 *F*
Hamilton, H M (W of Scotland) 1874 *E,* 1875 *E*
Hannah, R S M (W of Scotland) 1971 *I*
Harrower, P R (London Scottish) 1885 *W*
Hart, J G M (London Scottish) 1951 *SA*
Hart, T M (Glasgow U) 1930 *W, I*
Hart, W (Melrose) 1960 *SA*
Harvey, L (Greenock Wands) 1899 *I*
Hastie, A J (Melrose) 1961 *W, I, E,* 1964 *I, E,* 1965 *E, SA,* 1966 *F, W, I, E, A,* 1967 *F, W, I, NZ,* 1968 *F, W*

Hastie, I R (Kelso) 1955 *F,* 1958 *F, E,* 1959 *F, W, I*
Hastie, J D H (Melrose) 1938 *W, I, E*
Hastings, A G (Cambridge U, Watsonians, London Scottish) 1986 *F, W, E, I, R,* 1987 *I, F, W, E, [F, Z, R, NZ],* 1988 *I, F, W, E, A,* 1989 *Fj, R,* 1990 *I, F, W, E*
Hastings, S (Watsonians) 1986 *F, W, E, I, R,* 1987 *I, F, W, [R],* 1988 *I, F, W, A,* 1989 *W, E, I, F, Fj, R,* 1990 *I, F, W, E*
Hay, B H (Boroughmuir) 1975 *NZ, A,* 1976 *F,* 1978 *I, F, W, E, NZ,* 1979 *W, E, I, F, NZ,* 1980 *I, F, W, E,* 1981 *F, W, I, NZ 1,2*
Hay-Gordon, J R (Edinburgh Acads) 1875 *E,* 1877 *I, E*
Hegarty, C B (Hawick) 1978 *I, F, W, E*
Hegarty, J J (Hawick) 1951 *F,* 1953 *F, W, I, E,* 1955 *F*
Henderson, B C (Edinburgh Wands) 1963 *E,* 1964 *F, I, E,* 1965 *F, W, I, E,* 1966 *F, W, I, E*
Henderson, F W (London Scottish) 1900 *W, I*
Henderson, I C (Edinburgh Acads) 1939 *I, E,* 1947 *F, W, E, A,* 1948 *I, E*
Henderson, J H (Oxford U, Richmond) 1953 *F, W, I, E,* 1954 *F, W, I, E*
Henderson, J M (Edinburgh Acads) 1933 *W, E, I*
Henderson, J Y M (Watsonians) 1911 *E*
Henderson, M M (Dunfermline) 1937 *W, I, E*
Henderson, N F (London Scottish) 1892 *I*
Henderson, R G (Newcastle Northern) 1924 *I, E*
Hendrie, K G P (Heriot's FP) 1924 *F, W, I*
Hendry, T L (Clydesdale) 1893 *W, I, E,* 1895 *I*
Henriksen, E H (Royal HSFP) 1953 *I*
Hepburn, D P (Woodford) 1947 *A,* 1948 *F, W, I, E,* 1949 *F, W, I, E*
Heron, G (Glasgow Acads) 1874 *E,* 1875 *E*
Hill, C C P (St Andrew's U) 1912 *F, I*
Hinshelwood, A J W (London Scottish) 1966 *F, W, I, E, A,* 1967 *F, W, I, E, NZ,* 1968 *F, W, I, E, A,* 1969 *F, W, I, SA,* 1970 *F, W*
Hodgson, C G (London Scottish) 1968 *I, E*
Hogg, C G (Boroughmuir) 1978 *F (R), W (R)*
Holms, W F (RIE Coll) 1886 *W, E,* 1887 *I, E,* 1889 *W, I*
Horsburgh, G B (London Scottish) 1937 *W, I, E,* 1938 *W, I, E,* 1939 *W, I, E*
Howie, D D (Kirkcaldy) 1912 *F, W, I, E, SA,* 1913 *F, W*
Howie, R A (Kirkcaldy) 1924 *F, W, I, E,* 1925 *W, I, E*
Hoyer-Millar, G C (Oxford U) 1953 *I*
Huggan, J L (London Scottish) 1914 *E*
Hume, J (Royal HSFP) 1912 *F,* 1920 *F,* 1921 *F, W, I, E,* 1922 *F*
Hume, J W G (Oxford U, Edinburgh Wands) 1928 *I,* 1930 *F*
Hunter, F (Edinburgh U) 1882 *I*
Hunter, I G (Selkirk) 1984 *I (R),* 1985 *F (R), W, E*
Hunter, J M (Cambridge U) 1947 *F*
Hunter, M D (Glasgow High) 1974 *F*
Hunter, W J (Hawick) 1964 *F, NZ, W,* 1967 *F, W, I, E*
Hutchison, W R (Glasgow HSFP) 1911 *E*
Hutton, A H M (Dunfermline) 1932 *I*
Hutton, J E (Harlequins) 1930 *E,* 1931 *F*

Inglis, H M (Edinburgh Acads) 1951 *F, W, I, E, SA,* 1952 *W, I*
Inglis, J M (Selkirk) 1952 *E*
Inglis, W M (Cambridge U, Royal Engineers) 1937 *W, I, E,* 1938 *W, I, E*
Innes, J R S (Aberdeen GSFP) 1939 *W, I, E,* 1947 *A,* 1948 *F, W, I, E*
Ireland, J C H (Glasgow HSFP) 1925 *W, I, E,* 1926 *F, W, I, E,* 1927 *F, W, I, E*
Irvine, A R (Heriot's FP) 1972 *NZ,* 1973 *F, W, I, E, P,* 1974 *W, E, I, F,* 1975 *I, F, W, E, NZ, A,* 1976 *F, W, E, I,* 1977 *I, F, W,* 1978 *I, F, E, NZ,* 1979 *W, E, I, F, NZ,* 1980 *I, F, W, E,* 1981 *F, W, E, I, NZ 1,2, R, A,* 1982 *E, I, F, W, A 1,2*
Irvine, D R (Edinburgh Acads) 1878 *E,* 1879 *I, E*
Irvine, R W (Edinburgh Acads) 1871 *E,* 1872 *E,* 1873 *E,* 1874 *E,* 1875 *E,* 1876 *E,* 1877 *I, E,* 1878 *E,* 1879 *I, E,* 1880 *I, E*
Irvine, T W (Edinburgh Acads) 1885 *I1,2,* 1886 *W, I, E,* 1887 *I, W, E,* 1888 *W, I,* 1889 *I*

Jackson, K L T (Oxford U) 1933 *W, E, I,* 1934 *W*
Jackson, T G H (Army) 1947 *F, W, E, A,* 1948 *F, W, I, E,* 1949 *F, W, I, E*

Jackson, W D (Hawick) 1964 *I*, 1965 *E, SA*, 1968 *A*, 1969 *F, W, I, E*
Jamieson, J (W of Scotland) 1883 *W, I, E*, 1884 *W, I, E*, 1885 *W, I*1,2
Jeffrey, J (Kelso) 1984 *A*, 1985 *I, E*, 1986 *F, W, E, I, R*, 1987 *I, F, W, E, [F, Z, R]*, 1988 *I, W, A*, 1989 *W, E, I, F, Fj, R*, 1990 *I, F, W, E*
Johnston, D I (Watsonians) 1979 *NZ*, 1980 *I, F, W, E*, 1981 *R, A*, 1982 *E, I, F, W, A* 1,2, 1983 *I, F, W, NZ*, 1984 *W, E, I, F, R*, 1986 *F, W, E, I, R*
Johnston, H H (Edinburgh Collegian FP) 1877 *I, E*
Johnston, J (Melrose) 1951 *SA*, 1952 *F, W, I, E*
Johnston, W C (Glasgow HSFP) 1922 *F*
Johnston, W G S (Cambridge U) 1935 *W, I*, 1937 *W, I, E*

Junor, J E (Glasgow Acads) 1876 *E*, 1877 *I, E*, 1878 *E*, 1879 *I*, 1881 *I*

Keddie, R R (Watsonians) 1967 *NZ*
Keith, G J (Wasps) 1968 *F, W*
Keller, D H (London Scottish) 1949 *F, W, I, E*, 1950 *F, W, I*
Kelly, J R F (Watsonians) 1927 *A*, 1928 *F, W, E*
Kemp, J W Y (Glasgow HSFP) 1954 *W*, 1955 *F, W, I, E*, 1956 *F, W, I, E*, 1957 *F, W, I, E*, 1958 *F, W, A, I, E*, 1959 *F, W, I, E*, 1960 *F, W, I, E, SA*
Kennedy, A E (Watsonians) 1983 *NZ*, 1984 *W, E, A*
Kennedy, F (Stewart's Coll FP) 1920 *F, W, I, E*, 1921 *E*
Kennedy, N (W of Scotland) 1903 *W, I, E*
Ker, A B M (Kelso) 1988 *W, E*
Ker, H T (Glasgow Acads) 1887 *I, W, E*, 1888 *I*, 1889 *W*, 1890 *I, E*
Kerr, D S (Heriot's FP) 1923 *F, W*, 1924 *F*, 1926 *I, E*, 1927 *W, I, E*, 1928 *I, E*
Kerr, G C (Old Dunelmians, Edinburgh Wands) 1898 *I, E*, 1899 *I, W, E*, 1900 *I, E*
Kerr, J M (Heriot's FP) 1935 *NZ*, 1936 *I, E*, 1937 *W, I*
Kerr, W (London Scottish) 1953 *E*
Kidston, D W (Glasgow Acads) 1883 *W, E*
Kidston, W H (W of Scotland) 1874 *E*
Kilgour, I J (RMC Sandhurst) 1921 *F*
King, J H F (Selkirk) 1953 *F, W, E*, 1954 *E*
Kininmonth, P W (Oxford U, Richmond) 1949 *F, W, I, E*, 1950 *F, W, I, E*, 1951 *F, W, I, E, SA*, 1952 *F, W, I*, 1954 *F, NZ, I, E, W*
Kinnear, R M (Heriot's FP) 1926 *F, W, I*
Knox, J (Kelvinside Acads) 1903 *W, I, E*
Kyle, W E (Hawick) 1902 *W, I, E*, 1903 *W, I, E*, 1904 *W, I, E*, 1905 *W, I, E, NZ*, 1906 *W, I, E*, 1908 *E*, 1909 *W, I, E*, 1910 *W*

Laidlaw, A S (Hawick) 1897 *I*
Laidlaw, F A L (Melrose) 1965 *F, W, I, E, SA*, 1966 *F, W, I, E, A*, 1967 *F, W, I, E, NZ*, 1968 *F, W, I, A*, 1969 *F, W, I, E, SA*, 1970 *F, W, I, E, A*, 1971 *F, W, I*
Laidlaw, R J (Jedforest) 1980 *I, F, W, E*, 1981 *F, W, E, I, NZ* 1,2, *R, A*, 1982 *E, I, F, W, A* 1,2, 1983 *I, F, W, E, NZ*, 1984 *W, E, I, F, R, A*, 1985 *I, F*, 1986 *F, W, E, I, R*, 1987 *I, F, W, E, [F, R, NZ]*, 1988 *I, F, W, E*
Laing, A D (Royal HSFP) 1914 *W, I, E*, 1920 *F, W, I*, 1921 *F*
Lambie, I K (Watsonians) 1978 *NZ* (R), 1979 *W, E, NZ*
Lambie, L B (Glasgow HSFP) 1934 *W, I, E*, 1935 *W, I, E, NZ*
Lamond, G A W (Kelvinside Acads) 1899 *W, E*, 1905 *E*
Lang, D (Paisley) 1876 *E*, 1877 *I*
Langrish, R W (London Scottish) 1930 *F*, 1931 *F, W, I*
Lauder, W (Neath) 1969 *I, E, SA*, 1970 *F, W, I, A*, 1973 *I, F*, 1974 *W, E, I, F*, 1975 *I, F, NZ, A*, 1976 *F*, 1977 *E*
Laughland, I H P (London Scottish) 1959 *F*, 1960 *F, W, I, E*, 1961 *SA, W, I, E*, 1962 *F, W, I, E*, 1963 *F, W, I*, 1964 *F, NZ, W, I, E*, 1965 *F, W, I, E, SA*, 1966 *F, W, I, E*, 1967 *E*
Lawrie, J R (Melrose) 1922 *F, W, I, E*, 1923 *F, W, I, E*, 1924 *W, I, E*
Lawrie, K G (Gala) 1980 *F* (R), *W, E*
Lawson, A J M (Edinburgh Wands, London Scottish) 1972 *F* (R), *E*, 1973 *F*, 1974 *W, E*, 1976 *E, I*, 1977 *E*, 1978 *NZ*, 1979 *W, E, I, F, NZ*, 1980 *W* (R)
Lawther, T H B (Old Millhillians) 1932 *SA, W*
Ledingham, G A (Aberdeen GSFP) 1913 *F*

Lees, J B (Gala) 1947 *I, A*, 1948 *F, W, E*
Leggatt, H T O (Watsonians) 1891 *W, I, E*, 1892 *W, I*, 1893 *W, E*, 1894 *I, E*
Lely, W G (Cambridge U, London Scottish) 1909 *I*
Leslie, D G (Dundee HSFP, W of Scotland, Gala) 1975 *I, F, W, E, NZ, A*, 1976 *F, W, E, I*, 1978 *NZ*, 1980 *E*, 1981 *W, E, I, NZ* 1,2, *R, A*, 1982 *E*, 1983 *I, F, W, E*, 1984 *W, E, I, F, R*, 1985 *F, W, E*
Liddell, E H (Edinburgh U) 1922 *F, W, I*, 1923 *F, W, I, E*
Lind, H (Dunfermline) 1928 *I*, 1931 *F, W, I, E*, 1932 *SA, W, E*, 1933 *W, E, I*, 1934 *W, I, E*, 1935 *I*, 1936 *E*
Lindsay, A B (London Hospital) 1910 *I*, 1911 *I*
Lindsay, G C (London Scottish) 1884 *W*, 1885 *I* 1, 1887 *W, E*
Lindsay-Watson, R H (Hawick) 1909 *I*
Lineen, S R P (Boroughmuir) 1989 *W, E, I, F, Fj, R*, 1990 *I, F, W, E*
Little, A W (Hawick) 1905 *W*
Logan, W R (Edinburgh U, Edinburgh Wands) 1931 *E*, 1932 *SA, W, I*, 1933 *W, E, I*, 1934 *W, I, E*, 1935 *W, I, E, NZ*, 1936 *W, I, E*, 1937 *W, I, E*
Lorraine, H D B (Oxford U) 1933 *W, E, I*
Loudoun-Shand, E G (Oxford U) 1913 *E*
Lowe, J D (Heriot's FP) 1934 *W*
Lumsden, I J M (Bath, Watsonians) 1947 *F, W, A*, 1949 *F, W, I, E*
Lyall, G G (Gala) 1947 *A*, 1948 *F, W, I, E*
Lyall, W J C (Edinburgh Acads) 1871 *E*

Macarthur, J P (Waterloo) 1932 *E*
MacCallum, J C (Watsonians) 1905 *E, NZ*, 1906 *W, I, E, SA*, 1907 *W, I, E*, 1908 *W, I, E*, 1909 *W, I, E*, 1910 *F, W, I, E*, 1911 *F, I, E*, 1912 *F, W, I, E*
McClung, T (Edinburgh Acads) 1956 *I, E*, 1957 *W, I, E*, 1959 *F, W, I*, 1960 *W*
McClure, G B (W of Scotland) 1873 *E*
McClure, J H (W of Scotland) 1872 *E*
McCowan, D (W of Scotland) 1880 *I, E*, 1881 *I, E*, 1882 *I, E*, 1883 *I, E*, 1884 *I, E*
McCowat, R H (Glasgow Acads) 1905 *I*
McCrae, I G (Gordonians) 1967 *E*, 1968 *I*, 1969 *F* (R), *W*, 1972 *F, NZ*
McCrow, J W S (Edinburgh Acads) 1921 *I*
McDonald, C (Jedforest) 1947 *A*
Macdonald, D C (Edinburgh U) 1953 *F, W*, 1958 *I, E*
Macdonald, D S M (Oxford U, London Scottish, W of Scotland) 1977 *E, I, F, W*, 1978 *I, W, E*
Macdonald, J D (London Scottish, Army) 1966 *F, W, I, E*, 1967 *F, W*
Macdonald, J M (Edinburgh Wands) 1911 *W*
Macdonald, J S (Edinburgh U) 1903 *E*, 1904 *W, I, E*, 1905 *E*
Macdonald, K R (Stewart's Coll FP) 1956 *F, W, I*, 1957 *W, I, E*
Macdonald, R (Edinburgh U) 1950 *F, W, I, E*
McDonald, R (Edinburgh U) 1950 *F, W, I, E*
Macdonald, W A (Glasgow U) 1889 *W*, 1892 *I, E*
Macdonald, W G (London Scottish) 1969 *I* (R)
Macdougall, J B (Greenock Wands, Wakefield) 1913 *F*, 1914 *I*, 1921 *F, I, E*
McEwan, M C (Edinburgh Acads) 1886 *E*, 1887 *I, W, E*, 1888 *W, I*, 1889 *W, I*, 1890 *W, I, E*, 1891 *W, I, E*, 1892 *E*
MacEwan, N A (Gala, Highland) 1971 *F, W, I, E* (2[1C]), 1972 *F, W, E, NZ*, 1973 *F, W, I, E, P*, 1974 *W, E, I, F*, 1975 *W, E*
McEwan, W M C (Edinburgh Acads) 1894 *W, E*, 1895 *W, E*, 1896 *W, I, E*, 1897 *I, E*, 1898 *I, E*, 1899 *I, W, E*, 1900 *W, E*
MacEwen, R K G (Cambridge U, London Scottish) 1954 *F, NZ, I, W*, 1956 *F, W, I, E*, 1957 *F, W, I, E*, 1958 *W*
Macfarlan, D J (London Scottish) 1883 *W*, 1884 *W, I, E*, 1886 *W, I*, 1887 *I*, 1888 *I*
McFarlane, J L H (Edinburgh U) 1871 *E*, 1872 *E*, 1873 *E*
McGaughey, S K (Hawick) 1984 *R*
McGeechan, I R (Headingley) 1972 *NZ*, 1973 *F, W, I, E, P*, 1974 *W, E, I, F*, 1975 *I, F, W, E, NZ, A*, 1976 *F, W, E, I*, 1977 *E, I, F, W*, 1978 *I, F, W, NZ*, 1979 *W, E, I, F*
McGlashan, T P L (Royal HSFP) 1947 *F, I, E*, 1954 *F, NZ, I, E, W*

MacGregor, D G (Watsonians, Pontypridd) 1907 *W, I, E*
MacGregor, G (Cambridge U) 1890 *W, I, E*, 1891 *W, I, E*, 1893 *W, I, E*, 1894 *W, I, E*, 1896 *E*
MacGregor, I A A (Hillhead HSFP, Llanelli) 1955 *I, E*, 1956 *F, W, I, E*, 1957 *F, W, I*
MacGregor, J R (Edinburgh U) 1909 *I*
McGuinness, G M (W of Scotland) 1982 *A* 1,2, 1983 *I*, 1985 *I, F, W, E*
McHarg, A F (W of Scotland, London Scottish) 1968 *I, E, A*, 1969 *F, W, I, E*, 1971 *F, W, I, E* (2[1C]), 1972 *F, E, NZ*, 1973 *F, W, I, E, P*, 1974 *W, E, I, F*, 1975 *I, F, W, E, NZ, A*, 1976 *F, W, E, I*, 1977 *E, I, F, W*, 1978 *I, F, W, NZ*, 1979 *W, E*
McIndoe, F (Glasgow Acads) 1886 *W, I*
MacIntyre, I (Edinburgh Wands) 1890 *W, I, E*, 1891 *W, I, E*
Mackay, E B (Glasgow Acads) 1920 *W*, 1922 *E*
McKeating, E (Heriot's FP) 1957 *F, W*, 1961 *SA, W, I, E*
McKendrick, J G (W of Scotland) 1889 *I*
Mackenzie, A D G (Selkirk) 1984 *A*
Mackenzie, C J G (United Services) 1921 *E*
Mackenzie, D D (Edinburgh U) 1947 *W, I, E*, 1948 *F, W, I*
Mackenzie, D K A (Edinburgh, Wands) 1939 *I, E*
Mackenzie, J M (Edinburgh U) 1905 *NZ*, 1909 *W, I, E*, 1910 *W, I, E*, 1911 *W, I*
Mackenzie, R C (Glasgow Acads) 1877 *I, E*, 1881 *I, E*
Mackie, G Y (Highland) 1975 *A*, 1976 *F, W*, 1978 *F*
MacKinnon, A (London Scottish) 1898 *I, E*, 1899 *I, W, E*, 1900 *E*
Mackintosh, C E W C (London Scottish) 1924 *F*
Mackintosh, H S (Glasgow U, W of Scotland) 1929 *F, W, I, E*, 1930 *F, W, I, E*, 1931 *F, W, E, I*, 1932 *SA, W, I, E*
MacLachlan, L P (Oxford U, London Scottish) 1954 *NZ, I, E, W*
Maclagan, W E (Edinburgh Acads) 1878 *E*, 1879 *I, E*, 1880 *I, E*, 1881 *I, E*, 1882 *I, E*, 1883 *W, I, E*, 1884 *W, I, E*, 1885 *W, I*1,2, 1887 *I, W, E*, 1888 *W, I*, 1890 *W, I, E*
McLaren, A (Durham County) 1931 *F*
McLaren, E (London Scottish, Royal HSFP) 1923 *F, W, I, E*, 1924 *F*
McLauchlan, J (Jordanhill) 1969 *E, SA*, 1970 *F, W*, 1971 *F, W, I, E* (2[1C]), 1972 *F, W, E, NZ*, 1973 *F, W, I, E, P*, 1974 *W, E, I, F*, 1975 *I, F, W, E, NZ, A*, 1976 *F, W, E, I*, 1977 *W, I*, 1978 *I, F, W, E, NZ*, 1979 *W, E, I, F, NZ*
McLean, D I (Royal HSFP) 1947 *I, E*
Maclennan, W D (Watsonians) 1947 *F, I*
MacLeod, D A (Glasgow U) 1886 *I, E*
MacLeod, G (Edinburgh Acads) 1878 *E*, 1882 *I*
McLeod, H F (Hawick) 1954 *F, NZ, I, E, W*, 1955 *F, W, I, E*, 1956 *F, W, I, E*, 1957 *F, W, I, E*, 1958 *F, W, A, I, E*, 1959 *F, W, I, E*, 1960 *F, W, I, E, SA*, 1961 *F, SA, W, I, E*, 1962 *F, W, I, E*
MacLeod, K G (Cambridge U) 1905 *NZ*, 1906 *W, I, E, SA*, 1907 *W, I, E*, 1908 *I, E*
MacLeod, L M (Cambridge U) 1904 *W, I, E*, 1905 *W, I, NZ*
Macleod, W M (Fettesian-Lorettonians, Edinburgh Wands) 1886 *W, I*
McMillan, K H D (Sale) 1953 *F, W, I, E*
MacMillan, R G (London Scottish) 1887 *W, I, E*, 1890 *W, I, E*, 1891 *W, E*, 1892 *W, I, E*, 1893 *W, E*, 1894 *W, I, E*, 1895 *W, I, E*, 1897 *I, E*
MacMyn, D J (Cambridge U, London Scottish) 1925 *F, W, I, E*, 1926 *F, W, I, E*, 1927 *E, A*, 1928 *F*
McNeil, A S B (Watsonians) 1935 *I*
McPartlin, J J (Harlequins, Oxford U) 1960 *F, W*, 1962 *F, W, I, E*
Macphail, J A R (Edinburgh Acads) 1949 *E*, 1951 *SA*
Macpherson, D G (London Hospital) 1910 *I, E*
Macpherson, G P S (Oxford U, Edinburgh Acads) 1922 *F, W, I, E*, 1924 *W, E*, 1925 *F, W, E*, 1927 *F, W, I, E*, 1928 *F, W, E*, 1929 *I, E*, 1930 *F, W, I, E*, 1931 *W, E*, 1932 *SA, E*
Macpherson, N C (Newport, Mon) 1920 *W, I, E*, 1921 *F, E*, 1923 *I, E*
McQueen, S B (Waterloo) 1923 *F, W, I, E*
Macrae, D J (St Andrews U) 1937 *W, I, E*, 1938 *W, I,*

E, 1939 *W, I, E*
Mabon, J T (Jedforest) 1898 *I, E*, 1899 *I*, 1900 *I*
Madsen, D F (Gosforth) 1974 *W, E, I, F*, 1975 *I, F, W, E*, 1976 *F*, 1977 *E, I, F, W*, 1978 *I*
Mair, N G R (Edinburgh U) 1951 *F, W, I, E*
Maitland, G (Edinburgh Inst FP) 1885 *W, I*2
Maitland, R (Edinburgh Inst FP) 1881 *E*, 1882 *I, E*, 1884 *W*, 1885 *W*
Maitland, R P (Royal Artillery) 1872 *E*
Malcolm, A G (Glasgow U) 1888 *I*
Marsh, J (Edinburgh Inst FP) 1889 *W, I*
Marshall, A (Edinburgh Acads) 1875 *E*
Marshall, G R (Selkirk) 1988 *A* (R), 1989 *Fj*
Marshall, J C (London Scottish) 1954 *F, NZ, I, E, W*
Marshall, K W (Edinburgh Acads) 1934 *W, I, E*, 1935 *W, I, E*, 1936 *W*, 1937 *E*
Marshall, T R (Edinburgh Acads) 1871 *E*, 1872 *E*, 1873 *E*, 1874 *E*
Marshall, W (Edinburgh Acads) 1872 *E*
Martin, H (Edinburgh Acads, Oxford U) 1908 *W, I, E*, 1909 *W, E*
Masters, W H (Edinburgh Inst FP) 1879 *I*, 1880 *I, E*
Maxwell, F T (Royal Engineers) 1872 *E*
Maxwell, G H H P (Edinburgh Acads, RAF, London Scottish) 1913 *I, E*, 1914 *W, I, E*, 1920 *W, E*, 1921 *F, W, I, E*, 1922 *F, E*
Maxwell, J M (Langholm) 1957 *I*
Mein, J (Edinburgh Acads) 1871 *E*, 1872 *E*, 1873 *E*, 1874 *E*, 1875 *E*
Melville, C L (Army) 1937 *W, I, E*
Menzies, H F (W of Scotland) 1893 *W, I*, 1894 *W, E*
Methuen, A (London Scottish) 1889 *W, I*
Michie, E J S (Aberdeen U, Aberdeen GSFP) 1954 *F, NZ, I, E*, 1955 *W, I, E*, 1956 *F, W, I, E*, 1957 *F, W, I, E*
Millar, J N (W of Scotland) 1892 *W, I, E*, 1893 *W*, 1895 *I, E*
Millar, R K (London Scottish) 1924 *I*
Millican, J G (Edinburgh U) 1973 *W, I, E*
Milne, C J B (Fettesian-Lorettonians, W of Scotland) 1886 *W, I, E*
Milne, I G (Heriot's FP, Harlequins) 1979 *I, F, NZ*, 1980 *I, F*, 1981 *NZ* 1,2, *R, A*, 1982 *E, I, F, W, A* 1,2, 1983 *I, F, W, E, NZ*, 1984 *W, E, I, F, A*, 1985 *F, W, E*, 1986 *F, W, E, I, R*, 1987 *I, F, W, E, [F, Z, NZ]*, 1988 *A*, 1989 *W*
Milne, K S (Heriot's F P) 1989 *W, E, I, F, Fj, R*, 1990 *I, F, W, E*
Milne, W M (Glasgow Acads) 1904 *I, E*, 1905 *W, I*
Milroy, E (Watsonians) 1910 *W*, 1911 *E*, 1912 *W, I, E, SA*, 1913 *F, W, I, E*, 1914 *I, E*
Mitchell, G W E (Edinburgh Wands) 1967 *NZ*, 1968 *F, W*
Mitchell, J G (W of Scotland) 1885 *W, I*1,2
Moncreiff, F J (Edinburgh Acads) 1871 *E*, 1872 *E*, 1873 *E*
Monteith, H G (Cambridge U, London Scottish) 1905 *E*, 1906 *W, I, E, SA*, 1907 *W, I*, 1908 *E*
Monypenny, D B (London Scottish) 1899 *I, W, E*
Moodie, A R (St Andrew's U) 1909 *E*, 1910 *F*, 1911 *F*
Morgan, D W (Stewart's-Melville FP) 1973 *W, I, E, P*, 1974 *I, F*, 1975 *I, F, W, E, NZ, A*, 1976 *F, W*, 1977 *I, F, W*, 1978 *I, F, W*
Morrison, M C (Royal HSFP) 1896 *W, I, E*, 1897 *I, E*, 1898 *I, E*, 1899 *I, W, E*, 1900 *W, E*, 1901 *W, I, E*, 1902 *W, I, E*, 1903 *W, I*, 1904 *W, I, E*
Morrison, R H (Edinburgh U) 1886 *W, I, E*
Morrison, W H (Edinburgh Acads) 1900 *W*
Morton, D S (W of Scotland) 1887 *I, W, E*, 1888 *W, I*, 1889 *W, I*, 1890 *I, E*
Mowat, J G (Glasgow Acads) 1883 *W, E*
Muir, D E (Heriot's FP) 1950 *F, W, I, E*, 1952 *W, I, E*
Munnoch, N M (Watsonians) 1952 *F, W, I*
Munro, P (Oxford, London Scottish) 1905 *W, I, E, NZ*, 1906 *W, I, E, SA*, 1907 *I, E*, 1911 *F, W, I*
Munro, S (St Andrews U) 1871 *E*
Munro, S (Ayr, W of Scotland) 1980 *I, F*, 1981 *F, W, E, I, NZ* 1,2, *R*, 1984 *W*
Munro, W H (Glasgow HSFP) 1947 *I, E*
Murdoch, W C W (Hillhead HSFP) 1935 *E, NZ*, 1936 *W, I*, 1939 *E*, 1948 *F, W, I, E*
Murray, G M (Glasgow Acads) 1921 *I*, 1926 *W*
Murray, H M (Glasgow U) 1936 *W, I*

Murray, K T (Hawick) 1985 *I, F, W*
Murray, R O (Cambridge U) 1935 *W, E*
Murray, W A K (London Scottish) 1920 *F, I*, 1921 *F*

Napier, H M (W of Scotland) 1877 *I, E*, 1878 *E*, 1879 *I, E*
Neill, J B (Edinburgh Acads) 1963 *E*, 1964 *F, NZ, W, I, E*, 1965 *F*
Neill, R M (Edinburgh Acads) 1901 *E*, 1902 *I*
Neilson, G T (W of Scotland) 1891 *W, I, E*, 1892 *W, E*, 1893 *W*, 1894 *W, I*, 1895 *W, I, E*, 1896 *W, I, E*
Neilson, J A (Glasgow Acads) 1878 *E*, 1879 *E*
Neilson, R T (W of Scotland) 1898 *I, E*, 1899 *I, W*, 1900 *I, E*
Neilson, T (W of Scotland) 1874 *E*
Neilson, W (Merchiston, Cambridge U, London Scottish) 1891 *W, E*, 1892 *W, I, E*, 1893 *I, E*, 1894 *E*, 1895 *W, I, E*, 1896 *I*, 1897 *I, E*
Neilson, W G (Merchistonians) 1894 *E*
Nelson, J B (Glasgow Acads) 1925 *F, W, I, E*, 1926 *F, W, I, E*, 1927 *F, W, I, E*, 1928 *I, E*, 1929 *F, W, I, E*, 1930 *F, W, I, E*, 1931 *F, W, I*
Nelson, T A (Oxford U) 1898 *E*
Nichol, J A (Royal HSFP) 1955 *W, I, E*
Nimmo, C S (Watsonians) 1920 *E*

Ogilvy, C (Hawick) 1911 *I, E*, 1912 *I*
Oliver, G H (Hawick) 1987 *[Z]*
Oliver, G K (Gala) 1970 *A*
Orr, C E (W of Scotland) 1887 *I, E, W*, 1888 *W, I*, 1889 *W, I*, 1890 *W, I, E*, 1891 *W, I, E*, 1892 *W, I, E*
Orr, H J (London Scottish) 1903 *W, I, E*, 1904 *W, I*
Orr, J E (W of Scotland) 1889 *I*, 1890 *W, I, E*, 1891 *W, I, E*, 1892 *W, I, E*, 1893 *I, E*
Orr, J H (Edinburgh City Police) 1947 *F, W*
Osler, F L (Edinburgh U) 1911 *F, W*

Park, J (Royal HSFP) 1934 *W*
Paterson, D S (Gala) 1969 *SA*, 1970 *I, E, A*, 1971 *F, W, I, E* (2[1C]), 1972 *W*
Paterson, G Q (Edinburgh Acads) 1876 *E*
Paterson, J R (Birkenhead Park) 1924 *F, W, I, E*, 1926 *F, W, I, E*, 1927 *F, W, I, E, A*, 1928 *F, W, I, E*, 1929 *F, W, I, E*
Patterson, D (Hawick) 1896 *W*
Pattullo, G L (Panmure) 1920 *F, W, I, E*
Paxton, I A M (Selkirk) 1981 *NZ* 1,2, *R, A*, 1982 *E, I, F, W, A* 1,2, 1983 *I, E, NZ*, 1984 *W, E, I, F*, 1985 *I* (R), *F, W, E*, 1986 *W, E, I, R*, 1987 *I, F, W, E, [F, Z, R, NZ]*, 1988 *I, E, A*
Paxton, R E (Kelso) 1982 *I, A* 2 (R)
Pearson, J (Watsonians) 1909 *I, E*, 1910 *F, W, I, E*, 1911 *F*, 1912 *F, W, SA*, 1913 *I, E*
Pender, I M (London Scottish) 1914 *E*
Pender, N E K (Hawick) 1977 *I*, 1978 *F, W, E*
Penman, W M (RAF) 1939 *I*
Peterkin, W A (Edinburgh U) 1881 *E*, 1883 *I*, 1884 *W, I, E*, 1885 *W, I*1,2
Petrie, A G (Royal HSFP) 1873 *E*, 1874 *E*, 1875 *E*, 1876 *E*, 1877 *I, E*, 1878 *E*, 1879 *I, E*, 1880 *I, E*
Philp, A (Edinburgh Inst FP) 1882 *E*
Pocock, E I (Edinburgh Wands) 1877 *I, E*
Pollock, J A (Gosforth) 1982 *W*, 1983 *E, NZ*, 1984 *E* (R), *I, F, R*, 1985 *F*
Polson, A H (Gala) 1930 *E*
Purdie, W (Jedforest) 1939 *W, I, E*
Purves, A B H L (London Scottish) 1906 *W, I, E, SA*, 1907 *W, I, E*, 1908 *W, I, E*
Purves, W D C L (London Scottish) 1912 *F, W, I, SA*, 1913 *I, E*

Rea, C W W (W of Scotland, Headingley) 1968 *A*, 1969 *F, W, I, SA*, 1970 *F, W, I, A*, 1971 *F, W, E* (2[1C])
Reid, C (Edinburgh Acads) 1881 *I, E*, 1882 *I, E*, 1883 *W, I, E*, 1884 *W, I, E*, 1885 *W, I*1,2, 1886 *W, I, E*, 1887 *I, E*, 1888 *W, I*
Reid, J (Edinburgh Wands) 1874 *E*, 1875 *E*, 1876 *E*, 1877 *I, E*
Reid, J M (Edinburgh Acads) 1898 *I, E*, 1899 *I*
Reid, M F (Loretto) 1883 *I, E*
Reid-Kerr, J (Greenock Wand) 1909 *E*
Ralph, W K L (Stewart's Coll FP) 1955 *F, W, I, E*
Renny-Tailyour, H W (Royal Engineers) 1872 *E*
Renwick, J M (Hawick) 1972 *F, W, E, NZ*, 1973 *F,*

1974 *W, E, I, F*, 1975 *I, F, W, E, NZ, A*, 1976 *F, W, E*(R), 1977 *I, F, W*, 1978 *I, F, W, E, NZ*, 1979 *W, E, I, F, NZ*, 1980 *I, F, W, E*, 1981 *F, W, E, I, NZ* 1,2, *R, A*, 1982 *E, I, F, W*, 1983 *I, F, W, E*, 1984 *R*
Renwick, W L (London Scottish) 1989 *R*
Renwick, W N (London Scottish, Edinburgh Wands) 1938 *E*, 1939 *W*
Ritchie, G (Merchistonians) 1871 *E*
Ritchie, G F (Dundee HSFP) 1932 *E*
Ritchie, J M (Watsonians) 1933 *W, E, I*, 1934 *W, I, E*
Ritchie, W T (Cambridge U) 1905 *I, E*
Robb, G H (Glasgow U) 1881 *I*, 1885 *W*
Roberts, G (Watsonians) 1938 *W, I, E*, 1939 *W, E*
Robertson, A H (W of Scotland) 1871 *E*
Robertson, A W (Edinburgh Acads) 1897 *E*
Robertson, D (Edinburgh Acads) 1875 *E*
Robertson, D D (Cambridge U) 1893 *W*
Robertson, I (London Scottish, Watsonians) 1968 *E*, 1969 *E, SA*, 1970 *F, W, I, E, A*
Robertson, I P M (Watsonians) 1910 *F*
Robertson, J (Clydesdale) 1908 *E*
Robertson, K W (Melrose) 1978 *NZ*, 1979 *W, E, I, F, NZ*, 1980 *W, E*, 1981 *F, W, E, I, F, R, A*, 1982 *E, I, F, A* 1,2, 1983 *I, F, W, E*, 1984 *E, I, F, R, A*, 1985 *I, F, W, E*, 1986 *I*, 1987 *F* (R), *W, E, [F, Z, NZ]*, 1988 *E, A*, 1989 *E, I, F*
Robertson, L (London Scottish, United Services) 1908 *E*, 1911 *W*, 1912 *W, I, E, SA*, 1913 *W, I, E*
Robertson, M A (Gala) 1958 *F*
Robertson, R D (London Scottish) 1912 *F*
Robson, A (Hawick) 1954 *F*, 1955 *F, W, I, E*, 1956 *F, W, I, E*, 1957 *F, W, I, E*, 1958 *W, A, I, E*, 1959 *F, W, I, E*, 1960 *F*
Rodd, J A T (United Services, RN, London Scottish) 1958 *F, W, A, I, E*, 1960 *F, W*, 1962 *F, W*, 1964 *F, NZ, W*, 1965 *F, W, I*
Rogerson, J (Kelvinside Acads) 1894 *W*
Roland, E T (Edinburgh Acads) 1884 *I, E*
Rollo, D M D (Howe of Fife) 1959 *E*, 1960 *F, W, I, E, SA*, 1961 *F, SA, W, I, E*, 1962 *F, W, E*, 1963 *F, W, I, E*, 1964 *F, NZ, W, I, E*, 1965 *F, W, I, E, SA*, 1966 *F, W, I, E, A*, 1967 *F, W, E, NZ*, 1968 *F, W, I*
Rose, D M (Jedforest) 1951 *F, W, I, E, SA*, 1953 *F, W*
Ross, A (Kilmarnock) 1924 *F, W*
Ross, A (Royal HSFP) 1905 *W, I, E*, 1909 *W, I*
Ross, A R (Edinburgh U) 1911 *W*, 1914 *W, I, E*
Ross, E J (London Scottish) 1904 *W*
Ross, G T (Watsonians) 1954 *NZ, I, E, W*
Ross, I A (Hillhead HSFP) 1951 *F, W, I, E*
Ross, J (London Scottish) 1901 *W, I, E*, 1902 *W*, 1903 *E*
Ross, K I (Boroughmuir FP) 1961 *SA, W, I, E*, 1962 *F, W, I, E*, 1963 *F, W, E*
Ross, W A (Hillhead HSFP) 1937 *W, E*
Rottenburg, H (Cambridge U, London Scottish) 1899 *W, E*, 1900 *W, I, E*
Roughead, W N (Edinburgh Acads, London Scottish) 1927 *A*, 1928 *F, W, I, E*, 1930 *I, E*, 1931 *F, W, I, E*, 1932 *W*
Rowan, N A (Boroughmuir) 1980 *W, E*, 1981 *F, W, E, I*, 1984 *R*, 1985 *I*, 1987 *[R]*, 1988 *I, F, W, E*
Rowand, R (Glasgow HSFP) 1930 *F, W*, 1932 *E*, 1933 *W, E, I*, 1934 *W*
Roy, A (Waterloo) 1938 *W, I, E*, 1939 *W, I, E*
Russell, W L (Glasgow Acads) 1905 *NZ*, 1906 *W, I, E*
Rutherford, J Y (Selkirk) 1979 *W, E, I, F, NZ*, 1980 *I, F, E*, 1981 *F, W, E, I, NZ* 1,2, *A*, 1982 *E, I, F, W, A* 1,2, 1983 *E, NZ*, 1984 *W, E, I, F, R*, 1985 *I, F, E*, 1986 *F, W, E, I, R*, 1987 *I, F, W, E, [F]*

Sampson, R W F (London Scottish) 1939 *W*, 1947 *W*
Sanderson, G A (Royal HSFP) 1907 *W, I, E*, 1908 *I*
Sanderson, J L P (Edinburgh Acads) 1873 *E*
Schulze, D G (London Scottish) 1905 *E*, 1907 *I, E*, 1908 *W, I, E*, 1909 *W, I, E*, 1910 *W, I, E*, 1911 *W*
Scobie, R M (Royal Military Coll) 1914 *W, I, E*
Scotland, K J F (Heriot's FP, Cambridge U, Leicester) 1957 *F, W, I, E*, 1958 *E*, 1959 *F, W, I, E*, 1960 *F, W, I, E*, 1961 *F, SA, W, I, E*, 1962 *F, W, I, E*, 1963 *F, W, I, E*, 1965 *E*
Scott, D M (Langholm, Watsonians) 1950 *I, E*, 1951 *W, I, E, SA*, 1952 *F, W, I*, 1953 *F*
Scott, J M B (Edinburgh Acads) 1907 *E*, 1908 *W, I, E,*

1909 *W*, *I*, *E*, 1910 *F*, *W*, *I*, *E*, 1911 *F*, *W*, *I*, 1912 *W*, *I*, *E*, *SA*, 1913 *W*, *I*, *E*
Scott, J S (St Andrews U) 1950 *E*
Scott, J W (Stewart's Coll FP) 1925 *F*, *W*, *I*, *E*, 1926 *F*, *W*, *I*, *E*, 1927 *F*, *W*, *I*, *E*, *A*, 1928 *F*, *W*, *E*, 1929 *E*, 1930 *F*
Scott, R (Hawick) 1898 *I*, 1900 *I*, *E*
Scott, T (Langholm, Hawick) 1896 *W*, 1897 *I*, *E*, 1898 *I*, *E*, 1899 *I*, *W*, *E*, 1900 *W*, *I*, *E*
Scott, T M (Hawick) 1893 *E*, 1895 *W*, *I*, *E*, 1896 *W*, *E*, 1897 *I*, *E*, 1898 *I*, *E*, 1900 *W*, *I*
Scott, W P (W of Scotland) 1900 *I*, *E*, 1902 *I*, *E*, 1903 *W*, *I*, *E*, 1904 *W*, *I*, *E*, 1905 *W*, *I*, *E*, *NZ*, 1906 *W*, *I*, *E*, *SA*, 1907 *W*, *I*, *E*
Scoular, J G (Cambridge U) 1905 *NZ*, 1906 *W*, *I*, *E*, *SA*
Selby, J A R (Watsonians) 1920 *W*, *I*
Shackleton, J A P (London Scottish) 1959 *E*, 1963 *F*, *W*, 1964 *NZ*, *W*, 1965 *I*, *SA*
Sharp, G (Stewart's FP, Army) 1960 *F*, 1964 *F*, *NZ*, *W*
Shaw, G D (Sale) 1935 *NZ*, 1936 *W*, 1937 *W*, *I*, *E*, 1939 *I*
Shaw, I (Glasgow HSFP) 1937 *I*
Shaw, J N (Edinburgh Acads) 1921 *W*, *I*
Shaw, R W (Glasgow HSFP) 1934 *W*, *I*, *E*, 1935 *W*, *I*, *E*, *NZ*, 1936 *W*, *I*, *E*, 1937 *W*, *I*, *E*, 1938 *W*, *I*, *E*, 1939 *W*, *I*, *E*
Shedden, D (W of Scotland) 1972 *NZ*, 1973 *F*, *W*, *I*, *E*, *P*, 1976 *W*, *E*, *I*, 1977 *I*, *F*, *W*, 1978 *I*, *F*, *W*
Shillinglaw, R B (Gala, Army) 1960 *I*, *E*, *SA*, 1961 *F*, *SA*
Simmers, B M (Glasgow Acads) 1965 *F*, *W*, 1966 *A*, 1967 *F*, *W*, *I*, 1971 *F* (R)
Simmers, W M (Glasgow Acads) 1926 *W*, *I*, *E*, 1927 *F*, *W*, *I*, *E*, *A*, 1928 *F*, *W*, *I*, *E*, 1929 *F*, *W*, *I*, *E*, 1930 *F*, *W*, *I*, *E*, 1931 *F*, *W*, *I*, *E*, 1932 *SA*, *W*, *I*, *E*
Simpson, J W (Royal HSFP) 1893 *I*, *E*, 1894 *W*, *I*, *E*, 1895 *W*, *I*, *E*, 1896 *W*, *I*, 1897 *E*, 1899 *W*, *E*
Simpson, R S (Glasgow Acads) 1923 *I*
Simson, E D (Edinburgh U, London Scottish) 1902 *E*, 1903 *W*, *I*, *E*, 1904 *W*, *I*, *E*, 1905 *W*, *I*, *E*, *NZ*, 1906 *W*, *I*, *E*, 1907 *W*, *I*, *E*
Simson, J T (Watsonians) 1905 *NZ*, 1909 *W*, *I*, *E*, 1910 *F*, *W*, 1911 *I*
Simson, R F (London Scottish) 1911 *E*
Sloan, A T (Edinburgh Acads) 1914 *W*, 1920 *F*, *W*, *I*, *E*, 1921 *F*, *W*, *I*, *E*
Sloan, D A (Edinburgh Acads, London Scottish) 1950 *F*, *W*, 1951 *W*, *I*, *E*, 1953 *F*
Sloan, T (Glasgow Acads, Oxford U) 1905 *NZ*, 1906 *W*, *SA*, 1907 *W*, *E*, 1908 *W*, 1909 *I*
Smeaton, P W (Edinburgh Acads) 1881 *I*, 1883 *I*, *E*
Smith, A R (Oxford U) 1895 *W*, *I*, *E*, 1896 *W*, *I*, 1897 *I*, *E*, 1898 *I*, *E*, 1900 *I*, *E*
Smith, A R (Cambridge U, Gosforth, Ebbw Vale, Edinburgh Wands) 1955 *W*, *I*, *E*, 1956 *F*, *W*, *I*, *E*, 1957 *F*, *W*, *I*, *E*, 1958 *F*, *W*, *A*, *I*, 1959 *F*, *W*, *I*, *E*, 1960 *F*, *W*, *I*, *E*, *SA*, 1961 *F*, *SA*, *W*, *I*, *E*, 1962 *F*, *W*, *I*
Smith, D W C (London Scottish) 1949 *F*, *W*, *I*, *E*, 1950 *F*, *W*, *I*, 1953 *I*
Smith, E R (Edinburgh Acads) 1879 *I*
Smith, G K (Kelso) 1957 *I*, *E*, 1958 *F*, *W*, *A*, 1959 *F*, *W*, *I*, *E*, 1960 *F*, *W*, *I*, *E*, 1961 *F*, *SA*, *W*, *I*, *E*
Smith, H O (Watsonians) 1895 *W*, 1896 *W*, *I*, *E*, 1898 *I*, *E*, 1899 *W*, *I*, *E*, 1900 *E*, 1902 *E*
Smith, I S (Oxford U, Edinburgh U) 1924 *W*, *I*, *E*, 1925 *F*, *W*, *I*, *E*, 1926 *F*, *W*, *I*, *E*, 1927 *F*, *I*, *E*, 1929 *F*, *W*, *I*, *E*, 1930 *F*, *W*, *I*, 1931 *F*, *W*, *I*, *E*, 1932 *SA*, *W*, *I*, *E*, 1933 *W*, *E*, *I*
Smith, I S G (London Scottish) 1969 *SA*, 1970 *F*, *W*, *I*, *E*, 1971 *F*, *W*, *I*
Smith, M A (London Scottish) 1970 *W*, *I*, *E*, *A*
Smith, R T (Kelso) 1929 *F*, *W*, *I*, *E*, 1930 *F*, *W*, *I*
Smith, S H (Glasgow Acads) 1877 *I*, 1878 *E*
Smith, T J (Gala) 1983 *E*, *NZ*, 1985 *I*, *F*
Sole, D M B (Bath, Edinburgh Acads) 1986 *F*, *W*, 1987 *I*, *F*, *W*, *E*, [*F*, *Z*, *R*, *NZ*], 1988 *I*, *F*, *W*, *E*, *A*, 1989 *W*, *E*, *I*, *F*, *Fj*, *R*, 1990 *I*, *F*, *W*, *E*
Somerville, D (Edinburgh Inst FP) 1879 *I*, 1882 *I*, 1883 *W*, *I*, *E*, 1884 *W*
Speirs, L M (Watsonians) 1906 *SA*, 1907 *W*, *I*, *E*, 1908 *W*, *I*, *E*, 1910 *F*, *W*, *E*
Spence, K M (Oxford U) 1953 *I*

Spencer, E (Clydedale) 1898 *I*
Stagg, P K (Sale) 1965 *F*, *W*, *E*, *SA*, 1966 *F*, *W*, *I*, *E*, *A*, 1967 *F*, *W*, *I*, *E*, *NZ*, 1968 *F*, *W*, *I*, *E*, *A*, 1969 *F*, *W*, *I* (R), *SA*, 1970 *F*, *W*, *I*, *E*, *A*
Stanger, A G (Hawick) 1989 *Fj*, *R*, 1990 *I*, *F*, *W*, *E*
Steele, W C C (Langholm, Bedford, RAF, London Scottish) 1969 *E*, 1971 *F*, *W*, *I*, *E* (2[1*C*]), 1972 *F*, *W*, *E*, *NZ*, 1973 *F*, *W*, *I*, *E*, 1975 *I*, *F*, *W*, *E*, *NZ* (R), 1976 *W*, *E*, *I*, 1977 *E*
Stephen, A E (W of Scotland) 1885 *W*, 1886 *I*
Steven, P D (Heriot's FP) 1984 *A*, 1985 *F*, *W*, *E*
Steven, R (Edinburgh Wands) 1962 *I*
Stevenson, A K (Glasgow Acads) 1922 *F*, 1923 *F*, *W*, *E*
Stevenson, A M (Glasgow U) 1911 *F*
Stevenson, G D (Hawick) 1956 *E*, 1957 *F*, 1958 *F*, *W*, *A*, *I*, *E*, 1959 *W*, *I*, *E*, 1960 *W*, *I*, *E*, *SA*, 1961 *F*, *SA*, *W*, *I*, *E*, 1963 *F*, *W*, *I*, 1964 *E*, 1965 *F*
Stevenson, H J (Edinburgh Acads) 1888 *W*, *I*, 1889 *W*, *I*, 1890 *W*, *I*, *E*, 1891 *W*, *I*, *E*, 1892 *W*, *I*, *E*, 1893 *I*, *E*
Stevenson, L E (Edinburgh U) 1888 *W*
Stevenson, R C (London Scottish) 1897 *I*, *E*, 1898 *E*, 1899 *I*, *W*, *E*
Stevenson, R C (St Andrews U) 1910 *F*, *I*, *E*, 1911 *F*, *W*, *I*
Stevenson, W H (Glasgow Acads) 1925 *F*
Stewart, A K (Edinburgh U) 1874 *E*, 1876 *E*
Stewart, A M (Edinburgh Acads) 1914 *W*
Stewart, C A R (W of Scotland) 1880 *I*, *E*
Stewart, C E B (Kelso) 1960 *W*, 1961 *F*
Stewart, J (Glasgow HSFP) 1930 *F*
Stewart, J L (Edinburgh Acads) 1921 *I*
Stewart, M S (Stewart's Coll FP) 1932 *SA*, *W*, *I*, 1933 *W*, *E*, *I*, 1934 *W*, *I*, *E*
Stewart, W A (London Hospital) 1913 *F*, *W*, *I*, 1914 *W*
Steyn, S S L (Oxford U) 1911 *E*, 1912 *I*
Strachan, G M (Jordanhill) 1971 *E* (C) (R), 1973 *W*, *I*, *E*, *P*
Stronach, R S (Glasgow Acads) 1901 *W*, *E*, 1905 *W*, *I*, *E*
Stuart, C D (W of Scotland) 1909 *I*, 1910 *F*, *W*, *I*, *E*, 1911 *I*, *E*
Stuart, L M (Glasgow HSFP) 1923 *F*, *W*, *I*, *E*, 1924 *F*, 1928 *E*, 1930 *I*, *E*
Suddon, N (Hawick) 1965 *W*, *I*, *E*, *SA*, 1966 *A*, 1968 *E*, *A*, 1969 *F*, *W*, *I*, 1970 *I*, *E*, *A*
Sutherland, W R (Hawick) 1910 *W*, *E*, 1911 *F*, *E*, 1912 *F*, *W*, *E*, *SA*, 1913 *F*, *W*, *I*, *E*, 1914 *W*
Swan, J S (Army, London Scottish, Leicester) 1953 *E*, 1954 *F*, *NZ*, *I*, *E*, *W*, 1955 *F*, *W*, *I*, *E*, 1956 *F*, *W*, *I*, *E*, 1957 *F*, *W*, 1958 *F*
Swan, M W (Oxford U, London Scottish) 1958 *F*, *W*, *A*, *I*, *E*, 1959 *F*, *W*, *I*
Sweet, J B (Glasgow HSFP) 1913 *E*, 1914 *I*
Symington, A W (Cambridge U) 1914 *W*, *E*

Tait, A V (Kelso) 1987 [*F*(R), *Z*, *R*, *NZ*], 1988 *I*, *F*, *W*, *E*
Tait, J G (Edinburgh Acads) 1880 *I*, 1885 *I*2
Tait, P W (Royal HSFP) 1935 *E*
Taylor, E G (Oxford U) 1927 *W*, *A*
Taylor, R C (Kelvinside-West) 1951 *W*, *I*, *E*, *SA*
Telfer, C M (Hawick) 1968 *A*, 1969 *F*, *W*, *I*, *E*, 1972 *F*, *W*, *E*, 1973 *W*, *I*, *E*, *P*, 1974 *W*, *E*, *I*, 1975 *A*, 1976 *F*
Telfer, J W (Melrose) 1964 *F*, *NZ*, *W*, *I*, *E*, 1965 *F*, *W*, *I*, 1966 *F*, *W*, *I*, *E*, 1967 *W*, *I*, *E*, 1968 *E*, *A*, 1969 *F*, *W*, *I*, *E*, *SA*, 1970 *F*, *W*, *I*
Tennent, J M (W of Scotland) 1909 *W*, *I*, *E*, 1910 *F*, *W*, *E*
Thom, D A (London Scottish) 1934 *W*, 1935 *W*, *I*, *E*, *NZ*
Thom, G (Kirkcaldy) 1920 *F*, *W*, *I*, *E*
Thom, J R (Watsonians) 1933 *W*, *E*, *I*
Thomson, A E (United Services) 1921 *F*, *W*, *E*
Thomson, A M (St Andrews U) 1949 *I*
Thomson, B E (Oxford U) 1953 *F*, *W*, *I*
Thomson, I H M (Heriot's FP, Army) 1951 *W*, *I*, 1952 *F*, *W*, *I*, 1953 *I*, *E*
Thomson, J S (Glasgow Acads) 1871 *E*
Thomson, R H (London Scottish) 1960 *I*, *E*, *SA*, 1961 *F*, *SA*, *W*, *I*, *E*, 1963 *F*, *W*, *I*, *E*, 1964 *F*, *NZ*, *W*
Thomson, W H (W of Scotland) 1906 *SA*
Thomson, W J (W of Scotland) 1899 *W*, *E*, 1900 *W*
Timms, A B (Edinburgh U, Edinburgh Wands) 1896

W, 1900 *W*, *I*, 1901 *W*, *I*, *E*, 1902 *W*, *E*, 1903 *W*, *E*, 1904 *I*, *E*, 1905 *I*, *E*
Tod, H B (Gala) 1911 *F*
Tod, J (Watsonians) 1884 *W*, *I*, *E*, 1885 *W*, *I*1,2, 1886 *W*, *I*, *E*
Todd, J K (Glasgow Acads) 1874 *E*, 1875 *E*
Tolmie, J M (Glasgow HSFP) 1922 *E*
Tomes, A J (Hawick) 1976 *E*, *I*, 1977 *E*, 1978 *I*, *F*, *W*, *E*, *NZ*, 1979 *W*, *E*, *I*, *F*, *NZ*, 1980 *F*, *W*, *E*, 1981 *F*, *W*, *E*, *I*, *NZ* 1,2, *R*, *A*, 1982 *E*, *I*, *F*, *W*, *A* 1,2, 1983 *I*, *F*, *W*, 1984 *W*, *E*, *I*, *F*, *R*, *A*, 1985 *W*, *E*, 1987 *I*, *F*, *E* (R), [*F*, *Z*, *R*, *NZ*]
Torrie, T J (Edinburgh Acads) 1877 *E*
Tukalo, I (Selkirk) 1985 *I*, 1987 *I*, *F*, *W*, *E*, [*F*, *Z*, *R*, *NZ*], 1988 *F*, *W*, *E*, *A*, 1989 *W*, *E*, *I*, *F*, *Fj*, 1990 *I*, *F*, *W*, *E*
Turk, A S (Langholm) 1971 *E* (R)
Turnbull, D J (Hawick) 1987 [*NZ*], 1988 *F*, *E*, 1990 *E* (R)
Turnbull, F O (Kelso) 1951 *F*, *SA*
Turnbull, G O (W of Scotland) 1896 *I*, *E*, 1897 *I*, *E*, 1904 *W*
Turnbull, P (Edinburgh Acads) 1901 *W*, *I*, *E*, 1902 *W*, *I*, *E*
Turner, F H (Oxford U, Liverpool) 1911 *F*, *W*, *I*, *E*, 1912 *F*, *W*, *I*, *E*, *SA*, 1913 *F*, *W*, *I*, *E*, 1914 *I*, *E*
Turner, J W C (Gala) 1966 *W*, *A*, 1967 *F*, *W*, *I*, *E*, *NZ*, 1968 *F*, *W*, *I*, *E*, *A*, 1969 *F*, 1970 *E*, *A*, 1971 *F*, *W*, *I*, *E* (2[1C])

Usher, C M (United Services, Edinburgh Wands) 1912 *E*, 1913 *F*, *W*, *I*, *E*, 1914 *E*, 1920 *F*, *W*, *I*, *E*, 1921 *W*, *E*, 1922 *F*, *W*, *I*, *E*

Valentine, A R (RNAS, Anthorn) 1953 *F*, *W*, *I*
Valentine, D D (Hawick) 1947 *I*, *E*
Veitch, J P (Royal HSFP) 1882 *E*, 1883 *I*, 1884 *W*, *I*, *E*, 1885 *I*1,2, 1886 *E*
Villar, C (Edinburgh Wands) 1876 *E*, 1877 *I*, *E*

Waddell, G H (London Scottish, Cambridge U) 1957 *E*, 1958 *F*, *W*, *A*, *I*, *E*, 1959 *F*, *W*, *I*, *E*, 1960 *I*, *E*, *SA*, 1961 *F*, 1962 *F*, *W*, *I*, *E*
Waddell, H (Glasgow Acads) 1924 *F*, *W*, *I*, *E*, 1925 *I*, *E*, 1926 *F*, *W*, *I*, *E*, 1927 *F*, *W*, *I*, *A*, 1930 *W*
Wade, A L (London Scottish) 1908 *E*
Walker, A (W of Scotland) 1881 *I*, 1882 *E*, 1883 *W*, *I*, *E*
Walker, A W (Cambridge U, Birkenhead Park) 1931 *F*, *W*, *I*, *E*, 1932 *I*
Walker, J G (W of Scotland) 1882 *E*, 1883 *W*
Walker, M (Oxford U) 1952 *F*
Wallace, A C (Oxford U) 1923 *F*, 1924 *F*, *W*, *E*, 1925 *F*, *W*, *I*, *E*, 1926 *F*
Wallace, W M (Cambridge U) 1913 *E*, 1914 *W*, *I*, *E*
Walls, W A (Glasgow Acads) 1882 *E*, 1883 *W*, *I*, *E*, 1884 *W*, *I*, *E*, 1886 *W*, *I*, *E*
Walter, M W (London Scottish) 1906 *I*, *E*, *SA*, 1907 *W*, *I*, 1908 *W*, *I*, 1910 *I*
Warren, J R (Glasgow Acads) 1914 *I*
Warren, R C (Glasgow Acads) 1922 *W*, *I*, 1930 *W*, *I*, *E*
Waters, F H (Cambridge U, London Scottish) 1930 *F*, *W*, *I*, *E*, 1932 *SA*, *W*, *I*
Waters, J A (Selkirk) 1933 *W*, *E*, *I*, 1934 *W*, *I*, *E*, 1935 *W*, *I*, *E*, *NZ*, 1936 *W*, *I*, *E*, 1937 *W*, *I*, *E*
Waters, J B (Cambridge U) 1904 *I*, *E*
Watherston, J G (Edinburgh Wands) 1934 *I*, *E*
Watherston, W R A (London Scottish) 1963 *F*, *W*, *I*

Watson, D H (Glasgow Acads) 1876 *E*, 1877 *I*, *E*
Watson, W S (Boroughmuir) 1974 *W*, *E*, *I*, *F*, 1975 *NZ*, 1977 *I*, *F*, *W*, 1979 *I*, *F*
Watt, A G M (Edinburgh Acads) 1947 *F*, *W*, *I*, *A*, 1948 *F*, *W*
Weatherstone, T G (Stewart's Coll FP) 1952 *E*, 1953 *I*, *E*, 1954 *F*, *NZ*, *I*, *E*, *W*, 1955 *F*, 1958 *W*, *A*, *I*, *E*, 1959 *W*, *I*, *E*
Welsh, R (Watsonians) 1895 *W*, *I*, *E*, 1896 *W*
Welsh, R B (Hawick) 1967 *I*, *E*
Welsh, W B (Hawick) 1927 *A*, 1928 *F*, *W*, *I*, 1929 *I*, *E*, 1930 *F*, *W*, *I*, *E*, 1931 *F*, *W*, *I*, *E*, 1932 *SA*, *W*, *I*, *E*, 1933 *W*, *E*, *I*
Welsh, W H (Edinburgh U) 1900 *I*, *E*, 1901 *W*, *I*, *E*, 1902 *W*, *I*, *E*
Wemyss, A (Gala, Edinburgh Wands) 1914 *W*, *I*, 1920 *F*, *E*, 1922 *F*, *W*, *I*
West, L (Edinburgh U, West Hartlepool) 1903 *W*, *I*, *E*, 1905 *I*, *E*, *NZ*, 1906 *W*, *I*, *E*
Weston, V G (Kelvinside Acads) 1936 *I*, *E*
White, D B (Gala, London Scottish) 1982 *F*, *W*, *A* 1,2, 1987 *W*, *E*, [*F*, *R*, *NZ*], 1988 *I*, *F*, *W*, *E*, *A*, 1989 *W*, *E*, *I*, *F*, *Fj*, *R*, 1990 *I*, *F*, *W*, *E*
White, D M (Kelvinside Acads) 1963 *F*, *W*, *I*, *E*
White, T B (Edinburgh Acads) 1888 *W*, *I*, 1889 *W*
Whittington, T P (Merchistonians) 1873 *E*
Whitworth, R J E (London Scottish) 1936 *I*
Whyte, D J (Edinburgh Wands) 1965 *W*, *I*, *E*, *SA*, 1966 *F*, *W*, *I*, *E*, *A*, 1967 *F*, *W*, *I*, *E*
Will, J G (Cambridge U) 1912 *F*, *W*, *I*, *E*, 1914 *W*, *I*, *E*
Wilson, A W (Dunfermline) 1931 *F*, *I*, *E*
Wilson, G A (Oxford U) 1949 *F*, *W*, *E*
Wilson, G R (Royal HSFP) 1886 *E*, 1890 *W*, *I*, *E*, 1891 *I*
Wilson, J H (Watsonians) 1953 *I*
Wilson, J S (St Andrews U) 1931 *F*, *W*, *I*, *E*, 1932 *E*
Wilson, J S (United Services, London Scottish) 1908 *I*, 1909 *W*
Wilson, R (London Scottish) 1976 *E*, *I*, 1977 *E*, *I*, *F*, 1978 *I*, *F*, 1981 *R*, 1983 *I*
Wilson, R L (Gala) 1951 *F*, *W*, *I*, *E*, *SA*, 1953 *F*, *W*, *E*
Wilson, R W (W of Scotland) 1873 *E*, 1874 *E*
Wilson, S (Oxford U, London Scottish) 1964 *F*, *NZ*, *W*, *I*, *E*, 1965 *W*, *I*, *E*, *SA*, 1966 *F*, *W*, *I*, *A*, 1967 *F*, *W*, *I*, *E*, *NZ*, 1968 *F*, *W*, *I*, *E*
Wood, A (Royal HSFP) 1873 *E*, 1874 *E*, 1875 *E*
Wood, G (Gala) 1931 *W*, *I*, 1932 *W*, *I*, *E*
Woodburn, J C (Kelvinside Acads) 1892 *I*
Woodrow, A N (Glasgow Acads) 1887 *I*, *W*, *E*
Wotherspoon, W (W of Scotland) 1891 *I*, 1892 *I*, 1893 *W*, *E*, 1894 *W*, *I*, *E*
Wright, F A (Edinburgh Acads) 1932 *E*
Wright, H B (Watsonians) 1894 *W*
Wright, K M (London Scottish) 1929 *F*, *W*, *I*, *E*
Wright, R W J (Edinburgh Wands) 1973 *F*
Wright, S T H (Stewart's Coll FP) 1949 *E*
Wright, T (Hawick) 1947 *A*
Wyllie, D S (Stewart's-Melville FP) 1984 *A*, 1985 *W* (R), *E*, 1987 *I*, *F*, [*F*, *Z*, *R*, *NZ*], 1989 *R*

Young, A H (Edinburgh Acads) 1874 *E*
Young, E T (Glasgow Acads) 1914 *E*
Young, R G (Watsonians) 1970 *W*
Young, T E B (Durham) 1911 *F*
Young, W B (Cambridge U, London Scottish) 1937 *W*, *I*, *E*, 1938 *W*, *I*, *E*, 1939 *W*, *I*, *E*, 1948 *E*

SCOTTISH INTERNATIONAL RECORDS

Both team and individual records are for official Scotland international matches, up to 30 April 1990.

TEAM RECORDS

Highest score
60 v Zimbabwe (60-21) 1987 Wellington
v individual countries
24 v Australia (24-15) 1981 Murrayfield
33 v England (33-6) 1986 Murrayfield
38 v Fiji (38-17) 1989 Murrayfield
31 v France (31-3) 1912 Inverleith
37 v Ireland (37-21) 1989 Murrayfield
25 v N Zealand (25-25) 1983 Murrayfield
55 v Romania (55-28) 1987 Dunedin
10 v S Africa (10-18) 1960 Port Elizabeth
35 v Wales (35-10) 1924 Inverleith
60 v Zimbabwe (60-21) 1987 Wellington

Biggest winning points margin
39 v Zimbabwe (60-21) 1987 Wellington
v individual countries
 9 v Australia (24-15) 1981 Murrayfield
27 v England (33-6) 1986 Murrayfield
21 v Fiji (38-17) 1989 Murrayfield
28 v France (31-3) 1912 Inverleith
23 v Ireland (32-9) 1984 Dublin
No win v N Zealand
32 v Romania (32-0) 1989 Murrayfield
 6 v S Africa (6-0) 1906 Glasgow
25 v Wales (35-10) 1924 Inverleith
39 v Zimbabwe (60-21) 1987 Wellington

Highest score by opposing team
44 S Africa (0-44) 1951 Murrayfield
by individual countries
37 Australia (12-37) 1984 Murrayfield
30 England (18-30) 1980 Murrayfield
17 Fiji (38-17) 1989 Murrayfield
28 France (22-28) 1987 Parc des Princes
26 Ireland (8-26) 1953 Murrayfield
40 N Zealand (15-40) 1981 Auckland
28 Romania $\begin{cases} (22\text{-}28) \ 1984 \ \text{Bucharest} \\ (55\text{-}28) \ 1987 \ \text{Dunedin} \end{cases}$
44 S Africa (0-44) 1951 Murrayfield
35 Wales (12-35) 1972 Cardiff
21 Zimbabwe (60-21) 1987 Wellington

Biggest losing points margin
44 v S Africa (0-44) 1951 Murrayfield
v individual countries
25 v Australia (12-37) 1984 Murrayfield
20 v England (6-26) 1977 Twickenham
20 v France (3-23) 1977 Parc des Princes
21 v Ireland (0-21) 1950 Dublin
27 v N Zealand (3-30) 1987 Christchurch
 6 v Romania (22-28) 1984 Bucharest
44 v S Africa (0-44) 1951 Murrayfield
23 v Wales (12-35) 1972 Cardiff
No defeat v Fiji or Zimbabwe

Most tries by Scotland in an international
12 v Wales 1887 Raeburn Place
 (Edinburgh)

Most tries against Scotland in an international
9 by S Africa (0-44) 1951 Murrayfield

Most points by Scotland in International Championship in a season – 86
in season 1983-84

Most tries by Scotland in International Championship in a season – 17
in season 1924-25

INDIVIDUAL RECORDS

Most capped player
J M Renwick 52 1972-84
C T Deans 52 1978-87
in individual positions
Full-back
A R Irvine 47(51)[1] 1972-82

Wing
A R Smith 33 1955-62
Centre
J M Renwick 51(52)[2] 1972-84
Fly-half
J Y Rutherford 42 1979-87
Scrum-half
R J Laidlaw 47 1980-88
Prop
A B Carmichael 50 1967-78
Hooker
C T Deans 52 1978-87
Lock
A J Tomes 48 1976-87
Flanker
W I D Elliot 29 1947-54
No 8
I A M Paxton 27(36)[3] 1981-88
[1]*Irvine played 4 matches as a wing*
[2]*Renwick played once, as a replacement, on the wing*
[3]*Paxton played 9 matches as a lock*

Longest international career
W C W Murdoch 14 seasons 1935-48

Most internationals as captain
J McLauchlan 19 1973-79

Most points in internationals – 273
A R Irvine (51 matches) 1972-82

Most points in International Championship in a season – 52
A G Hastings (4 matches) 1985-86

Most points in an international – 27
A G Hastings v Romania 1987
   Dunedin

Most tries in internationals – 24
I S Smith (32 matches) 1924-33

Most tries in International Championship in a season – 8
I S Smith (4 matches) 1924-25

Most tries in an international – 5
G C Lindsay v Wales 1887 Raeburn Place
(Edinburgh)

Most conversions in internationals – 37
A G Hastings (24 matches) 1986-90

Most conversions in International Championship in a season – 8
P W Dods (4 matches) 1983-84

Most conversions in an international – 8
A G Hastings v Zimbabwe 1987 Wellington
A G Hastings v Romania 1987 Dunedin

Most dropped goals in internationals – 12
J Y Rutherford (42 matches) 1972-82

Most penalty goals in internationals – 61
A R Irvine (51 matches) 1972-82

Most penalty goals in International Championship in a season – 14
A G Hastings (4 matches) 1985-86

Most points on overseas tour – 56
W Lauder (5 appearances) Australia 1970
A R Irvine (4 appearances) N Zealand 1981
C D R Mair scored 100 points in the Far East in 1977, but this was not on a major tour

---

Most points in a tour match – 24
D W Morgan v Wellington 1975
   Wellington, (NZ)
A R Irvine v King Country 1981
   Taumarunui, (NZ)
A R Irvine v Wairarapa-Bush 1981
   Masterton, (NZ)
P W Dods scored 43 points v Alberta in 1985, but this was not on a major tour

---

Most tries in a tour match – 3
A R Smith v Eastern Transvaal 1960
   Springs, (SA)
K R F Bearne scored 5 tries v Ontario U in 1964, A J W Hinshelwood scored 5 v Quebec in 1964, and D E W Leckie scored 5 v Goshawks (Zimbabwe) in 1988, but these were not on a major tour

HARSH REALITY BANISHES FANTASY

THE 1989-90 SEASON IN IRELAND
Sean Diffley *Irish Independent*

Irish fortunes remained on the floor in 1989-90. There was a spate of grasping at straws, fantasy-land references to 'heroic resistance' against the all-conquering All Blacks in November, 'holding' England until into the second half at Twickenham, 'extending' the Scots at Lansdowne Road. The reality, of course, was that a sub-standard Ireland were really no match for any of the 'big boys', and only in their 14-8 win against Wales in Dublin did they meet a side that accommodated their own poor standards.

At the end of the season the beleaguered coach, Jimmy Davidson, decided that he would not allow his name to go forward for reappointment for next season. Ciaran Fitzgerald succeeds him. Ostensibly, the reason was what he considered to be a deliberate snub by the IRFU, who arranged a fitness testing session in Belfast in May under Dr Colin Boreham of Queen's University but did not consider it necessary to invite the reigning coach to attend. In fact, the writing had been on the wall for a long time. There had been rumours of a lack of confidence in Davidson on the part of several senior players.

Still, 1990 may well mark the turning-point in Ireland's fortunes; the year that the nettle was at last grasped and Ireland joined the other seven International Board countries in at last introducing a national competition for the leading clubs, the All-Ireland League. For many decades it has been clear that the Irish players lacked the benefits of real, honing, competitive rugby in the domestic game. So the All-Ireland League will commence in 1990-91 with two divisions comprising 19 leading clubs.

Nevertheless many clubs, finding themselves out in the cold, campaigned to the end to broaden the formula. They were backed mainly by Leinster and Connacht. And even when the IRFU formally confirmed the start of the All-Ireland this coming season, they announced at the same time that the following season the competition would comprise five divisions. So all of Ireland's 47 senior clubs will participate, their League positions depending on their finishing positions in their respective provincial leagues.

The highlight of the Irish scene was, of course, the pre-Christmas visit of the All Blacks and the impressive technique they deployed in disposing of the four provinces and of Ireland. But any hopes that the impeccable handling and all-round skill of Wayne Shelford and his men would influence the matches that Ireland faced after Christmas were not realised. At Twickenham the Irish were lucky to escape with a 23-0 defeat. Had England not been so inhibited for so long the reverse for the Irish could well have been horrendous.

Then, against Scotland at Lansdowne Road, Derek White romped over for two tries to put a better complexion on the visitors' 13-10 win than it deserved. Ireland disconcerted an easily disconcerted side, and few would have given the Scots much chance of a Grand Slam on that display. Next came the 31-12 defeat of Ireland in Paris by a French team that was still only a mere shadow of the country's better sides. Only Michael Kiernan's kicking – five penalty goals – kept some degree of respectability in the exchanges.

Finally, an Irish win in Dublin handed the Welsh a whitewash for the first time. Donal Lenihan, who had returned to captain Ireland against France when Willie Anderson was dropped, managed to improve the organisation and there were signs that Lenihan rather than the coach was calling the tune.

Ulster, the champion province, retained their title for the sixth consecutive season, providing some exhilarating football and moving the ball fluidly. Ballymena were the Irish club of the year for the second season, and again won the League and Cup double in Ulster. In Leinster the Wanderers club also brought off the League and Cup double in a most successful season.

WINNERS OF PROVINCIAL TOURNAMENTS
LEINSTER
Senior Cup: Wanderers Senior League: Wanderers Schools Senior Cup: Blackrock Schools Junior Cup: Presentation Bray
ULSTER
Senior Cup: Ballymena Senior League: Ballymena Schools Senior Cup: Methodist Schools Medallion: Ballyclare HS
MUNSTER
Senior Cup: Young Munster Senior League: Highfield Schools Senior Cup: Crescent Schools Junior Cup: CBC
CONNACHT
Senior Cup: Athlone Senior League: Galwegians Schools Senior Cup: Garbally Schools Junior Cup: St Joseph's Galway

INTER-PROVINCIAL TOURNAMENT 1989

14 October, Musgrave Park, Cork

Munster 10 (1G 1T) **Leinster 3** (1PG)
Munster: K Murphy (Constitution); J Galvin (Old Crescent), C Murphy (Constitution), P P A Danaher (Garryowen), C Haly (UCC); R P Keyes (Constitution), O Kiely (Shannon); J J Fitzgerald (Young Munster), T J Kingston (Dolphin), P M Clohessy (Young Munster), F Kearney (Sunday's Well), M J Galwey (Shannon), K O'Connell (Sunday's Well), P T J O'Hara (Sunday's Well), P C Collins (London Irish) (*capt*)
Scorers *Tries:* Kiely, Collins *Conversion:* K Murphy
Leinster: F J Dunlea (Lansdowne); J F Sexton (Lansdowne), B J Mullin (London Irish), V J G Cunningham (St Mary's Coll), P P Haycock (Terenure Coll); B A Smith (Oxford U), L F P Aherne (Lansdowne); N J Popplewell (Greystones), W Mulcahy (Skerries), D C Fitzgerald (Lansdowne), B J Rigney (Greystones), N P T Francis (Blackrock Coll), C Pim (Old Wesley), P Kenny (Wanderers), D Fanning (St Mary's Coll) (*capt*)
Scorer *Penalty Goal:* Smith
Referee D N Templeton

14 October, Galway

Connacht 3 (1PG) **Ulster 38** (3G 5T)
Connacht: J E Staples (London Irish); A Gillen (St Mary's Coll), M Cosgrave (Wanderers), R Hernan (UCD),

The Irish team which beat Wales in Dublin. L-R, back row:: J P McDonald, K J Hooks, D C Fitzgerald, W D McBride, N P Mannion, N P T Francis, P T J O'Hara, N J Popplewell (replacement), L F P Aherne (replacement), K Murphy, P P A Danaher (replacement); front row: K D Crossan, M T Bradley, B A Smith, K E Reid (manager), D G Lenihan (capt), J C Davidson (coach), M J Kiernan, B J Mullin, J J Fitzgerald.

E Guerin (Galwegians); E Elwood (Galwegians), S O'Beirne (St Mary's Coll); T P J Clancy (Lansdowne) (*capt*), J O'Riordan (Constitution), D Henshaw (Athlone), M M F Moylett (Shannon), A Higgins (London Irish), S Guerin (Galwegians), M Fitzgibbon (Shannon), N P Mannion (Corinthians)
Scorer *Penalty Goal:* O'Beirne
Ulster: P I Rainey (Ballymena); K J Hooks (Ards), D G Irwin (Instonians) (*capt*), J A Hewitt (London Irish), K D Crossan (Instonians); P Russell (Instonians), R Brady (Ballymena); M Reynolds (Malone), J P McDonald (Malone), J J McCoy (Bangor), P Johns (Dublin U), W A Anderson (Dungannon), P M Matthews (Wanderers), W D McBride (Malone), B F Robinson (Ballymena)
Scorers *Tries:* Hewitt (2), Crossan (2), Robinson (2), Hooks, Matthews   *Conversions:* Russell (3)
Referee R McDowell

21 October, Lansdowne Road

Leinster 6 (2PG)   **Ulster 14** (1PG 1DG 2T)
Leinster: F J Dunlea (Lansdowne); P P Haycock (Terenure Coll), B J Mullin (London Irish), V J G Cunningham (St Mary's Coll), P Purcell (Lansdowne); B A Smith (Oxford U), L F P Aherne (Lansdowne) (*capt*); N J Popplewell (Greystones), N Kearney (Old Wesley), D C Fitzgerald (Lansdowne), N P T Francis (Blackrock Coll), B J Rigney (Greystones), P Kenny (Wanderers), C Pim (Old Wesley), A Blair (Old Wesley)
Scorer *Penalty Goals:* Smith (2)
Ulster: C Wilkinson (Malone); K J Hooks (Ards), D G Irwin (Instonians) (*capt*), J A Hewitt (London Irish), K D Crossan (Instonians); P Russell (Instonians), R Brady (Ballymena); M Reynolds (Malone), S J Smith (Ballymena), J J McCoy (Bangor), W A Anderson (Dungannon), P Johns (Dublin U), P M Matthews (Wanderers), W D McBride (Malone), B F Robinson (Ballymena)
Scorers *Tries:* Crossan, Smith   *Penalty Goal:* Russell   *Dropped Goal:* Russell
Referee H A Smith

21 October, Galway

Connacht 10 (1G 1T)   **Munster 14** (2PG 2T)
Connacht: J E Staples (London Irish); D Holland (Corinthians), M Feely (Old Belvedere), M Cosgrave (Wanderers), E Guerin (Galwegians); E Elwood (Galwegians), S O'Beirne (St Mary's Coll); T P J Clancy (Lansdowne), J O'Riordan (Constitution), D Henshaw (Athlone), A Higgins (London Irish), Mark Feely (Old Belvedere), N McCarthy (St Mary's Coll) (*capt*), M Fitzgibbon (Shannon), N P Mannion (Corinthians)
Scorers *Tries:* Elwood, Guerin   *Conversion:* O'Beirne
Munster: K Murphy (Constitution); J Galvin (Old Crescent), C Murphy (Constitution), P P A Danaher (Garryowen), C Haly (UCC); R P Keyes (Constitution), O Kiely (Shannon); J J Fitzgerald (Young Munster), T J Kingston (Dolphin), P M Clohessy (Young Munster), P O'Grady (Shannon), M J Galwey (Shannon), K O'Connell (Sunday's Well), P T J O'Hara (Sunday's Well), P C Collins (London Irish) (*capt*)
Scorers *Tries:* C Murphy, Collins   *Penalty Goals:* Keyes (2)
Referee G Black

28 October, Ravenhill, Belfast

Ulster 13 (1G 1PG 1T)   **Munster 10** (1G 1T)
Ulster: P I Rainey (Ballymena); K J Hooks (Ards), D G Irwin (Instonians) (*capt*), J A Hewitt (London Irish), K D Crossan (Instonians); P Russell (Instonians), R Brady (Ballymena); M Reynolds (Malone), S J Smith (Ballymena), J J McCoy (Bangor), P Johns (Dublin U), W A Anderson (Dungannon), P M Matthews (Wanderers), W D McBride (Malone), B F Robinson (Dungannon)
Scorers *Tries:* Crossan (2)   *Conversion:* Russell   *Penalty Goal:* Russell
Munster: K Murphy (Constitution); J Galvin (Old Crescent), M J Kiernan (Dolphin), P P A Danaher (Garryowen), C Haly (UCC); R P Keyes (Constitution), O Kiely (Shannon); J J Fitzgerald (Young Munster), T J Kingston (Dolphin), P M Clohessy (Young Munster), D G Lenihan (Constitution), M J Galwey (Shannon), K O'Connell (Sunday's Well), P T J O'Hara (Sunday's Well), P C Collins (London Irish) (*capt*)
Scorers *Tries:* Kiernan, Lenihan   *Conversion:* Kiernan
Referee O E Doyle

28 October, Lansdowne Road

Leinster 16 (1G 2PG 1T)   **Connacht 12** (4PG)
Leinster: F J Dunlea (Lansdowne); N Farren (Old Wesley), B J Mullin (London Irish), P D Clinch (Lansdowne), P P Haycock (Terenure Coll); V J G Cunningham (St Mary's Coll), L F P Aherne (Lansdowne) (*capt*); N J Popplewell (Greystones), N Kearney (Old Wesley), D C Fitzgerald (Lansdowne), B J Rigney (Greystones), N P T Francis (Blackrock Coll), K Leahy (Wanderers), R Love (Old Wesley), A Blair (Old Wesley)
Scorers *Tries:* Mullin, Francis   *Penalty Goals:* Farren (2)   *Conversion:* Farren
Connacht: J E Staples (London Irish); D Holland (Corinthians), M Cosgrave (Wanderers), M Feely (Old Belvedere), E Guerin (Galwegians); C Cruess-Callaghan (Old Belvedere), S O'Beirne (St Mary's Coll); T P J Clancy (Lansdowne), J O'Riordan (Constitution), D Henshaw (Athlone), A Higgins (London Irish), Mark Feely (Old Belvedere), N McCarthy (St Mary's Coll) (*capt*), M Fitzgibbon (Shannon), N P Mannion (Corinthians)
Scorer *Penalty Goals:* O'Beirne (4)
Referee B W Stirling

IRISH INTERNATIONAL PLAYERS
(up to 30 April 1990)

ABBREVIATIONS

A – Australia; *C* – Canada; *E* – England; *F* – France; *It* – Italy; *M* – Maoris; *NZ* – New Zealand; *R* – Romania; *S* – Scotland; *SA* – South Africa; *Tg* – Tonga; *W* – Wales; *WS* – Western Samoa; *P* – Ireland v IRFU President's XV at Lansdowne Road in IRFU centenary season, 1974-75; (R) – Replacement. Entries in square brackets [ ] indicate appearances in the World Cup. NIFC – North of Ireland Football Club; CIYMS – Church of Ireland Young Men's Society; KCH – King's College Hospital

Note: Years given for Five Nations' matches are for second half of season; eg 1972 means season 1971-72. Years for all other matches refer to the actual year of the match. When a series has taken place, figures have been used to denote the particular matches in which players have featured. Thus 1981 *SA* 2 indicates that a player appeared in the second Test of the series. The abandoned game with Scotland at Belfast in 1885 is now included as a cap-match.

NB – The second of Ireland's two matches against France in 1972 was a non-championship match

Abraham, M (Bective Rangers) 1912 *E, S, W, SA,* 1914 *W*
Adams, C (Old Wesley) 1908 *E,* 1909 *E, F,* 1910 *F,* 1911 *E, S, W, F,* 1912 *S, W, SA,* 1913 *W, F,* 1914 *F, E, S*
Agar, R D (Malone) 1947 *F, E, S, W,* 1948 *F,* 1949 *S, W,* 1950 *F, E, W*
Agnew, P J (CIYMS) 1974 *F* (R), 1976 *A*
Ahearne, T (Queen's Coll, Cork) 1899 *E*
Aherne, L F P (Dolphin, Lansdowne) 1988 *E* 2, *WS, It,* 1989 *F, E, S, NZ,* 1990 *E, S, F, W* (R)
Alexander, R (NIFC, Police Union) 1936 *E, S, W,* 1937 *E, S, W,* 1938 *E, S,* 1939 *E, S, W*
Allen, C E (Derry, Liverpool) 1900 *E, S, W,* 1901 *E, S, W,* 1903 *S, W,* 1904 *E, S, W,* 1905 *E, S, W, NZ,* 1906 *E, S, W, SA,* 1907 *S, W*
Allen, G G (Derry, Liverpool) 1896 *E, S, W,* 1897 *E, S,* 1898 *E, S,* 1899 *E, W*
Allen, T C (NIFC) 1885 *E, S* 1
Allen, W S (Wanderers) 1875 *E*
Allison, J B (Edinburgh U) 1899 *E, S,* 1900 *E, S, W,* 1901 *E, S, W,* 1902 *E, S, W,* 1903 *S*
Anderson, F E (Queen's U, Belfast, NIFC) 1953 *F, E, S, W,* 1954 *NZ, F, E, S, W,* 1955 *F, E, S, W*
Anderson, H J (Old Wesley) 1903 *E, S,* 1906 *E, S*
Anderson, W A (Dungannon) 1984 *A,* 1985 *S, F, E,* 1986 *F, W, E, S, R,* 1987 *E, S, F, W,* [*W, C, Tg, A*], 1988 *S, F, W, E* 1,2, 1989 *F, W, E, NZ,* 1990 *E, S*
Andrews, G (NIFC) 1875 *E,* 1876 *E*
Andrews, H W (NIFC) 1888 *M,* 1889 *S, W*
Archer, A M (Dublin U, NIFC) 1879 *S*
Arigho, J E (Lansdowne) 1928 *F, E, W,* 1929 *F, E, S, W,* 1930 *F, E, S, W,* 1931 *F, E, S, W, SA*
Armstrong, W K (NIFC) 1960 *SA,* 1961 *W*
Arnott, D T (Lansdowne) 1876 *E*
Ash, W H (NIFC) 1875 *E,* 1876 *E,* 1877 *S*
Aston, H R (Dublin U) 1908 *E, W*
Atkins, A P (Bective Rangers) 1924 *F*
Atkinson, J M (NIFC) 1927 *F, A*
Atkinson, J R (Dublin U) 1882 *W, S*

Bagot, J C (Dublin U, Lansdowne) 1879 *S, E,* 1880 *E, S,* 1881 *S*
Bailey, A H (UC Dublin, Lansdowne) 1934 *W,* 1935 *E, S, W, NZ,* 1936 *E, S, W,* 1937 *E, S, W,* 1938 *E, S*
Bailey, N (Northampton) 1952 *E*
Bardon, M E (Bohemians) 1934 *E*
Barlow, M (Wanderers) 1875 *E*
Barnes, R J (Dublin U, Armagh) 1933 *W*
Barr, A (Methodist Coll, Belfast) 1898 *W,* 1899 *S,* 1901 *E, S*
Beamish, C E St J (RAF, Leicester) 1933 *W, S,* 1934 *S, W,* 1935 *E, S, W, NZ,* 1936 *E, S, W,* 1938 *W*
Beamish, G R (RAF, Leicester) 1925 *E, S, W,* 1928 *F, E, S, W,* 1929 *F, E, S, W,* 1930 *F, E, S, W,* 1931 *F, E, S, W, SA,* 1932 *E, S, W,* 1933 *E, W, S*
Beatty, W J (NIFC, Richmond) 1910 *F,* 1912 *F, W*
Becker, V A (Lansdowne) 1974 *F, W*
Beckett, G G P (Dublin U) 1908 *E, S, W*
Bell, R J (NIFC) 1875 *E,* 1876 *E*

Bell, W E (Belfast Collegians) 1953 *F, E, S, W*
Bennett, F (Belfast Collegians) 1913 *S*
Bent, G C (Dublin U) 1882 *W, E*
Berkery, P J (Lansdowne) 1954 *W,* 1955 *W,* 1956 *S, W,* 1957 *F, E, S, W,* 1958 *A, E, S*
Bermingham, J J C (Blackrock Coll) 1921 *E, S, W, F*
Blackham, J C (Queen's Coll, Cork) 1909 *S, W, F,* 1910 *E, S, W*
Blake-Knox, S E F (NIFC) 1976 *E, S,* 1977 *F* (R)
Blayney, J J (Wanderers) 1950 *S*
Bond, A T W (Derry) 1894 *S, W*
Bornemann, W W (Wanderers) 1960 *E, S, W, SA*
Bowen, D St J (Cork Const) 1977 *W, E, S*
Boyd, C A (Dublin U) 1900 *S,* 1901 *S, W*
Boyle, C V (Dublin U) 1935 *NZ,* 1936 *E, S, W,* 1937 *E, S, W,* 1938 *W,* 1939 *W*
Brabazon, H M (Dublin U) 1884 *E,* 1885 *S* 1, 1886 *E*
Bradley, M J (Dolphin) 1920 *W, F,* 1922 *E, S, W, F,* 1923 *E, S, W, F,* 1925 *F, S, W,* 1926 *F, E, S, W,* 1927 *F, W*
Bradley, M T (Cork Constitution) 1984 *A,* 1985 *S, F, W, E,* 1986 *F, W, E, S, R,* 1987 *E, S, F, W,* [*W, C, Tg, A*], 1988 *S, F, W, E* 1, 1990 *W*
Bradshaw, G (Belfast Collegians) 1903 *W*
Bradshaw, R M (Wanderers) 1885 *E, S* 1,2
Brady, A M (UC Dublin, Malone) 1966 *S,* 1968 *E, S, W*
Brady, J A (Wanderers) 1976 *E, S*
Brady, J R (CIYMS) 1951 *S, W,* 1953 *F, E, S, W,* 1954 *W,* 1956 *W,* 1957 *F, E, S*
Bramwell, T (NIFC) 1928 *F*
Brand, T N (NIFC) 1924 *NZ*
Brennan, J I (CIYMS) 1957 *S, W*
Bresnihan, F P K (UC Dublin, Lansdowne, London Irish) 1966 *E, W,* 1967 *A1, E, S, W, F,* 1968 *F, E, S, W, A,* 1969 *F, E, S, W,* 1970 *SA, F, E, S, W,* 1971 *F, E, S, W*
Brett, J T (Monkstown) 1914 *W*
Bristow, J R (NIFC) 1879 *E*
Brophy, N H (Blackrock Coll, UC Dublin, London Irish) 1957 *F, E,* 1959 *E, S, W, F,* 1960 *F, SA,* 1961 *S, W,* 1962 *E, S, W,* 1963 *E, W,* 1967 *E, S, W, F, A2*
Brown, E L (Instonians) 1958 *F*
Brown, G S (Monkstown, United Services) 1912 *S, W, SA*
Brown, H (Windsor) 1877 *E*
Brown, T (Windsor) 1877 *E, S*
Brown, W H (Dublin U) 1899 *E*
Brown, W J (Malone) 1970 *SA, F, S, W*
Brown, W S (Dublin U) 1893 *S, W,* 1894 *E, S, W*
Browne, A W (Dublin U) 1951 *SA*
Browne, D (Blackrock Coll) 1920 *F*
Browne, H C (United Services and RN) 1929 *E, S, W*
Browne, W F (United Services and Army) 1925 *E, S, W,* 1926 *S, W,* 1927 *F, E, S, W, A,* 1928 *E, S*
Browning, D R (Wanderers) 1881 *E, S*
Bruce, S A M (NIFC) 1883 *E, S,* 1884 *E*
Brunker, A A (Lansdowne) 1895 *E, W*
Bryant, C H (Cardiff) 1920 *E, S*
Buchanan, A McM (Dublin U) 1926 *E, S, W,* 1927 *S,*

W, A
Buchanan, J W B (Dublin U) 1882 *S*, 1884 *E, S*
Buckley, J H (Sunday's Well) 1973 *E, S*
Bulger, L Q (Lansdowne) 1896 *E, S, W*, 1897 *E, S*, 1898 *E, S, W*
Bulger, M J (Dublin U) 1888 *M*
Burges, J H (Rosslyn Park) 1950 *F, E*
Burgess, R B (Dublin U) 1912 *SA*
Burkitt, J C S (Queen's Coll, Cork) 1881 *E*
Burns, I J (Wanderers) 1980 *E* (R)
Butler, L G (Blackrock Coll) 1960 *W*
Butler, N (Bective Rangers) 1920 *E*
Byers, R M (NIFC) 1928 *S, W*, 1929 *E, S, W*
Byrne, E M J (Blackrock Coll) 1977 *S, F*, 1978 *F, W, E, NZ*
Byrne, N F (UC Dublin) 1962 *F*
Byrne, S J (UC Dublin, Lansdowne) 1953 *S, W*, 1955 *F*
Byron, W G (NIFC) 1896 *E, S, W*, 1897 *E, S*, 1898 *E, S, W*, 1899 *E, S, W*

Caddell, E D (Dublin U, Wanderers) 1904 *S*, 1905 *E, S, W, NZ*, 1906 *E, S, W, SA*, 1907 *E, S*, 1908 *S, W*
Cagney, S J (London Irish) 1925 *W*, 1926 *F, E, S, W*, 1927 *F*, 1928 *E, S, W*, 1929 *F, E, S, W*
Callan, C P (Lansdowne) 1947 *F, E, S, W*, 1948 *F, E, S, W*, 1949 *F, E*
Cameron, E D (Bective Rangers) 1891 *S, W*
Campbell, C E (Old Wesley) 1970 *SA*
Campbell, E F (Monkstown) 1899 *S, W*, 1900 *E, W*
Campbell, S B B (Derry) 1911 *E, S, W, F*, 1912 *F, E, S, W, SA*, 1913 *E, S*
Campbell, S O (Old Belvedere) 1976 *A*, 1979 *A* 1,2, 1980 *E, S, F, W*, 1981 *F, W, E, S, SA*1, 1982 *W, E, S, F*, 1983 *S, F, W, E*, 1984 *F, W*
Canniffe, D M (Lansdowne) 1976 *W, E*
Cantrell, J L (UC Dublin, Blackrock Coll) 1976 *A, F, W, E, S*, 1981 *S, SA* 1,2, *A*
Carpendale, M J (Monkstown) 1886 *S*, 1887 *W*, 1888 *W, S*
Carr, N J (Ards) 1985 *S, F, W, E*, 1986 *W, E, S, R*, 1987 *E, S, W*
Carroll, C (Bective Rangers) 1930 *F*
Carroll, R (Lansdowne) 1947 *F*, 1950 *S, W*
Casement, B N (Dublin U) 1875 *E*, 1876 *E*, 1879 *E*
Casement, F (Dublin U) 1906 *E, S, W*
Casey, J C (Young Munster) 1930 *S*, 1932 *E*
Casey, P J (UC Dublin, Lansdowne) 1963 *F, E, S, W, NZ*, 1964 *E, S, W, F*, 1965 *F, E, S*
Chambers, J (Dublin U) 1886 *E, S*, 1887 *E, S, W*
Chambers, R R (Instonians) 1951 *F, E, S, W*, 1952 *F, W*
Clancy, T P J (Lansdowne) 1988 *W, E* 1,2, *WS, It*, 1989 *F, W, E, S*
Clarke, J A B (Bective Rangers) 1922 *S, W, F*, 1923 *F*, 1924 *E, S, W*
Clegg, R J (Bangor) 1973 *F*, 1975 *E, S, F, W*
Clifford, J T (Young Munster) 1949 *F, E, S, W*, 1950 *F, E, S, W*, 1951 *F, E, S, SA*, 1952 *F, S, W*
Clinch, A D (Dublin U, Wanderers) 1892 *S*, 1893 *W*, 1895 *E, S, W*, 1896 *E, S, W*, 1897 *E, S*
Clinch, J D (Wanderers, Dublin U) 1923 *W*, 1924 *F, E, S, W, NZ*, 1925 *F, E, S*, 1926 *E, S, W*, 1927 *F*, 1928 *F, E, S, W*, 1929 *F, E, S, W*, 1930 *F, E, S, W*, 1931 *F, E, S, W, SA*
Clune, J J (Blackrock Coll) 1912 *SA*, 1913 *W, F*, 1914 *F, E, W*
Coffey, J J (Lansdowne) 1900 *E*, 1901 *W*, 1902 *E, S, W*, 1903 *E, S, W*, 1905 *E, S, W, NZ*, 1906 *E, S, W, SA*, 1907 *E*, 1908 *W*, 1910 *F*
Cogan, W St J (Queen's Coll, Cork) 1907 *E, S*
Collier, S R (Queen's Coll, Belfast) 1883 *S*
Collins, P C (Lansdowne, London Irish) 1987 *[C]*, 1990 *S* (R)
Collis, W R F (KCH, Harlequins) 1924 *F, W, NZ*, 1925 *F, E, S*, 1926 *F*
Collis, W S (Wanderers) 1884 *W*
Collopy, G (Bective Rangers) 1891 *S*, 1892 *S*
Collopy, R (Bective Rangers) 1923 *E, S, W, F*, 1924 *F, E, S, W, NZ*, 1925 *F, E, S, W*
Collopy, W P (Bective Rangers) 1914 *F, E, S, W*, 1921 *E, S, W, F*, 1922 *E, S, W, F*, 1923 *S, W, F*, 1924 *F, E, S, W*
Combe, A (NIFC) 1875 *E*
Condon, H C (London Irish) 1984 *S* (R)
Cook, H G (Lansdowne) 1884 *W*

Coote, P B (RAF, Leicester) 1933 *S*
Corcoran, J C (London Irish) 1947 *A*, 1948 *F*
Corken, T S (Belfast Collegians) 1937 *E, S, W*
Corley, H H (Dublin U, Wanderers) 1902 *E, S, W*, 1903 *E, S, W*, 1904 *E, S*
Cormac, H S T (Clontarf) 1921 *E, S, W*
Costello, P (Bective Rangers) 1960 *F*
Cotton, J (Wanderers) 1889 *W*
Coulter, H H (Queen's U, Belfast) 1920 *E, S, W*
Courtney, A W (UC Dublin) 1920 *S, W, F*, 1921 *E, S, W, F*
Cox, H L (Dublin U) 1875 *E*, 1876 *E*, 1877 *E, S*
Craig, R G (Queen's U, Belfast) 1938 *S, W*
Crawford, E C (Dublin U) 1885 *E, S* 1
Crawford, W E (Lansdowne) 1920 *E, S, W, F*, 1921 *E, S, W, F*, 1922 *E, S, W*, 1923 *E, S, W, F*, 1924 *F, E, W*, 1925 *F, E, S, W*, 1926 *F, E, S, W*, 1927 *F, E, S, W*
Crean, T J (Wanderers) 1894 *E, S, W*, 1895 *E, S, W*, 1896 *E, S, W*
Crichton, R Y (Dublin U) 1920 *E, S, W, F*, 1921 *F*, 1922 *E*, 1923 *W, F*, 1924 *F, E, S, W, NZ*, 1925 *E, S*
Croker, E W D (Limerick) 1878 *E*
Cromey, G E (Queen's U, Belfast) 1937 *E, S, W*, 1938 *E, S, W*, 1939 *E, S, W*
Cronyn, A P (Dublin U, Lansdowne) 1875 *E*, 1876 *E*, 1880 *S*
Crossan, K D (Instonians) 1982 *S*, 1984 *F, W, E, S*, 1985 *S, F, W, E*, 1986 *E, S, R*, 1987 *E, S, F, W*, *[W, C, Tg, A]*, 1988 *S, F, W, E* 1, *WS, It*, 1989 *W, S, NZ*, 1990 *E, S, F, W*
Crowe, J F (UC Dublin) 1974 *NZ*
Crowe, L (Old Belvedere) 1950 *E, S, W*
Crowe, M P (Lansdowne) 1929 *W*, 1930 *E, S, W*, 1931 *F, S, W, SA*, 1932 *S, W*, 1933 *W, S*, 1934 *E*
Crowe, P M (Blackrock Coll) 1935 *E*, 1938 *E*
Cullen, T J (UC Dublin) 1949 *F*
Cullen, W J (Monkstown and Manchester) 1920 *E*
Culliton, M G (Wanderers) 1959 *E, S, W, F*, 1960 *E, S, W, F, SA*, 1961 *E, S, W, F*, 1962 *S, F*, 1964 *E, S, W, F*
Cummins, W E A (Queen's Coll, Cork) 1879 *S*, 1881 *E*, 1882 *E*
Cunningham, D McC (NIFC) 1923 *E, S, W*, 1925 *F, E, W*
Cunningham, M J (UC Cork) 1955 *F, E, S, W*, 1956 *F, S, W*
Cunningham, V J G (St Mary's Coll) 1988 *E* 2, *It*
Cunningham, W A (Lansdowne) 1920 *W*, 1921 *E, S, W, F*, 1922 *E*, 1923 *S, W*
Cuppaidge, J L (Dublin U) 1879 *E*, 1880 *E, S*
Currell, J (NIFC) 1877 *S*
Curtis, A B (Oxford U) 1950 *F, E, S*
Cuscaden, W A (Dublin U, Bray) 1876 *E*
Cussen, D J (Dublin U) 1921 *E, S, W, F*, 1922 *E*, 1923 *E, S, W, F*, 1926 *F, E, S, W*, 1927 *F, E*

Daly, J C (London Irish) 1947 *F, E, S, W*, 1948 *E, S, W*
Daly, M J (Harlequins) 1938 *E*
Danaher, P P A (Lansdowne, Garryowen) 1988 *S, F, W, WS, It*, 1989 *F, NZ* (R), 1990 *F*
Dargan, M J (Old Belvedere) 1952 *S, W*
Davidson, C T (NIFC) 1921 *F*
Davidson, I G (NIFC) 1899 *E*, 1900 *S, W*, 1901 *E, S, W*, 1902 *E, S, W*
Davidson, J C (Dungannon) 1969 *F, E, S, W*, 1973 *NZ*, 1976 *NZ*
Davies, F E (Lansdowne) 1892 *S, W*, 1893 *E, S, W*
Davis, J L (Monkstown) 1898 *E, S*
Davis, W J N (Edinburgh U, Bessbrook) 1890 *S, W, E*, 1891 *E, S, W*, 1892 *E, S*, 1895 *S*
Davison, W (Belfast Academy) 1887 *W*
Davy, E O'D (UC Dublin, Lansdowne) 1925 *W*, 1926 *F, E, S, W*, 1927 *F, E, S, W, A*, 1928 *F, E, S, W*, 1929 *F, E, S, W*, 1930 *F, E, S, W*, 1931 *F, E, S, W, SA*, 1932 *E, S, W*, 1933 *E, W, S*, 1934 *E*
Dawson, A R (Wanderers) 1958 *A, E, S, W, F*, 1959 *E, S, W, F*, 1960 *F, SA*, 1961 *E, S, W, F, SA*, 1962 *S, F*, 1963 *F, E, S, W, NZ*, 1964 *E, S, F*
Dean, P M (St Mary's Coll) 1981 *SA* 1,2, *A*, 1982 *W, E, S, F*, 1984 *A*, 1985 *S, F, W, E*, 1986 *F, W, R*, 1987 *E, S, F, W*, *[W, A]*, 1988 *S, F, W, E*1,2, *WS, It*, 1989 *F, W, E, S*
Deane, E C (Monkstown) 1909 *E*
Deering, M J (Bective Rangers) 1929 *W*

Deering, S J (Bective Rangers) 1935 *E, S, W, NZ*, 1936 *E, S, W*, 1937 *E, S*
Deering, S M (Garryowen, St Mary's Coll) 1974 *W*, 1976 *F, W, E, S*, 1977 *W, E*, 1978 *NZ*
de Lacy, H (Harlequins) 1948 *E, S*
Delaney, M G (Bective Rangers) 1895 *W*
Dennison, S P (Garryowen) 1973 *F*, 1975 *E, S*
Dick, C J (Ballymena) 1961 *W, F, SA*, 1962 *W*, 1963 *F, E, S, W*
Dick, J S (Queen's U, Belfast) 1962 *E*
Dick, J S (Queen's Coll, Cork) 1887 *E, S, W*
Dickson, J A N (Dublin U) 1920 *E, W, F*
Doherty, A E (Old Wesley) 1974 *P* (R)
Doherty, W D (Guy's Hospital) 1920 *E, S, W*, 1921 *E, S, W, F*
Donaldson, J A (Belfast Collegians) 1958 *A, E, S, W*
Donovan, T M (Queen's Coll, Cork) 1889 *S*
Dooley, J F (Galwegians) 1959 *E, S, W*
Doran, B R W (Lansdowne) 1900 *S, W*, 1901 *E, S, W*, 1902 *E, S, W*
Doran, E F (Lansdowne) 1890 *S, W*
Doran, G P (Lansdowne) 1899 *S, W*, 1900 *E, S, W*, 1902 *S, W*, 1903 *W*, 1904 *E*
Douglas, A C (Instonians) 1923 *F*, 1924 *E, S*, 1927 *A*, 1928 *S*
Downing, A J (Dublin U) 1882 *W*
Dowse, J C A (Monkstown) 1914 *F, S, W*
Doyle, J A P (Greystones) 1984 *E, S*
Doyle, J T (Bective Rangers) 1935 *W*
Doyle, M G (Blackrock Coll, UC Dublin, Cambridge U, Edinburgh Wands) 1965 *F, E, S, W, SA*, 1966 *F, E, S, W*, 1967 *A 1, E, S, W, F, A 2*, 1968 *F, E, S, W, A*
Doyle, T J (Wanderers) 1968 *E, S, W*
Duggan, A T A (Lansdowne) 1963 *NZ*, 1964 *F*, 1966 *W*, 1967 *A 1, S, W, A 2*, 1968 *F, E, S, W*, 1969 *F, E, S*, 1970 *SA, F, E, S, W*, 1971 *F, E, S, W*, 1972 *F 2*
Duggan, W (UC Cork) 1920 *S, W*
Duggan, W P (Blackrock Coll) 1975 *E, S, F, W*, 1976 *A, F, W, S, NZ*, 1977 *W, E, S, F*, 1978 *S, F, W, E, NZ*, 1979 *E, S, A 1,2*, 1980 *E*, 1981 *F, W, E, S, SA 1,2, A*, 1982 *W, E, S*, 1983 *S, F, W, E*, 1984 *F, W, E, S*
Duncan, W R (Malone) 1984 *W, E*
Dunlea, F J (Lansdowne) 1989 *W, E, S*
Dunlop, R (Dublin U) 1889 *W*, 1890 *S, W, E*, 1891 *E, S, W*, 1892 *E, S*, 1893 *W*, 1894 *W*
Dunn, P E F (Bective Rangers) 1923 *S*
Dunn, T B (NIFC) 1935 *NZ*
Dunne, M J (Lansdowne) 1929 *F, E, S*, 1930 *F, E, S, W*, 1932 *E, S, W*, 1933 *E, W, S*, 1934 *E, S, W*
Dwyer, P J (UC Dublin) 1962 *W*, 1963 *F, NZ*, 1964 *S, W*

Edwards, H G (Dublin U) 1877 *E*, 1878 *E*
Edwards, R W (Malone) 1904 *W*
Edwards, T (Lansdowne) 1888 *M*, 1890 *S, W, E*, 1892 *W*, 1893 *E*
Edwards, W V (Malone) 1912 *F, E*
Egan, J D (Bective Rangers) 1922 *S*
Egan, J T (Cork Constitution) 1931 *F, E, SA*
Egan, M S (Garryowen) 1893 *E*, 1895 *S*
Ekin, W (Queen's Coll, Belfast) 1888 *W, S*
Elliott, W R J (Bangor) 1979 *S*
English, M A F (Lansdowne, Limerick Bohemians) 1958 *W, F*, 1959 *E, S, F*, 1960 *E, S*, 1961 *S, W, F*, 1962 *F, W*, 1963 *E, S, W, NZ*
Ennis, F N G (Wanderers) 1979 *A 1* (R)
Ensor, A H (Wanderers) 1973 *W, F*, 1974 *F, W, E, S, P, NZ*, 1975 *E, S, F, W*, 1976 *A, F, W, E, NZ*, 1977 *S, F, W, E*, 1978 *S, F, W, E*
Entrican, J C (Queen's U, Belfast) 1931 *S*

Fagan, G L (Kingstown School) 1878 *E*
Fagan, W B C (Wanderers) 1956 *F, E, S*
Farrell, J L (Bective Rangers) 1926 *F, E, S, W*, 1927 *F, E, S, W, A*, 1928 *F, E, S, W*, 1929 *F, E, S, W*, 1930 *F, E, S, W*, 1931 *F, E, S, W, SA*, 1932 *E, S, W*
Feddis, N (Lansdowne) 1956 *E*
Feighery, C F P (Lansdowne) 1972 *F 1, E, F2*
Feighery, T A O (St Mary's Coll) 1977 *W, E*
Ferris, H H (Queen's Coll, Belfast) 1901 *W*
Ferris, J H (Queen's Coll, Belfast) 1900 *E, S, W*
Finlay, J E (Queen's Coll, Belfast) 1913 *E, S, W*, 1920 *E, S, W*

Finlay, W (NIFC) 1876 *E*, 1877 *E, S*, 1878 *E*, 1879 *S, E*, 1880 *S*, 1882 *S*
Finn, M C (UC Cork, Cork Constitution) 1979 *E*, 1982 *W, E, S, F*, 1983 *S, F, W, E*, 1984 *E, S, A*, 1986 *F, W*
Finn, R G A (UC Dublin) 1977 *F*
Fitzgerald, C C (Glasgow U, Dungannon) 1902 *E*, 1903 *E, S*
Fitzgerald, C F (St Mary's Coll) 1979 *A 1,2*, 1980 *E, S, F, W*, 1982 *W, E, S, F*, 1983 *S, F, W, E*, 1984 *F, W, A*, 1985 *S, F, W, E*, 1986 *F, W, E, S*
Fitzgerald, D C (Lansdowne) 1984 *E, S*, 1986 *W, E, S, R*, 1987 *E, S, F, W*, [*W, C, A*], 1988 *S, F, W, E 1*, 1989 *NZ* (R), 1990 *E, S, F, W*
Fitzgerald, J (Wanderers) 1884 *W*
Fitzgerald, J J (Young Munster) 1988 *S, F*, 1990 *S, F, W*
Fitzpatrick, M P (Wanderers) 1978 *S*, 1980 *S, F, W*, 1981 *F, W, E, S, A*, 1985 *F* (R)
Fletcher, W W (Kingstown) 1882 *W, S*, 1883 *E*
Flood, R S (Dublin U) 1925 *W*
Flynn, M K (Wanderers) 1959 *F*, 1960 *F*, 1962 *E, S, F, W*, 1964 *E, S, W, F*, 1965 *F, E, S, W, SA*, 1966 *F, E, S*, 1972 *F 1, E, F 2*, 1973 *NZ*
Fogarty, T (Garryowen) 1891 *W*
Foley, B O (Shannon) 1976 *F, E*, 1977 *W* (R), 1980 *F, W*, 1981 *F, E, S, SA 1,2, A*
Forbes, R E (Malone) 1907 *E*
Forrest, A J (Wanderers) 1880 *E, S*, 1881 *E, S*, 1882 *W, E*, 1883 *S 2*
Forrest, E G (Wanderers) 1888 *M*, 1889 *S, W*, 1890 *S, E*, 1891 *E*, 1893 *S*, 1894 *E, S, W*, 1895 *W*, 1897 *E, S*
Forrest, H (Wanderers) 1893 *S, W*
Fortune, J J (Clontarf) 1963 *NZ*, 1964 *E*
Foster, A R (Derry) 1910 *E, S, F*, 1911 *E, S, W, F*, 1912 *F, E, S, W*, 1914 *E, S, W*, 1921 *E, S, W*
Francis, N P T (Blackrock Coll, London Irish) 1987 [*Tg, A*], 1988 *WS, It*, 1989 *S*, 1990 *E, F, W*
Franks, J G (Dublin U) 1898 *E, S*
Frazer, E F (Bective Rangers) 1891 *S*, 1892 *S*
Freer, A E (Lansdowne) 1901 *E, S, W*
Fulton, J (NIFC) 1895 *S, W*, 1896 *E*, 1897 *E*, 1898 *W*, 1899 *E*, 1900 *W*, 1901 *E*, 1902 *E, S, W*, 1903 *E, S, W*, 1904 *E, S*

Gaffikin, W (Windsor) 1875 *E*
Gage, J H (Queen's U, Belfast) 1926 *S, W*, 1927 *S, W*
Galbraith, E (Dublin U) 1875 *E*
Galbraith, H T (Belfast Acad) 1890 *W*
Galbraith, R (Dublin U) 1875 *E*, 1876 *E*, 1877 *E*
Ganly, J B (Monkstown) 1927 *F, E, S, W, A*, 1928 *F, E, S, W*, 1929 *F, S*, 1930 *F*
Gardiner, F (NIFC) 1900 *E, S*, 1901 *E, W*, 1902 *E, S, W*, 1903 *E, W*, 1904 *E, S, W*, 1906 *E, S, W*, 1907 *S, W*, 1908 *S, W*, 1909 *E, S, F*
Gardiner, J B (NIFC) 1923 *E, S, W, F*, 1924 *F, E, S, W, NZ*, 1925 *F, E, S, W*
Gardiner, S (Belfast Albion) 1893 *E, S*
Gardiner, W (NIFC) 1892 *E, S*, 1893 *E, S, W*, 1894 *E, S, W*, 1895 *E, S, W*, 1896 *E, S, W*, 1897 *E, S, W*, 1898 *W*
Garry, M G (Bective Rangers) 1909 *E, S, W*, 1911 *E, S, W*
Gaston, J T (Dublin U) 1954 *NZ, F, E, S, W*, 1955 *W*, 1956 *F, E*
Gavin, T J (Moseley, London Irish) 1949 *F, E*
Gibson, C M H (Cambridge U, NIFC) 1964 *E, S, W, F*, 1965 *F, E, S, W, SA*, 1966 *F, E, S, W*, 1967 *A 1, E, S, W, F, A 2*, 1968 *A, E, S, W, F*, 1969 *E, S, W*, 1970 *SA, F, E, S, W*, 1971 *F, E, S, W*, 1972 *F 1, E, F 2*, 1973 *NZ, E, S, W, F*, 1974 *F, W, E, S, P*, 1975 *E, S, F, W*, 1976 *A, F, W, E, S, NZ*, 1977 *W, E, S, F*, 1978 *F, W, E, NZ*, 1979 *S, A 1,2*
Gibson, M E (Lansdowne, London Irish) 1979 *F, W, E, S*, 1981 *W* (R), 1986 *R*, 1988 *S, F, W, E 2*
Gifford, H P (Wanderers) 1890 *S*
Gillespie, J C (Dublin U) 1922 *W, F*
Gilpin, F G (Queen's U, Belfast) 1962 *E, S, F*
Glass, D C (Belfast Collegians) 1958 *F*, 1960 *W*, 1961 *W, SA*
Glennon, J J (Skerries) 1980 *E, S*, 1987 *E, S, F*, [*W* (R)]
Godfrey, R P (UC Dublin) 1954 *S, W*
Goodall, K G (City of Derry and Newcastle U) 1967 *A 1, E, S, W, F, A 2*, 1968 *F, E, S, W, A*, 1969 *F, E, S*,

1970 *SA, F, E, S, W*
Gordon, A (Dublin U) 1884 *S*
Gordon, T G (NIFC) 1877 *E, S*, 1878 *E*
Gotto, R P C (NIFC) 1906 *SA*
Goulding, W J (Cork) 1879 *S*
Grace, T O (UC Dublin, St Mary's Coll) 1972 *F* 1, *E*, 1973 *NZ, E, S, W*, 1974 *E, S, P, NZ*, 1975 *E, S, F, W*, 1976 *A, F, W, E, S, NZ*, 1977 *W, E, S, F*, 1978 *S*
Graham, R I (Dublin U) 1911 *F*
Grant, E L (CIYMS) 1971 *F, E, S, W*
Grant, P J (Bective Rangers) 1894 *S, W*
Graves, C R A (Wanderers) 1934 *E, S, W*, 1935 *E, S, W, NZ*, 1936 *E, S, W*, 1937 *E, S*, 1938 *E, S, W*
Gray, R D (Old Wesley) 1923 *E, S*, 1925 *F*, 1926 *F*
Greene, E H (Dublin U, Kingstown) 1882 *W*, 1884 *W*, 1885 *E, S* 2, 1886 *E*
Greer, R (Kingstown) 1876 *E*
Greeves, T J (NIFC) 1907 *E, S, W*, 1909 *W, F*
Gregg, R J (Queen's U, Belfast) 1953 *F, E, S, W*, 1954 *F, E, S*
Griffin, C S (London Irish) 1951 *F, E*
Griffin, J L (Wanderers) 1949 *S, W*
Griffiths, W (Limerick) 1878 *E*
Grimshaw, C (Queen's U, Belfast) 1969 *E* (R)
Guerin, B N (Galwegians) 1956 *S*
Gwynn, A P (Dublin U) 1895 *W*
Gwynn, L H (Dublin U) 1893 *S*, 1894 *E, S, W*, 1897 *S*, 1898 *E, S*

Hakin, R F (CIYMS) 1976 *W, S, NZ*, 1977 *W, E, F*
Hall, R O N (Dublin U) 1884 *W*
Hall, W H (Instonians) 1923 *E, S, W, F*, 1924 *F, S*
Hallaran, C F G T (Royal Navy) 1921 *E, S, W*, 1922 *E, S, W*, 1923 *E, F*, 1924 *F, E, S, W*, 1925 *F*, 1926 *F, E*
Halpin, G F (Wanderers) 1990 *E*
Halpin, T (Garryowen) 1909 *W, F*, 1910 *E, S, W*, 1911 *E, S, W, F*, 1912 *F, E, S*
Hamilton, A J (Lansdowne) 1884 *W*
Hamilton, R L (NIFC) 1926 *F*
Hamilton, R W (Wanderers) 1893 *W*
Hamilton, W J (Dublin U) 1877 *E*
Hamlet, G T (Old Wesley) 1902 *E, S, W*, 1903 *E, S, W*, 1904 *S, W*, 1905 *E, S, W, NZ*, 1906 *SA*, 1907 *E, S, W*, 1908 *E, S, W*, 1909 *E, S, W, F*, 1910 *E, S, F*, 1911 *E, S, W, F*
Hanrahan, C J (Dolphin) 1926 *S, W*, 1927 *E, S, W, A*, 1928 *F, E, S*, 1929 *F, E, S, W*, 1930 *F, E, S, W*, 1931 *F*, 1932 *S, W*
Harbison, H T (Bective Rangers) 1984 *W* (R), *E, S*, 1986 *R*, 1987 *E, S, F, W*
Hardy, G G (Bective Rangers) 1962 *S*
Harman, G R A (Dublin U) 1899 *E, W*
Harper, J (Instonians) 1947 *F, E, S*
Harpur, T G (Dublin U) 1908 *E, S, W*
Harrison, T (Cork) 1879 *S*, 1880 *S*, 1881 *E*
Harvey, F M W (Wanderers) 1907 *W*, 1911 *F*
Harvey, G A D (Wanderers) 1903 *E, S*, 1904 *W*, 1905 *E, S*
Harvey, T A (Dublin U) 1900 *W*, 1901 *S, W*, 1902 *E, S, W*, 1903 *E, W*
Haycock, P P (Terenure Coll) 1989 *E*
Headon, T A (UC Dublin) 1939 *S, W*
Healey, P (Limerick) 1901 *E, S, W*, 1902 *E, S, W*, 1903 *E, S, W*, 1904 *S*
Heffernan, M R (Cork Constitution) 1911 *E, S, W, F*
Hemphill, R (Dublin U) 1912 *F, E, S, W*
Henderson, N J (Queen's U, Belfast, NIFC) 1949 *S, W*, 1950 *F*, 1951 *F, E, S, W, SA*, 1952 *F, S, W, E*, 1953 *F, E, S, W*, 1954 *NZ, F, E, S, W*, 1955 *F, E, S, W*, 1956 *S, W*, 1957 *F, E, S, W*, 1958 *A, E, S, W, F*, 1959 *E, S, W, F*
Henebrey, G J (Garryowen) 1906 *E, S, W, SA*, 1909 *W, F*
Heron, A G (Queen's Coll, Belfast) 1901 *E*
Heron, J (NIFC) 1877 *S*, 1879 *E*
Heron, W T (NIFC) 1880 *E, S*
Herrick, R W (Dublin U) 1886 *S*
Heuston, F S (Kingstown) 1882 *W*, 1883 *E, S*
Hewitt, D (Queen's U, Belfast, Instonians) 1958 *A, E, S, F*, 1959 *S, W, F*, 1960 *E, S, W, F*, 1961 *E, S, W, F*, 1962 *S, F*, 1965 *W*
Hewitt, F S (Instonians) 1924 *W, NZ*, 1925 *F, E, S*, 1926 *E*, 1927 *E, S, W*

Hewitt, J A (NIFC) 1981 *SA* 1 (R), 2 (R)
Hewitt, T R (Queen's U, Belfast) 1924 *W, NZ*, 1925 *F, E, S*, 1926 *F, E, S, W*
Hewitt, V A (Instonians) 1935 *S, W, NZ*, 1936 *E, S, W*
Hewitt, W J (Instonians) 1954 *E*, 1956 *S*, 1959 *W*, 1961 *SA*
Hewson, F T (Wanderers) 1875 *E*
Hickie, D J (St Mary's Coll) 1971 *F, E, S, W*, 1972 *F* 1, *E*
Higgins, J A D (Civil Service) 1947 *S, W, A*, 1948 *F, S, W*
Higgins, W W (NIFC) 1884 *E, S*
Hillary, M F (UC Dublin) 1952 *E*
Hingerty, D J (UC Dublin) 1947 *F, E, S, W*
Hinton, W P (Old Wesley) 1907 *W*, 1908 *E, S, W*, 1909 *E, S*, 1910 *E, S, W, F*, 1911 *E, S, W*, 1912 *F, E, W*
Hipwell, M L (Terenure Coll) 1962 *E, S*, 1968 *F, A*, 1969 *F* (R), *S* (R), *W*, 1971 *F, E, S, W*, 1972 *F* 2
Hobbs, T H M (Dublin U) 1884 *S*, 1885 *E*
Hobson, E W (Dublin U) 1876 *E*
Hogg, W (Dublin U) 1885 *S* 2
Holland, J J (Wanderers) 1981 *SA* 1,2, 1986 *W*
Holmes, G W (Dublin U) 1912 *SA*, 1913 *E, S*
Holmes, L J (Lisburn) 1889 *S, W*
Hooks, K J (Queen's U, Belfast, Ards) 1981 *S*, 1989 *NZ*, 1990 *F, W*
Horan, A K (Blackheath) 1920 *E, W*
Houston, K J (Oxford U, London Irish) 1961 *SA*, 1964 *S, W*, 1965 *F, E, SA*
Hughes, R W (NIFC) 1878 *E*, 1880 *E, S*, 1881 *S*, 1882 *E, S*, 1883 *E, S*, 1884 *E, S*, 1885 *E*, 1886 *E*
Hunt, E W F de Vere (Army, Rosslyn Park) 1930 *F*, 1932 *E, S, W*, 1933 *E*
Hunter, D V (Dublin U) 1885 *S* 2
Hunter, L (Civil Service) 1968 *W, A*
Hunter, W R (CIYMS) 1962 *E, S, W, F*, 1963 *F, E, S*, 1966 *F, E, S*
Hutton, S A (Malone) 1967 *S, W, F, A* 2

Ireland, J (Windsor) 1876 *E*, 1877 *E*
Irvine, H A S (Collegians) 1901 *S*
Irwin, D G (Queen's U, Belfast, Instonians) 1980 *F, W*, 1981 *F, W, E, S, SA* 1,2, *A*, 1982 *W*, 1983 *S, F, W, E*, 1984 *F, W*, 1987 *[Tg, A(R)]*, 1989 *F, W, E, S, NZ*, 1990 *E, S*
Irwin, J W S (NIFC) 1938 *E, S*, 1939 *E, S, W*
Irwin, S T (Queen's Coll, Belfast) 1900 *E, S, W*, 1901 *E, W*, 1902 *E, S, W*, 1903 *S*

Jack, H W (UC Cork) 1914 *S, W*, 1921 *W*
Jackson, A R V (Wanderers) 1911 *E, S, W, F*, 1913 *W, F*, 1914 *F, E, S, W*
Jackson, F (NIFC) 1923 *E*
Jackson, H W (Dublin U) 1877 *E*
Jameson, J S (Lansdowne) 1888 *M*, 1889 *S, W*, 1891 *W*, 1892 *E, W*, 1893 *S*
Jeffares, E W (Wanderers) 1913 *E, S*
Johnston, J (Belfast Acad) 1881 *S*, 1882 *S*, 1884 *S*, 1885 *S* 1,2, 1886 *E*, 1887 *E, S, W*
Johnston, M (Dublin U) 1880 *E, S*, 1881 *E, S*, 1882 *E*, 1884 *E, S*, 1886 *E*
Johnston, R (Wanderers) 1893 *E, W*
Johnston, R W (Dublin U) 1890 *S, W, E*
Johnston, T J (Queen's Coll, Belfast) 1892 *E, S, W*, 1893 *E, S*, 1895 *E*
Johnstone, W E (Dublin U) 1884 *W*
Johnstone-Smyth, T R (Lansdowne) 1882 *E*

Kavanagh, J R (UC Dublin, Wanderers) 1953 *F, E, S, W*, 1954 *NZ, S, W*, 1955 *F, E*, 1956 *E, S, W*, 1957 *F, E, S, W*, 1958 *A, E, S, W*, 1959 *E, S, W, F*, 1960 *E, S, W, F, SA*, 1961 *E, S, W, F, SA*, 1962 *F*
Kavanagh, P J (UC Dublin, Wanderers) 1952 *E*, 1955 *W*
Keane, M I (Lansdowne) 1974 *F, W, E, S, P, NZ*, 1975 *E, S, F, W*, 1976 *A, F, W, E, S, NZ*, 1977 *W, E, S, F*, 1978 *S, F, W, E, NZ*, 1979 *F, W, E, S, A* 1,2, 1980 *E, S, F, W*, 1981 *F, W, E, S*, 1982 *W, E, S, F*, 1983 *S, F, W, E*, 1984 *F, W, E, S*
Kearney, R K (Wanderers) 1982 *F*, 1984 *A*, 1986 *F, W*
Keeffe, E (Sunday's Well) 1947 *F, E, S, W, A*, 1948 *F*
Kelly, H C (NIFC) 1877 *E, S*, 1878 *E*, 1879 *S*, 1880 *E, S*
Kelly, J C (UC Dublin) 1962 *F, W*, 1963 *F, E, S, W*, *NZ*, 1964 *E, S, W, F*

McKee, W D (NIFC) 1947 *A*, 1948 *F, E, S, W*, 1949 *F, E, S, W*, 1950 *F, E*, 1951 *SA*
McKelvey, J M (Queen's U, Belfast) 1956 *F, E*
McKibbin, A R (Instonians, London Irish) 1977 *W, E, S*, 1978 *S, F, W, E, NZ*, 1979 *F, W, E, S*, 1980 *E, S*
McKibbin, C H (Instonians) 1976 *S* (R)
McKibbin, D (Instonians) 1950 *F, E, S, W*, 1951 *F, E, S, W*
McKibbin, H R (Queen's U, Belfast) 1938 *W*, 1939 *E, S, W*
McKinney, S A (Dungannon) 1972 *F* 1, *E, F* 2, 1973 *W, F*, 1974 *F, E, S, P, NZ*, 1975 *E, S*, 1976 *A, F, W, E, S, NZ*, 1977 *W, E, S*, 1978 *S* (R), *F, W, E*
McLaughlin, J H (Derry) 1887 *E, S*, 1888 *W, S*
McLean, R E (Dublin U) 1881 *S*, 1882 *W, E, S*, 1883 *E, S*, 1884 *E, S*, 1885 *E, S* 1
Maclear, B (Cork County, Monkstown) 1905 *E, S, W, NZ*, 1906 *E, S, W, SA*, 1907 *E, S, W*
McLennan, A C (Wanderers) 1977 *F*, 1978 *S, F, W, E, NZ*, 1979 *F, W, E, S*, 1980 *E, F*, 1981 *F, W, E, S, SA* 1,2
McLoughlin, F M (Northern) 1976 *A*
McLoughlin, G A J (Shannon) 1979 *F, W, E, S, A* 1,2, 1980 *E*, 1981 *SA* 1,2, 1982 *W, E, S, F*, 1983 *S, F, W, E*, 1984 *F*
McLoughlin, R J (UC Dublin, Blackrock Coll, Gosforth) 1962 *E, S, F*, 1963 *E, S, W, NZ*, 1964 *E, S*, 1965 *F, E, S, W, SA*, 1966 *F, E, S, W*, 1971 *F, E, S, W*, 1972 *F* 1, *E, F* 2, 1973 *NZ, E, S, W, F*, 1974 *F, W, E, S, P, NZ*, 1975 *E, S, F, W*
McMahon, L B (Blackrock Coll, UC Dublin) 1931 *E, SA*, 1933 *E*, 1934 *E*, 1936 *E, S, W*, 1937 *E, S, W*, 1938 *E, S*
McMaster, A W (Ballymena) 1972 *F* 1, *E, F* 2, 1973 *E, S, W, F*, 1974 *F, E, S, P*, 1975 *F, W*, 1976 *A, F, W, NZ*
McMordie, J (Queen's Coll, Belfast) 1886 *S*
McMorrow, A (Garryowen) 1951 *W*
McMullen, A R (Cork) 1881 *E, S*
McNamara, V (UC Cork) 1914 *E, S, W*
McNaughton, P P (Greystones) 1978 *S, F, W, E*, 1979 *F, W, E, S, A* 1,2, 1980 *E, S, F, W*, 1981 *F*
MacNeill, H P (Dublin U, Oxford U, Blackrock Coll, London Irish) 1981 *F, W, E, S, A*, 1982 *W, E, S, F*, 1983 *S, F, W, E*, 1984 *F, W, E, A*, 1985 *S, F, W, E*, 1986 *F, W, E, S, R*, 1987 *E, S, F, W*, [*W, C, Tg, A*], 1988 *S* (R), *E* 1,2
MacSweeney, D A (Blackrock Coll) 1955 *S*
McVicker, H (Army, Richmond) 1927 *E, S, W, A*, 1928 *F*
McVicker, J (Collegians) 1924 *F, E, S, W, NZ*, 1925 *F, E, S, W*, 1926 *F, E, S, W*, 1927 *F, E, S, W, A*, 1928 *W*, 1930 *F*
McVicker, S (Queen's U, Belfast) 1922 *E, S, W, F*
Madden, M N (Sunday's Well) 1955 *E, S, W*
Magee, J T (Bective Rangers) 1895 *E, S*
Magee, A M (Louis) (Bective Rangers, London Irish) 1895 *E, S, W*, 1896 *E, S W*, 1897 *E, S*, 1898 *E, S, W*, 1899 *E, S, W*, 1900 *E, S, W*, 1901 *E, S, W*, 1902 *E, S, W*, 1903 *E, S, W*, 1904 *W*
Maginiss, R M (Dublin U) 1875 *E*, 1876 *E*
Magrath, R M (Cork Constitution) 1909 *S*
Maguire, J F (Cork) 1884 *S*
Mahony, J (Dolphin) 1923 *E*
Malcolmson, G L (RAF, NIFC) 1935 *NZ*, 1936 *E, S, W*, 1937 *E, S, W*
Mannion N P (Corinthians) 1988 *WS, It*, 1989 *F, W, E, S, NZ*, 1990 *E, S, F, W*
Marshall, B D E (Queen's U, Belfast) 1963 *E*
Massey-Westropp, R H (Limerick, Monkstown) 1886 *E*
Matier, R N (NIFC) 1878 *E*, 1879 *S*
Matthews, P M (Ards, Wanderers) 1984 *A*, 1985 *S, F, W, E*, 1986 *F*, 1987 *E, S, F, W*, [*W, Tg, A*], 1988 *S, F, W, E* 1,2, *WS, It*, 1989 *F, W, E, S, NZ*, 1990 *E, S*
Mattsson, J (Wanderers) 1948 *E*
Mayne, R B (Queen's U, Belfast) 1937 *W*, 1938 *E, W*, 1939 *E, S, W*
Mayne, R H (Belfast Academy) 1888 *W, S*
Mayne, T (NIFC) 1921 *E, S, F*
Mays, K M A (UC Dublin) 1973 *NZ, E, S, W*
Meares, A W D (Dublin U) 1899 *S, W*, 1900 *E, W*
Megaw, J (Richmond, Instonians) 1934 *W*, 1938 *E*
Millar, A (Kingstown) 1880 *E, S*, 1883 *E*
Millar, H J (Monkstown) 1904 *W*, 1905 *E, S, W*

Millar, S (Ballymena) 1958 *F*, 1959 *E, S, W, F*, 1960 *E, S, W, F, SA*, 1961 *E, S, W, F, SA*, 1962 *E, S, F*, 1963 *F, E, S, W*, 1964 *F*, 1968 *F, E, S, W, A*, 1969 *F, E, S, W*, 1970 *SA, F, E, S, W*
Millar, W H J (Queen's U, Belfast) 1951 *E, S, W*, 1952 *S, W*
Miller, F H (Wanderers) 1886 *S*
Milliken, R A (Bangor) 1973 *E, S, W, F*, 1974 *F, W, E, S, P, NZ*, 1975 *E, S, F, W*
Millin, T J (Dublin U) 1925 *W*
Minch, J B (Bective Rangers) 1912 *SA*, 1913 *E, S*, 1914 *E, S*
Moffat, J (Belfast Academy) 1888 *W, S, M*, 1889 *S*, 1890 *S, W*, 1891 *S*
Moffatt, J E (Old Wesley) 1904 *S*, 1905 *E, S, W*
Moffett, J W (Ballymena) 1961 *E, S*
Molloy, M G (UC Galway, London Irish) 1966 *F, E*, 1967 *A* 1, *E, S, W, F, A* 2, 1968 *F, E, S, W, A*, 1969 *F, E, S, W*, 1970 *F, E, S, W*, 1971 *F, E, S, W*, 1973 *F*, 1976 *A*
Moloney, J J (St Mary's Coll) 1972 *F* 1, *E, F* 2, 1973 *NZ, E, S, W, F*, 1974 *F, W, E, S, P, NZ*, 1975 *E, S, F, W*, 1976 *S*, 1978 *S, F, W, E*, 1979 *A* 1,2, 1980 *S, W*
Moloney, L A (Garryowen) 1976 *W* (R), *S*, 1978 *S* (R), *NZ*
Molony, J U (UC Dublin) 1950 *S*
Monteith, J D E (Queen's U, Belfast) 1947 *E, S, W*
Montgomery, A (NIFC) 1895 *S*
Montgomery, F P (Queen's U, Belfast) 1914 *E, S, W*
Montgomery, R (Cambridge U) 1887 *E, S, W*, 1891 *E*, 1892 *W*
Moore, C M (Dublin U) 1887 *S*, 1888 *W, S*
Moore, D F (Wanderers) 1883 *E, S*, 1884 *E, W*
Moore, F W (Wanderers) 1884 *W*, 1885 *E, S* 2, 1886 *S*
Moore, H (Windsor) 1876 *E*, 1877 *S*
Moore, H (Queen's U, Belfast) 1910 *S*, 1911 *W, F*, 1912 *F, E, S, W, SA*
Moore, T A P (Highfield) 1967 *A* 2, 1973 *NZ, E, S, W, F*, 1974 *F, W, E, S, P, NZ*
Moore, W D (Queen's Coll, Belfast) 1878 *E*
Moran, F G (Clontarf) 1936 *E*, 1937 *E, S, W*, 1938 *S, W*, 1939 *E, S, W*
Morell, H B (Dublin U) 1881 *E, S*, 1882 *W, E*
Morgan, G J (Clontarf) 1934 *E, S, W*, 1935 *E, S, W, NZ*, 1936 *E, S, W*, 1937 *E, S, W*, 1938 *E, S, W*, 1939 *E, S, W*
Moriarty, C C H (Monkstown) 1899 *W*
Moroney, J C M (Garryowen) 1968 *W, A*, 1969 *F, E, S, W*
Moroney, R J M (Lansdowne) 1984 *F, W*, 1985 *F*
Moroney, T A (UC Dublin) 1964 *W*, 1967 *A* 1, *E, S*
Morphy, E McG (Dublin U) 1908 *E*
Morris, D P (Bective Rangers) 1931 *W*, 1932 *E*, 1935 *S, W, NZ*
Morrow, J W R (Queen's Coll, Belfast) 1882 *S*, 1883 *E, S*, 1884 *E, W*, 1885 *S* 1,2, 1886 *E, S*, 1888 *S*
Morrow R D (Bangor) 1986 *F, E, S*
Mortell, M (Bective Rangers, Dolphin) 1953 *F, E, S, W*, 1954 *NZ, F, E, S, W*
Morton, W A (Dublin U) 1888 *S*
Moyers, L W (Dublin U) 1884 *W*
Moylett, M M F (Shannon) 1988 *E* 1
Mulcahy, W A (UC Dublin, Bective Rangers, Bohemians) 1958 *A, E, S, W, F*, 1959 *E, S, W, F*, 1960 *E, S, W, SA*, 1961 *E, S, W, SA*, 1962 *E, S, F, W*, 1963 *F, E, S, W, NZ*, 1964 *E, S, W, F*, 1965 *F, E, S, W, SA*
Mullan, B (Clontarf) 1947 *F, E, S, W*, 1948 *F, E, S, W*
Mullane, J P (Limerick Bohemians) 1928 *W*, 1929 *F*
Mullen, K D (Old Belvedere) 1947 *F, E, S, W, A*, 1948 *F, E, S, W*, 1949 *F, E, S, W*, 1950 *F, E, S, W*, 1951 *F, E, S, W, SA*, 1952 *F, S, W*
Mulligan, A A (Wanderers) 1956 *F, E*, 1957 *F, E, S, W*, 1958 *A, E, S, F*, 1959 *E, S, W, F*, 1960 *E, S, W, F, SA*, 1961 *W, F, S*
Mullin, B J (Dublin U, Oxford U, Blackrock Coll, London Irish) 1984 *A*, 1985 *S, W, E*, 1986 *F, W, E, S, R*, 1987 *E, S, F, W*, [*W, C, Tg, A*], 1988 *S, F, W, E* 1,2, *WS, It*, 1989 *F, W, E, S, NZ*, 1990 *E, S, W*
Murphy, C J (Lansdowne) 1939 *E, S, W*, 1947 *F, E*
Murphy, J G M W (London Irish) 1951 *SA*, 1952 *S, W, E*, 1954 *NZ*, 1958 *W*
Murphy, J J (Greystones) 1981 *SA* 1, 1982 *W* (R), 1984 *S*

221

Murphy, K (Cork Constitution) 1990 *E, S, F, W*
Murphy, N A A (Cork Constitution) 1958 *A, E, S, W, F,* 1959 *E, S, W, F,* 1960 *E, S, W, F, SA,* 1961 *E, S, W,* 1962 *E,* 1963 *NZ,* 1964 *E, S, W, F,* 1965 *F, E, S, W, SA,* 1966 *F, E, S, W,* 1967 *A* 1, *E, S, W, F,* 1969 *F, E, S, W*
Murphy, N F (Cork Constitution) 1930 *E, W,* 1931 *F, E, S, W, SA,* 1932 *E, S, W,* 1933 *E*
Murphy-O'Connor, J (Bective Rangers) 1954 *E*
Murray, H W (Dublin) 1877 *S,* 1878 *E,* 1879 *E*
Murray, J B (UC Dublin) 1963 *F*
Murray, P F (Wanderers) 1927 *F,* 1929 *F, E, S,* 1930 *F, E, S, W,* 1931 *F, E, S, W, SA,* 1932 *E, S, W,* 1933 *E, W, S*
Murtagh, C W (Portadown) 1977 *S*
Myles, J (Dublin U) 1875 *E*

Nash, L C (Queen's Coll, Cork) 1889 *S,* 1890 *W, E,* 1891 *E, S, W*
Neely, M R (Collegians) 1947 *F, E, S, W*
Neill, H J (NIFC) 1885 *E, S* 1,2, 1886 *S,* 1887 *E, S, W,* 1888 *W, S*
Neill, J McF (Instonians) 1926 *F*
Nelson, J E (Malone) 1947 *A,* 1948 *E, S, W,* 1949 *F, E, S, W,* 1950 *F, E, S, W,* 1951 *F, E, W,* 1954 *F*
Nelson, R (Queen's Coll, Belfast) 1882 *E, S,* 1883 *S,* 1886 *S*
Nesdale, T J (Garryowen) 1961 *F*
Neville, W C (Dublin U) 1879 *S, E*
Nicholson, P C (Dublin U) 1900 *E, S, W*
Norton, G W (Bective Rangers) 1949 *F, E, S, W,* 1950 *F, E, S, W,* 1951 *F, E, S*
Notley, J R (Wanderers) 1952 *F, S*

O'Brien, B (Derry) 1893 *S, W*
O'Brien, B A P (Shannon) 1968 *F, E, S*
O'Brien, D J (London Irish, Cardiff, Old Belvedere) 1948 *E, S, W,* 1949 *F, E, S, W,* 1950 *F, E, S, W,* 1951 *F, E, S, W, SA,* 1952 *F, S, W, E*
O'Brien, K A (Broughton Park) 1980 *E,* 1981 *SA* 1 (R), 2
O'Brien-Butler, P E (Monkstown) 1897 *S,* 1898 *E, S,* 1899 *S, W,* 1900 *E*
O'Callaghan, C T (Carlow) 1910 *W, F,* 1911 *E, S, W, F,* 1912 *F*
O'Callaghan, M P (Sunday's Well) 1962 *W,* 1964 *E, F*
O' Callaghan, P (Dolphin) 1967 *A* 1, *E, A* 2, 1968 *F, E, S, W,* 1969 *F, E, S, W,* 1970 *SA, F, E, S, W,* 1976 *F, W, E, S, NZ*
O'Connell, P (Bective Rangers) 1913 *W, F,* 1914 *F, E, S, W*
O'Connell, W J (Lansdowne) 1955 *F*
O'Connor, H S (Dublin U) 1957 *F, E, S, W*
O'Connor, J (Garryowen) 1895 *S*
O'Connor, J H (Bective Rangers) 1888 *M,* 1890 *S, W, E,* 1891 *E, S,* 1892 *E, W,* 1893 *E, S,* 1894 *E, S, W,* 1895 *E,* 1896 *E, S, W*
O'Connor, J J (Garryowen) 1909 *F*
O'Connor, J J (UC Cork) 1933 *E, S, W,* 1934 *E, S, W,* 1935 *E, S, W, NZ,* 1936 *S, W,* 1938 *S*
O'Connor, P J (Lansdowne) 1887 *W*
Odbert, R V M (RAF) 1928 *F*
O'Donnell, R C (St Mary's Coll) 1979 *A* 1,2, 1980 *S, F, W*
O'Donoghue, P J (Bective Rangers) 1955 *F, E, S, W,* 1956 *W,* 1957 *F, E,* 1958 *A, E, S, W*
O'Driscoll, B J (Manchester) 1971 *F* (R), *E, S, W*
O'Driscoll, J B (London Irish, Manchester) 1978 *S,* 1979 *A* 1,2, 1980 *E, S, F, W,* 1981 *F, W, E, S, SA* 1,2, *A,* 1982 *W, E, S, F,* 1983 *S, F, W, E,* 1984 *F, W, E, S*
O'Flanagan, K P (London Irish) 1947 *A*
O'Flanagan, M (Lansdowne) 1948 *S*
O'Hanlon, B (Dolphin) 1947 *E, S, W,* 1948 *F, E, S, W,* 1949 *F, E, S, W,* 1950 *F*
O'Hara, P T J (Sunday's Well) 1988 *WS* (R), 1989 *F, W, E, NZ,* 1990 *E, S, F, W*
O'Leary, A (Cork Constitution) 1952 *S, W, E*
O'Loughlin, D B (UC Cork) 1938 *E, S, W,* 1939 *E, S, W*
O'Meara, J A (UC Cork, Dolphin) 1951 *F, E, S, W, SA,* 1952 *F, S, W, E,* 1953 *F, E, S, W,* 1954 *NZ, F, E, S,* 1955 *F, E,* 1956 *S, W,* 1958 *W*
O'Neill, H O'H (Queen's U, Belfast, UC Cork) 1930 *E, S, W,* 1933 *E, S, W*

O'Neill, J B (Queen's U, Belfast) 1920 *S*
O'Neill, W A (UC Dublin, Wanderers) 1952 *E,* 1953 *F, E, S, W,* 1954 *NZ*
O'Reilly, A J F (Old Belvedere, Leicester) 1955 *F, E, S, W,* 1956 *F, E, S, W,* 1957 *F, E, S, W,* 1958 *A, E, S, W, F,* 1959 *E, S, W, F,* 1960 *E,* 1961 *E, F, SA,* 1963 *F, S, W,* 1970 *E*
Orr, P A (Old Wesley) 1976 *F, W, E, S, NZ,* 1977 *W, E, S, F,* 1978 *S, F, W, E, NZ,* 1979 *F, W, E, S, A* 1,2, 1980 *E, S, F, W,* 1981 *F, W, E, S, SA* 1,2, *A,* 1982 *W, E, S, F,* 1983 *S, F, W, E,* 1984 *F, W, E, S, A,* 1985 *S, F, W, E,* 1986 *F, S, R,* 1987 *E, S, F, W,* [*W, C, A*]
O'Sullivan, A C (Dublin U) 1882 *S*
O'Sullivan, J M (Limerick) 1884 *S,* 1887 *S*
O'Sullivan, P J A (Galwegians) 1957 *F, E, S, W,* 1959 *E, S, W, F,* 1960 *SA,* 1961 *S,* 1962 *F, W,* 1963 *F, NZ*
O'Sullivan, W (Queen's Coll, Cork) 1895 *S*
Owens, R H (Dublin U) 1922 *E, S*

Parfrey, P (UC Cork) 1974 *NZ*
Parke, J C (Monkstown) 1903 *W,* 1904 *E, S, W,* 1905 *W, NZ,* 1906 *E, S, W, SA,* 1907 *E, S, W,* 1908 *E, S, W,* 1909 *E, S, W, F*
Parr, J S (Wanderers) 1914 *F, E, S, W*
Patterson, C S (Instonians) 1978 *NZ,* 1979 *F, W, E, S, A* 1,2, 1980 *E, S, F, W*
Patterson, R d'A (Wanderers) 1912 *F, S, W, SA,* 1913 *E, S, W, F*
Payne, C T (NIFC) 1926 *E,* 1927 *F, E, S, A,* 1928 *F, E, S, W,* 1929 *F, E, W,* 1930 *F, E, S, W*
Pedlow, A C (CIYMS) 1953 *W,* 1954 *NZ, F, E,* 1955 *F, E, S, W,* 1956 *F, E, S, W,* 1957 *F, E, S, W,* 1958 *A, E, S, W, F,* 1959 *E,* 1960 *E, S, W, F, SA,* 1961 *S,* 1962 *W,* 1963 *F*
Pedlow, J (Bessbrook) 1882 *S,* 1884 *W*
Pedlow, R (Bessbrook) 1891 *W*
Pedlow, T B (Queen's Coll, Belfast) 1889 *S, W*
Peel, T (Limerick) 1892 *E, S, W*
Peirce, W (Cork) 1881 *E*
Phipps, G C (Army) 1950 *E, W,* 1952 *F, W, E*
Pike, T O (Lansdowne) 1927 *E, S, W, A,* 1928 *F, E, S, W*
Pike, V J (Lansdowne) 1931 *E, S, W, SA,* 1932 *E, S, W,* 1933 *E, W, S,* 1934 *E, S, W*
Pike, W W (Kingstown) 1879 *E,* 1881 *E, S,* 1882 *E,* 1883 *S*
Pinion, G (Belfast Collegians) 1909 *E, S, W, F*
Piper, O J S (Cork Constitution) 1909 *E, S, W, F,* 1910 *E, S, W, F*
Polden, S E (Clontarf) 1913 *W, F,* 1914 *F,* 1920 *F*
Popham, I (Cork Constitution) 1922 *S, W, F,* 1923 *F*
Popplewell, N J (Greystones) 1989 *NZ*
Potterton, H N (Wanderers) 1920 *W*
Pratt, R H (Dublin U) 1933 *E, W, S,* 1934 *E, S*
Price, A H (Dublin U) 1920 *S, F*
Pringle, J C (NIFC) 1902 *S, W*
Purcell, N M (Lansdowne) 1921 *E, S, W, F*
Purdon, H (NIFC) 1879 *S, E,* 1880 *E,* 1881 *E, S*
Purdon, W B (Queen's Coll, Belfast) 1906 *E, S, W*
Purser, F C (Dublin U) 1898 *E, S, W*

Quinlan, S V J (Blackrock Coll) 1956 *F, E, W,* 1958 *W*
Quinn, B T (Old Belvedere) 1947 *F*
Quinn, F P (Old Belvedere) 1981 *F, W, E*
Quinn, J P (Dublin U) 1910 *E, S,* 1911 *E, S, W, F,* 1912 *E, S, W,* 1913 *E, W, F,* 1914 *F, E, S*
Quinn, K (Old Belvedere) 1947 *F, A,* 1953 *F, E, S*
Quinn, M A M (Lansdowne) 1973 *F,* 1974 *F, W, E, S, P, NZ,* 1977 *S, F,* 1981 *SA* 2
Quirke, J M T (Blackrock Coll) 1962 *E, S,* 1968 *S*

Rainey, P I (Ballymena) 1989 *NZ*
Rambaut, D F (Dublin U) 1887 *E, S, W,* 1888 *W*
Rea, H H (Edinburgh U) 1967 *A* 1, 1969 *F*
Read, H M (Dublin U) 1910 *S,* 1911 *E, S, W, F,* 1912 *F, E, S, W, SA,* 1913 *E, S*
Rearden, J V (Cork Constitution) 1934 *E, S*
Reid, C (NIFC) 1899 *S, W,* 1900 *E,* 1903 *W*
Reid, J L (Richmond) 1934 *S, W*
Reid, P J (Garryowen) 1947 *A,* 1948 *F, E, W*
Reid, T E (Garryowen) 1953 *E, S, W,* 1954 *F, NZ,* 1955 *E, S,* 1956 *F, E,* 1957 *F, E, S, W*
Reidy, C J (London Irish) 1937 *W*

Reidy, G F (Dolphin, Lansdowne) 1953 *W*, 1954 *F*, *E*, *S*, *W*

Richey, H A (Dublin U) 1889 *W*, 1890 *S*

Ridgeway, E C (Wanderers) 1932 *S*, *W*, 1935 *E*, *S*, *W*

Ringland, T M (Queen's U, Belfast, Ballymena) 1981 *A*, 1982 *W*, *E*, *F*, 1983 *S*, *F*, *W*, *E*, 1984 *F*, *W*, *E*, *S*, *A*, 1985 *S*, *F*, *W*, *E*, 1986 *F*, *W*, *E*, *S*, *R*, 1987 *E*, *S*, *F*, *W*, [*W*, *C*, *Tg*, *A*], 1988 *S*, *F*, *W*, *E* 1

Riordan, W F (Cork Constitution) 1910 *E*

Ritchie, J S (London Irish) 1956 *F*, *E*

Robb, C G (Queen's Coll, Belfast) 1904 *E*, *S*, *W*, 1905 *NZ*, 1906 *S*

Robbie, J C (Dublin U, Greystones) 1976 *A*, *F*, *NZ*, 1977 *S*, *F*, 1981 *F*, *W*, *E*, *S*

Robinson, T T H (Wanderers) 1904 *E*, *S*, 1905 *E*, *S*, *W*, *NZ*, 1906 *SA*, 1907 *E*, *S*, *W*

Roche, J (Wanderers) 1890 *S*, *W*, *E*, 1891 *E*, *S*, *W*, 1892 *W*

Roche, R E (UC Galway) 1955 *E*, *S*, 1957 *S*, *W*

Roche, W J (UC Cork) 1920 *E*, *S*, *F*

Roddy, P J (Bective Rangers) 1920 *S*, *F*

Roe, R (Lansdowne) 1952 *F*, 1953 *F*, *E*, *S*, *W*, 1954 *F*, *E*, *S*, *W*, 1955 *F*, *E*, *S*, *W*, 1956 *F*, *E*, *S*, *W*, 1957 *F*, *E*, *S*, *W*

Rooke, C V (Dublin U) 1891 *E*, *W*, 1892 *E*, *S*, *W*, 1893 *E*, *S*, *W*, 1894 *E*, *S*, *W*, 1895 *E*, *S*, *W*, 1896 *E*, *S*, *W*, 1897 *E*, *S*

Ross, D J (Belfast Academy) 1884 *E*, 1885 *S* 1,2, 1886 *E*, *S*

Ross, G R P (CIYMS) 1955 *W*

Ross, J F (NIFC) 1886 *S*

Ross, J P (Lansdowne) 1885 *E*, *S* 1,2, 1886 *E*, *S*

Ross, N G (Malone) 1927 *F*, *E*

Ross, W McC (Queen's U, Belfast) 1932 *E*, *S*, *W*, 1933 *E*, *W*, *S*, 1934 *E*, *S*, 1935 *NZ*

Russell, J (UC Cork) 1931 *F*, *E*, *S*, *W*, *SA*, 1933 *E*, *W*, *S*, 1934 *E*, *S*, *W*, 1935 *E*, *S*, *W*, 1936 *E*, *S*, *W*, 1937 *E*, *S*

Russell, P (Instonians) 1990 *E*

Rutherford, W G (Tipperary) 1884 *E*, *S*, 1885 *E*, *S* 1, 1886 *E*, 1888 *W*

Ryan, E (Dolphin) 1937 *W*, 1938 *E*, *S*

Ryan, J (Rockwell Coll) 1897 *E*, 1898 *E*, *S*, *W*, 1899 *E*, *S*, *W*, 1900 *S*, *W*, 1901 *E*, *S*, *W*, 1902 *E*, 1904 *E*

Ryan, J G (UC Dublin) 1939 *E*, *S*, *W*

Ryan, M (Rockwell Coll) 1897 *E*, *S*, 1898 *E*, *S*, *W*, 1899 *E*, *S*, *W*, 1900 *E*, *S*, *W*, 1901 *E*, *S*, *W*, 1903 *E*, 1904 *E*, *S*

Sayers, H J M (Lansdowne) 1935 *E*, *S*, *W*, 1936 *E*, *S*, *W*, 1938 *W*, 1939 *E*, *S*, *W*

Schute, F (Wanderers) 1878 *E*, 1879 *E*

Schute, F G (Dublin U) 1912 *SA*, 1913 *E*, *S*

Scott, D (Malone) 1961 *F*, *SA*, 1962 *S*

Scott, R D (Queen's U, Belfast) 1967 *E*, *F*, 1968 *F*, *E*, *S*

Scovell, R H (Kingstown) 1883 *E*, 1884 *E*

Scriven, G (Dublin U) 1879 *S*, *E*, 1880 *E*, *S*, 1881 *E*, 1882 *S*, 1883 *E*, *S*

Sealy, J (Dublin U) 1896 *E*, *S*, *W*, 1897 *S*, 1899 *E*, *S*, *W*, 1900 *E*, *S*

Sexton, J F (Dublin U, Lansdowne) 1988 *E* 2, *WS*, *It*, 1989 *F*

Sexton, W J (Garryowen) 1984 *A*, 1988 *S*, *E* 2

Shanahan, T (Lansdowne) 1885 *E*, *S* 1,2, 1886 *E*, 1888 *S*, *W*

Shaw, G M (Windsor) 1877 *S*

Sheehan, M D (London Irish) 1932 *E*

Sherry, B F (Terenure Coll) 1967 *A* 1, *E*, *S*, *A* 2, 1968 *F*, *E*

Sherry, M J A (Lansdowne) 1975 *F*, *W*

Siggins, J A E (Belfast Collegians) 1931 *F*, *E*, *S*, *W*, *SA*, 1932 *E*, *S*, *W*, 1933 *E*, *W*, *S*, 1934 *E*, *S*, *W*, 1935 *E*, *S*, *W*, *NZ*, 1936 *E*, *S*, *W*, 1937 *E*, *S*, *W*

Slattery, J F (UC Dublin, Blackrock Coll) 1970 *SA*, *F*, *E*, *S*, *W*, 1971 *F*, *E*, *S*, *W*, 1972 *F* 1, *E*, *F* 2, 1973 *NZ*, *E*, *S*, *W*, *F*, 1974 *F*, *W*, *E*, *S*, *P*, *NZ*, 1975 *E*, *S*, *F*, *W*, 1976 *A*, 1977 *S*, *F*, 1978 *S*, *F*, *W*, *E*, *NZ*, 1979 *F*, *W*, *E*, *S*, *A* 1,2, 1980 *E*, *S*, *F*, *W*, 1981 *F*, *W*, *E*, *S*, *SA* 1,2, *A*, 1982 *W*, *E*, *S*, *F*, 1983 *S*, *F*, *W*, *E*, 1984 *F*

Smartt, F N B (Dublin U) 1908 *E*, *S*, 1909 *E*

Smith, B A (Oxford U) 1989 *NZ*, 1990 *S*, *F*, *W*

Smith, J H (London Irish) 1951 *F*, *E*, *S*, *W*, *SA*, 1952 *F*, *S*, *W*, *E*, 1954 *NZ*, *W*, *F*

Smith, R E (Lansdowne) 1892 *E*

Smith, S J (Ballymena) 1988 *E* 2, *WS*, *It*, 1989 *F*, *W*, *E*, *S*, *NZ*, 1990 *E*

Smithwick, F F S (Monkstown) 1898 *S*, *W*

Smyth, J T (Queen's U, Belfast) 1920 *F*

Smyth, P J (Belfast Collegians) 1911 *E*, *S*, *F*

Smyth, R S (Dublin U) 1903 *E*, *S*, 1904 *E*

Smyth, T (Malone, Newport) 1908 *E*, *S*, *W*, 1909 *E*, *S*, *W*, 1910 *E*, *S*, *W*, *F*, 1911 *E*, *S*, *W*, 1912 *E*

Smyth, W S (Belfast Collegians) 1910 *W*, *F*, 1920 *E*

Solomons, B A H (Dublin U) 1908 *E*, *S*, *W*, 1909 *E*, *S*, *W*, *F*, 1910 *E*, *S*, *W*

Spain, A W (UC Dublin) 1924 *NZ*

Sparrow, W (Dublin U) 1893 *W*, 1894 *E*

Spillane, B J (Bohemians) 1985 *S*, *F*, *W*, *E*, 1986 *F*, *W*, *E*, 1987 *F*, *W*, [*W*, *C*, *A*(R)], 1989 *E* (R)

Spring, D E (Dublin U) 1978 *S*, *NZ*, 1979 *S*, 1980 *S*, *F*, *W*, 1981 *W*

Spring, R M (Lansdowne) 1979 *F*, *W*, *E*

Spunner, H F (Wanderers) 1881 *E*, *S*, 1884 *W*

Stack, C R R (Dublin U) 1889 *S*

Stack, G H (Dublin U) 1875 *E*

Steele, H W (Ballymena) 1976 *E*, 1977 *F*, 1978 *F*, *W*, *E*, 1979 *F*, *W*, *E*, *A* 1,2

Stephenson, G V (Queen's U, Belfast, London Hosp) 1920 *F*, 1921 *E*, *S*, *W*, *F*, 1922 *E*, *S*, *W*, *F*, 1923 *E*, *S*, *W*, *F*, 1924 *F*, *E*, *S*, *W*, *NZ*, 1925 *F*, *E*, *S*, *W*, 1926 *F*, *E*, *S*, *W*, 1927 *F*, *E*, *S*, *W*, *A*, 1928 *F*, *E*, *S*, *W*, 1929 *F*, *E*, *W*, 1930 *F*, *E*, *S*, *W*

Stephenson, H W V (United Services) 1922 *S*, *W*, *F*, 1924 *F*, *E*, *S*, *W*, *NZ*, 1925 *F*, *E*, *S*, *W*, 1927 *A*, 1928 *E*

Stevenson, J (Dungannon) 1888 *M*, 1889 *S*

Stevenson, J B (Instonians) 1958 *A*, *E*, *S*, *W*, *F*

Stevenson, R (Dungannon) 1887 *E*, *S*, *W*, 1888 *M*, 1889 *S*, *W*, 1890 *S*, *W*, *E*, 1891 *W*, 1892 *W*, 1893 *E*, *S*, *W*

Stevenson, T H (Belfast Acad) 1895 *E*, *W*, 1896 *E*, *S*, *W*, 1897 *E*, *S*

Stewart, A L (NIFC) 1913 *W*, *F*, 1914 *F*

Stewart, W J (Queen's U, Belfast, NIFC) 1922 *F*, 1924 *S*, 1928 *F*, *E*, *S*, *W*, 1929 *F*, *E*, *S*, *W*

Stoker, E W (Wanderers) 1888 *W*, *S*

Stoker, F O (Wanderers) 1886 *S*, 1888 *W*, *M*, 1889 *S*, 1891 *W*

Stokes, O S (Cork Bankers) 1882 *E*, 1884 *E*

Stokes, P (Garryowen) 1913 *E*, *S*, 1914 *F*, 1920 *E*, *S*, *W*, *F*, 1921 *E*, *S*, *F*, 1922 *W*, *F*

Stokes, R D (Queen's Coll, Cork) 1891 *S*, *W*

Strathdee, E (Queen's U, Belfast) 1947 *E*, *S*, *W*, *A*, 1948 *W*, *F*, 1949 *E*, *S*, *W*

Stuart, C P (Clontarf) 1912 *SA*

Stuart, I M B (Dublin U) 1924 *E*, *S*

Sugars, H S (Dublin U) 1905 *NZ*, 1906 *SA*, 1907 *S*

Sugden, M (Wanderers) 1925 *F*, *E*, *S*, *W*, 1926 *F*, *E*, *S*, *W*, 1927 *E*, *S*, *W*, *A*, 1928 *F*, *E*, *S*, *W*, 1929 *F*, *E*, *S*, *W*, 1930 *F*, *E*, *S*, *W*, 1931 *F*, *E*, *S*, *W*

Sullivan, D B (UC Dublin) 1922 *E*, *S*, *W*, *F*

Sweeney, J A (Blackrock Coll) 1907 *E*, *S*, *W*

Symes, G R (Monkstown) 1895 *E*

Synge, J S (Lansdowne) 1929 *S*

Taggart, T (Dublin U) 1887 *W*

Taylor, A S (Queen's Coll, Belfast) 1910 *E*, *S*, *W*, 1912 *F*

Taylor, D R (Queen's Coll, Belfast) 1903 *E*

Taylor, J (Belfast Collegians) 1914 *E*, *S*, *W*

Taylor, J W (NIFC) 1879 *S*, 1880 *E*, *S*, 1881 *S*, 1882 *E*, *S*, 1883 *E*, *S*

Tector, W R (Wanderers) 1955 *F*, *E*, *S*

Tedford, A (Malone) 1902 *E*, *S*, *W*, 1903 *E*, *S*, *W*, 1904 *E*, *S*, *W*, 1905 *E*, *S*, *W*, *NZ*, 1906 *E*, *S*, *W*, *SA*, 1907 *E*, *S*, *W*, 1908 *E*, *S*, *W*

Teehan, C (UC Cork) 1939 *E*, *S*, *W*

Thompson, C (Belfast Collegians) 1907 *E*, *S*, 1908 *E*, *S*, *W*, 1909 *E*, *S*, *W*, *F*, 1910 *E*, *S*, *W*, *F*

Thompson, J A (Queen's Coll, Belfast) 1885 *S* 1,2

Thompson, J K S (Dublin U) 1921 *W*, 1922 *E*, *S*, *F*, 1923 *E*, *S*, *W*, *F*

Thompson, R G (Lansdowne) 1882 *W*

Thompson, R H (Instonians) 1951 *SA*, 1952 *F*, 1954 *NZ*, *F*, *E*, *S*, *W*, 1955 *F*, *S*, *W*, 1956 *W*

Thornhill, T (Wanderers) 1892 *E*, *S*, *W*, 1893 *E*

Thrift, H (Dublin U) 1904 *W*, 1905 *E*, *S*, *W*, *NZ*, 1906 *E*, *W*, *SA*, 1907 *E*, *S*, *W*, 1908 *E*, *S*, *W*, 1909 *E*, *S*, *W*, *F*

Tierney, D (UC Cork) 1938 *S*, *W*, 1939 *E*

Tillie, C R (Dublin U) 1887 *E, S*, 1888 *W, S*
Todd, A W P (Dublin U) 1913 *W, F*, 1914 *F*
Torrens, J D (Bohemians) 1938 *W*, 1939 *E, S, W*
Tucker, C C (Shannon) 1979 *F, W*, 1980 *F* (R)
Tuke, B B (Bective Rangers) 1890 *E*, 1891 *E, S*, 1892 *E*, 1894 *E, S, W*, 1895 *E, S*
Turley, N (Blackrock Coll) 1962 *E*
Tydings, J J (Young Munster) 1968 *A*
Tyrrell, W (Queen's U, Belfast) 1910 *F*, 1913 *E, S, W, F*, 1914 *F, E, S, W*

Uprichard, R J H (Harlequins, RAF) 1950 *S, W*

Waide, S L (Oxford U, NIFC) 1932 *E, S, W*, 1933 *E, W*
Waites, J (Bective Rangers) 1886 *S*, 1888 *M*, 1889 *W*, 1890 *S, W, E*, 1891 *E*
Waldron, O C (Oxford U, London Irish) 1966 *S, W*, 1968 *A*
Walker, S (Instonians) 1934 *E, S*, 1935 *E, S, W, NZ*, 1936 *E, S, W*, 1937 *E, S, W*, 1938 *E, S, W*
Walkington, D B (NIFC) 1887 *E, W*, 1888 *W*, 1890 *W, E*, 1891 *E, S, W*
Walkington, R B (NIFC) 1875 *E*, 1876 *E*, 1877 *E, S*, 1878 *E*, 1879 *S*, 1880 *E, S*, 1882 *E, S*
Wall, H (Dolphin) 1965 *S, W*
Wallace, Jas (Wanderers) 1904 *E, S*
Wallace, Jos (Wanderers) 1903 *S, W*, 1904 *E, S, W*, 1905 *E, S, W, NZ*, 1906 *W*
Wallace, T H (Cardiff) 1920 *E, S, W*
Wallis, A K (Wanderers) 1892 *E, S, W*, 1893 *E, W*
Wallis, C O'N (Old Cranleighans, Wanderers) 1935 *NZ*
Wallis, T G (Wanderers) 1921 *F*, 1922 *E, S, W, F*
Wallis, W A (Wanderers) 1880 *S*, 1881 *E, S*, 1882 *W*, 1883 *S*
Walmsley, G (Bective Rangers) 1894 *E*
Walpole, A (Dublin U) 1888 *S, M*
Walsh, E J (Lansdowne) 1887 *E, S, W*, 1892 *E, S, W*, 1893 *E*
Walsh, H D (Dublin U) 1875 *E*, 1876 *E*
Walsh, J C (UC Cork, Sunday's Well) 1960 *S, SA*, 1961 *E, S, F, SA*, 1963 *E, S, W, NZ*, 1964 *E, S, W, F*, 1965 *F, S, W, SA*, 1966 *F, S, W*, 1967 *E, S, W, F, A* 2

Ward, A J P (Garryowen, St Mary's Coll, Greystones) 1978 *S, F, W, E, NZ*, 1979 *F, W, E, S*, 1981 *W, E, S, A*, 1983 *E* (R), 1984 *E, S*, 1986 *S*, 1987 [*C, Tg*]
Warren, J P (Kingstown) 1883 *E*
Warren, R G (Lansdowne) 1884 *W*, 1885 *E, S* 1,2, 1886 *E*, 1887 *E, S, W*, 1888 *W, S, M*, 1889 *S, W*, 1890 *S, W, E*
Watson, R (Wanderers) 1912 *SA*
Wells, H G (Bective Rangers) 1891 *S, W*, 1894 *E, S*
Westby, A J (Dublin U) 1876 *E*
Wheeler, G H (Queen's Coll, Belfast) 1884 *S*, 1885 *E*
Wheeler, J R (Queen's U, Belfast) 1922 *E, S, W, F*, 1924 *E*
Whelan, P C (Garryowen) 1975 *E, S*, 1976 *NZ*, 1977 *W, E, S, F*, 1978 *S, F, W, E, NZ*, 1979 *F, W, E, S*, 1981 *F, W, E*
White, M (Queen's Coll, Cork) 1906 *E, S, W, SA*, 1907 *E, W*
Whitestone, A M (Dublin U) 1877 *E*, 1879 *S, E*, 1880 *E*, 1883 *S*
Whittle, D (Bangor) 1988 *F*
Wilkinson, R W (Wanderers) 1947 *A*
Williamson, F W (Dolphin) 1930 *E, S, W*
Willis, W J (Lansdowne) 1879 *E*
Wilson, F (CIYMS) 1977 *W, E, S*
Wilson, H G (Glasgow U, Malone) 1905 *E, S, W, NZ*, 1906 *E, S, W, SA*, 1907 *E, S, W*, 1908 *E, S, W*, 1909 *E, S, W*, 1910 *W*
Wilson, W H (Bray) 1877 *E, S*
Withers, H H C (Army, Blackheath) 1931 *F, E, S, W, SA*
Wolfe, E J (Armagh) 1882 *E*
Wood, G H (Dublin U) 1913 *W*, 1914 *F*
Wood, B G M (Garryowen) 1954 *E, S*, 1956 *F, E, S, W*, 1957 *F, E, S, W*, 1958 *A, E, S, W, F*, 1959 *E, S, W, F*, 1960 *E, S, W, F, SA*, 1961 *E, S, W, F, SA*
Woods, D C (Bessbrook) 1888 *M*, 1889 *S*
Wright, R A (Monkstown) 1912 *S*

Yeates, R A (Dublin U) 1889 *S, W*
Young, G (UC Cork) 1913 *E*
Young, R M (Collegians) 1965 *F, E, S, W, SA*, 1966 *F, E, S, W*, 1967 *W, F*, 1968 *W, A*, 1969 *F, E, S, W*, 1970 *SA, F, E, S, W*, 1971 *F, E, S, W*

IRISH INTERNATIONAL RECORDS

Both team and individual records are for official Ireland international matches up to 30 April 1990.

TEAM RECORDS

Highest score
60 v Romania (60-0) 1986 Dublin
v individual countries
27 v Australia (27-12) 1979 Brisbane
46 v Canada (46-19) 1987 Dunedin
26 v England (26-21) 1974 Twickenham
25 v France { (25-5) 1911 Cork
              (25-6) 1975 Dublin
31 v Italy (31-15) 1988 Dublin
10 v N Zealand (10-10) 1973 Dublin
60 v Romania (60-0) 1986 Dublin
15 v S Africa (15-23) 1981 Cape Town
26 v Scotland (26-8) 1953 Murrayfield
32 v Tonga (32-9) 1987 Brisbane
21 v Wales { (21-24) 1979 Cardiff
             (21-7) 1980 Dublin
             (21-9) 1985 Cardiff
49 v W Samoa (49-22) 1988 Dublin

37 Scotland (21-37) 1989 Murrayfield
9 Tonga (32-9) 1987 Brisbane
34 Wales (9-34) 1976 Dublin
22 W Samoa (49-22) 1988 Dublin

Biggest losing points margin
38 v S Africa (0-38) 1912 Dublin
v individual countries
18 v Australia (15-33) 1987 Sydney
32 v England (3-35) 1988 Twickenham
23 v France (3-26) 1976 Paris
17 v N Zealand (6-23) 1989 Dublin
38 v S Africa (0-38) 1912 Dublin
23 v Scotland (9-32) 1984 Dublin
29 v Wales (0-29) 1907 Cardiff
No defeats v Canada, Italy, Romania, Tonga or W Samoa

Biggest winning points margin
60 v Romania (60-0) 1986 Dublin
v individual countries
15 v Australia (27-12) 1979 Brisbane
27 v Canada (46-19) 1987 Dunedin
22 v England (22-0) 1947 Dublin
24 v France (24-0) 1913 Cork
16 v Italy (31-15) 1988 Dublin
No win v N Zealand
60 v Romania (60-0) 1986 Dublin
3 v S Africa (9-6) 1965 Dublin
21 v Scotland (21-0) 1950 Dublin
23 v Tonga (32-9) 1987 Brisbane
16 v Wales (19-3) 1925 Belfast
27 v W Samoa (49-22) 1988 Dublin

Most tries by Ireland in an international
10 v Romania (60-0) 1986 Dublin

Most tries against Ireland in an international
10 by S Africa (0-38) 1912 Dublin

Most points by Ireland in International Championship in a season – 71
in season 1982-83

Most tries by Ireland in International Championship in a season – 12
in seasons 1927-28 and 1952-53

Highest score by opposing team
38 S Africa (0-38) 1912 Dublin
by individual countries
33 Australia (15-33) 1987 Sydney
19 Canada (46-19) 1987 Dunedin
36 England (14-36) 1938 Dublin
31 France (12-31) 1990 Paris
15 Italy (31-15) 1988 Dublin
23 N Zealand (6-23) 1989 Dublin
0 Romania (60-0) 1986 Dublin
38 S Africa (0-38) 1912 Dublin

INDIVIDUAL RECORDS

Most capped player
C M H Gibson   69   1964-79
in individual positions
Full-back
T J Kiernan   54   1960-73
Wing
T M Ringland   34   1981-88

Centre
C M H Gibson   40(69)[1]   1964-79
Fly-half
J W Kyle   46   1947-58
Scrum-half
M Sugden   28   1925-31
Prop
P A Orr   58   1976-87
Hooker
K W Kennedy   45   1965-75
Lock
W J McBride   63   1962-75
Flanker
J F Slattery   61   1970-84
No 8
W P Duggan   39(41)[2]   1975-84

[1]*Gibson won 40 caps as a centre, 25 at fly-half and 4 as a wing. G V Stephenson, 42 caps, won 37 as a centre and 5 on the wing. N J Henderson, 40 caps, won 35 as a centre and 5 at full-back and M J Kiernan, 41 caps, has won 33 as a centre and 8 as a wing.*
[2]*Duggan won 39 caps at No 8 and 2 as a flanker*

Longest international career
A J F O'Reilly 16 seasons 1955-70
C M H Gibson 16 seasons 1964-79
Gibson's career ended during a Southern Hemisphere season

Most internationals as captain
T J Kiernan   24   1963-73

Most points in internationals – 283
M J Kiernan (41 matches) 1982-90

Most points in International Championship in a season – 52
S O Campbell (4 matches) 1982-83

Most points in an international – 21
S O Campbell v Scotland 1982 Dublin
S O Campbell v England 1983 Dublin

Most tries in internationals – 14
G V Stephenson (42 matches) 1920-30

Most tries in International Championship in a season – 5
J E Arigho (3 matches) 1927-28

Most tries in an international – 3
R Montgomery v Wales 1887 Birkenhead

J P Quinn v France 1913 Cork
E O'D Davy v Scotland 1930 Murrayfield
S J Byrne v Scotland 1953 Murrayfield
K D Crossan v Romania 1986 Dublin
B J Mullin v Tonga 1987 Brisbane

Most conversions in internationals – 40
M J Kiernan (41 matches) 1982-90

Most conversions in International Championship in a season – 7
R A Lloyd (4 matches) 1912-13

Most conversions in an international – 7
M J Kiernan v Romania 1986 Dublin

Most dropped goals in internationals – 7
R A Lloyd (19 matches) 1910-20
S O Campbell (22 matches) 1976-84

Most penalty goals in internationals – 55
M J Kiernan (41 matches) 1982-90

Most penalty goals in International Championship in a season – 14
S O Campbell (4 matches) 1982-83

Most points for Ireland on overseas tour – 60
S O Campbell (5 appearances) 1979 Australia
M J Kiernan scored 65 points in Japan 1985, but this was not on a major tour

Most points in any match on tour – 19
A J P Ward v Australian Capital Territory 1979 Canberra
S O Campbell v Australia 1979 Brisbane
M J Kiernan scored 25 points in the second match against Japan 1985, but this was not on a major tour

Most tries in any match on tour – 3
A T A Duggan v Victoria 1967 Melbourne
J F Slattery v SA President's XV 1981 East London
M J Kiernan v Gold Cup XV 1981 Oudtshoorn, SA
T M Ringland scored 3 tries v Japan at Osaka 1985, but this was not on a major tour

A NATION IN TURMOIL

THE 1989-90 SEASON IN WALES

John Billot *Western Mail*

It was the rack and thumbscrews for Welsh rugby in every respect during the most turbulent and humiliating season in the history of the WRU. The president and the secretary resigned at the start of the season, and although Clive Rowlands was persuaded to resume his presidential duties, with massive support from the clubs, David East, after just eight months in the secretary's chair, declined to reconsider his decision. The crisis grew from the undercover methods used to persuade some Welsh players to join the world team for South Africa's Centenary celebrations. Originally, six of the ten Welsh players who eventually made the trip had said they would not go. After hurriedly leaving a WRU committee meeting, Mr East explained that he had resigned on a point of principle. 'Other people had gone behind the scenes', he said. 'I was not prepared to tolerate that.'

R H Williams, a national selector who was due to become president in 1991, resigned because he had brought criticism on the WRU by stating that he would not be going to South Africa when he knew that arrangements for the trip had already been made for him. Gwilym Treharne and Terry Vaux resigned as Welsh representatives on the IRB when the WRU passed a resolution by a large majority expressing lack of confidence in them and the committees associated with the IRB. The WRU, bitterly resentful of South Africa's methods of persuasion, recommended that their clubs reverse the 1984 decision and sever links with South Africa. This action was approved by 276 votes to 113 with six abstentions on 6 October 1989 behind closed doors at Port Talbot Civic Centre. Later, a four-man committee of inquiry was set up by the WRU to investigate all aspects of the involvement of the ten Welsh players and six officials in the South African celebrations.

The turmoil off the field was bad enough, but events for Wales on it were infinitely worse. Never before had a Five Nations tournament resulted in a whitewash for the Welsh team. Lack of high-level fitness and basic skills proved a keen disappointment to John Ryan, and he stood down as national coach after his team fell apart at Twickenham. As the seventh WRU national coach, in succession to David Nash, Clive Rowlands, John Dawes, John Lloyd, John Bevan and Tony Gray, he had only two victories to look back on in nine matches at the helm, during which his team had scored just 11 tries to 24 against them. It was enough to make a proud man embrace the Trappist Order! With Robert Jones, the Swansea scrum-half and captain, assuming the mantle of Wales skipper, more vision had been expected from the team. Despite the drain of talent to rugby league, there was a strong residue of emerging talent, lacking only in experience. But experience is essential against such battle-hardened opponents as New Zealand and France, and those were the first two engagements for a team trying desperately to re-establish confidence and fluency of operation.

Bridgend defeated the Welsh XV 24-17 in one of the two warm-up matches, and that grim portent was followed by defeat at the hands of the All Blacks 34-9 (although the result was considerably closer than many had feared) and France 29-19 after Kevin Moseley was sent off for stamping and banned for 32 weeks. Never had Wales scored as many as 19 points and lost! The selection of Llanelli heavyweight lock Phil Davies as blind-side wing forward for that match was widely criticised. He played the same role against England, but afterwards new coach Ron Waldron, whose game plan demands total mobility, instantly switched the Llanelli captain back into the second row.

The trauma of Twickenham demanded change: that 34-6 defeat rocked the Welsh nation to its very foundations. Thank the gods that Llywelyn the Last, great warrior king, had not been about to witness it! Waldron, manager of the most successful team in Wales, immediately decided to rebuild around the framework of his club side and brought in his props, not noted scrummagers but dynamic drivers. Five Neath forwards faced Scotland and their club-mate, Allan Bateman, won his first cap in the centre. Loose head prop Brian Williams, only 13 stone 7 pounds, was outstanding all season with his astonishing upper-body strength and jolting charges. But Wales could not hold the Scottish scrum in Cardiff in spite of a defiant display, their best of the season. 'Performance is important, but victory is everything', summed up a bitterly disappointed Waldron.

Nevertheless, the improvement gave hope that a first whitewash could be averted in Dublin against opponents who hardly inspired confidence. Martyn Morris, yet another Neath stalwart, was recalled to the national side after five years and Steve Ford, the Cardiff wing, was brought in to win a first cap less than two years after the lifting of a life ban for playing in a Rugby League trial. It was a shoot-out for the dreaded wooden spoon, both teams without a victory, and Ireland deserved their 14-8 success. Wales had conceded a record 90 points in four Championship games and Jeff Squire and David Burcher quit as national selectors because they were not in agreement with the thoughts of coach Waldron.

The time had come for the whole structure of Welsh rugby administration to be reviewed, as had been urged in many quarters. So in April 1990 the WRU issued their 106-page plan, containing 78 initiatives, called 'The Quest for Excellence'. The main points were the creation of three new key posts to embrace coaching, marketing and refereeing, namely a national technical director to oversee coaching, a commercial manager and a referees' development officer. The job of technical director was to be advertised worldwide, and a Wales team

The Welsh team which lost to France in Cardiff. L–R, back row: F A Howard (referee), M Griffiths, P T Davies, K Moseley, A G Allen, M A Jones, G Jones, A Emyr; front row: K H Phillips, M G Ring, D Young, D W Evans, R N Jones (capt), M R Hall, M H Titley, P H Thorburn.

manager, who would also be national team coach, would be appointed. Coach Waldron stressed that he would set up a network of assessors in the regions to report on players and tap the knowledge of advisers on a number of issues from fitness to diet.

The major clubs, despite the continued reluctance of a number of detractors, accepted the introduction of National Leagues for 1990-91 after a long wrangle with the WRU, and Heineken became the sponsors. Neath achieved a unique treble success as Schweppes Cup winners, Western Mail Welsh club champions and Whitbread Merit Table title-holders, losing only three matches (to Bath, Llanelli and New Zealand). Llanelli, runners-up in the Championship and the Merit Table, set a new club scoring record with 1,666 points.

WESTERN MAIL CLUB CHAMPIONSHIP 1989-90

	W	D	L	F	A	Avge
Neath	34	0	3	1377	347	91.89
Llanelli	35	0	8	1249	675	81.39
Pontypool	28	2	11	1071	565	70.73
Bridgend	26	0	13	865	530	66.66
Glam Wands	22	1	12	785	638	64.28
Swansea	22	1	12	946	666	64.28
Newbridge	24	0	14	852	525	63.15
Pontypridd	21	0	16	929	639	56.75
Maesteg	21	0	17	635	753	55.26
Cardiff	19	2	19	904	761	50.00
Abertillery	17	2	20	607	765	46.15
Cross Keys	15	0	18	426	543	45.45
Ebbw Vale	15	1	27	614	1012	36.04
Newport	13	1	26	645	913	33.75
London Welsh	10	1	21	509	717	32.81
SW Police	12	1	28	613	919	30.48
Aberavon	9	0	30	484	849	23.07
Tredegar	6	1	26	364	934	19.69
Penarth	4	1	29	322	1370	13.23

WHITBREAD WELSH MERIT TABLE 1989-90

	W	D	L	F	A	Avge
Neath	26	0	1	1046	228	96.30
Llanelli	19	0	4	685	302	82.60
Pontypool	23	2	7	916	390	75.00
Newbridge	21	0	8	684	374	72.41
Glam Wands	17	1	9	561	445	64.81
Swansea	15	1	8	703	486	64.58
Bridgend	19	0	11	628	391	63.33
Pontypridd	17	0	12	737	482	58.62
Abertillery	16	1	12	492	524	56.90
Maesteg	15	0	15	472	612	50.00
Cardiff	10	1	11	508	441	47.72
Cross Keys	12	0	17	337	504	41.38
Newport	10	0	17	485	588	37.03
Ebbw Vale	10	1	22	454	774	31.81
SW Police	6	1	21	318	682	23.20
Aberavon	7	0	25	388	680	21.87
Tredegar	2	1	22	225	752	10.00
Penarth	1	1	23	170	1115	6.00

SNELLING SEVENS 1989-90
26 August 1989, Rodney Parade, Newport

Preliminary round: Newbridge 15, Pontypool 12; Aberavon 16, Ebbw Vale 4
First round: Llanelli 26, Maesteg 4; Bridgend 20, Pontypridd 16;
Glamorgan Wanderers 26, Neath 6; Newport 18, Tredegar 6; Cardiff 12, Abertillery 10;
South Wales Police 16, Cross Keys 8; Swansea 36, Penarth 4; Newbridge 18, Aberavon 12
Second round: Bridgend 26, Glamorgan Wanderers 12; Newport 22, Cardiff 6;
Swansea 26, South Wales Police 6; Llanelli 18, Newbridge 10
Semi-finals: Bridgend 22, Llanelli 12; Swansea 16, Newport 0
Final: Swansea 22, Bridgend 16
Teams in the Final
Swansea: T Michael; S Parfitt, M H Titley, A Williams (*capt*); A Reynolds, W J James, S Williams
Bridgend: R V Wintle; A Martin, A Williams, B Roach; O Williams (*capt*), S Penry-Ellis, J Cooper
Referee G Simmonds (Cardiff)

SCHWEPPES CHALLENGE CUP 1989-90

John Billot *Western Mail*

5 May, Cardiff Arms Park
Neath 16 (1G 1PG 1DG 1T)   Bridgend 10 (2DG 1T)

A sun-soaked crowd of some 53,000 watched Neath and Bridgend locked in a tedious kicking contest, which was marred by the first sending-off in a Schweppes Cup final. Referee Clive Norling, who was alerted by the touch-judge, despatched Andrew Kembery, the 6 foot 8 inch line-out jumper, for the dreaded early bath midway through the second half. Interestingly, touch-judge Les Peard, who witnessed Kembery stamping after he had already been warned by the referee for grappling, had merely sent Neath No 8 Mark Jones to the sin-bin in the 1989 final for the same offence.

Bridgend, who had defeated a Welsh XV in the national side's build-up to their clash with New Zealand, again made a tremendous effort. Few gave them any chance of curbing Neath's momentum, but they tackled with sustained defiance and never allowed the Cup-holders to break out. 'Obviously, Bridgend had assessed the type of game we play and did a very good job of disrupting it', observed Neath team manager Ron Waldron. So Neath, who needed four tries to top the world record aggregate of 345 they established the previous season, were never able to swamp the Bridgend defence with the quick-fire succession of drives that had overwhelmed virtually all opponents during a great season of success. Tactical kicking ruled supreme, which was especially surprising from Bridgend, whose emergency coach, Meredydd James, called in just 11 days before the final on the resignation of Brian Nicholas, had promised flexible game plan.

We will never know what would have happened had Bridgend let their runners loose. Anyway, they were within striking distance of a shock result – only 10-12 behind into the closing stages, which was a significant achievement for the underdogs. Neath opened the scoring when Martyn Morris escaped from a maul to dart away and dive for a momentum try midway through the first half. Thorburn converted and put over a penalty goal, and Jason Ball added a dropped goal to give Neath a 12-0 lead. But Bridgend hit back with a try from Ellis, breaking on the open-side of a scrum five, and in the second half Aled Williams put over two dropped goals from scrums. Finally, Ellis, who was named player of the match for the Lloyd Lewis Memorial Award, lost possession on his goal-line at a badly-released pressure scrum, and Chris Bridges pounced for a gift try to seal Neath's victory.

Neath: P H Thorburn; J Ball, C Laity, A G Bateman, A Edmunds; P Williams, C Bridges; B R Williams, K H Phillips (*capt*), J D Pugh, G O Llewellyn, A Kembery, R Phillips, M A Jones, M S Morris *Replacement* D Joseph for Pugh

Scorers *Tries:* Morris, Bridges *Conversion:* Thorburn *Penalty Goal:* Thorburn
Dropped Goal: Ball
Bridgend: A Parry; G M C Webbe, J Apsee (*capt*), L Evans, R Diplock; A Williams,
K Ellis; D Austin, W H Hall, P Edwards, P Kawulok, N Spender, S Bryant, O Williams,
M Budd
Scorers *Try:* Ellis *Dropped Goals:* Williams (2)
Referee C Norling (Birchgrove, Swansea)

Neither Neath nor Bridgend impressed in winning their semi-final ties.
Bridgend out-scored Aberavon 3-0 on tries (each of them from close-up
scrums) to win by 12-6 the first semi-final to be staged at Stradey Park,
while Neath wore down Swansea 24-16 at Cardiff Arms Park. Neath
pounced for both their tries following charged kicks and operated on a
narrow front to triumph after the lead had swung five times.

Neath sent Cardiff crashing out of the Cup 22-6 in the sixth round at
the Gnoll, and there was a shock at Aberavon when the home side
accounted for Pontypool 18-12. A late Swansea onslaught ensured a
28-14 home success over Newport while Bridgend, although short of
possession against a spirited Tumble pack, collected five tries for a 31-4
victory at the Brewery Field.

Phil Davies, the Llanelli captain, urged that the fifth round tie
against Cardiff at the Arms Park be postponed because of the wet
ground – the field was dotted with pools of water. Referee Derek Bevan
pointed out he had controlled matches in worse conditions, so the tie
went ahead and Llanelli, their runners bogged down, lost 15-4. Unlucky
Phil Davies lost the ball in the act of scoring between the posts and then
gave away a simple penalty goal. It was not his day! Ebbw Vale were
unfortunate to lose a battle of penalty kicks to Pontypool 12-9, Swansea
came back from 9-3 down to defeat Glamorgan Wanderers 15-9 at
waterlogged St Helen's, and Aberavon surprised Newbridge to win
15-9. The Newport-Pontypridd tie was twice postponed before Gary
Abraham played his finest game for Newport, kicking three goals, and
his side won 12-3.

Mark Ring, dropped from the Wales squad after the defeat by New
Zealand, gave an immediate response with a dynamic display for Cardiff
in the fourth round to score 18 points in their 38-16 victory over
Bridgend Athletic. Swansea defended desperately in the mud at Treorchy
to hold out 16-6, and Pontypridd had two forwards sin-binned during
their 24-16 victory at Llandeilo. Neath crushed Ystrad Rhondda and
Bridgend swamped Dunvant.

Maesteg went out in the third round in a 19-19 draw because their
opponents, Bonymaen, scored three tries to their two. Cross Keys fell
victim 19-10 at Blaina while Maesteg Celtic won 10-4 against South
Wales Police. Penarth were knocked out in the second round, 23-19 at
Treherbert.

RESULTS

Third Round

Aberaman 6, Neath 46; Aberavon Quins 15, Pontyberem 18; Abercynon 11, Rumney 3; Blaina 19, Cross Keys 10; *Bonymaen 19, Maesteg 19; Carmarthen Quins 9, Aberavon 30; Cilfynydd 13, Cardiff 26; Croesyceiliog 12, Swansea 46; Dunvant 20, Cwmbran 9; Ebbw Vale 34, Gowerton 12; Glamorgan Wanderers 17, UC Cardiff 14; Glynneath 3, Pontypridd 15; Hartridge HSOB 18, Senghenydd 19; Hendy 7, Abertillery 25; Kenfig Hill 12, Llanelli 33; Llandeilo 9, Pill Harriers 6; Llandybie 12, Llandovery 18; Llanharan 36, Nelson 6; Llantrisant 27, Vardre 16; Mountain Ash 16, Porthcawl 25; Newbridge 34, Seven Sisters 4; Newport 38, Beddau 19; Pontypool United 9, Bridgend Athletic 13; Ruthin 3, Pontypool 47; South Wales Police 4, Maesteg Celtic 10; Taffs Well 3, Tonyrefail 0; Talywain 3, Tumble 20; Tondu 9, Treherbert 12; Tredegar 6, Bridgend 35; Treorchy 38, St Peter's 10; Trimsaran 13, †Laugharne 13; Ystrad Rhondda 18, Garndiffaith 3

*Winners on 'most tries' rule
†Winners on 'away team' rule

Fourth Round

Aberavon 13, Laugharne 3; Abertillery 12, *Maesteg Celtic 12; Bonymaen 11, Tumble 13; Bridgend 33, Dunvant 6; Cardiff 38, Bridgend Athletic 16; Ebbw Vale 22, Porthcawl 0; Llandeilo 16, Pontypridd 24; Llanharan 4, Blaina 3; Newbridge 28, Llantrisant 9; Pontyberem 6, Llandovery 7; Pontypool 34, Abercynon 10; Senghenydd 12, Llanelli 62; Taffs Well 9, Glamorgan Wanderers 14; Treherbert 8, Newport 31; Ystrad Rhondda 3, Neath 57; Treorchy 6, Swansea 16

*Winners on 'most tries' rule

Fifth Round

Aberavon 15, Newbridge 9; Bridgend 30, Llandovery 4; Cardiff 15, Llanelli 4; Ebbw Vale 9, Pontypool 12; Maesteg Celtic 6, Neath 19; Newport 12, Pontypridd 3; Swansea 15, Glamorgan Wanderers 9; Tumble 19, Llanharan 6

Sixth Round

Aberavon 18, Pontypool 12; Bridgend 31, Tumble 4; Neath 22, Cardiff 6; Swansea 28, Newport 14

Semi-finals

Neath 24 Swansea 16
  (at Cardiff Arms Park)
Bridgend 12 Aberavon 6
  (at Llanelli)

FINAL (at Cardiff Arms Park)
Neath 16 Bridgend 10

Previous finals

(all at Cardiff Arms Park)

1972	Neath 15	Llanelli 9
1973	Llanelli 30	Cardiff 7
1974	Llanelli 12	Aberavon 10
1975	Llanelli 15	Aberavon 6
1976	Llanelli 15	Swansea 4
1977	Newport 16	Cardiff 15
1978	Swansea 13	Newport 9
1979	Bridgend 18	Pontypridd 12
1980	Bridgend 15	Swansea 9
1981	Cardiff 14	Bridgend 6
1982*	Cardiff 12	Bridgend 12
1983	Pontypool 18	Swansea 6
1984	Cardiff 24	Neath 19
1985	Llanelli 15	Cardiff 14
1986	Cardiff 28	Newport 21
1987	Cardiff 16	Swansea 15
1988	Llanelli 28	Neath 13
1989	Neath 14	Llanelli 13

*Winners on 'most tries' rule

WELSH INTERNATIONAL PLAYERS
(*up to 30 April 1990*)

ABBREVIATIONS

A – Australia; *C* – Canada; *E* – England; *F* – France; *Fj* – Fiji; *I* – Ireland; *M* – Maoris; *NZ* – New Zealand; *NZA* – New Zealand Army; *R* – Romania; *S* – Scotland; *SA* – South Africa; *Tg* – Tonga; *US* – United States; *WS* – Western Samoa; (R) – Replacement. Entries in square brackets [ ] indicate appearances in the World Cup.

Note: Years given for Five Nations' matches are for second half of season; eg 1972 means season 1971-72. Years for all other matches refer to the actual year of the match. When a series has taken place, figures have been used to denote the particular matches in which players have featured. Thus 1969 *NZ* 2 indicates that a player appeared in the second Test of the series.

Ackerman, R A (Newport, London Welsh) 1980 *NZ*, 1981 *E, S, A*, 1982 *I, F, E, S*, 1983 *S, I, F, R*, 1984 *S, I, F, E, A*, 1985 *S, I, F, E, Fj*
Alexander, E P (Llandovery Coll, Cambridge U) 1885 *S*, 1886 *E, S*, 1887 *E, I*
Alexander, W H (Llwynypia) 1898 *I, E*, 1899 *E, S, I*, 1901 *S, I*
Allen, A G (Newbridge) 1990 *F, E, I*
Allen, C P (Oxford U, Beaumaris) 1884 *E, S*
Andrews, F (Pontypool) 1912 *SA*, 1913 *E, S, I*
Andrews, F G (Swansea) 1884 *E, S*
Andrews, G E (Newport) 1926 *E, S*, 1927 *E, F, I*
Anthony, L (Neath) 1948 *E, S, F*
Arnold, W R (Swansea) 1903 *S*
Arthur, C S (Cardiff) 1888 *I, M*, 1891 *E*
Arthur, T (Neath) 1927 *S, F, I*, 1929 *E, S, F, I*, 1930 *E, S, I, F*, 1931 *E, S, F, I, SA*, 1933 *E, S*
Ashton, C (Aberavon) 1959 *E, S, I*, 1960 *E, S, I*, 1962 *I*
Attewell, S L (Newport) 1921 *E, S, F*

Badger, O (Llanelli) 1895 *E, S, I*, 1896 *E*
Baker, A (Neath) 1921 *I*, 1923 *E, S, F, I*
Baker, A M (Newport) 1909 *S, F*, 1910 *S*
Bancroft, J (Swansea) 1909 *E, S, F, I*, 1910 *F, E, S, I*, 1911 *E, F, I*, 1912 *E, S, I*, 1913 *I*, 1914 *E, S, F*
Bancroft, W J (Swansea) 1890 *S, E, I*, 1891 *E, S, I*, 1892 *E, S, I*, 1893 *E, S, I*, 1894 *E, S, I*, 1895 *E, S, I*, 1896 *E, S, I*, 1897 *E*, 1898 *I, E*, 1899 *E, S, I*, 1900 *E, S, I*, 1901 *E, S, I*
Barlow, T M (Cardiff) 1884 *I*
Barrell, R J (Cardiff) 1929 *S, F, I*, 1933 *I*
Bartlett, J D (Llanelli) 1927 *S*, 1928 *E, S*
Bassett, A (Cardiff) 1934 *I*, 1935 *E, S, I*, 1938 *E, S*
Bassett, J A (Penarth) 1929 *E, S, F, I*, 1930 *E, S, I*, 1931 *E, S, F, I, SA*, 1932 *E, S, I*
Bateman, A G (Neath) 1990 *S, I*
Bayliss, G (Pontypool) 1933 *S*
Bebb, D I E (Carmarthen TC, Swansea) 1959 *E, S, I, F*, 1960 *E, S, I, F, SA*, 1961 *E, S, I, F*, 1962 *E, S, F, I*, 1963 *E, F, NZ*, 1964 *E, S, F, SA*, 1965 *E, S, I, F*, 1966 *F, A*, 1967 *S, I, F, E*
Beckingham, G (Cardiff) 1953 *E, S*, 1958 *F*
Bennett, I (Aberavon) 1937 *I*
Bennett, P (Cardiff Harlequins) 1891 *E, S*, 1892 *E, S*
Bennett, P (Llanelli) 1969 *F* (R), 1970 *SA, S, F*, 1972 *S* (R), *NZ*, 1973 *E, S, I, F, A*, 1974 *S, I, F, E*, 1975 *S* (R), *I*, 1976 *E, S, I, F*, 1977 *I, F, E, S*, 1978 *E, S, I, F*
Bergiers, R T E (Cardiff Coll of Ed, Llanelli) 1972 *E, S, F, NZ*, 1973 *E, S, I, F, A*, 1974 *E*, 1975 *I*
Bevan, G W (Llanelli) 1947 *E*
Bevan, J A (Cambridge U) 1881 *E*
Bevan, J C (Cardiff, Cardiff Coll of Ed) 1971 *E, S, I, F*, 1972 *E, S, F, NZ*, 1973 *E, S*
Bevan, J D (Aberavon) 1975 *F, E, S, A*
Bevan, S (Swansea) 1904 *I*
Beynon, B (Swansea) 1920 *E, S*
Beynon, G E (Swansea) 1925 *F, I*
Biggs, N W (Cardiff) 1888 *M*, 1889 *I*, 1892 *I*, 1893 *E, S, I*, 1894 *E, S*
Biggs, S H (Cardiff) 1895 *E, S*, 1896 *S*, 1897 *E*, 1898 *I, E*, 1899 *S, I*, 1900 *I*
Birch, J (Neath) 1911 *S, F*
Birt, F W (Newport) 1911 *E, S*, 1912 *E, S, I, SA*, 1913 *E*

Bishop, D J (Pontypool) 1984 *A*
Bishop, E H (Swansea) 1889 *S*
Blackmore, J H (Abertillery) 1909 *E*
Blackmore, S W (Cardiff) 1987 *I*, [*Tg*(R), *C, A*]
Blake, J (Cardiff) 1899 *E, S, I*, 1900 *E, S, I*, 1901 *E, S, I*
Blakemore, R E (Newport) 1947 *E*
Bland, A F (Cardiff) 1887 *E, S, I*, 1888 *S, I, M*, 1890 *S, E, I*
Blyth, L (Swansea) 1951 *SA*, 1952 *E, S*
Blyth, W R (Swansea) 1974 *E*, 1975 *S* (R), 1980 *F, E, S, I*
Boon, R W (Cardiff) 1930 *S, F*, 1931 *E, S, F, I, SA*, 1932 *E, S, I*, 1933 *E, I*
Booth, J (Pontymister) 1898 *I*
Boots, J G (Newport) 1898 *I, E*, 1899 *I*, 1900 *E, S, I*, 1901 *E, S, I*, 1902 *E, S, I*, 1903 *E, S, I*, 1904 *E*
Boucher, A W (Newport) 1892 *E, S, I*, 1893 *E, S, I*, 1894 *E*, 1895 *E, S, I*, 1896 *E, I*, 1897 *E*
Bowcott, H M (Cardiff, Cambridge U) 1929 *S, F, I*, 1930 *E*, 1931 *E, S*, 1933 *E, I*
Bowdler, F A (Cross Keys) 1927 *A*, 1928 *E, S, I, F*, 1929 *E, S, F, I*, 1930 *E*, 1931 *SA*, 1932 *E, S, I*, 1933 *I*
Bowen, B (S Wales Police, Swansea) 1983 *R*, 1984 *S, I, F, E*, 1985 *S, I, F, Fj, Tg, WS*, 1987 [*C, E, NZ*], *US*, 1988 *E, S, I, F, WS*, 1989 *S, I*
Bowen, C A (Llanelli) 1896 *E, S, I*, 1897 *E*
Bowen, D H (Llanelli) 1883 *E*, 1886 *E, S*, 1887 *E*
Bowen, G E (Swansea) 1887 *S, I*, 1888 *S, I*
Bowen, W (Swansea) 1921 *S, F*, 1922 *E, S, I, F*
Bowen, Wm A (Swansea) 1886 *E, S*, 1887 *E, S, I*, 1888 *M*, 1889 *S, I*, 1890 *S, E, I*, 1891 *E, S*
Brace, D O (Llanelli, Oxford U) 1956 *E, S, I, F*, 1957 *E*, 1960 *S, I, F*, 1961 *I*
Braddock, K J (Newbridge) 1966 *A*, 1967 *S, I*
Bradshaw, K (Bridgend) 1964 *E, S, I, F, SA*, 1966 *E, S, I, F*
Brewer, T J (Newport) 1950 *E*, 1955 *E, S*
Brice, A B (Aberavon) 1899 *S, I*, 1900 *E, S, I*, 1901 *E, S, I*, 1902 *E, S, I*, 1903 *E, S, I*, 1904 *E, S, I*
Bridie, R H (Newport) 1882 *I*
Britton, G R (Newport) 1961 *S*
Broughton, A S (Treorchy) 1927 *A*, 1929 *S*
Brown, A (Newport) 1921 *I*
Brown, J (Cardiff) 1925 *I*
Brown, J A (Cardiff) 1907 *E, S, I*, 1908 *E, S, F*, 1909 *E*
Brown, M (Pontypool) 1983 *R*, 1986 *E, S, Fj* (R), *Tg, WS*
Bryant, D J (Bridgend) 1988 *NZ* 1,2, *WS, R*, 1989 *S, I, F, E*
Buchanan, A (Llanelli) 1987 [*Tg, E, NZ, A*], 1988 *I*
Burcher, D H (Newport) 1977 *I, F, E, S*
Burgess, R C (Ebbw Vale) 1977 *I, F, E, S*, 1981 *I, F*, 1982 *F, E, S*
Burnett, R (Newport) 1953 *E*
Burns, J (Cardiff) 1927 *F, I*
Bush, P F (Cardiff) 1905 *NZ*, 1906 *E, SA*, 1907 *I*, 1908 *E, S*, 1910 *S, I*
Butler, E T (Pontypool) 1980 *F, E, S, I, NZ* (R), 1982 *S*, 1983 *E, S, I, F, R*, 1984 *S, I, F, E, A*

Cale, W R (Newbridge, Pontypool) 1949 *E, S, I*, 1950 *E, S, I, F*
Cattell, A (Llanelli) 1883 *E, S*
Challinor, C (Neath) 1939 *E*

1889 *S*, 1890 *S, I*, 1893 *E, S, I*, 1894 *E, S, I*
Hinam, S (Cardiff) 1925 *I*, 1926 *E, S, I, F*
Hinton, J T (Cardiff) 1884 *I*
Hirst, G L (Newport) 1912 *S*, 1913 *S*, 1914 *E, S, F, I*
Hodder, W (Pontypool) 1921 *E, S, F*
Hodges, J J (Newport) 1899 *E, S, I*, 1900 *E, S, I*, 1901
E, S, 1902 *E, S, I*, 1903 *E, S, I*, 1904 *E, S*, 1905 *E, S, I*,
NZ, 1906 *E, S, I*
Hodgson, G T R (Neath) 1962 *I*, 1963 *E, S, I, F, NZ*,
1964 *E, S, I, F, SA*, 1966 *S, I, F*, 1967 *I*
Hollingdale, H (Swansea) 1912 *SA*, 1913 *E*
Hollingdale, T H (Neath) 1927 *A*, 1928 *E, S, I, F*,
1930 *E*
Holmes, T D (Cardiff) 1978 *A* 2, *NZ*, 1979 *S, I, F, E*,
1980 *F, E, S, I, NZ*, 1981 *A*, 1982 *I, F, E*, 1983 *E, S, I*,
F, 1984 *E*, 1985 *S, I, F, Fj*
Hopkin, W H (Newport) 1937 *S*
Hopkins, K (Cardiff, Swansea) 1985 *E*, 1987 *F, E, S*,
[Tg, C(R)], US
Hopkins, P L (Swansea) 1908 *A*, 1909 *E, I*, 1910 *E*
Hopkins, R (Maesteg) 1970 *E* (R)
Hopkins, T (Swansea) 1926 *E, S, I, F*
Hopkins, W J (Aberavon) 1925 *E, S*
Howells, B (Llanelli) 1934 *E*
Howells, W G (Llanelli) 1957 *E, S, I, F*
Howells, W H (Swansea) 1888 *S, I*
Hughes, D (Newbridge) 1967 *NZ*, 1969 *NZ* 2, 1970
SA, S, E, I
Hughes, G (Penarth) 1934 *E, S, I*
Hughes, H (Cardiff) 1887 *S*, 1889 *S*
Hughes, K (Cambridge U, London Welsh) 1970 *I*,
1973 *A*, 1974 *S*
Hullin, W (Cardiff) 1967 *S*
Hurrell, J (Newport) 1959 *F*
Hutchinson, F (Neath) 1894 *I*, 1896 *S, I*
Huxtable, R (Swansea) 1920 *F, I*
Huzzey, H V P (Cardiff) 1898 *I, E*, 1899 *E, S, I*
Hybart, A J (Cardiff) 1887 *E*

Ingledew, H M (Cardiff) 1890 *I*, 1891 *E, S*
Isaacs, I (Cardiff) 1933 *E, S*

Jackson, T H (Swansea) 1895 *E*
James, B (Bridgend) 1968 *E*
James, C R (Llanelli) 1958 *A, F*
James, D (Swansea) 1891 *I*, 1892 *S, I*, 1899 *E*
James, D R (Treorchy) 1931 *F, I*
James, E (Swansea) 1890 *S*, 1891 *I*, 1892 *S, I*, 1899 *E*
James, M (Cardiff) 1947 *A*, 1948 *E, S, F, I*
James, T O (Aberavon) 1935 *I*, 1937 *S*
James, W J (Aberavon) 1983 *E, S, I, F, R*, 1984 *S*,
1985 *S, I, F, E, Fj*, 1986 *E, S, I, F, Fj, Tg, WS*, 1987
E, S, I
James, W P (Aberavon) 1925 *E, S*
Jarman, H (Newport) 1910 *E, S, I*, 1911 *E*
Jarrett, K S (Newport) 1967 *E*, 1968 *E, S*, 1969 *S, I, F,
E, NZ* 1,2, *A*
Jeffery, J J (Cardiff Coll of Ed, Newport) 1967 *NZ*
Jenkin, A M (Swansea) 1895 *I*, 1896 *E*
Jenkins, A (Llanelli) 1920 *E, S, F, I*, 1921 *S, F*, 1922
F, 1923 *E, S, F, I*, 1924 *NZ*, 1928 *S, I*
Jenkins, D M (Treorchy) 1926 *E, S, I, F*
Jenkins, D R (Swansea) 1927 *A*, 1929 *E*
Jenkins, E (Newport) 1910 *S, I*
Jenkins, E M (Aberavon) 1927 *S, F, I, A*, 1928 *E, S, I,
F*, 1929 *F*, 1930 *S, I, F*, 1931 *E, S, F, I, SA*, 1932 *E,
S, I*
Jenkins, J C (London Welsh) 1906 *SA*
Jenkins, J L (Aberavon) 1923 *S, F*
Jenkins, L H (Mon TC, Newport) 1954 *I*, 1956 *E, S, I,
F*
Jenkins, V G J (Oxford U, Bridgend, London Welsh)
1933 *E, I*, 1934 *S, I*, 1935 *E, S, NZ*, 1936 *E, S, I*, 1937
E, 1938 *E, S*, 1939 *E*
Jenkins, W (Cardiff) 1912 *I, F*, 1913 *S, I*
John, B (Llanelli, Cardiff) 1966 *A*, 1967 *S, NZ*, 1968 *E,
S, I, F*, 1969 *S, I, F, E, NZ* 1,2, *A*, 1970 *SA, S, E, I*,
1971 *E, S, I, F*, 1972 *E, S, F*
John, D A (Llanelli) 1925 *I*, 1928 *E, S, I*
John D E (Llanelli) 1923 *F, I*, 1928 *E, S, I*
John, E R (Neath) 1950 *E, S, I, F*, 1951 *E, S, I, F, SA*,
1952 *E, S, I, F*, 1953 *E, S, I, F, NZ*, 1954 *E*
John, G (St Luke's Coll, Exeter) 1954 *E, F*

John, J H (Swansea) 1926 *E, S, I, F*, 1927 *E, S, F, I*
Johnson, T A (Cardiff) 1921 *E, F, I*, 1923 *E, S, F*,
1924 *E, S, NZ*, 1925 *E, S, F*
Johnson, W D (Swansea) 1953 *E*
Jones, A E (known as Emyr) (Swansea) 1989 *E, NZ*,
1990 *F, E, S, I*
Jones, A H (Cardiff) 1933 *E, S*
Jones, B (Abertillery) 1914 *E, S, F, I*
Jones, Bert (Llanelli) 1934 *S, I*
Jones, Bob (Llwynypia) 1901 *I*
Jones, B J (Newport) 1960 *I, F*
Jones, B Lewis (Devonport Services, Llanelli) 1950 *E,
S, I, F*, 1951 *E, S, SA*, 1952 *E, S, F*
Jones, C W (Cambridge U, Cardiff) 1934 *E, S, I*, 1935
E, S, I, NZ, 1936 *E, S, I*, 1938 *E, S, F*
Jones, C W (Bridgend) 1920 *E, S, F*
Jones, D (Neath) 1927 *A*
Jones, D (Aberavon) 1897 *E*
Jones, D (Swansea) 1947 *E, F, I*, 1949 *E, S, I, F*
Jones, D (Treherbert) 1902 *E, S, I*, 1903 *E, S, I*, 1905
E, S, I, NZ, 1906 *E, S, SA*
Jones, D (Newport) 1926 *E, S, I, F*, 1927 *E*
Jones, D (Llanelli) 1948 *E*
Jones, D K (Llanelli, Cardiff) 1962 *E, S, F, I*, 1963 *E,
F, NZ*, 1964 *E, S, SA*, 1966 *E, S, I, F*
Jones, D P (Pontypool) 1907 *I*
Jones, E H (Neath) 1929 *E, S*
Jones, E L (Llanelli) 1930 *I*, 1933 *E, S, I*, 1935 *E*
Jones, Elvet L (Llanelli) 1939 *S*
Jones, G (Ebbw Vale) 1963 *S, I, F*
Jones, G (Llanelli) 1988 *NZ*2, 1989 *F, E, NZ*, 1990 *F*
Jones, G G (Cardiff) 1930 *S*, 1933 *I*
Jones, H (Penygraig) 1902 *S, I*
Jones, H (Neath) 1904 *I*
Jones, H (Swansea) 1930 *I, F*
Jones, Iorwerth (Llanelli) 1927 *A*, 1928 *E, S, I, F*
Jones, I C (London Welsh) 1968 *I*
Jones, Ivor E (Llanelli) 1924 *E, S*, 1927 *S, F, I, A*,
1928 *E, S, I, F*, 1929 *E, S, F, I*, 1930 *E, S*
Jones, J (Aberavon) 1901 *E*
Jones, J (Swansea) 1924 *F*
Jones, Jim (Aberavon) 1919 *NZA*, 1920 *E, S*, 1921 *S,
F, I*
Jones, J A (Cardiff) 1883 *S*
Jones, J P (Tuan) (Pontypool) 1913 *S*
Jones, J P (Pontypool) 1908 *A*, 1909 *E, S, F, I*, 1910 *F,
E*, 1912 *E, F*, 1913 *F, I*, 1920 *F, I*, 1921 *E*
Jones, K D (Cardiff) 1960 *SA*, 1961 *E, S, I*, 1962 *E, F*,
1963 *E, S, I, NZ*
Jones, K J (Newport) 1947 *E, S, F, I, A*, 1948 *E, S, F,
I*, 1949 *E, S, I, F*, 1950 *E, S, I, F*, 1951 *E, S, I, F, SA*,
1952 *E, S, I, F*, 1953 *E, S, I, F, NZ*, 1954 *E, I, F, S*,
1955 *E, S, I, F*, 1956 *E, S, I, F*, 1957 *S*
Jones, K W J (Oxford U, London Welsh) 1934 *E*
Jones, M A (Neath) 1987 *S*, 1988 *NZ*2(R), 1989 *S, I,
F, E, NZ*, 1990 *F, E, S, I*
Jones, P (Newport) 1912 *SA*, 1913 *E, S, F*, 1914 *E, S,
F, I*
Jones, P B (Newport) 1921 *S*
Jones, R (Swansea) 1901 *I*, 1902 *E*, 1904 *E, S, I*, 1905
E, 1908 *F, I, A*, 1909 *E, S, F, I*, 1910 *F, E*
Jones, R (London Welsh) 1929 *E*
Jones, R (Northampton) 1926 *E, S, F*
Jones, R (Swansea) 1927 *A*, 1928 *F*
Jones, R B (Cambridge U) 1933 *E, S*
Jones, R E (Coventry) 1967 *E*, 1968 *S, I, F*
Jones, R N (Swansea) 1986 *E, S, I, F, Fj, Tg, WS*,
1987 *F, E, S, I, [I, Tg, E, NZ, A], US*, 1988 *E, S, I, F,
NZ*1, *WS, R*, 1989 *I, F, E, NZ*, 1990 *F, E, S, I*
Jones, S T (Pontypool) 1983 *S, I, F, R*, 1984 *S*, 1988
*E, S, F, NZ*1,2
Jones, Tom (Newport) 1922 *E, S, I, F*, 1924 *E, S*
Jones, T B (Newport) 1882 *I*, 1883 *E, S*, 1884 *S*, 1885
E, S
Jones, W (Cardiff) 1898 *I, E*
Jones, W (Mountain Ash) 1905 *I*
Jones, W I (Llanelli, Cambridge U) 1925 *E, S, F, I*
Jones, W J (Llanelli) 1924 *I*
Jones, W K (Cardiff) 1967 *NZ*, 1968 *E, S, I, F*
Jones-Davies, T E (London Welsh) 1930 *E, I*, 1931 *E,
S*
Jordan, H M (Newport) 1885 *E, S*, 1889 *S*
Joseph, W (Swansea) 1902 *E, S, I*, 1903 *E, S, I*, 1904

E, *S*, 1905 *E*, *S*, *I*, *NZ*, 1906 *E*, *S*, *I*, *SA*
Jowett, W F (Swansea) 1903 *E*
Judd, S (Cardiff) 1953 *E*, *S*, *I*, *F*, *NZ*, 1954 *E*, *F*, *S*, 1955 *E*, *S*
Judson, J H (Llanelli) 1883 *E*, *S*

Kedzlie, Q D (Cardiff) 1888 *S*, *I*
Keen, L (Aberavon) 1980 *F*, *E*, *S*, *I*
Knill, F M D (Cardiff) 1976 *F* (R)

Lane, S M (Cardiff) 1978 *A* 1 (R), 2, 1979 *I* (R), 1980 *S*, *I*
Lang, J (Llanelli) 1931 *F*, *I*, 1934 *S*, *I*, 1935 *E*, *S*, *I*, *NZ*, 1936 *E*, *S*, *I*, 1937 *E*
Lawrence, S (Bridgend) 1925 *S*, *I*, 1926 *S*, *I*, *F*, 1927 *S*
Law, V J (Newport) 1939 *I*
Legge, W S G (Newport) 1937 *I*, 1938 *I*
Leleu, J (London Welsh, Swansea) 1959 *E*, *S*, 1960 *F*, *SA*
Lemon, A (Neath) 1929 *I*, 1930 *S*, *I*, *F*, 1931 *E*, *S*, *F*, *I*, *SA*, 1932 *E*, *S*, *I*, 1933 *I*
Lewis, A J L (Ebbw Vale) 1970 *F*, 1971 *E*, *I*, *F*, 1972 *E*, *S*, *F*, 1973 *E*, *S*, *I*, *F*
Lewis, A R (Abertillery) 1966 *E*, *S*, *I*, *F*, *A*, 1967 *I*
Lewis, B R (Swansea, Cambridge U) 1912 *I*, 1913 *I*
Lewis, C P (Llandovery Coll) 1882 *I*, 1883 *E*, *S*, 1884 *E*, *S*
Lewis, D H (Cardiff) 1886 *E*, *S*
Lewis, E J (Llandovery) 1881 *E*
Lewis, G W (Richmond) 1960 *E*, *S*
Lewis, H (Swansea) 1913 *S*, *F*, *I*, 1914 *E*
Lewis, J G (Llanelli) 1887 *I*
Lewis, J M C (Cardiff, Cambridge U) 1912 *E*, 1913 *S*, *F*, *I*, 1914 *E*, *S*, *F*, *I*, 1921 *I*, 1923 *E*, *S*
Lewis, J R (S Glam Inst, Cardiff) 1981 *E*, *S*, *I*, *F*, 1982 *F*, *E*, *S*
Lewis, M (Treorchy) 1913 *F*
Lewis, P I (Llanelli) 1984 *A*, 1985 *S*, *I*, *F*, *E*, 1986 *E*, *S*, *I*
Lewis, T W (Cardiff) 1926 *E*, 1927 *E*, *S*
Lewis, W (Llanelli) 1925 *F*
Lewis, W H (London Welsh, Cambridge U) 1926 *I*, 1927 *E*, *F*, *I*, *A*, 1928 *F*
Llewellyn, D B (Newport, Llanelli) 1970 *SA*, *S*, *E*, *I*, *F*, 1971 *E*, *S*, *I*, *F*, 1972 *E*, *S*, *F*, *NZ*
Llewellyn, G O (Neath) 1989 *NZ*, 1990 *E*, *S*, *I*
Llewellyn, P D (Swansea) 1973 *I*, *F*, *A*, 1974 *S*, *E*
Llewellyn, W (Llwynypia) 1899 *E*, *S*, *I*, 1900 *E*, *S*, *I*, 1901 *E*, *S*, *I*, 1902 *E*, *S*, *I*, 1903 *I*, 1904 *E*, *S*, *I*, 1905 *E*, *S*, *I*, *NZ*
Lloyd, D J (Bridgend) 1966 *E*, *S*, *I*, *F*, *A*, 1967 *S*, *I*, *F*, *E*, 1968 *S*, *I*, *F*, 1969 *S*, *I*, *F*, *E*, *NZ* 1, *A*, 1970 *F*, 1972 *E*, *S*, *F*, 1973 *E*, *S*
Lloyd, E (Llanelli) 1895 *S*
Lloyd, G L (Newport) 1896 *I*, 1899 *S*, *I*, 1900 *E*, *S*, 1901 *E*, *S*, 1902 *S*, *I*, 1903 *E*, *S*, *I*
Lloyd, P (Llanelli) 1890 *S*, *E*, 1891 *E*, *I*
Lloyd, R A (Pontypool) 1913 *S*, *F*, *I*, 1914 *E*, *S*, *F*, *I*
Lloyd, T (Maesteg) 1953 *I*, *F*
Lloyd, T C (Neath) 1909 *F*, 1913 *F*, *I*, 1914 *E*, *S*, *F*, *I*
Lockwood, T W (Newport) 1887 *E*, *S*, *I*
Long, E C (Swansea) 1936 *E*, *S*, *I*, 1937 *E*, *S*, 1939 *S*, *I*
Lyne, H S (Newport) 1883 *S*, 1884 *E*, *S*, *I*, 1885 *E*

McCall, B E W (Welch Regt, Newport) 1936 *E*, *S*, *I*
McCarley, A (Neath) 1938 *E*, *S*, *I*
McCutcheon, W M (Swansea) 1891 *E*, 1892 *E*, *S*, 1893 *E*, *S*, *I*, 1894 *E*
Maddock, H T (London Welsh) 1906 *E*, *S*, *I*, 1907 *E*, *S*, 1910 *F*
Maddocks, K (Neath) 1957 *E*
Main, D R (London Welsh) 1959 *E*, *S*, *I*, *F*
Mainwaring, H J (Swansea) 1961 *F*
Mainwaring, W T (Aberavon) 1967 *S*, *I*, *F*, *E*, *NZ*, 1968 *E*
Major, W C (Maesteg) 1949 *F*, 1950 *S*
Male, B O (Cardiff) 1921 *F*, 1923 *S*, 1924 *S*, *I*, 1927 *E*, *S*, *F*, *I*, 1928 *S*, *I*, *F*
Manfield, L (Mountain Ash, Cardiff) 1939 *S*, *I*, 1947 *A*, 1948 *E*, *S*, *F*, *I*
Mann, B B (Cardiff) 1881 *E*
Mantle, J T (Loughborough Colls, Newport) 1964 *E*, *SA*

Margrave, F L (Llanelli) 1884 *E*, *S*
Marsden-Jones, D (Cardiff) 1921 *E*, 1924 *NZ*
Martin, A J (Aberavon) 1973 *A*, 1974 *S*, *I*, 1975 *F*, *E*, *S*, *I*, *A*, 1976 *E*, *S*, *I*, *F*, 1977 *I*, *F*, *E*, *S*, 1978 *E*, *S*, *I*, *F*, *A* 1,2, *NZ*, 1979 *S*, *I*, *F*, *E*, 1980 *F*, *E*, *S*, *I*, *NZ*, 1981 *I*, *F*
Martin, W J (Newport) 1912 *I*, *F*, 1919 *NZA*
Mason, J (Pontypridd) 1988 *NZ*2(R)
Mathews, Rev A A (Lampeter) 1886 *S*
Mathias, R (Llanelli) 1970 *F*
Matthews, C (Bridgend) 1939 *I*
Matthews, J (Cardiff) 1947 *E*, *A*, 1948 *E*, *S*, *F*, 1949 *E*, *S*, *I*, *F*, 1950 *E*, *S*, *I*, *F*, 1951 *E*, *S*, *I*, *F*
May, P S (Llanelli) 1988 *E*, *S*, *I*, *F*, *NZ*1,2
Meredith, A (Devonport Services) 1949 *E*, *S*, *I*
Meredith, B V (St Luke's Coll, London Welsh, Newport) 1954 *F*, *S*, 1955 *E*, *S*, *I*, *F*, 1956 *E*, *S*, *I*, *F*, 1957 *E*, *S*, *I*, *F*, 1958 *A*, *E*, *S*, *I*, 1959 *E*, *S*, *I*, *F*, 1960 *E*, *S*, *F*, *SA*, 1961 *E*, *S*, *I*, 1962 *E*, *S*, *F*, *I*
Meredith, C C (Neath) 1953 *S*, *NZ*, 1954 *E*, *I*, *F*, *S*, 1955 *E*, *S*, *I*, *F*, 1956 *E*, *I*, 1957 *E*, *S*
Meredith, J (Swansea) 1888 *S*, *I*, 1890 *S*, *E*
Merry, A E (Pill Harriers) 1912 *I*, *F*
Michael, G (Swansea) 1923 *E*, *S*
Michaelson, R C B (Aberavon, Cambridge U) 1963 *E*
Miller, F (Mountain Ash) 1896 *I*, 1900 *E*, *S*, *I*, 1901 *E*, *S*, *I*
Mills, F M (Swansea, Cardiff) 1892 *E*, *S*, *I*, 1893 *E*, *S*, *I*, 1894 *E*, *S*, *I*, 1895 *E*, *S*, *I*, 1896 *E*
Moore, W J (Bridgend) 1933 *I*
Morgan, C H (Llanelli) 1957 *I*, *F*
Morgan, C I (Cardiff) 1951 *I*, *F*, *SA*, 1952 *E*, *S*, *I*, 1953 *S*, *I*, *F*, *NZ*, 1954 *E*, *I*, *S*, 1955 *E*, *S*, *I*, *F*, 1956 *E*, *S*, *I*, *F*, 1957 *E*, *S*, *I*, *F*, 1958 *E*, *S*, *I*, *F*
Morgan, D (Swansea) 1885 *S*, 1886 *E*, *S*, 1887 *E*, *S*, *I*, 1889 *I*
Morgan, D (Llanelli) 1895 *I*, 1896 *E*
Morgan, D R R (Llanelli) 1962 *E*, *S*, *F*, *I*, 1963 *E*, *S*, *I*, *F*, *NZ*
Morgan, E (Llanelli) 1920 *I*, 1921 *E*, *S*, *F*
Morgan, Edgar (Swansea) 1914 *E*, *S*, *F*, *I*
Morgan, E T (London Welsh) 1902 *E*, *S*, *I*, 1903 *I*, 1904 *E*, *S*, *I*, 1905 *E*, *S*, *I*, *NZ*, 1906 *E*, *S*, *I*, *SA*, 1908 *F*
Morgan, F L (Llanelli) 1938 *E*, *S*, *I*, 1939 *E*
Morgan, H J (Abertillery) 1958 *E*, *S*, *I*, *F*, 1959 *I*, *F*, 1960 *E*, 1961 *E*, *S*, *I*, *F*, 1962 *E*, *S*, *F*, *I*, 1963 *S*, *I*, *F*, 1965 *E*, *S*, *I*, *F*, 1966 *E*, *S*, *I*, *F*, *A*
Morgan, H P (Newport) 1956 *E*, *S*, *I*, *F*
Morgan, I (Swansea) 1908 *A*, 1909 *E*, *S*, *F*, *I*, 1910 *F*, *E*, *S*, *I*, 1911 *E*, *F*, *I*, 1912 *S*
Morgan, J L (Llanelli) 1912 *SA*, 1913 *E*
Morgan, M E (Swansea) 1938 *E*, *S*, *I*, 1939 *E*
Morgan, N (Newport) 1960 *S*, *I*, *F*
Morgan, P E J (Aberavon) 1961 *E*, *S*, *F*
Morgan, P J (Llanelli) 1980 *S* (R), *I*, *NZ* (R), 1981 *I*
Morgan, R (Newport) 1984 *S*
Morgan, T (Llanelli) 1889 *I*
Morgan, W G (Cambridge U) 1927 *F*, *I*, 1929 *E*, *S*, *F*, *I*, 1930 *I*, *F*
Morgan, W L (Cardiff) 1910 *S*
Moriarty, R D (Swansea) 1981 *A*, 1982 *I*, *F*, *E*, *S*, 1983 *E*, 1984 *S*, *I*, *F*, *E*, 1985 *S*, *I*, *F*, 1986 *Fj*, *Tg*, *WS*, 1987 [*I*, *Tg*, *C*(R), *E*, *NZ*, *A*]
Moriarty, W P (Swansea) 1986 *I*, *F*, *Fj*, *Tg*, *WS*, 1987 *F*, *E*, *S*, *I*, [*I*, *Tg*, *C*, *E*, *NZ*, *A*], *US*, 1988 *E*, *S*, *I*, *F*, *NZ*1
Morley, J C (Newport) 1929 *E*, *S*, *F*, *I*, 1930 *E*, *I*, 1931 *E*, *S*, *F*, *I*, *SA*, 1932 *E*, *S*, *I*
Morris, G L (Swansea) 1882 *I*, 1883 *E*, *S*, 1884 *E*, *S*
Morris, H T (Cardiff) 1951 *F*, 1955 *I*, *F*
Morris, J I T (Swansea) 1924 *E*, *S*
Morris, M S (S Wales Police, Neath) 1985 *S*, *I*, *F*, 1990 *I*
Morris, R R (Swansea, Bristol) 1933 *S*, 1937 *S*
Morris, S (Cross Keys) 1920 *E*, *S*, *F*, *I*, 1922 *E*, *S*, *I*, *F*, 1923 *E*, *S*, *F*, *I*, 1924 *E*, *S*, *F*, *NZ*, 1925 *E*, *S*, *F*
Morris, W (Abertillery) 1919 *NZA*, 1920 *F*, 1921 *I*
Morris, W (Llanelli) 1896 *S*, *I*, 1897 *E*
Morris, W D (Neath) 1967 *F*, *E*, 1968 *E*, *S*, *I*, *F*, 1969 *S*, *I*, *F*, *E*, *NZ* 1,2, *A*, 1970 *SA*, *S*, *E*, *I*, *F*, 1971 *E*, *S*, *I*, *F*, 1972 *E*, *S*, *F*, *NZ*, 1973 *E*, *S*, *I*, *A*, 1974 *S*, *I*, *F*, *E*
Morris, W J (Newport) 1965 *S*, 1966 *F*
Morris, W J (Pontypool) 1963 *S*, *I*

239

Thompson, J F (Cross Keys) 1923 *E*
Thorburn, P H (Neath) 1985 *F, E, Fj,* 1986 *E, S, I, F,* 1987 *F, [I, Tg, C, E, NZ, A],* US, 1988 *S, I, F, WS, R*(R), 1989 *S, I, F, E, NZ,* 1990 *F, E, S, I*
Titley, M H (Bridgend, Swansea) 1983 *R,* 1984 *S, I, F, E, A,* 1985 *S, I, Fj,* 1986 *F, Fj, Tg, WS,* 1990 *F, E*
Towers, W H (Swansea) 1887 *I,* 1888 *M*
Travers, G (Pill Harriers) 1903 *E, S, I,* 1905 *E, S, I, NZ,* 1906 *E, S, I, SA,* 1907 *E, S, I,* 1908 *E, S, F, I, A,* 1909 *E, S, I,* 1911 *S, F, I*
Travers, W H (Newport) 1937 *S, I,* 1938 *E, S, I,* 1939 *E, S, I,* 1949 *E, S, I, F*
Treharne, E (Pontypridd) 1881 *E,* 1883 *E*
Trew, W J (Swansea) 1900 *E, S, I,* 1901 *E, S,* 1903 *S,* 1905 *S,* 1906 *S,* 1907 *E, S,* 1908 *E, S, F, I, A,* 1909 *E, S, F, I,* 1910 *E, S,* 1911 *E, S, F, I,* 1912 *S,* 1913 *S, F, I,* 1910 *F, E, S, I, F,* 1911 *E, S, F, I,* 1912 *S,* 1913 *S, F*
Trott, R F (Cardiff) 1948 *E, S, F, I,* 1949 *E, S, I, F*
Truman, W H (Llanelli) 1934 *E,* 1935 *E*
Trump, L C (Newport) 1912 *E, S, I, F*
Turnbull, B R (Cardiff) 1925 *I,* 1927 *E, S,* 1928 *E, F,* 1930 *S*
Turnbull, M J L (Cardiff) 1933 *E, I*
Turner, P (Newbridge) 1989 *I*(R), *F, E*

Uzzell, H (Newport) 1912 *E, S, I, F,* 1913 *S, F, I,* 1914 *E, S, F, I,* 1920 *E, S, F, I*
Uzzell, J R (Newport) 1963 *NZ,* 1965 *E, S, I, F*

Vickery, W E (Aberavon) 1938 *E, S, I,* 1939 *E*
Vile, T H (Newport) 1908 *E, S,* 1910 *I,* 1912 *I, F, SA,* 1913 *E,* 1921 *S*
Vincent, H C (Bangor) 1882 *I*

Wakeford, J D M (S Wales Police) 1988 *WS, R*
Waldron, R (Neath) 1965 *E, S, I, F*
Waller, P D (Newport) 1908 *A,* 1909 *E, S, F, I,* 1910 *F*
Walters, N (Llanelli) 1902 *E*
Wanbon, R (Aberavon) 1968 *E*
Ward, W S (Cross Keys) 1934 *S, I*
Warlow, J (Llanelli) 1962 *I*
Waters D R (Newport) 1986 *E, S, I, F*
Watkins, D (Newport) 1963 *E, S, I, F, NZ,* 1964 *E, S, I, F, SA,* 1965 *E, S, I, F,* 1966 *E, S, I, F,* 1967 *I, F, E*
Watkins, E (Neath) 1924 *E, S, I, F*
Watkins, E (Blaina) 1926 *S, I, F*
Watkins, E (Cardiff) 1935 *NZ,* 1937 *S, I,* 1938 *E, S, I,* 1939 *E, S*
Watkins, H (Llanelli) 1904 *S, I,* 1905 *E, S, I,* 1906 *E*
Watkins, I J (Ebbw Vale) 1988 *E*(R), *S, I, F, NZ2, R,* 1989 *S, I, F, E*
Watkins, L (Oxford U, Llandaff) 1881 *E*
Watkins, M J (Newport) 1984 *I, F, E, A*
Watkins, S J (Newport, Cardiff) 1964 *S, I, F,* 1965 *E, S, I, F,* 1966 *E, S, I, F,* 1967 *S, I, F, E, NZ,* 1968 *E, S,* 1969 *S, I, F, E, NZ 1,* 1970 *E, I*
Watkins, W R (Newport) 1959 *F*
Watts, D (Maesteg) 1914 *E, S, F, I*
Watts, J (Llanelli) 1907 *E, S, I,* 1908 *E, S, F, I, A,* 1909 *S, F, I*
Watts, W (Llanelli) 1914 *E*
Watts, W H (Newport) 1892 *E, S, I,* 1893 *E, S, I,* 1894 *E, S, I,* 1895 *E, I,* 1896 *E*
Weaver, D (Swansea) 1964 *E*
Webb, J (Abertillery) 1907 *S,* 1908 *E, S, F, I, A,* 1909 *E, S, F, I,* 1910 *F, E, S, I,* 1911 *E, S, F, I,* 1912 *E, S*
Webb, J E (Newport) 1888 *M,* 1889 *S*
Webbe, G M C (Bridgend) 1986 *Tg* (R), *WS,* 1987 *F, E, S, [Tg], US,* 1988 *F*(R), *NZ1, R*
Webster, R E (Swansea) 1987 *[A]*
Wells, G T (Cardiff) 1955 *E, S,* 1957 *I, F,* 1958 *A, E, S*
Westacott, D (Cardiff) 1906 *I*
Wetter, H (Newport) 1912 *SA,* 1913 *E*
Wetter, J J (Newport) 1914 *S, F, I,* 1920 *E, S, F, I,* 1921 *E,* 1924 *I, NZ*
Wheel, G A D (Swansea) 1974 *I, E* (R), 1975 *F, E, I, A,* 1976 *E, S, I, F,* 1977 *I, F, E, S,* 1978 *E, S, I, F, A 1,2, NZ,* 1979 *S, I,* 1980 *F, E, S, I,* 1981 *E, S, I, F, A,* 1982 *I*
Wheeler, P J (Aberavon) 1967 *NZ,* 1968 *E*
Whitefoot, J (Cardiff) 1984 *A* (R), 1985 *S, I, F, E, Fj,* 1986 *E, S, I, F, Fj, Tg, WS,* 1987 *F, E, S, I, [I, C]*
Whitfield, J (Newport) 1919 *NZA,* 1920 *E, S, F, I,* 1921 *E,* 1922 *E, S, I, F,* 1924 *S, I*

Whitson, G K (Newport) 1956 *F,* 1960 *S, I*
Williams, B (Llanelli) 1920 *S, F, I*
Williams, B L (Cardiff) 1947 *E, S, F, I, A,* 1948 *E, S, F, I,* 1949 *E, S, I,* 1951 *I, SA,* 1952 *S,* 1953 *E, S, I, F, NZ,* 1954 *S,* 1955 *E*
Williams, B R (Neath) 1990 *S, I*
Williams, C (Llanelli) 1924 *NZ,* 1925 *E*
Williams, C (Aberavon, Swansea) 1977 *E, S,* 1980 *F, E, S, I, NZ,* 1983 *E*
Williams, C D (Cardiff, Neath) 1955 *F,* 1956 *F*
Williams, D (Ebbw Vale) 1963 *E, S, I, F,* 1964 *E, S, I, F, SA,* 1965 *E, S, I, F,* 1966 *E, S, I, A,* 1967 *F, E, NZ,* 1968 *E,* 1969 *S, I, F, E, NZ 1,2, A,* 1970 *SA, S, E, I,* 1971 *E, S, I, F*
Williams, D B (Newport, Swansea) 1978 *A 1,* 1981 *E, S*
Williams, E (Neath) 1924 *NZ,* 1925 *F*
Williams, E (Aberavon) 1925 *E, S*
Williams, F L (Cardiff) 1929 *S, F, I,* 1930 *E, S, I, F,* 1931 *F, I, SA,* 1932 *E, S, I,* 1933 *I*
Williams G (Aberavon) 1936 *E, S, I*
Williams G (London Welsh) 1950 *I, F,* 1951 *E, S, I, F, SA,* 1952 *E, S, I, F,* 1953 *NZ,* 1954 *E*
Williams, G (Bridgend) 1981 *I, F,* 1982 *E* (R), *S*
Williams, G P (Bridgend) 1980 *NZ,* 1981 *E, S, A,* 1982 *I*
Williams, J (Blaina) 1920 *E, S, F, I,* 1921 *S, F, I*
Williams, J F (London Welsh) 1905 *I, NZ,* 1906 *S, SA*
Williams, J J (Llanelli) 1973 *F* (R), *A,* 1974 *S, I, F, E,* 1975 *F, E, S, I, A,* 1976 *E, S, I, F,* 1977 *I, F, E, S,* 1978 *E, S, I, F, A 1,2, NZ,* 1979 *S, I, F, E*
Williams, J L (Cardiff) 1906 *SA,* 1907 *E, S, I,* 1908 *E, S, I, A,* 1909 *E, S, F, I,* 1910 *I,* 1911 *E, S, F, I*
Williams, J P R (London Welsh, Bridgend) 1969 *S, I, F, E, NZ 1,2, A,* 1970 *SA, S, E, I, F,* 1971 *E, S, I, F,* 1972 *E, S, F, NZ,* 1973 *E, S, I, F, A,* 1974 *S, I, F,* 1975 *F, E, S, I, A,* 1976 *E, S, I, F,* 1977 *I, F, E, S,* 1978 *E, S, I, F, A 1,2, NZ,* 1979 *S, I, F, E,* 1980 *NZ,* 1981 *E, S*
Williams, L (Llanelli, Cardiff) 1947 *E, S, F, I, A,* 1948 *I,* 1949 *E*
Williams, L H (Cardiff) 1957 *S, I, F,* 1958 *E, S, I, F,* 1959 *E, S, I,* 1961 *F,* 1962 *E, S*
Williams, M (Newport) 1923 *F*
Williams, O (Llanelli) 1947 *E, S, A,* 1948 *E, S, F, I*
Williams, R (Llanelli) 1954 *S,* 1957 *F,* 1958 *A*
Williams, R D G (Newport) 1881 *E*
Williams, R F (Cardiff) 1912 *SA,* 1913 *E, S,* 1914 *I*
Williams, R H (Llanelli) 1954 *I, F, S,* 1955 *S, I, F,* 1956 *E, S, I,* 1957 *E, S, I, F,* 1958 *A, E, S, I, F,* 1959 *E, S, I, F,* 1960 *E*
Williams, S (Llanelli) 1947 *E, S, F, I,* 1948 *S, F*
Williams, S A (Aberavon) 1939 *E, S, I*
Williams, T (Pontypridd) 1882 *I*
Williams, T (Swansea) 1888 *S, I*
Williams, T (Swansea) 1912 *I,* 1913 *F,* 1914 *E, S, F, I*
Williams, Tudor (Swansea) 1921 *F*
Williams, T G (Cross Keys) 1935 *S, I, NZ,* 1936 *E, S, I,* 1937 *S, I*
Williams, W A (Crumlin) 1927 *E, S, F, I*
Williams, W A (Newport) 1952 *I, F,* 1953 *E*
Williams, W E O (Cardiff) 1887 *S, I,* 1889 *S,* 1890 *S, E*
Williams, W H (Pontymister) 1900 *E, S, I,* 1901 *E*
Williams, W O G (Swansea, Devonport Services) 1951 *F, SA,* 1952 *E, S, I, F,* 1953 *E, S, I, F, NZ,* 1954 *E, I, F, S,* 1955 *E, S, I, F,* 1956 *E, S, I*
Williams, W P J (Neath) 1974 *I, F*
Williams-Jones, H (S Wales Police) 1989 *S*(R), 1990 *F*(R), *I*
Willis, W R (Cardiff) 1950 *E, S, I, F,* 1951 *E, S, I, F, SA,* 1952 *E, S,* 1953 *S, NZ,* 1954 *E, I, F, S,* 1955 *E, S, I, F*
Wiltshire, M L (Aberavon) 1967 *NZ,* 1968 *E, S, F*
Windsor, R W (Pontypool) 1973 *A,* 1974 *S, I, F, E,* 1975 *F, E, S, I, A,* 1976 *E, S, I, F,* 1977 *I, F, E, S,* 1978 *E, S, I, F, A 1,2, NZ,* 1979 *S, I, F*
Winfield, H B (Cardiff) 1903 *I,* 1904 *E, S, I,* 1905 *NZ,* 1906 *E, S, I,* 1907 *S, I,* 1908 *E, S, F, I, A*
Winmill, S (Cross Keys) 1921 *E, S, I, F*
Wintle, R V (London Welsh) 1988 *WS*(R)
Wooller, W (Sale, Cambridge U, Cardiff) 1933 *E, S, I,* 1935 *E, S, I, NZ,* 1936 *E, S, I,* 1937 *E, S, I,* 1938 *S, I,* 1939 *E, S, I*
Wyatt, M A (Swansea) 1983 *E, S, I, F,* 1984 *A,* 1985 *S,*

I, 1987 *E, S, I*

Young, D (Swansea, Cardiff) 1987 [*E, NZ*], *US*, 1988
*E, S, I, F, NZ*1,2, *WS, R*, 1989 *S, NZ*, 1990 *F*

Young, G A (Cardiff) 1886 *E, S*

Young, J (Harrogate, RAF, London Welsh) 1968 *S, I,
F*, 1969 *S, I, F, E, NZ* 1, 1970 *E, I, F*, 1971 *E, S, I, F*,
1972 *E, S, F, NZ*, 1973 *E, S, I, F*

Martyn Morris, who regained his place on the Welsh flank during the season, dives to score a spectacular try for Neath in the Schweppes/WRU Cup final at Cardiff.

WELSH INTERNATIONAL RECORDS

Both team and individual records are for official Welsh international matches up to 30 April 1990.

TEAM RECORDS

Highest score
49 v France (49-14) 1910 Swansea
v individual countries
28 v Australia (28-3) 1975 Cardiff
40 v Canada (40-9) 1987 Invercargill
34 v England (34-21) 1967 Cardiff
49 v France (49-14) 1910 Swansea
40 v Fiji (40-3) 1985 Cardiff
34 v Ireland (34-9) 1976 Dublin
16 v N Zealand (16-19) 1972 Cardiff
 9 v Romania (9-15) 1988 Cardiff
35 v Scotland (35-12) 1972 Cardiff
 6 v S Africa (6-6) 1970 Cardiff
29 v Tonga (29-16) 1987 Palmerston North
46 v United States (46-0) 1987 Cardiff
32 v W Samoa (32-14) 1986 Apia

Biggest winning points margin
46 v United States (46-0) 1987 Cardiff
v individual countries
25 v Australia (28-3) 1975 Cardiff
31 v Canada (40-9) 1987 Invercargill
25 v England (25-0) 1905 Cardiff
42 v France (47-5) 1909 Colombes
37 v Fiji (40-3) 1985 Cardiff
29 v Ireland (29-0) 1907 Cardiff
 5 v N Zealand (13-8) 1953 Cardiff
23 v Scotland (35-12) 1972 Cardiff
13 v Tonga (29-16) 1987 Palmerston North
46 v United States (46-0) 1987 Cardiff
22 v W Samoa (28-6) 1988 Cardiff
No wins v Romania or South Africa

Highest score by opposing team
54 N Zealand (9-54) 1988 Auckland
v individual countries
28 Australia (9-28) 1984 Cardiff
 9 Canada (40-9) 1987 Invercargill
34 England (6-34) 1990 Twickenham
31 France (12-31) 1989 Paris
15 Fiji (22-15) 1986 Suva
21 Ireland {
  (24-21) 1979 Cardiff
  (7-21) 1980 Dublin
  (9-21) 1985 Cardiff
}
54 N Zealand (9-54) 1988 Auckland
24 Romania (6-24) 1983 Bucharest
35 Scotland (10-35) 1924 Inverleith
24 S Africa (3-24) 1964 Durban
16 Tonga (29-16) 1987 Palmerston North
 0 United States (46-0) 1987 Cardiff
14 W Samoa (32-14) 1986 Apia

Biggest losing points margin
49 v N Zealand (3-52) 1988 Christchurch
v individual countries
19 v Australia (9-28) 1984 Cardiff
28 v England (6-34) 1990 Twickenham
19 v France (12-31) 1989 Paris
16 v Ireland (3-19) 1925 Belfast
49 v N Zealand (3-52) 1988 Christchurch
18 v Romania (6-24) 1983 Bucharest
25 v Scotland (10-35) 1924 Inverleith
21 v S Africa (3-24) 1964 Durban
No defeats v Canada, Fiji, Tonga, United States or Western Samoa

Most tries by Wales in an international
11 v France (47-5) 1909 Colombes

Most tries against Wales in an international
13 by England 1881 Blackheath

Most points by Wales in International Championship in a season – 102
in season 1975-76

Most tries by Wales in International Championship in a season – 21
in season 1909-10

INDIVIDUAL RECORDS

Most capped player
J P R Williams 55 1969-81
in individual positions
Full-back
J P R Williams 54(55)[1] 1969-81
Wing
K J Jones 44[2] 1947-57
Centre
S P Fenwick 30 1975-81

Fly-half
C I Morgan 29[3] 1951-58
Scrum-half
G O Edwards 53 1967-78
Prop
G Price 41 1975-83
Hooker
B V Meredith 34 1954-62
Lock
A J Martin 34 1973-81
R L Norster 34 1982-89
Flanker
W D Morris 32(34)[4] 1967-74
No 8
T M Davies 38 1969-76

[1]*Williams won one cap as a flanker*
[2]*T G R Davies, 46 caps, won 35 as a wing, 11 as a centre*
[3]*P Bennett, 29 caps, played 25 times as a fly-half*
[4]*Morris won his first two caps as a No 8*

Longest international career
W J Trew
14 seasons 1899-1900 to 1912-13
T H Vile
14 seasons 1907-08   to 1920-21
H Tanner
14 seasons 1935-36   to 1948-49

Most internationals as captain
A J Gould 18 1889-97

Most points in internationals – 227
P H Thorburn (29 matches) 1985-90

**Most points in International
Championship in a season – 52**
P H Thorburn (4 matches) 1985-86

Most points in an international – 19
J Bancroft v France 1910 Swansea
K S Jarrett v England 1967 Cardiff
P Bennett   v Ireland 1976 Dublin

Most tries in internationals – 20
G O Edwards (53 matches) 1967-78
T G R Davies (46 matches) 1966-78

**Most tries in International
Championship in a season – 6**
R A Gibbs (4 matches) 1907-08
M C R Richards (4 matches) 1968-69

Most tries in an international – 4
W M Llewellyn* v England 1899 Swansea
R A Gibbs v France 1908 Cardiff
M C R Richards v England 1969 Cardiff
I C Evans v Canada 1987 Invercargill
on first appearance

Most conversions in internationals – 38
J Bancroft (18 matches) 1909-1914

**Most conversions in International
Championship in a season – 11**
J Bancroft (4 matches) 1908-09

Most conversions in an international – 8
J Bancroft v France 1910 Swansea

Most dropped goals in internationals – 13
J Davies (27 matches) 1985-88

Most penalty goals in internationals – 53
P H Thorburn (29 matches) 1985-90

**Most penalty goals in International
Championship in a season – 16**
P H Thorburn (4 matches) 1985-86

Most points on overseas tour – 55
S P Fenwick (7 matches) Australia 1978
*P Bennett scored 63 points in the Far East in 1975, but this
was not on a major tour*

Most points in a tour match – 21
J Davies v Hawke's Bay 1988 Napier, NZ
*P Bennett scored 34 points v Japan in Tokyo in 1975, but
this was not on a major tour*

Most tries in a tour match – 3
M C R Richards v Otago 1969 Dunedin,
  NZ
Several others have scored 3 in matches on non-major tours

FRENCH DIVIDED IN DEFEAT
THE 1989-90 SEASON IN FRANCE
Bob Donahue *International Herald Tribune*

Jacques Fouroux, chairman of selectors and head coach, could still hope at the start of the season that most of his veterans would serve until the World Cup, that new blood could be injected slowly and that a smooth build-up to 1991 was possible. By February those hopes had been dashed. The final humiliation came in May, when Romania beat France in Fouroux's home town of Auch. So a rebuilding job needed to be started in Australia in June.

Three victories and five defeats in 1989-90 made the worst tally since 1981-82. Strains within the squad, first evident in New Zealand, led in February to the dropping of the captain, Pierre Berbizier. An awkward transition of another sort loomed when Albert Ferrasse, president of the Fédération Française de Rugby since 1968, declared in March that he would not seek a seventh four-year term in 1992. Opposition to his preferred successor, the acerbic and increasingly powerful vice-president Fouroux, was strengthened by the poor results.

The FFR began the season with just over 200,000 registered players (and some 30,000 officials) in 1,740 clubs. Fouroux was in charge of a drive to reach 300,000 players by 1992. For the third time, the league phase of the club championship was played in two radically different stages. The first grouped the 80 clubs of the first division in 16 leagues of five. The average gate at these 320 matches was a mere 750. The top two in each league qualified for the serious stage: four leagues of eight, 224 matches and an average gate of 1,880.

A leading rugby league club, Le Pontet, switched to the Union code. Ferrasse had to weather allegations of professionalism as rumours about money swelled in tandem with swelling sponsorship. A desultory Provinces Cup attracted scant interest. Amid gaudy theatrics on the first Wednesday night of October a Home Unions XV won 29-27 against an experimental French team in which Laurent Rodriguez's fellow forwards boasted only 16 caps between them. It was France's first defeat at the Parc des Princes since 1982.

Next came tours by Fiji, Western Samoa and Australia, totalling 15 matches, all at different venues. In Strasbourg, the first Test against the Wallabies was lost 32-15, the biggest French losing margin at home since 1952, when the Springboks beat France 25-3. Out went Serge Blanco, Jean Condom, Rodriguez and Berbizier, with 230 caps between them. Victory in Lille in the second Test, with Henri Sanz as scrum-half and captain, silenced Fouroux's critics for a while. But tension continued to grow: friction over sponsorship policy set Ferrasse against his old side-kick Guy Basquet. Ferrasse temporarily sacked another companion, Marcel Martin, in a murky dispute involving French television rights for the World Cup. Fouroux recalled his veterans, and

The French team beaten by England in Paris. L-R, back row: P Ondarts, J-P Garuet, L Armary, L Rodriguez, D Erbani, E Champ, T Devergie, O Roumat; front row: M Andrieu, P Sella, S Blanco, P Berbizier (capt), F Mesnel, D Charvet, P Lagisquet.

an historic eighth consecutive win over Wales was welcome news.

Ticket requests for the England match in February exceeded 100,000, according to the new secretary general, Francis Senegas. A violent wind felled scores of trees in the Bois de Boulogne as the All Whites swept the French off the pitch. On the Monday morning, *L'Equipe* informed the country that the torch of supremacy in Europe had passed from France to England. *Midi Olympique* sadly acknowledged 'the wind of history'.

The remainder of the international season – disgrace at Murrayfield, revival at home against Ireland, collapse against Romania – made a confused prelude to the rebuilding mission in Australia. Of the 30 players who had toured New Zealand, only 15 were in the squad that flew to Sydney in May. Daniel Dubroca became assistant coach.

League play ended with Bayonne, La Rochelle, Lourdes, Nice, Tarbes and Perpignan among the 16 clubs failing to qualify for the knock-out phase. Nîmes, Béziers, Castres, Brive, Colomiers, Auch, Bègles and Biarritz fell in the eighth-finals. In the quarter-finals, reigning champions Toulouse beat Narbonne, Racing Club de France beat Grenoble, Agen beat Toulon and Montferrand beat Dax. Racing surprised everyone by knocking out Toulouse in a semi-final at Béziers, and Agen out-kicked Montferrand at Toulouse. The Paris club went into the final as unfancied underdog.

Two nice touches brightened the end of a troubled season. The experienced Blanco, with 75 caps and 30 international tries to his credit, was named captain for the Australia tour. Back in February he had considered retiring. And then, in the club final, Racing's backs wore pink bow ties and garish shorts, sipped champagne at half-time, did their utmost to play champagne rugby – and won the match in extra time, 22-12. The Brennus Shield belonged to Paris for the first time since 1959. In some respects, however, it was an ugly final. The two packs spent the evening exchanging petulant fouls, while the referee tolerated 21 collapsed scrums. The crowd, as it had done at the England match, chanted for Ferrasse to resign. This seemed unfair on the day, but also symptomatic of a growing malaise in French rugby.

FRENCH CLUB CHAMPIONSHIP FINAL 1990
26 May, Parc des Princes

Racing Club de France 22 (1G 4PG 1T) **Agen 12** (3PG 1DG)

Racing Club de France: J-B Lafond; P Guillard, F Mesnel, E Blanc, G Abadie; D Pouyau, J-P Saffore; L Benezech, J-P Genet, P Voisin, M Tachdjian, P Serrière (*capt*), X Blond, L Cabannes, C Deslandes *Replacements* M Dawson for Voisin; B Dalle for Blond
Scorers *Tries:* Cabannes, Abadie *Conversion:* Pouyau
Penalty Goals: Pouyau (2), Lafond, Abadie

Agen: B Lacombe; O Campan, P Sella, P Schattel, E Gleyze; P Montlaur, Pierre Berbizier (*capt*); J-L Tolot, Philippe Berbizier, L Seigne, A Benazzi, B Mazzer, J Gratton, P Benetton, D Erbani *Replacements* P Pujade for Benazzi; G Lascube for Philippe Berbizier
Scorers *Penalty Goals:* Campan, Montlaur (2) *Dropped Goal:* Montlaur
Referee C Debat (Pyrenées)

FRENCH INTERNATIONAL PLAYERS
(*up to 30 April 1990*)

ABBREVIATIONS

A – Australia; *Arg* – Argentina; *B* – British Forces and Home Union Teams; *Cz* – Czechoslovakia; *E* – England; *Fj* – Fiji; *G* – Germany; *I* – Ireland; *It* – Italy; *J* – Japan; *K* – New Zealand Services; *M* – Maoris; *NZ* – New Zealand; *R* – Romania; *S* – Scotland; *SA* – South Africa; *US* – United States of America; *W* – Wales; *Z* – Zimbabwe; (R) – Replacement. Entries in square brackets [ ] indicate appearances in the World Cup

Club Abbreviations: ASF-Association Sportive Française; BEC-Bordeaux Etudiants Club; CASG-Club Athlétique des Sports Généraux; PUC-Paris Université Club; RCF-Racing Club de France; SB-Stade Bordelais; SBUC-Stade Bordelais Université Club; SCUF-Sporting Club Universitaire de France; SF-Stade Français; SOE-Stade Olympien des Etudiants; TOEC-Toulouse Olympique Employés Club.

Note: Years given for Five Nations' matches are for second half of season, eg 1972 refers to season 1971-72. Years for all other matches refer to the actual year of the match. When a series has taken place, or more than one match has been played against a country in the same year, figures have been used to denote the particular matches in which players have featured. Thus 1967 *SA* 2,4 indicates that a player appeared in the second and fourth Tests of the 1967 series against South Africa. This list includes only those players who have appeared in FFR International Matches '*donnant droit au titre d'international*'.

Abadie, A (Pau) 1964 *I*
Abadie, A (Graulhet) 1965 *R*, 1967 *SA* 1, 3, 4, *NZ*, 1968 *S, I*
Abadie, L (Tarbes) 1963 *R*
Aguerre, R (Biarritz O) 1979 *S*
Aguilar, D (Pau) 1937 *G*
Aguirre, J-M (Bagnères) 1971 *A* 2, 1972 *S*, 1973 *W, I, J, R*, 1974 *I, W, Arg* 2, *R, SA* 1, 1976 *W* (R), *E, US, A* 2, *R*, 1977 *W, E, S, I, Arg* 1, 2, *NZ* 1, 2, *R*, 1978 *E, S, I, W, R*, 1979 *I, W, E, S, NZ* 1, 2, *R*, 1980 *W, I*
Ainciart, E (Bayonne) 1933 *G*, 1934 *G*, 1935 *G*, 1937 *G, It*, 1938 *G* 1
Albaladejo, P (Dax) 1954 *E, It*, 1960 *W, I, It, R*, 1961 *S, SA, E, W, I, NZ* 1, 2, *A*, 1962 *S, E, W, I*, 1963 *S, I, E, W, It*, 1964 *S, NZ, W, It, I, SA, Fj*
Alvarez, A-J (Tyrosse) 1945 *B* 2, 1946 *B, I, K, W*, 1947 *S, I, W, E*, 1948 *I, A, S, W, E*, 1949 *I, E, W*, 1951 *S, E, W*
Amand, H (SF) 1906 *NZ*
Ambert, A (Toulouse) 1930 *S, I, E, G, W*
Amestoy, J-B (Mont-de-Marsan) 1964 *NZ, E*
André, G (RCF) 1913 *SA, E, W, I*, 1914 *I, W, E*
Andrieu, M (Nîmes) 1986 *Arg* 2, *NZ* 1, *R* 2, *NZ* 2, 1987 [*R, Z*], *R*, 1988 *E, S, I, W, Arg* 1, 2, 3, 4, *R*, 1989 *I, W, E, S, NZ* 2, *B, A* 2, 1990 *W, E, I* (R)
Anduran, J (SCUF) 1910 *W*
Araou, R (Narbonne) 1924 *R*
Arcalis, R (Brive) 1950 *S, I*, 1951 *I, E, W*
Arino, M (Agen) 1962 *R*
Aristouy, P (Pau) 1948 *S*, 1949 *Arg* 2, 1950 *S, I, E, W*
Armary, L (Lourdes) 1987 [*R*], *R*, 1988 *S, I, W, Arg* 3, 4, *R*, 1989 *W, S, A* 1, 2, 1990 *W, E, S, I*
Arnal, J-M (RCF) 1914 *I, W*
Arnaudet, M (Lourdes) 1964 *I*, 1967 *It, W*
Arotca, R (Bayonne) 1938 *R*
Arrieta, J (SF) 1953 *E, W*
Arthapignet, P (Tarbes) 1988 *Arg* 4 (R)
Astre, R (Béziers) 1971 *R*, 1972 *I* 1, 1973 *E* (R), 1975 *E, S, I, SA* 1, 2, *Arg* 2, 1976 *A* 2, *R*
Augé, J (Dax) 1929 *S, W*
Augras, L (Agen) 1931 *I, S, W*
Averous, J-L (La Voulte) 1975 *S, I, SA* 1, 2, 1976 *I, W, E, US, A* 1, 2, *R*, 1977 *W, E, S, I, Arg* 1, *R*, 1978 *E, S, I*, 1979 *NZ* 1, 2, 1980 *E, S*, 1981 *A* 2
Azarete, J-L (Dax, St Jean-de-Luz) 1969 *W, R*, 1970 *S, I, W, R*, 1971 *S, I, E, W, A* 2, *R*, 1972 *E, W, I* 2, *A* 1, *R*, 1973 *NZ, W, I, R*, 1974 *I, R, SA* 1, 2, 1975 *W*

Bader, E (Primevères) 1926 *M*, 1927 *I, S*
Badin, C (Chalon) 1973 *W, I*, 1975 *Arg* 1
Baillette, M (Perpignan) 1925 *I, NZ, S*, 1926 *W, M*, 1927 *I, W, G* 2, 1929 *G*, 1930 *S, I, E, G*, 1931 *I, S, E*, 1932 *G*
Baladie, G (Agen) 1945 *B* 1, 2, *W*, 1946 *B, I, K*
Ballarin, J (Tarbes) 1924 *E*, 1925 *NZ, S*
Baquet, J (Toulouse) 1921 *I*

Barbazanges, A (Roanne) 1932 *G*, 1933 *G*
Barrau, M (Beaumont, Toulouse) 1971 *S, E, W*, 1972 *E, W, A* 1, 2, 1973 *S, NZ, E, I, J, R*, 1974 *I, S*
Barrère, P (Toulon) 1929 *G*, 1931 *W*
Barrière, R (Béziers) 1960 *R*
Barthe, E (SBUC) 1925 *W, E*
Barthe, J (Lourdes) 1954 *Arg* 1, 2, 1955 *S*, 1956 *I, W, It, E, Cz*, 1957 *S, I, E, W, R* 1, 2, 1958 *S, E, A, W, It, I, SA* 1, 2, 1959 *S, E, It, W*
Basauri, R (Albi) 1954 *Arg* 1
Bascou, P (Bayonne) 1914 *E*
Basquet, G (Agen) 1945 *W*, 1946 *B, I, K, W*, 1947 *S, I, W, E*, 1948 *I, A, S, W, E*, 1949 *S, I, E, W, Arg* 1, 1950 *S, I, E, W*, 1951 *S, I, E, W*, 1952 *S, I, SA, W, E, It*
Bastiat, J-P (Dax) 1969 *R*, 1970 *S, I, W*, 1971 *S, I, SA* 2, 1972 *A* 1, 1973 *E*, 1974 *Arg* 1, 2, *SA* 2, 1975 *W, Arg* 1, 2, *R*, 1976 *S, I, W, E, A* 1, 2, *R*, 1977 *W, E, S, I*, 1978 *E, S, I, W*
Baudry, N (Montferrand) 1949 *S, I, W, Arg* 1, 2
Baulon, R (Vienne, Bayonne) 1954 *S, NZ, W, E, It*, 1955 *I, E, W, It*, 1956 *S, I, W, It, E, Cz*, 1957 *S, I, It*
Baux, J-P (Lannemezan) 1968 *NZ* 1, 2, *SA* 1, 2
Bavozet, J (Lyon) 1911 *S, E, W*
Bayard, J (Toulouse) 1923 *S, W, E*, 1924 *W, R, US*
Bayardon, J (Chalon) 1964 *S, NZ, E*
Beaurin, C (SF) 1907 *E*, 1908 *E*
Bégu, J (Dax) 1982 *Arg* 2 (R), 1984 *E, S*
Béguerie, C (Agen) 1979 *NZ* 1
Beguet, L (RCF) 1922 *I*, 1923 *S, W, E, I*, 1924 *S, I, E, R, US*
Behoteguy, A (Bayonne, Cognac) 1923 *E*, 1924 *S, I, E, W, R, US*, 1926 *E*, 1927 *E, G* 1, 2, 1928 *A, I, E, G, W*, 1929 *S, W, E*
Behoteguy, H (RCF, Cognac) 1923 *W*, 1928 *A, I, E, G, W*
Belascain, C (Bayonne) 1977 *R*, 1978 *E, S, I, W, R*, 1979 *I, W, E, S*, 1982 *W, E, S, I*, 1983 *E, S, I, W*
Belletante, G (Nantes) 1951 *I, E, W*
Bénésis, R (Narbonne) 1969 *W, R*, 1970 *S, I, W, E, R*, 1971 *S, I, E, W, A* 2, *R*, 1972 *S, I* 1, *E, W, I* 2, *A* 1, *R*, 1973 *NZ, E, W, I, J, R*, 1974 *I, W, E, S*
Benetière, J (Roanne) 1954 *It, Arg* 1
Benetton, P (Agen) 1989 *B*
Berbizier, P (Lourdes, Agen) 1981 *S, I, W, E, NZ* 1, 2, 1982 *I, R*, 1983 *S, I*, 1984 *S* (R), *NZ* 1, 2, 1985 *Arg* 1, 2, 1986 *S, I, W, E, R* 1, *Arg* 1, *A*, *NZ* 1, *R* 2, *NZ* 2, 3, 1987 *W, E, S, I, [S, R, Fj, A, NZ]*, *R*, 1988 *E, S, I, W, Arg* 1, 2, 1989 *I, W, E, S, NZ* 1, 2, *B, A* 1, 1990 *W, E*
Berejnoi, J-C (Tulle) 1963 *R*, 1964 *S, W, It, I, SA, Fj, R*, 1965 *S, I, E, W, It, R*, 1966 *S, I, E, W, It, R*, 1967 *S, A, E, It, W, I, R*
Berges, B (Toulouse) 1926 *I*
Berges-Cau, R (Lourdes) 1976 *E* (R)
Bergeze, F (Bayonne) 1936 *G* 2, 1937 *G, It*, 1938 *G* 1, *R, G* 2
Bergougnan, Y (Toulouse) 1945 *B* 1, *W*, 1946 *B, I, K,*

248

W, 1947 S, I, W, E, 1948 S, W, E, 1949 S, E, Arg 1, 2
Bernard, R (Bergerac) 1951 S, I, E, W
Bernon, J (Lourdes) 1922 I, 1923 S
Bérot, J-L (Toulouse) 1968 NZ 3, A, 1969 S, I, 1970 E, R, 1971 S, I, E, W, SA 1, 2, A 1, 2, R, 1972 S, I 1, E, W, A 1, 1974 I
Bérot, P (Agen), 1986 R 2, NZ 2, 3, 1987 W, E, S, I, R, 1988 E, S, I, Arg 1, 2, 3, 4, R, 1989 S, NZ 1, 2
Bertrand, P (Bourg) 1951 I, E, W, 1953 S, I, E, W, It
Bertranne, R (Bagnères) 1971 E, W, SA 2, A 1, 2, 1972 S, I 1, 1973 NZ, E, J, R, 1974 I, W, E, S, Arg 1, 2, SA 1, 2, 1975 W, E, S, I, SA 1, 2, Arg 1, 2, R, 1976 S, I, W, E, US, A 1, 2, 1977 W, E, S, I, Arg 1, 2, NZ 1, 2, R, 1978 E, S, I, W, R, 1979 I, W, E, S, R, 1980 W, E, S, I, SA, R, 1981 S, I, W, E, R, NZ 1, 2
Berty, D (Toulouse) 1989 A 1(R)
Besset, E (Grenoble) 1924 S
Besset, L (SCUF) 1914 W, E
Besson, M (CASG) 1924 I, 1925 I, E, 1926 S, W, 1927 I
Besson, P (Brive) 1963 S, I, E, 1965 W, 1968 SA 1
Bianchi, J (Toulon) 1986 Arg 1
Bichendaritz, J (Biarritz O) 1954 It, Arg 1, 2
Bidart, L (La Rochelle) 1953 W
Biemouret, P (Agen) 1969 E, W, 1970 I, W, E, 1971 W, SA 1, 2, A 1, 1972 E, W, I 2, A 2, R, 1973 S, NZ, E, W, I
Biénès, R (Cognac) 1950 S, I, E, W, 1951 S, I, E, W, 1952 S, I, SA, W, E, It, 1953 S, I, E, 1954 S, I, NZ, W, E, Arg 1, 2, 1956 S, I, W, It, E
Bigot, C (Quillan) 1930 S, E, 1931 I, S
Bilbao, L (St Jean de Luz) 1978 I, 1979 I
Billac, E (Bayonne) 1920 S, E, W, I, US, 1921 S, W, 1922 W, 1923 E
Billière, M (Toulouse) 1968 NZ 3
Bioussa, A (Toulouse) 1924 W, US, 1925 I, NZ, S, E, 1926 S, I, E, 1928 E, G, W, 1929 I, S, W, E, 1930 S, I, E, G, W
Bioussa, C (Toulouse) 1913 W, I, 1914 I
Biraben, M (Dax) 1920 I, US, 1921 S, W, E, I, 1922 S, E, I
Blain, A (Carcassonne) 1934 G
Blanco, S (Biarritz O) 1980 SA, R, 1981 S, W, E, A 1, 2, R, NZ 1, 2, 1982 W, E, S, I, R, Arg 1, 2, 1983 E, S, I, W, 1984 I, W, E, S, NZ 1, 2, R, 1985 E, S, I, W, Arg 1, 2, 1986 S, I, W, E, R 1, Arg 2, A, NZ 1, R 2, NZ 2, 3, 1987 W, E, S, I, [S, R, Fj, A, NZ], R, 1988 E, S, I, W, Arg 1, 2, 3, 4, R, 1989 I, W, E, S, NZ 1, 2, B, A 1, 1990 E, S, I
Blond, J (SF) 1935 G, 1936 G 2, 1937 G, 1938 G 1, R, G 2
Boffelli, V (Aurillac) 1971 A 2, R, 1972 S, I 1, 1973 J, R, 1974 I, W, E, S, Arg 1, 2, R, SA 1, 2, 1975 W, S, I, 2, R, 1969 S, I, E, R, 1970 W, E
Bonal, J-M (Toulouse) 1968 E, W, Cz, NZ 2, 3, SA 1, 2, R, 1969 S, I, E, R, 1970 W, E
Bonamy, R (SB) 1928 A, I
Boniface, A (Mont-de-Marsan) 1954 I, NZ, W, E, Arg 1, 2, 1955 S, I, 1956 S, I, W, It, Cz, 1957 S, I, W, R 2, 1958 S, E, 1959 E, 1961 NZ 1, 3, A, R, 1962 E, W, I, It, R, 1963 S, I, E, W, It, R, 1964 S, NZ, E, W, It, 1965 W, It, R, 1966 S, I, E, W
Boniface, G (Mont-de-Marsan) 1960 W, I, It, R, Arg 1, 2, 3, 1961 S, SA, E, W, It, NZ 1, 2, 3, A, R, 1962 R, 1963 S, I, E, W, It, R, 1964 S, 1965 S, I, E, W, It, R, 1966 S, I, E, W
Bonnes, E (Narbonne) 1924 W, R, US
Bonneval, E (Toulouse) 1984 NZ 2 (R), 1985 W, Arg 1, 1986 W, E, R 1, Arg 1, 2, A, R 2, NZ 2, 3, 1987 W, E, S, I, [Z], 1988 E
Bonnus, F (Toulon) 1950 S, I, E, W
Bonnus, M (Toulon) 1937 It, 1938 G 1, R, G 2, 1940 R
Bontemps, D (La Rochelle) 1968 SA 2
Borchard, G (RCF) 1908 E, 1909 E, W, I, 1911 I
Borde, F (RCF) 1920 I, US, 1921 S, W, E, 1922 S, W, 1923 S, I, 1924 E, 1925 I, 1926 E
Bordenave, L (Toulon) 1948 A, S, W, E, 1949 S
Boubee, J (Tarbes) 1921 S, E, I, 1922 E, W, 1923 E, I, 1925 NZ, S
Boudreau, R (SCUF) 1910 W, S
Bouet, D (Dax) 1989 NZ 1, 2, B, A 2
Bouguyon, G (Grenoble) 1961 SA, E, W, It, I, NZ 1, 2, 3, A

1962 S, E, W, I
Bourdeu, J R (Lourdes) 1952 S, I, SA, W, E, It, 1953 S, I, E
Bourgarel, R (Toulouse) 1969 R, 1970 S, I, E, R, 1971 W, SA 1, 2, 1973 S
Bourguignon, G (Narbonne) 1988 Arg 3, 1989 I, E, B, A 1
Bousquet, A (Béziers) 1921 E, I, 1924 R
Bousquet, R (Albi) 1926 M, 1927 I, S, W, E, G 1, 1929 W, E, 1930 W
Boyau, M (SBUC) 1912 I, S, W, E, 1913 W, I
Boyer, P (Toulon) 1935 G
Branca, G (SF) 1928 S, 1929 I, S
Branlat, A (RCF) 1906 NZ, E, 1908 W
Brejassou, R (Tarbes) 1952 S, I, SA, W, E, 1953 W, E, 1954 S, I, NZ, 1955 S, I, E, W, It
Brethes, R (St Sever) 1960 Arg 2
Bringeon, A (Biarritz O) 1925 W
Brun, G (Vienne) 1950 E, W, 1951 S, E, W, 1952 S, I, SA, W, E, It, 1953 E, W, It
Bruneau, M (SBUC) 1910 W, E, 1913 SA, E
Brunet, Y (Perpignan) 1975 SA 1, 1977 Arg 1
Buchet, E (Nice) 1980 E, W, 1982 E, R (R), Arg 1, 2
Buisson, H (Béziers) 1931 E, G
Buonomo, Y (Béziers) 1971 A 2, R, 1972 I 1
Burgun, M (RCF) 1909 I, 1910 W, S, I, 1911 S, E, 1912 I, S, 1913 S, E, 1914 E
Bustaffa, D (Carcassonne) 1977 Arg 1, 2, NZ 1, 2, 1978 W, R, 1980 W, E, S, SA, R
Buzy, C-E (Lourdes) 1946 K, W, 1947 S, I, W, E, 1948 I, A, S, W, E, 1949 S, I, E, W, Arg 1, 2

Cabanier, J-M (Montauban) 1963 R, 1964 S, Fj, 1965 S, I, W, It, R, 1966 S, I, E, W, It, R, 1967 S, A, E, It, W, I, SA 1, 3, NZ, R, 1968 S, I
Cabrol, H (Béziers) 1972 A 1 (R), A 2, 1973 J, 1974 SA 2
Cadenat, J (SCUF) 1910 S, E, 1911 W, I, 1912 W, E, 1913 I
Cahuc, F (St Girons) 1922 S
Cals, R (RCF) 1938 G 1
Calvo, G (Lourdes) 1961 NZ 1, 3
Camberabero, D (La Voulte, Béziers) 1982 R, Arg 1, 2, 1983 E, W, 1987 [R(R),Z, Fj(R), A, NZ], 1988 I, 1989 B, A 1, 1990 W, S, I
Camberabero, G (La Voulte) 1961 NZ 3, 1962 R, 1964 R, 1967 A, E, It, W, I, SA 1, 3, 4, 1968 S, E, W
Camberabero, L (La Voulte) 1964 R, 1965 S, I, 1966 E, W, 1967 A, E, It, W, I, 1968 S, E, W
Cambré, T (Oloron) 1920 E, W, I, US
Camel, A (Toulouse) 1928 S, A, I, E, G, W, 1929 W, E, G, 1930 S, I, E, G, W, 1935 G
Camel, M (Toulouse) 1929 S, W, E
Camicas, F (Tarbes) 1927 G 2, 1928 S, I, E, G, W, 1929 I, S, W, E
Camo, E (Villeneuve) 1931 I, S, W, E, G, 1932 G
Campaes, A (Lourdes) 1965 W, 1967 NZ, 1968 S, I, E, W, Cz, NZ 1, 2, A, 1969 S, W, 1972 R, 1973 NZ
Cantoni, J (Béziers) 1970 W, R, 1971 S, I, E, W, SA 1, 2, A 1, R, 1972 S, I 1, 1973 S, NZ, W, I, 1975 W (R)
Capdouze, J (Pau) 1964 SA, Fj, R, 1965 S, I, E
Capendeguy, J-M (Begles) 1967 NZ, R
Capitani, P (Toulon) 1954 Arg 1, 2
Capmau, J-L (Toulouse) 1914 E
Carabignac, J (Agen) 1951 S, I, 1952 SA, W, E, 1953 S, I
Carbonne, J (Perpignan) 1927 W
Carminati, A (Béziers) 1986 R 2, NZ 2, 1987 [R, Z], 1988 I, W, Arg 1, 2, 1989 I, W, S, NZ 1(R), 2, A 2, 1990 S
Caron, L (Lyon O, Castres) 1947 E, 1948 I, A, W, E, 1949 S, I, E, W, Arg 1
Carpentier, M (Lourdes) 1980 E, SA, R, 1981 S, I, A 1, 1982 E, S
Carrère, C (Toulon) 1966 R, 1967 S, A, E, W, I, SA 1, 3, 4, NZ, R, 1968 S, I, E, W, Cz, NZ 3, A, R, 1969 S, I, 1970 S, I, W, E, 1971 E, W
Carrère, J (Vichy, Toulon) 1956 S, 1957 E, W, R 2, 1958 S, A 1, 2, 1959 I
Carrère, R (Mont-de-Marsan) 1953 E, It
Casaux, L (Tarbes) 1959 I, It, 1962 S
Cassagne, P (Pau) 1957 It
Cassayet, A (Tarbes, Narbonne) 1920 S, E, W, US, 1921 W, E, I, 1922 S, E, W, 1923 S, W, E, I, 1924 S, E, W, R, US, 1925 I, NZ, S, W, 1926 S, I, E, W, M, 1927

249

I, S, W
Cassiède, M (Dax) 1961 *NZ* 3, *A, R*
Castets, J (Toulon) 1923 *W, E, I*
Caujolle, J (Tarbes) 1909 *E*, 1913 *SA, E*, 1914 *W, E*
Caunègre, R (SB) 1938 *R, G* 2
Caussade, A (Lourdes) 1978 *R*, 1979 *I, W, E, NZ* 1, 2, *R*, 1980 *W, E, S*, 1981 *S* (R), *I*
Caussarieu, G (Pau) 1929 *I*
Cayrefourcq, E (Tarbes) 1921 *E*
Cazals, P (Mont-de-Marsan) 1961 *NZ* 1, *A, R*
Cazenave, A (Pau) 1927 *E, G* 1, 1928 *S, A, G*
Cazenave, F (RCF) 1950 *E*, 1952 *S*, 1954 *I, NZ, W, E*
Cecillon, M (Bourgoin) 1988 *I, W, Arg* 2, 3, 4, *R*, 1989 *I, E, NZ* 1, 2, *A* 1
Celaya, M (Biarritz O, SBUC) 1953 *E, W, It*, 1954 *I, E, It, Arg* 1, 2, 1955 *S, I, E, W, It*, 1956 *S, I, W, It, E, Cz*, 1957 *S, I, E, W, R* 2, 1958 *S, E, A, W, It*, 1959 *S, E*, 1960 *S, E, W, I, R, Arg* 1, 2, 3, 1961 *S, SA, E, W, It, I, NZ* 1, 2, 3, *A, R*
Celhay, M (Bayonne) 1935 *G*, 1936 *G* 1, 1937 *G, It*, 1938 *G* 1, 1940 *B*
Cessieux, N (Lyon) 1906 *NZ*
Cester, E (TOEC, Valence) 1966 *S, I, E*, 1967 *W*, 1968 *S, I, E, W, Cz, NZ* 1, 3, *A, SA* 1, 2, *R*, 1969 *S, I, E, W*, 1970 *S, I, W, E*, 1971 *A* 1, 1972 *R*, 1973 *S, NZ, W, I, J, R*, 1974 *I, W, E, S*
Chaban-Delmas, J (CASG) 1945 *B* 2
Chabowski, H (Nice, Bourgoin) 1985 *Arg* 2 1986 *R* 2, *NZ* 2, 1989 *B*(R)
Chadebech, P (Brive) 1982 *R, Arg* 1, 2, 1986 *S, I*
Champ, E (Toulon) 1985 *Arg* 1, 2, 1986 *I, W, E, R* 1, *Arg* 1, 2, *A, NZ* 1, *R* 2, *NZ* 2, 3, 1987 *W, E, S, I*, [*S, R, Fj, A, NZ*], *R*, 1988 *E, S, Arg* 1, 3, 4, *R*, 1989 *W, S, A* 1, 2, 1990 *W, E*
Chapuy, L (SF) 1926 *S*
Charpentier, G (SF) 1911 *E*, 1912 *W, E*
Charton, P (Montferrand) 1940 *B*
Charvet, D (Toulouse) 1986 *W, E, R* 1, *Arg* 1, *A, NZ* 1, 3, 1987 *W, E, S, I*, [*S, R, Z, Fj, A, NZ*], *R*, 1989 *E*(R), 1990 *W, E*
Chassagne, J (Montferrand) 1938 *G* 1
Chatau, A (Bayonne) 1913 *SA*
Chaud, E (Toulon) 1932 *G*, 1934 *G*, 1935 *G*
Chenevay, C (Grenoble) 1968 *SA* 1
Chevallier, B (Montferrand) 1952 *S, I, SA, W, E, It*, 1953 *E, W, It*, 1954 *S, I, NZ, W, Arg* 1, 1955 *S, I, E, W, It*, 1956 *S, I, W, It, E, Cz*, 1957 *S*
Chiberry, J (Chambéry) 1955 *It*
Chilo, A (RCF) 1920 *S, W*, 1925 *I, NZ*
Cholley, G (Castres) 1975 *E, S, I, SA* 1, 2, *Arg* 1, 2, *R*, 1976 *S, I, W, E, A* 1, 2, *R*, 1977 *W, E, S, I, Arg* 1, 2, *NZ* 1, 2, *R*, 1978 *E, S, I, W, R*, 1979 *I, S*
Choy, J (Narbonne) 1930 *S, I, E, G, W*, 1931 *I*, 1933 *G*, 1934 *G*, 1935 *G*, 1936 *G* 2
Cimarosti, J (Castres) 1976 *US* (R)
Clady, A (Lezignan) 1929 *G*, 1931 *I, S, E, G*
Clarrac, H (St Girons) 1938 *G* 1
Claudel, R (Lyon) 1932 *G*, 1934 *G*
Clauzel, F (Béziers) 1924 *E, W*, 1925 *W*
Clave, J (Agen) 1936 *G* 2, 1938 *R, G* 2
Claverie, H (Lourdes) 1954 *NZ, W*
Clement, G (RCF) 1931 *W*
Clement, J (RCF) 1921 *S, W, E*, 1922 *S, E, W, I*, 1923 *S, W, I*
Clemente, M (Oloron) 1978 *R*, 1980 *S, I*
Cluchague, L (Biarritz O) 1924 *S*, 1925 *E*
Coderc, J (Chalon) 1932 *G*, 1933 *G*, 1934 *G*, 1935 *G*, 1936 *G* 1
Codorniou, D (Narbonne) 1979 *NZ* 1, 2, *R*, 1980 *W, E, S, I*, 1981 *S, W, E, A* 2, 1983 *E, S, I, W, A* 1, 2, *R*, 1984 *I, W, E, S, NZ* 1, 2, *R*, 1985 *E, S, I, W, Arg* 1, 2, 1986 *S, I, W, E, R* 1, *Arg* 1, 2, *NZ* 1, *R* 2, *NZ*
Cognet, L (Montferrand) 1932 *G*, 1936 *G* 1, 2, 1937 *G, It*
Colombier, J (St Junien) 1952 *SA, W, E*
Colomine, G (Narbonne) 1979 *NZ* 1
Combe, J (SF) 1910 *S, E, I*, 1911 *S*
Combes, G (Fumel) 1945 *B* 2
Communeau, M (SF) 1906 *NZ, E*, 1907 *E*, 1908 *E, W*, 1909 *E, W, I*, 1910 *S, E, I*, 1911 *S, E, I*, 1912 *I, S, W, E*, 1913 *SA, E, W*
Condom, J (Boucau, Biarritz) 1982 *R*, 1983 *E, S, I, W, A* 1, 2, *R*, 1984 *I, W, E, S, NZ* 1, 2, *R*, 1985 *E, S, I, W, Arg* 1, 2, 1986 *S, I, W, E, R* 1, *Arg* 1, 2, *NZ* 1, *R* 2, *NZ*

2, 3, 1987 *W, E, S, I*, [*S, R, Z, A, NZ*], *R*, 1988 *E, S, W, Arg* 1, 2, 3, 4, *R*, 1989 *I, W, E, S, NZ* 1, 2, *A* 1, 1990 *I*
Conilh de Beyssac, J (SBUC) 1912 *I, S*, 1914 *I, W, E*
Constant, G (Perpignan) 1920 *W*
Coscolla, G (Béziers) 1921 *S, W*
Costantino, J (Montferrand) 1973 *R*
Costes, F (Montferrand) 1979 *E, S, NZ* 1, 2, *R*, 1980 *W, I*
Coulon, E (Grenoble) 1928 *S*
Crabos, R (RCF) 1920 *S, E, W, I, US*, 1921 *S, W, E, I*, 1922 *S, E, W, I*, 1923 *S, I*, 1924 *S, I*
Crampagne, J (Begles) 1967 *SA* 4
Crancee, R (Lourdes) 1960 *Arg* 3, 1961 *S*
Crauste, M (RCF, Lourdes) 1957 *R* 1, 2, 1958 *S, E, A, W, It, I*, 1959 *E, It, W, I*, 1960 *S, E, W, I, It, R, Arg* 1, 3, 1961 *S, SA, E, W, It, I, NZ* 1, 2, 3, *A, R*, 1962 *S, E, W, I, It, R*, 1963 *S, I, E, W, It, R*, 1964 *S, NZ, E, W, It, I, SA, Fj, R*, 1965 *S, I, E, W, It, R*, 1966 *S, I, E, W, It*
Cremaschi, M (Lourdes) 1980 *R*, 1981 *R, NZ* 1, 2, 1982 *W, S*, 1983 *A* 1, 2, *R*, 1984 *I, W*
Crichton, W H (Le Havre) 1906 *NZ, E*
Cristina, J (Montferrand) 1979 *R*
Cussac, P (Biarritz O) 1934 *E*
Cutzach, A (Quillan) 1929 *G*

Daguerre, F (Biarritz O) 1936 *G* 1
Daguerre, J (CASG) 1933 *G*
Dalmaso, M (Mont-de-Marsan) 1988 *R*(R)
Danion, J (Toulon) 1924 *I*
Danos, P (Toulon, Béziers) 1954 *Arg* 1, 2, 1957 *R* 2, 1958 *S, E, W, It, I, SA* 1, 2, 1959 *S, E, It, W, I*, 1960 *S, E*
Darbos, P (Dax) 1969 *R*
Darracq, R (Dax) 1957 *It*
Darrieussecq, A (Biarritz O) 1973 *E*
Darrieussecq, J (Mont-de-Marsan) 1953 *It*
Darrouy, C (Mont-de-Marsan) 1957 *I, E, W, It, R* 1, 1959 *E*, 1961 *R*, 1963 *S, I, E, W, It*, 1964 *NZ, E, W, It, I, SA, Fj, R*, 1965 *S, I, E, It, R*, 1966 *S, I, E, W, It, R*, 1967 *S, A, E, It, W, I, SA* 1, 2, 4
Daudignon, G (SF) 1928 *S*
Dauga, B (Mont-de-Marsan) 1964 *S, NZ, E, W, It, I, SA, Fj, R*, 1965 *S, I, E, W, It, R*, 1966 *S, I, E, W, It*, 1967 *S, A, E, It, W, I, SA* 1, 2, 3, 4, *NZ, R*, 1968 *S, I, NZ* 1, 2, 3, *A, SA* 1, 2, *R*, 1969 *S, I, E, R*, 1970 *S, I, W, E, R*, 1971 *S, I, E, W, SA* 1, 2, *A* 1, 2, *R*, 1972 *S, I* 1, *W*
Dauger, J (Bayonne) 1945 *B* 1, 2, 1953 *S*
Daulouede, P (Tyrosse) 1937 *G, It*, 1938 *G* 1, 1940 *B*
Decamps, P (RCF) 1911 *S*
Dedet, J (SF) 1910 *S, E, I*, 1911 *W, I*, 1912 *S*, 1913 *E, I*
Dedeyn, P (RCF) 1906 *NZ*
Dedieu, P (Béziers) 1963 *E, It*, 1964 *W, It, I, SA, Fj, R*, 1965 *S, I, E, W*
De Gregorio, J (Grenoble) 1960 *S, E, W, I, It, R, Arg* 1, 2, 1961 *S, SA, E, W, It, I*, 1962 *S, E, W*, 1963 *S, W, It*, 1964 *NZ, E*
Dehez, J-L (Agen) 1967 *SA* 2, 1969 *R*
De Jouvencel, E (SF) 1909 *W, I*
De Laborderie, M (RCF) 1921 *I*, 1922 *I*, 1925 *W, E*
Delage, C (Agen) 1983 *S, I*
De Malherbe, H (CASG) 1932 *G*, 1933 *G*
De Malmann, R (RCF) 1908 *E, W*, 1909 *E, W, I*, 1910 *E, I*
De Muizon, J J (SF) 1910 *I*
Delaigue, G (Toulon) 1973 *J, R*
Delque, A (Toulouse) 1937 *It*, 1938 *G* 1, *R, G* 2
Descamps, (SB) 1927 *G* 2
Desclaux, F (RCF) 1949 *Arg* 1, 2, 1953 *It*
Desclaux, J (Perpignan) 1934 *G*, 1935 *G*, 1936 *G* 1, 2, 1937 *G, It*, 1938 *G* 1, *R, G* 2, 1945 *B* 1
Desnoyer, L (Brive) 1974 *R*
Destarac, L (Tarbes) 1926 *S, I, E, W, M*, 1927 *W, E, G* 1, 2
Desvouges, R (SF) 1914 *W*
Detrez, P-E (Nîmes) 1983 *A* 2 (R), 1986 *Arg* 1 (R), 2, *A* (R), *NZ* 1
Devergie, T (Nîmes) 1988 *R*, 1989 *NZ* 1, 2, *B, A* 2, 1990 *W, E, S, I*
Deygas, M (Vienne) 1937 *It*
Dintrans, P (Tarbes) 1979 *NZ* 1, 2, *R*, 1980 *E, S, I*,

SA, R, 1981 *S, I, W, E, A* 1, 2, *R, NZ* 1, 2, 1982 *W, E, S, I, R, Arg* 1, 2, 1983 *E, W, A* 1, 2, *R*, 1984 *I, W, E, S, NZ* 1,2, *R*, 1985 *E, S, I, W, Arg* 1, 2, 1987 [*R*], 1988 *Arg* 1, 2, 3, 1989 *W, E, S*

Dizabo, P (Tyrosse) 1948 *A, S, E*, 1949 *S, I, E, W, Arg* 2, 1950 *S, I*, 1960 *Arg* 1, 2, 3

Domec, A (Carcassonne) 1929 *W*

Domec, H (Lourdes) 1953 *W, It*, 1954 *S, I, NZ, W, E, It*, 1955 *S, I, E, W*, 1956 *I, W, It*, 1958 *E, A, W, It, I*

Domenech, A (Vichy, Brive) 1954 *W, E, It*, 1955 *S, I, E, W*, 1956 *S, I, W, It, E, Cz*, 1957 *S, I, E, W, It, R* 1, 2, 1958 *S, E, It*, 1959 *It*, 1960 *S, E, W, I, It, R, Arg* 1, 2, 3, 1961 *S, SA, E, W, It, I, NZ* 1, 2, 3, *A, R*, 1962 *S, E, W, I, It, R*, 1963 *W, It*

Domercq, J (Bayonne) 1912 *I, S*

Dorot, J (RCF) 1935 *G*

Dospital, P (Bayonne) 1977 *R*, 1980 *I*, 1981 *S, I, W, E*, 1982 *I, R, Arg* 1, 2, 1983 *E, S, I, W*, 1984 *E, S, NZ* 1,2, *R*, 1985 *E, S, I, W, Arg* 1

Dourthe, C (Dax) 1966 *R*, 1967 *S, A, E, W, I, SA* 1, 2, 3, *NZ*, 1968 *W, NZ* 3, *SA* 1, 2, 1969 *W*, 1971 *SA* 2 (R), *R*, 1972 *I* 1, 2, *A* 1, 2, *R*, 1973 *S, NZ, E*, 1974 *I, Arg* 1, 2, *SA* 1, 2, 1975 *W, E, S*, 1927 *W, E, S*

Dousseau, E (Angoulême) 1938 *R*

Droitecourt, M (Montferrand) 1972 *R*, 1973 *NZ* (R), *E*, 1974 *E, S, Arg* 1, *SA* 2, 1975 *SA* 1, 2, *Arg* 1, 2, *R*, 1976 *S, I, W, A* 1, 1977 *Arg* 2

Dubertrand, A (Montferrand) 1971 *A* 2, *R*, 1972 *I* 2, 1974 *I, W, E, SA* 2, 1975 *Arg* 1, 2, *R*, 1976 *S, US*

Dubois, D (Begles) 1971 *S*

Dubroca, D (Agen) 1979 *NZ* 2, 1981 *NZ* 2 (R), 1982 *E, S*, 1984 *W, E, S*, 1985 *Arg* 2, 1986 *S, I, W, E, R* 1, *Arg* 2, *A, NZ* 1, *R* 2, *NZ* 2, 3, 1987 *W, E, S, I*, [*S, Z, Fj, A, NZ*], *R*, 1988 *E, S, I, W*

Duche (Limoges) 1929 *W*

Duclos, A (Lourdes) 1931 *S*

Ducousso, J (Tarbes) 1925 *S, W, E*

Dufau, G (RCF) 1948 *I, A*, 1949 *I, W*, 1950 *S, E, W*, 1951 *S, I, E, W*, 1952 *SA, W*, 1953 *S, I, E, W*, 1954 *S, I, NZ, W, E, It*, 1955 *S, I, E, W, It*, 1956 *S, I, W, It*, 1957 *S, I, E, W, It, R* 1

Dufau, J (Biarritz) 1912 *I, S, W, E*

Duffaut, Y (Agen) 1954 *Arg* 1, 2

Dufour, R (Tarbes) 1911 *W*

Dufourcq, J (SBUC) 1906 *NZ, E*, 1907 *E*, 1908 *W*

Duhard, Y (Bagnères) 1980 *E*

Duhau, J (SF) 1928 *I*, 1930 *I, G*, 1931 *I, S, W*, 1933 *G*

Dulaurens, C (Toulouse) 1926 *I*, 1928 *S*, 1929 *W*

Duluc, A (Béziers) 1934 *G*

Du Manoir, Y LeP (RCF) 1925 *I, NZ, S, W, E*, 1926 *S*, 1927 *I, S*

Dupont, C (Lourdes) 1923 *S, W, I*, 1924 *S, I, W, R, US*, 1925 *S*, 1927 *E, G* 1, 2, 1928 *A, G, W*, 1929 *I*

Dupont, J-L (Agen) 1983 *S*

Dupont, L (RCF) 1934 *G*, 1935 *G*, 1936 *G* 1, 2, 1938 *R, G* 2

Dupouy, A (SB) 1924 *W, R*

Duprat, B (Bayonne) 1966 *E, W, It, R*, 1967 *S, A, E, SA* 2, 3, 1968 *S, I*, 1972 *E, W, I* 2, *A* 1

Dupré, P (RCF) 1909 *W*

Dupuy, J (Tarbes) 1956 *S, I, W, It, E, Cz*, 1957 *S, I, E, W, It, R* 2, 1958 *S, E, SA* 1, 2, 1959 *S, E, It, W, I*, 1960 *W, I, It, Arg* 1, 3, 1961 *S, SA, E, NZ* 2, *R*, 1962 *S, E, W, I, It*, 1963 *W, It, R*, 1964 *S*

Du Souich, C J (SCUF) 1911 *W, I*

Dutin, B (Mont-de-Marsan) 1968 *NZ* 2, *A, SA* 2, *R*

Dutour, F X (Toulouse) 1911 *E, I*, 1912 *S, W, E*, 1913 *S*

Dutrain, H (Toulouse) 1945 *W*, 1946 *B, I*, 1947 *E*, 1949 *I, E, W, Arg* 1

Dutrey, J (Lourdes) 1940 *B*

Duval, R (SF) 1908 *E, W*, 1909 *E*, 1911 *E, W, I*

Echave, L (Agen) 1961 *S*

Elissalde, E (Bayonne) 1936 *G* 2, 1940 *B*

Elissalde, J-P (La Rochelle) 1980 *SA, R*, 1981 *A* 1, 2, *R*

Erbani, D (Agen) 1981 *A* 1, 2, *NZ* 1, 2, 1982 *Arg* 1, 2, 1983 *S* (R), *I, W, A* 1, 2, *R*, 1984 *W, E, R*, 1985 *E, W*(R), *Arg* 2, 1986 *S, I, W, E, R* 1, *Arg* 2, *NZ* 1, 2 (R), 3, 1987 *W, E, S, I*, [*S, R, Fj, A, NZ*], 1988 *E, S*, 1989 *I*(R), *W, E, S, NZ* 1, 2, 1990 *W, E*

Escaffre, P (Narbonne) 1933 *G*, 1934 *G*

Escommier, M (Montelimar) 1955 *It*

Esponda, J-M (RCF) 1967 *SA* 1, 2, *R*, 1968 *NZ* 1, 2,

SA 2, *R*, 1969 *S, I* (R), *E*

Estève, A (Béziers) 1971 *SA* 1, 1972 *I* 1, *E, W, I* 2, *A* 2, *R*, 1973 *S, NZ, E, I*, 1974 *I, W, E, S, R, SA* 1, 2, 1975 *W, E*

Estève, P (Narbonne, Lavelanet) 1982 *R, Arg* 1, 2, 1983 *E, S, I, W, A* 1, 2, *R*, 1984 *I, W, E, S, NZ* 1,2, *R*, 1985 *E, S, I, W*, 1986 *S, I*, 1987 [*S, Z*]

Etcheberry, J (Rochefort, Cognac) 1923 *W, I*, 1924 *S, I, E, W, R, US*, 1926 *S, I, E, M*, 1927 *I, S, W, G* 2

Etchenique, J (Biarritz O) 1974 *R, SA* 1, 1975 *E, Arg* 2

Etchepare, A (Bayonne) 1922 *I*

Etcheverry, M (Pau) 1971 *S, I*

Eutrope, A (SCUF) 1913 *I*

Fabre, E (Toulouse) 1937 *It*, 1938 *G* 1, 2

Fabre, J (Toulouse) 1963 *S, I, E, W, It*, 1964 *S, NZ, E*

Fabre, L (Lezignan) 1930 *G*

Fabre, M (Béziers) 1981 *A* 1, *R, NZ* 1, 2, 1982 *I, R*

Failliot, P (RCF) 1911 *S, W, I*, 1912 *I, S, E*, 1913 *E, W*

Fargues, G (Dax) 1923 *I*

Faure, P (Tarbes) 1914 *I, W, E*

Fauvel, J-P (Tulle) 1980 *R*

Favre, M (Lyon) 1913 *E, W*

Ferrand, L (Chalon) 1940 *B*

Ferrien, R (Tarbes) 1950 *S, I, E, W*

Finat, R (CASG) 1932 *G*, 1933 *G*

Fite, R (Brive) 1963 *W, It*

Forestier, J (SCUF) 1912 *W*

Forgues, F (Bayonne) 1911 *S, E, W*, 1912 *I, W, E*, 1913 *S, SA, W*, 1914 *I, E*

Fort, J (Agen) 1967 *It, W, I, SA* 1, 2, 3, 4

Fourcade, G (BEC) 1909 *E, W*

Foures, H (Toulouse) 1951 *S, I, E, W*

Fournet, F (Montferrand) 1950 *W*

Fouroux, J (La Voulte) 1972 *I* 2, *R*, 1974 *W, E, Arg* 1, 2, *R, SA* 1, 2, 1975 *W, Arg* 1, 1976 *S, I, W, E, US, A* 1, 1977 *W, E, S, I, Arg* 1, 2, *NZ* 1, 2, *R*

Franquenelle, A (Vaugirard) 1911 *S*, 1913 *W, I*

Furcade, R (Perpignan) 1952 *S*

Gabernet, S (Toulouse) 1980 *E, S*, 1981 *S, I, W, E, A* 1, 2, *R, NZ* 1, 2, 1982 *I*, 1983 *A* 2, *R*

Gachassin, J (Lourdes) 1961 *S, I*, 1963 *R*, 1964 *S, NZ, E, W, It, I, SA, Fj, R*, 1965 *S, I, E, W, It, R*, 1966 *S, I, E, W*, 1967 *S, A, It, W, I, NZ*, 1968 *I, E*, 1969 *S, I*

Galau, H (Toulouse) 1924 *S, I, E, W, US*

Galia, J (Quillan) 1927 *E, G* 1, 2, 1928 *S, A, I, E, W*, 1929 *I, E, G*, 1930 *S, I, E, G, W*, 1931 *S, W, E, G*

Gallion, J (Toulon) 1978 *E, S, I, W*, 1979 *I, W, E, S, NZ* 2, *R*, 1980 *W, E, S, I*, 1983 *A* 1, 2, *R*, 1984 *I, W, E, S, R* 1985 *E, S, I, W*, 1986 *Arg* 2

Galy, J (Perpignan) 1953 *W*

Garuet, J-P (Lourdes) 1983 *A* 1, 2, *R*, 1984 *I, NZ* 1,2, *R*, 1985 *E, S, I, W, Arg* 1, 1986 *S, I, W, E, R* 1, *Arg* 1, *NZ* 1, *NZ* 2, 3, 1987 *W, E, S, I*, [*S, R, Fj, A, NZ*], 1988 *E, S, Arg*1,2, *R*, 1989 *E*(*R*), *S, NZ* 1, 2, 1990 *W, E*

Gasc, J (Graulhet) 1977 *NZ* 2

Gasparotto, G (Montferrand) 1976 *A* 2, *R*

Gauby, G (Perpignan) 1956 *Cz*

Gaudermen, P (RCF) 1906 *E*

Gayraud, W (Toulouse) 1920 *I*

Geneste, R (BEC) 1945 *B* 1, 1949 *Arg* 2

Gensane, R (Béziers) 1962 *S, E, W, I, It, R*, 1963 *S*

Gerald, G (RCF) 1927 *E, G* 2, 1928 *S, A, I, E, W, G*, 1930 *S, I, E, G, W*, 1931 *S, I, E, G*

Gerintes, G (CASG) 1924 *R*, 1925 *I*, 1926 *W*

Geschwind, P (RCF) 1936 *G* 1, 2

Giacardy, M (SBUC) 1907 *E*

Gommes, J (RCF) 1909 *I*

Gonnet, C-A (Albi) 1921 *E, I*, 1922 *E, W*, 1924 *S, E*, 1926 *S, I, E, W, M*, 1927 *I, S, W, E, G* 1

Got, R (Perpignan) 1920 *I, US*, 1921 *S, W*, 1922 *S, E, W, I*, 1924 *I, E, W, R, US*

Gourdon, J-F (RCF, Bagnères) 1974 *S, Arg* 1, 2, *R, SA* 1, 2, 1975 *W, E, S, I, R*, 1976 *S, I, W, E*, 1978 *E, S*, 1979 *W, E, S, R*, 1980 *I*

Goyard, A (Lyon U) 1936 *G* 1, 2, 1937 *G, It*, 1938 *G* 1, *R, G* 2

Graciet, R (SBUC) 1926 *I, W*, 1927 *S, G* 1, 1929 *E*, 1930 *W*

Gratton, J (Agen) 1984 *NZ* 2, *R*, 1985 *E, S, I, W, Arg* 1, 2, 1986 *S, NZ* 1

Graule, V (Arl Perpignan) 1926 *I, E, W*, 1927 *S, W*, 1931 *G*

251

Lepatey, J (Mazamet) 1954 *It*, 1955 *S, I, E, W*
Lepatey, L (Mazamet) 1924 *S, I, E*
Lescarboura, J-P (Dax) 1982 *W, E, S, I*, 1983 *A* 1, 2, *R*, 1984 *I, W, E, S, NZ* 1,2, *R*, 1985 *E, S, I, W, Arg* 1, 2, 1986 *Arg* 2, *A, NZ* 1, *R* 2, *NZ* 2, 1988 *S, W*
Lesieur, E (SF) 1906 *E*, 1908 *E, W*, 1909 *E, W, I*, 1910 *S, E, I*, 1911 *E, I*, 1912 *W*
Leuvielle, M (SBUC) 1908 *W*, 1913 *S, SA, E, W*, 1914 *W, E*
Levasseur, R (SF) 1925 *W, E*
Levee, H (RCF) 1906 *NZ*
Lewis, E W (Le Havre) 1906 *E*
Lhermet, J-M (Montferrand) 1990 *S, I*
Libaros, G (Tarbes) 1936 *G* 1, 1940 *B*
Lira, M (La Voulte) 1962 *R*, 1963 *I, E, W, It, R*, 1964 *W, It, I, SA*, 1965 *S, I, R*
Llary, (Carcassonne) 1926 *W*
Lobies, J (RCF) 1921 *S, W, E*
Lombard, F (Narbonne) 1934 *G*, 1937 *It*
Lombarteix, R (Montferrand) 1938 *R, G* 2
Londios, J (Montauban) 1967 *SA* 3
Lorieux, A (Grenoble, Aix) 1981 *A* 1, *R, NZ* 1, 2, 1982 *W*, 1983 *A* 2, *R*, 1984 *I, W, E*, 1985 *Arg* 1, 2 (R), 1986 *R* 2, *NZ* 2, 3, 1987 *W, E, [S, Z, Fj, A, NZ]*, 1988 *S, I, W, Arg* 1, 2, 4, 1989 *W, A* 2
Loury, A (RCF) 1927 *E, G* 1, 2, 1928 *S, A, I*
Loustau, M (Dax) 1923 *E*
Lubin-Lebrère, M-F (Toulouse) 1914 *I, W, E*, 1920 *S, E, W, I, US*, 1921 *S*, 1922 *S, E, W*, 1924 *W, US*, 1925 *I*
Lubrano, A (Béziers) 1972 *A* 2, 1973 *S*
Lux, J-P (Tyrosse, Dax) 1967 *E, It, W, I, SA* 1, 2, 4, *R*, 1968 *I, E, Cz, NZ* 3, *A, SA* 1, 2, 1969 *S, I, E*, 1970 *S, I, W, E, R*, 1971 *S, I, E, W, A* 1, 2, 1972 *S, I* 1, *E, W, I* 2, *A* 1, 2, *R*, 1973 *S, NZ, E*, 1974 *I, W, E, S, Arg* 1, 2, 1975 *W*

Maclos, P (SF) 1906 *E*, 1907 *E*
Magnanou, C (RCF) 1923 *E*, 1925 *W, E*, 1926 *S*, 1929 *S, W*, 1930 *S, I, E, W*
Magnol, L (Toulouse) 1928 *S*, 1929 *S, W, E*
Magois, H (La Rochelle) 1968 *SA* 1, 2, *R*
Majerus, R (SF) 1928 *W*, 1929 *I, S*, 1930 *S, I, E, G, W*
Malbet, J-C (Agen) 1967 *SA* 2, 4
Maleig, A (Oloron) 1979 *W, E, NZ* 2, 1980 *W, E, SA, R*
Malquier, Y (Narbonne) 1979 *S*
Manterola, T (Lourdes) 1955 *It*, 1957 *R* 1
Mantoulan, C (Pau) 1959 *I*
Marcet, J (Albi) 1925 *I, NZ, S, W, E*, 1926 *I, E*
Marchal, J-F (Lourdes) 1979 *S, R*, 1980 *W, S, I*
Marchand, R (Poitiers) 1920 *S, W*
Marocco, P (Montferrand) 1986 *S, I, W, E, R* 1, *Arg* 1, 2, *A*, 1988 *Arg* 4, 1989 *I*, 1990 *R*
Marot, A (Brive) 1969 *R*, 1970 *S, I, W*, 1971 *SA* 1, 1972 *I* 2, 1976 *A* 1
Marquesuzaa, A (RCF) 1958 *It, SA* 1, 2, 1959 *S, E, It, W*, 1960 *S, E, Arg* 1
Marracq, H (Pau) 1961 *R*
Martin, C (Lyon) 1909 *I*, 1910 *W, S*
Martin, H (SBUC) 1907 *E*, 1908 *W*
Martin, J-L (Béziers) 1971 *A* 2, *R*, 1972 *S, I* 1
Martin, L (Pau) 1948 *I, A, S, W, E*, 1950 *S*
Martine, R (Lourdes) 1952 *S, I, It*, 1953 *I, S*, 1954 *S, I, NZ, W, E, It, Arg* 2, 1955 *S, I, W*, 1958 *A, W, It, I, SA* 1, 2, 1960 *S, E, Arg* 3, 1961 *S, It*
Martinez, G (Toulouse) 1982 *W, E, S, Arg* 1, 2, 1983 *E, W*
Mas, F (Béziers) 1962 *R*, 1963 *S, I, E, W*
Maso, J (Perpignan, Narbonne) 1966 *It, R*, 1967 *S, R*, 1968 *S, W, Cz, NZ* 1, 2, 3, *A, R*, 1969 *S, I, W*, 1971 *S, I, R*, 1972 *E, W, A* 2, 1973 *W, I, J, R*
Massare, J (PUC) 1945 *B* 1, 2, *W*, 1946 *B, I, W*
Masse, A (SBUC) 1908 *W*, 1909 *E, W*, 1910 *W, S, E, I*
Masse, H (Grenoble) 1937 *G*
Matheu, J (Agen) 1945 *W*, 1946 *B, I, K, W*, 1947 *S, I, W, E*, 1948 *I, A, S, W, E*, 1949 *S, I, E, W, Arg* 1, 2, 1950 *E, W*, 1951 *S, I*
Mauduy, G (Périgueux) 1957 *It, R* 1, 2, 1958 *S, E*, 1961 *W, It*
Mauran, J (Castres) 1952 *SA, W, E, It*, 1953 *I, E*
Mauriat, P (Lyon) 1907 *E*, 1908 *E, W*, 1909 *W, I*, 1910 *W, S, E, I*, 1911 *S, E, W, I*, 1912 *I, S*, 1913 *S, SA, W, I*
Maurin, G (ASF) 1906 *E*

Maury, A (Toulouse) 1925 *I, NZ, S, W, E*, 1926 *S, I, E*
Maysonnie, A (Toulouse) 1908 *E, W*, 1910 *W*
Melville, R (Toulon) 1990 *J*(R)
Menrath, R (SCUF) 1910 *W*
Menthiller, Y (Romans) 1964 *W, It, SA, R*, 1965 *E*
Meret, F (Tarbes) 1940 *B*
Mericq, S (Agen) 1959 *I*, 1960 *S, E, W*, 1961 *I*
Merquey, J (Toulon) 1950 *S, I, E, W*
Mesnel, F (RCF) 1986 *NZ* 2 (R), 3, 1987 *W, E, S, I, [S, Z, Fj, A, NZ], R*, 1988 *E, Arg*1, 2, 3, 4, *R*, 1989 *I, W, E, S, NZ* 1, *A* 1, 2, 1990 *E, S, I*
Mesny, P (RCF, Grenoble) 1979 *NZ* 1, 2, 1980 *SA, R*, 1981 *I, W* (R), *A* 1, 2, *R, NZ* 1, 2, 1982 *I, Arg* 1, 2
Meyer, G-S (Périgueux) 1960 *S, E, It, R, Arg* 2
Meynard, J (Cognac) 1954 *Arg* 1, 1956 *Cz*
Mias, L (Mazamet) 1951 *S, I, E, W*, 1952 *I, SA, W, E, It*, 1953 *S, I, W, It*, 1954 *S, I, NZ, W*, 1957 *R* 2, 1958 *S, E, A, W, I, SA* 1, 2, 1959 *S, It, W, I*
Milliand, P (Grenoble) 1936 *G* 2, 1937 *G, It*
Minjat, R (Lyon) 1945 *B* 1
Mir, J-H (Lourdes) 1967 *R*, 1968 *I*
Mir, J-P (Lourdes) 1967 *A*
Modin, R (Brive) 1987 *[Z]*
Moga, A-M-A (Begles) 1945 *B* 1, 2, *W*, 1946 *B, I, K, W*, 1947 *S, I, W, E*, 1948 *I, A, S, W, E*, 1949 *S, I, E, W, Arg* 1, 2
Mommejat, B (Cahors, Albi) 1958 *It, I, SA* 1, 2, 1959 *S, E, It, W, I*, 1960 *S, E, I, R*, 1962 *S, E, W, I, It, R*, 1963 *S, I, W*
Moncla, F (RCF, Pau) 1956 *Cz*, 1957 *I, E, W, It, R* 1, 1958 *SA* 1, 2, 1959 *S, E, It, W, I*, 1960 *S, E, W, I, It, R, Arg* 1, 2, 3, 1961 *S, SA, E, W, I, NZ* 1, 2, 3
Monie, R (Perpignan) 1956 *Cz*, 1957 *E*
Monier, R (SBUC) 1911 *I*, 1912 *S*
Monniot, M (RCF) 1912 *W, E*
Montade, A (Perpignan) 1925 *I, NZ, S, W*, 1926 *W*
Moraitis, B (Toulon) 1969 *E, W*
Morel, A (Grenoble) 1954 *Arg* 2
Morere, J (Toulouse) 1927 *E, G* 1, 1928 *S, A*
Mouiq, P (Toulouse) 1911 *S, E, W, I*, 1912 *I, E*, 1913 *S, SA, E*
Moure, H (SCUF) 1908 *E*
Moureu, P (Béziers) 1920 *I, US*, 1921 *W, E, I*, 1922 *S, W, I*, 1923 *S, W, E, I*, 1924 *S, I, E, W*, 1925 *E*
Mournet, A (Bagnères) 1981 *A* 1 (R)
Mouronval, F (SF) 1909 *I*
Muhr, A H (RCF) 1906 *NZ, E*, 1907 *E*
Murillo, G (Dijon) 1954 *It, Arg* 1

Namur, R (Toulon) 1931 *E, G*
Noble, J-C (La Voulte) 1968 *E, W, Cz, NZ* 3, *A, R*
Normand, A (Toulouse) 1957 *R* 1
Novès, G (Toulouse) 1977 *NZ* 1, 2, *R*, 1978 *W, R*, 1979 *I, W*

Olive, D (Montferrand) 1951 *I*, 1952 *I*
Ondarts, P (Biarritz O) 1986 *NZ* 3, 1987 *W, E, S, I, [S, Z, Fj, A, NZ], R*, 1988 *E, I, W, Arg*1, 2, 3, 4, *R*, 1989 *I, W, E, NZ* 1, 2, *A* 2, 1990 *W, E, S, I*
Orso, J-C (Nice, Toulon) 1982 *Arg* 1, 2, 1983 *E, S, A* 1, 1984 *E* (R), *S, NZ* 1, 1985 *I* (R), *W*, 1988 *I*
Othats, J (Dax) 1960 *Arg* 2, 3

Paco, L (Béziers) 1974 *Arg* 1, 2, *R, SA* 1, 2, 1975 *W, E, Arg* 1, 2, *R*, 1976 *S, I, W, E, US, A* 1, 2, *R*, 1977 *W, E, S, I, NZ* 1, 2, *R*, 1978 *E, S, I, W, R*, 1979 *I, W, E, S, S, I, NZ* 1, 2, *R*, 1978 *E, S, I, W, R*, 1979 *I, W, E, S, S*, 1980 *W*
Palat, J (Perpignan) 1938 *G* 2
Palmié, M (Béziers) 1975 *SA* 1, 2, *Arg* 1, 2, *R*, 1976 *S, I, W, E, US*, 1977 *W, E, S, I, Arg* 1, 2, *NZ* 1, 2, *R*, 1978 *E, S, I, W*
Paoli, R (SF) 1911 *I*, 1912 *I, S*
Paparemborde, R (Pau) 1975 *SA* 1, 2, *Arg* 1, 2, *R*, 1976 *S, I, W, E, US, A* 1, 2, *R*, 1977 *W, E, S, I, Arg* 1, NZ 1, 2, 1978 *E, S, I, W, R*, 1979 *I, W, E, S, NZ* 1, 2, *R*, 1980 *W, E, S, SA, R*, 1981 *S, I, W, E, A* 1, 2, *R, NZ* 1, 2, 1982 *W, I, R, Arg* 1, 2, 1983 *E, S, I, W*
Pardo, L (Hendaye) 1924 *I, E*
Pardo, L (Bayonne) 1980 *SA, R*, 1981 *S, I, W, E, A* 1, 1982 *W, E, S*, 1983 *A* 1 (R), 1985 *S, I, Arg* 2
Pargade, J-H (Lyon U) 1953 *I*
Paries, L (Biarritz O) 1968 *SA* 2, *R*, 1970 *S, I, W*, 1975 *E, S, I*

253

I, W, Arg 1, 2, 3, 4, *R*, 1989 *I, W, E, S, NZ* 1, 2, *B, A* 1, 2, 1990 *W, E, S, I*
Semmartin, J (SCUF) 1913 *W, I*
Senal, G (Béziers) 1974 *Arg* 1, 2, *R, SA* 1, 2, 1975 *W*
Sentilles, J (Tarbes) 1912 *W, E*, 1913 *S, SA*
Serin, L (Béziers) 1928 *E*, 1929 *W, E, G*, 1930 *S, I, E, G, W*, 1931 *I, W, E*
Serre, P (Perpignan) 1920 *S, E*
Serrière, P (RCF) 1986 *A*, 1987 *R*, 1988 *E*
Servole, L (Toulon) 1931 *I, S, W, E, G*, 1934 *G*, 1935 *G*
Sicart, N (Perpignan) 1922 *I*
Sillières, J (Tarbes) 1968 *R*, 1970 *S, I*, 1971 *S, I, E*, 1972 *E, W*
Siman, M (Montferrand) 1948 *E*, 1949 *S*, 1950 *S, I, E, W*
Sitjar, M (Agen) 1964 *W, It, I, R*, 1965 *It, R*, 1967 *A, E, It, W, I, SA* 1, 2
Skréla, J-C (Toulouse) 1971 *SA* 2, *A* 1, 2, 1972 *I* 1 (R), *E, W, I* 2, *A* 1, 1973 *W, J, R*, 1974 *W, E, S, Arg* 1, *R*, 1975 *W* (R), *E, S, I, SA* 1, 2, *Arg* 1, 2, *R*, 1976 *S, I, W, E, US, A* 1, 2, *R*, 1977 *W, E, S, I, Arg* 1, 2, *NZ* 1, 2, *R*, 1978 *E, S, I, W*
Soler, M (Quillan) 1929 *G*
Soro, R (Lourdes, Romans) 1945 *B* 1, 2, *W*, 1946 *B, I, K*, 1947 *S, I, W, E*, 1948 *I, A, S, W, E*, 1949 *S, I, E, W, Arg* 1, 2
Sorrondo, L-M (Montauban) 1946 *K*, 1947 *S, I, W, E*, 1948 *I*
Soulié, E (CASG) 1920 *E, I, US*, 1921 *S, E, I*, 1922 *E, W, I*
Sourgens, J (Begles) 1926 *M*
Spanghero, C (Narbonne) 1971 *E, W, SA* 1, 2, *A* 1, 2, *R*, 1972 *S, E, W, I* 2, *A* 1, 2, 1974 *I, W, E, S, R, SA* 1, 1975 *E, S, I*
Spanghero, W (Narbonne) 1964 *SA, Fj, R*, 1965 *S, I, E, W, It, R*, 1966 *S, I, E, W, It, R*, 1967 *S, A, E, SA* 1, 2, 3, 4, *NZ*, 1968 *S, I, E, W, NZ* 1, 2, 3, *A, SA* 1, 2, *R*, 1969 *S, I, W*, 1970 *R*, 1971 *E, W, SA* 1, 1972 *E, I* 2, *A* 1, 2, *R*, 1973 *S, NZ, E, W, I*
Stener, G (PUC) 1956 *S, I, E*, 1958 *SA* 1, 2
Struxiano, P (Toulouse) 1913 *W, I*, 1920 *S, E, W, I, US*
Sutra, G (Narbonne) 1967 *SA* 2, 1969 *W*, 1970 *S, I*
Swierczinski, C (Begles) 1969 *E*, 1977 *Arg* 2

Taffary, M (RCF) 1975 *W, E, S, I*
Taillantou, J (Pau) 1930 *I, G, W*
Tarricq, P (Lourdes) 1958 *A, W, It, I*
Tavernier, H (Toulouse) 1913 *I*
Terreau, M-M (Bourg) 1945 *W*, 1946 *B, I, K, W*, 1947 *S, I, W, E*, 1948 *I, A, W, E*, 1949 *S, Arg* 1, 2, 1951 *S*
Theuriet, A (SCUF) 1909 *E, W*, 1910 *S*, 1911 *W*, 1913 *E*
Thevenot, M (SCUF) 1910 *W, E, I*
Thierry, R (RCF) 1920 *S, E, W, US*
Thiers, P (Montferrand) 1936 *G* 1, 2, 1937 *G, It*, 1938

G 1, 2, 1940 *B*, 1945 *B* 1, 2
Thil, P (Nantes) 1912 *W, E*, 1913 *S, SA, E, W*
Tignol, P (Toulouse) 1953 *S, I*
Tolot, J-L (Agen) 1987 [*Z*]
Torreilles, S (Perpignan) 1956 *S*
Tourte, R (St Girons) 1940 *B*
Trillo, J (Begles) 1967 *SA* 3, 4, *NZ, R*, 1968 *S, I, NZ* 1, 2, 3, *A*, 1969 *I, E, W, R*, 1970 *E, R*, 1971 *S, I, SA* 1, 2, *A* 1, 2, 1972 *S, A* 1, 2, *R*, 1973 *S, E*
Triviaux, R (Cognac) 1931 *E, G*
Tucoo-Chala, M (PUC) 1940 *B*

Ugartemendia, J-L (St Jean-de-Luz) 1975 *S, I*

Vaills, G (Perpignan) 1928 *A*, 1929 *G*
Vallot, C (SCUF) 1912 *S*
Vannier, M (RCF, Chalon) 1953 *W*, 1954 *S, I, Arg* 1, 2, 1955 *S, I, E, W, It*, 1956 *S, I, W, It, E*, 1957 *S, I, E, W, It, R* 1, 2, 1958 *S, E, A, W, It, I*, 1960 *S, E, W, I, It, R, Arg* 1, 3, 1961 *SA, E, W, It, I, NZ* 1, *A*
Vaquer, F (Perpignan) 1921 *S, W*, 1922 *W*
Vaquerin, A (Béziers) 1971 *R*, 1972 *S, I* 1, *A* 1, 1973 *S*, 1974 *W, E, S, Arg* 1, 2, *R, SA* 1, 2, 1975 *W, E, S, I*, 1976 *US, A* 1 (R), 2, *R*, 1977 *Arg* 2, 1979 *W, E*, 1980 *S, I*
Vareilles, C (SF) 1907 *E*, 1908 *E, W*, 1910 *S, E*
Varenne, F (RCF) 1952 *S*
Varvier, T (RCF) 1906 *E*, 1909 *E, W*, 1911 *E, W*, 1912 *I*
Vassal, G (Carcassonne) 1938 *R, G* 2
Vaysse, J (Albi) 1924 *US*, 1926 *M*
Vellat, E (Grenoble) 1927 *I, E, G* 1, 2, 1928 *A*
Verger, A (SF) 1927 *W, E, G* 1, 1928 *I, E, G, W*
Verges, L (SF) 1906 *NZ, E*, 1907 *E*
Viard, G (Narbonne) 1969 *W*, 1970 *S, R*, 1971 *S, I*
Vigerie, M (Agen) 1931 *W*
Vigier, R (Montferrand) 1956 *S, W, It, E, Cz*, 1957 *S, E, W, It, R* 1, 2, 1958 *S, E, A, W, It, I, SA* 1, 2, 1959 *S, E, It, W, I*
Vigneau, A (Bayonne) 1935 *G*
Vignes, C (RCF) 1957 *R* 1, 2, 1958 *S, E*
Villa, E (Tarbes) 1926 *M*
Villagra, J (Vienne) 1945 *B* 2
Villepreux, P (Toulouse) 1967 *It, I, SA* 2, *NZ*, 1968 *I, Cz, NZ* 1, 2, 3, *A*, 1969 *S, I, E, W, R*, 1970 *S, I, W, E, R*, 1971 *S, I, E, W, A* 1, 2, *R*, 1972 *S, I* 1, *E, W, I* 2, *A* 1, 2
Viviès, B (Agen) 1978 *E, S, I, W*, 1980 *SA, R*, 1981 *S, A* 1, 1983 *A* 1 (R)
Volot, M (SF) 1945 *W*, 1946 *B, I, K, W*

Weller, S (Grenoble) 1989 *A* 1, 2
Wolff, J-P (Béziers) 1980 *SA, R*, 1981 *A* 2, 1982 *E*

Yachvili, M (Tulle, Brive) 1968 *E, W, Cz, NZ* 3, *A, R*, 1969 *S, I, R*, 1971 *E, SA* 1, 2, *A* 1, 1972 *R*, 1975 *SA* 2

Zago, F (Montauban) 1963 *I, E*

FRENCH INTERNATIONAL RECORDS

Both team and individual records are for official French international matches, up to 30 April 1990.

TEAM RECORDS

Highest score
70 v Zimbabwe (70-12) 1987 Auckland
v individual countries
37 v Argentina (37-3) 1960 Buenos Aires
34 v Australia (34-6) 1976 Parc des Princes
28 v Czechoslovakia (28-3) 1956 Toulouse
37 v England (37-12) 1972 Colombes
31 v Fiji (31-16) 1987 Auckland
38 v Germany (38-17) 1933 Parc des Princes
31 v Ireland (31-12) 1990 Parc des Princes
60 v Italy (60-13) 1967 Toulon
30 v Japan (30-18) 1973 Bordeaux
24 v N Zealand (24-19) 1979 Auckland
59 v Romania (59-3) 1924 Colombes
28 v Scotland (28-22) 1987 Parc des Princes
25 v S Africa (25-38) 1975 Bloemfontein
33 v United States (33-14) 1976 Chicago
31 v Wales (31-12) 1989 Parc des Princes
70 v Zimbabwe (70-12) 1987 Auckland

Biggest winning points margin
58 v Zimbabwe (70-12) 1987 Auckland
v individual countries
34 v Argentina (37-3) 1960 Buenos Aires
28 v Australia (34-6) 1976 Parc des Princes
25 v Czechoslovakia (28-3) 1956 Toulouse
25 v England (37-12) 1972 Colombes
18 v Fiji (21-3) 1964 Colombes
34 v Germany (34-0) 1931 Colombes
23 v Ireland (26-3) 1976 Parc des Princes
47 v Italy (60-13) 1967 Toulon
12 v Japan (30-18) 1973 Bordeaux
13 v N Zealand (16-3) 1986 Nantes
56 v Romania (59-3) 1924 Colombes
20 v Scotland (23-3) 1977 Parc des Princes
5 v S Africa (19-14) 1967 Johannesburg
19 v United States (33-14) 1976 Chicago
19 v Wales (31-12) 1989 Parc des Princes
58 v Zimbabwe (70-12) 1987 Auckland

Highest score by opposing team
49 Wales (14-49) 1910 Swansea
S Africa beat 'France' 55-6 at Parc des Princes on 3 January 1907, but it is not regarded as an official international match

by individual countries
27 Argentina (31-27) 1974 Buenos Aires
32 Australia (15-32) 1989 Strasbourg
6 Czechoslovakia (19-6) 1968 Prague
41 England (13-41) 1907 Richmond
16 Fiji (31-16) 1987 Auckland
17 Germany { (16-17) 1927 Frankfurt / (38-17) 1933 Parc des Princes
25 Ireland { (5-25) 1911 Cork / (6-25) 1975 Dublin
13 Italy (60-13) 1967 Toulon
18 Japan (30-18) 1973 Bordeaux
38 N Zealand (8-38) 1906 Parc des Princes
15 Romania   on several occasions
31 Scotland (3-31) 1912 Inverleith
38 S Africa { (5-38) 1913 Bordeaux / (25-38) 1975 Bloemfontein
17 United States (3-17) 1924 Colombes
49 Wales (14-49) 1910 Swansea
12 Zimbabwe (70-12) 1987 Auckland

Biggest losing points margin
42 v Wales (5-47) 1909 Colombes
The 6-55 defeat by S Africa in Paris in 1907 is regarded as unofficial
v individual countries
12 v Argentina (6-18) 1988 Buenos Aires
17 v Australia (15-32) 1989 Strasbourg
37 v England (0-37) 1911 Twickenham
3 v Germany (0-3) 1938 Frankfurt
24 v Ireland (0-24) 1913 Cork
30 v N Zealand (8-38) 1906 Parc des Princes
15 v Romania (0-15) 1980 Bucharest
28 v Scotland (3-31) 1912 Inverleith
33 v S Africa (5-38) 1913 Bordeaux
14 v United States (3-17) 1924 Colombes
42 v Wales (5-47) 1909 Colombes
No defeats v Czechoslovakia, Fiji, Italy, Japan or Zimbabwe

Most tries by France in an international
13 v Romania (59-3) 1924 Paris

Most tries against France in an international
11 by Wales (5-47) 1909 Colombes

Most points by France in International Championship in a season – 98
in season 1985-86

Most tries by France in International Championship in a season – 13
in seasons 1975-76 and 1985-86

INDIVIDUAL RECORDS

Most capped player
S Blanco 75 1980-90
in individual positions
Full-back
S Blanco 63(75)[1] 1980-90
Wing
C Darrouy 40[2] 1957-67
Centre
P Sella 60(67)[3] 1982-90
Fly-half
J-P Romeu 33(34)[4] 1972-77
Scrum-half
P Berbizier 52 1981-90
Prop
R Paparemborde 55 1975-83
Hooker
P Dintrans 49 1979-89
Lock
J Condom 58[5] 1982-90
Flanker
J-P Rives 59[5] 1975-84
No 8
G Basquet 33[5] 1945-52
[1] *S Blanco has won 12 caps as a wing*
[2] *J Dupuy, 40 caps, played once in the centre and 39 times on the wing*
[3] *Sella has won 6 caps as wing and one as a full-back. R Bertranne, 69 caps, played 52 times as a centre*
[4] *Romeu was capped once as a replacement full-back*
[5] *B Dauga and M Crauste, 63 caps each, are France's most-capped forwards. Dauga was capped as a lock and No 8; Crauste as flanker and No 8*

Longest international career
F Haget 14 seasons 1974-87

Most internationals as captain
J-P Rives 34 1978-84

Most points in internationals – 265
J-P Romeu (34 matches) 1972-77

Most points in International Championship in a season – 54
J-P Lescarboura (4 matches) 1983-84

Most points in an international – 30
D Camberabero v Zimbabwe 1987 Auckland

Most tries in internationals – 30
S Blanco (75 matches) 1980-90

Most tries in International Championship in a season – 5
P Estève (4 matches) 1982-83
E Bonneval (4 matches) 1986-87

Most tries in an international – 4
A Jauréguy v Romania 1924 Colombes
M Celhay v Italy 1937 Parc des Princes

Most conversions in internationals – 45
M Vannier (43 matches) 1953-61

Most conversions in International Championship in a season – 7
P Villepreux (4 matches) 1971-72

Most conversions in an international – 9
G Camberabero v Italy 1967 Toulon
D Camberabero v Zimbabwe 1987 Auckland
Father and son

Most dropped goals in internationals – 15
J-P Lescarboura (27 matches) 1982-88

Most penalty goals in internationals – 56
J-P Romeu (34 matches) 1972-77

Most penalty goals in international Championship in a season – 10
J-P Lescarboura (4 matches) 1983-84

Most points on overseas tour – 84
P Bérot (6 matches) 1988 South America

Most points in any match on tour – 28
P Lagisquet v Paraguayan XV 1988
  Ascunción
P Estève scored 32 points against East Japan in 1984, but this was not on a major tour

Most tries in a tour match – 7
P Lagisquet v Paraguayan XV 1988
  Ascunción
P Estève scored 8 tries v East Japan in 1984, but this was not on a major tour

Philippe Sella, France's most-capped centre, and still the key man in the French back division, powers in for a try against Australia in the 1987 World Cup semi-final.

THE 'BIG SIX' WERE NOT AMUSED

THE 1989 SEASON IN SOUTH AFRICA
Reg Sweet

Somewhere along the line, it had seemed clear enough in recent seasons, there would be a major confrontation in South African rugby between the provincial unions, whose good fortune it is to own the grounds on which international matches are played, and those of lesser affluence. Unhappily, the balloon went up in the very season in which the SA Rugby Board celebrated its Centenary and threatened the very core of the Board itself. Fundamental to the squabble was the question of whether the so-called 'Test match unions', whose incomes unquestionably generate the funds that keep the game financially secure, should enjoy freedom from relegation from Section A of the Currie Cup, the most prestigious competition in South African rugby and, in terms of the turnstiles, its very backbone.

The 'big six' clearly felt that they had earned this right. The smaller unions disagreed. Indeed, they came to the SA Board with a proposal that not only rejected entrenchment but at the same time severely curtailed the influence of the Test unions on the Board's affairs. The six were not amused. Orange Free State president Steve Strydom told the Board that since the Test unions provided its major income they would consider withdrawing and setting up on their own if promotion and relegation challenge matches again became the rule. Earlier, the Board had in fact entrenched the position of Eastern Province, a Test union, which had occupied last place in the Currie Cup standings for 1989. In the season just completed, one report claimed the six had between them brought in R4.4 million (appreciably more than £1 million) and the remaining provinces less than R200,000 in total. Very soon, it was said, the Board would face bankruptcy.

The threatened split caused the Test unions to call a meeting of their own. A new element emerged when Transvaal's Dr Louis Luyt implicated Dr Danie Craven in the proposals to restructure the Board in a manner which would severely restrict the six. There was a delicate confrontation on television. 'If I am standing in the way of rugby progress then I must go', said Dr Craven. The Test match unions were basically in agreement but in the finer detail Western Province, Northern Transvaal and Natal were clearly more conservative than the more adamant Transvaal, Free State and Eastern Province. And on the Dr Craven issue Dr Nic Labuschagne, president of Natal and former England international, crystallised the conservative standpoint when he said: 'There is no question of Natal wanting Dr Craven out of rugby, and this has always been my union's view'.

The SA Board met again and took three relevant decisions. It reaffirmed the principle of strength versus strength, at the same time shelving the motion calling for the restructuring of the Board, the germ of the rift, and it resolved to take another look at the promotion-relegation system. In the end, South West Africa emerged as the catalyst when it was withdrawn from Currie Cup competition as a result of the approaching independence of Namibia. Conveniently, therefore, Western Transvaal replaced SWA in Section A of the Currie Cup and the question of Eastern Province facing a promotion-relegation challenge became irrelevant. Effectively this meant a truce within the SA Board.

However, there was more to the Centenary season than the domestic upset. True to its word, the IB sanctioned the tour by an invited international side which was to set the seal on the celebration. And on the face of it the victories of the South African side, led by Transvaal No 8 Jannie Breedt, in the representative matches, 20-19 at Newlands and 22-16 at Ellis Park, brought a measure of satisfaction. But there could be no doubt that something of the fine edge was missing from the Springbok game, unquestionably the legacy of several recent seasons without the regular spur of true international competition. The conclusion of this short series marked the retirement of Dr Cecil Moss as Springbok coach following a distinguished run of ten victories in 12 international matches. He will remain available as a selector.

At the season's end, Currie Cup rugby took a turn no one had dared forecast. With much the more impressive record, Northern Transvaal contested the final with Western Province at Newlands and were held to a 16-16 draw. Indeed, Western Province alone seemed capable of matching Northern, for they won the provincial knock-out, the Lion Cup, against the same side by a 21-16 margin. The Yardley Gold Cup, an invitation tournament at Ellis Park, went for the second successive season to Natal. The Toyota-sponsored National Club Championship at King's Park, Durban, saw a Transvaal club victorious for the first time in the event's history when Roodepoort beat Goudstad Teachers' Training College 29-22 in an entertaining final, leaving a string of more highly-fancied former champions such as Pretoria and Stellenbosch Universities, Despatch and Shimlas trailing in their wake.

CURRIE CUP SECTION A	P	W	D	L	F	A	Pts
Northern Transvaal	14	14	0	0	530	195	28
Western Province	14	10	0	4	429	258	20
Free State	14	8	0	6	336	272	16
Transvaal	14	7	0	7	408	369	14
Natal	14	7	0	7	327	313	14
South West Africa	14	4	0	10	248	434	8
Northern Orange Free State	14	3	0	11	262	434	6
Eastern Province	14	3	0	11	211	476	6

Currie Cup final: Western Province 16, Northern Transvaal 16 (at Newlands); **Lion Cup final:** Western Province 21, Northern Transvaal 16 (at Newlands); **Yardley Gold Cup final:** Natal 30, Eastern Province 12 (at Ellis Park); **Toyota National Club Championship final:** Roodepoort 29, Goudstad TTC 22 (at King's Park, Durban)

SOUTH AFRICAN INTERNATIONAL PLAYERS *(up to 30 April 1990)*

ABBREVIATIONS

A – Australia; *BI* – British Isles teams; *Cv* – New Zealand Cavaliers; *E* – England; *F* – France; *I* – Ireland; *NZ* – New Zealand; *S* – Scotland; *S Am* – South America; *US* – United States of America; *W* – Wales; *Wld* – World Invitation XV; (R) – Replacement

PROVINCIAL ABBREVIATIONS

Bor – Border; Bol – Boland; EP – Eastern Province; GW – Griqualand West; N – Natal; NT – Northern Transvaal; OFS – Orange Free State; R – Rhodesia; SET – South East Transvaal; SWA – South West Africa; SWD – South West Districts; Tvl – Transvaal; WP – Western Province; WT – Western Transvaal; Z-R – Zimbabwe-Rhodesia

Note: When a series has taken place, figures denote the particular matches in which players featured. Thus 1968 *BI* 1,2,4 indicates that a player appeared in the first, second and fourth Tests of the 1968 series against the British Isles.

Ackermann, D S P (WP) 1955 *BI* 2,3,4, 1956 *A* 1,2, *NZ* 1,3, 1958 *F* 2
Albertyn, P K (SWD) 1924 *BI* 1,2,3,4
Alexander, E (GW) 1891 *BI* 1,2
Allen, P B (EP) 1960 *S*
Allport, P (WP) 1910 *BI* 2,3
Anderson, J A (WP) 1903 *BI* 3
Anderson, J H (WP) 1896 *BI* 1,3,4
Andrew, J B (Tvl) 1896 *BI* 2
Antelme, M J G (Tvl) 1960 *NZ* 1,2,3,4, 1960-61 *F*
Apsey, J T (WP) 1933 *A* 4,5, 1938 *BI* 2
Ashley, S (WP) 1903 *BI* 2
Aston, F T D (Tvl) 1896 *BI* 1,2,3,4
Aucamp, J (WT) 1924 *BI* 1,2

Baard, A P (WP) 1960-61 *I*
Babrow, L (WP) 1937 *A* 1,2, *NZ* 1,2,3
Barnard, A S (EP) 1984 *S Am* 1,2, 1986 *Cv* 1,2
Barnard, J H (Tvl) 1965 *S*, *A* 1,2, *NZ* 3,4
Barnard, R W (Tvl) 1970 *NZ* 2(R)
Barnard, W H M (NT) 1949 *NZ* 4, 1951-52 *W*
Barry, J (WP) 1903 *BI* 1,2,3
Bartmann, W J (Tvl) 1986 *Cv* 1,2,3,4
Bastard, W E (N) 1937 *A* 1, *NZ* 1,2,3, 1938 *BI* 1,3
Bates, A J (WT) 1969-70 *E*, 1970 *NZ* 1,2, 1972 *E*
Bayvel, P C R (Tvl) 1974 *BI* 2,4, *F* 1,2, 1975 *F* 1,2, 1976 *NZ* 1,2,3,4
Beck, J J (WP) 1981 *NZ* 2(R), 3(R), *US*
Bedford, T P (N) 1963 *A* 1,2,3,4, 1964 *W*, *F*, 1965 *I*, *A* 1,2, 1968 *BI* 1,2,3,4, *F* 1,2, 1969 *A* 1,2,3,4, 1969-70 *S*, *E*, *I*, *W*, 1971 *F* 1,2
Bekker, H J (WP) 1981 *NZ* 1,3
Bekker, H P J (NT) 1951-52 *E*, *F*, 1953 *A* 1,2,3,4, 1955 *BI* 2,3,4, 1956 *A* 1,2, *NZ* 1,2,3,4
Bekker, M J (NT) 1960 *S*
Bekker, R P (NT) 1953 *A* 3,4
Bergh, W F (SWD) 1931-32 *W*, *I*, *E*, *S*, 1933 *A* 1, 2,3,4,5, 1937 *A* 1,2, *NZ* 1,2,3, 1938 *BI* 1,2,3
Bestbier, A (OFS) 1974 *F* 2(R)
Bester, J J N (WP) 1924 *BI* 2,4
Bester, J L A (WP) 1938 *BI* 2,3
Beswick, A M (Bor) 1896 *BI* 2,3,4
Bezuidenhoudt, C E (NT) 1962 *BI* 2,3,4
Bezuidenhoudt, N S E (NT) 1972 *E*, 1974 *BI* 2,3,4, *F* 1,2, 1975 *F* 1,2, 1977 *Wld*
Bierman, J N (Tvl) 1931-32 *I*
Bisset, W M (WP) 1891 *BI* 1,3
Blair, R (WP) 1977 *Wld*
Bosch, G R (Tvl) 1974 *BI* 2, *F* 1,2, 1975 *F* 1,2, 1976 *NZ* 1,2,3,4
Bosman, N J S (Tvl) 1924 *BI* 2,3,4
Botha, D S (NT) 1981 *NZ* 1
Botha, H E (NT) 1980 *S Am* 1,2, *BI* 1,2,3,4, *S Am* 3,4, *F*, 1981 *I* 1,2, *NZ* 1,2,3, *US*, 1982 *S Am* 1,2, 1986 *Cv* 1,2,3,4, 1989 *Wld* 1,2
Botha, J (Tvl) 1903 *BI* 3
Botha, J P F (NT) 1962 *BI* 2,3,4
Botha, P H (Tvl) 1965 *A* 1,2
Boyes, H C (GW) 1891 *BI* 1,2
Brand, G H (WP) 1928 *NZ* 2,3, 1931-32 *W*, *I*, *E*, *S*,

Bredenkamp, M (GW) 1896 *BI* 1,3
Breedt, J C (Tvl) 1986 *Cv* 1,2,3,4, 1989 *Wld* 1,2
Brewis, J D (NT) 1949 *NZ* 1,2,3,4, 1951-52 *S*, *I*, *W*, *E*, *F*, 1953 *A* 1
Briers, T P D (WP) 1955 *BI* 1,2,3,4, 1956 *NZ* 2,3,4
Brink, D J (WP) 1906 *S*, *W*, *E*,
Brooks, D (Bor) 1906 *S*
Brown, C (WP) 1903 *BI* 1,2,3
Brynard, G S (WP) 1965 *A* 1, *NZ* 1,2,3, 1968 *BI* 3,4
Buchler, J U (Tvl) 1951-52 *S*, *I*, *W*, *E*, *F*, 1953 *A* 1,2,3,4, 1956 *A* 2
Burdett, A F (WP) 1906 *S*, *I*
Burger, J M (WP) 1989 *Wld* 1,2
Burger, M B (NT) 1980 *BI* 2(R), *S Am* 3, 1981 *US* (R)
Burger, S W P (WP) 1984 *E* 1,2, 1986 *Cv* 1,2,3,4
Burger, W A G (Bor) 1906 *S*, *I*, *W*, 1910 *BI* 2

Carelse, G (EP) 1964 *W*, *F*, 1965 *I*, *S*, 1967 *F* 1,2,3, 1968 *F* 1,2, 1969 *A* 1,2,3,4, 1969-70 *S*
Carlson, R A (WP) 1972 *E*
Carolin, H W (WP) 1903 *BI* 3, 1906 *S*, *I*
Castens, H H (WP) 1891 *BI* 1
Chignell, T W (WP) 1891 *BI* 3
Cilliers, G D (OFS) 1963 *A* 1,3,4
Claassen, J T (WT) 1955 *BI* 1,2,3,4, 1956 *A* 1,2, *NZ* 1,2,3,4, 1958 *F* 1,2, 1960 *S*, *NZ* 1,2,3, 1960-61 *W*, *I*, *E*, *S*, *F*, 1961 *I*, *A* 1,2, 1962 *BI* 1,2,3,4
Claassen, W (N) 1981 *I* 1,2, *NZ* 2,3, *US*, 1982 *S Am* 1,2
Clarke, W H (Tvl) 1933 *A* 3
Clarkson, W A (N) 1921 *NZ* 1,2, 1924 *BI* 1
Cloete, H A (WP) 1896 *BI* 4
Cockrell, C H (WP) 1969-70 *S*, *I*, *W*
Cockrell, R J (WP) 1974 *F* 1,2, 1975 *F* 1,2, 1976 *NZ* 1,2, 1977 *Wld*, 1981 *NZ* 1,2(R),3, *US*
Coetzee, J H H (WP) 1974 *BI* 1, 1975 *F* 2(R), 1976 *NZ* 1,2,3,4
Cope, D (Tvl) 1896 *BI* 2
Cotty, W (GW) 1896 *BI* 3
Crampton, G (GW) 1903 *BI* 2
Craven, D H (WP) 1931-32 *W*, *I*, *S*, 1933 *A* 1,2,3,4,5, 1937 *A* 1,2, *NZ* 1,2,3, 1938 *BI* 1,2,3
Cronje, P A (Tvl) 1971 *F* 1,2, *A* 1,2,3, 1974 *BI* 3,4
Crosby, J H (Tvl) 1896 *BI* 2
Crosby, N J (Tvl) 1910 *BI* 1,3
Currie, C (GW) 1903 *BI* 2

D'Alton, G (WP) 1933 *A* 1
Daneel, G M (WP) 1928 *NZ* 1,2,3,4, 1931-32 *W*, *I*, *E*, *S*
Daneel, H J (WP) 1906 *S*, *I*, *W*, *E*
Davidson, M (EP) 1910 *BI* 1
De Bruyn, J (OFS) 1974 *BI* 3
De Jongh, H P K (WP) 1928 *NZ* 3
De Klerk, I J (Tvl) 1969-70 *E*, *I*, *W*
De Klerk, K B H (Tvl) 1974 *BI* 1,2,3(R), 1975 *F* 1,2, 1976 *NZ* 2(R),3,4, 1980 *S Am* 1,2, *BI* 2, 1981 *I* 1,2
De Kock, A (GW) 1891 *BI* 2
De Kock, J S (WP) 1921 *NZ* 3, 1924 *BI* 3
Delport, W H (EP) 1951-52 *S*, *I*, *W*, *E*, *F*, 1953 *A*

261

1,2,3,4
De Melker, S C (GW) 1903 *BI* 2, 1906 *E*
Devenish, C (GW) 1896 *BI* 2
Devenish, G St L (Tvl) 1896 *BI* 2
Devenish, M (Tvl) 1891 *BI* 1
De Villiers, D I (Tvl) 1910 *BI* 1,2,3
De Villiers, D J (WP, Bol) 1962 *BI* 2,3, 1965 *I, NZ*
1,3,4, 1967 *F* 1,2,3,4, 1968 *BI* 1,2,3,4, *F* 1,2, 1969 *A*
1,4, 1969-70 *E, I, W,* 1970 *NZ* 1,2,3,4
De Villiers, H A (WP) 1906 *S, W, E*
De Villiers, H O (WP) 1967 *F* 1,2,3,4, 1968 *F* 1,2, 1969
A 1,2,3,4, 1969-70 *S, E, I, W*
De Villiers, P du P (WP) 1928 *NZ* 1,3,4, 1931-32 *E,*
1933 *A* 4, 1937 *A* 1,2, *NZ* 1
Devine, D (Tvl) 1924 *BI* 3, 1928 *NZ* 2
De Vos, D J J (WP) 1965 *S,* 1969 *A* 3, 1969-70 *S*
De Waal, A N (WP) 1967 *F* 1,2,3,4
De Waal, P (WP) 1896 *BI* 4
De Wet, A E (WP) 1969 *A* 3,4, 1969-70 *E*
De Wet, P (WP) 1938 *BI* 1,2,3
Dinkelmann, E E (NT) 1951-52 *S, I, E, F,* 1953 *A* 1,2
Dirksen, C W (NT) 1963 *A* 4, 1964 *W,* 1965 *I, S,* 1967
F 1,2,3,4, 1968 *BI* 1,2
Dobbin, F J (GW) 1903 *BI* 1,2, 1906 *S, W, E,* 1910 *BI*
1, 1912-13 *S, I, W*
Dobie, J A R (Tvl) 1928 *NZ* 2
Dormehl, P J (WP) 1896 *BI* 3,4
Douglass, F W (EP) 1896 *BI* 1
Dryburgh, R G (WP) 1955 *BI* 2,3,4, 1956 *A* 2, *NZ* 1,4,
1960 *NZ* 1,2
Duff, B (WP) 1891 *BI* 1,2,3
Duffy, B A (Bor) 1928 *NZ* 1
Du Plessis, C J (WP) 1982 *S Am* 1,2, 1984 *E* 1,2, *S Am*
1,2, 1986 *Cv* 1,2,3,4, 1989 *Wld* 1,2
Du Plessis, D C (NT) 1977 *Wld,* 1980 *S Am* 2
Du Plessis, F (Tvl) 1949 *NZ* 1,2,3
Du Plessis, M (WP) 1971 *A* 1,2,3, 1974 *BI* 1,2, *F* 1,2,
1975 *F* 1,2, 1976 *NZ* 1,2,3,4, 1977 *Wld,* 1980 *S Am* 1,2,
BI 1,2,3,4, *S Am* 4, *F*
Du Plessis, M J (WP) 1984 *S Am* 1,2, 1986 *Cv* 1,2,3,4,
1989 *Wld* 1,2
Du Plessis, N J (WT) 1921 *NZ* 2,3, 1924 *BI* 1,2,3
Du Plessis, P G (NT) 1972 *E*
Du Plessis, T D (NT) 1980 *S Am* 1,2
Du Plessis, W (WP) 1980 *S Am* 1,2, *BI* 1,2,3,4, *S Am*
3,4, *F,* 1981 *NZ* 1,2,3, 1982 *S Am* 1,2
Du Plooy, A J J (EP) 1955 *BI* 1
Du Preez, F C H (NT) 1960-61 *E, S,* 1961 *A* 1,2, 1962
BI 1,2,3,4, 1963 *A* 1, 1964 *W, F,* 1965 *A* 1,2, *NZ*
1,2,3,4, 1967 *F* 4, 1968 *BI* 1,2,3,4, *F* 1,2, 1969 *A* 1,2,
1969-70 *S, I, W,* 1970 *NZ* 1,2,3,4, 1971 *F* 1,2, *A* 1,2,3
Du Preez, J G H (WP) 1956 *NZ* 1
Du Rand, J A (R, NT) 1949 *NZ* 2,3, 1951-52 *S, I, W,*
E, F, 1953 *A* 1,2,3,4, 1955 *BI* 1,2,3,4, 1956 *A* 1,2, *NZ*
1,2,3,4
Du Toit, A F (WP) 1928 *NZ* 3,4
Du Toit, B A (Tvl) 1938 *BI* 1,2,3
Du Toit, P A (NT) 1949 *NZ* 2,3,4, 1951-52 *S, I, W, E, F*
Du Toit, P G (WP) 1981 *NZ* 1, 1982 *S Am* 1,2, 1984 *E*
1,2
Du Toit, P S (WP) 1958 *F* 1,2, 1960 *NZ* 1,2,3,4,
1960-61 *W, I, E, S, F,* 1961 *I, A* 1,2
Duvenhage, F P (GW) 1949 *NZ* 1,3

Edwards, P (NT) 1980 *S Am* 1,2
Ellis, J H (SWA) 1965 *NZ* 1,2,3,4, 1967 *F* 1,2,3,4,
1968 *BI* 1,2,3,4, *F* 1,2, 1969 *A* 1,2,3,4, 1969-70 *S, I,*
W, 1970 *NZ* 1,2,3,4, 1971 *F* 1,2, *A* 1,2,3, 1972 *E,* 1974
BI 1,2,3,4, *F* 1,2, 1976 *NZ* 1
Ellis, M (Tvl) 1921 *NZ* 2,3, 1924 *BI* 1,2,3,4
Engelbrecht, J P (WP) 1960 *S,* 1960-61 *W, I, E, S, F,*
1961 *A* 1,2, 1962 *BI* 2,3,4, 1963 *A* 2,3, 1964 *W, F,* 1965
I, S, A 1,2, *NZ* 1,2,3,4, 1967 *F* 1,2,3,4, 1968 *BI* 1,2, *F*
1,2, 1969 *A* 1,2
Erasmus, F S (NT, EP) 1986 *Cv* 3,4, 1989 *Wld* 2
Etlinger, T E (WP) 1896 *BI* 4

Ferreira, C (OFS) 1986 *Cv* 1,2
Ferreira, P S (WP) 1984 *S Am* 1,2
Ferris, H H (Tvl) 1903 *BI* 3
Forbes, H H (Tvl) 1896 *BI* 2
Fourie, C (EP) 1974 *F* 1,2, 1975 *F* 1,2
Fourie, T T (SET) 1974 *BI* 3

Fourie, W L (SWA) 1958 *F* 1,2
Francis, J A J (Tvl) 1912-13 *S, I, W, E, F*
Frederickson, C A (Tvl) 1974 *BI* 2, 1980 *S Am* 1,2
Frew, A (Tvl) 1903 *BI* 1
Froneman, D C (OFS) 1977 *Wld*
Froneman, I L (Bor) 1933 *A* 1
Fry, S P (WP) 1951-52 *S, I, W, E, F,* 1953 *A* 1,2,3,4,
1955 *BI* 1,2,3,4

Gage, J H (OFS) 1933 *A* 1
Gainsford, J L (WP) 1960 *S, NZ* 1,2,3,4, 1960-61 *W,*
I, E, S, F, 1961 *A* 1,2, 1962 *BI* 1,2,3,4, 1963 *A* 1,2,3,4,
1964 *W, F,* 1965 *I, S, A* 1,2, *NZ* 1,2,3,4, 1967 *F* 1,2,3
Geel, P J (OFS) 1949 *NZ* 3
Geere, V (Tvl) 1933 *A* 1,2,3,4,5
Geffin, A O (Tvl) 1949 *NZ* 1,2,3,4, 1951-52 *S, I, W*
Geldenhuys, S B (NT) 1981 *NZ* 2,3, *US,* 1982 *S Am*
1,2, 1989 *Wld* 1,2
Gentles, T A (WP) 1955 *BI* 1,2,4, 1956 *NZ* 2,3, 1958 *F* 2
Geraghty, E M (Bor) 1949 *NZ* 4
Gerber, D M (EP) 1980 *S Am* 3,4, *F,* 1981 *I* 1,2, *NZ*
1,2,3, *US,* 1982 *S Am* 1,2, 1984 *E* 1,2, *S Am* 1,2, 1986
Cv 1,2,3,4
Gerber, M C (EP) 1958 *F* 1,2, 1960 *S*
Gericke, F W (Tvl) 1960 *S*
Germishuys, J S (OFS, Tvl) 1974 *BI* 2, 1976 *NZ*
1,2,3,4, 1977 *Wld,* 1980 *S Am* 1,2, *BI* 1,2,3,4, *S Am*
3,4, *F,* 1981 *I* 1,2, *NZ* 2,3, *US*
Gibbs, B (GW) 1903 *BI* 2
Goosen, C P (OFS) 1965 *NZ* 2
Gorton, H C (Tvl) 1896 *BI* 1
Gould, R L (N) 1968 *BI* 1,2,3,4
Gray, B G (WP) 1931-32 *W, E, S,* 1933 *A* 5
Greenwood, C M (WP) 1961 *I*
Greyling, P J F (OFS) 1967 *F* 1,2,3,4, 1968 *BI* 1, *F* 1,2,
1969 *A* 1,2,3,4, 1969-70 *S, E, I, W,* 1970 *NZ* 1,2,3,4,
1971 *F* 1,2, *A* 1,2,3, 1972 *E*
Grobler, C J (OFS) 1974 *BI* 4, 1975 *F* 1,2
Guthrie, F H (WP) 1891 *BI* 1,3, 1896 *BI* 1

Hahn, C H L (Tvl) 1910 *BI* 1,2,3
Hamilton, F (EP) 1891 *BI* 1
Harris, T A (Tvl) 1937 *NZ* 2,3, 1938 *BI* 1,2,3
Hartley, A J (WP) 1891 *BI* 3
Hattingh, L B (OFS) 1933 *A* 2
Heatlie, B H (WP) 1891 *BI* 2,3, 1896 *BI* 1,4, 1903 *BI*
1,3
Hepburn, T (WP) 1896 *BI* 4
Heunis, J W (NT) 1981 *NZ* 3(R), *US,* 1982 *S Am* 1,2,
1984 *E* 1,2, *S Am* 1,2, 1986 *Cv* 1,2,3,4, 1989 *Wld* 1,2
Hill, R A (R) 1960-61 *W, I,* 1961 *I, A* 1,2, 1962 *BI* 4,
1963 *A* 3
Hirsch, J G (EP) 1906 *I,* 1910 *BI* 1
Hobson, T E C (WP) 1903 *BI* 3
Hoffman, R S (Bol) 1953 *A* 3
Holton, D N (EP) 1960 *S*
Hopwood, D J (WP) 1960 *S, NZ* 3,4, 1960-61 *W, E, S,*
F, 1961 *I, A* 1,2, 1962 *BI* 1,2,3,4, 1963 *A* 1,2,4, 1964
W, F, 1965 *S, NZ* 3,4
Howe, B F (Bor) 1956 *NZ* 1,4
Howe-Browne, N R F G (WP) 1910 *BI* 1,2,3
Hugo, D P (WP) 1989 *Wld* 1,2

Immelman, J H (WP) 1912-13 *F*

Jackson, D C (WP) 1906 *I, W, E*
Jackson, J S (WP) 1903 *BI* 2
Jansen, E (OFS) 1981 *NZ* 1
Jansen, J S (OFS) 1970 *NZ* 1,2,3,4, 1971 *F* 1,2, *A*
1,2,3, 1972 *E*
Jennings, C B (Bor) 1937 *NZ* 1
Johnstone, P G A (WP) 1951-52 *S, I, W, E, F,* 1956 *A*
1, *NZ* 1,2,4
Jones, C H (Tvl) 1903 *BI* 1,2
Jones, P S T (WP) 1896 *BI* 1,3,4
Jordaan, R P (NT) 1949 *NZ* 1,2,3,4
Joubert, A J (OFS) *Wld* 1 (R)
Joubert, S J (WP) 1906 *I, W, E*

Kahts, W J H (NT) 1980 *BI* 1,2,3, *S Am* 3,4, *F,* 1981 *I*
1,2, *NZ* 2, 1982 *S Am* 1,2
Kaminer, J (Tvl) 1958 *F* 2

263

1,2, *NZ* 3
Van Vuuren, T F (EP) 1912-13 *S, I, W, E, F*
Van Wyk, C J (Tvl) 1951-52 *S, I, W, E, F,* 1953 *A*
1,2,3,4, 1955 *BI* 1
Van Wyk, J F B (NT) 1970 *NZ* 1,2,3,4, 1971 *F* 1,2, *A*
1,2,3, 1972 *E*, 1974 *BI* 1,3,4, 1976 *NZ* 3,4
Van Wyk, S P (WP) 1928 *NZ* 1,2
Van Zyl, B P (WP) 1961 *I*
Van Zyl, C G P (OFS) 1965 *NZ* 1,2,3,4
Van Zyl, G H (WP) 1958 *F* 1, 1960 *S, NZ* 1,2,3,4,
1960-61 *W, I, E, S, F*, 1961 *I, A* 1,2, 1962 *BI* 1,3,4
Van Zyl, H J (Tvl) 1960 *NZ* 1,2,3,4, 1960-61 *I, E, S,*
1961 *I, A* 1,2
Van Zyl, P J (Bol) 1961 *I*
Veldsman, P E (WP) 1977 *Wld*
Venter, F D (Tvl) 1931-32 *W, S,* 1933 *A* 3
Versfeld, C (WP) 1891 *BI* 3
Versfeld, M (WP) 1891 *BI* 1,2,3
Vigne, J T (Tvl) 1891 *BI* 1,2,3
Viljoen, J F (GW) 1971 *F* 1,2, *A* 1,2,3, 1972 *E*
Viljoen, J T (N) 1971 *A* 1,2,3
Villet, J V (WP) 1984 *E* 1,2
Visagie, P J (GW) 1967 *F* 1,2,3,4, 1968 *BI* 1,2,3,4, *F*
1,2, 1969 *A* 1,2,3,4, 1969-70 *S, E,* 1970 *NZ* 1,2,3,4,
1971 *F* 1,2, *A* 1,2,3
Visagie, R G (OFS) 1984 *E* 1,2, *S Am* 1,2
Visser, J de V (WP) 1981 *NZ* 2, *US*
Visser, P J (Tvl) 1933 *A* 2
Viviers, S S (OFS) 1956 *A* 1,2, *NZ* 2,3,4
Vogel, M L (OFS) 1974 *BI* 2(R)

Wagenaar, C (NT) 1977 *Wld*
Wahl, J J (WP) 1949 *NZ* 1
Walker, A P (N) 1921 *NZ* 1,3, 1924 *BI* 1,2,3,4
Walker, H N (OFS) 1953 *A* 3, 1956 *A* 2, *NZ* 1,4
Walker, H W (Tvl) 1910 *BI* 1,2,3
Walton, D C (N) 1964 *F*, 1965 *I, S, NZ* 3,4, 1969 *A*
1,2, 1969-70 *E*
Waring, F W (WP) 1931-32 *I, E*, 1933 *A* 1,2,3,4,5
Wessels, J J (WP) 1896 *BI* 1,2,3
Whipp, P J M (WP) 1974 *BI* 1,2, 1975 *F* 1, 1976 *NZ*
1,3,4, 1980 *S Am* 1,2
White, J (Bor) 1931-32 *W*, 1933 *A* 1,2,3,4,5, 1937 *A*
1,2, *NZ* 1,2
Williams, A E (GW) 1910 *BI* 1
Williams, A P (WP) 1984 *E* 1,2
Williams, D O (WP) 1937 *A* 1,2, *NZ* 1,2,3, 1938 *BI*
1,2,3
Williams, J G (NT) 1971 *F* 1,2, *A* 1,2,3, 1972 *E*, 1974
BI 1,2,4, *F* 1,2, 1976 *NZ* 1,2
Wilson, L G (WP) 1960 *NZ* 3,4, 1960-61 *W, I, E, F,*
1961 *I, A* 1,2, 1962 *BI* 1,2,3,4, 1963 *A* 1,2,3,4, 1964 *W,*
F, 1965 *I, S, A* 1,2, *NZ* 1,2,3,4
Wolmarans, B J (OFS) 1977 *Wld*
Wright, G D (EP, Tvl) 1986 *Cv* 3,4, 1989 *Wld* 1,2
Wyness, M R K (WP) 1962 *BI* 1,2,3,4, 1963 *A* 2

Zeller, W C (N) 1921 *NZ* 2,3
Zimerman, M (WP) 1931-32 *W, I, E, S*

SOUTH AFRICAN INTERNATIONAL RECORDS

Both team and individual records are for official South African international matches, up to 30 April 1990.

TEAM RECORDS

Highest score
50 v S America (50-18) 1982 Pretoria
v individual countries
30 v Australia (30-11) 1969 Johannesburg
34 v B Isles (34-14) 1962 Bloemfontein
35 v England (35-9) 1984 Johannesburg
38 v France ⎰(38-5) 1913 Bordeaux
⎱(38-25) 1975 Bloemfontein
38 v Ireland (38-0) 1912 Dublin
24 v N Zealand (24-12) 1981 Wellington
33 v NZ Cavaliers (33-18) 1986 Pretoria
50 v S America (50-18) 1982 Pretoria
44 v Scotland (44-0) 1951 Murrayfield
38 v United States (38-7) 1981 New York
24 v Wales (24-3) 1964 Durban

Biggest winning points margin
44 v Scotland (44-0) 1951 Murrayfield
v individual countries
25 v Australia (28-3) 1961 Johannesburg
20 v B Isles (34-14) 1962 Bloemfontein
26 v England (35-9) 1984 Johannesburg
33 v France (38-5) 1913 Bordeaux
38 v Ireland (38-0) 1912 Dublin
17 v N Zealand (17-0) 1928 Durban
15 v NZ Cavaliers (33-18) 1986 Pretoria
32 v S America (50-18) 1982 Pretoria
44 v Scotland (44-0) 1951 Murrayfield
31 v United States (38-7) 1981 New York
21 v Wales (24-3) 1964 Durban

Highest score by opposing team
28 B Isles (9-28) 1974 Pretoria
by individual countries
21 Australia (6-21) 1933 Durban
28 B Isles (9-28) 1974 Pretoria
18 England (9-18) 1972 Johannesburg
25 France (38-25) 1975 Bloemfontein
15 Ireland (23-15) 1981 Cape Town
25 N Zealand (22-25) 1981 Auckland
19 NZ Cavaliers (18-19) 1986 Durban
21 S America (12-21) 1982 Bloemfontein
10 Scotland (18-10) 1960 Port Elizabeth
7 United States (38-7) 1981 New York
6 Wales (6-6) 1970 Cardiff

Biggest losing points margin
19 v B Isles (9-28) 1974 Pretoria
v individual countries
15 v Australia (6-21) 1933 Durban
19 v B Isles (9-28) 1974 Pretoria
9 v England (9-18) 1972 Johannesburg
5 v France (14-19) 1967 Johannesburg
3 v Ireland (6-9) 1965 Dublin
17 v N Zealand (3-20) 1965 Auckland
1 v NZ Cavaliers (18-19) 1986 Durban
9 v S America (12-21) 1982 Bloemfontein
6 v Scotland (0-6) 1906 Glasgow
No defeats v United States or Wales

Most tries by South Africa in an international
10 v Ireland (38-0) 1912 Dublin

Most tries against South Africa in an international
⎧ by B Isles (22-23) 1955 Johannesburg
5 ⎨ by N Zealand (3-20) 1965 Auckland
⎩ by B Isles (9-28) 1974 Pretoria

Most points on overseas tour (all matches)
753 in Australia/N Zealand (26 matches) 1937

Most tries on overseas tour (all matches)
161 in Australia/N Zealand (26 matches) 1937

INDIVIDUAL RECORDS

Most capped player
F C H du Preez ⎱ 38 ⎰ 1960-71
J H Ellis ⎰ ⎱ 1965-76
in individual positions
Full-back
L G Wilson   27   1960-65
Wing
J P Engelbrecht   33   1960-69

Centre
J L Gainsford   33   1960-67
Fly-half
P J Visagie   25   1967-71
Scrum-half
D J de Villiers   25   1962-70
Prop
J F K Marais   35   1963-74
Hooker
G F Malan   18   1958-65
Lock
F C H du Preez   31(38)[1]   1960-71
Flanker
J H Ellis   38   1965-76
No 8
D J Hopwood   22[2]   1960-65

[1]*du Preez won 7 caps as a flanker*
[2]*T P Bedford, 25 caps, won 19 at No 8 and 6 as a flanker*

Longest international career
J M Powell   13 seasons   1891-1903
B H Heatlie   13 seasons   1891-1903

Most internationals as captain
D J de Villiers   22   1965-70

Most points in internationals – 268
H E Botha (23 matches) 1980-89

Most points in an international – 22
G R Bosch v France 1975 Pretoria

Most tries in internationals – 15
D M Gerber (19 matches) 1980-86

Most tries in an international – 3
E E McHardy v Ireland 1912 Dublin
J A Stegmann v Ireland 1912 Dublin
K T van Vollenhoven v B Isles
  1955 Cape Town
H J van Zyl v Australia 1961 Johannesburg
R H Mordt v New Zealand 1981 Auckland
R H Mordt v United States
  1981 New York
D M Gerber v S America 1982 Pretoria
D M Gerber v England 1984 Johannesburg

Most conversions in internationals – 43
H E Botha (23 matches) 1980-89

Most conversions in an international – 7
A Geffin v Scotland 1951 Murrayfield

Most dropped goals in internationals – 15
H E Botha (23 matches) 1980-89

Most penalty goals in internationals – 43
H E Botha (23 matches) 1980-89

Most points in international series – 69
H E Botha (4 appearances) v
  NZ Cavaliers 1986

**Most points in international series
on tour – 35**
H E Botha (3 appearances)
  1981 N Zealand

**Most tries in international series
on tour – 6**
E E McHardy (5 appearances) 1912-13
  B Isles/France

Most points on overseas tour – 190
G H Brand (20 appearances) 1937
  Australia/N Zealand

Most tries on overseas tour – 22
J A Loubser (20 appearances) 1906-07
  B Isles/France

Most points in a tour match – 35
W J de Wet Ras v British Schools OB
  1980 Montevideo

Most tries in a tour match – 6
R G Dryburgh v Queensland 1956
  Brisbane

LAST QUARTER DOMINANCE AND RUTHLESSNESS

THE 1989 SEASON IN NEW ZEALAND
Donald Cameron *New Zealand Herald*

Someone seeking an illustration of the All Blacks' recent dominance of world rugby, which carried them unbeaten in seven internationals and 12 other matches in 1989, described them as the Mike Tyson of rugby. Yet even Tyson was eventually floored, and the analogy was not quite accurate in another respect. The All Blacks were unbeaten and seldom seriously challenged. They were ruthless. But in 1989 there developed a marked pattern to their play which suggested, in boxing terms, the 15-round points victory rather than the first-round knock-out. Future opponents should study the All Black pattern of 1989, for it offers, if not a hint of vulnerability, at least a chink in their armour which challengers might try to exploit. For in 1989 the All Blacks were very often under pressure for three-quarters of the game, and only demonstrated their superiority during the last quarter. That superiority, then, while based on a very solid and dependable playing pattern, depends just as much on their greater fitness.

Not surprisingly, there were many instances in 1989 when the All Blacks were at full stretch. Their pattern had become common knowledge in world rugby, and thus easier to counter. Nonetheless, in many cases they got home in reasonably good order in the last quarter. In the first international against France on their short tour the All Blacks had only fingertip control as France pulled up to 17-18 with 27 minutes left. However, the All Blacks got the late points when they needed them for a 25-17 win. Fourteen minutes into the second half of the second Test France led 20-19, but the All Blacks closed down the game with 14 points in the last quarter. Even the Pumas, slaughtered 9-60 in the first international, held the All Blacks to 15-12 at half-time in the second international. Australia, in the single international for the Bledisloe Cup, were highly competitive at 12-18 with 18 minutes to play, but in the vital last phase of the game the All Blacks managed more control, and recorded a 24-12 win.

During the tour of Wales and Ireland the pattern was often the same. Teams such as Neath, Ireland, Llanelli and Cardiff hustled and bustled the All Blacks for two-thirds of the game, but at the sharp end of the match the All Blacks were the only side scoring points. So the fitness methods devised a few years ago by Glaswegian Jim Blair, and adopted in turn by Canterbury, Auckland and the All Blacks, represent a priceless legacy. However, there were hints that one remorseless enemy, time, was catching up with the All Blacks, and that another unbeaten year was taking its toll.

On the home front Auckland continued their incredible Ranfurly Shield saga which began in late 1985, and which now consists of 33 consecutive defences of the precious trophy. Auckland again took the shield on tour, to challenges at Thames Valley and Mid-Canterbury. The first was a stunning success for the challengers, even if Auckland won 58-7. The second, for the smallish town of Ashburton, represented one of the great achievements of the rugby year. The whole area became organised around the match and Ashburton staged a magnificent parade before the game.

During the year there were short tours by France and Argentina, and a one-off Test against Australia. The French sometimes delighted, sometimes disappointed, seldom escaping the frustration that Jacques Fouroux's directions brought to a team of aristocrats who too often played like peasants. The Pumas were given a ridiculously hard itinerary, but they won four matches, as many as the French.

The NZRFU administration continued to flourish, at least in the arranging of hefty sponsorship backing and in keeping the national championship running smoothly. But very soon the NZRFU may have to persuade some of the weaker unions to amalgamate and take on new strengths. On the east coast of the North Island, on the west coast of the South Island and around North Otago rugby is facing a continual battle simply to survive. At a time when the game is flourishing beyond measure in so many areas the playing poverty here is a jarring note.

NATIONAL CHAMPIONSHIP
First Division

	P	W	D	L	F	A	Pts
Auckland	10	9	1	0	348	87	38
Canterbury	10	8	1	1	287	168	34
North Harbour	10	7	1	2	272	164	31
Waikato	10	7	0	3	335	124	29
Otago	10	4	1	5	243	161	21
Bay of Plenty	10	4	1	5	189	231	18
Wellington	10	4	0	6	169	245	17
North Auckland	10	3	1	6	195	255	15
Counties	10	3	0	7	139	319	13
Taranaki	10	2	0	8	156	372	9
Hawke's Bay	10	1	0	9	140	345	4

Hawke's Bay relegated, Southland promoted

Second Division

	P	W	D	L	F	A	Pts
Southland	7	6	0	1	195	80	25
Manawatu	7	6	0	1	220	65	25
King Country	7	5	0	2	137	108	22
Marlborough	7	4	0	3	109	144	17
Wairarapa-Bush	7	3	0	4	99	132	12
Poverty Bay	7	2	0	5	87	151	9
Mid-Canterbury	7	1	1	5	92	199	7
Thames Valley	7	0	1	6	63	123	4

Wanganui promoted, Thames Valley relegated

Third Division

	P	W	D	L	F	A	Pts
Wanganui	7	7	0	0	273	73	28
Sth Canterbury	7	5	0	2	276	76	22
Horowhenua	7	5	0	2	159	103	21
Nelson Bays	7	4	0	3	100	136	17
Buller	7	4	0	3	90	145	17
East Coast	7	2	0	5	68	203	8
North Otago	7	1	0	6	64	158	7

RANFURLY SHIELD CHAMPIONSHIP

Auckland 58 (7G 4PG 1T), Thames Valley 7 (1PG 1T); Auckland 44 (4G 4PG 2T), Taranaki 15 (1G 3PG); Auckland 66 (8G 2PG 3T), Mid-Canterbury 0; Auckland 84 (11G 2PG 3T), Counties 3 (1PG); Auckland 34 (3G 4PG 1T), Bay of Plenty 21 (2G 3PG); Auckland 22 (1G 4PG 1T), Waikato 9 (3PG); Auckland 29 (2G 3PG 2T), Wellington 6 (1G)

NEW ZEALAND INTERNATIONAL PLAYERS *(up to 30 April 1990)*

ABBREVIATIONS

A – Australia; *Arg* – Argentina; *AW* – Anglo-Welsh; *BI* – British Isles teams; *E* – England; *F* – France; *Fj* – Fiji; *I* – Ireland; *It* – Italy; *R* – Romania; *S* – Scotland; *SA* – South Africa; *US* – United States of America; *W* – Wales; (R) – Replacement. Entries in square brackets [ ] indicate appearances in the Rugby World Cup

Note: When a series has taken place, figures denote the particular matches in which players featured. Thus 1959 *BI* 2,4 indicates that a player appeared in the second and fourth Tests of the 1959 series against the British Isles.

Abbott, H L (Taranaki) 1906 *F*
Aitken, G G (Wellington) 1921 *SA* 1,2
Allen, F R (Auckland) 1946 *A* 1,2, 1947 *A* 1,2, 1949 *SA* 1,2
Allen, N H (Counties) 1980 *A* 3, *W*
Alley, G T (Canterbury) 1928 *SA* 1,2,3
Anderson, A (Canterbury) 1983 *S, E*, 1984 *A* 1,2,3, 1987 [*Fj*]
Anderson, B L (Wairarapa-Bush) 1986 *A* 1
Archer, W R (Otago, Southland) 1955 *A* 1,2, 1956 *SA* 1,3
Argus, W G (Canterbury) 1946 *A* 1,2, 1947 *A* 1,2
Arnold, D A (Canterbury) 1963 *I, W*, 1964 *E, F*
Arnold, K D (Waikato) 1947 *A* 1,2
Ashby, D L (Southland) 1958 *A* 2
Asher, A A (Auckland) 1903 *A*
Ashworth, B G (Auckland) 1978 *A* 1,2
Ashworth, J C (Canterbury, Hawke's Bay) 1978 *A* 1,2,3, 1980 *A* 1,2,3, 1981 *SA* 1,2,3, 1982 *A* 1,2, 1983 *BI* 1,2,3,4, *A*, 1984 *F* 1,2, *A* 1,2,3, 1985 *E* 1,2, *A*
Atkinson, H (West Coast) 1913 *A* 1
Avery, H E (Wellington) 1910 *A* 1,2,3

Bachop, G T M (Canterbury) 1989 *W, I*
Badeley, C E O (Auckland) 1921 *SA* 1,2
Baird, J A S (Otago) 1913 *A* 2
Ball, N (Wellington) 1931 *A*, 1932 *A* 2,3, 1935 *W*, 1936 *E*
Barrett, J (Auckland) 1913 *A* 2,3
Barry, E F (Wellington) 1934 *A* 2
Batty, G B (Wellington, Bay of Plenty) 1972 *W, S*, 1973 *E* 1, *I, F, E* 2, 1974 *A* 1,3, *I*, 1975 *S*, 1976 *SA* 1,2,3,4, 1977 *BI* 1
Batty, W (Auckland) 1930 *BI* 1,3,4, 1931 *A*
Beatty, G E (Taranaki) 1950 *BI* 1
Bell, R H (Otago) 1951 *A* 3, 1952 *A* 1,2
Belliss, E A (Wanganui) 1921 *SA* 1,2,3
Bennet, R (Otago) 1905 *A*
Berghan, T (Otago) 1938 *A* 1,2,3
Berry, M J (Wairarapa-Bush) 1986 *A* 3(R)
Bevan, V D (Wellington) 1949 *A* 1,2, 1950 *BI* 1,2,3,4
Birtwistle, W M (Canterbury) 1965 *SA* 1,2,3,4, 1967 *E, W, S*
Black, J E (Canterbury) 1977 *F* 1, 1979 *A*, 1980 *A* 3
Black, N W (Auckland) 1949 *SA* 3
Black, R S (Otago) 1914 *A* 1
Blake, A W (Wairarapa) 1949 *A* 1
Boggs, E G (Auckland) 1946 *A* 2, 1949 *SA* 1
Bond, J G (Canterbury) 1949 *A* 2
Booth, E E (Otago) 1906 *F*, 1907 *A* 1,3
Boroevich, K G (Wellington) 1986 *F* 1, *A* 1, *F* 3(R)
Botica, F M (North Harbour) 1986 *F* 1, *A* 1,2,3, *F* 2,3, 1989 *Arg* 1 (R)
Bowden, N J G (Taranaki) 1952 *A* 2
Bowers, R G (Wellington) 1954 *I, F*
Bowman, A W (Hawke's Bay) 1938 *A* 1,2,3
Braid, G J (Bay of Plenty) 1983 *S, E*
Bremner, S G (Auckland, Canterbury) 1952 *A* 2, 1956 *SA* 2
Brewer, M R (Otago) 1986 *F* 1, *A* 1,2,3, *F* 2,3, 1988 *A* 1, 1989 *A*, *W, I*
Briscoe, K C (Taranaki) 1959 *BI* 2, 1960 *SA* 1,2,3,4, 1963 *I, W*, 1964 *E, S*
Brooke, Z V (Auckland) 1987 [*Arg*], 1989 *Arg* 2 (R)
Brooke-Cowden, M (Auckland) 1986 *F* 1, *A* 1, 1987 [*W*]
Brown, C (Taranaki) 1913 *A* 2,3
Brown, R H (Taranaki) 1955 *A* 3, 1956 *SA* 1,2,3,4, 1957 *A* 1,2, 1958 *A* 1,2,3, 1959 *BI* 1,3, 1961 *F* 1,2,3,

1962 *A* 1
Brownlie, C J (Hawke's Bay) 1924 *W*, 1925 *E, F*
Brownlie, M J (Hawke's Bay) 1924 *I, W*, 1925 *E, F*, 1928 *SA* 1,2,3,4
Bruce, J A (Auckland) 1914 *A* 1,2
Bruce, O D (Canterbury) 1976 *SA* 1,2,4, 1977 *BI* 2,3,4, *F* 1,2, 1978 *A* 1,2, *I, W, E, S*
Bryers, R F (King Country) 1949 *A* 1
Budd, T A (Southland) 1946 *A* 2, 1949 *A* 2
Bullock-Douglas, G A H (Wanganui) 1932 *A* 1,2,3, 1934 *A* 1,2
Burgess, G A J (Auckland) 1981 *SA* 2
Burgess, G F (Southland) 1905 *A*
Burgess, R E (Manawatu) 1971 *BI* 1,2,3, 1972 *A* 3, *W*, 1973 *I, F*
Burke, P S (Taranaki) 1955 *A* 1, 1957 *A* 1,2
Burns, P J (Canterbury) 1908 *AW* 2, 1910 *A* 1,2,3, 1913 *A* 3
Bush, R G (Otago) 1931 *A*
Bush, W K (Canterbury) 1974 *A* 1,2, 1975 *S*, 1976 *I, SA* 2,4, 1977 *BI* 2,3,4(R), 1978 *I, W*, 1979 *A*
Buxton, J B (Canterbury) 1955 *A* 3, 1956 *SA* 1

Cain, M J (Taranaki) 1913 *US*, 1914 *A* 1,2,3
Callesen, J A (Manawatu) 1974 *A* 1,2,3, 1975 *S*
Cameron, D (Taranaki) 1908 *AW* 1,2,3
Cameron, L M (Manawatu) 1980 *A* 3, 1981 *SA* 1(R),2,3, *R*
Carleton, S R (Canterbury) 1928 *SA* 1,2,3, 1929 *A* 1,2,3
Carrington, K R (Auckland) 1971 *BI* 1,3,4
Casey, S T (Otago) 1905 *S, I, E, W*, 1907 *A* 1,2,3, 1908 *AW* 1
Catley, E H (Waikato) 1946 *A* 1, 1947 *A* 1,2, 1949 *SA* 1,2,3,4
Caughey, T H C (Auckland) 1932 *A* 1,3, 1934 *A* 1,2, 1935 *S, I*, 1936 *E*, *A*1, 1937 *SA* 3
Caulton, R W (Wellington) 1959 *BI* 2,3,4, 1960 *SA* 1,4, 1961 *F* 2, 1963 *E* 1,2, *I, W*, 1964 *E, S, F, A* 1,2,3
Cherrington, N P (North Auckland) 1950 *BI* 1
Christian, D L (Auckland) 1949 *SA* 4
Clamp, M (Wellington) 1984 *A*2,3
Clark, D W (Otago) 1964 *A* 1,2
Clark, W H (Wellington) 1953 *W*, 1954 *I, E, S*, 1955 *A* 1,2, 1956 *SA* 2,3,4
Clarke, A H (Auckland) 1958 *A* 3, 1959 *BI* 4, 1960 *SA* 1
Clarke, D B (Waikato) 1956 *SA* 3,4, 1957 *A* 1,2, 1958 *A* 1,3, 1959 *BI* 1,2,3,4, 1960 *SA* 1,2,3,4, 1961 *F* 1,2,3, 1962 *A* 1,2,3,4,5, 1963 *E* 1,2, *I, W*, 1964 *E, S, F, A* 2,3
Clarke, I J (Waikato) 1953 *W*, 1955 *A* 1,2,3, 1956 *SA* 1,2,3,4, 1957 *A* 1,2, 1958 *A* 1,3, 1959 *BI* 1,2, 1960 *SA* 2,4, 1961 *F* 1,2,3, 1962 *A* 1,2,3, 1963 *E* 1,2
Clarke, R L (Taranaki) 1932 *A* 2,3
Cobden, D G (Canterbury) 1937 *SA* 1
Cockerill, M S (Taranaki) 1951 *A* 1,2,3
Cockroft, E A P (South Canterbury) 1913 *A* 3, 1914 *A* 2,3
Codlin, B W (Counties) 1980 *A* 1,2,3
Collins, A H (Taranaki) 1932 *A* 2,3, 1934 *A* 1
Collins, J L (Poverty Bay) 1964 *A* 1, 1965 *SA* 1,4
Colman, J T H (Taranaki) 1907 *A* 1,2, 1908 *AW* 1,3
Connor, D M (Auckland) 1961 *F* 1,2,3, 1962 *A* 1,2,3, 4,5, 1963 *E* 1,2, 1964 *A* 2,3
Conway, R J (Otago, Bay of Plenty) 1959 *BI* 2,3,4, 1960 *SA* 1,3,4, 1965 *SA* 1,2,3,4
Cooke, A E (Auckland, Wellington) 1924 *I, W*, 1925 *E, F*, 1930 *BI* 1,2,3,4
Cooke, R J (Canterbury) 1903 *A*
Cooper, G J L (Auckland) 1986 *F* 1, *A* 1,2

Corner, M M N (Auckland) 1930 *BI* 2,3,4, 1931 *A*, 1934 *A* 1, 1936 *E*
Cossey, R R (Counties) 1958 *A* 1
Cottrell, A I (Canterbury) 1929 *A* 1,2,3, 1930 *BI* 1,2, 3,4, 1931 *A*, 1932 *A* 1,2,3
Cottrell, W D (Canterbury) 1968 *A* 1,2, *F* 2,3, 1970 *SA* 1, 1971 *BI* 1,2,3,4
Couch, M B R (Wairarapa) 1947 *A* 1, 1949 *A* 1,2
Coughlan, T D (South Canterbury) 1958 *A* 1
Creighton, J N (Canterbury) 1962 *A* 4
Crichton, S (Wellington) 1983 *S, E*
Cross, T (Canterbury) 1904 *BI*, 1905 *A*
Crowley, K J (Taranaki) 1985 *E* 1,2, *A, Arg* 1,2, 1986 *A* 3, *F* 2,3, 1987 [*Arg*]
Crowley, P J B (Auckland) 1949 *SA* 3,4, 1950 *BI* 1,2,3,4
Cummings, W (Canterbury) 1913 *A* 2,3
Cundy, R T (Wairarapa) 1929 *A* 2(R)
Cunningham, G R (Auckland) 1979 *A, S, E*, 1980 *A* 1,2
Cunningham, W (Auckland) 1905 *S, I*, 1906 *F*, 1907 *A* 1,2,3, 1908 *AW* 1,2,3
Cupples, L F (Bay of Plenty) 1924 *I, W*
Currie, C J (Canterbury) 1978 *I, W*
Cuthill, J E (Otago) 1913 *A* 1, US

Dalley, W C (Canterbury) 1924 *I*, 1928 *SA* 1,2,3,4
Dalton, A G (Counties) 1977 *F* 2, 1978 *A* 1,2,3, *I, W, E, S*, 1979 *F* 1,2, *S*, 1981 *S* 1,2, *SA* 1,2,3, *R, F* 1,2, 1982 *A* 1,2,3, 1983 *BI* 1,2,3,4,4, *A*, 1984 *F* 1,2, *A* 1,2,3, 1985 *E* 1,2, *A*
Dalton, D (Hawke's Bay) 1935 *I, W*, 1936 *A* 1,2, 1937 *SA* 1,2,3, 1938 *A* 1,2
Dalton, R A (Wellington) 1947 *A* 1,2
Dalzell, G N (Canterbury) 1953 *W*, 1954 *I, E, S, F*
Davie, M G (Canterbury) 1983 *E* (R)
Davies, W A (Auckland, Otago) 1960 *SA* 4, 1962 *A* 4,5
Davis, K (Auckland) 1952 *A* 2, 1953 *W*, 1954 *I, E, S, F*, 1955 *A* 2, 1958 *A* 1,2,3
Davis, L J (Canterbury) 1976 *I*, 1977 *BI* 3,4
Davis, W L (Hawke's Bay) 1967 *A, E, W, F, S*, 1968 *A* 1,2, *F* 1, 1969 *W* 1,2, 1970 *SA* 2
Deans, I B (Canterbury) 1988 *W* 1,2, *A* 1,2,3, 1989 *F* 1,2, *Arg* 1,2, *A*
Deans, R G (Canterbury) 1905 *S, I, E, W*, 1908 *AW* 3
Deans, R M (Canterbury) 1983 *S, E*, 1984 *A* 1(R),2,3
Delamore, G W (Wellington) 1949 *SA* 4
Dewar, H (Taranaki) 1913 *A* 1, US
Diack, E S (Otago) 1959 *BI* 2
Dick, J (Auckland) 1937 *SA* 1,2, 1938 *A* 3
Dick, M J (Auckland) 1963 *I, W*, 1964 *E, S, F*, 1965 *SA* 3, 1966 *BI* 4, 1967 *A, E, W, F*, 1969 *W* 1,2, 1970 *SA* 1,4
Dixon, M J (Canterbury) 1954 *I, E, S, F*, 1956 *SA* 1,2,3,4, 1957 *A* 1,2
Dobson, R L (Auckland) 1949 *A* 1
Dodd, E H (Wellington) 1905 *A*
Donald, A J (Wanganui) 1983 *S, E*, 1984 *F* 1,2, *A* 1,2,3
Donald, J G (Wairarapa) 1921 *SA* 1,2
Donald, Q (Wairarapa) 1924 *I, W*, 1925 *E, F*
Donaldson, M W (Manawatu) 1977 *F* 1,2, 1978 *A* 1, 2,3, *I, E, S*, 1979 *F* 1,2, *A, S* (R), 1981 *SA* 3(R)
Dougan, J P (Wellington) 1972 *A* 1, 1973 *E* 2
Downing, A J (Auckland) 1913 *A* 1, US, 1914 *A* 1,2,3
Drake, J A (Auckland) 1986 *F* 2,3, 1987 [*Fj, Arg, S, W, F*], *A*
Duff, R H (Canterbury) 1951 *A* 1,2,3, 1952 *A* 1,2, 1955 *A* 2,3, 1956 *SA* 1,2,3,4
Duncan, J (Otago) 1903 *A*
Duncan, M G (Hawke's Bay) 1971 *BI* 3(R), 4
Duncan, W D (Otago) 1921 *SA* 1,2,3
Dunn, E J (North Auckland) 1979 *S*, 1981 *S* 1
Dunn, I T W (North Auckland) 1983 *BI* 1,4, *A*
Dunn, J M (Auckland) 1946 *A* 1

Earl, A T (Canterbury) 1986 *F* 1, *A* 1, *F* 3(R), 1987 [*Arg*], 1989 *W, I*
Eastgate, B P (Canterbury) 1952 *A* 1,2, 1954 *S*
Elliott, K G (Wellington) 1946 *A* 1,2
Elsom, A E G (Canterbury) 1952 *A* 1,2, 1953 *W*, 1955 *A* 1,2,3
Elvidge, R R (Otago) 1946 *A* 1,2, 1949 *SA* 1,2,3,4, 1950 *BI* 1,2,3

Erceg, C P (Auckland) 1951 *A* 1,2,3, 1952 *A* 1
Evans, D A (Hawke's Bay) 1910 *A* 2
Eveleigh, K A (Manawatu) 1976 *SA* 2,4, 1977 *BI* 1,2

Fanning, A H N (Canterbury) 1913 *A* 3
Fanning, B J (Canterbury) 1903 *A*, 1904 *BI*
Farrell, C P (Auckland) 1977 *BI* 1,2
Fawcett, C L (Auckland) 1976 *SA* 2,3
Fea, W R (Otago) 1921 *SA* 3
Finlay, B E L (Manawatu) 1959 *BI* 1
Finlay, J (Manawatu) 1946 *A* 1
Finlayson, I (North Auckland) 1928 *SA* 1,2,3,4, 1930 *BI* 1,2
Fitzgerald, J T (Wellington) 1952 *A* 1
Fitzpatrick, B B J (Wellington) 1953 *W*, 1954 *I, F*
Fitzpatrick, S B T (Auckland) 1986 *F* 1, *A* 1, *F* 2,3, 1987 [*It, Fj, Arg, S, W, F*], *A*, 1988 *W* 1,2, *A* 1,2,3, 1989 *F* 1,2, *Arg* 1,2, *A, W, I*
Fleming, J K (Wellington) 1979 *S, E*, 1980 *A* 1,2,3
Fletcher, C J C (North Auckland) 1921 *SA* 3
Fogarty, R (Taranaki) 1921 *SA* 1,3
Ford, B R (Marlborough) 1977 *BI* 3,4, 1978 *I*, 1979 *E*
Fox, G J (Auckland) 1985 *Arg* 1, 1987 [*It, Fj, Arg, S, W, F*], *A*, 1988 *W* 1,2, *A* 1,2,3, 1989 *F* 1,2, *Arg* 1,2, *A, W, I*
Francis, A R H (Auckland) 1905 *A*, 1907 *A* 1,2,3, 1908 *AW* 1,2,3, 1910 *A* 1,2,3
Francis, W C (Wellington) 1913 *A* 2,3, 1914 *A* 1,2,3
Fraser, B G (Wellington) 1979 *S, E*, 1980 *A* 3, *W*, 1981 *S* 1,2, *SA* 1,2,3, *R, F*1, 2, 1982 *A* 1,2,3, 1983 *BI* 1,2,3,4, *A, S, E*, 1984 *A* 1
Frazer, H F (Hawke's Bay) 1946 *A* 1,2, 1947 *A* 1,2, 1949 *SA* 2
Fryer, F C (Canterbury) 1907 *A* 1,2,3, 1908 *AW* 2
Fuller, W B (Canterbury) 1910 *A* 1,2
Furlong, B D M (Hawke's Bay) 1970 *SA* 4

Gallagher, J A (Wellington) 1987 [*It, Fj, S, W, F*], *A*, 1988 *W* 1,2, *A* 1,2,3, 1989 *F* 1,2, *Arg* 1,2, *A, W, I*
Gallaher, D (Auckland) 1903 *A*, 1904 *BI*, 1905 *S, E, W*, 1906 *F*
Gard, P C (North Otago) 1971 *BI* 4
Gardiner, A J (Taranaki) 1974 *A* 3
Geddes, J H (Southland) 1929 *A* 1
Geddes, W McK (Auckland) 1913 *A* 2
Gemmell, B McL (Auckland) 1974 *A* 1,2
George, V L (Southland) 1938 *A* 1,2,3
Gilbert, G D M (West Coast) 1935 *S, I, W*, 1936 *E*
Gillespie, C T (Wellington) 1913 *A* 2
Gillespie, W D (Otago) 1958 *A* 3
Gillett, G A (Canterbury, Auckland) 1905 *S, I, E, W*, 1907 *A* 2,3, 1908 *AW* 1,3
Gillies, C C (Otago) 1936 *A* 2
Gilray, C M (Otago) 1905 *A*
Glasgow, F T (Taranaki, Southland) 1905 *S, I, E, W*, 1906 *F*, 1908 *AW* 3
Glenn, W S (Taranaki) 1904 *BI*, 1906 *F*
Goddard, M P (South Canterbury) 1946 *A* 2, 1947 *A* 1,2, 1949 *SA* 3,4
Going, S M (North Auckland) 1967 *A, F*, 1968 *F* 3, 1969 *W* 1,2, 1970 *SA* 1(R), 4, 1971 *BI* 1,2,3,4, 1972 *A* 1,2,3, *W, S*, 1973 *E* 1, *I, F, E* 2, 1974 *I*, 1975 *S*, 1976 *I* (R), *SA* 1,2,3,4, 1977 *BI* 1,2
Graham, D J (Canterbury) 1958 *A* 1,2, 1960 *SA* 2,3, 1961 *F* 1,2,3, 1962 *A* 1,2,3,4,5, 1963 *E* 1,2, *I, W*, 1964 *E, S, F*, *A* 1,2,3
Graham, J B (Otago) 1913 *US*, 1914 *A* 1,3
Graham, W G (Otago) 1979 *F* 1(R)
Grant, L A (South Canterbury) 1947 *A* 1,2, 1949 *SA* 1,2
Gray, G D (Canterbury) 1908 *AW* 2, 1913 *A* 1, US
Gray, K F (Wellington) 1963 *I, W*, 1964 *E, S, F, A* 1,2,3, 1965 *SA* 1,2,3,4, 1966 *BI* 1,2,3,4, 1967 *W, F, S*, 1968 *A* 1, *F* 2,3, 1969 *W* 1,2
Gray, W N (Bay of Plenty) 1955 *A* 2,3, 1956 *SA* 1,2,3,4
Green, C I (Canterbury) 1983 *S*(R), *E*, 1984 *A* 1,2,3, 1985 *E* 1,2, *A*, *Arg* 1,2, 1986 *A* 2,3, *F* 2,3, 1987 [*It, Fj, S, W, F*], *A*
Grenside, B A (Hawke's Bay) 1928 *SA* 1,2,3,4, 1929 *A* 2,3
Griffiths, J L (Wellington) 1934 *A* 2, 1935 *S, I, W*, 1936 *A* 1,2, 1938 *A* 3
Guy, R A (North Auckland) 1971 *BI* 1,2,3,4

271

McAtamney, F S (Otago) 1956 *SA* 2
McCahill, B J (Auckland) 1987 [*Arg*, *S*(R), *W*(R)], 1989 *Arg* 1(R), 2(R)
McCaw, W A (Southland) 1951 *A* 1,2,3, 1953 *W*, 1954 *F*
McCool, M J (Wairarapa-Bush) 1979 *A*
McCormick, W F (Canterbury) 1965 *SA* 4, 1967 *E*, *W*, *F*, *S*, 1968 *A* 1,2, *F* 1,2,3, 1969 *W* 1,2, 1970 *SA* 1,2,3, 1971 *BI* 1
McCullough, J F (Taranaki) 1959 *BI* 2,3,4
McDonald, A (Otago) 1905 *S*, *I*, *E*, *W*, 1907 *A* 1, 1908 *AW* 1, 1913 *A* 1, *US*
Macdonald, H H (Canterbury, North Auckland) 1972 *W*, *S*, 1973 *E* 1, *I*, *F*, *E* 2, 1974 *I*, 1975 *S*, 1976 *I*, *SA* 1,2,3
McDowell, S C (Auckland, Bay of Plenty) 1985 *Arg* 1,2, 1986 *A* 2,3, *F* 2,3, 1987 [*It*, *Fj*, *S*, *W*, *F*], *A*, 1988 *W* 1,2, *A* 1,2,3, 1989 *F* 1,2, *Arg* 1,2, *A*, *W*, *I*
McEldowney, J T (Taranaki) 1977 *BI* 3,4
MacEwan, I N (Wellington) 1956 *SA* 2, 1957 *A* 1,2, 1958 *A* 1,2,3, 1959 *BI* 1,2,3, 1960 *SA* 1,2,3,4, 1961 *F* 1,2,3, 1962 *A* 1,2,3,4
McGrattan, B (Wellington) 1983 *S*, *E*, 1985 *Arg* 1,2, 1986 *F* 1, *A* 1
McGregor, A J (Auckland) 1913 *A* 1, *US*
McGregor, D (Canterbury, Southland) 1903 *A*, 1904 *BI*, 1905 *E*, *W*
McGregor, N P (Canterbury) 1924 *W*, 1925 *E*
McGregor, R W (Auckland) 1903 *A*, 1904 *BI*
McHugh, M J (Auckland) 1946 *A* 1,2, 1949 *SA* 3
McIntosh, D N (Wellington) 1956 *SA* 1,2, 1957 *A* 1,2
McKay, D W (Auckland) 1961 *F* 1,2,3, 1963 *E* 1,2
McKechnie, B J (Southland) 1977 *F* 1,2, 1978 *A* 2(R),3, *W*(R), *E*, *S*, 1979 *A*, 1981 *SA* 1(R), *F* 1
McKellar, G F (Wellington) 1910 *A* 1,2,3
McKenzie, R J (Wellington) 1913 *A* 1, *US*, 1914 *A* 2,3
McKenzie, R McC (Manawatu) 1934 *A* 1, 1935 *S*, 1936 *A* 1, 1937 *SA* 1,2,3, 1938 *A* 1,2,3
McLachlan, J S (Auckland) 1974 *A* 2
McLaren, H C (Waikato) 1952 *A* 1
McLean, A L (Bay of Plenty) 1921 *SA* 2,3
McLean, H F (Wellington, Auckland) 1930 *BI* 3,4, 1932 *A* 1,2,3, 1934 *A* 1, 1935 *I*, *W*, 1936 *E*
McLean, J K (King Country, Auckland) 1947 *A* 1, 1949 *A* 2
McLeod, B E (Counties) 1964 *A* 1,2,3, 1965 *SA* 1,2,3,4, 1966 *BI* 1,2,3,4, 1967 *E*, *W*, *F*, *S*, 1968 *A* 1,2, *F* 1,2,3, 1969 *W* 1,2, 1970 *SA* 1,2
McMinn, A F (Wairarapa, Manawatu) 1903 *A*, 1905 *A*
McMinn, F A (Manawatu) 1904 *BI*
McMullen, R F (Auckland) 1957 *A* 1,2, 1958 *A* 1,2,3, 1959 *BI* 1,2,3, 1960 *SA* 2,3,4
McNab, J R (Otago) 1949 *SA* 1,2,3, 1950 *BI* 1,2,3
McNaughton, A M (Bay of Plenty) 1971 *BI* 1,2,3
McNeece, J (Southland) 1913 *A* 2,3, 1914 *A* 1,2,3
McPhail, B E (Canterbury) 1959 *BI* 1,4
Macpherson, D G (Otago) 1905 *A*
MacPherson, G L (Otago) 1986 *F* 1
MacRae, I R (Hawke's Bay) 1966 *BI* 1,2,3,4, 1967 *A*, *E*, *W*, *F*, *S*, 1968 *F* 1,2, 1969 *W* 1,2, 1970 *SA* 1,2,3,4
McRae, J A (Southland) 1946 *A* 1(R),2
McWilliams, R G (Auckland) 1928 *SA* 2,3,4, 1929 *A* 1,2,3, 1930 *BI* 1,2,3,4
Mackrell, W H C (Auckland) 1906 *F*
Macky, J V (Auckland) 1913 *A* 2
Maguire, J R (Auckland) 1910 *A* 1,2,3
Mahoney, A (Bush) 1935 *S*, *I*, *W*, 1936 *E*
Mains, L W (Otago) 1971 *BI* 2,3,4, 1976 *I*
Major, J (Taranaki) 1967 *A*
Manchester, J E (Canterbury) 1932 *A* 1,2,3, 1934 *A* 1,2, 1935 *S*, *I*, *W*, 1936 *E*
Mason, D F (Wellington) 1947 *A* 2(R)
Masters, R R (Canterbury) 1924 *I*, *W*, 1925 *E*, *F*
Mataira, H K (Hawke's Bay) 1934 *A* 2
Matheson, J D (Otago) 1972 *A* 1,2,3, *W*, *S*
Max, D S (Nelson) 1931 *A*, 1934 *A* 1,2
Meads, C E (King Country) 1957 *A* 1,2, 1958 *A* 1,2,3, 1959 *BI* 2,3,4, 1960 *SA* 1,2,3,4, 1961 *F* 1,2,3, 1962 *A* 1,2,3,5, 1963 *E* 1,2, *I*, *W*, 1964 *E*, *S*, *F*, *A* 1,2,3, 1965 *SA* 1,2,3,4, 1966 *BI* 1,2,3,4, 1967 *A*, *E*, *W*, *F*, *S*, 1968 *A* 1,2, *F* 1,2,3, 1969 *W* 1,2, 1970 *SA* 3,4, 1971 *BI* 1,2,3,4
Meads, S T (King Country) 1961 *F* 1, 1962 *A* 4,5, 1963

I, 1964 *A* 1,2,3, 1965 *SA* 1,2,3,4, 1966 *BI* 1,2,3,4
Meates, K F (Canterbury) 1952 *A* 1,2
Meates, W A (Otago) 1949 *SA* 2,3,4, 1950 *BI* 1,2,3,4
Metcalfe, T C (Southland) 1931 *A*, 1932 *A* 1
Mexted, G G (Wellington) 1950 *BI* 4
Mexted, M G (Wellington) 1979 *S*, *E*, 1980 *A* 1,2,3, *W*, 1981 *S* 1,2, *SA* 1,2,3, *R*, *F* 1,2, 1982 *A* 1,2,3, 1983 *BI* 1,2,3,4, *A*, *S*, *E*, 1984 *F* 1,2, *A* 1,2,3, 1985 *E* 1,2, *A*, *Arg* 1,2
Mill, J J (Hawke's Bay, Wairarapa) 1924 *W*, 1925 *E*, *F*, 1930 *BI* 1
Milliken, H M (Canterbury) 1938 *A* 1,2,3
Milner, H P (Wanganui) 1970 *SA* 3
Mitchell, N A (Southland, Otago) 1935 *S*, *I*, *W*, 1936 *E*, *A* 2, 1937 *SA* 3, 1938 *A* 1,2
Mitchell, T W (Canterbury) 1976 *SA* 4(R)
Mitchell, W J (Canterbury) 1910 *A* 2,3
Mitchinson, F E (Wellington) 1907 *A* 1,2,3, 1908 *AW* 1,2,3, 1910 *A* 1,2,3, 1913 *A* 1(R), *US*
Moffitt, J E (Wellington) 1921 *SA* 1,2,3
Moore, G J T (Otago) 1949 *A* 1
Moreton, R C (Canterbury) 1962 *A* 3,4, 1964 *A* 1,2,3, 1965 *SA* 2,3
Morgan, J E (North Auckland) 1974 *A* 3, *I*, 1976 *SA* 2,3,4
Morris, T J (Nelson Bays) 1972 *A* 1,2,3
Morrison, T C (South Canterbury) 1938 *A* 1,2,3
Morrison, T G (Otago) 1973 *E* 2(R)
Morrissey, P J (Canterbury) 1962 *A* 3,4,5
Mourie, G N K (Taranaki) 1977 *BI* 3,4, *F* 1,2, 1978 *I*, *W*, *E*, *S*, 1979 *F* 1,2, *A*, *S*, *E*, 1980 *W*, 1981 *S* 1,2, *F* 1,2, 1982 *A* 1,2,3
Muller, B L (Taranaki) 1967 *A*, *E*, *W*, *F*, 1968 *A* 1, *F* 1, 1969 *W* 1, 1970 *SA* 1,2,4, 1971 *BI* 1,2,3,4
Mumm, W J (Buller) 1949 *A* 1
Murdoch, K (Otago) 1970 *SA* 4, 1972 *A* 3, *W*
Murdoch, P H (Auckland) 1964 *A* 2,3, 1965 *SA* 1,2,3
Murray, H V (Canterbury) 1913 *A* 1, *US*, 1914 *A* 2,3
Murray, P C (Wanganui) 1908 *AW* 2
Myers, R G (Waikato) 1978 *A* 3
Mynott, H J (Taranaki) 1905 *I*, *W*, 1906 *F*, 1907 *A* 1,2,3, 1910 *A* 1,3

Nathan, W J (Auckland) 1962 *A* 1,2,3,4,5, 1963 *E* 1,2, *W*, 1964 *F*, 1966 *BI* 1,2,3,4, 1967 *A*
Nelson, K A (Otago) 1962 *A* 4,5
Nepia, G (Hawke's Bay, East Coast) 1924 *I*, *W*, 1925 *E*, *F*, 1929 *A* 1, 1930 *BI* 1,2,3,4
Nesbit, S R (Auckland) 1960 *SA* 2,3
Newton, F (Canterbury) 1905 *E*, *W*, 1906 *F*
Nicholls, H E (Wellington) 1921 *SA* 1
Nicholls, M F (Wellington) 1921 *A* 1,2,3, 1924 *I*, *W*, 1925 *E*, *F*, 1928 *SA* 4, 1930 *BI* 2,3
Nicholson, G W (Auckland) 1903 *A*, 1904 *BI*, 1907 *A* 2,3
Norton, R W (Canterbury) 1971 *BI* 1,2,3,4, 1972 *A* 1,2,3, *W*, *S*, 1973 *E* 1, *I*, *F*, *E* 2, 1974 *A* 1,2,3, *I*, 1975 *S*, 1976 *I*, *SA* 1,2,3,4, 1977 *BI* 1,2,3,4

O'Brien, J G (Auckland) 1914 *A* 1
O'Callaghan, M W (Manawatu) 1968 *F* 1,2,3
O'Callaghan, T R (Wellington) 1949 *A* 2
O'Donnell, D H (Wellington) 1949 *A* 2
Old, G H (Manawatu) 1981 *SA* 3, *R*(R), 1982 *A* 1(R)
O'Leary, M J (Auckland) 1910 *A* 1,3, 1913 *A* 2,3
Oliver, C J (Canterbury) 1929 *A* 1,2, 1934 *A* 1, 1935 *S*, *I*, *W*, 1936 *E*
Oliver, D J (Wellington) 1930 *BI* 1,2
Oliver, D O (Otago) 1954 *I*, *F*
Oliver, F J (Southland, Otago, Manawatu) 1976 *SA* 4, 1977 *BI* 1,2,3,4, *F* 1,2, 1978 *A* 1,2,3, *I*, *W*, *E*, *S*, 1979 *F* 1,2, 1981 *SA* 2
Orr, R W (Otago) 1949 *A* 1
Osborne, W M (Wanganui) 1975 *S*, 1976 *SA* 2(R), 4(R), 1977 *BI* 1,3,4, *F* 1(R), 2, 1978 *I*, *W*, *E*, *S*, 1980 *W*, 1982 *A* 1,3
O'Sullivan, J M (Taranaki) 1905 *S*, *I*, *E*, *W*, 1907 *A* 3
O'Sullivan, T P A (Taranaki) 1960 *SA* 1, 1961 *F* 1, 1962 *A* 1,2

Page, J R (Wellington) 1931 *A*, 1932 *A* 1,2,3, 1934 *A* 1,2
Palmer, B P (Auckland) 1929 *A* 2, 1932 *A* 2,3

273

Tetzlaff, P L (Auckland) 1947 *A* 1,2
Thimbleby, N W (Hawke's Bay) 1970 *SA* 3
Thomas, B T (Auckland, Wellington) 1962 *A* 5, 1964 *A* 1,2,3
Thomson, H D (Wellington) 1908 *AW* 1
Thorne, G S (Auckland) 1968 *A* 1,2, *F* 1,2,3, 1969 *W* 1, 1970 *SA* 1,2,3,4
Thornton, N H (Auckland) 1947 *A* 1,2, 1949 *SA* 1
Tilyard, J T (Wellington) 1913 *A* 3
Tindill, E W T (Wellington) 1936 *E*
Townsend, L J (Otago) 1955 *A* 1,3
Tremain, K R (Canterbury, Hawke's Bay) 1959 *BI* 2,3,4, 1960 *SA* 1,2,3,4, 1961 *F* 2,3, 1962 *A* 1,2,3, 1963 *E* 1,2, *I, W,* 1964 *E, S, F, A* 1,2,3, 1965 *SA* 1,2,3,4, 1966 *BI* 1,2,3,4, 1967 *A, E, W, S,* 1968 *A* 1, *F* 1,2,3
Trevathan, D (Otago) 1937 *SA* 1,2,3
Tuck, J M (Waikato) 1929 *A* 1,2,3
Turtill, H S (Canterbury) 1905 *A*
Twigden, T M (Auckland) 1980 *A* 2,3
Tyler, G A (Auckland) 1903 *A,* 1904 *BI,* 1905 *S, I, E, W,* 1906 *F*

Udy, D K (Wairarapa) 1903 *A*
Urbahn, R J (Taranaki) 1959 *BI* 1,3,4
Urlich, R A (Auckland) 1970 *SA* 3,4
Uttley, I N (Wellington) 1963 *E* 1,2

Vincent, P B (Canterbury) 1956 *SA* 1,2
Vodanovich, I M H (Wellington) 1955 *A* 1,2,3

Wallace, W J (Wellington) 1903 *A,* 1904 *BI,* 1905 *S, I, E, W,* 1906 *F,* 1907 *A* 1,2,3, 1908 *AW* 2
Walsh, P T (Counties) 1955 *A* 1,2,3, 1956 *SA* 1,2,4, 1957 *A* 1,2, 1958 *A* 1,2,3, 1959 *BI* 1, 1963 *E* 2
Ward, R H (Southland) 1936 *A* 2, 1937 *SA* 1,3
Waterman, A C (North Auckland) 1929 *A* 1,2
Watkins, E L (Wellington) 1905 *A*
Watt, B A (Canterbury) 1962 *A* 1,4, 1963 *E* 1,2, *W,* 1964 *E, S, A* 1
Watt, J M (Otago) 1936 *A* 1,2
Watt, J R (Wellington) 1958 *A* 2, 1960 *SA* 1,2,3,4, 1961 *F* 1,3, 1962 *A* 1,2
Watts, M G (Taranaki) 1979 *F* 1,2, 1980 *A* 1,2,3(R)
Webb, D S (North Auckland) 1959 *BI* 2
Wells, J (Wellington) 1936 *A* 1,2
West, A H (Taranaki) 1921 *SA* 2,3
Whetton, A J (Auckland) 1984 *A* 1(R), 3(R), 1985 *A*(R), *Arg* 1(R), 1986 *A* 2, 1987 [*It, Fj, Arg, S, W, F*], *A,* 1988 *W* 1,2, *A* 1,2,3, 1989 *F* 1,2, *Arg* 1,2, *A*
Whetton, G W (Auckland) 1981 *SA* 3, *R, F* 1,2, 1982 *A* 3, 1983 *BI* 1,2,3,4, 1984 *F* 1,2, *A* 1,2,3, 1985 *E* 1,2, *A, Arg* 2, 1986 *A* 2,3, *F* 2,3 1987 [*It, Fj, Arg, S, W, F*], *A,*

1988 *W* 1,2, *A* 1,2,3, 1989 *F* 1,2, *Arg* 1,2, *A, W, I*
Whineray, W J (Canterbury, Waikato, Auckland) 1957 *A* 1,2, 1958 *A* 1,2,3, 1959 *BI* 1,2,3,4, 1960 *SA* 1,2,3,4, 1961 *F* 1,2,3, 1962 *A* 1,2,3,4,5, 1963 *E* 1,2, *I, W,* 1964 *E, S, F,* 1965 *SA* 1,2,3,4
White, A (Southland) 1921 *SA* 1, 1924 *I,* 1925 *E, F*
White, H L (Auckland) 1954 *I, E, F,* 1955 *A* 3
White, R A (Poverty Bay) 1949 *A* 1,2, 1950 *BI* 1,2,3,4, 1951 *A* 1,2,3, 1952 *A* 1,2, 1953 *W,* 1954 *I, E, S, F,* 1955 *A* 1,2,3, 1956 *SA* 1,2,3,4
White, R M (Wellington) 1946 *A* 1,2, 1947 *A* 1,2
Whiting, G J (King Country) 1972 *A* 1,2, *S,* 1973 *E* 1, *I, F*
Whiting, P J (Auckland) 1971 *BI* 1,2,4, 1972 *A* 1,2,3, *W, S,* 1973 *E* 1, *I, F,* 1974 *A* 1,2,3, *I,* 1976 *I, SA* 1,2,3,4
Williams, B G (Auckland) 1970 *SA* 1,2,3,4, 1971 *BI* 1,2,4, 1972 *A* 1,2,3, *W, S,* 1973 *E* 1, *I, F, E* 2, 1974 *A* 1,2,3, *I,* 1975 *S,* 1976 *I, SA* 1,2,3,4, 1977 *BI* 1,2,3,4, *F* 1, 1978 *A* 1,2,3, *I*(R), *W, E, S*
Williams, G C (Wellington) 1967 *E, W, F, S,* 1968 *A* 2
Williams, P (Otago) 1913 *A* 1
Williment, M (Wellington) 1964 *A* 1, 1965 *SA* 1,2,3, 1966 *BI* 1,2,3,4, 1967 *A*
Willocks, C (Otago) 1946 *A* 1,2, 1949 *SA* 1,3,4
Wilson, B W (Otago) 1977 *BI* 3,4, 1978 *A* 1,2,3, 1979 *F* 1,2, *A*
Wilson, D D (Canterbury) 1954 *E, S*
Wilson, H W (Otago) 1949 *A* 1, 1950 *BI* 4, 1951 *A* 1,2,3
Wilson, N A (Wellington) 1908 *AW* 1,2, 1910 *A* 1,2,3, 1913 *A* 2,3, 1914 *A* 1,2,3
Wilson, N L (Otago) 1951 *A* 1,2,3
Wilson, R G (Canterbury) 1979 *S, E*
Wilson, S S (Wellington) 1977 *F* 1,2, 1978 *A* 1,2,3, *I, W, E, S,* 1979 *F* 1,2, *A, S, E,* 1980 *A* 1, *W,* 1981 *S* 1,2, *SA* 1,2,3, *R, F* 1,2, 1982 *A* 1,2,3, 1983 *BI* 1,2,3,4, *A, S, E*
Wolfe, T N (Wellington, Taranaki) 1961 *F* 1,2,3, 1962 *A* 2,3, 1963 *E* 1
Wood, M E (Canterbury, Auckland) 1903 *A,* 1904 *BI*
Woodman, F A (North Auckland) 1981 *SA* 1,2, *F* 2
Wrigley, E (Wairarapa) 1905 *A*
Wright, T J (Auckland) 1986 *F* 1, *A* 1, 1987 [*Arg*], 1988 *W* 1,2, *A* 1,2,3, 1989 *F* 1,2, *Arg* 1,2, *A, W, I*
Wylie, J T (Auckland) 1913 *A* 1, *US*
Wyllie, A J (Canterbury) 1970 *SA* 2,3, 1971 *BI* 2,3,4, 1972 *W, S,* 1973 *E* 1, *I, F, E* 2

Yates, V M (North Auckland) 1961 *F* 1,2,3
Young, D (Canterbury) 1956 *SA* 2, 1958 *A* 1,2,3, 1960 *SA* 1,2,3,4, 1961 *F* 1,2,3, 1962 *A* 1,2,3,5, 1963 *E* 1,2, *I, W,* 1964 *E, S, F*

NEW ZEALAND INTERNATIONAL RECORDS

Both team and individual records are for official New Zealand international matches, up to 30 April 1990.

TEAM RECORDS

Highest score
74 v Fiji (74-13) 1987 Christchurch
v individual countries
60 v Argentina (60-9) 1989 Dunedin
38 v Australia (38-3) 1972 Auckland
38 v B Isles (38-6) 1983 Auckland
42 v England (42-15) 1985 Wellington
74 v Fiji (74-13) 1987 Christchurch
38 v France (38-8) 1906 Paris
23 v Ireland (23-6) 1989 Dublin
70 v Italy (70-6) 1987 Auckland
14 v Romania (14-6) 1981 Bucharest
25 v S Africa (25-22) 1981 Auckland
40 v Scotland (40-15) 1981 Auckland
51 v United States (51-3) 1913 Berkeley
54 v Wales (54-9) 1988 Auckland

Biggest winning points margin
64 v Italy (70-6) 1987 Auckland
v individual countries
51 v Argentina (60-9) 1989 Dunedin
35 v Australia (38-3) 1972 Auckland
32 v B Isles (38-6) 1983 Auckland
27 v England (42-15) 1985 Wellington
61 v Fiji (74-13) 1987 Christchurch
30 v France (38-8) 1906 Paris
17 v Ireland (23-6) 1989 Dublin
64 v Italy (70-6) 1987 Auckland
 8 v Romania (14-6) 1981 Bucharest
17 v S Africa (20-3) 1965 Auckland
27 v Scotland (30-3) 1987 Christchurch
48 v United States (51-3) 1913 Berkeley
49 v Wales (52-3) 1988 Christchurch

Highest score by opposing team
30 Australia (16-30) 1978 Auckland
by individual countries
21 Argentina (21-21) 1985 Buenos Aires
30 Australia (16-30) 1978 Auckland
17 B Isles (18-17) 1959 Dunedin
16 England (10-16) 1973 Auckland

13 Fiji (74-13) 1987 Christchurch
24 France (19-24) 1979 Auckland
10 Ireland (10-10) 1973 Dublin
 6 Italy (70-6) 1987 Auckland
 6 Romania (14-6) 1981 Bucharest
24 S Africa (12-24) 1981 Wellington
25 Scotland (25-25) 1983 Edinburgh
 3 United States (51-3) 1913 Berkeley
16 Wales (19-16) 1972 Cardiff

Biggest losing points margin
17 v S Africa (0-17) 1928 Durban
v individual countries
16 v Australia (10-26) 1980 Sydney
10 v B Isles (3-13) 1971 Wellington
13 v England (0-13) 1936 Twickenham
13 v France (3-16) 1986 Nantes
17 v S Africa (0-17) 1928 Durban
 5 v Wales (8-13) 1953 Cardiff
No defeats v Argentina, Fiji, Ireland, Italy, Romania, Scotland or United States

---

Most tries by New Zealand in an international
13 v United States (51-3) 1913 Berkeley

Most tries against New Zealand in an international
5 by { S Africa (6-17) 1937 Auckland
       { Australia (16-30) 1978 Auckland

Most points on overseas tour (all matches)
868 in B Isles/France (33 matches) 1905-06

Most tries on overseas tour (all matches)
215 in B Isles/France (33 matches) 1905-06

INDIVIDUAL RECORDS

Most capped player
C E Meads   55   1957-71
in individual positions
Full-back
D B Clarke   31   1956-64
Wing
B G Williams   36(38)[1]   1970-78
Centre (includes 2nd five-eighth)
B J Robertson   34   1972-81
1st five-eighth
G J Fox   20   1985-89
Scrum-half
S M Going   29   1967-77
Prop
G A Knight   36   1977-86
Hooker
A G Dalton   35   1977-85
Lock
C E Meads   48(55)[2]   1957-71
Flanker
K R Tremain   36(38)[3]   1959-68
I A Kirkpatrick   36(39)[4]   1967-77
No 8
M G Mexted   34   1979-85
[1]*Williams won 2 caps as a centre*
[2]*Meads won 5 caps as a flanker, 2 as a No 8*
[3]*Tremain won 2 caps as a No 8*
[4]*Kirkpatrick won 3 caps as a No 8*

Longest international career
E Hughes   15 seasons   1907-21
C E Meads   15 seasons   1957-71

Most internationals as captain
W J Whineray   30   1958-65

Most points in internationals – 331
G J Fox (20 matches) 1985-89

Most points in an international – 26
A R Hewson v Australia 1982 Auckland
G J Fox v Fiji 1987 Christchurch

Most tries in internationals – 25
J J Kirwan (30 matches) 1984-89

Most tries in an international – 4
D McGregor v England 1905 Crystal Palace
C I Green v Fiji 1987 Christchurch

J A Gallagher v Fiji 1987 Christchurch
J J Kirwan v Wales 1988 Christchurch

Most conversions in internationals – 77
G J Fox (20 matches) 1985-89

Most conversions in an international – 10
G J Fox v Fiji 1987 Christchurch

Most dropped goals in internationals – 5
D B Clarke (31 matches) 1956-64

Most penalty goals in internationals – 56
G J Fox (20 matches) 1985-89

Most points in international series – 46
A R Hewson (4 appearances) v B Isles 1983

Most points in international series on tour – 37
G J Fox (3 appearances) 1988
   Australia

Most tries in international series on tour – 5
K Svenson (4 appearances) 1924-25
   B Isles/France
Svenson scored in each match of the international series

Most points on tour – 230
W J Wallace (25 appearances) 1905-06
   B Isles/France

Most tries on tour – 42
J Hunter (23 appearances) 1905-06
   B Isles/France

Most points in a tour match – 43
R M Deans v South Australia 1984
   Adelaide

Most tries in a tour match – 8
T R Heeps v Northern NSW 1962
   Quirindi

OUT OF THE SUBURBS, INTO THE CENTRE

THE 1989 SEASON IN AUSTRALIA
Greg Campbell *The Australian*

Australia's 1989 season was highlighted by two record victories, one each against the British Lions and France, yet the unimpressive overall Test record (P6, W2) clearly underlined the annoying inconsistency and uncertainty of a promising team striving for excellence. What made the year even more frustrating was the fact that in both Test series Australia outscored the opposition in both points and tries and yet failed to win either. But despite the disappointments, Australia enters the 1990s comforted by the knowledge that it has a wealth of talented and experienced players eager for international success following the blooding of 11 new caps. Perhaps the greatest victory of all took place off the field when the suburban Concord Oval was abandoned as Sydney's major Test match venue. The recommendation of ARFU president Mr Joe French was endorsed in time for the Lions' Sydney Tests to be held at the magnificent 40,000-capacity all-seater Sydney Football Stadium. The public responded in force, and Test sell-outs resulted in a match atmosphere never previously witnessed.

Australia's debut at the SFS was a tremendous performance. The Wallabies scored a comprehensive 30-12 (four tries to nil) victory over the Lions, and the eventual Rugby Writers' Schweppes Player of the Year, fly-half Michael Lynagh, controlled the game superbly. Extricating themselves from their plight, the Lions squared the series with a controversial 19-12 second Test victory at Ballymore where the weaknesses of the Australian forwards were revealed. As hard as Australia attempted to withstand the commitment and superior technique of the Lions pack, the deciding third Test was settled by a reckless in-goal pass by Wallaby winger David Campese which allowed the Lions to snatch a gripping 19-18 victory. Australia's desperation to reassemble a new pack containing strength, mobility and hunger led to widespread changes for the Bledisloe Cup match against New Zealand. And although the young, inexperienced Wallaby team fought like tigers against the all-conquering All Blacks, to the point where a draw could have been the final result, the All Blacks jumped decisively clear with a late try.

The arduous Wallaby tour of Canada and France was a recipe for disaster given that up to 15 of Australia's leading players made themselves unavailable. Although the final tour record was five wins and five losses, the slashing 32-15 first Test victory over France by a young side demonstrated the potential within the team. Unfortunately, this effort could not be repeated in the second Test, which a desperate French team won by 25-19. Australia's disappointments were also reflected in the sevens game. Australia were beaten 22-10 by New Zealand in the 1989 Cathay Pacific-Hong Kong Bank Sevens final and were eliminated in the Sydney International Sevens semi-finals by the eventual champions, New Zealand.

The year's overall record led to several challengers for Bob Dwyer's national coaching position. But in the final ballot Dwyer was returned ahead of Alec Evans, Paul Dalton and Dick Laffan. In an unprecedented move designed to maintain coaching continuity, the ARFU decided to reappoint Dwyer until the completion of the 1991 World Cup. Off the field, rugby had its share of controversy involving courts, banks and, again, South Africa. The Sydney Rugby Union sought action in the Equity Division of the New South Wales Supreme Court, compelling its parent body, the New South Wales Rugby Union, to prepare an audited statement outlining the 'total amounts of emoluments and other benefits paid to its directors and each director of a subsidiary'. The application, which centred on payments made to former NSWRU executive director Mr Ken Elphick, was dismissed.

The ARFU's decision to play Test matches at the SFS was one of the main reasons for former Wallaby player, manager and ARFU administrator Mr Ross Turnbull's resignation from the ARFU and as chairman of the NSWRU. Mr Turnbull had been one of the prime movers behind the development of Concord Oval. The development plan was a major factor in the NSWRU's losses of $3.7 million in 1988, taking its total liabilities to $15.8 million. A debenture scheme was later established by the new NSWRU administration to help make the union solvent.

Six players – Greg Martin, Ian Williams, Bill Campbell, Rod McCall, Mark Hartill and Tom Lawton – plus assistant Wallaby coach Bob Templeton all accepted invitations to tour South Africa with a World team after several players, including captain Nick Farr-Jones and David Campese, had rejected initial approaches.

On the domestic front, Queensland swept to 31-3 and 31-0 victories over New South Wales in the inter-state series, despite NSW's stunning 16-11 win over the previously-dominant Auckland team in the South Pacific Championship. Auckland were again victorious, with NSW and Queensland the respective runners-up. Randwick qualified for their 14th Sydney grand final and won their third successive title, beating Eastwood 19-6, while Queensland University won the Brisbane title by defeating Southern Districts 34-9. Randwick successfully defended the Australian club championship with a 30-15 victory over Queensland University.

AUSTRALIAN INTERNATIONAL PLAYERS *(up to 30 April 1990)*

ABBREVIATIONS

Arg – Argentina; *BI* – British Isles teams; *C* – Canada; *E* – England; *F* – France; *Fj* – Fiji; *I* – Ireland; *It* – Italy; *J* – Japan; *M* – Maoris; *NZ* – New Zealand; *S* – Scotland; *SA* – South Africa; *SK* – South Korea; *Tg* – Tonga; *US* – United States of America; *W* – Wales; (R) – Replacement. Entries in square brackets [ ] indicate appearances in the Rugby World Cup

STATE ABBREVIATIONS

ACT – Australian Capital Territory; NSW – New South Wales; Q – Queensland; V – Victoria; WA – Western Australia

N.B. In the summer of 1986, the ARU retrospectively granted full Australian Test status to the five international matches played by the 1927-28 touring team to Europe. In 1988 Test status was extended to all those who played overseas in the 1920s.

Note: When a series has taken place, figures denote the particular matches in which players featured. Thus 1963 *SA* 2,4 indicates that a player appeared in the second and fourth Tests of the 1963 series against South Africa.

Abrahams, A M F (NSW) 1967 *NZ*, 1968 *NZ* 1, 1969 *W*
Adams, N J (NSW) 1955 *NZ* 1
Adamson, R W (NSW) 1912 *US*
Allan, T (NSW) 1946 *NZ* 1, *M*, *NZ* 2, 1947 *NZ* 2, *S*, *I*, *W*, 1948 *E*, *F*, 1949 *M* 1,2,3, *NZ* 1,2
Anlezark, E A (NSW) 1905 *NZ*
Armstrong, A R (NSW) 1923 *NZ* 1,2
Austin, L R (NSW) 1963 *E*

Baker, R L (NSW) 1904 *BI* 1,2
Baker, W H (NSW) 1914 *NZ* 1,2,3
Ballesty, J P (NSW) 1968 *NZ* 1,2, *F*, *I*, *S*, 1969 *W*, *SA* 2,3,4
Bannon, D P (NSW) 1946 *M*
Bardsley, E J (NSW) 1928 *NZ* 1, 3, *M* (R)
Barker, H S (NSW) 1952 *Fj* 1,2, *NZ* 1,2, 1953 *SA* 4, 1954 *Fj* 1,2
Barnett, J T (NSW) 1907 *NZ* 1,2,3, 1908 *W*, 1909 *E*
Barry, M J (Q) 1971 *SA* 3
Barton, R F D (NSW) 1899 *BI* 3
Batch, P G (Q) 1975 *S*, *W*, 1976 *E*, *Fj* 1,2,3, *F* 1,2, 1978 *W* 1,2, *NZ* 1,2,3, 1979 *Arg* 2
Batterham, R P (NSW) 1967 *NZ*, 1970 *S*
Battishall, B R (NSW) 1973 *E*
Baxter, A J (NSW) 1949 *M* 1,2,3, *NZ* 1,2, 1951 *NZ* 1,2, 1952 *NZ* 1,2
Baxter, T J (Q) 1958 *NZ* 3
Beith, B McN (NSW) 1914 *NZ* 3
Bell, K R (Q) 1968 *S*
Bennett, W G (Q) 1931 *M*, 1933 *SA* 1,2,3
Bermingham, J V (Q) 1934 *NZ* 1,2, 1937 *SA* 1
Berne, J E (NSW) 1975 *S*
Besomo, K S (NSW) 1979 *I* 2
Betts, T N (Q) 1951 *NZ* 2,3, 1954 *Fj* 2
Biilmann, R R (NSW) 1933 *SA* 1,2,3,4
Birt, R (Q) 1914 *NZ* 2
Black, J W (NSW) 1985 *C* 1,2, *NZ*, *Fj* 1
Blackwood, J G (NSW) 1923 *NZ* 1,2,3, 1925 *NZ*, 1927 *I*, *W*, *S*, 1928 *E*, *F*
Blair, M R (NSW) 1928 *F*, 1931 *M*, *NZ*
Bland, G V (NSW) 1928 *NZ* 3, *M*, 1932 *NZ* 1,2,3, 1933 *SA* 1,2,4,5
Blomley, J (NSW) 1949 *M* 1,2,3, *NZ* 1,2, 1950 *BI* 1,2
Boland, S B (Q) 1899 *BI* 3,4, 1903 *NZ*
Bond, J H (NSW) 1921 *NZ*
Bonis, E T (Q) 1929 *NZ* 1,2,3, 1930 *BI*, 1931 *M*, *NZ*, 1932 *NZ* 1,2,3, 1933 *SA* 1,2,3,4,5, 1934 *NZ* 1,2, 1936 *NZ* 1,2, *M*, 1937 *SA* 1, 1938 *NZ* 1
Bosler, J M (NSW) 1953 *SA* 1
Bouffler, R G (NSW) 1899 *BI* 3
Bourke, T K (Q) 1947 *NZ* 2
Bowers, A J A (NSW) 1923 *NZ* 3, 1925 *NZ*, 1927 *I*
Boyce, E S (NSW) 1962 *NZ* 1,2, 1964 *NZ* 1,2,3, 1965 *SA* 1,2, 1966 *W*, *S*, 1967 *E*, *I* 1, *F*, *I* 2
Boyce, J S (NSW) 1962 *NZ* 3,4,5, 1963 *E*, *SA* 1,2,3,4, 1964 *NZ* 1,3, 1965 *SA* 1,2

Boyd, A (NSW) 1899 *BI* 3
Boyd, A F McC (Q) 1958 *M* 1
Brass, J E (NSW) 1966 *BI* 2, *W*, *S*, 1967 *E*, *I* 1, *F*, *I* 2, *NZ*, 1968 *NZ* 1, *F*, *I*, *S*
Breckenridge, J W (NSW) 1927 *I*, *W*, *S*, 1928 *E*, *F*, 1929 *NZ* 1,2,3; 1930 *BI*
Bridle, O L (V) 1931 *M*, 1932 *NZ* 1,2,3, 1933 *SA* 3,4,5, 1934 *NZ* 1,2, 1936 *NZ* 1,2, *M*
Broad, E G (Q) 1949 *M* 1
Brockhoff, J D (NSW) 1949 *M* 2,3, *NZ* 1,2, 1950 *BI* 1,2, 1951 *NZ* 2,3
Brown, B R (Q) 1972 *NZ* 1,3
Brown, J V (NSW) 1956 *SA* 1,2, 1957 *NZ* 1,2, 1958 *W*, *I*, *E*, *S*, *F*
Brown, R C (NSW) 1975 *E* 1,2
Brown, S W (NSW) 1953 *SA* 2,3,4
Bryant, H (NSW) 1925 *NZ*
Buchan, A J (NSW) 1946 *NZ* 1,2, 1947 *NZ* 1,2, *S*, *I*, *W*, 1948 *E*, *F*, 1949 *M* 3
Bull, D (NSW) 1928 *M*
Buntine, H (NSW) 1923 *NZ* 1 (R)
Burdon, A (NSW) 1903 *NZ*, 1904 *BI* 1,2, 1905 *NZ*
Burge, A B (NSW) 1907 *NZ* 3, 1908 *W*
Burge, P H (NSW) 1907 *NZ* 1,2,3
Burge, R (NSW) 1928 *NZ* 1,2,3 (R), *M* (R)
Burke, B T (NSW) 1988 *S* (R)
Burke, C T (NSW) 1946 *NZ* 2, 1947 *NZ* 1,2, *S*, *I*, *W*, 1948 *E*, *F*, 1949 *M* 2,3, *NZ* 1,2, 1950 *BI* 1,2, 1951 *NZ* 1,2,3, 1953 *SA* 2,3,4, 1954 *Fj* 1, 1955 *NZ* 1,2,3, 1956 *SA* 1,2
Burke, M P (NSW) 1984 *E* (R), *I*, 1985 *C* 1,2, *NZ*, *Fj* 1,2, 1986 *It* (R), *F*, *Arg* 1,2, *NZ* 1,2,3, 1987 *SK*, [*US*, *J*, *I*, *F*, *W*], *NZ*, *Arg* 1,2
Burnet, D R (NSW) 1972 *F* 1,2, *NZ* 1,2,3, *Fj*
Butler, O F (NSW) 1969 *SA* 1,2, 1970 *S*, 1971 *SA* 2,3, *F* 1,2

Calcraft, W J (NSW) 1985 *C* 1, 1986 *It*, *Arg* 2
Caldwell, B C (NSW) 1928 *NZ* 3
Cameron, A S (NSW) 1951 *NZ* 1,2,3, 1952 *Fj* 1,2, *NZ* 1,2, 1953 *SA* 1,2,3,4, 1954 *Fj* 1,2, 1955 *NZ* 1,2,3, 1956 *SA* 1,2, 1957 *NZ* 1, 1958 *I*
Campbell, J D (NSW) 1910 *NZ* 1,2,3
Campbell, W A (Q) 1984 *Fj*, 1986 *It*, *F*, *Arg* 1,2, *NZ* 1,2,3, 1987 *SK*, [*E*, *US*, *J* (R), *I*, *F*], *NZ*, 1988 *E*, 1989 *BI* 1,2,3, *NZ*
Campese, D I (ACT, NSW) 1982 *NZ* 1,2,3, 1983 *US*, *Arg* 1,2, *NZ*, *It*, *F* 1,2, 1984 *Fj*, *NZ* 1,2,3, *E*, *I*, *W*, *S*, 1985 *Fj* 1,2, 1986 *It*, *F*, *Arg* 1,2, *NZ* 1,2,3, 1987 [*E*, *US*, *J*, *I*, *F*, *W*], *NZ*, 1988 *E* 1,2, *NZ* 1,2,3, *E*, *S*, *It*, 1989 *BI* 1,2,3, *NZ*, *F* 1,2
Canniffe, W D (Q) 1907 *NZ* 2
Carberry, C M (NSW, Q) 1973 *Tg* 2, *E*, 1976 *I*, *US*, *Fj* 1,2,3, 1981 *F* 1,2, *I*, *W*, *S*, 1982 *E*
Cardy, A M (NSW) 1966 *BI* 1,2, *W*, *S*, 1967 *E*, *I* 1, *F*, 1968 *NZ* 1,2
Carew, P J (Q) 1899 *BI* 1,2,3,4

Carmichael, P (Q) 1904 *BI* 2, 1907 *NZ* 1, 1908 *W*, 1909 *E*
Carpenter, M G (V) 1938 *NZ* 1,2
Carr, E T A (NSW) 1913 *NZ* 1,2,3, 1914 *NZ* 1,2,3
Carr, E W (NSW) 1921 *NZ* 1 (R)
Carroll, D B (NSW) 1908 *W*, 1912 *US*
Carroll, J C (NSW) 1953 *SA* 1
Carroll, J H (NSW) 1958 *M* 2,3, *NZ* 1,2,3, 1959 *BI* 1,2
Carson, J (NSW) 1899 *BI* 1
Carson, P J (NSW) 1979 *NZ*, 1980 *NZ* 3
Carter, D G (NSW) 1988 *E* 1,2, *NZ* 1, 1989 *F* 1,2
Casey, T V (NSW) 1963 *SA* 2,3,4, 1964 *NZ* 1,2,3
Catchpole, K W (NSW) 1961 *Fj* 1,2,3, *SA* 1,2, *F*, 1962 *NZ* 1,2,4, 1963 *SA* 2,3,4, 1964 *NZ* 1,2,3, 1965 *SA* 1,2, 1966 *BI* 1,2, *W*, *S*, 1967 *E*, *I* 1, *F*, *I*2, *NZ*, 1968 *NZ* 1
Cawsey, R M (NSW) 1949 *M* 1, *NZ* 1,2
Cerutti, W H (NSW) 1928 *NZ* 1,2,3, *M*, 1929 *NZ* 1,2,3, 1930 *BI*, 1931 *M*, *NZ*, 1932 *NZ* 1,2,3, 1933 *SA* 1,2,3,4,5, 1936 *M*, 1937 *SA* 1,2
Challoner, R L (NSW) 1899 *BI* 2
Chapman, G A (NSW) 1962 *NZ* 3,4,5
Clark, J G (Q) 1931 *M*, *NZ*, 1932 *NZ* 1,2, 1933 *SA* 1
Clarken, J C (NSW) 1905 *NZ*, 1910 *NZ* 1,2,3
Cleary, M A (NSW) 1961 *Fj* 1,2,3, *SA* 1,2, *F*
Clements, P (NSW) 1982 *NZ* 3
Clifford, M (NSW) 1938 *NZ* 3
Cobb, W G (NSW) 1899 *BI* 3,4
Cocks, M R (NSW, Q) 1972 *F* 1,2, *NZ* 2,3, *Fj*, 1973 *Tg* 1,2, *W*, *E*, 1975 *J* 1
Codey, D (NSW Country, Q) 1983 *Arg* 1, 1984 *E*, *W*, *S*, 1985 *C* 2, *NZ*, 1986 *F*, *Arg* 1, 1987 [*US*, *J*, *F*(R), *W*], *NZ*
Cody, E W (NSW) 1913 *NZ* 1,2,3
Coker, T (Q) 1987 [*E*, *US*, *F*, *W*]
Colbert, R (NSW) 1952 *Fj* 2, *NZ* 1,2, 1953 *SA* 2,3,4
Cole, J W (NSW) 1968 *NZ* 1,2, *F*, *I*, *S*, 1969 *W*, *SA* 1,2,3,4, 1970 *S*, 1971 *SA* 1,2,3, *F* 1,2, 1972 *NZ* 1,2,3, 1973 *Tg* 1,2, 1974 *NZ* 1,2,3
Collins, P K (NSW) 1937 *SA* 2, 1938 *NZ* 2,3
Colton, A J (Q) 1899 *BI* 1,3
Colton, T (Q) 1904 *BI* 1,2
Comrie-Thomson, I R (NSW) 1928 *NZ* 1,2,3, *M*
Connor, D M (Q) 1958 *W*, *I*, *E*, *S*, *F*, *M* 2,3, *NZ* 1,2,3, 1959 *BI* 1,2
Cook, M T (Q) 1986 *F*, 1987 *SK*, [*J*], 1988 *E* 1,2, *NZ* 1,2,3, *E*, *S*, *It*
Cooke, B P (Q) 1979 *I* 1
Cooke, G M (Q) 1932 *NZ* 1,2,3, 1933 *SA* 1,2,3, 1946 *NZ* 2, 1947 *NZ* 2, *S*, *I*, *W*, 1948 *E*, *F*
Coolican, J E (NSW) 1982 *NZ* 1, 1983 *It*, *F* 1,2
Corfe, A C (Q) 1899 *BI* 2
Cornelsen, G (NSW) 1974 *NZ* 2,3, 1975 *J* 2, *S*, *W*, 1976 *E*, *F* 1,2, 1978 *W* 1,2, *NZ* 1,2,3, 1979 *I* 1,2, *NZ*, *Arg* 1,2, 1980 *NZ* 1,2,3, 1981 *I*, *W*, *S*, 1982 *E*
Cornes, J R (Q) 1972 *Fj*
Cornforth, R G W (NSW) 1947 *NZ* 1, 1950 *BI* 2
Costello, P P S (Q) 1950 *BI* 2
Cottrell, N V (Q) 1949 *M* 1,2,3, *NZ* 1,2, 1950 *BI* 1,2, 1951 *NZ* 1,2,3, 1952 *Fj* 1,2, *NZ* 1,2
Cowper, D L (V) 1931 *NZ*, 1932 *NZ* 1,2,3, 1933 *SA* 1,2,3,4,5
Cox, B P (NSW) 1952 *Fj* 1,2, *NZ* 1,2, 1954 *Fj* 2, 1955 *NZ* 1, 1956 *SA* 2, 1957 *NZ* 1,2
Cox, M H (NSW) 1981 *W*, *S*
Cox, P A (NSW) 1979 *Arg* 1,2, 1980 *Fj*, *NZ* 1,2, 1981 *W* (R), *S*, 1982 *S* 1,2, *NZ* 1,2,3, 1984 *Fj*, *NZ* 1,2,3
Craig, R R (NSW) 1908 *W*
Crakanthorp, J S (NSW) 1923 *NZ* 3
Cremin, J F (NSW) 1946 *NZ* 1,2, 1947 *NZ* 1
Crittle, C P (NSW) 1962 *NZ* 4,5, 1963 *SA* 2,3,4, 1964 *NZ* 1,2,3, 1965 *SA* 1,2, 1966 *BI* 1,2, *S*, 1967 *E*, *I*
Croft, B H D (NSW) 1928 *M*
Cross, J R (NSW) 1955 *NZ* 1,2,3
Cross, K A (NSW) 1949 *M* 1, *NZ* 1,2, 1950 *BI* 1,2, 1951 *NZ* 2,3, 1952 *NZ* 1, 1953 *SA* 1,2,3,4, 1954 *Fj* 1,2, 1955 *NZ* 3, 1956 *SA* 1,2, 1957 *NZ* 1,2
Crossman, O C (NSW) 1925 *NZ*, 1929 *NZ* 2, 1930 *BI*
Crowe, P J (NSW) 1976 *F* 2, 1978 *W* 1,2, 1979 *I* 2, *NZ*, *Arg* 1
Crowley, D (Q) 1989 *BI* 1,2,3
Curley, T G P (NSW) 1957 *NZ* 1,2, 1958 *W*, *I*, *E*, *S*, *F*, *M* 1, *NZ* 1,2,3
Curran, D J (NSW) 1980 *NZ* 3, 1981 *F* 1,2, *W*, 1983 *Arg* 1

Currie, E W (Q) 1899 *BI* 2
Cutler, S A G (NSW) 1982 *NZ* 2(R), 1984 *NZ* 1,2,3, *E*, *I*, *W*, *S*, 1985 *C* 1,2, *NZ*, *Fj* 1,2, 1986 *It*, *F*, *NZ* 1,2,3, 1987 *SK*, [*E*, *J*, *I*, *F*, *W*], *NZ*, *Arg* 1,2, 1988 *E* 1,2, *NZ* 1,2,3, *E*, *S*, *It*, 1989 *BI* 1,2,3, *NZ*

Daly, A J (NSW) 1989 *NZ*, *F* 1,2
D'Arcy, A M (Q) 1980 *Fj*, *NZ* 3, 1981 *F* 1,2, *I*, *W*, *S*, 1982 *E*, *S* 1,2
Darveniza, P (NSW) 1969 *W*, *SA* 2,3,4
Davidson, R A L (NSW) 1952 *Fj* 1,2, *NZ* 1,2, 1953 *SA* 1, 1957 *NZ* 1,2, 1958 *W*, *I*, *E*, *S*, *F*, *M* 1
Davis, C C (NSW) 1949 *NZ* 1, 1951 *NZ* 1,2,3
Davis, E H (V) 1947 *S*, *W*, 1949 *M* 1,2
Davis, G V (NSW) 1963 *E*, *SA* 1,2,3,4, 1964 *NZ* 1,2,3, 1965 *SA* 1, 1966 *BI* 1,2, *W*, *S*, 1967 *E*, *I* 1, *F*, *I* 2, *NZ*, 1968 *NZ* 1,2, *F*, *I*, *S*, 1969 *W*, *SA* 1,2,3,4, 1970 *S*, 1971 *SA* 1,2,3, *F* 1,2, 1972 *F* 1,2, *NZ* 1,2,3
Davis, G W G (NSW) 1955 *NZ* 2,3
Davis, R A (NSW) 1974 *NZ* 1,2,3
Davis, T S R (NSW) 1921 *NZ*, 1923 *NZ* 1,2,3
Davis, W (NSW) 1899 *BI* 1,3,4
Dawson, W L (NSW) 1946 *NZ* 1,2
Diett, L J (NSW) 1959 *BI* 1,2
Dix, W (NSW) 1907 *NZ* 1,2,3, 1909 *E*
Dixon, E J (Q) 1904 *BI* 3
Donald, K J (Q) 1957 *NZ* 1, 1958 *W*, *I*, *E*, *S*, *M* 2,3, 1959 *BI* 1,2
Dore, E (Q) 1904 *BI* 1
Dore, M J (Q) 1905 *NZ*
Dorr, R W (V) 1936 *M*, 1937 *SA* 1
Douglas, J A (V) 1962 *NZ* 3,4,5
Dowse, J H (NSW) 1961 *Fj* 1,2, *SA* 1,2
Dunbar, A R (NSW) 1910 *NZ* 1,2,3, 1912 *US*
Dunlop, E E (V) 1932 *NZ* 3, 1934 *NZ* 1
Dunn, P K (NSW) 1958 *NZ* 1,2,3, 1959 *BI* 1,2
Dunn, V A (NSW) 1921 *NZ*
Dunworth, D A (Q) 1971 *F* 1,2, 1972 *F* 1,2, 1976 *Fj* 2
Dwyer, L J (NSW) 1910 *NZ* 1,2,3, 1912 *US*, 1913 *NZ* 3, 1914 *NZ* 1,2,3

Eastes, C C (NSW) 1946 *NZ* 1,2, 1947 *NZ* 1,2, 1949 *M* 1,2
Ella, G A (NSW) 1982 *NZ* 1,2, 1983 *F* 1,2, 1988 *E* 2, *NZ* 1
Ella, G J (NSW) 1982 *S* 1, 1983 *It*, 1985 *C* 2 (R), *Fj* 2
Ella, M G (NSW) 1980 *NZ* 1,2,3, 1981 *F* 2, *S*, 1982 *E*, *S* 1, *NZ* 1,2,3, 1983 *US*, *Arg* 1,2, *NZ*, *It*, *F* 1,2, 1984 *Fj*, *NZ* 1,2,3, *E*, *I*, *W*, *S*
Ellem, M A (NSW) 1976 *Fj* 3 (R)
Elliott, F M (NSW) 1957 *NZ* 1
Elliott, R E (NSW) 1921 *NZ*, 1923 *NZ* 1,2,3
Ellis, C S (NSW) 1899 *BI* 1,2,3,4
Ellis, K J (NSW) 1958 *NZ* 1,2,3, 1959 *BI* 1,2
Ellwood, B J (NSW) 1958 *NZ* 1,2,3, 1961 *Fj* 2,3, *SA* 1, *F*, 1962 *NZ* 1,2,3,4,5, 1963 *SA* 1,2,3,4, 1964 *NZ* 3, 1965 *SA* 1,2, 1966 *BI* 1
Emanuel, D M (NSW) 1957 *NZ* 2, 1958 *W*, *I*, *E*, *S*, *F*, *M* 1,2,3
Emery, N A (NSW) 1947 *NZ* 2, *S*, *I*, *W*, 1948 *E*, *F*, 1949 *M* 2,3, *NZ* 1,2
Erasmus, D J (NSW) 1923 *NZ* 1,2
Erby, A B (NSW) 1923 *NZ* 2,3
Evans, L J (Q) 1903 *NZ*, 1904 *BI* 1,3
Evans, W T (Q) 1899 *BI* 1,2

Fahey, E J (NSW) 1912 *US*, 1913 *NZ* 1,2, 1914 *NZ* 3
Fairfax, R L (NSW) 1971 *F* 1,2, 1972 *F* 1,2, *NZ* 1, *Fj*, 1973 *W*, *E*
Farmer, E H (Q) 1910 *NZ* 1
Farr-Jones, N C (NSW) 1984 *E*, *I*, *W*, *S*, 1985 *C* 1,2, *NZ*, *Fj* 1,2, 1986 *It*, *F*, *Arg* 1,2, *NZ* 1,2,3, 1987 *SK*, [*E*, *I*, *F*, *W*(R)], *NZ*, *Arg* 2, 1988 *E* 1,2, *NZ* 1,2,3, *E*, *S*, *It*, 1989 *BI* 1,2,3, *NZ*, *F* 1,2
Fay, G (NSW) 1971 *SA* 2, 1972 *NZ* 1,2,3, 1973 *Tg* 1,2, *W*, *E*, 1974 *NZ* 1,2,3, 1975 *E* 1,2, *J* 1, *S*, *W*, 1976 *I*, *US*, 1978 *W* 1,2, *NZ* 1,2,3, 1979 *I* 1
Fenwicke, P T (NSW) 1957 *NZ* 1, 1958 *W*, *I*, *E*, 1959 *BI* 1,2
Ferguson, R T (NSW) 1923 *NZ* 3
Fihelly, J A (Q) 1907 *NZ* 2
Finlay, A N (NSW) 1927 *I*, *W*, *S*, 1928 *E*, *F*, 1929 *NZ* 1,2,3, 1930 *BI*

Greg Martin, finding his feet in international rugby as Australia's full-back, holds off the Lions forwards during the second Test in Brisbane in 1989.

AUSTRALIAN INTERNATIONAL RECORDS

Both team and individual records are for official Australian international matches, up to 30 April 1990.

TEAM RECORDS

Highest score
65 v South Korea (65-18) 1987 Brisbane

v individual countries
39 v Argentina (39-19) 1986 Brisbane
30 v British Isles (30-12) 1989 Sydney
59 v Canada (59-3) 1985 Sydney
30 v England (30-21) 1975 Brisbane
52 v Fiji (52-28) 1985 Brisbane
32 v France (32-15) 1989 Strasbourg
33 v Ireland (33-15) 1987 Sydney
55 v Italy (55-6) 1988 Rome
50 v Japan (50-25) 1975 Brisbane
30 v N Zealand (30-16) 1978 Auckland
37 v Scotland (37-12) 1984 Murrayfield
21 v South Africa (21-6) 1933 Durban
65 v South Korea (65-18) 1987 Brisbane
30 v Tonga (30-12) 1973 Sydney
49 v United States (49-3) 1983 Sydney
28 v Wales (28-9) 1984 Cardiff

Biggest winning points margin
56 v Canada (59-3) 1985 Sydney

v individual countries
26 v Argentina (26-0) 1986 Sydney
18 v British Isles (30-12) 1989 Sydney
56 v Canada (59-3) 1985 Sydney
20 v England (28-8) 1988 Sydney
24 v Fiji (52-28) 1985 Brisbane
17 v France (32-15) 1989 Strasbourg
18 v Ireland (33-15) 1987 Sydney
49 v Italy (55-6) 1988 Rome
30 v Japan (37-7) 1975 Sydney
16 v N Zealand (26-10) 1980 Sydney
25 v Scotland (37-12) 1984 Murrayfield
15 v South Africa (21-6) 1933 Durban
47 v South Korea (65-18) 1987 Brisbane
18 v Tonga (30-12) 1973 Sydney
46 v United States (49-3) 1983 Sydney
19 v Wales (28-9) 1984 Cardiff

Highest score by opposing team
38 { N Zealand (13-38) 1936 Dunedin
     { N Zealand (3-38) 1972 Auckland

by individual countries
27 Argentina (19-27) 1987 Buenos Aires
31 British Isles (0-31) 1966 Brisbane
15 Canada (43-15) 1985 Brisbane
28 England (19-28) 1988 Twickenham
28 Fiji (52-28) 1985 Brisbane
34 France (6-34) 1976 Paris
27 Ireland (12-27) 1979 Brisbane
18 Italy (39-18) 1986 Brisbane
25 Japan (50-25) 1975 Brisbane
38 { N Zealand (13-38) 1936 Dunedin
     { N Zealand (3-38) 1972 Auckland
24 Scotland (15-24) 1981 Murrayfield
30 South Africa (11-30) 1969 Johannesburg
18 South Korea (65-18) 1987 Brisbane
16 Tonga (11-16) 1973 Brisbane
12 United States (47-12) 1987 Brisbane
28 Wales (3-28) 1975 Cardiff

Biggest losing points margin
35 v N Zealand (3-38) 1972 Auckland

v individual countries
15 v Argentina (3-18) 1983 Brisbane
31 v British Isles (0-31) 1966 Brisbane
17 v England { (3-20) 1973 Twickenham
               { (6-23) 1976 Twickenham
2 v Fiji { (15-17) 1952 Sydney
          { (16-18) 1954 Sydney
28 v France (6-34) 1976 Paris
15 v Ireland (12-27) 1979 Brisbane
35 v New Zealand (3-38) 1972 Auckland
9 v Scotland (15-24) 1981 Murrayfield
25 v South Africa (3-28) 1961 Johannesburg
5 v Tonga (11-16) 1973 Brisbane
25 v Wales (3-28) 1975 Cardiff
No defeats v Canada, Italy, Japan, South Korea or United States.

Most tries by Australia in an international
13 v South Korea (65-18) 1987 Brisbane

Most tries against Australia in an international
9 by New Zealand (13-38) 1936 Dunedin

Most points on overseas tour (all matches)
500 in B Isles/France (35 matches) 1947-48

**Most tries on overseas tour
(all matches)**
115 in B Isles/France (35 matches)
  1947-48

INDIVIDUAL RECORDS

Most capped player
S P Poidevin 51 1980-89
in individual positions
Full-back
R G Gould 25 1980-87
Wing
D I Campese 37(48)[1] 1982-89
Centre
A G Slack 39 1978-87
Fly-half
M P Lynagh 28(36)[2] 1984-89
Scrum-half
J N B Hipwell 36 1968-82
N C Farr-Jones 36(37)[3] 1984-89
Prop
A J McIntyre 38 1982-89
Hooker
P G Johnson 42 1959-71
Lock
S A G Cutler 39 1982-89
Flanker
S P Poidevin 51 1980-89
No 8
S N Tuynman 28(33)[4] 1983-89
[1]*Campese has played 11 times as a full-back*
[2]*Lynagh has played 7 times as a centre and once as a replacement full-back*
[3]*Farr-Jones was capped once as a replacement wing*
[4]*Tuynman played 5 times as a flanker*

Longest international career
G M Cooke 16 seasons 1932-1947/8
A R Miller 16 seasons 1952-1967
Cooke's career ended during a Northern hemisphere season

Most internationals as captain
J E Thornett 16   1962-67
G V Davis   16   1969-72

Most points in internationals – 456
M P Lynagh (36 matches) 1984-89

Most points in an international – 23
M P Lynagh v Canada 1985 Sydney
M P Lynagh v France 1986 Sydney
M P Lynagh v Argentina 1986 Brisbane

M P Lynagh v Italy 1988 Rome

Most tries in internationals – 34
D I Campese (48 matches) 1982-89

Most tries in an international – 4
G Cornelsen v N Zealand 1978 Auckland
D I Campese v United States 1983 Sydney

Most conversions in internationals – 80
M P Lynagh (36 matches) 1984-89

Most conversions in an international – 8
M P Lynagh v Italy 1988 Rome

Most dropped goals in internationals – 9
P F Hawthorne (21 matches) 1962-67

Most penalty goals in internationals – 85
M P Lynagh (36 matches) 1984-89

**Most points in international series
on tour – 42**
M P Lynagh (4 appearances) 1984
  B Isles

**Most tries in international series on tour
– 4**
G Cornelsen (3 appearances) 1978
  N Zealand
M G Ella (4 appearances) 1984
  B Isles
Ella scored in each match of the international series

Most points on overseas tour – 154
P E McLean (18 appearances) B Isles
  1975-76

Most tries on overseas tour – 23
C J Russell B Isles 1908-09

Most points in a tour match – 26
A J Leeds v Buller 1986 Westport

Most tries in a tour match – 6
J S Boyce v Wairarapa (NZ) 1962
  Masterton

INTERNATIONAL MATCH APPEARANCES FOR BRITISH ISLES TEAMS *(up to 30 April 1990)*

From 1910 onwards, when British Isles teams first became officially representative of the four Home Unions. (*Uncapped when first selected to play in a Test match for the British Isles.)

ABBREVIATIONS

A – Australia; *NZ* – New Zealand; *SA* – South Africa; (R) – Replacement.

CLUB ABBREVIATIONS

NIFC – North of Ireland Football Club; CIYMS – Church of Ireland Young Men's Society

Note: When a series has taken place, figures have been used to denote the particular matches in which players have featured. Thus 1962 *SA* 1,4 indicates that a player appeared in the first and fourth Tests of a series.

Aarvold, C D (Cambridge U, Blackheath and England) 1930 *NZ* 1,2,3,4, *A*
Ackerman, R A (London Welsh and Wales) 1983 *NZ* 1,4(R)
Ackford, P J (Harlequins and England) 1989 *A* 1,2,3
Alexander, R (NIFC and Ireland) 1938 *SA* 1,2,3
Andrew, C R (Wasps and England) 1989 *A* 2,3
Arneil, R J (Edinburgh Acads and Scotland) 1968 *SA* 1,2,3,4
Ashcroft, A (Waterloo and England) 1959 *A* 1, *NZ* 2

Bainbridge, S J (Gosforth and England) 1983 *NZ* 3,4
Baird, G R T (Kelso and Scotland) 1983 *NZ* 1,2,3,4
Baker, A M (Newport and Wales) 1910 *SA* 3
Baker, D G S (Old Merchant Taylors' and England) 1955 *SA* 3,4
Bassett, J (Penarth and Wales) 1930 *NZ* 1,2,3,4, *A*
Beamish, G R (Leicester, RAF and Ireland) 1930 *NZ* 1,2,3,4, *A*
Beattie, J R (Glasgow Acads and Scotland) 1983 *NZ* 2(R)
Beaumont, W B (Fylde and England) 1977 *NZ* 2,3,4, 1980 *SA* 1,2,3,4
Bebb, D I E (Swansea and Wales) 1962 *SA* 2,3, 1966 *A* 1,2, *NZ* 1,2,3,4
Bennett, P (Llanelli and Wales) 1974 *SA* 1,2,3,4, 1977 *NZ* 1,2,3,4
Bevan, J C (Cardiff Coll of Ed, Cardiff and Wales) 1971 *NZ* 1
Black, A W (Edinburgh U and Scotland) 1950 *NZ* 1,2
Black, B H (Oxford U, Blackheath and England) 1930 *NZ* 1,2,3,4, *A*
Blakiston, A F (Northampton and England) 1924 *SA* 1,2,3,4
Bowcott, H M (Cambridge U, Cardiff and Wales) 1930 *NZ* 1,2,3,4, *A*
Boyle, C V (Dublin U and Ireland) 1938 *SA* 2,3
Brand, T N (NIFC and *Ireland) 1924 *SA* 1,2
Bresnihan, F P K (UC Dublin and Ireland) 1968 *SA* 1,2,4
Brophy, N H (UC Dublin and Ireland) 1962 *SA* 1,4
Brown, G L (W of Scotland and Scotland) 1971 *NZ* 3,4, 1974 *SA* 1,2,3, 1977 *NZ* 2,3,4
Budge, G M (Edinburgh Wands and Scotland) 1950 *NZ* 4
Burcher, D H (Newport and Wales) 1977 *NZ* 3
Butterfield, J (Northampton and England) 1955 *SA* 1,2,3,4

Calder, F (Stewart's-Melville FP and Scotland) 1989 *A* 1,2,3
Calder, J H (Stewart's-Melville FP and Scotland) 1983 *NZ* 3
Cameron, A (Glasgow HSFP and Scotland) 1955 *SA* 1,2
Campbell, S O (Old Belvedere and Ireland) 1980 *SA* 2(R), 3,4, 1983 *NZ* 1,2,3,4
Campbell-Lamerton, M J (Halifax, Army and Scotland) 1962 *SA* 1,2,3,4, 1966 *A* 1,2, *NZ* 1,3

Carleton, J (Orrell and England) 1980 *SA* 1,2,4, 1983 *NZ* 2,3,4
Chalmers, C M (Melrose and Scotland) 1989 *A* 1
Cleaver, W B (Cardiff and Wales) 1950 *NZ* 1,2,3
Clifford, T (Young Munster and Ireland) 1950 *NZ* 1,2,3, *A* 1,2
Cobner, T J (Pontypool and Wales) 1977 *NZ* 1,2,3
Colclough, M J (Angoulême and England) 1980 *SA* 1,2,3,4, 1983 *NZ* 1,2,3,4
Connell, G C (Trinity Acads and Scotland) 1968 *SA* 4
Cotton, F E (Loughborough Colls, Coventry and England) 1974 *SA* 1,2,3,4, 1977 *NZ* 2,3,4
Coulman, M J (Moseley and England) 1968 *SA* 3
Cove-Smith, R (Old Merchant Taylors' and England) 1924 *SA* 1,2,3,4
Cowan, R C (Selkirk and Scotland) 1962 *SA* 4
Cromey, G E (Queen's U, Belfast and Ireland) 1938 *SA* 3
Cunningham, W A (Lansdowne and Ireland) 1924 *SA* 3

Dancer, G T (Bedford) 1938 *SA* 1,2,3
Davies, C (Cardiff and Wales) 1950 *NZ* 4
Davies, D M (Somerset Police and Wales) 1950 *NZ* 3,4, *A* 1
Davies, D S (Hawick and Scotland) 1924 *SA* 1,2,3,4
Davies, H J (Newport and Wales) 1924 *SA* 2
Davies, T G R (Cardiff, London Welsh and Wales) 1968 *SA* 3, 1971 *NZ* 1,2,3,4
Davies, T J (Llanelli and Wales) 1959 *NZ* 2,4
Davies, T M (London Welsh, Swansea and Wales) 1971 *NZ* 1,2,3,4, 1974 *SA* 1,2,3,4
Davies, W G (Cardiff and Wales) 1980 *SA* 2
Davies, W P C (Harlequins and England) 1955 *SA* 1,2,3
Dawes, S J (London Welsh and Wales) 1971 *NZ* 1,2,3,4
Dawson, A R (Wanderers and Ireland) 1959 *A* 1,2, *NZ* 1,2,3,4
Dixon, P J (Harlequins and England) 1971 *NZ* 1,2,4
Dodge, P W (Leicester and England) 1980 *SA* 3,4
Dooley, W A (Preston Grasshoppers and England) 1989 *A* 2,3
Doyle, M G (Blackrock Coll and Ireland) 1968 *SA* 1
Drysdale, D (Heriot's FP and Scotland) 1924 *SA* 1,2,3,4
Duckham, D J (Coventry and England) 1971 *NZ* 2,3,4
Duggan, W P (Blackrock Coll and Ireland) 1977 *NZ* 1,2,3,4
Duff, P L (Glasgow Acads and Scotland) 1938 *SA* 2,3

Edwards, G O (Cardiff and Wales) 1968 *SA* 1,2, 1971 *NZ* 1,2,3,4, 1974 *SA* 1,2,3,4
Evans, G (Maesteg and Wales) 1983 *NZ* 3,4
Evans, G L (Newport and Wales) 1977 *NZ* 2,3,4
Evans, I C (Llanelli and Wales) 1989 *A* 1,2,3
Evans, R T (Newport and Wales) 1950 *NZ* 1,2,3,4, *A* 1,2
Evans, T P (Swansea and Wales) 1977 *NZ* 1
Evans, W R (Cardiff and Wales) 1959 *A* 2, *NZ* 1,2,3

Farrell, J L (Bective Rangers and Ireland) 1930 *NZ* 1,2,3,4, *A*
Faull, J (Swansea and Wales) 1959 *A* 1, *NZ* 1,3,4
Fenwick, S P (Bridgend and Wales) 1977 *NZ* 1,2,3,4
Fitzgerald, C F (St Mary's Coll and Ireland) 1983 *NZ* 1,2,3,4
Foster, A R (Queen's U, Belfast and Ireland) 1910 *SA* 1,2

Gibson, C M H (Cambridge U, NIFC and Ireland) 1966 *NZ* 1,2,3,4, 1968 *SA* 1(R),2,3,4, 1971 *NZ* 1,2,3,4
Giles, J L (Coventry and England) 1938 *SA* 1,3
Gravell, R W R (Llanelli and Wales) 1980 *SA* 1 (R),2,3,4
Graves, C R A (Wanderers and Ireland) 1938 *SA* 1,3
Greenwood, J T (Dunfermline and Scotland) 1955 *SA* 1,2,3,4
Grieve, C F (Oxford U and Scotland) 1938 *SA* 2,3
Griffiths, G M (Cardiff and Wales) 1955 *SA* 2,3,4
Griffiths, V M (Newport and Wales) 1924 *SA* 3,4
Guscott, J C (Bath and England) 1989 *A* 2,3

Hall, M R (Bridgend and Wales) 1989 *A* 1
Handford, F G (Manchester and England) 1910 *SA* 1,2,3
Harding, W R (Cambridge U, Swansea and Wales) 1924 *SA* 2,3,4
Harris, S W (Blackheath and England) 1924 *SA* 3,4
Hastings, A G (London Scottish and Scotland) 1989 *A* 1,2,3
Hastings, S (Watsonians and Scotland) 1989 *A* 2,3
Hay, B H (Boroughmuir and Scotland) 1980 *SA* 2,3,4
Hayward, D J (Newbridge and Wales) 1950 *NZ* 1,2,3
Henderson, N J (Queen's U, Belfast, NIFC and Ireland) 1950 *NZ* 3
Henderson, R G (Northern and Scotland) 1924 *SA* 3,4
Hendrie K G P (Heriot's FP and Scotland) 1924 *SA* 2
Hewitt, D (Queen's U, Belfast, Instonians and Ireland) 1959 *A* 1,2, *NZ* 1,3,4, 1962 *SA* 4
Higgins, R (Liverpool and England) 1955 *SA* 1
Hinshelwood, A J W (London Scottish and Scotland) 1966 *NZ* 2,4, 1968 *SA* 2
Hodgson, J McD (Northern and *England) 1930 *NZ* 1,3
Holmes, T D (Cardiff and Wales) 1983 *NZ* 1
Hopkins, R (Maesteg and Wales) 1971 *NZ* 1(R)
Horrocks-Taylor, J P (Leicester and England) 1959 *NZ* 3
Horton, A L (Blackheath and England) 1968 *SA* 2,3,4
Howard, W G (Old Birkonians) 1938 *SA* 1
Howie, R A (Kirkcaldy and Scotland) 1924 *SA* 1,2,3,4

Irvine, A R (Heriot's FP and Scotland) 1974 *SA* 3,4, 1977 *NZ* 1,2,3,4, 1980 *SA* 2,3,4
Irwin, D G (Instonians and Ireland) 1983 *NZ* 1,2,4
Isherwood, G A M (Old Alleynians, Sale) 1910 *SA* 1,2,3

Jackson, P B (Coventry and England) 1959 *A* 1,2, *NZ* 1,3,4
Jarman, H (Newport and Wales) 1910 *SA* 1,2,3,
Jeeps, R E G (Northampton and *England) 1955 *SA* 1,2,3,4, 1959 *A* 1,2, *NZ* 1,2,3, 1962 *SA* 1,2,3,4
Jenkins, V G J (Oxford U, London Welsh and Wales) 1938 *SA* 1
John, B (Cardiff and Wales) 1968 *SA* 1, 1971 *NZ* 1,2,3,4
John, E R (Neath and Wales) 1950 *NZ* 1,2,3,4, *A* 1,2
Jones, B L (Devonport Services, Llanelli and Wales) 1950 *NZ* 4, *A* 1,2
Jones, D K (Llanelli, Cardiff and Wales) 1962 *SA* 1,2,3, 1966 *A* 1,2, *NZ* 1
Jones, E L (Llanelli and *Wales) 1938 *SA* 1,3
Jones, Ivor (Llanelli and Wales) 1930 *NZ* 1,2,3,4, *A*
Jones, J P (Newport and Wales) 1910 *SA* 1,2,3
Jones, K D (Cardiff and Wales) 1962 *SA* 1,2,3,4
Jones, K J (Newport and Wales) 1950 *NZ* 1,2,4
Jones, R N (Swansea and Wales) 1989 *A* 1,2,3
Jones, S T (Pontypool and Wales) 1983 *NZ* 2,3,4

Keane, M I (Lansdowne and Ireland) 1977 *NZ* 1
Kennedy, K W (CIYMS, London Irish and Ireland) 1966 *A* 1,2, *NZ* 1,4
Kiernan, M J (Dolphin and Ireland) 1983 *NZ* 2,3,4

Kiernan, T J (Cork Const and Ireland) 1962 *SA* 3, 1968 *SA* 1,2,3,4
Kininmonth, P W (Oxford U, Richmond and Scotland) 1950 *NZ* 1,2,4
Kinnear, R M (Heriot's FP and *Scotland) 1924 *SA* 1,2,3,4
Kyle, J W (Queen's U, Belfast, NIFC and Ireland) 1950 *NZ* 1,2,3,4, *A* 1,2

Laidlaw, F A L (Melrose and Scotland) 1966 *NZ* 2,3
Laidlaw, R J (Jedforest and Scotland) 1983 *NZ* 1(R), 2,3,4
Lamont, R A (Instonians and Ireland) 1966 *NZ* 1,2,3,4
Lane, M F (UC Cork and Ireland) 1950 *NZ* 4, *A* 2
Larter, P J (Northampton, RAF and England) 1968 *SA* 2
Lewis, A R (Abertillery and Wales) 1966 *NZ* 2,3,4
Lynch, J F (St Mary's Coll and Ireland) 1971 *NZ* 1,2,3,4

McBride, W J (Ballymena and Ireland) 1962 *SA* 3,4, 1966 *NZ* 2,3,4, 1968 *SA* 1,2,3,4, 1971 *NZ* 1,2,3,4, 1974 *SA* 1,2,3,4
Macdonald, R (Edinburgh U and Scotland) 1950 *NZ* 1, *A* 2
McFadyean, C W (Moseley and England) 1966 *NZ* 1,2,3,4
McGeechan, I R (Headingley and Scotland) 1974 *SA* 1,2,3,4, 1977 *NZ* 1,2,3(R),4
McKay, J W (Queen's U, Belfast and Ireland) 1950 *NZ* 1,2,3,4, *A* 1,2
McKibbin, H R (Queen's U, Belfast and Ireland) 1938 *SA* 1,2,3
McLauchlan, J (Jordanhill and Scotland) 1971 *NZ* 1,2,3,4, 1974 *SA* 1,2,3,4
McLeod, H F (Hawick and Scotland) 1959 *A* 1,2, *NZ* 1,2,3,4
McLoughlin, R J (Gosforth, Blackrock Coll and Ireland) 1966 *A* 1,2, *NZ* 4
MacNeill, H P (Oxford U and Ireland) 1983 *NZ* 1, 2,4(R)
Macpherson, N C (Newport and Scotland) 1924 *SA* 1,2,3,4
Macrae, D J (St Andrew's U and Scotland) 1938 *SA* 1
McVicker, J (Collegians and Ireland) 1924 *SA* 1,3,4
Marques, R W D (Harlequins and England) 1959 *A* 2, *NZ* 2
Marsden-Jones, D (London Welsh and Wales) 1924 *SA* 1,2
Martin, A J (Aberavon and Wales) 1977 *NZ* 1
Martindale, S A (Kendal and England) 1930 *A*
Matthews, J (Cardiff and Wales) 1950 *NZ* 1,2,3,4, *A* 1,2
Maxwell, R B (Birkenhead Park) 1924 *SA* 1
Mayne, R B (Queen's U, Belfast and Ireland) 1938 *SA* 1,2,3
Meredith, B V (Newport and Wales) 1955 *SA* 1,2,3,4, 1962 *SA* 1,2,3,4
Meredith, C C (Neath and Wales) 1955 *SA* 1,2,3,4
Millar, S (Ballymena and Ireland) 1959 *A* 1,2, *NZ* 2, 1962 *SA* 1,2,3,4, 1968 *SA* 1,2
Milliken, R A (Bangor and Ireland) 1974 *SA* 1,2,3,4
Moore, B C (Nottingham and England) 1989 *A* 1,2,3
Morgan, C I (Cardiff and Wales) 1955 *SA* 1,2,3,4
Morgan, D W (Stewart's-Melville FP and Scotland) 1977 *NZ* 3(R),4
Morgan, G J (Clontarf and Ireland) 1938 *SA* 3
Morgan, H J (Abertillery and Wales) 1959 *NZ* 3,4, 1962 *SA* 2,3
Morgan, M E (Swansea and Wales) 1938 *SA* 1,2
Morley, J C (Newport and Wales) 1930 *NZ* 1,2,3
Mulcahy, W A (UC Dublin and Ireland) 1959 *A* 1, *NZ* 4, 1962 *SA* 1,2,3,4
Mullen, K D (Old Belvedere and Ireland) 1950 *NZ* 1,2, *A* 2
Mulligan, A A (Wanderers, London Irish and Ireland) 1959 *NZ* 4
Mullin, B J (London Irish and Ireland) 1989 *A* 1
Murphy, N A A (Cork Const and Ireland) 1959 *A* 2, *NZ* 1,2,4, 1966 *A* 1,2, *NZ* 2,3
Murray, P F (Wanderers and Ireland) 1930 *NZ* 1,2,4, *A*

Neale, M E (Bristol, Blackheath and *England) 1910 SA 1,2,3
Neary, A (Broughton Park and England) 1977 NZ 4
Nelson, J E (Malone and Ireland) 1950 NZ 3,4, A 1,2
Nicholson, B E (Harlequins and England) 1938 SA 2
Norris, C H (Cardiff and Wales) 1966 NZ 1,2,3
Norster, R L (Cardiff and Wales) 1983 NZ 1,2, 1989 A 1
Novis, A L (Blackheath and England) 1930 NZ 2,4, A

O'Donnell, R C (St Mary's Coll and Ireland) 1980 SA 1
O'Driscoll, J B (London Irish and Ireland) 1980 SA 1,2,3,4, 1983 NZ 2,4
O'Neill, H O'H (Queen's U, Belfast and Ireland) 1930 NZ 1,2,3,4, A
O'Reilly, A J F (Old Belvedere and Ireland) 1955 SA 1,2,3,4, 1959 A 1,2, NZ 1,2,3,4
Orr, P A (Old Wesley and Ireland) 1977 NZ 1
O'Shea, J P (Cardiff and Wales) 1968 SA 1

Parker, D (Swansea and Wales) 1930 NZ 1,2,3,4, A
Pask, A E I (Abertillery and Wales) 1962 SA 1,2,3, 1966 A 1,2, NZ 1,3,4
Patterson, C S (Instonians and Ireland) 1980 SA 1,2,3
Patterson, W M (Sale and *England) 1959 NZ 2
Paxton, I A M (Selkirk and Scotland) 1983 NZ 1,2,3,4
Pedlow, A C (CIYMS and Ireland) 1955 SA 1,4
Pillman, C H (Blackheath and England) 1910 SA 2,3
Piper, O J S (Cork Const and Ireland) 1910 SA 1,2
Poole, H (Cardiff) 1930 NZ 3
Preece, I (Coventry and England) 1950 NZ 1
Prentice, F D (Leicester and England) 1930 NZ 2, A
Price, B (Newport and Wales) 1966 A 1,2, NZ 1,4
Price, G (Pontypool and Wales) 1977 NZ 1,2,3,4, 1980 SA 1,2,3,4, 1983 NZ 1,2,3,4
Price, M J (Pontypool and Wales) 1959 A 1,2, NZ 1,2,3
Prosser, T R (Pontypool and Wales) 1959 NZ 4
Pullin, J V (Bristol and England) 1968 SA 2,3,4, 1971 NZ 1,2,3,4

Quinnell, D L (Llanelli and *Wales) 1971 NZ 3, 1977 NZ 2,3, 1980 SA 1,2

Ralston, C W (Richmond and England) 1974 SA 4
Rees, H E (Neath and *Wales) 1977 NZ 4
Reeve, J S R (Harlequins and England) 1930 NZ 1,3,4, A
Reid, T E (Garryowen and Ireland) 1955 SA 2,3
Renwick, J M (Hawick and Scotland) 1980 SA 1
Rew, H (Blackheath, Army and England) 1930 NZ 1,2,3,4
Reynolds, F J (Old Cranleighans and England) 1938 SA 1,2
Richards, D (Leicester and England) 1989 A 1,2,3
Richards, D S (Swansea and Wales) 1980 SA 1
Richards, M C R (Cardiff and Wales) 1968 SA 1,3,4
Richards, T J (Bristol and Australia) 1910 SA 1,2
Rimmer, G (Waterloo and England) 1950 NZ 3
Ringland, T M (Ballymena and Ireland) 1983 NZ 1
Risman, A B W (Loughborough Colls and England) 1959 A 1,2, NZ 1,4
Robbie, J C (Greystones and Ireland) 1980 SA 4
Robins, J D (Birkenhead Park and Wales) 1950 NZ 1,2,3, A 1,2
Robins, R J (Pontypridd and Wales) 1955 SA 1,2,3,4
Rogers, D P (Bedford and England) 1962 SA 1,4
Rowlands, K A (Cardiff and Wales) 1962 SA 1,2,4
Rutherford, D (Gloucester and England) 1966 A 1
Rutherford, J Y (Selkirk and Scotland) 1983 NZ 3

Savage, K F (Northampton and England) 1968 SA 1,2,3,4
Scotland, K J F (Cambridge U, Heriot's FP and Scotland) 1959 A 1,2, NZ 1,3,4
Sharp, R A W (Oxford U, Redruth and England) 1962 SA 3,4
Slattery, J F (Blackrock Coll and Ireland) 1974 SA 1,2,3,4
Slemen, M A C (Liverpool and England) 1980 SA 1
Smith, A R (Edinburgh Wands, London Scottish and Scotland) 1962 SA 1,2,3
Smith, D F (Richmond and England) 1910 SA 1,2,3

Smith, D W C (London Scottish and Scotland) 1950 A 1
Smith, G K (Kelso and Scotland) 1959 A 1,2, NZ 1,3
Smith, I S (Oxford U, London Scottish and Scotland) 1924 SA 1,2
Smyth, T (Malone, Newport and Ireland) 1910 SA 2,3
Sole, D M B (Edinburgh Acads and Scotland) 1989 A 1,2,3
Spong, R S (Old Millhillians and England) 1930 NZ 1,2,3,4, A
Spoors, J A (Bristol) 1910 SA 1,2,3
Squire, J (Newport, Pontypool and Wales) 1977 NZ 4, 1980 SA 1,2,3,4, 1983 NZ 1
Squires, P J (Harrogate and England) 1977 NZ 1
Stagg, P K (Oxford U, Sale and Scotland) 1968 SA 1,3,4
Steele, W C C (Bedford, RAF and Scotland) 1974 SA 1,2
Stephens, I (Bridgend and Wales) 1983 NZ 1
Stephens, J R G (Neath and Wales) 1950 A 1,2
Stevenson, R C (St Andrew's U and Scotland) 1910 SA 1,2,3

Tanner, H (Swansea and Wales) 1938 SA 2
Taylor, A R (Cross Keys and Wales) 1938 SA 1,2
Taylor, J (London Welsh and Wales) 1971 NZ 1,2,3,4
Taylor, R B (Northampton and England) 1968 SA 1,2,3,4
Teague, M C (Gloucester and England) 1989 A 2,3
Telfer, J W (Melrose and Scotland) 1966 A 1,2, NZ 1,2,4, 1968 SA 2,3,4
Thomas, M C (Devonport Services, Newport and Wales) 1950 NZ 2,3,4, A 1, 1959 NZ 2
Thomas, R C C (Swansea and Wales) 1955 SA 3,4
Thomas, W D (Llanelli and *Wales) 1966 NZ 2,3, 1968 SA 3 (R),4, 1971 NZ 1,2,4 (R)
Thompson, R H (Instonians, London Irish and Ireland) 1955 SA 1,2,4
Travers, W H (Newport and Wales) 1938 SA 2,3
Tucker, C C (Shannon and Ireland) 1980 SA 3,4
Turner, J W C (Gala and Scotland) 1968 SA 1,2,3,4

Underwood, R (RAF, Leicester and England) 1989 A 1,2,3
Unwin, E J (Rosslyn Park, Army and England) 1938 SA 1,2
Uttley, R M (Gosforth and England) 1974 SA 1,2,3,4

Voyce, A T (Gloucester and England) 1924 SA 3,4

Waddell, G H (Cambridge U, London Scottish and Scotland) 1962 SA 1,2
Waddell, H (Glasgow Acads and Scotland) 1924 SA 1,2,4
Walker, S (Instonians and Ireland) 1938 SA 1,2,3
Wallace, W (Percy Park) 1924 SA 1
Waller, P D (Newport and Wales) 1910 SA 1,2,3
Ward, A J P (Garryowen and Ireland) 1980 SA 1
Waters, J A (Selkirk and Scotland) 1938 SA 3
Watkins, D (Newport and Wales) 1966 A 1,2, NZ 1,2,3,4
Watkins, S J (Newport and Wales) 1966 A 1,2, NZ 3
Webb, J (Abertillery and Wales) 1910 SA 1,2,3
Welsh, W B (Hawick and Scotland) 1930 NZ 4
Weston, M P (Richmond, Durham City and England) 1962 SA 1,2,3,4, 1966 A 1,2
Wheeler, P J (Leicester and England) 1977 NZ 2,3,4, 1980 SA 1,2,3,4
White, D B (London Scottish and Scotland) 1989 A 1
Whitley, H (Northern and *England) 1924 SA 1,3,4
Willcox, J G (Oxford U, Harlequins and England) 1962 SA 1,2,4
Williams, B L (Cardiff and Wales) 1950 NZ 2,3,4, A 1,2
Williams, C (Swansea and Wales) 1980 SA 1,2,3,4
Williams, D (Ebbw Vale and Wales) 1966 A 1,2, NZ 1,2,4
Williams, D B (Cardiff and *Wales) 1977 NZ 1,2,3
Williams, J J (Llanelli and Wales) 1974 SA 1,2,3,4, 1977 NZ 1,2,3
Williams, J P R (London Welsh and Wales) 1971 NZ 1,2,3,4, 1974 SA 1,2,3,4
Williams, R H (Llanelli and Wales) 1955 SA 1,2,3,4,

291

1959 *A* 1,2, *NZ* 1,2,3,4
Williams, S H (Newport and *England) 1910 *SA* 1,2,3
Williams, W O G (Swansea and Wales) 1955 *SA* 1,2,3,4
Willis, W R (Cardiff and Wales) 1950 *NZ* 4, *A* 1,2
Wilson, S (London Scottish and Scotland) 1966 *A* 2, *NZ* 1,2,3,4
Windsor, R W (Pontypool and Wales) 1974 *SA* 1,2,3,4, 1977 *NZ* 1
Winterbottom, P J (Headingley and England) 1983 *NZ* 1,2,3,4
Wood, B G M (Garryowen and Ireland) 1959 *NZ* 1,3

Wood, K B (Leicester) 1910 *SA* 1,3
Woodward, C R (Leicester and England) 1980 *SA* 2,3

Young, A T (Cambridge U, Blackheath and England) 1924 *SA* 2
Young, D (Cardiff and Wales) 1989 *A* 1,2,3
Young, J (Harrogate, RAF and Wales) 1968 *SA* 1
Young, J R C (Oxford U, Harlequins and England) 1959 *NZ* 2
Young, R M (Queen's U, Belfast, Collegians and Ireland) 1966 *A* 1,2, *NZ* 1, 1968 *SA* 3

The 1989 Lions Test front row of David Young, Brian Moore and David Sole. Several months after the tour, Young signed for Leeds rugby league club.

RESULTS OF BRITISH ISLES MATCHES
(up to 30 April 1990)
From 1910 onwards – the tour to South Africa in that year was the first fully representative one in which the four Home Unions cooperated.

v SOUTH AFRICA
Played 30   British Isles won 8, South Africa won 18, Drawn 4

1910 *1* Johannesburg **South Africa** 1G 3T (14) to 1DG 2T (10)	*3* Cape Town **South Africa** 1G 1PG (8) to 1DG (3)
2 Port Elizabeth **British Isles** 1G 1T (8) to 1T (3)	*4* Bloemfontein **South Africa** 5G 2PG 1T (34) to 1G 1PG 2T (14)
3 Cape Town **South Africa** 3G 1PG 1T (21) to 1G (5) *South Africa won series 2-1*	*South Africa won series 3-0, with 1 draw*
1924 *1* Durban **South Africa** 1DG 1T (7) to 1T (3)	1968 *1* Pretoria **South Africa** 2G 4PG 1T (25) to 1G 5PG (20)
2 Johannesburg **South Africa** 1G 1PG 3T (17) to 0	*2* Port Elizabeth **Drawn** 2PG (6) each
3 Port Elizabeth **Drawn** 1T (3) each	*3* Cape Town **South Africa** 1G 2PG (11) to 2PG (6)
4 Cape Town **South Africa** 1DG 4T (16) to 1PG 2T (9) *South Africa won series 3-0, with 1 draw*	*4* Johannesburg **South Africa** 2G 1DG 2T (19) to 2PG (6) *South Africa won series 3-0, with 1 draw*
1938 *1* Johannesburg **South Africa** 4G 2PG (26) to 4PG (12)	1974 *1* Cape Town **British Isles** 3PG 1DG (12) to 1DG (3)
2 Port Elizabeth **South Africa** 2G 2PG 1T (19) to 1T (3)	*2* Pretoria **British Isles** 1G 1PG 1DG 4T (28) to 2PG 1DG (9)
3 Cape Town **British Isles** 1G 1PG 1DG 3T (21) to 2G 1PG 1T (16) *South Africa won series 2-1*	*3* Port Elizabeth **British Isles** 1G 2PG 2DG 2T (26) to 3PG (9)
1955 *1* Johannesburg **British Isles** 4G 1T (23) to 2G 2PG 2T (22)	*4* Johannesburg **Drawn** British Isles 1G 1PG 1T (13) South Africa 3PG 1T (13) *British Isles won series 3-0, with 1 draw*
2 Cape Town **South Africa** 2G 5T (25) to 1PG 2T (9)	1980 *1* Cape Town **South Africa** 3G 2T (26) to 5PG 1DG 1T (22)
3 Pretoria **British Isles** 1PG 1DG 1T (9) to 2PG (6)	*2* Bloemfontein **South Africa** 2G 2PG 2T (26) to 1G 3PG 1T (19)
4 Port Elizabeth **South Africa** 2G 1DG 3T (22) to 1G 1T (8) *Series drawn 2-2*	*3* Port Elizabeth **South Africa** 1G 1PG 1DG (12) to 2PG 1T (10)
1962 *1* Johannesburg **Drawn** 1T (3) each	*4* Pretoria **British Isles** 1G 1PG 2T (17) to 3PG 1T (13) *South Africa won series 3-1*
2 Durban **South Africa** 1PG (3) to 0	

v NEW ZEALAND
Played 28   British Isles won 5, New Zealand won 21, Drawn 2

1930 *1* Dunedin **British Isles** 2T (6) to 1T (3)	*2* Christchurch **New Zealand** 2G 1GM (13) to 2G (10)

293

3 Auckland
New Zealand 1G 1DG 2T (15)
to 2G (10)

4 Wellington
New Zealand 2G 4T (22) to 1G 1PG (8)
New Zealand won series 3-1

1950 *1* Dunedin
Drawn 1PG 2T (9) each

2 Christchurch
New Zealand 1G 1T (8) to 0

3 Wellington
New Zealand 1PG 1T (6) to 1PG (3)

4 Auckland
New Zealand 1G 1DG 1T (11)
to 1G 1PG (8)
New Zealand won series 3-0, with 1 draw

1959 *1* Dunedin
New Zealand 6PG (18)
to 1G 1PG 3T (17)

2 Wellington
New Zealand 1G 2T (11) to 1G 1PG (8)

3 Christchurch
New Zealand 2G 1PG 1DG 2T (22)
to 1G 1PG (8)

4 Auckland
British Isles 3T (9) to 2PG (6)
New Zealand won series 3-1

1966 *1* Dunedin
New Zealand 1G 2PG 1DG 2T (20)
to 1PG (3)

2 Wellington
New Zealand 2G 1PG 1T (16)
to 3PG 1DG (12)

3 Christchurch
New Zealand 2G 2PG 1T (19) to 2T (6)

4 Auckland
New Zealand 3G 1PG 1DG 1T (24)
to 1G 1PG 1T (11)
New Zealand won series 4-0

1971 *1* Dunedin
British Isles 2PG 1T (9) to 1PG (3)

2 Christchurch
New Zealand 2G 1PG 3T (22)
to 1PG 1DG 2T (12)

3 Wellington
British Isles 2G 1DG (13) to 1T (3)

4 Auckland
Drawn British Isles 1G 2PG 1DG (14)
New Zealand 1G 2PG 1T (14)
British Isles won series 2-1, with 1 draw

1977 *1* Wellington
New Zealand 2G 1T (16) to 4PG (12)

2 Christchurch
British Isles 3PG 1T (13) to 3PG (9)

3 Dunedin
New Zealand 1G 2PG 1DG 1T (19)
to 1PG 1T (7)

4 Auckland
New Zealand 2PG 1T (10) to 1G 1PG (9)
New Zealand won series 3-1

1983 *1* Christchurch
New Zealand 3PG 1DG 1T (16)
to 3PG (12)

2 Wellington
New Zealand 1G 1PG (9) to 0

3 Dunedin
New Zealand 1G 3PG (15) to 2T (8)

4 Auckland
New Zealand 4G 2PG 2T (38) to 2PG (6)
New Zealand won series 4-0

v AUSTRALIA
Played 10   British Isles won 8, Australia won 2, Drawn 0

1930 Sydney
Australia 2T (6) to 1G (5)

1950 *1* Brisbane
British Isles 2G 2PG 1DG (19)
to 2PG (6)

2 Sydney
British Isles 3G 1PG 2T (24) to 1T (3)
British Isles won series 2-0

1959 *1* Brisbane
British Isles 1G 2PG 1DG 1T (17)
to 2PG (6)

2 Sydney
British Isles 3G 1PG 2T (24) to 1PG (3)
British Isles won series 2-0

1966 *1* Sydney
British Isles 1G 1PG 1T (11)
to 1G 1PG (8)

2 Brisbane
British Isles 5G 1PG 1DG (31) to 0
British Isles won series 2-0

1989 *1* Sydney
Australia 4G 1PG 1DG (30)
to 3PG 1DG (12)

2 Brisbane
British Isles 1G 2PG 1DG 1T (19)
to 1G 2PG (12)

3 Sydney
British Isles 5PG 1T (19) to 1G 4PG (18)
British Isles won series 2-1

BRITISH ISLES RECORDS
(*up to 30 April 1990*)

From 1910 onwards – the tour to South Africa in that year was the first fully representative one in which the four Home Unions cooperated.

TEAM RECORDS

Highest score
31 v Australia (31-0) 1966 Brisbane
v individual countries
28 v S Africa (28-9) 1974 Pretoria
17 v New Zealand (17-18) 1959 Dunedin
31 v Australia (31-0) 1966 Brisbane

Biggest winning points margin
31 v Australia (31-0) 1966 Brisbane
v individual countries
19 v S Africa (28-9) 1974 Pretoria
10 v New Zealand (13-3) 1971 Wellington
31 v Australia (31-0) 1966 Brisbane

Highest score by opposing team
38 New Zealand (6-38) 1983 Auckland
by individual countries
34 S Africa (14-34) 1962 Bloemfontein
38 New Zealand (6-38) 1983 Auckland
30 Australia (12-30) 1989 Sydney

Biggest losing points margin
32 v New Zealand (6-38) 1983 Auckland
v individual countries
20 v S Africa (14-34) 1962 Bloemfontein
32 v New Zealand (6-38) 1983 Auckland
18 v Australia (12-30) 1989 Sydney

Most tries by B Isles in an international
5 ⎰ v Australia (24-3) 1950 Sydney
⎱ v S Africa (23-22) 1955 Johannesburg
⎱ v Australia (24-3) 1959 Sydney
⎱ v Australia (31-0) 1966 Brisbane
⎱ v S Africa (28-9) 1974 Pretoria

Most tries against B Isles in an international
7 by South Africa (9-25) 1955 Cape Town

Most points on overseas tour (all matches)
842 in Australia, New Zealand and Canada (33 matches) 1959
(includes 582 points in 25 matches in New Zealand)

Most tries on overseas tour (all matches)
165 in Australia, New Zealand and Canada (33 matches) 1959
(includes 113 tries in 25 matches in New Zealand)

INDIVIDUAL RECORDS

Most capped player
W J McBride 17 1962-74
in individual positions
Full-back
J P R Williams 8[1] 1971-74
Wing
A J F O'Reilly 9 (10)[2] 1955-59
Centre
C M H Gibson 8 (12)[3] 1966-71
Fly-half
P Bennett 8 1974-77
Scrum-half
R E G Jeeps 13 1955-62
Prop
G Price 12 1977-83
Hooker
B V Meredith 8 1955-62
Lock
W J McBride 17 1962-74
Flanker
N A A Murphy 8 1959-66
No 8
T M Davies 8[4] 1971-74

[1] A R Irvine, 9 Tests, played 7 times at full-back and twice as a wing
[2] O'Reilly played once as a centre
[3] Gibson played 4 times as a fly-half. I R McGeechan, 8 Tests, played 7 times as a centre and once, as a replacement, on the wing
[4] Both A E I Pask and J W Telfer (8 Tests each), played 4 Tests at No 8 and 4 Tests at flanker

Longest international career
W J McBride   13 seasons   1962-74

Most internationals as captain – 6
A R Dawson 1959

Most points in internationals – 44
P Bennett (8 appearances) 1974-77

Most points in an international – 18
A J P Ward v S Africa 1980 Cape Town

Most tries in internationals – 6
A J F O'Reilly (10 appearances) 1955-59

Most tries in an international – 2
C D Aarvold v New Zealand 1930
   Christchurch
J E Nelson v Australia 1950 Sydney
M J Price v Australia 1959 Sydney
M J Price v New Zealand 1959 Dunedin
D K Jones v Australia 1966 Brisbane
T G R Davies v New Zealand 1971
   Christchurch
J J Williams v S Africa 1974 Pretoria
J J Williams v S Africa 1974 Port Elizabeth

Most conversions in internationals – 6
S Wilson (5 matches) 1966

Most conversions in an international – 5
S Wilson v Australia 1966 Brisbane

Most dropped goals in internationals – 2
D Watkins (6 matches) 1966
B John (5 matches) 1968-71
P Bennett (8 matches) 1974-77
(P F Bush also dropped 2 goals in tests played by British teams prior to 1910)

Most penalty goals in internationals – 11
T J Kiernan (5 matches) 1962-68

Most points for B Isles on overseas tour – 188
B John (17 appearances) 1971 Australia/
   N Zealand
(includes 180 points in 16 appearances in
   N Zealand)

Most tries for B Isles on overseas tour – 22*
A J F O'Reilly (23 appearances) 1959
   Australia/N Zealand/Canada
(includes 17* tries in 17 appearances in
   N Zealand)
Includes one penalty try

Most points for B Isles in international series – 35
T J Kiernan (4 appearances) 1968 S Africa

Most tries for B Isles in international series – 4
J J Williams (4 appearances) 1974 S Africa

Most points for B Isles in any match on tour – 37
A G B Old v South Western Districts
   1974 Mossel Bay, SA

Most tries for B Isles in any match on tour – 6
D J Duckham v West Coast-Buller 1971
   Greymouth NZ
J J Williams v South Western Districts
   1974 Mossel Bay, SA
(A R Irvine scored 5 tries from full-back
   v King Country-Wanganui 1977
   Taumarunui, NZ)

LEADING CAP-WINNERS
(up to 30 April 1990)

ENGLAND

A Neary	43	C T Deans	52
J V Pullin	42	A R Irvine	51
P J Wheeler	41	A B Carmichael	50
R Underwood	38	A J Tomes	48
D J Duckham	36	R J Laidlaw	47
G S Pearce	35	A F McHarg	44
P J Winterbottom	35	K W Robertson	44
D P Rogers	34	J McLauchlan	43
W B Beaumont	34	J Y Rutherford	42
J P Scott	34	I G Milne	42
W A Dooley	34	H F McLeod	40
P W Dodge	32	D M D Rollo	40
W W Wakefield	31	J MacD Bannerman	37
F E Cotton	31	I A M Paxton	36
M A C Slemen	31	A R Smith	33
C R Andrew	31	I S Smith	32
E Evans	30	F A L Laidlaw	32
R Cove-Smith	29	I R McGeechan	32
C R Jacobs	29	D G Leslie	32
M P Weston	29	N S Bruce	31
P J Squires	29	I H P Laughland	31
J Butterfield	28	G L Brown	30
S J Smith	28	W I D Elliot	29
A T Voyce	27	W M Simmers	28
J S Tucker	27	P K Stagg	28
P A G Rendall	27	J Jeffrey	28
J Carleton	26	J W Y Kemp	27
C N Lowe	25	K J F Scotland	27
J D Currie	25	P C Brown	27
M S Phillips	25	J H Calder	27
C B Stevens	25	D I Johnston	27
W H Hare	25	G R T Baird	27
M J Colclough	25	W E Maclagan	26
R E G Jeeps	24	D Drysdale	26
P J Larter	24	J C McCallum	26
A G Ripley	24	G P S Macpherson	26
J MacG K Kendall-Carpenter	23	F Calder	26
R W D Marques	23	J B Nelson	25
R M Uttley	23	J P Fisher	25
B C Moore	23	J R Beattie	25
W J A Davies	22	J W Telfer	25
P E Judd	22	D M B Sole	25
C W Ralston	22		
P J Dixon	22	**IRELAND**	
J G G Birkett	21	C M H Gibson	69
H G Periton	21	W J McBride	63
C R Woodward	21	J F Slattery	61
G H Davies	21	P A Orr	58
P B Jackson	20	T J Kiernan	54
N E Horton	20	M I Keane	51
G W Rees	20	J W Kyle	46
D Richards	20	D G Lenihan	46
		K W Kennedy	45
SCOTLAND		G V Stephenson	42
J M Renwick	52	N A A Murphy	41

297

W P Duggan	41
M J Kiernan	41
N J Henderson	40
R J McLoughlin	40
S Millar	37
H P MacNeill	37
J R Kavanagh	35
W A Mulcahy	35
E O'D Davy	34
T M Ringland	34
K D Crossan	33
P M Dean	32
B J Mullin	32
A C Pedlow	30
G T Hamlet	30
W E Crawford	30
J D Clinch	30
J L Farrell	29
B G M Wood	29
A J F O'Reilly	29
M Sugden	28
J S McCarthy	28
A M Magee	27
A R Dawson	27
M G Molloy	27
J J Moloney	27
W A Anderson	27
P M Matthews	27
J C Walsh	26
R M Young	26
J B O'Driscoll	26
G R Beamish	25
K D Mullen	25
F P K Bresnihan	25
A T A Duggan	25
B J McGann	25
T O Grace	25
S A McKinney	25
C F Fitzgerald	25
D G Irwin	25

WALES

J P R Williams	55
G O Edwards	53
T G R Davies	46
K J Jones	44
G Price	41
T M Davies	38
D Williams	36
R M Owen	35
B V Meredith	34
D I E Bebb	34
W D Morris	34
A J Martin	34
R L Norster	34
W J Bancroft	33
B Price	32
J R G Stephens	32
G A D Wheel	32
R N Jones	32
J J Williams	30
S P Fenwick	30

W J Trew	29
C I Morgan	29
P Bennett	29
J Squire	29
P H Thorburn	29
R W Windsor	28
A J Gould	27
W C Powell	27
M C Thomas	27
H J Morgan	27
A M Hadley	27
J Davies	27
R C C Thomas	26
A E I Pask	26
S J Watkins	26
J Taylor	26
G Travers	25
H Tanner	25
B John	25
N R Gale	25
W D Thomas	25
T D Holmes	25
P T Davies	25

FRANCE

S Blanco	75
R Bertranne	69
P Sella	67
M Crauste	63
B Dauga	63
J-P Rives	59
J Condom	58
R Paparemborde	55
L Rodriguez	55
A Domenech	52
P Berbizier	52
J Prat	51
W Spanghéro	51
J-L Joinel	51
M Celaya	50
P Dintrans	49
A Boniface	48
J-P Lux	47
J-C Skréla	46
D Erbani	46
M Vannier	43
J-P Garuet	42
J Dupuy	40
C Darrouy	40
F Haget	40
J-M Aguirre	39
P Lagisquet	39
G Dufau	38
G Boniface	35
E Cester	35
A Paco	35
E Champ	35
E Ribère	34
J Bouquet	34
P Villepreux	34
J Iraçabal	34
J-P Romeu	34

G Basquet	33
C Lacaze	33
C Dourthe	33
D Dubroca	33
J Gachassin	32
J-P Bastiat	32
A Cassayet	31
A Jauréguy	31
M Prat	31
F Moncla	31
G Cholley	31
D Codorniou	31
P Albaladéjo	30
A Roques	30
R Bénésis	30
A Lorieux	30
R Biénès	29
L Mias	29
P Ondarts	29
J Trillo	28
F Mesnel	28
H Rancoule	27
P Lacroix	27
J-C Berejnoi	27
C Carrère	27
J Fouroux	27
J Gallion	27
J-P Lescarboura	27
B Chevallier	26
J Barthe	26
J-M Cabanier	26
A Gruarin	26
J-L Azarète	26
A Vaquerin	26
M Andrieu	26
R Martine	25
J Maso	25
J-L Averous	25
P Estève	25

SOUTH AFRICA

F C H Du Preez	38
J H Ellis	38
J F K Marais	35
J P Engelbrecht	33
J L Gainsford	33
J T Claassen	28
F du T Roux	27
L G Wilson	27
T P Bedford	25
D J de Villiers	25
P J F Greyling	25
S H Nomis	25
P J Visagie	25
L C Moolman	24
H E Botha	23
D J Hopwood	22
A C Koch	22
M Du Plessis	22
J A du Rand	21
M T S Stofberg	21
J S Germishuys	20

NEW ZEALAND

C E Meads	55
A M Haden	41
G W Whetton	41
I A Kirkpatrick	39
K R Tremain	38
B G Williams	38
G A Knight	36
A G Dalton	35
B J Robertson	34
S S Wilson	34
M G Mexted	34
W J Whineray	32
D B Clarke	31
M W Shaw	30
J J Kirwan	30
S M Going	29
R W Norton	27
M J Pierce	26
B J Lochore	25
J T Stanley	25
B E McLeod	24
K F Gray	24
I J Clarke	24
J C Ashworth	24
D S Loveridge	24
W T Taylor	24
S C McDowell	24
R A White	23
B G Fraser	23
S B T Fitzpatrick	23
D J Graham	22
D Young	22
A J Whetton	22
G N K Mourie	21
M J B Hobbs	21
K L Skinner	20
C R Laidlaw	20
I N MacEwan	20
P J Whiting	20
C I Green	20
G J Fox	20
W T Shelford	20

AUSTRALIA

S P Poidevin	51
D I Campese	48
P G Johnson	42
A R Miller	41
T A Lawton	41
G V Davis	39
A G Slack	39
S A G Cutler	39
A J McIntyre	38
J E Thornett	37
N C Farr-Jones	37
J N B Hipwell	36
A A Shaw	36
M P Lynagh	36
B J Moon	35
S N Tuynman	33

N M Shehadie	30	J W Cole	24
P E McLean	30	G Fay	24
M E Loane	28	R Phelps	23
S A Williams	28	M P Burke	23
K W Catchpole	27	R A Smith	22
G A Shaw	27	J E C Meadows	22
C T Burke	26	E T Bonis	21
E E Rodriguez	26	P F Hawthorne	21
R B Prosser	25	R J Heming	21
G Cornelsen	25	A N McGill	21
M G Ella	25	W H Cerutti	21
R G Gould	25	A S Cameron	20
P C Grigg	25	B J Ellwood	20
M J Hawker	25	C J Windon	20
J K Lenehan	24	J S Miller	20
J P L White	24	W A Campbell	20

WORLD'S LEADING CAP-WINNERS
(up to 30 April 1990)

For purposes of comparison, the following list includes appearances for individual countries in major international matches.

S Blanco	France	75	T J Kiernan	Ireland	54
C M H Gibson	Ireland	69	G O Edwards	Wales	53
R Bertranne	France	69	A Domenech	France	52
P Sella	France	67	J M Renwick	Scotland	52
M Crauste	France	63	C T Deans	Scotland	52
W J McBride	Ireland	63	P Berbizier	France	52
B Dauga	France	63	J Prat	France	51
J F Slattery	Ireland	61	W Spanghero	France	51
J-P Rives	France	59	A R Irvine	Scotland	51
P A Orr	Ireland	58	M I Keane	Ireland	51
J Condom	France	58	J-L Joinel	France	51
C E Meads	New Zealand	55	S P Poidevin	Australia	51
J P R Williams	Wales	55	M Celaya	France	50
R Paparemborde	France	55	A B Carmichael	Scotland	50
L Rodriguez	France	55			

The following list incorporates appearances by home countries' players for British Isles teams (the Lions) in International matches against New Zealand, Australia and South Africa (up to 30 April 1990). The number of Lions' appearances is shown in brackets.

C M H Gibson	Ireland	81	(12)	L Rodriguez	France	55	
W J McBride	Ireland	80	(17)	J M Renwick	Scotland	53	(1)
S Blanco	France	75		G Price	Wales	53	(12)
R Bertranne	France	69		A Domenech	France	52	
P Sella	France	67		C T Deans	Scotland	52	
J F Slattery	Ireland	65	(4)	J W Kyle	Ireland	52	(6)
G O Edwards	Wales	63	(10)	M I Keane	Ireland	52	(1)
J P R Williams	Wales	63	(8)	P Berbizier	France	52	
M Crauste	France	63		J Prat	France	51	
B Dauga	France	63		W Spanghero	France	51	
A R Irvine	Scotland	60	(9)	T G R Davies	Wales	51	(5)
T J Kiernan	Ireland	59	(5)	J McLauchlan	Scotland	51	(8)
J-P Rives	France	59		J-L Joinel	France	51	
P A Orr	Ireland	59	(1)	S P Poidevin	Australia	51	
J Condom	France	58		M Celaya	France	50	
C E Meads	New Zealand	55		A B Carmichael	Scotland	50	
R Paparemborde	France	55					

Most appearances for the Lions are by W J McBride 17, R E G Jeeps (England) 13, C M H Gibson 12, G Price 12, and A J F O'Reilly (Ireland), R H Williams (Wales), and G O Edwards 10 each, up to 30 April 1990.

INTERNATIONAL REFEREES 1989-90

Leading Referees

Up to 30 April 1990, in major international matches. These include all matches for which full members of the International Board have awarded caps, and also all matches played in the World Cup final stages.

12 or more internationals

K D Kelleher	Ireland	23	D I H Burnett	Ireland	15
D G Walters	Wales	23	C H Gadney	England	15
M Joseph	Wales	22	K V J Fitzgerald	Australia	15
R C Williams	Ireland	21	I David	Wales	14
C Norling	Wales	21	Dr I R Vanderfield	Australia	14
A M Hosie	Scotland	19	R Hourquet	France	14
Capt M J Dowling	Ireland	18	R G Byres	Australia	13
A E Freethy	Wales	18	J P Murphy	New Zealand	13
R C Quittenton	England	18	N R Sanson	Scotland	13
J R West	Ireland	18	F A Howard	England	13
D P D'Arcy	Ireland	17	R F Johnson	England	12
F Palmade	France	17	T D Schofield	Wales	12
B S Cumberlege	England	16	T H Vile	Wales	12
J B Anderson	Scotland	16	W Williams	England	12

Major international match appearances 1989-90

Matches controlled between 30 April 1989 and 30 April 1990

1989

R v E	**J B Anderson** (Scotland)
NZ v F(2)	**F A Howard** (England)
A v BI	**K H Lawrence** (New Zealand)
A v BI(2)	**R Hourquet** (France)
NZ v Arg(2)	**C Norling** (Wales)
NZ v A	**S R Hilditch** (Ireland)
SA v Wld(2)	**K V J Fitzgerald** (Australia)
F v B	**J B Anderson** (Scotland)
S v Fj	**P Robin** (France)
W v NZ	**A R MacNeill** (Australia)
E v Fj	*****B W Stirling** (Ireland)
F v A(2)	*****F Burger** (South Africa)
I v NZ	**A R MacNeill** (Australia)
S v R	**S R Hilditch** (Ireland)

1990

E v I	**P Robin** (France)
W v F	**F A Howard** (England)
F v E	**O E Doyle** (Ireland)
I v S	**C Norling** (Wales)
E v W	*****D Leslie** (Scotland)
S v F	**F A Howard** (England)
F v I	*****K W McCartney** (Scotland)
W v S	**R Hourquet** (France)
S v E	**D J Bishop** (New Zealand)
I v W	**D J Bishop** (New Zealand)

* Denotes debut in a major international

Referees dismissing players in a major international

A E Freethy	E v NZ	1925	K V J Fitzgerald	NZ v W	1987
K D Kelleher	S v NZ	1967	F A Howard	A v W	1987
R T Burnett	A v E	1975	K V J Fitzgerald	Fj v E	1988
W M Cooney	A v Fj	1976	O E Doyle	Arg v F	1988
N R Sanson (two)	W v I	1977	B W Stirling (two)	E v Fj	1989
D I H Burnett	E v W	1980	F A Howard	W v F	1990
C Norling	F v I	1984	F A Howard	S v F	1990

INTERNATIONAL REFEREES

The list which follows shows referees who have controlled major internationals (i.e. games for which a member country of the IB has awarded caps, or the final stages of the official World Cup) since 1876, when referees were first appointed, up to 30 April, 1990.

ABBREVIATIONS

A – Australia; *Arg* – Argentina; *AW* – Anglo-Welsh; *B* – British Forces' and Home Union Teams; *BI* – British Isles; *C* – Canada; *Cv* – New Zealand Cavaliers; *Cz* – Czechoslovakia; *E* – England; *F* – France; *Fj* – Fiji; *GB* – Great Britain; *G* – Germany; *I* – Ireland; *It* – Italy; *J* – Japan; *K* – New Zealand Kiwis; *M* – New Zealand Maoris; *NZ* – New Zealand; *NZA* – New Zealand Army; *P* – President's XV; *R* – Romania; *S* – Scotland; *SA* – South Africa; *SAm* – South America; *SK* – South Korea; *Tg* – Tonga; *US* – United States of America; *W* – Wales; *Wld* – World XV; *WS* – Western Samoa; *Z* – Zimbabwe; (C) – Special Centenary Match; (R) – Replacement. Entries in square brackets [ ] indicate matches in the World Cup final stages.

N.B. The Australian Rugby Union now recognises the internationals played by the New South Wales touring teams of the 1920s as cap matches.

Ackermann, C J (South Africa) 1953 *SA v A* (2), 1955 *SA v BI*, 1958 *SA v F*
Acton, W H (Ireland) 1926 *W v E, E v S*
Alderson, F H R (England) 1903 *S v I*
Allan, M A (Scotland) 1931 *I v W, I v SA*, 1933 *E v I, I v W*, 1934 *I v E*, 1935 *E v I, I v W*, 1936 *I v E*, 1937 *I v W*, 1947 *I v E*, 1948 *I v W*
Allen, J W (Ireland) 1906 *W v S, S v E*
Anderson, C (Scotland) 1928 *I v F*
Anderson, J B (Scotland) 1981 *W v E, I v A*, 1982 *R v F*, 1983 *I v E, A v NZ*, 1984 *E v W*, 1986 *W v F, NZ v A*, 1987 [*A v US, A v I, F v A*], 1988 *A v NZ* (2), 1989 *I v F, R v E, F v B*
Anderson, J H (South Africa) 1903 *SA v GB*
Angus, A W (Scotland) 1924 *W v E*, 1927 *I v A*
Ashmore, H L (England) 1890 *S v I*, 1891 *S v W*, 1892 *S v I*, 1894 *I v S*, 1895 *S v I*
Austin, A W C (Scotland) 1952 *W v F*, 1953 *I v E*, 1954 *I v W*
Austry, R (France) 1972 *E v I*

Badger, Dr (England) 1900 *I v S*
Baise, M (South Africa) 1967 *SA v F* (2), 1968 *SA v BI* (2), 1969 *SA v A*, 1974 *SA v BI* (2)
Baise, S (South Africa) 1969 *SA v A*
Barnes, P (Australia) 1938 *A v NZ*
Baxter, J (England) 1913 *F v S, S v I*, 1914 *I v S*, 1920 *S v I*, 1921 *W v S, I v S*, 1923 *W v S*, 1925 *W v S, I v W*
Bean, A S (England) 1939 *W v S*, 1945 *W v F*, 1946 *F v W*, 1947 *F v W, W v A*, 1948 *S v F, W v F*, 1949 *S v I*
Beattie, R A (Scotland) 1937 *E v W*, 1938 *W v E*, 1945 *B v F*, 1947 *W v E, I v A*, 1948 *E v W*, 1949 *I v E*, 1950 *E v I, I v W*
Beattie, W H (Australia) 1899 *A v GB*, 1904 *A v GB*
Bell, T (Ireland) 1932 *S v W*, 1933 *E v W*
Bevan, W D (Wales) 1985 *E v R*, 1986 *F v E, NZ v A* (2), 1987 [*NZ v Fj, F v Z*], *A v NZ*, 1988 *I v WS*
Beves, G (South Africa) 1896 *SA v GB*
Bezuidenhout, G P (South Africa) 1976 *SA v NZ* (3)
Bishop, D J (New Zealand) 1986 *Fj v W, R v F, I v R*, 1987 [*W v Tg, W v C*], 1988 *A v E*, (2), *E v A, S v A*, 1990 *S v E, I v W*
Bissett, W M (South Africa) 1896 *SA v GB*
Bonnet, J-P (France) 1979 *W v E*, 1980 *S v E, SA v BI* (2), 1981 *I v E, Arg v E* (2), 1982 *W v S*
Bott, J G (England) 1931 *W v S*, 1933 *W v S*
Boundy, L M (England) 1955 *S v I*, 1956 *W v S*, 1957 *F v S, I v F, S v I, R v F*, 1958 *S v F*, 1959 *S v I*, 1961 *S v SA*
Bowden, G (Scotland) 1910 *F v E*
Bowen, D H (Wales) 1905 *E v S*
Bradburn, T J (England) 1928 *F v A*, 1929 *F v G*
Bressy, Y (France) 1988 *W v S*
Brook, P G (England) 1963 *F v W*, 1964 *W v S*, 1965 *W v I, I v SA*, 1966 *F v I, It v F, R v F*
Brown, A (Australia) 1907 *A v NZ*
Brown, D A (England) 1960 *I v W, It v F*
Brunton, J (England) 1924 *W v NZ*
Buchanan, A (Scotland) 1877 *I v S*, 1880 *S v I*

Bullerwell, I M (England) 1988 *W v R*
Burger, F (South Africa) 1989 *F v A* (2)
Burmeister, R D (South Africa) 1949 *SA v NZ* (2), 1953 *SA v A*, 1955 *SA v BI* (2), 1960 *SA v NZ* (2), 1961 *SA v A*
Burnand, F W (England) 1890 *I v W*
Burnet, W (Scotland) 1932 *I v E*, 1934 *W v I*
Burnett, D I H (Ireland) 1977 *W v E*, 1979 *F v W*, 1980 *E v W*, 1981 *S v W, E v S*, 1982 *W v F, F v Arg*, 1983 *E v F*, 1984 *S v E, A v NZ*, 1985 *E v F, NZ v A*, 1986 *S v F*, 1987 [*S v Z, NZ v S*]
Burnett, R T (Australia) 1973 *A v Tg*, 1974 *A v NZ*, 1975 *A v E, A v J*, 1978 *A v W*
Burrell, G (Scotland) 1958 *E v I*, 1959 *W v I*
Burrell, R P (Scotland) 1966 *I v W*, 1967 *I v F, F v NZ*, 1969 *I v E, F v W*
Butt, C C (Australia) 1914 *A v NZ*
Byres, R G (Australia) 1976 *A v Fj*, 1978 *A v W*, 1979 *A v I* (2), *A v NZ*, 1980 *A v NZ*, 1981 *NZ v S*, 1982 *A v S* (2), 1983 *NZ v BI* (2), 1984 *I v W, W v F*

Calitz, M (South Africa) 1961 *SA v I*
Calmet, R (France) 1970 *E v W*
Calver, E W (England) 1914 *F v I*
Camardon, J (Argentina) 1960 *Arg v F*
Campbell, A (New Zealand) 1908 *NZ v AW* (2)
Carlson, K R V (South Africa) 1962 *SA v BI*
Cartwright, V H (England) 1906 *I v S*, 1909 *S v I*, 1910 *I v S, F v I*, 1911 *S v I*
Castens, H H (South Africa) 1891 *SA v GB*
Chambers, J (Ireland) 1888 *W v S, I v M*, 1890 *S v E*, 1891 *E v S*
Chapman, W S (Australia) 1938 *A v NZ* (2)
Charman, R (England) 1919 *W v NZA*
Chevrier, G (France) 1980 *I v S*
Chiene, Dr J (Scotland) 1879 *I v S*
Clark, K H (Ireland) 1973 *E v F*, 1974 *S v F*, 1976 *F v E*
Cochrane, C B (Australia) 1907 *A v NZ*
Coffey, J J (Ireland) 1912 *S v F*
Coles, P (England) 1903 *W v I*, 1905 *S v I*
Collett, C K (Australia) 1981 *NZ v S*
Combe, A (Ireland) 1876 *I v E*
Cook, H G (Ireland) 1886 *S v E*
Cooney, R C (Australia) 1929 *A v NZ*, 1930 *A v BI*, 1932 *A v NZ*, 1934 *A v NZ*
Cooney, W M (Australia) 1972 *A v F*, 1975 *A v E, A v J*, 1976 *A v Fj*
Cooper, Dr P F (England) 1952 *I v W*, 1953 *S v W, W v I, F v It, W v NZ*, 1954 *I v NZ, W v S, It v F*, 1956 *F v I, W v F, It v F*, 1957 *F v W*
Corley, H H (Ireland) 1906 *S v SA*, 1908 *S v E*
Corr, W S (Australia) 1899 *A v GB* (2)
Costello, J (Fiji) 1972 *Fj v A*
Craven, W S D (Ireland) 1920 *F v W*
Crawford, S H (Ireland) 1913 *W v E, S v W*, 1920 *S v W*, 1921 *S v E*
Cross, W (Scotland) 1877 *S v E*
Crowe, K J (Australia) 1965 *A v SA*, 1966 *A v BI*, 1968 *A v NZ*, 1976 *A v Fj*

Cumberlege, B S (England) 1926 *S v I*, *W v I*, 1927 *S v F*, *I v S*, *I v W*, 1928 *S v I*, 1929 *F v I*, *S v F*, *I v S*, 1930 *I v F*, *S v I*, 1931 *I v S*, 1932 *S v SA*, *S v I*, 1933 *I v S*, 1934 *S v I*
Cunningham, J G (Scotland) 1913 *W v I*, 1921 *F v I*
Cuny, Dr A (France) 1976 *W v S*
Curnow, J (Canada) 1976 *US v F*
Currey, F I (England) 1887 *S v W*

Dallas, J D (Scotland) 1905 *W v NZ*, 1908 *I v W*, 1909 *W v E*, *I v E*, 1910 *E v W*, *I v W*, 1911 *I v E*, 1912 *I v W*
D'Arcy, D P (Ireland) 1967 *E v F*, *E v S*, *F v W*, *F v R*, 1968 *E v W*, *S v E*, *F v SA*, 1969 *E v F*, *W v E*, 1970 *W v S*, 1971 *W v E*, 1973 *F v NZ*, *F v W*, *F v R*, 1975 *E v S*, *F v Arg*, *W v A*
David, I (Wales) 1938 *E v S*, 1939 *S v E*, 1947 *E v S*, 1952 *S v F*, *I v S*, *E v I*, 1953 *S v I*, 1954 *S v F*, *E v NZ*, *S v NZ*, *F v NZ*, *F v E*, 1955 *I v F*, 1956 *F v E*
Davidson, I G (Ireland) 1911 *S v W*
Day, H L V (England) 1934 *S v W*
Day, P W (South Africa) 1903 *SA v GB*
Dedet, L (France) 1906 *F v NZ*, *F v E*
De Bruyn, C J (South Africa) 1969 *SA v A*, 1974 *SA v BI* (2)
Delany, M G (Ireland) 1899 *S v W*, 1900 *S v E*
Dickie, A I (Scotland) 1954 *F v I*, *E v I*, *W v F*, 1955 *I v E*, *W v I*, 1956 *E v I*, *I v W*, 1957 *W v E*, *I v E*, 1958 *W v A*, *W v F*
Dodds, J (Ireland) 1898 *S v E*
Domercq, G (France) 1972 *S v NZ*, 1973 *W v E*, 1976 *E v W*, 1977 *S v W*, 1978 *I v W*
Donaldson, S (Ireland) 1937 *S v E*
Donaldson, W P (Scotland) 1903 *SA v GB*
Don Wauchope, A R (Scotland) 1889 *W v I*, 1890 *E v I*, 1893 *I v E*
Doocey, T F (New Zealand) 1976 *NZ v I*, 1983 *E v S*, *F v W*
Douglas, W M (Wales) 1891 *I v E*, 1894 *E v I*, 1896 *S v E*, 1903 *E v S*
Doulcet, J-C (France) 1989 *S v W*
Dowling, M J (Ireland) 1947 *S v W*, 1950 *W v S*, *S v E*, *W v F*, 1951 *W v E*, *S v W*, *F v W*, *E v S*, *S v SA*, 1952 *W v S*, *F v SA*, *S v E*, 1953 *W v E*, *E v S*, 1954 *E v W*, 1955 *S v W*, 1956 *S v F*, *S v E*
Downes, A D (New Zealand) 1913 *NZ v A*
Doyle, O E (Ireland) 1984 *W v S*, *R v S*, *W v A*, 1987 *E v S*, 1988 *F v E*, *Arg v F* (2), *W v WS*, 1989 *F v S*, 1990 *F v E*
Drennan, V (Ireland) 1914 *W v S*
Duffy, B (New Zealand) 1977 *NZ v BI*
Duncan, J (New Zealand) 1908 *NZ v AW*
Durand, C (France) 1969 *F v S*, 1970 *I v S*, 1971 *E v S*

Eckhold, A E (New Zealand) 1923 *NZ v A*
Elliott, H B (England) 1955 *F v S*, *F v It*, 1956 *I v S*
Engelbrecht, Dr G K (South Africa) 1964 *SA v W*
Evans, F T (New Zealand) 1904 *NZ v GB*
Evans, G (England) 1905 *E v NZ*, 1908 *W v A*
Evans, W J (Wales) 1958 *I v A*, *F v E*
Farquhar, A B (New Zealand) 1961 *NZ v F* (3), 1962 *NZ v A* (2), 1964 *NZ v A*
Faull, J W (Wales) 1936 *E v NZ*, *S v I*, 1937 *E v I*
Ferguson, C F (Australia) 1963 *A v E*, 1965 *A v SA*, 1968 *A v F*, 1969 *A v W*, 1971 *A v SA* (2)
Ferguson, P (Australia) 1914 *A v NZ*
Findlay, D G (Scotland) 1895 *I v E*, 1896 *E v W*, *E v I*, 1897 *I v E*, 1898 *E v I*, 1899 *I v E*, 1900 *E v I*, 1901 *I v E*, 1907 *I v E*
Findlay, J C (Scotland) 1902 *I v W*, 1903 *I v E*, 1904 *E v W*, *I v W*, 1905 *I v NZ*, 1911 *I v F*
Finlay, A K (Australia) 1961 *A v Fj*, 1962 *A v NZ*
Fitzgerald, K V J (Australia) 1985 *I v F*, *W v I*, *NZ v E* (2), *Arg v NZ* (2), 1987 [*I v W*, *E v US*, *NZ v W*, *NZ v F*], 1988 *Fj v E*, 1989 *S v I*, *W v E*, *SA v Wld* (2)
Fleming, G R (Scotland) 1879 *S v E*
Fleming, J M (Scotland) 1985 *I v E*, 1986 *A v Arg* (2), 1987 *E v F*, [*A v J*, *Fj v Arg*], *F v R*, 1989 *F v W*
Fleury, A L (New Zealand) 1959 *NZ v BI*
Fong, A S (New Zealand) 1946 *NZ v A*, 1950 *NZ v BI*
Fordham, R J (Australia) 1986 *E v W*, *F v I*, *Arg v F* (2), 1987 [*NZ v It*, *F v R*]
Fornès, E (Argentina) 1954 *Arg v F* (2)
Forsyth, R A (New Zealand) 1958 *NZ v A*
Frames, P R (South Africa) 1891 *SA v GB*

Francis, R C (New Zealand) 1984 *E v A*, *I v A*, 1985 *Arg v F* (2), 1986 *W v S*, *S v E*, *WS v W*
Freeman, W L (Ireland) 1932 *E v SA*
Freethy, A E (Wales) 1923 *F v E*, 1924 *E v F*, *I v NZ*, *F v US*, 1925 *E v NZ*, *I v S*, *S v E*, *F v E*, 1926 *E v F*, 1927 *F v E*, 1928 *I v E*, *E v F*, 1929 *E v I*, *F v E*, 1930 *I v E*, *E v F*, 1931 *E v I*, *F v E*
Fright, W H (New Zealand) 1956 *NZ v SA* (2)
Frood, J (New Zealand) 1952 *NZ v A*
Fry, H A (England) 1945 *F v B*
Furness, D C (Australia) 1952 *A v Fj* (2), 1954 *A v Fj*

Gadney, C H (England) 1935 *S v NZ*, *W v NZ*, 1936 *S v W*, *W v I*, 1937 *W v S*, 1938 *S v W*, *S v I*, 1939 *I v S*, 1940 *F v B*, 1946 *F v B*, 1947 *F v S*, *S v I*, 1948 *F v A*, *I v S*
Games, J (Wales) 1909 *E v A*, 1913 *E v F*, 1914 *F v E*
Gardiner, F (Ireland) 1912 *S v E*
Gardner, J A (Scotland) 1884 *E v W*, 1887 *W v I*
Garling, A F (Australia) 1981 *A v NZ* (2)
Garrard, W G (New Zealand) 1899 *A v GB*
Gilchrist, N R (New Zealand) 1936 *M v A*
Gillespie, J I (Scotland) 1907 *W v E*, 1911 *W v E*
Gilliard, P (England) 1902 *W v S*
Gillies, C R (New Zealand) 1958 *NZ v A* (2), 1959 *NZ v BI* (2)
Gilliland, R W (Ireland) 1964 *It v F*, 1965 *S v W*, *E v F*, *F v W*, *F v R*, 1966 *E v W*, 1967 *F v A*
Gillmore, W N (England) 1956 *F v Cz*, 1958 *I v S*, *It v F*
Glasgow, O B (Ireland) 1953 *F v S*, *F v W*, 1954 *S v E*, 1955 *W v E*, *F v W*
Goulding, W J (Ireland) 1882 *I v W*
Gourlay, I W (South Africa) 1976 *SA v NZ*
Gouws, Dr J (South Africa) 1977 *SA v Wld*
Greenlees, Dr J R C (Scotland) 1913 *I v E*, 1914 *E v W*
Grierson, T F E (Scotland) 1970 *I v SA*, 1971 *F v R*, 1972 *F v E*, 1973 *W v I*, 1975 *E v F*
Griffin, Dr (South Africa) 1891 *SA v GB*
Griffiths, A A (New Zealand) 1946 *M v A*, 1952 *NZ v A*
Guillemard, A G (England) 1877 *E v I*, 1878 *E v S*, 1879 *E v I*, 1880 *E v S*, 1881 *I v E*, *E v W*
Gurdon, E T (England) 1898 *I v S*, 1899 *S v I*

Hamilton, F M (Ireland) 1902 *S v E*
Harland, R W (Ireland) 1922 *E v W*, 1925 *W v F*, 1926 *F v W*, 1928 *W v E*, *S v W*, *F v W*, 1929 *E v W*, 1931 *W v F*
Harnett, G H (England) 1896 *W v S*, 1901 *S v I*, *W v I*
Harris, G A (Ireland) 1910 *S v F*
Harrison, G L (New Zealand) 1980 *Fj v A*, 1981 *A v F*, 1983 *A v US*, *F v A* (2) 1984 *Fj v A*
Harrison, H C (England) 1922 *F v S*
Hartley, A (England) 1900 *W v S*
Haslett, F W (Ireland) 1934 *W v E*, *E v S*, 1935 *E v W*, *W v S*, 1936 *W v E*
Haydon, N V (Australia) 1957 *A v NZ*
Helliwell, D (England) 1926 *S v W*, 1927 *W v A*, 1929 *W v S*, 1930 *F v S*, *W v I*, *G v F*, *F v W*
Herbert, D (Wales) 1883 *W v E*
Herck, M (Romania) 1938 *F v G*
High, C J (England) 1987 *F v W*, *W v US*
Hilditch, S R (Ireland) 1984 *S v A*, 1985 *W v Fj*, 1987 [*R v Z*, *S v R*], 1988 *E v W*, 1989 *E v F*, *NZ v A*, *S v R*
Hill, A (England) 1902 *I v S*
Hill, E D (New Zealand) 1949 *NZ v A*
Hill, G R (England) 1883 *S v W*, 1884 *S v I*, *W v I*, 1885 *S v W*, 1886 *S v I*, 1887 *W v E*, *I v S*, 1888 *I v W*, 1889 *E v M*, 1891 *I v S*, 1893 *I v S*
Hill, W W (Australia) 1913 *US v NZ*
Hinton, W P (Ireland) 1921 *S v F*
Hodgson, J (England) 1892 *W v S*
Hofmeyr, E W (South Africa) 1949 *SA v NZ* (2), 1961 *SA v A*, 1963 *SA v A*
Hollander, S (New Zealand) 1930 *NZ v BI* (3), 1931 *NZ v A*
Hollis, M (England) 1931 *F v G*
Holmes, E (England) 1931 *W v SA*, 1932 *W v I*
Holmes, E B (England) 1892 *I v W*, 1894 *W v S*, 1895 *S v W*, *W v I*, 1896 *I v S*, *I v W*, 1897 *S v I*
Horak, A T (South Africa) 1938 *SA v BI*
Hosie, A M (Scotland) 1973 *I v E*, 1974 *F v I*, 1975 *W v E*, 1976 *E v I*, *F v A*, 1977 *F v E*, *I v F*, 1979 *W v I*, *I v E*, 1980 *W v F*, *F v I*, 1981 *E v F*, *R v NZ*, 1982 *E v*

Neilson, A E (New Zealand) 1921 *NZ v SA* (2)
Neser, V H (South Africa) 1924 *SA v BI*, 1928 *SA v NZ* (4), 1933 *SA v A* (4)
Neville, Dr W C (Ireland) 1882 *I v E*
Nicholls, E G (Wales) 1909 *E v S*
Nicholls, F (England) 1904 *W v S*
Nicholson, G W (New Zealand) 1913 *NZ v A*
Noon, O (Argentina) 1949 *Arg v F*
Norling, C (Wales) 1978 *I v NZ*, 1979 *E v S*, 1980 *F v E*, 1981 *I v F*, *NZ v SA* (2), *F v NZ*, 1982 *I v S*, 1983 *A v Arg* (2), 1984 *F v I*, 1985 *E v S*, 1986 *E v I*, 1987 *I v F*, [*C v Tg*, *F v Fj*], 1988 *E v I*, *R v F*, 1989 *NZ v Arg* (2), 1990 *I v S*
Nugent, G P (Ireland) 1888 *I v E*

Oakley, L D (South Africa) 1924 *SA v BI*
O'Callaghan, B J (Australia) 1959 *A v BI*
O'Leary, J (Australia) 1958 *A v M*

Palmade, F (France) 1973 *F v S* (R), *S v W*, 1974 *I v S*, 1975 *I v E*, 1977 *I v E*, 1978 *E v I*, 1979 *S v W*, 1980 *SA v BI* (2), 1981 *W v I*, *SA v I* (2), 1982 *E v W*, 1983 *NZ v BI* (2), 1985 *W v E*, 1986 *I v S*
Parfitt, V J (Wales) 1953 *E v F*, 1954 *I v S*
Parkes, Dr N M (England) 1958 *W v S*, *F v A*, *I v W*, *F v I*, 1959 *F v It*, *F v W*, 1960 *W v F*, 1961 *F v W*, 1962 *W v S*, *I v S*
Parkinson, F G M (New Zealand) 1955 *NZ v A*, 1956 *NZ v SA* (2)
Paton, R J (New Zealand) 1931 *M v A*
Pattinson, K A (England) 1973 *F v S*, *W v A*, 1974 *I v W*, *R v F*, 1975 *F v W*, 1976 *S v F*
Pattisson, A S (Scotland) 1883 *E v S*
Pauling, T G (Australia) 1904 *A v GB* (2), 1914 *A v NZ*
Peake, J F (New Zealand) 1923 *NZ v A*
Pearce, T N (England) 1948 *F v I*, *W v S*, 1949 *F v S*, *I v F*, *W v I*, 1950 *F v I*, *I v S*, 1951 *F v S*, *I v F*, *S v I*, 1952 *F v I*
Peard, L J (Wales) 1989 *I v E*
Petrie, A G (Scotland) 1882 *S v I*
Phillips, T H (Wales) 1936 *E v S*
Phillips, W D (Wales) 1887 *I v E*, 1889 *I v S*
Pontin, A C (USA) 1976 *US v A*
Pozzi, S (Italy) 1957 *F v R*, 1960 *R v F*
Pretorius, N F (South Africa) 1938 *SA v BI*
Price, F G (Wales) 1963 *I v F*
Prideaux, L (England) 1980 *W v S*, *I v W*, *SAm v SA* (2), 1981 *S v I*, *NZ v SA*, 1985 *F v S*
Priest, T E (England) 1952 *It v F*, 1953 *I v F*
Pring, J P G (New Zealand) 1966 *NZ v BI*, 1967 *NZ v A*, 1968 *NZ v F*, 1971 *NZ v BI* (4), 1972 *NZ v A*
Purcell, N M (Ireland) 1927 *S v E*

Quittenton, R C (England) 1977 *Arg v F* (2), 1978 *W v NZ*, 1979 *I v F*, *F v S*, *S v NZ*, 1981 *S v A*, 1982 *NZ v A*, 1983 *S v W*, *F v R*, 1984 *A v NZ* (2), 1986 *R v S*, 1987 *S v I*, [*Arg v It*, *NZ v Arg*], 1988 *I v S*, 1989 *W v I*

Rainie, R D (Scotland) 1890 *E v W*, 1891 *W v E*, 1894 *I v W*
Rea, M D M (Ireland) 1978 *R v F*, 1981 *S v R*, 1982 *F v E*
Reading, L S (England) 1912 *US v A*
Reilly, J R (Australia) 1972 *A v F*
Richards, A (Wales) 1980 *R v F*, 1981 *A v F*, 1982 *E v A*, 1983 *F v S*
Richards, A R (South Africa) 1896 *SA v GB*
Robbertse, P (South Africa) 1967 *SA v F*, 1969 *SA v A*, 1970 *SA v NZ* (2)
Roberts, E (Wales) 1924 *F v S*
Roberts, R A (England) 1924 *F v W*
Robertson, W A (Scotland) 1920 *E v F*, *I v E*
Robin, P (France) 1988 *It v A*, 1989 *S v Fj*, 1990 *E v I*
Robinson, H L (Ireland) 1882 *E v S*
Robson, C F (New Zealand) 1963 *NZ v E*
Roca, J (France) 1937 *F v It*
Rowlands, K (Wales) 1980 *SA v SAm* (2), 1981 *F v S*, 1982 *S v E*, 1986 *SA v Cv* (4)
Rowsell, A (England) 1891 *W v I*
Royds, P M R (England) 1921 *W v F*, 1923 *F v I*

Rutherford, C F (Scotland) 1908 *F v E*
Rutter, A (England) 1876 *E v S*

St Guilhem, J (France) 1974 *S v E*, 1975 *W v I*
Sanson, N R (Scotland) 1974 *W v F*, *F v SA*, 1975 *I v P*(C), *SA v F* (2), *F v R*, 1976 *I v A*, *I v W*, 1977 *W v I*, 1978 *F v E*, *E v W*, *E v NZ*, 1979 *E v NZ*
Schoeman, J P J (South Africa) 1968 *SA v BI*
Schofield, T D (Wales) 1907 *E v S*, 1908 *E v I*, 1910 *E v I*, 1911 *E v S*, 1912 *E v I*, *F v E*, 1913 *E v S*, 1914 *E v I*, *S v E*, 1920 *E v S*, 1921 *E v I*, 1922 *S v I*
Schwoenberg, M (Germany) 1938 *R v F*
Scott, J M B (Scotland) 1923 *E v W*
Scott, R L (Scotland) 1927 *F v I*, *E v W*
Scriven, G (Ireland) 1884 *E v S*
Short, J A (Scotland) 1979 *F v R*, 1982 *I v W*
Simpson, J W (Scotland) 1906 *I v W*
Simpson, R L (New Zealand) 1913 *NZ v A*, 1921 *NZ v A*, 1923 *NZ v A*
Slabber, M J (South Africa) 1955 *SA v BI*, 1960 *SA v NZ*
Smith, J A (Scotland) 1892 *E v I*, 1894 *E v W*, 1895 *W v E*
Stanton, R W (South Africa) 1910 *SA v GB* (3)
Steyn, M (Germany) 1932 *G v F*
Stirling, B W (Ireland) 1989 *E v Fj*
Strasheim, Dr E A (South Africa) 1958 *SA v F*, 1960 *SA v S*, *SA v NZ*, 1962 *SA v BI* (2), 1964 *SA v F*, 1967 *SA v F*, 1968 *SA v BI*
Strasheim, Dr J J (South Africa) 1938 *SA v BI*
Strydom, S (South Africa) 1979 *Arg v A* (2), 1982 *SA v SAm*, 1985 *S v I*, *F v W*, 1986 *F v NZ* (2)
Sturrock, J C (Scotland) 1921 *E v W*, *F v E*, 1922 *W v I*
Sullivan, G (New Zealand) 1950 *NZ v BI*
Sutherland, F E (New Zealand) 1925 *NZ v A*, 1928 *NZ v A* (2), 1930 *NZ v BI*
Swainston, E (England) 1878 *I v E*

Tagnini, S (Italy) 1968 *Cz v F*
Taylor, A R (New Zealand) 1968 *NZ v SA* (R), 1972 *NZ v A*
Taylor, J A S (Scotland) 1957 *W v I*, 1960 *E v W*, *F v E*, *W v SA*, 1961 *F v It*, 1962 *E v W*, *F v I*, *I v W*
Tennent, J M (Scotland) 1920 *I v F*, 1921 *I v W*, 1922 *W v E*, *E v F*, *I v F*, *I v E*, 1923 *I v W*
Thomas, C (Wales) 1979 *S v I*, 1980 *E v I*
Thomas, C G P (Wales) 1977 *F v NZ*, 1978 *S v F*, *F v I*
Tierney, A T (Australia) 1957 *A v NZ*, 1958 *A v M*, 1959 *A v BI*
Tindill, E W T (New Zealand) 1950 *NZ v BI* (2), 1955 *NZ v A*
Titcomb, M H (England) 1966 *W v S*, 1967 *W v I*, *W v NZ*, 1968 *I v W*, *S v A*, 1971 *S v W*, *E v P* (C), 1972 *W v F*
Tolhurst, H A (Australia) 1951 *A v NZ* (2)
Tomalin, L C (Australia) 1947 *A v NZ*, 1949 *A v M* (2) 1950 *A v BI*
Treharne, G J (Wales) 1960 *I v SA*, 1961 *E v SA*, *I v E*, *I v F*, 1963 *S v I*
Trigg, J A F (England) 1981 *F v R*, 1982 *S v F*, 1983 *W v I*
Tulloch, J T (Scotland) 1906 *I v SA*, *E v SA*, 1907 *I v E*, 1908 *E v W*, 1912 *E v W*, 1913 *E v SA*, 1914 *I v W*, 1920 *W v E*, 1924 *W v I*
Turnbull, A (Scotland) 1898 *I v W*, 1899 *W v E*, *W v I*, 1900 *E v W*, *I v W*, 1901 *W v E*

Vanderfield, Dr I R (Australia) 1956 *A v SA*, 1958 *A v M*, 1961 *A v Fj* (2), *A v F*, 1962 *A v NZ*, 1966 *A v BI*, 1967 *A v I*, 1968 *A v NZ*, 1970 *A v S*, 1971 *A v SA*, 1973 *A v Tg*, 1974 *A v NZ* (2)
Van der Horst, A W (South Africa) 1933 *SA v A*
Van der Merwe, A (South Africa) 1936 *G v F*
Vile, T H (Wales) 1923 *S v F*, *E v I*, *I v S*, *S v E*, 1924 *I v E*, *S v I*, *E v S*, 1925 *E v I*, 1927 *E v I*, 1928, *E v A*, *E v S*, 1931 *F v I*

Waldron, C A (Australia) 1986 *F v R*, 1987 *A v SK*
Waldron, H (England) 1957 *F v It*
Walsh, L (New Zealand) 1949 *NZ v A*
Walters, D G (Wales) 1959 *F v S*, *I v E*, *E v S*, *I v F*, 1960 *S v F*, *E v I*, *I v S*, *F v I*, 1961 *F v SA*, *E v F*, 1962 *E v I*, *F v E*, 1963 *E v S*, *F v R*, 1964 *E v I*, *F v E*, *I v S*,

305

A sad moment for Andrew Kembery of Neath as Clive Norling points to the dressing-room during the Schweppes/WRU Cup final.

WORLD INTERNATIONAL RECORDS

Both team and individual records are for official International matches played by full members of the International Board, up to 30 April 1990.

TEAM RECORDS

Highest score – 74
New Zealand (74-13) v Fiji 1987
   Christchurch

Biggest winning margin – 64
New Zealand (70-6) v Italy 1987 Auckland

Most tries in an international – 13
England v Wales 1881 Blackheath
New Zealand v United States 1913 Berkeley
France v Romania 1924 Paris
France v Zimbabwe 1987 Auckland

Most conversions in an international – 10
New Zealand v Fiji 1987 Christchurch

Most penalty goals in an international – 7
South Africa v France 1975 Pretoria

**Most consecutive international
   victories – 17**
New Zealand between 1965 and 1969

**Most consecutive internationals
   undefeated – 19**
New Zealand between 1987 and 1989

**Most points in an international
   series – 109**
New Zealand v Argentina (2 matches)
   1989 in New Zealand

Most tries in an international series – 18
New Zealand v Wales (2 matches) 1988
   in New Zealand

**Most points in Five Nations
Championship in a season – 102**
Wales 1975-76

**Most tries in Five Nations
Championship in a season – 21**
Wales 1909-10

**Most points on an overseas tour
(all matches) – 868**
New Zealand to B Isles/France
   (33 matches) 1905-06

**Most tries on an overseas tour
(all matches) – 215**
New Zealand to B Isles/France
   (33 matches) 1905-06

**Biggest win on a major tour
(all matches)**
117-6 New Zealand v S Australia 1974
   Adelaide

INDIVIDUAL RECORDS
including appearances for British Isles, shown in brackets

Most capped player
C M H Gibson (Ireland) 81(12)[1]1964-79
in individual positions
Full-back
S Blanco (France) 63[2] 1980-90
Wing
K J Jones (Wales) 47(3)[3] 1947-57
Centre (includes 2nd five-eighth)
P Sella (France) 60[4] 1982-90
Fly-half (includes 1st five-eighth)
J W Kyle (Ireland) 52(6) 1947-58
Scrum-half
G O Edwards (Wales) 63(10) 1967-78
Prop
P A Orr (Ireland) 59(1) 1976-87
Hooker
C T Deans (Scotland) 52 1978-87
Lock
W J McBride (Ireland) 80(17) 1962-75

Flanker
J F Slattery (Ireland) 65(4) 1970-84
No 8
T M Davies (Wales) 46(8)[5] 1969-76
[1]*Gibson played 48 of his matches at centre, 29 at fly-half, and 4 on the wing.*
[2]*Blanco has also played 12 times as a wing. J P R Williams, 63 caps in all, played once as a flanker.*
[3]*T G R Davies (Wales), 51(5), won 39 caps as a wing, 12 as a centre and Campese, 48 caps, has won 37 as a wing.*
[4]*Sella has also played 6 times on the wing and once at full-back. R Bertranne, 69 caps in all, played 17 times as a wing.*
[5]*Several French utility forwards have won more caps than Davies, but none has played as frequently at No 8*

Most consecutive internationals for a country – 53
G O Edwards (Wales) 1967-78

Most internationals as captain – 34
J-P Rives (France) 1979-84

Most points in internationals – 456
M P Lynagh (Australia) (36 matches) 1984-89

Most points in an international – 30
D Camberabero (France) v Zimbabwe 1987 Auckland

Most tries in internationals – 34
D I Campese (Australia) (48 matches) 1982-89

Most tries in an international – 5
G C Lindsay (Scotland) v Wales 1887 Edinburgh
D Lambert (England) v France 1907 Richmond
R Underwood (England) v Fiji 1989 Twickenham

Most conversions in internationals – 80
M P Lynagh (Australia) (36 matches) 1984-89

Most conversions in an international – 10
G J Fox (New Zealand) v Fiji 1987 Christchurch

Most dropped goals in internationals – 15
J-P Lescarboura (France) (27 matches) 1982-88

Most dropped goals in an international – 3
P Albaladejo (France) v Ireland 1960 Paris
P F Hawthorne (Australia) v England 1967 Twickenham
H E Botha (South Africa) v S America 1980 Durban
H E Botha (South Africa) v Ireland 1981 Durban
J-P Lescarboura (France) v England 1985 Twickenham
J-P Lescarboura (France) v New Zealand 1986 Christchurch

Most penalty goals in internationals – 85
M P Lynagh (Australia) 36 matches 1984-89

Most penalty goals in an international – 6
D B Clarke (NZ) v B Isles 1959 Dunedin
G R Bosch (SA) v France 1975 Pretoria
J-M Aguirre (France) v Argentina 1977 Buenos Aires
G Evans (Wales) v France 1982 Cardiff
S O Campbell (Ireland) v Scotland 1982 Dublin
*K J Crowley (NZ) v England 1985 Christchurch
C R Andrew (England) v Wales 1986 Twickenham
* A G Hastings (Scotland) v France 1986 Murrayfield
M P Lynagh (Australia) v France 1986 Sydney
G J Fox (NZ) v Argentina 1987 Wellington
G J Fox (NZ) v Scotland 1987 Christchurch
M P Lynagh (Australia) v England 1988 Brisbane
on international debut

Fastest player to 100 points in internationals
G J Fox (New Zealand) in his 6th match

Fastest player to 200 points in internationals
G J Fox (New Zealand) in his 13th match

Fastest player to 300 points in internationals
G J Fox (New Zealand) in his 18th match

Most points in Five Nations Championship in a season – 54
J-P Lescarboura (France) (4 appearances)
  1983-84

Most tries in Five Nations Championship in a season – 8
C N Lowe (England) (4 appearances)
  1913-14
I S Smith (Scotland) (4 appearances)
  1924-25

Tries in each match of a Five Nations Championship
H C Catcheside (England) 1923-24
A C Wallace (Scotland) 1924-25
P Estève (France) 1982-83
P Sella (France) 1985-86

Most penalty goals in Five Nations Championship in a season – 16
P H Thorburn (Wales) (4 appearances)
  1985-86

Most conversions in Five Nations Championship in a season – 11
J Bancroft (Wales) (4 appearances)
  1908-09

Most dropped goals in Five Nations Championship in a season – 5
G Camberabero (France) (3 appearances)
  1966-67
J-P Lescarboura (France) dropped a goal in each Championship match 1983-84, a feat never performed before.

Most points on an overseas tour – 230
W J Wallace (NZ) (25 appearances) in
  B Isles/France 1905-06

Most tries on an overseas tour – 42
J Hunter (NZ) (23 appearances) in
  B Isles/France 1905-06

Most points in any match on tour – 43
R M Deans (NZ) v South Australia 1984
  Adelaide

Most tries in any match on tour – 8
T R Heeps (NZ) v Northern NSW 1962
P Estève scored 8 for France v East Japan in 1984, but this was not on a major tour

---

PARTNERSHIP RECORDS
Centre threequarters
B J Mullin and M J Kiernan (Ireland) 21
Half-backs
J Y Rutherford and R J Laidlaw
  (Scotland) 35
Front row
R Paparemborde, A Paco and G Cholley
  (France) 21
Second row
A J Martin and G A D Wheel (Wales) 27
Back row
J Matheu, G Basquet and J Prat (France) 22

INTERNATIONAL TOURS SINCE 1945
(*up to 30 April 1990*)

*Indicates replacement during tour, throughout this section

BRITISH ISLES TEAMS TO AUSTRALIA AND NEW ZEALAND

1950

Full record	Played 29	Won 22	Lost 6	Drawn 1	Points for 570	Against 214
in New Zealand	Played 23	Won 17	Lost 5	Drawn 1	Points for 420	Against 162
in Australia	Played 6	Won 5	Lost 1	Drawn 0	Points for 150	Against 52

International record

v New Zealand	Played 4	Lost 3	Drawn 1
v Australia	Played 2	Won 2	

International details

v New Zealand	May 27	New Zealand 9	British Isles 9	(Dunedin)
	Jun 10	New Zealand 8	British Isles 0	(Christchurch)
	Jul 1	New Zealand 6	British Isles 3	(Wellington)
	Jul 29	New Zealand 11	British Isles 8	(Auckland)
v Australia	Aug 19	Australia 6	British Isles 19	(Brisbane)
	Aug 26	Australia 3	British Isles 24	(Sydney)

Players

Full-backs: G W Norton (Bective Rangers), W B Cleaver (Cardiff), B Lewis Jones* (Devonport Services and Llanelli)
Threequarters: D W C Smith (London Scottish), M F Lane (U C Cork), K J Jones (Newport), M C Thomas (Devonport Services and Newport), B L Williams (Cardiff), J Matthews (Cardiff), N J Henderson (Queen's U, Belfast), R Macdonald (Edinburgh U)
Half-backs: J W Kyle (Queen's U, Belfast), I Preece (Coventry), W R Willis (Cardiff), G Rimmer (Waterloo), A W Black (Edinburgh U)
Forwards: V G Roberts (Penryn), J S McCarthy (Dolphin), R T Evans (Newport), J W McKay (Queen's U, Belfast), J R G Stephens (Neath), E R John (Neath), P W Kininmonth (Oxford U and Richmond), J E Nelson (Malone), D J Hayward (Newbridge), J D Robins (Birkenhead Park), T Clifford (Young Munster), C Davies (Cardiff), G M Budge (Edinburgh Wanderers), D M Davies (Somerset Police), Dr K D Mullen (Old Belvedere)
Captain Dr K D Mullen **Manager** Surgeon-Captain (D) L B Osborne (RN)
Assistant Manager E L Savage

1959

Full record	Played 31	Won 25	Lost 6	Drawn 0	Points for 756	Against 336
in Australia	Played 6	Won 5	Lost 1	Drawn 0	Points for 174	Against 70
in New Zealand	Played 25	Won 20	Lost 5	Drawn 0	Points for 582	Against 266

International record

v Australia	Played 2	Won 2	
v New Zealand	Played 4	Won 1	Lost 3

International details

v Australia	Jun 6	Australia 6	British Isles 17	(Brisbane)
	Jun 13	Australia 3	British Isles 24	(Sydney)
v New Zealand	Jul 18	New Zealand 18	British Isles 17	(Dunedin)
	Aug 15	New Zealand 11	British Isles 8	(Wellington)
	Aug 29	New Zealand 22	British Isles 8	(Christchurch)
	Sep 19	New Zealand 6	British Isles 9	(Auckland)

Players

Full-backs: T J Davies (Llanelli), K J F Scotland (Cambridge U)
Threequarters: J R C Young (Oxford U), P B Jackson (Coventry),
A J F O'Reilly (Old Belvedere), N H Brophy (UC Dublin), M J Price (Pontypool),
W M Patterson* (Sale), D Hewitt (Queen's U, Belfast), J Butterfield (Northampton),
M C Thomas (Newport), G H Waddell (Cambridge U)
Half-backs: J P Horrocks-Taylor* (Leicester), A B W Risman (Manchester U),
M A F English (Limerick Bohemians), R E G Jeeps (Northampton),
S Coughtrie (Edinburgh Acads), A A Mulligan* (Wanderers, London Irish)
Forwards: B V Meredith (Newport), R Prosser (Pontypool), A R Dawson (Wanderers),
H F McLeod (Hawick), G K Smith (Kelso), S Millar (Ballymena),
B G M Wood (Garryowen), R H Williams (Llanelli), W A Mulcahy (UC Dublin),
W R Evans (Cardiff), R W D Marques (Harlequins), A Ashcroft (Waterloo),
N A A Murphy (Cork Constitution), H J Morgan (Abertillery), J Faull (Swansea)
Captain A R Dawson **Manager** A Wilson **Assistant Manager** O B Glasgow

1966

Full record	Played 33	Won 22	Lost 8	Drawn 3	Points for 502	Against 329
in Australia	Played 8	Won 7	Lost 0	Drawn 1	Points for 202	Against 48
in New Zealand	Played 25	Won 15	Lost 8	Drawn 2	Points for 300	Against 281
International record						
v Australia	Played 2	Won 2				
v New Zealand	Played 4	Lost 4				

International details

v Australia	May 28	Australia	8	British Isles 11	(Sydney)
	Jun 4	Australia	0	British Isles 31	(Brisbane)
v New Zealand	Jul 16	New Zealand 20		British Isles 3	(Dunedin)
	Aug 6	New Zealand 16		British Isles 12	(Wellington)
	Aug 27	New Zealand 19		British Isles 6	(Christchurch)
	Sep 10	New Zealand 24		British Isles 11	(Auckland)

Players

Full-backs: D Rutherford (Gloucester), S Wilson (London Scottish), T G Price* (Llanelli)
Threequarters: D I E Bebb (Swansea), A J W Hinshelwood (London Scottish),
K F Savage (Northampton), S J Watkins (Newport), D K Jones (Cardiff),
F P K Bresnihan* (UC Dublin), M P Weston (Durham City),
C W McFadyean (Moseley), J C Walsh (Sunday's Well)
Half-backs: C M H Gibson (Cambridge U), D Watkins (Newport),
A R Lewis (Abertillery), R M Young (Queen's U, Belfast)
Forwards: R A Lamont (Instonians), A E I Pask (Abertillery),
N A A Murphy (Cork Constitution), D Grant (Hawick), G J Prothero (Bridgend),
J W Telfer (Melrose), W J McBride (Ballymena), M J Campbell-Lamerton
(London Scottish), W D Thomas (Llanelli), B Price (Newport), R J McLoughlin
(Gosforth), D L Powell (Northampton), C H Norris (Cardiff), D Williams
(Ebbw Vale), K W Kennedy (CIYMS), F A L Laidlaw (Melrose)
Captain M J Campbell-Lamerton **Manager** D J O'Brien
Assistant Manager J D Robins

1971

Full record	Played 26	Won 23	Lost 2	Drawn 1	Points for 580	Against 231
in Australia	Played 2	Won 1	Lost 1	Drawn 0	Points for 25	Against 27
in New Zealand	Played 24	Won 22	Lost 1	Drawn 1	Points for 555	Against 204
International record						
v New Zealand	Played 4	Won 2	Lost 1	Drawn 1		

International details

v New Zealand	Jun 26	New Zealand 3	British Isles 9	(Dunedin)
	Jul 10	New Zealand 22	British Isles 12	(Christchurch)
	Jul 31	New Zealand 3	British Isles 13	(Wellington)
	Aug 14	New Zealand 14	British Isles 14	(Auckland)

Players

Full-backs: R Hiller (Harlequins), J P R Williams (London Welsh)
Threequarters: D J Duckham (Coventry), A G Biggar (London Scottish), T G R Davies (London Welsh), J C Bevan (Cardiff Coll of Education), A J Lewis (Ebbw Vale), J S Spencer (Headingley), S J Dawes (London Welsh), C W W Rea (Headingley)
Half-backs: C M H Gibson (North of Ireland), B John (Cardiff), G O Edwards (Cardiff), R Hopkins (Maesteg)
Forwards: T M Davies (London Welsh), P J Dixon (Harlequins), J Taylor (London Welsh), J F Slattery (U C Dublin), M L Hipwell (Terenure Coll), D L Quinnell (Llanelli), R J Arneil* (Leicester), W D Thomas (Llanelli), W J McBride (Ballymena), M G Roberts (London Welsh), G L Brown (West of Scotland), T G Evans* (London Welsh), A B Carmichael (West of Scotland), R J McLoughlin (Blackrock Coll), J McLauchlan (Jordanhill Coll), J F Lynch (St Mary's Coll), C B Stevens* (Harlequins and Penzance-Newlyn), J V Pullin (Bristol), F A L Laidlaw (Melrose)
Captain S J Dawes   **Manager** Dr D W C Smith   **Assistant Manager** C R James

1977 (New Zealand and Fiji only)

Full record	Played 26	Won 21	Lost 5	Drawn 0	Points for 607	Against 320
in New Zealand	Played 25	Won 21	Lost 4	Drawn 0	Points for 586	Against 295
in Fiji	Played 1	Won 0	Lost 1	Drawn 0	Points for 21	Against 25

International record

v New Zealand	Played 4	Won 1	Lost 3

International details

v New Zealand	Jun 18	New Zealand 16	British Isles 12	(Wellington)
	Jul 9	New Zealand 9	British Isles 13	(Christchurch)
	Jul 30	New Zealand 19	British Isles 7	(Dunedin)
	Aug 13	New Zealand 10	British Isles 9	(Auckland)

Players

Full-backs: A R Irvine (Heriot's FP), B H Hay (Boroughmuir)
Threequarters: P J Squires (Harrogate), H E Rees (Neath), J J Williams (Llanelli), G L Evans (Newport), C M H Gibson (North of Ireland FC), S P Fenwick (Bridgend), D H Burcher (Newport), I R McGeechan (Headingley)
Half-backs: P Bennett (Llanelli), J D Bevan (Aberavon), D W Morgan (Stewart's Melville FP), D B Williams (Cardiff), A D Lewis* (Cambridge U & London Welsh)
Forwards: W P Duggan (Blackrock Coll), J Squire (Newport), T J Cobner (Pontypool), T P Evans (Swansea), A Neary (Broughton Park), D L Quinnell (Llanelli), G L Brown (West of Scotland), N E Horton (Moseley), A J Martin (Aberavon), M I Keane (Lansdowne), W B Beaumont* (Fylde), F E Cotton (Sale), P A Orr (Old Wesley), G Price (Pontypool), C Williams (Aberavon), A G Faulkner* (Pontypool), R W Windsor (Pontypool), P J Wheeler (Leicester)
Captain P Bennett   **Manager** G Burrell   **Assistant Manager** S J Dawes

1983 (New Zealand only)

Full record	Played 18	Won 12	Lost 6	Drawn 0	Points for 478	Against 276
International record	Played 4	Lost 4				
International details	Jun 4	New Zealand 16	British Isles 12	(Christchurch)		
	Jun 18	New Zealand 9	British Isles 0	(Wellington)		
	Jul 2	New Zealand 15	British Isles 8	(Dunedin)		
	Jul 16	New Zealand 38	British Isles 6	(Auckland)		

Players
Full-backs: H P MacNeill (Oxford U), W H Hare (Leicester), G Evans (Maesteg)
Threequarters: J Carleton (Orrell), G R T Baird (Kelso), T M Ringland (Ballymena),
D G Irwin (Instonians), M J Kiernan (Dolphin), R A Ackerman (London Welsh),
C R Woodward (Leicester)
Half-backs: S O Campbell (Old Belvedere), J Y Rutherford (Selkirk), T D Holmes
(Cardiff), R J Laidlaw (Jedforest), N D Melville* (Wasps), S J Smith* (Sale)
Forwards: S T Jones (Pontypool), I Stephens (Bridgend), G A J McLoughlin* (Shannon),
G Price (Pontypool), I G Milne (Heriot's FP), C T Deans (Hawick), C F Fitzgerald
(St Mary's Coll), S B Boyle (Gloucester), R L Norster (Cardiff), M J Colclough
(Angoulême), D G Lenihan* (Cork Const), S J Bainbridge (Gosforth), J H Calder
(Stewart's-Melville FP), J B O'Driscoll (London Irish), P J Winterbottom (Headingley),
J Squire (Pontypool), N C Jeavons* (Moseley), J R Beattie (Glasgow Acads),
I A M Paxton (Selkirk), E T Butler* (Pontypool)
Captain C F Fitzgerald **Manager** W J McBride **Assistant Manager** J W Telfer

1989 (Australia only)

Full record	Played 12 Won 11 Lost 1 Drawn 0 Points for 360 Against 192			
International record	Played 3 Won 2 Lost 1			
International details	Jul 1	Australia 30	British Isles 12	(Sydney)
	Jul 8	Australia 12	British Isles 19	(Brisbane)
	Jul 15	Australia 18	British Isles 19	(Sydney)

Players
Full-backs: A G Hastings (London Scottish), P W Dods (Gala)
Threequarters: I C Evans (Llanelli), M R Hall (Bridgend), C Oti (Wasps), R Underwood
(Leicester & RAF), J A Devereux (Bridgend), J C Guscott (Bath), S Hastings
(Watsonians), B J Mullin (London Irish)
Half-backs: C M Chalmers (Melrose), P M Dean (St Mary's Coll), C R Andrew* (Wasps),
A Clement* (Swansea), R N Jones (Swansea), G Armstrong (Jedforest)
Forwards: B C Moore (Nottingham), S J Smith (Ballymena), D M B Sole (Edinburgh
Acads), M Griffiths (Bridgend), G J Chilcott (Bath), D Young (Cardiff), D G Lenihan
(Cork Const), W A Dooley (Preston Grasshoppers), P J Ackford (Harlequins),
R L Norster (Cardiff), J Jeffrey (Kelso), R A Robinson (Bath), M C Teague (Gloucester),
D Richards (Leicester), D B White (London Scottish), F Calder (Stewart's-Melville FP)
Captain F Calder **Manager** D C T Rowlands **Coach** I R McGeechan

BRITISH ISLES TEAMS TO SOUTH AFRICA

1955

Full record	Played 24 Won 18 Lost 5 Drawn 1 Points for 418 Against 271			
International record	Played 4 Won 2 Lost 2			
International details	Aug 6	South Africa 22	British Isles 23	(Johannesburg)
	Aug 20	South Africa 25	British Isles 9	(Cape Town)
	Sep 3	South Africa 6	British Isles 9	(Pretoria)
	Sep 24	South Africa 22	British Isles 8	(Port Elizabeth)

Players
Full-backs: A Cameron (Glasgow HSFP), A G Thomas (Llanelli)
Threequarters: A R Smith (Cambridge U), F D Sykes (Northampton),
H Morris (Cardiff), A C Pedlow (Queen's U, Belfast), J Butterfield
(Northampton), W P C Davies (Harlequins), A J F O'Reilly (Old Belvedere),
J P Quinn (New Brighton), G Griffiths* (Cardiff)
Half-backs: C I Morgan (Cardiff), D G S Baker (Old Merchant Taylors),
J E Williams (Old Millhillians), R E G Jeeps (Northampton), T Lloyd (Maesteg)
Forwards: R H Thompson (Instonians), C C Meredith (Neath),
B V Meredith (Newport), H F McLeod (Hawick), W O Williams (Swansea),

R Roe (Lansdowne), T Elliot (Gala), E J S Michie (Aberdeen U),
T E Reid (Garryowen), R H Williams (Llanelli), J T Greenwood (Dunfermline),
R J Robins (Pontypridd), R Higgins (Liverpool), D S Wilson
(Metropolitan Police), R C C Thomas (Swansea)
Captain R H Thompson **Manager** J A E Siggins **Assistant Manager** D E Davies

1962

Full record	Played 24 Won 15 Lost 5 Drawn 4 Points for 351 Against 208			
International record	Played 4 Lost 3 Drawn 1			
International details	Jun 23	South Africa 3	British Isles 3	(Johannesburg)
	Jul 21	South Africa 3	British Isles 0	(Durban)
	Aug 4	South Africa 8	British Isles 3	(Cape Town)
	Aug 25	South Africa 34	British Isles 14	(Bloemfontein)

Players
Full-backs: T J Kiernan (UC Cork), J G Willcox (Oxford U)
Threequarters: N H Brophy (Blackrock), D I E Bebb (Swansea), R C Cowan (Selkirk),
A R Smith (Edinburgh Wands), J M Dee (Hartlepool Rovers), W R Hunter (CIYMS),
M P Weston (Durham City), D K Jones (Llanelli), D Hewitt (Queen's U, Belfast)
Half-backs: R A W Sharp (Oxford U), R E G Jeeps (Northampton), G H Waddell
(London Scottish), A O'Connor (Aberavon), H J C Brown★ (RAF, Blackheath)
Forwards: S Millar (Ballymena), K D Jones (Cardiff), D M D Rollo (Howe of Fife),
T P Wright (Blackheath), B V Meredith (Newport), A E I Pask (Abertillery),
S A M Hodgson (Durham City), M J Campbell-Lamerton (Army, Halifax),
W J McBride (Ballymena), W A Mulcahy (Bohemians), K A Rowlands (Cardiff),
H J Morgan (Abertillery), D P Rogers (Bedford), J Douglas (Stewart's Coll FP),
D Nash (Ebbw Vale), H O Godwin★ (Coventry), G D Davidge★ (Newport)
Captain A R Smith **Manager** Instructor-Commander D B Vaughan RN
Assistant Manager H R McKibbin

1968

Full record	Played 20 Won 15 Lost 4 Drawn 1 Points for 377 Against 181			
International record	Played 4 Lost 3 Drawn 1			
International details	Jun 8	South Africa 25	British Isles 20	(Pretoria)
	Jun 22	South Africa 6	British Isles 6	(Port Elizabeth)
	Jul 13	South Africa 11	British Isles 6	(Cape Town)
	Jul 27	South Africa 19	British Isles 6	(Johannesburg)

Players
Full-backs: T J Kiernan (Cork Constitution), R Hiller (Harlequins)
Threequarters: A J W Hinshelwood (London Scottish), W K Jones (Cardiff),
M C R Richards (Cardiff), K F Savage (Northampton), F P K Bresnihan (UC Dublin),
T G R Davies (Cardiff), K S Jarrett (Newport), W H Raybould (London Welsh),
J W C Turner (Gala)
Half-backs: C M H Gibson (North of Ireland), B John (Cardiff), G O Edwards
(Cardiff), R M Young (Queen's U, Belfast), G C Connell★ (London Scottish)
Forwards: A L Horton (Blackheath), M J Coulman (Moseley), S Millar (Ballymena),
J P O'Shea (Cardiff), P J Larter (Northampton), W J McBride (Ballymena),
P K Stagg (Sale), W D Thomas (Llanelli), J V Pullin (Bristol), J Young (Harrogate),
M G Doyle (Blackrock Coll), J Taylor (London Welsh), K G Goodall★ (City of Derry),
R J Arneil (Edinburgh Acads), R B Taylor (Northampton), J W Telfer (Melrose),
B R West★ (Northampton)
Captain T J Kiernan **Manager** D K Brooks **Assistant Manager** A R Dawson

1974

Full record	Played 22 Won 21 Lost 0 Drawn 1 Points for 729 Against 207
International record	Played 4 Won 3 Drawn 1

International details

	Jun 8	South Africa 3	British Isles 12	(Cape Town)
	Jun 22	South Africa 9	British Isles 28	(Pretoria)
	Jul 13	South Africa 9	British Isles 26	(Port Elizabeth)
	Jul 27	South Africa 13	British Isles 13	(Johannesburg)

Players

Full-backs: A R Irvine (Heriot's FP), J P R Williams (London Welsh)
Threequarters: T O Grace (St Mary's Coll, Dublin), C F W Rees (London Welsh),
W C C Steele (Bedford and RAF), J J Williams (Llanelli), A J Morley★ (Bristol),
R T E Bergiers (Llanelli), G W Evans (Coventry), I R McGeechan (Headingley),
R A Milliken (Bangor, N Ireland)
Half-backs: P Bennett (Llanelli), A G B Old (Leicester), C M H Gibson★
(North of Ireland FC), G O Edwards (Cardiff), J J Moloney (St Mary's Coll, Dublin)
Forwards: T M Davies (Swansea), A G Ripley (Rosslyn Park), T P David (Llanelli),
S A McKinney (Dungannon), A Neary (Broughton Park), J F Slattery (Blackrock Coll),
G L Brown (West of Scotland), W J McBride (Ballymena), C W Ralston (Richmond),
R M Uttley (Gosforth), M A Burton (Gloucester), A B Carmichael (West of Scotland),
F E Cotton (Coventry), J McLauchlan (Jordanhill), K W Kennedy (London Irish),
R W Windsor (Pontypool)
Captain W J McBride   **Manager** A G Thomas   **Assistant Manager** S Millar

1980

Full record	Played 18 Won 15 Lost 3 Drawn 0 Points for 401 Against 244			
International record	Played 4 Won 1 Lost 3			
International details	May 31	South Africa 26	British Isles 22	(Cape Town)
	Jun 14	South Africa 26	British Isles 19	(Bloemfontein)
	Jun 28	South Africa 12	British Isles 10	(Port Elizabeth)
	Jul 12	South Africa 13	British Isles 17	(Pretoria)

Players

Full-backs: B H Hay (Boroughmuir), R C O'Donnell (St Mary's Coll, Dublin),
A R Irvine★ (Heriot's FP)
Threequarters: J Carleton (Orrell), H E Rees (Neath), M A C Slemen (Liverpool),
P Morgan (Llanelli), R W R Gravell (Llanelli), J M Renwick (Hawick),
D S Richards (Swansea), C R Woodward (Leicester), P W Dodge★ (Leicester)
Half-backs: S O Campbell (Old Belvedere), W G Davies (Cardiff),
A J P Ward★ (Garryowen), T D Holmes (Cardiff), C S Patterson (Instonians),
J C Robbie★ (Greystones), S J Smith★ (Sale)
Forwards: J R Beattie (Glasgow Acads), D L Quinnell (Llanelli), S M Lane (Cardiff),
J B O'Driscoll (London Irish), J Squire (Pontypool), C C Tucker (Shannon),
G P Williams★ (Bridgend), W B Beaumont (Fylde), M J Colclough (Angoulême),
A J Martin (Aberavon), A J Tomes (Hawick), P J Blakeway (Gloucester),
G Price (Pontypool), F E Cotton (Sale), C Williams (Swansea), I Stephens★ (Bridgend),
P A Orr★ (Old Wesley), A J Phillips (Cardiff), P J Wheeler (Leicester)
Captain W B Beaumont   **Manager** S Millar   **Assistant Manager** N A A Murphy

NEW ZEALAND TO BRITISH ISLES AND FRANCE

1953-54

Full record	Played 31 Won 25 Lost 4 Drawn 2 Points for 446 Against 129			
in B Isles	Played 29 Won 25 Lost 2 Drawn 2 Points for 438 Against 115			
in France	Played 2 Won 0 Lost 2 Drawn 0 Points for 8 Against 14			
International record	Played 5 Won 3 Lost 2			
International details	Dec 19	Wales 13	New Zealand 8	(Cardiff)
	Jan 9	Ireland 3	New Zealand 14	(Dublin)
	Jan 30	England 0	New Zealand 5	(Twickenham)
	Feb 13	Scotland 0	New Zealand 3	(Murrayfield)
	Feb 27	France 3	New Zealand 0	(Paris, Colombes)

Players
Full-backs: J W Kelly (Auckland), R W H Scott (Auckland)
Threequarters: M J Dixon (Canterbury), A E G Elsom (Canterbury),
W S S Freebairn (Manawatu), R A Jarden (Wellington), J T Fitzgerald (Wellington),
J M Tanner (Auckland)
Five-eighths: B B J Fitzpatrick (Wellington), C J Loader (Wellington),
D D Wilson (Canterbury), R G Bowers (Wellington), L S Haig (Otago)
Scrum-halves: V D Bevan (Wellington), K Davis (Auckland)
Forwards: W A McCaw (Southland), R C Stuart (Canterbury),
W H Clark (Wellington), P F Jones (North Auckland), R J O'Dea (Thames Valley),
O D Oliver (Otago), K P Bagley (Manawatu), G N Dalzell (Canterbury),
R A White (Poverty Bay), I J Clarke (Waikato), B P Eastgate (Canterbury),
K L Skinner (Otago), H L White (Auckland), R C Hemi (Waikato),
C A Woods (Southland)
Captain R C Stuart **Manager** N Millard **Assistant Manager** A E Marslin

1963-64

Full record	Played 34	Won 32	Lost 1	Drawn 1	Points for 568	Against 153
in B Isles	Played 30	Won 28	Lost 1	Drawn 1	Points for 508	Against 137
in France	Played 4	Won 4	Lost 0	Drawn 0	Points for 60	Against 16
International record	Played 5	Won 4	Drawn 1			
International details	Dec 7	Ireland	5	New Zealand	6	(Dublin)
	Dec 21	Wales	0	New Zealand	6	(Cardiff)
	Jan 4	England	0	New Zealand	14	(Twickenham)
	Jan 18	Scotland	0	New Zealand	0	(Murrayfield)
	Feb 8	France	3	New Zealand	12	(Paris, Colombes)

Players
Full-back: D B Clarke (Waikato)
Threequarters: R W Caulton (Wellington), W L Davis (Hawke's Bay), M J Dick
(Auckland), I S T Smith (Otago), P F Little (Auckland), I R MacRae (Hawke's Bay)
Five-eighths: D A Arnold (Canterbury), P T Walsh (Counties),
M A Herewini (Auckland), E W Kirton (Otago), B A Watt (Canterbury)
Scrum-halves: K C Briscoe (Taranaki), C R Laidlaw (Otago)
Forwards: I J Clarke (Waikato), K F Gray (Wellington), J M Le Lievre (Canterbury),
W J Whineray (Auckland), D Young (Canterbury), J Major (Taranaki),
R H Horsley (Manawatu), C E Meads (King Country), A J Stewart (Canterbury),
S T Meads (King Country), K E Barry (Thames Valley), D J Graham (Canterbury),
W J Nathan (Auckland), K R Tremain (Hawke's Bay), B J Lochore (Wairarapa),
K A Nelson (Otago)
Captain W J Whineray **Manager** F D Kilby **Assistant Manager** N J McPhail

1967

Full record	Played 15	Won 14	Lost 0	Drawn 1	Points for 294	Against 129
in B Isles	Played 11	Won 10	Lost 0	Drawn 1	Points for 207	Against 78
in France	Played 4	Won 4	Lost 0	Drawn 0	Points for 87	Against 51
International record	Played 4	Won 4				
International details	Nov 4	England	11	New Zealand	23	(Twickenham)
	Nov 11	Wales	6	New Zealand	13	(Cardiff)
	Nov 25	France	15	New Zealand	21	(Paris, Colombes)
	Dec 2	Scotland	3	New Zealand	14	(Murrayfield)

Players
Full-back: W F McCormick (Canterbury)
Threequarters: M J Dick (Auckland), W M Birtwistle (Waikato), A G Steel (Canterbury),
P H Clarke (Marlborough), G S Thorne (Auckland), W L Davis (Hawke's Bay)

Five-eighths: I R MacRae (Hawke's Bay), G F Kember (Wellington),
W D Cottrell (Canterbury), E W Kirton (Otago), M A Herewini (Auckland)
Scrum-halves: C R Laidlaw (Otago), S M Going (North Auckland)
Forwards: B J Lochore (Wairarapa), I A Kirkpatrick (Canterbury),
W J Nathan (Auckland), K R Tremain (Hawke's Bay), G C Williams (Wellington),
M C Wills (Taranaki), C E Meads (King Country), A G Jennings (Bay of Plenty),
S C Strahan (Manawatu), A E Smith (Taranaki), A E Hopkinson (Canterbury),
E J Hazlett (Southland), B L Muller (Taranaki), K F Gray (Wellington),
B E McLeod (Counties), J Major (Taranaki)
Captain B J Lochore **Manager** C K Saxton **Assistant Manager** F R Allen

1972-73

Full record	Played 30	Won 23	Lost 5	Drawn 2	Points for 568	Against 254
in Britain and						
Ireland	Played 26	Won 20	Lost 4	Drawn 2	Points for 521	Against 227
in France	Played 4	Won 3	Lost 1	Drawn 0	Points for 47	Against 27
International record	Played 5	Won 3	Lost 1	Drawn 1		
International details	Dec 2	Wales 16	New Zealand 19	(Cardiff)		
	Dec 16	Scotland 9	New Zealand 14	(Murrayfield)		
	Jan 6	England 0	New Zealand 9	(Twickenham)		
	Jan 20	Ireland 10	New Zealand 10	(Dublin)		
	Feb 10	France 13	New Zealand 6	(Parc des Princes)		

Players
Full-backs: J F Karam (Wellington), T J Morris (Nelson-Bays)
Threequarters: B G Williams (Auckland), G B Batty (Wellington),
D A Hales (Canterbury), G R Skudder (Waikato), B J Robertson (Counties),
I A Hurst (Canterbury)
Five-eighths: R M Parkinson (Poverty Bay), M Sayers (Wellington),
R E Burgess (Manawatu), I N Stevens (Wellington)
Scrum-halves: S M Going (North Auckland), G L Colling (Otago)
Forwards: A R Sutherland (Marlborough), A J Wyllie (Canterbury),
B Holmes (North Auckland), I A Kirkpatrick (Poverty Bay), K W Stewart (Southland),
A I Scown (Taranaki), H H Macdonald (Canterbury), I M Eliason (Taranaki),
A M Haden (Auckland), P J Whiting (Auckland), K Murdoch (Otago),
J D Matheson (Otago), K K Lambert (Manawatu), G J Whiting (King Country),
R A Urlich (Auckland), R W Norton (Canterbury), L A Clark* (Otago),
A L R McNicol* (Wanganui)
Captain I A Kirkpatrick **Manager** E L Todd **Assistant Manager** R H Duff

1974 (to Ireland and UK)

Full record	Played 8	Won 7	Lost 0	Drawn 1	Points for 127	Against 50
in Ireland	Played 6	Won 6	Lost 0	Drawn 0	Points for 102	Against 34
International record	Played 1	Won 1				
International details	Nov 23	Ireland 6	New Zealand 15	(Dublin)		

Players
Full-backs: J F Karam (Wellington), K T Going (North Auckland)
Threequarters: T W Mitchell (Canterbury), B G Williams (Auckland),
G Batty (Wellington), B J Robertson (Counties), I A Hurst (Canterbury),
J E Morgan (North Auckland), G M Kane (Waikato)
Half-backs: D J Robertson (Otago), O D Bruce (Canterbury),
S M Going (North Auckland), I N Stevens (Wellington)
Forwards: A R Leslie (Wellington), L G Knight (Auckland),
I A Kirkpatrick (Poverty Bay), K W Stewart (Southland), K A Eveleigh (Manawatu),
P J Whiting (Auckland), H H Macdonald (Canterbury), J A Callesen (Manawatu),

K J Tanner (Canterbury), A J Gardiner (Taranaki), W K Bush (Canterbury),
K K Lambert (Manawatu), R W Norton (Canterbury), G M Crossman (Bay of Plenty)
Captain A R Leslie   **Manager** N H Stanley   **Assistant Manager** J J Stewart

1977 (France only, except for one match in Italy)

Full record	Played 9	Won 8	Lost 1	Drawn 0	Points for 216	Against 86
in Italy	Played 1	Won 1	Lost 0	Drawn 0	Points for 17	Against 9
in France	Played 8	Won 7	Lost 1	Drawn 0	Points for 199	Against 77
International record	Played 2	Won 1	Lost 1			
International details	Nov 11	France 18	New Zealand 13	(Toulouse)		
	Nov 19	France 3	New Zealand 15	(Parc des Princes)		

Players
Full-back: B W Wilson (Otago)
Threequarters: B G Williams (Auckland), B R Ford (Marlborough),
B J Robertson (Counties), S S Wilson (Wellington), N M Taylor (Bay of Plenty),
W M Osborne (Wanganui), B Hegarty* (Wellington & Biarritz)
Half-backs: O D Bruce (Canterbury), B J McKechnie (Southland),
M W Donaldson (Manawatu), K M Green (Waikato)
Forwards: G N K Mourie (Taranaki), K A Eveleigh (Manawatu),
L G Knight (Poverty Bay), G A Seear (Otago), R G Myers (Waikato),
R L Stuart (Hawke's Bay), F J Oliver (Southland), A M Haden (Auckland),
G A Knight (Manawatu), B R Johnstone (Auckland), J C Ashworth (Canterbury),
J T McEldowney (Taranaki), A G Dalton (Counties), J E Black (Canterbury)
Captain G N K Mourie   **Manager** R M Don   **Assistant Manager** J Gleeson

1978 (no matches in France)

Full record	Played 18	Won 17	Lost 1	Drawn 0	Points for 364	Against 147
International record	Played 4	Won 4				
International details	Nov 4	Ireland 6	New Zealand 10	(Dublin)		
	Nov 11	Wales 12	New Zealand 13	(Cardiff)		
	Nov 25	England 6	New Zealand 16	(Twickenham)		
	Dec 9	Scotland 9	New Zealand 18	(Murrayfield)		

Players
Full-backs: C J Currie (Canterbury), B J McKechnie (Southland),
R G Wilson* (Canterbury)
Threequarters: B R Ford (Marlborough), B G Williams (Auckland),
S S Wilson (Wellington), R Kururangi (Counties), B J Robertson (Counties),
Five-eighths: J L Jaffray (Otago), W M Osborne (Wanganui), N M Taylor
(Bay of Plenty), O D Bruce (Canterbury), E J Dunn (North Auckland),
Scrum-halves: M W Donaldson (Manawatu), D S Loveridge (Taranaki)
Forwards: G A Seear (Otago), A A McGregor (Southland), G N K Mourie (Taranaki),
B G Ashworth (Auckland), L M Rutledge (Southland), W G Graham (Otago),
A M Haden (Auckland), F J Oliver (Otago), J K Loveday (Manawatu),
J K Fleming (Wellington), W K Bush (Canterbury), J C Ashworth (Canterbury),
G A Knight (Manawatu), B R Johnstone (Auckland), A G Dalton (Counties),
J E Black (Canterbury)
Captain G N K Mourie   **Manager** R W Thomas   **Assistant Manager** J Gleeson

1979 (to England and Scotland only, except for one match in Italy)

Full record	Played 11	Won 10	Lost 1	Drawn 0	Points for 192	Against 95
International record (in UK)	Played 2	Won 2				
International details	Nov 10	Scotland 6	New Zealand 20	(Murrayfield)		
	Nov 24	England 9	New Zealand 10	(Twickenham)		

Players
Full-backs: R G Wilson (Canterbury), A R Hewson (Wellington)
Threequarters: S S Wilson (Wellington), B R Ford (Marlborough),
B G Fraser (Wellington), G R Cunningham (Auckland), T M Twigden (Auckland)
Five-eighths: K J Keane (Canterbury), E Dunn (North Auckland),
M B Taylor (Waikato)
Scrum-halves: M W Donaldson (Manawatu), D S Loveridge (Taranaki)
Forwards: M G Mexted (Wellington), G N K Mourie (Taranaki),
K W Stewart (Southland), M Burgoyne (North Auckland), V E Stewart (Canterbury),
A M Haden (Auckland), J K Fleming (Wellington), B R Johnstone (Auckland),
B A Thompson (Canterbury), R C Ketels (Counties), J E Speirs (Counties),
A G Dalton (Counties), P H Sloane (North Auckland)
Captain G N K Mourie   **Manager** R W Thomas   **Assistant Manager** E A Watson

1980 (to Wales only, except for two matches in North America)

Full record	Played 7	Won 7	Lost 0	Drawn 0	Points for 197	Against 41
in Wales	Played 5	Won 5	Lost 0	Drawn 0	Points for 101	Against 25

International record   Played 1   Won 1
International details   Nov 1   Wales 3   New Zealand 23   (Cardiff)
Players
Full-backs: B W Codlin (Counties), D L Rollerson (Manawatu)
Threequarters: S S Wilson (Wellington), B G Fraser (Wellington),
F A Woodman (North Auckland), B J Robertson (Counties)
Five-eighths: W M Osborne (Wanganui), M B Taylor (Waikato), N H Allen (Counties)
Scrum-halves: M W Donaldson (Manawatu), D S Loveridge (Taranaki)
Forwards: G H Old (Manawatu), M G Mexted (Wellington), G N K Mourie (Taranaki),
G R Hines (Waikato), M W Shaw (Manawatu), G Higginson (Canterbury),
F J Oliver (Manawatu), A M Haden (Auckland), R C Ketels (Counties),
G A Knight (Manawatu), J E Spiers (Counties), J C Ashworth (Canterbury),
H R Reid (Bay of Plenty), A G Dalton (Counties)
Captain G N K Mourie   **Manager** R A Harper   **Assistant Manager** E A Watson

1981 (to France only, except for two matches in Romania)

Full record	Played 10	Won 8	Lost 1	Drawn 1	Points for 170	Against 108
in Romania	Played 2	Won 2	Lost 0	Drawn 0	Points for 39	Against 15
in France	Played 8	Won 6	Lost 1	Drawn 1	Points for 131	Against 93

International record
v Romania   Played 1   Won 1
v France   Played 2   Won 2
International details
v Romania   Oct 24   Romania 6   New Zealand 14   (Bucharest)
v France   Nov 14   France 9   New Zealand 13   (Toulouse)
  Nov 21   France 6   New Zealand 18   (Parc des Princes)
Players
Full-back: A R Hewson (Wellington)
Threequarters: B G Fraser (Wellington), S S Wilson (Wellington),
F A Woodman (North Auckland), J L B Salmon (Wellington), A M Stone (Waikato),
L M Cameron (Manawatu)
Five-eighths: S T Pokere (Southland), D L Rollerson (Manawatu),
B J McKechnie (Southland), J Boe* (Waikato)
Scrum-halves: D S Loveridge (Taranaki), A Donald (Wanganui)
Forwards: M G Mexted (Wellington), G H Old (Manawatu), G N K Mourie (Taranaki),
F K Shelford (Bay of Plenty), M W Shaw (Manawatu), B Morrissey* (Waikato),
A M Haden (Auckland), G W Whetton (Auckland), J Ross (Mid-Canterbury),
R C Ketels (Counties), W Neville (North Auckland), J E Spiers (Counties),

319

P T Koteka (Waikato), H R Reid (Bay of Plenty), A G Dalton (Counties)
Captain G N K Mourie   **Manager** P Gill   **Assistant Manager** P Burke

1983 (to England and Scotland only)

Full record	Played 8 Won 5 Lost 2 Drawn 1 Points for 162 Against 116			
International record	Played 2 Lost 1 Drawn 1			
International details	Nov 12 Scotland 25 New Zealand 25 (Murrayfield)			
	Nov 19 England 15 New Zealand 9 (Twickenham)			

Players
Full-backs: K J Crowley (Taranaki), R M Deans (Canterbury)
Threequarters: S S Wilson (Wellington), B G Fraser (Wellington), B W Smith (Waikato),
C I Green (Canterbury), S T Pokere (Southland), W T Taylor (Canterbury)
Half-backs: I T Dunn (North Auckland), W R Smith (Canterbury),
A J Donald (Wanganui), D E Kirk (Otago)
Forwards: K G Boroevich (King Country), S A Crichton (Wellington),
M G Davie (Canterbury), B McGrattan (Wellington), H R Reid (Bay of Plenty),
B H Wilson (Counties), A Anderson (Canterbury), G J Braid (Bay of Plenty),
A G Robinson (North Auckland), M J Hobbs (Canterbury), M W Shaw (Manawatu),
F N K Shelford (Hawke's Bay), M G Mexted (Wellington), G H Old (Manawatu)
Captain S S Wilson   **Manager** P W Mitchell   **Assistant Manager** D B Rope

1986 (to France only)

Full record	Played 8 Won 7 Lost 1 Drawn 0 Points for 218 Against 87
International record	Played 2 Won 1 Lost 1
International details	Nov 8 France 7 New Zealand 19 (Toulouse)
	Nov 15 France 16 New Zealand 3 (Nantes)

Players
Full-backs: K J Crowley (Taranaki), J A Gallagher (Wellington)
Threequarters: J J Kirwan (Auckland), C I Green (Canterbury), T J Wright (Auckland),
M J Berry (Wairarapa-Bush), J T Stanley (Auckland), A M Stone (Bay of Plenty)
Half-backs: F M Botica (North Harbour), G J Fox (Auckland), D J Kenny (Otago),
D E Kirk (Auckland)
Forwards: K G Boroevich (Wellington), J A Drake (Auckland), S C McDowell (Auckland),
S B T Fitzpatrick (Auckland), H R Reid (Bay of Plenty), G W Whetton (Auckland),
M W Speight (Waikato), M J Pierce (Wellington), A T Earl (Canterbury), M J B Hobbs
(Canterbury), M W Shaw (Hawke's Bay), M Brooke-Cowden (Auckland), M R Brewer
(Otago), W T Shelford (North Harbour)
Captain M J B Hobbs   **Manager** R A Guy   **Assistant Manager** B J Lochore

1989 (to Canada, Wales and Ireland, and one match at Twickenham)

Full record	Played 14 Won 14 Lost 0 Drawn 0 Points for 454 Against 122
in UK and Ireland	Played 13 Won 13 Lost 0 Drawn 0 Points for 406 Against 119
International record	Played 2 Won 2
International details	Nov 4 Wales 9 New Zealand 34 (Cardiff)
	Nov 18 Ireland 6 New Zealand 23 (Dublin)

Players
Full-backs: J A Gallagher (Wellington), M J Ridge (Auckland)
Threequarters: V L Tuigamala (Auckland), J J Kirwan (Auckland), T J Wright
(Auckland), C R Innes (Auckland), B J McCahill (Auckland), J T Stanley (Auckland),
W K Little (North Harbour), N J Schuster (Wellington), J K R Timu* (Otago)
Half-backs: F M Botica (North Harbour), G J Fox (Auckland), I B Deans (Canterbury),
G T M Bachop (Canterbury)
Forwards: S B T Fitzpatrick (Auckland), W D Gatland (Waikato), R O Williams (North
Harbour), G H Purvis (Waikato), R W Loe (Waikato), S C McDowell (Auckland),

G W Whetton (Auckland), I D Jones (North Auckland), S B Gordon (Waikato),
M J Pierce (Wellington), A J Whetton (Auckland), P W Henderson (Otago), M R Brewer
(Otago), A T Earl (Canterbury), K J Schuler* (Manawatu), W T Shelford
(North Harbour), Z V Brooke (Auckland)
Captain W T Shelford **Manager** J A Sturgeon **Coach** A J Wyllie

NEW ZEALAND TO SOUTH AFRICA
1949

Full record	Played 24 Won 14 Lost 7 Drawn 3 Points for 230 Against 146			
International record	Played 4 Lost 4			
International details	Jul 16	South Africa 15	New Zealand 11	(Cape Town)
	Aug 13	South Africa 12	New Zealand 6	(Johannesburg)
	Sep 3	South Africa 9	New Zealand 3	(Durban)
	Sep 17	South Africa 11	New Zealand 8	(Port Elizabeth)

Players
Full-backs: J W Goddard (South Canterbury), R W H Scott (Auckland)
Threequarters: E G Boggs (Auckland), I J Botting (Otago), P Henderson (Wanganui),
W A Meates (Otago), Dr R R Elvidge (Otago), M P Goddard (South Canterbury)
Five-eighths: F R Allen (Auckland), K E Gudsell (Wanganui), N W Black (Auckland),
G W Delamore (Wellington), J C Kearney (Otago)
Scrum-halves: W J Conrad (Waikato), L T Savage (Canterbury)
Forwards: L A Grant (South Canterbury), N H Thornton (Auckland), P J B Crowley
(Auckland), P Johnstone (Otago), J R McNab (Otago), H F Frazer
(Hawke's Bay), L R Harvey (Otago), M J McHugh (Auckland), C Willocks (Otago),
D L Christian (Auckland), R A Dalton (Otago), J G Simpson (Auckland),
K L Skinner (Otago), E H Catley (Waikato), N L Wilson (Otago)
Captain F R Allen **Manager** J H Parker **Assistant Manager** A McDonald

1960

Full record	Played 26 Won 20 Lost 4 Drawn 2 Points for 441 Against 164			
International record	Played 4 Won 1 Lost 2 Drawn 1			
International details	Jun 25	South Africa 13	New Zealand 0	(Johannesburg)
	Jul 23	South Africa 3	New Zealand 11	(Cape Town)
	Aug 13	South Africa 11	New Zealand 11	(Bloemfontein)
	Aug 27	South Africa 8	New Zealand 3	(Port Elizabeth)

Players
Full-backs: D B Clarke (Waikato), W A Davies (Auckland)
Threequarters: D H Cameron (Mid-Canterbury), R W Caulton (Wellington),
K F Laidlaw (Southland), R F McMullen (Auckland), T P A O'Sullivan (Taranaki),
J R Watt (Wellington)
Five-eighths: S G Bremner (Canterbury), A H Clarke (Auckland),
T R Lineen (Auckland), S R Nesbit (Auckland)
Scrum-halves: K C Briscoe (Taranaki), R J Urbahn (Taranaki)
Forwards: E J Anderson (Bay of Plenty), R J Boon* (Taranaki),
Dr H C Burry (Canterbury), I J Clarke (Waikato), R J Conway (Otago),
W D Gillespie (Otago), D J Graham (Canterbury), R C Hemi (Waikato),
R H Horsley (Wellington), M W Irwin (Otago), P F Jones (North Auckland),
I N MacEwan (Wellington), C E Meads (King Country), E A R Pickering (Waikato),
K R Tremain (Canterbury), W J Whineray (Auckland), D Young (Canterbury)
Captain W J Whineray **Manager** T H Pearce **Assistant Manager** J L Sullivan

1970

Full record	Played 24 Won 21 Lost 3 Drawn 0 Points for 687 Against 228
International record	Played 4 Won 1 Lost 3

International details

Jul 25	South Africa 17	New Zealand	6	(Pretoria)
Aug 8	South Africa 8	New Zealand	9	(Cape Town)
Aug 29	South Africa 14	New Zealand	3	(Port Elizabeth)
Sep 12	South Africa 20	New Zealand	17	(Johannesburg)

Players

Full-back: W F McCormick (Canterbury)

Threequarters: M J Dick (Auckland), B A Hunter (Otago), B G Williams (Auckland), G S Thorne (Auckland), W L Davis (Hawke's Bay), H P Milner (Wanganui)

Five-eighths: I R MacRae (Hawke's Bay), W D Cottrell (Canterbury), E W Kirton (Otago), B D M Furlong (Hawke's Bay), G F Kember (Wellington)

Scrum-halves: C R Laidlaw (Otago), S M Going (North Auckland)

Forwards: B J Lochore (Wairarapa), A R Sutherland (Marlborough), I A Kirkpatrick (Poverty Bay), A J Wyllie (Canterbury), T N Lister (South Canterbury), B Holmes (North Auckland), C E Meads (King Country), S C Strahan (Manawatu), A E Smith (Taranaki), J F Burns (Canterbury), B L Muller (Taranaki), K Murdoch (Otago), A E Hopkinson (Canterbury), N W Thimbleby (Hawke's Bay), B E McLeod (Counties), R A Urlich (Auckland)

Captain B J Lochore **Manager** R L Burk **Assistant Manager** I M H Vodanovich

1976

Full record	Played 24	Won 18	Lost 6	Drawn 0	Points for 610	Against 291
International record	Played 4	Won 1	Lost 3			
International details	Jul 24	South Africa 16	New Zealand 7	(Durban)		
	Aug 14	South Africa 9	New Zealand 15	(Bloemfontein)		
	Sep 4	South Africa 15	New Zealand 10	(Cape Town)		
	Sep 18	South Africa 15	New Zealand 14	(Johannesburg)		

Players

Full-backs: L W Mains (Otago), C L Fawcett (Auckland)

Threequarters: B G Williams (Auckland), N A Purvis (Otago), B J Robertson (Counties), W M Osborne (Wanganui), G B Batty (Bay of Plenty), T W Mitchell (Canterbury)

Five-eighths: J E Morgan (North Auckland), J L Jaffray (Otago), D J Robertson (Otago), O D Bruce (Canterbury)

Scrum-halves: L J Davis (Canterbury), S M Going (North Auckland)

Forwards: A R Leslie (Wellington), A R Sutherland (Marlborough), K A Eveleigh (Manawatu), L G Knight (Poverty Bay), I A Kirkpatrick (Poverty Bay), K W Stewart (Southland), P J Whiting (Auckland), G A Seear (Otago), F J Oliver (Southland), H H Macdonald (North Auckland), K K Lambert (Manawatu), W K Bush (Canterbury), K J Tanner (Canterbury), B R Johnstone (Auckland), P C Harris* (Manawatu), R W Norton (Canterbury), G M Crossman (Bay of Plenty)

Captain A R Leslie **Manager** N H Stanley **Assistant Manager** J J Stewart

SOUTH AFRICA TO BRITISH ISLES AND FRANCE

1951-52

Full record	Played 31	Won 30	Lost 1	Drawn 0	Points for 562	Against 167
in B Isles	Played 27	Won 26	Lost 1	Drawn 0	Points for 499	Against 143
in France	Played 4	Won 4	Lost 0	Drawn 0	Points for 63	Against 24
International record	Played 5	Won 5				
International details	Nov 24	Scotland 0	South Africa 44	(Murrayfield)		
	Dec 8	Ireland 5	South Africa 17	(Dublin)		
	Dec 22	Wales 3	South Africa 6	(Cardiff)		
	Jan 5	England 3	South Africa 8	(Twickenham)		
	Feb 16	France 3	South Africa 25	(Paris, Colombes)		

Players
Full-backs: J Buchler (TVL), A C Keevy (E TVL)
Threequarters: J K Ochse (WP), F P Marais (Bol), M J Saunders (Bor), P Johnstone (WP),
M T Lategan (WP), R A M van Schoor (R), D J Sinclair (TVL), S S Viviers (OFS)
Half-backs: J D Brewis (N TVL), D J Fry (WP), J S Oelofse (TVL),
P A du Toit (N TVL)
Forwards: P W Wessels (OFS), W H Delport (EP), A C Koch (Bol), A Geffin (TVL),
H P J Bekker (N TVL), F E van der Ryst (TVL), E E Dinkelmann (N TVL), J A Pickard
(WP), G Dannhauser (TVL), W H M Barnard (GW), S P Fry (WP), C J van Wyk (TVL),
B Myburgh (E TVL), J A du Rand (R), B J Kenyon (Bor), H S Muller (TVL)
Captain B J Kenyon   **Manager** F W Mellish   **Assistant Manager** Dr D H Craven

1960-61

Full record	Played 34	Won 31	Lost 1	Drawn 2	Points for 567	Against 132
in B Isles	Played 30	Won 28	Lost 1	Drawn 1	Points for 476	Against 110
in France	Played 4	Won 3	Lost 0	Drawn 1	Points for 91	Against 22
International record	Played 5	Won 4	Drawn 1			

International details	Dec 3	Wales	0	South Africa	3	(Cardiff)
	Dec 17	Ireland	3	South Africa	8	(Dublin)
	Jan 7	England	0	South Africa	5	(Twickenham)
	Jan 21	Scotland	5	South Africa	12	(Murrayfield)
	Feb 18	France	0	South Africa	0	(Paris, Colombes)

Players
Full-backs: L G Wilson (WP), G J Wentzel (EP)
Threequarters: H J van Zyl (TVL), M J G Antelme (TVL), J P Engelbrecht (WP),
F du T Roux (WP), B P van Zyl* (WP), A I Kirkpatrick (GW), J L Gainsford (WP),
D A Stewart (WP), B B van Niekerk (OFS)
Half-backs: K Oxlee (N), C F Nimb (WP), R J Lockyear (GW), P de W Uys (N TVL)
Forwards: P S du Toit (WP), S P Kuhn (TVL), J L Myburgh (N TVL),
D N Holton (EP), G F Malan (WP), R A Hill (R), R G Johns* (WP),
A S Malan (TVL), J T Claassen (W TVL), H S van der Merwe (N TVL),
P J van Zyl (Bol), H J M Pelser (TVL), G H van Zyl (WP), J P F Botha (N TVL),
F C H du Preez (N TVL), D J Hopwood (WP), A P Baard (WP)
Captain A S Malan   **Manager** W F Bergh   **Assistant Manager** M M (Boy) Louw

1965 (Ireland and Scotland only)

Full record	Played 5	Won 0	Lost 4	Drawn 1	Points for 37	Against 53
International record	Played 2	Lost 2				

International details	Apr 10	Ireland	9	South Africa	6	(Dublin)
	Apr 17	Scotland	8	South Africa	5	(Murrayfield)

Players
Full-back: L G Wilson (WP)
Threequarters: C D Cilliers (OFS), C W Dirksen (N TVL), J P Engelbrecht (WP),
J L Gainsford (WP), W J Mans (WP), D A Stewart (WP)
Half-backs: J H Barnard (TVL), K Oxlee (N), S C Conradie* (WP),
D J de Villiers (WP), D J J de Vos (WP)
Forwards: S P Kuhn (TVL), J F K Marais (WP), J B Neethling (WP), D C Walton (N),
J W Wessels (OFS), G Carelse (EP), F C H du Preez (N TVL), A S Malan (TVL),
J Schoeman (WP), M R Suter (N), T P Bedford (N), D J Hopwood (WP)
Captain A S Malan   **Manager** B M Medway   **Assistant Manager** M M Louw

1968 (France only)

Full record	Played 6	Won 5	Lost 1	Drawn 0	Points for 84	Against 43
International record	Played 2	Won 2				

International details Nov 9 France 9 South Africa 12 (Bordeaux)
Nov 16 France 11 South Africa 16 (Paris, Colombes)

Players
Full-backs: H O de Villiers (WP), R L Gould (N)
Threequarters: J P Engelbrecht (WP), S H Nomis (TVL), E Olivier (WP),
F du T Roux (WP), O A Roux (N TVL)
Half-backs: P J Visagie (GW), M A Menter (N TVL), D J de Villiers (WP),
P de W Uys (N TVL)
Forwards: J F K Marais (WP), J L Myburgh (N TVL), J B Neethling (WP), G Pitzer
(N TVL), D C Walton (N), F C H du Preez (N TVL), J P Naude (WP), G Carelse (EP),
J H Ellis (SWA), P J F Greyling (OFS), M J Lourens (N TVL), T P Bedford (N)
Captain D J de Villiers **Manager** F C Eloff **Assistant Manager** J T Claassen

1969-70 (British Isles only)

Full record Played 24 Won 15 Lost 5 Drawn 4 Points for 323 Against 157
International record Played 4 Lost 2 Drawn 2
International details Dec 6 Scotland 6 South Africa 3 (Murrayfield)
Dec 20 England 11 South Africa 8 (Twickenham)
Jan 10 Ireland 8 South Africa 8 (Dublin)
Jan 24 Wales 6 South Africa 6 (Cardiff)

Players
Full-backs: H O de Villiers (WP), P J Durand (WP)
Threequarters: R N Grobler (N TVL), G H Muller (WP), S H Nomis (TVL),
A E van der Watt (WP), E Olivier (WP), O A Roux (N TVL),
J P van der Merwe (WP), P J van der Schyff (W TVL), F du T Roux★ (GW)
Half-backs: M J Lawless (WP), P J Visagie (GW), D J de Villiers (Bol),
D J J de Vos (W TVL)
Forwards: J L Myburgh (N TVL), J B Neethling (WP), J F K Marais (EP),
R Potgieter (N TVL), G Carelse (EP), A E de Wet (WP), F C H du Preez
(N TVL), G Pitzer (N TVL), D C Walton (N), M C J van Rensburg (N),
A J Bates (W TVL), J H Ellis (SWA), P J F Greyling (TVL), P I van Deventer (GW),
T P Bedford (N), M W Jennings (Bol), I J de Klerk★ (TVL), C H Cockrell★ (WP),
R Barnard★ (TVL)
Captain D J de Villiers **Manager** C A J Bornman **Assistant Manager** A S Malan

1974 (France only)

Full record Played 9 Won 8 Lost 1 Drawn 0 Points for 170 Against 74
International record Played 2 Won 2
International details Nov 23 France 4 South Africa 13 (Toulouse)
Nov 30 France 8 South Africa 10 (Paris, Parc des Princes)

Players
Full-backs: I W Robertson (R), D S L Snyman (WP)
Threequarters: C Fourie (EP), W P Stapelberg (N TVL), C F Pope (WP),
P J M Whipp (WP), J J Oosthuizen (WP), J A van Staden (N TVL)
Half-backs: J C P Snyman (OFS), G R Bosch (TVL), P C R Bayvel (TVL),
R J McCallum (WP)
Forwards: M du Plessis (WP), J L Kritzinger (TVL), J H Ellis (SWA),
T T Fourie (SE TVL), C J Grobler (OFS), J L van Heerden (N TVL),
J G Williams (N TVL), K B H De Klerk (TVL), J De Bruyn (OFS),
J F K Marais (EP), N S E Bezuidenhoudt (TVL), J C J Stander (OFS),
D S van Den Berg (N), A Bestbier (OFS), R J Cockrell (WP)
Captain J F K Marais **Manager** J Z le Roux
Assistant Managers J T Claassen & A I Kirkpatrick★

SOUTH AFRICA TO AUSTRALIA AND NEW ZEALAND

1956

Full record

	Played 29	Won 22	Lost 6	Drawn 1	Points for 520	Against 203
in Australia	Played 6	Won 6	Lost 0	Drawn 0	Points for 150	Against 26
in New Zealand	Played 23	Won 16	Lost 6	Drawn 1	Points for 370	Against 177

International record

in Australia	Played 2	Won 2	
in New Zealand	Played 4	Won 1	Lost 3

International details

v Australia	May 26	Australia	0	South Africa	9	(Sydney)
	Jun 2	Australia	0	South Africa	9	(Brisbane)
v New Zealand	Jul 14	New Zealand	10	South Africa	6	(Dunedin)
	Aug 4	New Zealand	3	South Africa	8	(Wellington)
	Aug 18	New Zealand	17	South Africa	10	(Christchurch)
	Sep 1	New Zealand	11	South Africa	5	(Auckland)

Players

Full-backs: J U Buchler (TVL), S S Viviers (OFS)

Threequarters: K T van Vollenhoven (N TVL), P G Johnstone (TVL),
R G Dryburgh (N), J du Preez (WP), T P Briers* (WP), W Rosenberg (TVL),
P E Montini (WP), A I Kirkpatrick (GW), J J Nel (WP)

Half-backs: C A Ulyate (TVL), B F Howe (Bor), B D Pfaff (WP), T A Gentles (WP),
C F Strydom (OFS)

Forwards: H P J Bekker (N TVL), A C Koch (Bol), P S du Toit (WP), H N Walker
(W TV), A J van der Merwe (Bol), M Hanekom (Bol), J A du Rand (N TVL),
J T Claassen (W TVL), C J de NYsschen (N), J A Pickard (WP), C J van Wyk (TVL),
D S P Ackermann (WP), C J De Wilzem (OFS), G P Lochner (WPI), D F Retief
(N TVL), J J Starke* (Stellenbosch)

Captain S S Viviers   **Manager** Dr D H Craven   **Assistant Manager** D J de Villiers

1965

Full record

	Played 30	Won 22	Lost 8	Drawn 0	Points for 669	Against 285
in Australia	Played 6	Won 3	Lost 3	Drawn 0	Points for 184	Against 53
in New Zealand	Played 24	Won 19	Lost 5	Drawn 0	Points for 485	Against 232

International record

v Australia	Played 2	Lost 2	
v New Zealand	Played 4	Won 1	Lost 3

International details

v Australia	Jun 19	Australia	18	South Africa	11	(Sydney)
	Jun 26	Australia	12	South Africa	8	(Brisbane)
v New Zealand	Jul 31	New Zealand	6	South Africa	3	(Wellington)
	Aug 21	New Zealand	13	South Africa	0	(Dunedin)
	Sep 4	New Zealand	16	South Africa	19	(Christchurch)
	Sep 18	New Zealand	20	South Africa	3	(Auckland)

Players

Full-backs: L G Wilson (WP), C G Mulder (E TVL)

Threequarters: J P Engelbrecht (WP), F du T Roux (GW), J L Gainsford (WP),
E Olivier* (WP), G Brynard (WP), J T Truter (N), S H Nomis (TVL),
W J Mans (WP), C J C Cronje (E TVL)

Half-backs: K Oxlee (N), J H Barnard (TVL), D J de Villiers (WP), C M Smith (OFS)

Forwards: D J Hopwood (WP), J A Nel (W TVL), J Schoeman (WP),
F C H du Preez (N TVL), J P Naude (WP), J H Ellis (SWA), A W MacDonald (Rho),
G F Malan (TVL), C P van Zyl (OFS), D C Walton (N), C P Goosen (OFS),

T P Bedford (N), L J Slabber★ (OFS), P H Botha (TVL), A Janson (WP),
W H Parker (EP), J F Marais (EP)
Captain D J de Villiers **Manager** J F Louw **Assistant Manager** H S (Hennie) Muller

1971 (Australia only)

Full record	Played 13	Won 13	Lost 0	Drawn 0	Points for 396	Against 102
International record	Played 3	Won 3				
International details	Jul 17	Australia 11	South Africa 19	(Sydney)		
	Jul 31	Australia 6	South Africa 14	(Brisbane)		
	Aug 7	Australia 6	South Africa 18	(Sydney)		

Players
Full-backs: I D McCallum (WP), O A Roux (N TVL)
Threequarters: G H Muller (WP), S H Nomis (TVL), J T Viljoen (N),
P A Cronje (TVL), J S Jansen (OFS), P S Swanson (TVL), A E van der Watt★ (WP)
Half-backs: P J Visagie (GW), D S L Snyman (WP), J F Viljoen (GW),
D J J de Vos (W TVL)
Forwards: J F K Marais (EP), M J Louw (TVL), J T Sauermann (TVL),
J F B van Wyk (N TVL), R W Barnard (TVL), F C H du Preez (N TVL),
J J Spies (N TVL), J G Williams (N TVL), J H Ellis (SWA), P J F Greyling (TVL),
M J Lourens (N TVL), T P Bedford (N), M du Plessis (WP), A J Bates★ (W TVL),
Captain J F K Marais **Manager** G P Lochner **Assistant Manager** J T Claassen

1981 (New Zealand only, except for three matches in USA)

Full record	Played 17	Won 14	Lost 2	Drawn 1	Points for 535	Against 190
in New Zealand	Played 14	Won 11	Lost 2	Drawn 1	Points for 410	Against 171
in USA	Played 3	Won 3	Lost 0	Drawn 0	Points for 125	Against 19
International record						
v New Zealand	Played 3	Won 1	Lost 2			
v USA	Played 1	Won 1				
International details						
v New Zealand	Aug 15	New Zealand 14	South Africa 9	(Christchurch)		
	Aug 29	New Zealand 12	South Africa 24	(Wellington)		
	Sep 12	New Zealand 25	South Africa 22	(Auckland)		
v USA	Sep 26	USA 7	South Africa 38	(Glenville, NY)		

Players
Full-backs: Z M J Pienaar (OFS), J W Heunis (N TVL)
Threequarters: J S Germishuys (TVL), D S Botha (N TVL) E F W Krantz (OFS),
R H Mordt (TVL), C J du Plessis (WP), W du Plessis (WP), E G Tobias (Bol),
D M Gerber (EP)
Half-backs: H E Botha (N TVL), J J Beck (WP), D J Serfontein (WP), B J Wolmarans
(OFS), G Visagie★ (N)
Forwards: W Claassen (N), J H Marias (N TVL), M B Burger (N TVL),
S B Geldenhuys (N TVL), E Jansen (OFS), R J Louw (WP), H J Bekker (WP),
L C Moolman (N TVL), M T S Stofberg (N TVL), J de V Visser (WP), P G du Toit (WP),
O W Oosthuizen (N TVL), H J van Aswegen (WP), P R van der Merwe (S W Districts),
R J Cockrell (WP), W J H Kahts (N TVL), S Povey★ (WP)
Captain W Claassen **Manager** J T Claassen
Assistant Managers C M Smith & A Williams

AUSTRALIA TO BRITISH ISLES AND FRANCE

1947-48

Full record	Played 35	Won 29	Lost 6	Drawn 0	Points for 500	Against 243
in B Isles	Played 30	Won 25	Lost 5	Drawn 0	Points for 429	Against 197
in France	Played 5	Won 4	Lost 1	Drawn 0	Points for 71	Against 46

International record	Played 5	Won 3	Lost 2		
International details	Nov 22	Scotland 7	Australia 16	(Murrayfield)
	Dec 6	Ireland 3	Australia 16	(Dublin)
	Dec 20	Wales 6	Australia 0	(Cardiff)
	Jan 3	England 0	Australia 11	(Twickenham)
	Jan 11	France 13	Australia 6	(Paris, Colombes)

Players

Full-backs: B J C Piper (NSW), C J Windsor (Queensland)
Threequarters: C C Eastes (NSW), A E J Tonkin (NSW), J W T MacBride (NSW),
T K Bourke (Queensland), T Allan (NSW), M L Howell (NSW), A K Walker (NSW)
Five-eighths: J F Cremin (NSW), N A Emery (NSW), E G Broad (Queensland)
Scrum-halves: C T Burke (NSW), R M Cawsey (NSW)
Forwards: W M McLean (Queensland), A J Buchan (NSW), C J Windon (NSW),
J O Stenmark (NSW), K C Winning (Queensland), J G Fuller (NSW),
G M Cooke (Queensland), P A Hardcastle (NSW), D F Kraefft (NSW),
N Shehadie (NSW), R E McMaster (Queensland), E Tweedale (NSW),
D H Keller (NSW), E H Davis (Victoria), K H Kearney (NSW), W L Dawson (NSW)
Captain W M McLean **Manager** A J Tancred **Assistant Manager** J Noseda

1957-58

Full record	Played 34	Won 16	Lost 15	Drawn 3	Points for 285	Against 244
in B Isles	Played 30	Won 14	Lost 13	Drawn 3	Points for 248	Against 203
in France	Played 4	Won 2	Lost 2	Drawn 0	Points for 37	Against 41
International record	Played 5	Lost 5				
International details	Jan 4	Wales 9	Australia 3	(Cardiff)		
	Jan 18	Ireland 9	Australia 6	(Dublin)		
	Feb 1	England 9	Australia 6	(Twickenham)		
	Feb 15	Scotland 12	Australia 8	(Murrayfield)		
	Mar 9	France 19	Australia 0	(Paris, Colombes)		

Players

Full-backs: T G Curley (NSW), J K Lenehan (NSW)
Threequarters: K J Donald (Queensland), R Phelps (NSW), A R Morton (NSW),
O G Fox (NSW), J A Phipps (NSW), G D Bailey (NSW), J M Potts (NSW),
S W White (NSW)
Half-backs: R Harvey (NSW), A Summons (NSW), D Logan (NSW),
D M Connor (Queensland)
Forwards: R A L Davidson (NSW), P T Fenwicke (NSW), N M Hughes (NSW),
W J Gunther (NSW), J E Thornett (NSW), K Yanz (NSW), E M Purkis (NSW),
A R Miller (NSW), A S Cameron (NSW), D M Emanuel (NSW), S Scotts (NSW),
N Shehadie (NSW), G N Vaughan (Victoria), K J Ryan (Queensland),
J V Brown (NSW), R Meadows (NSW)
Captain R A L Davidson **Manager** T H McClenaghan
Assistant Manager D L Cowper

1966-67

Full record	Played 34	Won 17	Lost 14	Drawn 3	Points for 348	Against 322
in B Isles	Played 30	Won 15	Lost 13	Drawn 2	Points for 303	Against 280
in France	Played 4	Won 2	Lost 1	Drawn 1	Points for 45	Against 42
International record	Played 5	Won 2	Lost 3			
International details	Dec 3	Wales 11	Australia 14	(Cardiff)		
	Dec 17	Scotland 11	Australia 5	(Murrayfield)		
	Jan 7	England 11	Australia 23	(Twickenham)		
	Jan 21	Ireland 15	Australia 8	(Dublin)		
	Feb 11	France 20	Australia 14	(Paris, Colombes)		

Players

Full-backs: J K Lenehan (NSW), P F Ryan (NSW)
Threequarters: E S Boyce (NSW), P V Smith (NSW), R Webb (Victoria)
R J Marks (Queensland), J E Brass (NSW), A M Cardy (NSW), J A Francis (NSW)
Five-eighths: P R Gibbs (Victoria), A M C Moore (NSW), P F Hawthorne (NSW)
Scrum-halves: J N B Hipwell (NSW), K W Catchpole (NSW)
Forwards: J E Thornett (NSW), R Cullen (Queensland), R B Prosser (NSW),
R G Teitzel (Queensland), R J Heming (NSW), R D Tulloch (Victoria),
J O'Gorman (NSW), G V Davis (NSW), C P Crittle (NSW), P G Johnson (NSW),
A R Miller (NSW), J M Miller (NSW), D A O'Callaghan (NSW),
D A Taylor (Queensland), M P Purcell (Queensland), J Guerassimoff (Queensland),
R Taylor★ (NSW)
Captain J E Thornett   **Manager** R E M McLaughlin   **Assistant Manager** A S Roper

1968 (Ireland and Scotland only)

Full record	Played 5	Won 2	Lost 3	Drawn 0	Points for 38 Against 40
International record	Played 2	Lost 2			
International details	Oct 26	Ireland 10	Australia 3	(Dublin)	
	Nov 2	Scotland 9	Australia 3	(Murrayfield)	

Players

Full-back: A N McGill (NSW)
Threequarters: T R Forman (NSW), R P Batterham (NSW), J W Cole (NSW),
B D Honan (Queensland), A M Pope (Queensland), P V Smith (NSW),
J E Brass (NSW)
Five-eighth: J P Ballesty (NSW)
Scrum-halves: M J Barry (Queensland), J N B Hipwell (NSW)
Forwards: P G Johnson (NSW), P Darveniza (NSW), R B Prosser (NSW),
R V Turnbull (NSW), N P Reilly (Queensland), S C Gregory (Queensland),
K R Bell (Queensland), A J Skinner (NSW), D A Taylor (Queensland),
H A Rose (NSW), G V Davis (NSW)
Captain P G Johnson   **Manager** J H Lord   **Assistant Manager** D M Connor

1971 (France only)

Full record	Played 8	Won 4	Lost 4	Drawn 0	Points for 110 Against 101
International record	Played 2	Won 1	Lost 1		
International details	Nov 20	France 11	Australia 13	(Toulouse)	
	Nov 27	France 18	Australia 9	(Paris, Colombes)	

Players

Full-back: A N McGill (NSW)
Threequarters: J W Cole (NSW), R P Batterham (NSW), L Monaghan (NSW),
J J McLean (Queensland), D L'Estrange (Queensland), D Rathie (Queensland),
G A Shaw (NSW)
Half-backs: G C Richardson (Queensland), R L Fairfax (NSW), J N B Hipwell (NSW),
G Grey (NSW)
Forwards: G V Davis (NSW), M Flynn (Queensland), P D Sullivan (NSW),
R McLean (NSW), O Butler (NSW), S Gregory (Queensland), B Stumbles (NSW),
R Smith (NSW), D Dunworth (Queensland), R B Prosser (NSW),
B Brown (Queensland), P G Johnson (NSW), R Thompson (WA)
Captain G V Davis   **Manager** J French   **Assistant Manager** R I Templeton

1973 (England and Wales only)

Full record	Played 8	Won 2	Lost 5	Drawn 1	Points for 85 Against 131
International record	Played 2	Lost 2			

International details   Nov 10   Wales 24   Australia 0   (Cardiff)
                                   Nov 17   England 20 Australia 3   (Twickenham)

Players
Full-back: A N McGill (NSW), R L Fairfax (NSW) (utility back)
Threequarters: L E Monaghan (NSW), O Stephens (NSW), J J McLean (Queensland),
D R Burnet (NSW), R D L'Estrange (Queensland), G A Shaw (NSW)
Half-backs: G C Richardson (Queensland), P G Rowles (NSW), J N B Hipwell (NSW),
R G Hauser (South Australia)
Forwards: K G McCurrach (NSW), A A Shaw (Queensland), P D Sullivan (NSW),
B R Battishall (NSW), M R Cocks (Queensland), G Fay (NSW), R A Smith (NSW),
S C Gregory (NSW), J L Howard (NSW), R Graham (NSW), S G Macdougall (NSW),
M E Freney (Queensland), C M Carberry (NSW)
Captain P D Sullivan   **Manager** J E Freedman   **Assistant Manager** R I Templeton

1975-76 (including one match in USA)

Full record	Played 26	Won 19	Lost 6	Drawn 1	Points for 496	Against 349
in B Isles	Played 25	Won 18	Lost 6	Drawn 1	Points for 472	Against 337
in USA	Played 1	Won 1	Lost 0	Drawn 0	Points for 24	Against 12
International record	Played 5	Won 2	Lost 3			
International details	Dec 6	Scotland 10	Australia 3	(Murrayfield)		
	Dec 20	Wales 28	Australia 3	(Cardiff)		
	Jan 3	England 23	Australia 6	(Twickenham)		
	Jan 17	Ireland 10	Australia 20	(Dublin)		
	Jan 31	USA 12	Australia 24	(Los Angeles)		

Players
Full-back: M A Fitzgerald (NSW)
Threequarters: J R Ryan (NSW), L E Monaghan (NSW), P G Batch (Queensland),
L J Weatherstone (ACT), G A Shaw (NSW), W A McKid (NSW),
R D L'Estrange (Queensland), J Berne (NSW)
Half-backs: K J Wright (NSW), P E McLean (Queensland), J C Hindmarsh (NSW),
J N B Hipwell (NSW), R G Hauser (Queensland), G O Grey★ (NSW)
Forwards: A A Shaw (Queensland), M E Loane (Queensland), R A Price (NSW),
G K Pearse (NSW), J K Lambie (NSW), G Cornelsen (NSW), R A Smith (NSW),
B W Mansfield (NSW), D W Hillhouse (Queensland), G S Eisenhauer (NSW[C]),
G Fay★ (NSW), J E C Meadows (Victoria), S G Macdougall (ACT),
S C Finnane (NSW), R Graham (NSW), P A Horton (NSW), C M Carberry (NSW)
Captain J N B Hipwell   **Manager** R V Turnbull   **Assistant Manager** J D Brockhoff

1976 (France only, except for one match in Italy)

Full record	Played 10	Won 4	Lost 6	Drawn 0	Points for 114	Against 163
in France	Played 9	Won 3	Lost 6	Drawn 0	Points for 98	Against 148
in Italy	Played 1	Won 1	Lost 0	Drawn 0	Points for 16	Against 15
International record	Played 2	Lost 2				
International details	Oct 24	France 18	Australia 15	(Bordeaux)		
	Oct 30	France 34	Australia 6	(Paris, Parc des Princes)		

Players
Full-back: P E McLean (Queensland)
Threequarters: P G Batch (Queensland), L E Monaghan (NSW), J R Ryan (NSW),
P J Crowe (NSW), G A Shaw (NSW), W A McKid (NSW),
G G Shambrook (Queensland)
Half-backs: K J Wright (NSW), J C Hindmarsh (NSW), R G Hauser (Queensland),
G O Grey (NSW)
Forwards: M E Loane (Queensland), A A Shaw (Queensland), G Cornelsen (NSW),

G K Pearse (NSW), B R Battishall (NSW), R A Smith (NSW), D W Hillhouse
(Queensland), G S Eisenhauer (NSW), K S Besomo (NSW), R Graham (NSW),
S C Finnane (NS), J E C Meadows (Victoria), D A Dunworth (Queensland),
C M Carberry (NSW), P A Horton (NSW), A M Gelling* (NSW)
Captain G A Shaw   **Manager** J G Bain   **Assistant Manager** R I Templeton

1981-82

Full record	Played 23	Won 16	Lost 6	Drawn 1	Points for 431	Against 219
International record	Played 4	Won 1	Lost 3			
International details	Nov 21	Ireland	12	Australia 16	(Dublin)	
	Dec 5	Wales	18	Australia 13	(Cardiff)	
	Dec 19	Scotland	24	Australia 15	(Murrayfield)	
	Jan 2	England	15	Australia 11	(Twickenham)	

Players
Full-backs: R G Gould (Queensland), G J Ella (NSW)
Threequarters: B J Moon (Queensland), M C Martin (NSW), P C Grigg (Queensland),
G A Ella (NSW), A G Slack (Queensland), M D O'Connor (Queensland),
M H Cox (NSW), M J Hawker (NSW)
Half-backs: P E McLean (Queensland), M G Ella (NSW), J N B Hipwell (NSW),
A J Parker (Queensland), P A Cox* (NSW)
Forwards: M E Loane (Queensland), D Hall (Queensland), A A Shaw (Queensland),
C Roche (Queensland), S P Poidevin (NSW), G Cornelsen (NSW), P W Lucas (NSW),
S A Williams (NSW), M J Mathers (NSW), P W McLean (Queensland), S J Pilecki
(Queensland), J E C Meadows (Victoria), A M D'Arcy (Queensland), D J Curran
(NSW), B P Malouf (NSW), C M Carberry (Queensland), L R Walker* (NSW)
Captain A A Shaw   **Manager** Sir Nicholas Shehadie, OBE
Assistant Manager R I Templeton

1983 (to France only, except for two matches in Italy)

Full record	Played 11	Won 6	Lost 3	Drawn 2	Points for 190	Against 157
in Italy	Played 2	Won 2	Lost 0	Drawn 0	Points for 55	Against 7
in France	Played 9	Won 4	Lost 3	Drawn 2	Points for 135	Against 150
International record	Played 3	Won 1	Lost 1	Drawn 1		
International details	Oct 22	Italy	7	Australia 29	(Rovigo)	
	Nov 13	France	15	Australia 15	(Clermont-Ferrand)	
	Nov 19	France	15	Australia 6	(Parc des Princes)	

Players
Full-backs: G J Ella (NSW), R G Gould (Queensland)
Threequarters: D I Campese (ACT), R G Hanley (Queensland), B J Moon (Queensland),
G A Ella (NSW), M J Hawker (NSW), A G Slack (Queensland)
Half-backs: M G Ella (NSW), A J Parker (Queensland), D Vaughan (NSW),
M P Lynagh (Queensland), T A Lane* (Queensland)
Forwards: J E Coolican (NSW), O B Hall (NSW), M A Harding (NSW),
A J McIntyre (Queensland), T A Lawton (Queensland), M I McBain (Queensland),
S A G Cutler (NSW), D W Hillhouse (Queensland), N C Holt (Queensland),
S A Williams (NSW), J S Miller (Queensland), S P Poidevin (NSW),
C Roche (Queensland), D Hall (Queensland), S N Tuynman (NSW), R Crerar* (NSW)
Captain M G Ella   **Manager** Dr C R Wilson   **Assistant Manager** R Dwyer

1984

Full record	Played 18	Won 13	Lost 4	Drawn 1	Points for 400	Against 232
International record	Played 4	Won 4				
International details	Nov 3	England	3	Australia 19	(Twickenham)	
	Nov 10	Ireland	9	Australia 16	(Dublin)	

| Nov 24 | Wales | 9 | Australia 28 | (Cardiff) |
| Dec 8 | Scotland | 12 | Australia 37 | (Murrayfield) |

Players

Full-back: R G Gould (Queensland)

Threequarters: D I Campese (ACT), P C Grigg (Queensland), B J Moon (Queensland), R G Hanley (Queensland), J W Black (NSW), M P Burke (NSW), T A Lane (Queensland), M J Hawker (NSW), A G Slack (Queensland), I M Williams* (NSW)

Half-backs: M G Ella (NSW), M P Lynagh (Queensland), P A Cox (NSW), N C Farr-Jones (NSW)

Forwards: C A Lillicrap (Queensland), A J McIntyre (Queensland), S Pilecki (Queensland), E E Rodriguez (NSW), G H Burrow* (NSW), T A Lawton (Queensland), M I McBain (Queensland), S A Williams (NSW), W A Campbell (Queensland), N G Holt (Queensland), S A G Cutler, (NSW), C Roche (Queensland), W J Calcraft (NSW), D Codey (Queensland), S P Poidevin (NSW), R J Reynolds (NSW), S N Tuynman (NSW)

Captain A G Slack **Manager** Dr C R Wilson **Assistant Manager** A B Jones

1988 (to England, Scotland, Wales and Italy)

Full record	Played 15	Won 11	Lost 4	Drawn 0	Points for 438	Against 236
in Britain	Played 13	Won 9	Lost 4	Drawn 0	Points for 357	Against 212
in Italy	Played 2	Won 2	Lost 0	Drawn 0	Points for 81	Against 24
International record	Played 3	Won 2	Lost 1			
International details	Nov 5	England 28	Australia 19	(Twickenham)		
	Nov 19	Scotland 13	Australia 32	(Murrayfield)		
	Dec 3	Italy 6	Australia 55	(Rome)		

Players

Full-back: A J Leeds (NSW)

Threequarters: D I Campese (NSW), P V Carozza (Queensland), M T Cook (Queensland), P Cornish (ACT), B Girvan (ACT), J C Grant (NSW), A S Niuqila (NSW), R C Toombs (Queensland), L F Walker (NSW)

Half-backs: M P Lynagh* (Queensland), S L James (NSW), D J Knox (NSW), B T Burke (NSW), N C Farr-Jones (NSW)

Forwards: M N Hartill (NSW), R Lawton (Queensland), A J McIntyre (Queensland), E J A McKenzie (NSW), M I McBain (Queensland), T A Lawton (Queensland), W A Campbell (Queensland), S A G Cutler (NSW), D Frawley (NSW), B T Gavin (NSW), R J McCall (Queensland), D G Carter (NSW), J M Gardner (Queensland), S R Gourley (Eastwood), J S Miller (Queensland), S N Tuynman (NSW)

Captain N C Farr-Jones **Manager** A J Conway **Coach** R S F Dwyer

1989 (to France only, except for one match in Canada)

Full record	Played 9	Won 4	Lost 5	Drawn 0	Points for 192	Against 155
in France	Played 8	Won 3	Lost 5	Drawn 0	Points for 149	Against 140
International record	Played 2	Won 1	Lost 1			
International details	Nov 4	France 15	Australia 32	(Strasbourg)		
	Nov 11	France 25	Australia 19	(Lille)		

Players

Full-backs: G J Martin (Queensland), M Roebuck (NSW)

Threequarters: D I Campese (NSW), B Girvan (ACT), A G Herbert (Queensland), T J Horan (Queensland), D K Junee (NSW), J Little (Queensland), D Maguire (Queensland), I M Williams (NSW)

Half-backs: M P Lynagh (Queensland), M Palm (Queensland), P Slattery (Queensland), N C Farr-Jones (NSW)

Forwards: P N Kearns (NSW), T A Lawton (Queensland), D J Crowley (Queensland), A J Daly (NSW), M N Hartill (NSW), E J A McKenzie (NSW), D P A Dix (NSW),

P FitzSimons (NSW), T P Kava (NSW), M A McInnes (ACT), D G Carter (NSW),
R J McCall (Queensland), B Nasser (Queensland), D J Wilson (Queensland),
S Scott-Young (Queensland), B T Gavin (NSW)
Captain N C Farr-Jones **Manager** A J Conway
Coaches R S F Dwyer & R I Templeton

AUSTRALIA TO SOUTH AFRICA

1953

Full record	Played 27 Won 16 Lost 10 Drawn 1 Points for 450 Against 413			
International record	Played 4 Won 1 Lost 3			
International details	Aug 22	South Africa 25	Australia 3	(Johannesburg)
	Sep 5	South Africa 14	Australia 18	(Cape Town)
	Sep 19	South Africa 18	Australia 8	(Durban)
	Sep 26	South Africa 22	Australia 9	(Port Elizabeth)

Players
Full-backs: T Sweeney (Queensland), R Colbert (NSW)
Threequarters: E Stapleton (NSW), G Jones (Queensland), S W White (NSW),
G Horsley (Queensland), H S Barker (NSW), J Blomley (NSW), H J Solomon (NSW),
J A Phipps (NSW)
Half-backs: S W Brown (NSW), M Tate (NSW), C T Burke (NSW), J Bosler (NSW)
Forwards: N Shehadie (NSW), E Morey (NSW), A S Cameron (NSW),
A R Miller (NSW), C F Forbes (Queensland), R A L Davidson (NSW),
J C Carroll (NSW), F M Elliott (NSW), J J Walsh (NSW), J Bain (NSW),
K A Cross (NSW), R Outterside (NSW), C Windon (NSW), D Brockhoff (NSW),
B B Johnson (NSW), N McL Hughes (NSW)
Captain H J Solomon **Manager** J W Breckenridge **Assistant Manager** A C Wallace

1961 (Short)

Full record	Played 6 Won 3 Lost 2 Drawn 1 Points for 90 Against 80			
International record	Played 2 Lost 2			
International details	Aug 5	South Africa 28	Australia 3	(Johannesburg)
	Aug 12	South Africa 23	Australia 11	(Port Elizabeth)

Players
Full-back: J Lenehan (NSW)
Threequarters: M Cleary (NSW), E Magrath (NSW), R Phelps (NSW),
B Ellwood (NSW), J Lisle (NSW)
Half-backs: J Dowse (NSW), H Roberts (Queensland), O Edwards (Queensland),
K Catchpole (NSW)
Forwards: T Reid (NSW), E Heinrich (NSW), J O'Gorman (NSW), R Heming (NSW),
J Thornett (NSW), R Thornett (NSW), G Macdougall (NSW), A Miller (NSW),
J White (NSW), D McDeed (NSW), P Johnson (NSW)
Captain K Catchpole **Manager** B J Halvorsen

1963

Full record	Played 24 Won 15 Lost 8 Drawn 1 Points for 303 Against 233			
International record	Played 4 Won 2 Lost 2			
International details	Jul 13	South Africa 14	Australia 3	(Pretoria)
	Aug 10	South Africa 5	Australia 9	(Cape Town)
	Aug 24	South Africa 9	Australia 11	(Johannesburg)
	Sep 7	South Africa 22	Australia 6	(Port Elizabeth)

Players
Full-backs: T Casey (NSW), P Ryan (NSW)
Threequarters: K Walsham (NSW), J Williams (NSW), J Boyce (NSW),

J Wolfe (Queensland), R Marks (Queensland), I Moutray (NSW), P Jones (NSW),
B Ellwood (NSW)
Half-backs: P Hawthorne (NSW), J Klem (NSW), K Catchpole (NSW),
K McMullen (NSW)
Forwards: J Guerassimoff (Queensland), D O'Neill (Queensland), G Davis (NSW),
D Shepherd (Victoria), E Heinrich (NSW), J O'Gorman (NSW), R Heming (NSW),
J M Miller (NSW), P Crittle (NSW), J Thornett (NSW), J White (NSW),
L Austin (NSW), J Freedman (NSW), B Bailey (NSW), P Johnson (NSW),
M Jenkinson (NSW)
Captain J Thornett   **Manager** R E M McLaughlin   **Assistant Manager** A S Roper

1969

Full record	Played 26 Won 15 Lost 11 Drawn 0 Points for 465 Against 353
International record	Played 4 Lost 4
International details	Aug 2 South Africa 30 Australia 11 (Johannesburg)
	Aug 16 South Africa 16 Australia 9 (Durban)
	Sep 6 South Africa 11 Australia 3 (Cape Town)
	Sep 20 South Africa 19 Australia 8 (Bloemfontein)

Players
Full-backs: A N McGill (NSW), B A Weir (NSW)
Threequarters: T R Forman (NSW), R P Batterham (NSW), J W Cole (NSW),
P D Moore (Queensland), S O Knight (NSW), P V Smith (NSW),
B D Honan (Queensland), G A Shaw (NSW)
Half-backs: J P Ballesty (NSW), R G Rosenblum (NSW), J N B Hipwell (NSW),
M J Barry (Queensland)
Forwards: J R Roxburgh (NSW), J L Howard (NSW), R B Prosser (NSW),
S S Sullivan (Queensland), B S Taafe (NSW), P Darveniza (NSW),
S C Gregory (Queensland), A M Abrahams (NSW), N P Reilly (Queensland),
O F Butler (NSW), G V Davis (NSW), M R Cocks (NSW), B McDonald (NSW),
R J Kelleher (Queensland), H A Rose (NSW), A J Skinner (NSW),
R Wood* (Queensland)
Captain G V Davis   **Manager** C C Eastes   **Assistant Manager** D M Connor

ENGLAND TO AUSTRALIA, NEW ZEALAND AND FIJI

1963 (New Zealand and Australia only)

Full record	Played 6 Won 1 Lost 5 Drawn 0 Points for 54 Against 91
in New Zealand	Played 5 Won 1 Lost 4 Drawn 0 Points for 45 Against 73
in Australia	Played 1 Won 0 Lost 1 Drawn 0 Points for 9 Against 18
International record	
v New Zealand	Played 2 Lost 2
v Australia	Played 1 Lost 1
International details	May 25 New Zealand 21 England 11 (Auckland)
	Jun 1 New Zealand 9 England 6 (Christchurch)
	Jun 4 Australia 18 England 9 (Sydney)

Players
Full-back: R W Hosen (Northampton)
Threequarters: M S Phillips (Fylde), F D Sykes (Northampton), M P Weston
(Durham City), J C Gibson (United Services), J M Ranson (Rosslyn Park),
J M Dee (Hartlepool Rovers)
Half-backs: R F Read (Harlequins), J P Horrocks-Taylor (Leicester),
T C Wintle (St Mary's Hospital), S J S Clarke (Cambridge U)
Forwards: P E Judd (Coventry), J E Highton (United Services),

C R Jacobs (Northampton), H O Godwin (Coventry), J D Thorne (Bristol),
J E Owen (Coventry), T A Pargetter (Coventry), A M Davis (Torquay Athletic),
D P Rogers (Bedford), D G Perry (Bedford), B J Wightman (Coventry),
V R Marriott (Harlequins)
Captain M P Weston   **Manager** J T W Berry
Assistant Manager M R Steele-Bodger

1973 (Fiji and New Zealand only)

Full record	Played 5	Won 2	Lost 3	Drawn 0	Points for 60	Against 72
in Fiji	Played 1	Won 1	Lost 0	Drawn 0	Points for 13	Against 12
in New Zealand	Played 4	Won 1	Lost 3	Drawn 0	Points for 47	Against 60

International record
  v New Zealand   Played 1   Won 1
International details   Sep 15   New Zealand 10   England 16   (Auckland)
Players
Full-backs: P A Rossborough (Coventry), A M Jorden (Blackheath)
Threequarters: D J Duckham (Coventry), P M Knight (Bristol), P J Squires (Harrogate),
J P A G Janion (Richmond), G W Evans (Coventry), P S Preece (Coventry)
Half-backs: A G B Old (Leicester), M J Cooper (Moseley), S J Smith (Sale),
J G Webster (Moseley)
Forwards: M A Burton (Gloucester), C B Stevens (Penzance-Newlyn),
F E Cotton (Loughborough Colls and Coventry), J V Pullin (Bristol), J White (Bristol),
C W Ralston (Richmond), N O Martin (Bedford), R M Uttley (Gosforth),
R M Wilkinson (Cambridge U and Bedford), P J Hendy (St Ives),
A Neary (Broughton Park), J A Watkins (Gloucester), A G Ripley (Rosslyn Park)
Captain J V Pullin   **Manager** D L Sanders   **Assistant Manager** J Elders

1975 (Australia only)

Full record	Played 8	Won 4	Lost 4	Drawn 0	Points for 217	Against 110
International record	Played 2	Lost 2				
International details	May 24	Australia 16	England 9	(Sydney)		
	May 31	Australia 30	England 21	(Brisbane)		

Players
Full-backs: P E Butler (Gloucester), A J Hignell (Cambridge U)
Threequarters: P J Squires (Harrogate), A J Morley (Bristol), D M Wyatt (Bedford),
P S Preece (Coventry), K Smith (Roundhay), A W Maxwell (New Brighton),
J P A G Janion★ (Richmond)
Half-backs: W N Bennett (Bedford), A J Wordsworth (Cambridge U),
A G B Old★ (Middlesbrough), W B Ashton (Orrell), P Kingston (Gloucester),
I N Orum★ (Roundhay)
Forwards: A G Ripley (Rosslyn Park), D M Rollitt (Bristol), A Neary (Broughton Park),
S R Callum (Upper Clapton), P J Dixon★ (Gosforth), R M Uttley (Gosforth),
W B Beaumont (Fylde), R M Wilkinson (Bedford), N D Mantell (Rosslyn Park),
F E Cotton (Coventry), M A Burton (Gloucester), P J Blakeway (Gloucester),
B G Nelmes★ (Cardiff), J V Pullin (Bristol), J A G D Raphael (Northampton)
Captain A Neary   **Manager** A O Lewis   **Assistant Manager** J Burgess

1985 (New Zealand only)

Full record	Played 7	Won 4	Lost 3	Drawn 0	Points for 146	Against 123
International record	Played 2	Lost 2				
International details	Jun 1	New Zealand 18	England 13	(Christchurch)		
	Jun 8	New Zealand 42	England 15	(Wellington)		

Players

Full-backs: C R Martin (Bath), I R Metcalfe (Moseley)

Threequarters: M E Harrison (Wakefield), S T Smith (Wasps), J M Goodwin (Moseley),
P W Dodge (Leicester), J L B Salmon (Harlequins), B Barley (Wakefield)

Half-backs: G H Davies (Wasps), S Barnes (Bristol), R J Hill (Bath),
N D Melville (Wasps)

Forwards: R P Huntsman (Headingley), M Preedy (Gloucester), G S Pearce
(Northampton), A Sheppard (Bristol), S E Brain (Coventry), A W Simpson (Sale),
W A Dooley (Preston Grasshoppers), J Orwin (Gloucester, RAF), S Bainbridge
(Gosforth), D H Cooke (Harlequins), G W Rees (Nottingham), J P Hall (Bath),
M C Teague (Gloucester), R Hesford (Bristol)

Captain P W Dodge   **Manager** W G D Morgan   **Assistant Manager** M J Green

1988 (Australia and Fiji only)

Full record	Played 9	Won 6	Lost 3	Drawn 0	Points for 203	Against 136
in Australia	Played 8	Won 5	Lost 3	Drawn 0	Points for 178	Against 124
in Fiji	Played 1	Won 1	Lost 0	Drawn 0	Points for 25	Against 12

International record

v Australia	Played 2	Lost 2
v Fiji	Played 1	Won 1

International details

v Australia	May 29	Australia 22	England 16	(Brisbane)
	Jun 12	Australia 28	England 8	(Sydney)
v Fiji	Jun 17	Fiji 12	England 25	(Suva)

Players

Full-backs: R Adamson (Wakefield), J M Webb (Bristol)

Threequarters: R Underwood (Leicester & RAF), J Bentley (Sale), B J Evans
(Leicester), B Barley (Wakefield), S J Halliday (Bath), J R B Buckton (Saracens),
T Buttimore★ (Leicester), W D C Carling★ (Harlequins & Army)

Half-backs: S Barnes (Bath), C R Andrew (Wasps), S Robson (Moseley), R M Harding
(Bristol)

Forwards: P A G Rendall (Wasps), G J Chilcott (Bath), J A Probyn (Wasps), G S Pearce
(Northampton), B C Moore (Nottingham), R G R Dawe (Bath), N C Redman (Bath),
J Orwin (Bedford), W A Dooley (Preston Grasshoppers), R A Robinson (Bath),
D W Egerton (Bath), G W Rees (Nottingham), M G Skinner (Harlequins), D Richards
(Leicester)

Captain J Orwin   **Manager** G Cooke   **Coaches** A B C Davies & D Robinson

ENGLAND TO SOUTH AFRICA
1972

Full record	Played 7	Won 6	Lost 0	Drawn 1	Points for 166	Against 58

International record	Played 1	Won 1

International details	Jun 3	South Africa 9	England 18	(Johannesburg)

Players

Full-backs: S A Doble (Moseley), D F Whibley (Leicester)

Threequarters: P M Knight (Bristol), A A Richards (Fylde), J P A G Janion (Bedford),
A J Morley (Bristol), J S Spencer (Headingley), P S Preece (Coventry)

Half-backs: A G B Old (Middlesbrough), T Palmer (Gloucester), L E Weston
(West of Scotland), J B Webster (Mosely), S J Smith★ (Loughborough Colls)

Forwards: M A Burton (Gloucester), F E Cotton (Loughborough Colls),
C B Stevens (Harlequins and Penzance-Newlyn), J V Pullin (Bristol),
A V Boddy (Metropolitan Police), P J Larter (RAF and Northampton),

C W Ralston (Richmond), D E J Watt (Bristol), T A Cowell (Rugby),
A Neary (Broughton Park), J A Watkins (Gloucester), J Barton (Coventry),
A G Ripley (Rosslyn Park)
Captain J V Pullin   **Manager** A O Lewis   **Assistant Manager** J Elders

1984

Full record	Played 7 Won 4 Lost 2 Drawn 1 Points for 156 Against 145
International record	Played 2 Lost 2
International details	Jun 2 South Africa 33 England 15 (Port Elizabeth)
	Jun 9 South Africa 35 England 9 (Johannesburg)

Players
Full-backs: W H Hare (Leicester), N C Stringer (Wasps)
Threequarters: M D Bailey (Cambridge U), A H Swift (Swansea), D M Trick (Bath),
P W Dodge (Leicester), J A Palmer (Bath), S B Burnhill (Loughborough U),
B Barley* (Wakefield), G H Davies (Wasps)
Half-backs: J P Horton (Bath), N G Youngs (Leicester), R J Hill (Bath)
Forwards: P J Blakeway (Gloucester), G S Pearce (Northampton),
M Preedy (Gloucester), P A G Rendall (Wasps), S G F Mills (Gloucester), S E Brain
(Coventry), J P Scott (Cardiff), D A Cusani (Orrell), J H Fidler (Gloucester), G W Rees
(Nottingham), P J Winterbottom (Headingley), J P Hall (Bath),
C J S Butcher (Harlequins), M C Teague (Gloucester)
Captain J P Scott   **Manager** C R Jacobs
Assistant Managers W G D Morgan & J R H Greenwood

SCOTLAND TO SOUTH AFRICA

1960

Full record	Played 3 Won 2 Lost 1 Drawn 0 Points for 61 Against 45
International record	Played 1 Lost 1
International details	Apr 30 South Africa 18 Scotland 10 (Port Elizabeth)

Players
Full-back: R W T Chisholm (Melrose)
Threequarters: A R Smith (Cambridge U, Edinburgh Wands),
R H Thomson (London Scottish), R C Cowan (Selkirk), G D Stevenson (Hawick),
T McClung (Edinburgh Acads), P J Burnet (London Scottish)
Half-backs: G H Waddell (London Scottish), R B Shillinglaw (Gala and Army),
A J Hastie (Melrose)
Forwards: H F McLeod (Hawick), J B Neill (Edinburgh Acads), D M D Rollo
(Howe of Fife), N S Bruce (Blackheath), T O Grant (Hawick), J W Y Kemp
(Glasgow HSFP), F H ten Bos (Oxford U, London Scottish), W Hart (Melrose),
D B Edwards (Heriot's FP), R M Tollervey (Heriot's FP), C E B Stewart (Kelso)
Captain G H Waddell   **Managers** R W Shaw & C W Drummond

SCOTLAND TO AUSTRALIA

1970

Full record	Played 6 Won 3 Lost 3 Drawn 0 Points for 109 Against 94
International record	Played 1 Lost 1
International details	Jun 6 Australia 23 Scotland 3 (Sydney)

Players
Full-back: I S G Smith (London Scottish)
Threequarters: M A Smith (London Scottish), J N M Frame (Gala), J W C Turner (Gala),
C W Rea (West of Scotland), A G Biggar (London Scottish), A D Gill (Gala)

Half-backs: I Robertson (Watsonians), C M Telfer (Hawick), D S Paterson (Gala),
G C Connell (London Scottish) .
Forwards: F A L Laidlaw (Melrose), D T Deans (Hawick), N Suddon (Hawick),
J McLauchlan (Jordanhill Coll), A B Carmichael (West of Scotland), P K Stagg (Sale),
G L Brown (West of Scotland), P C Brown (Gala), T G Elliott (Langholm),
W Lauder (Neath), G K Oliver (Gala), R J Arneil (Leicester)
Captain F A L Laidlaw   **Managers** H S P Monro & G Burrell

1982

Full record	Played 9 Won 6 Lost 3 Drawn 0 Points for 220 Against 113
International record	Played 2 Won 1 Lost 1
International details	Jul 4 Australia 7 Scotland 12 (Brisbane)
	Jul 10 Australia 33 Scotland 9 (Sydney)

Players

Full-backs: P W Dods (Gala), A R Irvine (Heriot's FP)
Threequarters: G R T Baird (Kelso), J A Pollock (Gosforth), R J Gordon
(London Scottish), D I Johnston (Watsonians), K W Robertson (Melrose),
C J Williamson (West of Scotland)
Half-backs: B M Gossman (West of Scotland), J Y Rutherford (Selkirk), I G Hunter
(Selkirk), R J Laidlaw (Jedforest)
Forwards: J Aitken (Gala), G M McGuinness (West of Scotland), I G Milne (Heriot's FP),
N A Rowan (Boroughmuir), R F Cunningham (Bath), C T Deans (Hawick),
W Cuthbertson (Kilmarnock), I D McKie (Sale), A J Tomes (Hawick), F Calder
(Stewart's Melville FP), J H Calder (Stewart's Melville FP), I A M Paxton (Selkirk),
D B White (Gala), R E Paxton (Kelso), John Calder* (Stewart's Melville FP)
Captain A R Irvine   **Manager** I A A MacGregor   **Assistant Manager** J W Telfer

SCOTLAND TO NEW ZEALAND
1975

Full record	Played 7 Won 4 Lost 3 Drawn 0 Points for 157 Against 104
International record	Played 1 Lost 1
International details	Jun 14 New Zealand 24 Scotland 0 (Auckland)

Players

Full-backs: A R Irvine (Heriot's FP), B H Hay (Boroughmuir)
Threequarters: W C C Steele (RAF and London Scottish), L G Dick (Jordanhill),
J N M Frame (Gala), D L Bell (Watsonians), G A Birkett (Harlequins),
J M Renwick (Hawick)
Half-backs: I R McGeechan (Headingley), C M Telfer (Hawick),
A J M Lawson (London Scottish), D W Morgan (Stewart's Melville FP)
Forwards: D G Leslie (Dundee HSFP), G Y Mackie (Highland),
W S Watson (Boroughmuir), W Lauder (Neath), M A Biggar (London Scottish),
A J Tomes (Hawick), I A Barnes (Hawick), A F McHarg (London Scottish),
N A K Pender (Hawick), A B Carmichael (West of Scotland),
J McLauchlan (Jordanhill), D F Madsen (Gosforth), C D Fisher (Waterloo)
Captain J McLauchlan   **Manager** G Burrell   **Assistant Manager** W Dickinson

1981

Full record	Played 8 Won 5 Lost 3 Drawn 0 Points for 189 Against 125
International record	Played 2 Lost 2
International details	Jun 13 New Zealand 11 Scotland 4 (Dunedin)
	Jun 20 New Zealand 40 Scotland 15 (Auckland)

Players
Full-backs: A R Irvine (Heriot's FP), P W Dods (Gala)
Threequarters: S Munro (Ayr), B H Hay (Boroughmuir), G R T Baird (Kelso),
R W Breakey (Gosforth), A G Cranston (Hawick), J M Renwick (Hawick)
Half-backs: J Y Rutherford (Selkirk), R Wilson (London Scottish), R J Laidlaw
(Jedforest), I G Hunter (Selkirk), A J M Lawson★ (London Scottish, Heriot's FP)
Forwards: D B White (Gala), I A M Paxton (Selkirk), P M Lillington★ (Durham U),
J H Calder (Stewart's Melville FP), G Dickson (Gala), D G Leslie (Gala),
W Cuthbertson (Kilmarnock), T J Smith (Gala), A J Tomes (Hawick), J Aitken (Gala),
G M McGuinness (West of Scotland), I G Milne (Heriot's FP),
N A Rowan (Boroughmuir), C T Deans (Hawick), K G Lawrie (Gala)
Captain A R Irvine   **Manager** G K Smith   **Assistant Manager** J W Telfer

IRELAND TO SOUTH AFRICA

1961

Full record	Played 4	Won 3	Lost 1	Drawn 0	Points for 59	Against 36
International record	Played 1	Lost 1				
International details	May 13	South Africa 24	Ireland 8	(Cape Town)		

Players
Full-back: T J Kiernan (UC Cork, Cork Constitution)
Threequarters: A J F O'Reilly (Old Belvedere, Leicester), N H Brophy (UC Dublin),
J C Walsh (UC Cork, Sunday's Well), K J Houston (London Irish, Oxford U),
W J Hewitt (Instonians), J F Dooley (Galwegians)
Half-backs: W G Tormey (UC Dublin), D C Glass (Belfast Collegians),
A A Mulligan (Cambridge U, London Irish), T J Cleary (Limerick)
Forwards: S Millar (Ballymena), B G M Wood (Garryowen), J N Thomas (Blackrock),
A R Dawson (Wanderers), J S Dick (Queen's U, Belfast),
W A Mulcahy (UC Dublin, Bective Rangers), M G Culliton (Wanderers),
C J Dick (Ballymena), N A A Murphy (Cork Constitution), D Scott (Malone),
J R Kavanagh (UC Dublin, Wanderers), T McGrath (Garryowen)
Captain A R Dawson   **Manager** N F Murphy   **Assistant Manager** T A O'Reilly

1981

Full record	Played 7	Won 3	Lost 4	Drawn 0	Points for 207	Against 90
International record	Played 2	Lost 2				
International details	May 30	South Africa 23	Ireland 15	(Cape Town)		
	Jun 6	South Africa 12	Ireland 10	(Durban)		

Players
Full-backs: J J Murphy (Greystones), K A O'Brien (Broughton Park)
Threequarters: K D Crossan (Instonians), T J Kennedy (St Mary's Coll),
M J Kiernan (Dolphin), A C McLennan (Wanderers), J A Hewitt (North of Ireland FC),
A W Irwin (Queen's U, Belfast), D G Irwin (Queen's U, Belfast)
Half-backs: S O Campbell (Old Belvedere), P M Dean (St Mary's Coll),
M A M Quinn★ (Lansdowne), J C Robbie (Greystones), R J M McGrath (Wanderers),
J B O'Connor★ (Palmerston)
Forwards: W P Duggan (Blackrock Coll), R K Kearney (Wanderers), J F Slattery
(Blackrock Coll), J B O'Driscoll (London Irish), A F O'Leary (Cork Constitution),
B O Foley (Shannon), J J Holland (Wanderers), G H Wallace (Old Wesley),
D C Fitzgerald (Dublin U), G A J McLoughlin (Shannon), P A Orr (Old Wesley),
J L Cantrell (Blackrock Coll), H T Harbison (UC Dublin)
Captain J F Slattery   **Manager** P F Madigan   **Assistant Manager** T J Kiernan

IRELAND TO AUSTRALIA
1967

Full record	Played 6	Won 4	Lost 2	Drawn 0	Points for 119	Against 80
International record	Played 1	Won 1				
International details	May 13	Australia 5	Ireland 11	(Sydney)		

Players

Full-backs: T J Kiernan (Cork Constitution)

Threequarters: A T A Duggan (Lansdowne), F P K Bresnihan (UC Dublin),
J C Walsh (UC Cork), N H Brophy (UC Dublin), P J McGrath (UC Cork),
J B Murray (UC Dublin)

Half-backs: C M H Gibson (NIFC), B F Sherry (Terenure), L Hall (UC Cork)

Forwards: S A Hutton (Malone), K W Kennedy (London Irish), S MacHale
(Lansdowne), P O'Callaghan (Dolphin), W J McBride (Ballymena), M G Molloy
(UC Galway), K G Goodall (City of Derry), T A Moore (Highfield),
M G Doyle (UC Dublin), L G Butler (Blackrock), J M Flynn (Wanderers),
D J Hickie (St Mary's College)

Captain T J Kiernan   **Manager** E O'D Davy   **Assistant Manager** D McKibbin

1979

Full record	Played 8	Won 7	Lost 1	Drawn 0	Points for 184	Against 75
International record	Played 2	Won 2				
International details	Jun 3	Australia 12	Ireland 27	(Brisbane)		
	Jun 16	Australia 3	Ireland 9	(Sydney)		

Players

Full-backs: F N G Ennis (Wanderers), R C O'Donnell (St Mary's Coll)

Threequarters: C M H Gibson (North of Ireland FC), T J Kennedy (St Mary's Coll),
A C McLennan (Wanderers), P A J Andreucetti (St Mary's Coll), D G Irwin
(Queen's U, Belfast), P P McNaughton (Greystones)

Half-backs: S O Campbell (Old Belvedere), A J P Ward (Garryowen), J J Moloney
(St Mary's Coll), C S Patterson (Instonians)

Forwards: W P Duggan (Blackrock Coll), C D Cantillon (Cork Constitution),
A J McLean (Ballymena), J B O'Driscoll (London Irish), J F Slattery (Blackrock Coll),
B O Foley (Shannon), M I Keane (Lansdowne), H W Steele (Ballymena), E M J Byrne
(Blackrock Coll), M P Fitzpatrick* (Wanderers), G A J McLoughlin (Shannon),
P A Orr (Old Wesley), C F Fitzgerald (St Mary's Coll), P C Whelan (Garryowen)

Captain J F Slattery   **Manager** J F Coffey   **Assistant Manager** N A A Murphy

IRELAND TO NEW ZEALAND AND FIJI
1976

Full record	Played 8	Won 5	Lost 3	Drawn 0	Points for 96	Against 68
in New Zealand	Played 7	Won 4	Lost 3	Drawn 0	Points for 88	Against 68
in Fiji	Played 1	Won 1	Lost 0	Drawn 0	Points for 8	Against 0
International record	Played 1	Lost 1				
International details	Jun 5	New Zealand 11	Ireland 3	(Wellington)		

Players

Full-backs: A H Ensor (Wanderers), L A Moloney (Garryowen)

Threequarters: T O Grace (St Mary's Coll), A W McMaster (Ballymena), J A Brady
(Wanderers), C M H Gibson (North of Ireland FC), J A McIlrath (Ballymena)

Half-backs: B J McGann (Cork Constitution), M A Quinn (Lansdowne),
D M Canniffe (Lansdowne), J C Robbie (Dublin U), R J M McGrath* (Wanderers)

Forwards: W P Duggan (Blackrock Coll), H W Steele (Ballymena),
S A McKinney (Dungannon), S M Deering (Garryowen), J C Davidson*
(Dungannon), R F Hakin (CIYMS), M I Keane (Lansdowne), B O Foley

(Shannon), E J O'Rafferty (Wanderers), T A O Feighery (St Mary's Coll),
P O'Callaghan (Dolphin), P A Orr (Old Wesley), R J Clegg (Bangor),
J L Cantrell (UC Dublin), P C Whelan (Garryowen)
Captain T O Grace **Manager** K J Quilligan **Assistant Manager** T W Meates

WALES TO SOUTH AFRICA

1964

Full record   Played 4   Won 2· Lost 2   Drawn 0   Points for 43   Against 58
International record   Played 1   Lost 1
International details   May 23   South Africa 24   Wales 3   (Durban)
Players
Full-backs: G T R Hodgson (Neath), H J Davies (London Welsh)
Threequarters: D I Bebb (Carmarthen TC, Swansea), S J Watkins (Newport),
P M Rees (Newport), K Bradshaw (Bridgend), D K Jones (London Welsh, Cardiff),
S J Dawes (London Welsh)
Half-backs: D Watkins (Newport), M Young (Bridgend), D C T Rowlands (Pontypool),
A R Lewis (Abertillery)
Forwards: L J Cunningham (Aberavon), D Williams (Ebbw Vale), R G Waldron
(Neath), N R Gale (Llanelli), J Isaacs (Swansea), B E Thomas (Neath), B Price
(Newport), J T Mantle (Loughborough Colls), D J Hayward (Cardiff),
H J Morgan (Abertillery), G J Prothero (Bridgend), A E I Pask (Abertillery)
Captain D C T Rowlands   **Manager** D J Phillips
Assistant Manager Alun G Thomas

WALES TO AUSTRALIA, NEW ZEALAND AND FIJI

1969

Full record   Played 7   Won 4   Lost 2   Drawn 1   Points for 112 Against 103
  in New Zealand   Played 5   Won 2   Lost 2   Drawn 1   Points for 62 Against 76
  in Australia   Played 1   Won 1   Lost 0   Drawn 0   Points for 19 Against 16
  in Fiji   Played 1   Won 1   Lost 0   Drawn 0   Points for 31 Against 11
International record
  v New Zealand   Played 2   Lost 2
  v Australia   Played 1   Won 1
International details
  v New Zealand   May 31   New Zealand 19   Wales 0   (Christchurch)
                   Jun 14   New Zealand 33   Wales 12   (Auckland)
  v Australia   Jun 21   Australia   16   Wales 19   (Sydney)
Players
Full-back: J P R Williams (London Welsh)
Threequarters: S J Watkins (Newport), A P Skirving (Newport), M C R Richards
(Cardiff), S J Dawes (London Welsh), T G R Davies (Cardiff), K S Jarrett (Newport)
Half-backs: B John (Cardiff), P Bennett (Llanelli), G O Edwards (Cardiff),
R Hopkins (Maesteg)
Forwards: T M Davies (London Welsh), D Hughes (Newbridge), W D Morris (Neath),
J Taylor (London Welsh), B Price (Newport), B E Thomas (Neath), W D Thomas
(Llanelli), D B Llewelyn (Newport), D J Lloyd (Bridgend), D Williams
(Ebbw Vale), N R Gale (Llanelli), J Young (Harrogate), V C Perrins* (Newport)
Captain B Price   **Manager** H C Rogers   **Assistant Manager** D C T Rowlands

1978 (Australia only)

Full record   Played 9   Won 5   Lost 4   Drawn 0   Points for 227   Against 106
International record   Played 2   Lost 2
International details   Jun 11   Australia 18   Wales 8   (Brisbane)
                              Jun 17   Australia 19   Wales 17   (Sydney)

Players
Full-back: J P R Williams (Bridgend)
Threequarters: T G R Davies (Cardiff), G L Evans (Newport), J J Williams (Llanelli),
P C T Daniels (Cardiff), A J Donovan (Swansea), S P Fenwick (Bridgend),
R W R Gravell (Llanelli)
Half-backs: W G Davies (Cardiff), D S Richards (Swansea), T D Holmes (Cardiff),
D B Williams (Newport)
Forwards: C Davis (Newbridge), D L Quinnell (Llanelli), J Squire (Newport),
T J Cobner (Pontypool), S M Lane (Cardiff), B G Clegg (Swansea), A J Martin
(Aberavon), G A D Wheel (Swansea), A G Faulkner (Pontypool), G Price (Pontypool),
S J Richardson (Aberavon), M J Watkins (Cardiff), R W Windsor (Pontypool)
Captain T J Cobner   **Manager** D C T Rowlands   **Assistant Manager** S J Dawes

1988 (New Zealand only)

Full record	Played 8	Won 2	Lost 5	Drawn 1	Points for 135	Against 243
International record	Played 2	Lost 2				
International details	May 28	New Zealand 52	Wales 3	(Christchurch)		
	Jun 11	New Zealand 54	Wales 9	(Auckland)		

Players
Full-backs: A Clement (Swansea), S Bowling (Llanelli), J Mason* (Pontypridd)
Threequarters: I C Evans (Llanelli), G M C Webbe (Bridgend), C Davies (Llanelli),
J A Devereux (Bridgend), B Bowen (S Wales Police), M R Hall (Cambridge U &
Bridgend), M G Ring (Pontypool), N G Davies (Llanelli)
Half-backs: J Davies (Llanelli), R N Jones (Swansea), J L Griffiths (Llanelli)
Forwards: S T Jones (Pontypool), D A Buchanan (Llanelli), D Young (Swansea),
J D Pugh (Neath), M Pugh* (S Wales Police), I J Watkins (Ebbw Vale), K H Phillips
(Neath), R L Norster (Cardiff), P S May (Llanelli), K Moseley (Pontypool),
S Sutton* (S Wales Police), R Phillips (Neath), W P Moriarty (Swansea), R G Collins
(S Wales Police), G Jones* (Llanelli), T Fauvel (Aberavon), D J Bryant (Bridgend),
M A Jones* (Neath)
Captain B Bowen   **Manager** R Morgan   **Coach** A J Gray

FRANCE TO SOUTH AFRICA

1958

Full record	Played 10	Won 5	Lost 3	Drawn 2	Points for 137	Against 124
International record	Played 2	Won 1	Drawn 1			
International details	Jul 26	South Africa 3	France 3	(Cape Town)		
	Aug 16	South Africa 5	France 9	(Johannesburg)		

Players
Full-backs: M Vannier (Racing Club de France), P Lacaze (FC Lourdais)
Threequarters: J Dupuy (S Tarbais), H Rancoule (FC Lourdais), J Lepatey
(SC Mazamet), L Rogé (AS Béziers), A Marquesuzaa (Racing Club de France),
G Stener (Paris U), L Casaux (S Tarbais)
Half-backs: R Martine (FC Lourdais), A Haget (Paris UC), P Danos (AS Béziers),
P Lacroix (S Montois)
Forwards: J Barthe (FC Lourdais), M Celaya (Biarritz), J Carrère (RC Toulonnais),
L Mias (SC Mazamet), B Mommejat (S Cadurcien), R Baulon (A Bayonnais),
F Moncla (Racing Club de France), L Echavé (SU Agen), A Roques (S Cadurcien),
R Barrière (AS Béziers), A Quaglio (SC Mazamet), R Vigier (AS Montferrand),
A Fremaux (Paris U), J de Gregorio (FC Grenoble)
Captain M Celaya   **Manager** S Saulnier   **Assistant Manager** M Laurent

1964

Full record	Played 6	Won 5	Lost 1	Drawn 0	Points for 117	Against 55

International record   Played 1   Won 1
International details   Jul 25   South Africa 6   France 8 (Springs)
Players
Full-back: P Dedieu (AS Béziers)
Threequarters: J Gachassin (FC Lourdais), C Darrouy (S Montois), M Arnaudet (FC Lourdais), R Halçaren (FC Lourdais), J Dupuy (S Tarbais), J Piqué (S Paloise)
Half-backs: P Albaladejo (US Dacquoise), J Capdouze (S Paloise), J-C Hiquet (SU Agen), J-C Lasserre (US Dax), C Laborde (RCF)
Forwards: W Spanghero (RC Narbonne), M Crauste (FC Lourdais), M Lira (La Voulte S), M Sitjar (SU Agen), J-J Rupert (US Tyrosse), B Dauga (S Montois), E Cester (Toulouse OEC), A Herrero (RC Toulonnais), A Gruarin (RC Toulonnais), J C Berejnoi (SC Tulle), M Etcheverry (S Paloise), Y Menthiller (US Romans), J M Cabanier (US Montauban)
Captain M Crauste   **Manager** S Saulnier   **Assistant Manager** J Prat

1967

Full record	Played 13	Won 8	Lost 4	Drawn 1	Points for 209	Against 161
International record	Played 4	Won 1	Lost 2	Drawn 1		
International details	Jul 15	South Africa 26	France 3	(Durban)		
	Jul 22	South Africa 16	France 3	(Bloemfontein)		
	Jul 29	South Africa 14	France 19	(Johannesburg)		
	Aug 12	South Africa 6	France 6	(Cape Town)		

Players
Full-backs: C Lacaze (SC Angoulême), P Villepreux (S Toulousain), J Crampagne (CA Beglais)
Threequarters: C Darrouy (S Montois), J Londios (US Montauban), B Duprat (A Bayonnais), J-P Lux (US Tyrosse), C Dourthe (US Dax), J Trillo (CA Beglais), J Saby (SC Graulhet), J-P Mir (FC Lourdais)
Half-backs: G Camberabero (La Voulte S), J-L Dehez (SU Agen), J-C Roques (CA Brive), M Puget (CA Brive), G Sutra (RC Narbonne)
Forwards: A Abadie (SC Graulhet), J-M Esponda (Racing Club de France), M Lasserre (SU Agen), B Cardebat (US Montauban), J-M Cabanier (US Montauban), J-C Malbet (SU Agen), B Dauga (S Montois), W Spanghero (RC Narbonne), J Fort (SU Agen), A Plantefol (Racing Club de France), C Carrère (RC Toulonnais), M Sitjar (SU Agen), A Quilis (RC Narbonne), G Viard (RC Narbonne)
Captain C Darrouy   **Manager** M Laurent   **Assistant Manager** A Garrigues

1971

Full record	Played 9	Won 7	Lost 1	Drawn 1	Points for 228	Against 92
International record	Played 2	Lost 1	Drawn 1			
International details	Jun 12	South Africa 22	France 9	(Bloemfontein)		
	Jun 19	South Africa 8	France 8	(Durban)		

Players
Full-back: P Villepreux (S Toulousain)
Threequarters: R Bertranne (S Bagnerais), R Bourgarel (S Toulousain), J Cantoni (AS Béziers), C Dourthe (US Dax), A Marot (CA Brive), J Maso (RC Narbonne), J Sillières (S Tarbais), J Trillo (CA Beglais)
Half-backs: M Barrau (S Beaumontois), J-L Berot (S Toulousain), G Pardiès* (SU Agen), M Pebeyre (AS Montferrand)
Forwards: J-L Azarète (St Jean-de-Luz Ol), J-P Bastiat (US Dax), P Biemouret (SU Agen), C Carrère (RC Toulonnais), B Dauga (S Montois), A Estève (AS Béziers), M Etcheverry (S Paloise), J Iraçabal (A Bayonnais), M Lasserre (SU Agen), J le Droff (FC Auch), J-C Skrela (S Toulousain), C Spanghero (RC Narbonne), W Spanghero (RC Narbonne),

C Swierczinski (CA Beglais), M Yachvili (CA Brive)
Captain C Carrère **Manager** E Pebeyre
Assistant Managers F Cazenave & M Celaya

1975

Full record	Played 11	Won 6	Lost 4	Drawn 1	Points for 282	Against 190
International record	Played 2	Lost 2				
International details	Jun 21	South Africa 38	France 25	(Bloemfontein)		
	Jun 28	South Africa 33	France 18	(Pretoria)		

Players
Full-backs: J M Aguirre (S Bagnerais), M Droitecourt (AS Montferrand)
Threequarters: J-C Amade (Biarritz Ol), J-L Averous (La Voulte Sp),
D Harize (S Cahors), M Dupey (FC Auch), C Badin (CA Brive),
R Bertranne (S Bagnerais), J-M Etchenique (Biarritz Ol), F Sangalli (RC Narbonne)
Half-backs: J-P Romeu (AS Montferrand), J P Pesteil (AS Béziers),
R Astre (AS Béziers), J Fouroux (La Voulte Sp)
Forwards: Y Brunet (USA Perpignan), J Costantino (AS Montferrand),
D Revallier (UA Gaillac), R Paparemborde (S Paloise), B Forestier (CA Beglais),
G Cholley (Castres Ol), J-P Decrae (Racing Club de France), F Haget (SU Agen),
A Guilbert (RC Toulon), M Julian (Castres Ol), M Yachvili (CA Brive),
J-C Skréla (S Toulousain), P Peron (Racing Club de France), S Lassoujade (SU Agen),
G Rousset (AS Béziers), J-L Joinel (CA Brive), M Palmie* (AS Béziers)
Captains (joint) R Astre & J Fouroux **Manager** M Batigne
Assistant Managers M Celaya & F Cazenave

1980

Full record	Played 4	Won 3	Lost 1	Drawn 0	Points for 90	Against 95
International record	Played 1	Lost 1				
International details	Nov 8	South Africa 37	France 15	(Pretoria)		

Players
Full-backs: S Gabernet (Toulouse), S Blanco (Biarritz)
Threequarters: D Bustaffa (Carcassonne), C Martinez (Béziers), J-C Castagnet (Pau),
L Pardo (Bayonne), R Bertranne (Bagnères), P Mesny (Grenoble)
Half-backs: B Viviès (Agen), P Fort (Béziers), J Gallion (Toulon),
J-P Elissalde (La Rochelle)
Forwards: J-L Joinel (Brive), M Carpentier (Lourdes), T Sinico (Valence),
J-P Rives (Toulouse), P Lacans (Béziers), J-P Wolff (Béziers), A Maleig (Tarbes),
J-P Fauvel (SC de Tulle), D Dubroca (Agen), R Paparemborde (Pau),
P Dospital (Bayonne), B Herrero (Nice), P Dintrans (Tarbes)
Captain J-P Rives **Manager** Y Noé **Assistant Managers** M Celaya & J Piqué

FRANCE TO AUSTRALIA AND NEW ZEALAND
1961

Full record	Played 15	Won 8	Lost 7	Drawn 0	Points for 180	Against 169
in New Zealand	Played 13	Won 6	Lost 7	Drawn 0	Points for 150	Against 149
in Australia	Played 2	Won 2	Lost 0	Drawn 0	Points for 30	Against 20
International record						
v New Zealand	Played 3	Lost 3				
v Australia	Played 1	Won 1				
International details						
v New Zealand	Jul 22	New Zealand 13	France 6	(Auckland)		
	Aug 5	New Zealand 5	France 3	(Wellington)		
	Aug 19	New Zealand 32	France 3	(Christchurch)		
v Australia	Aug 26	Australia 8	France 15	(Sydney)		

Players
Full-backs: M Vannier (RC Chalon), J Meynard (US Cognac)
Threequarters: S Plantey (Racing Club de France), G Boniface (S Montois),
H Rancoule (RC Toulon), J Dupuy (S Tarbais), G Calvo (FC Lourdais),
J Piqué (S Paloise), J Bouquet (CS Vienne), A Boniface (S Montois)
Half-backs: C Lacaze (FC Lourdais), G Camberabero (La Voulte S),
P Albaladejo (US Dacquoise), P Lacroix (SU Agen), L Camberabero (La Voulte S),
J Serin (SC Mazamet)
Forwards: M Celaya (S Bordelais), S Meyer (CA Perigueux), R Lefèvre (CA Brive),
M Crauste (FC Lourdais), F Moncla (S Paloise), C Vidal (SC Mazamet),
M Cassiede (US Dax), J P Saux (S Paloise), A Domenech (CA Brive),
A Bianco (FC Auch), G Bouguyon (FC Grenoble) P Cazals (S Montois),
J Laudouar (AS Soustons), J Rollet (A Bayonnais)
Captain F Moncla   **Manager** M Laurent   **Assistant Manager** G Basquet

1968

Full record	Played 14	Won 9	Lost 5	Drawn 0	Points for 195	Against 142
in New Zealand	Played 12	Won 8	Lost 4	Drawn 0	Points for 154	Against 120
in Australia	Played 2	Won 1	Lost 1	Drawn 0	Points for 41	Against 22

International record

v New Zealand	Played 3	Lost 3
v Australia	Played 1	Lost 1

International details

v New Zealand	Jul 13	New Zealand 12	France 9	(Christchurch)
	Jul 27	New Zealand 9	France 3	(Wellington)
	Aug 10	New Zealand 19	France 12	(Auckland)
v Australia	Aug 17	Australia 11	France 10	(Sydney)

Players
Full-backs: P Villepreux (S Toulousain), C Lacaze (Angoulême)
Threequarters: A Campaes (FC Lourdais), J M Bonal (S Toulousain),
P Besson (CA Brive), A Piazza (US Montauban), J-P Lux (US Tyrosse),
C Dourthe (US Dax), J Trillo (CA Beglais), J Maso (US Perpignan)
Half-backs: J Andrieu (SC Graulhet), C Boujet (Grenoble), J-L Berot (S Toulousain),
M Puget (CA Brive)
Forwards: M Greffe (Grenoble), W Spanghero (RC Narbonne),
M Billiere (S Toulousain), J Salut (Toulouse, OEC), C Carrère (RC Toulonnais),
B Dutin (Mont de Marsan), C Chenevay (Grenoble), B Dauga (Mont de Marsan),
A Plantefol (SU Agen), E Cester (Toulouse OEC), J-M Esponda (US Perpignan),
M Lasserre (SU Agen), J-C Noble (La Voulte S), J Iraçabal (A Bayonnais),
M Yachvili (SC Tulle), J-P Baux (CA Lannemezan)
Captain C Carrère   **Manager** J-C Bourrier   **Assistant Manager** A Garrigues

1972 (Australia only)

Full record	Played 9	Won 8	Lost 0	Drawn 1	Points for 254	Against 122
International record	Played 2	Won 1	Drawn 1			
International details	Jun 17	Australia 14	France 14	(Sydney)		
	Jun 25	Australia 15	France 16	(Brisbane)		

Players
Full-backs: P Villepreux (S Toulousain), H Cabrol (AS Béziers)
Threequarters: B Duprat (A Bayonnais), J Cantoni (AS Béziers), G Lavagne
(AS Béziers), J Trillo (CA Beglais), C Dourthe (US Dax), J-P Lux (US Dax),
J Maso (RC Narbonne)
Half-backs: J-L Berot (S Toulousain), A Marot (CA Briviste), M Barrau (S Beaumontois),
J Fouroux (La Voulte Sp)
Forwards: J-C Skrela (S Toulousain), P Biemouret (SU Agen), O Saisset (AS Béziers),

W Spanghero (RC Narbonne), B Vinsonneau (US Dax), C Spanghero (RC Narbonne),
J-P Bastiat (US Dax), A Estève (AS Béziers), J Iraçabal (A Bayonnais),
J-L Azarète (St Jean de Luz), A Vaquerin (AS Béziers), J-C Rossignol (CA Briviste),
A Lubrano (AS Béziers), R Bénésis (SU Agen)
Captain W Spanghero **Manager** R Dasse
Assistant Managers M Celaya & F Cazenave

1979 (New Zealand only, except one match in Fiji)

Full record	Played 9	Won 6	Lost 3	Drawn 0	Points for 168	Against 116
in New Zealand	Played 8	Won 5	Lost 3	Drawn 0	Points for 155	Against 112

International record (in NZ)

International details	Played 2	Won 1	Lost 1	
	Jul 7	New Zealand 23	France 9	(Christchurch)
	Jul 14	New Zealand 19	France 24	(Auckland)

Players

Full-backs: J-M Aguirre (Bagnères), S Blanco (Biarritz)
Threequarters: F Costes (Montferrand), J-L Averous (La Voulte), D Bustaffa
(Carcassonne), D Codorniou (Narbonne), P Mesny* (Racing Club de France),
M Duffranc (Tyrosse), L Pardo (Tarbes)
Half-backs: A Caussade (Lourdes), G Laporte (Graulhet), J Gallion (Toulon),
Y Laffarge (Montferrand)
Forwards: Y Malquier (Narbonne), C Beguerie (Agen), J-L Joinel (Brive),
J-P Rives (Toulouse), F Haget (Biarritz), P Salas (Narbonne), J-F Marchal (Lourdes),
A Maleig (Oloron), G Colomine (Narbonne), D Dubroca (Agen), R Paparemborde (Pau),
P Dintrans (Tarbes), J-F Perche (Bourg)
Captain J-P Rives **Manager** Y Noé **Assistant Managers** F Cazenave & J Desclaux

1981 (Australia only)

Full record	Played 9	Won 6	Lost 3	Drawn 0	Points for 189	Against 112
International record	Played 2	Lost 2				

International details	Jul 5	Australia 17	France 15	(Brisbane)
	Jul 11	Australia 24	France 14	(Sydney)

Players

Full-backs: S Gabernet (Toulouse), S Blanco (Biarritz)
Threequarters: M Bruel (Pau), M Fabre (Béziers), J-L Averous (La Voulte),
P Chadebech (Brive), D Codorniou (Narbonne), P Mesny (Grenoble),
L Pardo (Bayonne)
Half-backs: B Viviès (Agen), M Sallefranque (Dax), P Berbizier (Lourdes),
J-P Elissalde (La Rochelle), A Mournet* (Bagnères)
Forwards: M Carpentier (Lourdes), D Erbani (Agen), J-P Rives (Toulouse),
P Lacans (Béziers), L Rodriguez (Mont-de-Marsan), O Derghali (Bagnères),
D Revallier (Graulhet), A Lorieux (Grenoble), P Salas (Narbonne),
R Paparemborde (Pau), M Crémaschi (Lourdes), J-P Wolff (Béziers),
J-L Dupont (Agen), P Dintrans (Tarbes)
Captain J-P Rives **Manager** Y Noé **Assistant Managers** J Fouroux & J Piqué

1984 (New Zealand only)

Full record	Played 8	Won 6	Lost 2	Drawn 0	Points for 224	Against 138
International record	Played 2	Lost 2				

International details	Jun 16	New Zealand 10	France 9	(Christchurch)
	Jun 23	New Zealand 31	France 18	(Auckland)

Players

Full-backs: S Blanco (Biarritz), B Viviès (Agen)
Threequarters: P Estève (Narbonne), P Lagisquet (Bayonne), M Andrieu (Nîmes),

L Pardo (Montferrand), D Codorniou (Narbonne), P Sella (Agen), E Bonneval (Toulouse)
Half-backs: J-P Lescarboura (Dax), G Laporte (Graulhet), P Berbizier (Lourdes), H Sanz (Graulhet)
Forwards: P Dospital (Bayonne), J-P Garuet (Lourdes), P-E Detrez (Nîmes), D Dubroca (Agen), B Herrero (Nice), P Dintrans (Tarbes), A Lorieux (Grenoble), F Haget (Biarritz), J Condom (Boucau), P Lacans (Béziers), L Rodriguez (Mont-de-Marsan), J-C Orso (Nice), J-L Joinel (Brive), J Grattan (Agen)
Captain P Dintrans   **Manager** Y Noé   **Assistant Manager** J Fouroux

1986 (including three matches in Argentina)

Full record	Played 8	Won 4	Lost 3	Drawn 1	Points for 199	Against 139
in Argentina	Played 3	Won 2	Lost 1	Drawn 0	Points for 80	Against 48
in Australia	Played 3	Won 1	Lost 1	Drawn 1	Points for 80	Against 54
in New Zealand	Played 2	Won 1	Lost 1	Drawn 0	Points for 39	Against 37
International record						
v Argentina	Played 2	Won 1	Lost 1			
v Australia	Played 1	Lost 1				
v New Zealand	Played 1	Lost 1				

International details					
v Argentina	May 31	Argentina	15	France 13	(Buenos Aires)
	Jun 7	Argentina	9	France 22	(Buenos Aires)
v Australia	Jun 21	Australia	27	France 14	(Sydney)
v New Zealand	Jun 28	New Zealand	18	France 9	(Christchurch)

Players
Full-backs: J Bianchi (Toulon), S Blanco (Biarritz)
Threequarters: M Andrieu (Nîmes), P Bérot (Agen), E Bonneval (Toulouse), P Lagisquet (Bayonne), P Chadebach (Brive), P Sella (Agen), J-B Lafond (RCF), D Charvet (Toulouse)
Half-backs: J-P Lescarboura (Dax), G Laporte (Graulhet), J Gallion (Toulon), P Berbizier (Agen), R Modin* (Brive)
Forwards: P-E Detrez (Nîmes), J-P Garuet (Lourdes), P Marocco (Montferrand), C Portolan (Toulouse), D Dubroca (Agen), B Herrero (Toulon), J Condom (Boucau), F Haget (Biarritz), J-C Orso (Nice), T Picard (Montferrand), P Serriere (RCF), M Cecillon (Bourgoin), E Champ (Toulon), D Erbani (Agen), J Gratton (Agen), J-L Joinel (Brive), L Rodriguez (Mont-de-Marsan)
Captain D Dubroca   **Manager** Y Noé   **Assistant Manager** J Fouroux

1989 (New Zealand only)

Full record	Played 8	Won 4	Lost 4	Drawn 0	Points for 180	Against 170
International record	Played 2	Lost 2				
International details	Jun 17	New Zealand 25	France 17	(Christchurch)		
	Jul 1	New Zealand 34	France 20	(Auckland)		

Players
Full-backs: S Blanco (Biarritz), J-B Lafond (RCF)
Threequarters: P Lagisquet (Bayonne), P Bérot (Agen), S Weller (Grenoble), P Hontas (Biarritz), P Sella (Agen), D Charvet (Toulouse), M Andrieu (Nîmes)
Half-backs: F Mesnel (RCF), J-M Lescure (Narbonne), P Rougé-Thomas (Toulouse), P Berbizier (Agen), H Sanz (Narbonne)
Forwards: D Bouet (Dax), P Gallard (Béziers), J-P Garuet (Lourdes), P Ondarts (Biarritz), M Pujolle (Nice), H Chabowski (Bourgoin), T Devergie (Nîmes), J Condom (Biarritz), O Roumat (Dax), D Erbani (Agen), J-F Tordo (Toulon), P Beraud (Dax), P Benetton (Agen), M Cecillon (Bourgoin), A Carminati (Béziers), L Rodriguez (Dax)
Captain P Berbizier   **Manager** J Fouroux   **Assistant Manager** D Dubroca

TOP SCORERS 1989-1990

Peter Jackson *Daily Mail*

John Liley beat Dusty Hare's single season record for Leicester by one point at the first attempt. He has only to keep it up for another 17 seasons to overtake his predecessor's ultimate achievement. Hare's 7,000-plus world record may be just about the most untouchable landmark in sport, but the new Leicester full-back has wasted no time in proving that he can match the old Tiger kick for kick, at least over one full season. However, Liley, a Yorkshireman from Wakefield who spent a 'probationary' season at Welford Road playing second fiddle to Hare, did an awful lot more than land the goals. He also scored 18 tries, more than any other Leicester player, and that all-round quality was good enough to earn him promotion to the England party for the summer trip to Argentina.

Alan Edmunds, second in the tries list in 1988-89, went one better to finish as the leading try-scorer in senior British and Irish competition. His total of 41 for Neath, among them one against the 'other' All Blacks, would have been even more imposing but for occasional interruptions through injury.

Eddie Saunders and Brendan Hanavan chased him home in a season in which Ballymena supplied two of the most consistent scorers in the game, Derek McAleese, third in the points chart, and David Smyth, joint fifth in the tries list with 29.

POINTS

439 – John Liley (Leicester); **372** – Arwel Parry (Bridgend); **337** – Derek McAleese (Ballymena); **336** – Martin Strett (Orrell); **333** – Andy Green (Exeter); **318** – Steve Burnage (Fylde); **315** – Simon Hodgkinson (Nottingham), Calum McDonald (Stirling County); **307** – John Steele (Northampton); **306** – Robbie Stewart (Kilmarnock); **301** – Martin Livesey (Richmond); **300** – Michael Kiernan (Dolphin); **295** – John Graves (Rosslyn Park); **288** – Andy Higgin (Vale of Lune); **281** – Kevin O'Brien (Broughton Park); **278** – Rodney Pow (Selkirk); **269** – Tim Smith (Gloucester); **267** – Matthew Silva (Pontypool); **264** – Alistair Donaldson (Currie); **261** – Ian Aitchison (London Irish); **257** – Craig Chalmers (Melrose); **256** – Mark Wyatt (Swansea); **255** – Paul Thorburn (Neath); **252** – Dave Barrett (West of Scotland); **251** – David Pears (Harlequins); **250** – Dan Pulfrey (Edinburgh Wanderers); **243** – Byron Hayward (Newbridge); **242** – Colin Stephens (Llanelli); **234** – Andrew Ker (Kelso), Paul Williams (Neath); **224** – Graeme Spearman (Gosforth); **223** – Stuart Barnes (Bath), Chris Howard (Rugby); **217** – Johnny Pearse (Shannon), Murry Walker (Boroughmuir); **216** – Russell Hensley (Nuneaton); **212** – Scott Welsh (Hawick); **207** – Robbie Kemp (Ayr); **203** – Tosh Askew (Liverpool St Helens), Gavin Hastings (London Scottish); **201** – Gregor McKechnie (Jedforest); **198** – Carl Mogford (Abertillery); **194** – Rob Andrew (Wasps); **193** – Mark Smith (Lydney); **188** – Andy Phillips (Pontypridd); **182** – Jeff Bird (Llanelli)

TRIES

41 – Alan Edmunds (Neath); **37** – Eddie Saunders (Rugby); **35** – Brendan Hanavan (Fylde); **31** – Rory Underwood (Leicester); **29** – Rupert Moon (Neath), David Smyth

Leicester's John Liley, who beat Dusty Hare's single season record at the first attempt with 439 points.

(Ballymena); **27** – Graeme Stirling (Edinburgh Wanderers), Tony Swift (Bath); **26** – Roger Bidgood (Pontypool), Carwyn Davies (Llanelli); **25** – Steve Bowling (Llanelli), Keith Orrell (Pontypool), Simon Povoas (Leicester), Mark Titley (Swansea); **24** – Mike Harrison (Wakefield), Mark Sephton (Liverpool St Helens), Aled Williams (Bridgend); **23** – Mike DeBusk (Boroughmuir), Iwan Tukalo (Selkirk); **22** – Mike Murtagh (Wakefield), David Michie (Glasgow High/Kelvinside), Phil Manning (Ayr); **21** – Graham Agnew (Kilmarnock), Allan Bateman (Neath), Kevin Ellis (Bridgend), Gary McGregor (Corstorphine), Mark Thomas (Ebbw Vale); **20** – Simon Davies (Llanelli), Rowland Phillips (Neath), Tony Stanger (Hawick); **19** – Paul Collings (Bristol), Martin Lightbody (Glasgow Academicals), Derek Morgan (Gloucester), Graeme MacGregor (Glasgow Academicals), Steve Walklin (Plymouth Albion), Barry Whitehead (Bristol), Huw Woodland (Maesteg); **18** – Steve Fealey (Newbridge), Scott Forrester (Currie), Alun Harries (Newbridge), Peter Hewitt (Heriot's FP), John Liley (Leicester), Alex Moore (Edinburgh Academicals), Craig Stirling (Edinburgh Wanderers); **17** – Steve Brown (Broughton Park), Nigel Davies (Llanelli), Barry Evans (Leicester), Ian Hemburrow (SW Police), Brian Hughes (Jedforest), Keith Johnston (Selkirk), Richard Mogg (Gloucester), Bright Sodje (Blackheath), Simon Smith (Wasps), Raphael Tsagane (Wasps)

Figures are based on all first-class fixtures, Cup ties, County Championships, Barbarian, representative and international matches

348

CLUBS SECTION

(Records of most-capped players are complete up to 30 April 1990)

ENGLAND
Bath

Year of formation 1865
Grounds Recreation Ground, London Road, Bath   Tel: Bath (0225) 429227;
Horse Show Ground, London Road, Bath   Tel: Bath (0225) 330365
Colours Blue, white and black
Most capped player D M B Sole (Scotland) 25 caps
Captain 1989-90 S Barnes
1st XV 1989-90 P42 W35 D1 L6 F1116 A363
Courage Leagues Div 1 3rd   **Pilkington Cup** *Winners* Beat Gloucester 48-6 (final)
Top scorer S Barnes (223)   **Most tries** A Swift (26)

League Record in 1989-90

Date	Venue	Opponents	Result	Scorers
9 Sept	H	Harlequins	32–12	*T:* Hall, Callard, Hoskin, Robinson, Barnes (2) *C:* Barnes (4)
23 Sept	A	Gloucester	6–13	*T:* Egerton *C:* Barnes
14 Oct	H	Rosslyn Park	34–6	*T:* Swift (2), Hall, Halliday, Barnes, Callard *C:* Barnes (5)
28 Oct	A	Bristol	14–13	*T:* Swift, Blackett *PG:* Barnes (2)
11 Nov	H	Moseley	27–9	*T:* Halliday (2), Ubogu, Swift *C:* Barnes (4) *PG:* Barnes
18 Nov	A	Orrell	9–6	*PG:* Barnes (3)
25 Nov	A	Wasps	18–9	*T:* Swift (2), Blackett, Dawe *C:* Barnes
13 Jan	H	Bedford	76–0	*T:* Guscott (4), Callard (3), Swift (4), Hall, Ubogu, Barnes *C:* Barnes (10)
10 Mar	A	Nottingham	9–12	*T:* Barnes *C:* Barnes *PG:* Barnes
31 Mar	A	Saracens	7–9	*T:* Egerton *PG:* Callard
28 Apr	H	Leicester	26–15	*T:* Adebayo (2), Callard, Withey, Barnes *C:* Barnes (3)

Bedford

Year of formation 1886
Ground Goldington Road, Bedford   Tel: Bedford (0234) 59160/54619
Colours Wide hoops in Oxford and Cambridge blues
Most capped player D P Rogers (England) 34 caps
Captain 1989-90 Mark Howe
1st XV 1989-90 P38 W6 D1 L31 F388 A1083
Courage Leagues Div 1 12th *relegated* **Pilkington Cup** Lost 7-12 to Richmond
(3rd round) **Top scorer** A Moffat (49) **Most tries** D Francombe (6)

League Record in 1989-90

Date	Venue	Opponents	Result	Scorers
9 Sept	H	Saracens	3–22	*DG:* Finnie
23 Sept	A	Leicester	3–60	*PG:* Finnie
14 Oct	H	Harlequins	8–71	*T:* Harris, Cullen
28 Oct	A	Gloucester	6–37	*PG:* Vaudin (2)
11 Nov	H	Orrell	7–25	*T:* Howe *PG:* Vaudin
18 Nov	H	Nottingham	16–47	*T:* Howe (2), Francombe *C:* Greed (2)

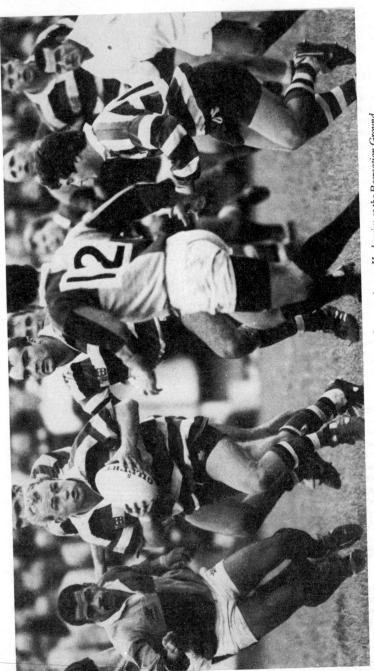

Andy Robinson of Bath warns off potential tacklers during Bath's early-season League win over Harlequins at the Recreation Ground.

25 Nov	H	Moseley	0–24	
13 Jan	A	Bath	0–76	
10 Mar	H	Wasps	9–44	*PG:* Greed (3)
31 Mar	A	Rosslyn Park	12–45	*T:* Clark, Egan *C:* Frost (2)
28 Apr	H	Bristol	6–16	*T:* Egan *C:* Frost

Blackheath

Year of formation 1858
Ground Rectory Field, Blackheath, London SE3   Tel: 081-858 1578 and 3677
Colours Red and black hoops
Most capped player C N Lowe (England) 25 caps
Captain 1989-90 T Fenby
1st XV 1989-90   P33   W16   D4   L13   F713   A540
Courage Leagues Div 2 10th   **Pilkington Cup** Lost 16-26 to Sale (3rd round)
Top scorer C Parker (171)   **Most tries** B Sodje (17)

League Record in 1989–90

Date	Venue	Opponents	Result	Scorers
9 Sept	H	Rugby	0–21	
23 Sept	A	Gosforth	12–12	*T:* Mercer *C:* Parker *PG:* Parker (2)
14 Oct	H	Plymouth Albion	9–37	*T:* Annous *C:* Parker *PG:* Parker
28 Oct	A	Headingley	12–31	*T:* Smith, Jones *C:* Parker (2)
12 Nov	A	Richmond	15–15	*T:* King *C:* Parker *PG:* Parker (2) *DG:* King
18 Nov	H	Coventry	16–21	*T:* Jones, Scott *C:* Parker *PG:* Parker (2)
25 Nov	A	Waterloo	19–10	*T:* Harris, King, McIntyre *C:* Harris (2) *PG:* Harris
13 Jan	H	Northampton	9–10	*PG:* Harris (2) *DG:* King
10 Mar	A	Liverp'l St H	3–16	*PG:* Scott
31 Mar	A	Sale	18–14	*T:* Harris *C:* Parker *PG:* Parker (4)
28 Apr	H	London Irish	28–18	*T:* Parker, King, Sodje, Swain *C:* Parker (3) *DG:* King (2)

Bristol

Year of formation 1888
Ground Memorial Ground, Filton Avenue, Horfield, Bristol BS7 0AG
Tel: Bristol (0272) 514448
Colours Blue and white
Most capped player J V Pullin (England) 42 caps
Captain 1989-90 A F Dun
1st XV 1989-90   P44   W27   D1   L16   F1012   A550
Courage Leagues Div 1 9th   **Pilkington Cup** Lost 13-15 to Moseley (quarter-final)
Top scorer J Webb (121)   **Most tries** P Collings, B Whitehead (19)

League Record in 1989–90

Date	Venue	Opponents	Result	Scorers
9 Sept	A	Orrell	15–12	*PG:* Webb (5)
23 Sept	H	Nottingham	13–9	*T:* Woodman *PG:* Webb (3)
14 Oct	A	Moseley	16–10	*T:* Knibbs, Hull *C:* Webb *PG:* Webb (2)
28 Oct	H	Bath	13–14	*T:* Collings *PG:* Webb (3)
11 Nov	H	Harlequins	7–13	*T:* Harding *PG:* Webb
18 Nov	H	Gloucester	6–13	*PG:* Webb, Hogg
25 Nov	H	Rosslyn Park	6–15	*T:* Hogg *C:* Hogg
13 Jan	A	Saracens	12–17	*T:* Collings, Whitehead, Hull

10 Mar	H	Leicester	11–13	*T:* Davis, Smith *PG:* Painter
31 Mar	H	Wasps	21–22	*T:* Davis *C:* Tainton *PG:* Tainton (5)
28 Apr	A	Bedford	16–6	*T:* Duggan, Thiller *C:* Tainton *PG:* Tainton (2)

Coventry

Year of formation 1874
Ground Coundon Road, Coventry   Tel: Coventry (0203) 591274
Colours Navy and white hoops, navy shorts
Most capped player D J Duckham (England) 36 caps
Captain 1989-90 S Thomas
1st XV 1989-90   P41   W20   D1   L20   F738   A693
Courage Leagues Div 2 4th   **Pilkington Cup** Lost 6-17 to Liverpool St Helens (2nd round)   **Top scorer** M Fairn (89)   **Most tries** S Hall (14)

League Record in 1989–90

Date	Venue	Opponents	Result	Scorers
9 Sept	H	London Irish	18–25	*T:* S Thomas, Medford *C:* S Thomas (2) *PG:* S Thomas *DG:* Rowan
23 Sept	A	Sale	22–24	*T:* Travers *PG:* S Thomas (6)
14 Oct	H	Rugby	18–10	*T:* S Thomas *C:* S Thomas *PG:* S Thomas, M Thomas (2) *DG:* Rowan
28 Oct	A	Gosforth	16–0	*T:* S Thomas, Hall (2), Travers
11 Nov	H	Liverp'l St H	13–13	*T:* S Thomas (2) *C:* Mitchell *DG:* Mitchell
18 Nov	A	Blackheath	21–16	*T:* Medford *C:* Mitchell *PG:* Mitchell (5)
25 Nov	H	Richmond	21–18	*T:* Robbins, Hall, Mitchell, Farrington *C:* S Thomas *PG:* Mitchell
13 Jan	H	Waterloo	22–12	*T:* Robbins (3), P Thomas *C:* S Thomas (3)
10 Mar	A	Northampton	18–24	*PG:* S Thomas (5) *DG:* Rowan
31 Mar	A	Headingley	22–30	*T:* S Thomas, McKenzie, Hickey, Hall, Fairn *C:* S Thomas
28 Apr	H	Plymouth Albion	15–13	*T:* Hickey *C:* Fairn *PG:* Fairn (3)

Gloucester

Year of formation 1873
Ground Kingsholm, Kingsholm Road, Gloucester GL1 3AX
Tel: Gloucester (0452) 20901 (office); 28385 (club)
Colours Cherry and white
Most capped player A T Voyce (England) 27 caps
Captain 1989-90 M Hamlin
1st XV 1989-90   P46   W34   D2   L10   F1090   A665
Courage Leagues Div 1 2nd   **Pilkington Cup** Lost 6-48 to Bath (final)
Top scorer T Smith (259)   **Most tries** D Morgan (19)

League Record in 1989–90

Date	Venue	Opponents	Result	Scorers
9 Sept	A	Moseley	16–12	*T:* Gadd *PG:* T Smith (3) *DG:* Hamlin
23 Sept	H	Bath	13–6	*T:* Dunn *PG:* T Smith (3)
14 Oct	A	Wasps	4–29	*T:* Gadd
28 Oct	H	Bedford	37–6	*T:* Caskie (2), Morgan (2), Hamlin, Marment, Brain, Clark *C:* Hamlin *PG:* T Smith
11 Nov	H	Rosslyn Park	41–12	*T:* Morgan (3), Price (2), T Smith, Hannaford, Hawker *C:* T Smith, Hamlin (2) *PG:* T Smith

18 Nov	A	Bristol	13–6	T: Pascall, Marment C: Marment
				PG: Marment
25 Nov	H	Saracens	21–21	T: Morgan, Hamlin, Breeze, Hannaford
				C: Marment PG: Marment
13 Jan	A	Leicester	26–16	T: Mogg, Hannaford (2), Brain C: T Smith (2)
				PG: T Smith (2)
10 Mar	H	Harlequins	24–9	T: Dunn C: T Smith PG: T Smith (6)
31 Mar	H	Orrell	16–10	T: T Smith, Price C: T Smith PG: T Smith (2)
28 Apr	A	Nottingham	3–12	PG: T Smith

Gosforth

Year of formation 1877
Ground New Ground, Great North Road, Gosforth, Newcastle upon Tyne NE3 2DT
Tel: Newcastle (0632) 856915
Colours Green and white hoops, white shorts, green and white hooped stockings
Most capped player R J McLoughlin (Ireland) 40 caps
Captain 1989-90 D Briggs
1st XV 1989-90 P40 W11 D1 L22 F526 A724
Courage Leagues Div 2 12th **Pilkington Cup** Lost 15-26 to Gloucester (4th round)
Top scorer G Spearman (252) **Most tries** G Spearman (13)

League Record in 1989-90

Date	Venue	Opponents	Result	Scorers
9 Sept	A	Liverp'l St H	11–16	T: Douglas, Spearman PG: Spearman
23 Sept	H	Blackheath	12–12	PG: Spearman (4)
14 Oct	A	Richmond	3–36	PG: Clarke
28 Oct	H	Coventry	0–16	
11 Nov	A	Rugby	9–49	T: Wilkinson C: Spearman PG: Spearman
18 Nov	H	London Irish	6–27	PG: Spearman (2)
25 Nov	A	Plymouth Albion	13–28	T: Flowers, Frazer C: Spearman
				PG: Spearman
13 Jan	A	Headingley	10–17	T: Short PG: Spearman DG: Markham
10 Mar	H	Sale	22–18	T: Parker, Frankland, Campbell C: Spearman
				PG: Spearman (2)
31 Mar	H	Northampton	15–22	T: Winham C: Spearman PG: Spearman (3)
28 Apr	A	Waterloo	7–25	T: Lesley PG: Spearman

Harlequins

Year of formation 1866
Grounds Stoop Memorial Ground, Craneford Way, Twickenham, Middlesex and
RFU Ground, Twickenham   Tel: 081-892 0822 (Stoop)
Colours Light blue, magenta, chocolate, French grey, black and light green
Most capped player W W Wakefield (England) 31 caps
Captain 1989-90 J Olver
1st XV 1989-90 P35 W22 D0 L13 F693 A610
Courage Leagues Div 1 7th **Pilkington Cup** Lost 0-9 to Bath (3rd round)
Top scorer D Pears (183) **Most tries** R Glenister (14)

League Record in 1989-90

Date	Venue	Opponents	Result	Scorers
9 Sept	A	Bath	12–32	T: Thompson C: Dudman PG: Dudman (2)
23 Sept	H	Wasps	12–9	PG: Pears (4)

14 Oct	A	Bedford	71–8	T: Wedderburn (3), Pears (2), Glenister (2), Luxton (2), Skinner, Langhorn C: Pears (8) PG: Pears
28 Oct	H	Orrell	15–9	PG: Pears (5)
11 Nov	H	Bristol	13–7	T: Luxton (2) C: Pears PG: Pears
18 Nov	A	Saracens	9–15	T: Ackford C: Pears DG: Pears
25 Nov	H	Leicester	15–12	T: Glenister C: Pears PG: Pears (2) DG: Pears
13 Jan	H	Rosslyn Park	19–15	T: Glenister, Carling C: Pears PG: Pears (3)
10 Mar	A	Gloucester	9–24	PG: Pears (3)
31 Mar	H	Nottingham	22–27	T: Thompson, Thresher, Davis, Luxton PG: Pears DG: Pears
28 Apr	A	Moseley	21–22	T: Wood, Tupman C: Pears (2) PG: Pears (3)

Headingley

Year of formation 1878
Ground Bridge Road, Kirkstall, Leeds 5   Tel: Leeds (0532) 755029
Colours Green, black and white jerseys, blue shorts
Most capped player I R McGeechan (Scotland) 32 caps
Captain 1989-90 P Huntsman
1st XV 1989-90 P42 W17 D1 L24 F627 A747
Courage Leagues Div 2 8th   **Pilkington Cup** Lost 3-25 to Bath (4th round)
Top scorer S Irving (159)   **Most tries** D Kennell (14)

League Record in 1989–90

Date	Venue	Opponents	Result	Scorers
9 Sept	A	Waterloo	6–9	T: Sumner C: Irving
23 Sept	H	Northampton	15–3	T: Summers (2), Joyce PG: Irving
14 Oct	A	Liverp'l St H	4–10	T: Kennell
28 Oct	H	Blackheath	31–12	T: Pepper (2), Swales, Atkinson, Kennell C: Irving PG: Irving (3)
11 Nov	A	London Irish	19–25	T: Kennell, Johnson C: Haworth PG: Haworth (3)
18 Nov	H	Sale	3–9	PG: Haworth
25 Nov	A	Rugby	8–31	T: Atkinson, Kennell
13 Jan	H	Gosforth	17–10	T: Irving, Kennell, Hill C: Irving PG: Irving
10 Mar	A	Plymouth Albion	20–9	T: Pepper, Kennell, Johnson C: Johnson PG: Johnson (2)
31 Mar	H	Coventry	30–22	T: Pepper (2), Kennell, Johnson C: Johnson PG: Johnson (4)
28 Apr	A	Richmond	8–86	T: Kennell, Hill

Leicester

Year of formation 1880
Ground The Clubhouse, Aylestone Road, Leicester LE2 7LF
Tel: Leicester (0533) 540276
Colours Scarlet, green and white
Most capped player P J Wheeler (England) 41 caps
Captain 1989-90 P W Dodge/L Cusworth
1st XV 1989-90 P36 W27 D0 L9 F1031 A480
Courage Leagues Div 1 5th   **Pilkington Cup** Lost 7-23 to Northampton (5th round)
Top scorer J Liley (439)   **Most tries** S Povoas (24)

Wayne Richardson of Leicester exerts fingertip control on events, but his side were well beaten by Gloucester in the Division 1 match at Welford Road.

League Record in 1989–90

Date	Venue	Opponents	Result	Scorers
9 Sept	A	Wasps	12–29	T: Kardooni C: Liley PG: Liley (2)
23 Sept	H	Bedford	60–3	T: Liley (3), R Underwood (2), Wells (2), I Smith, Bates, T Underwood, Povoas C: Liley (5) PG: Liley DG: Cusworth
14 Oct	A	Orrell	10–33	T: T Underwood PG: Liley DG: Harris
28 Oct	H	Nottingham	15–6	T: Redfern, pen C: Liley (2) PG: Liley
11 Nov	H	Saracens	34–6	T: R Underwood, T Underwood, Thacker, Povoas, Liley (2) C: Liley (2) PG: Liley (2)
18 Nov	A	Rosslyn Park	23–9	T: Evans (2), Sandford (2), Povoas PG: Liley
25 Nov	A	Harlequins	12–15	PG: Liley (4)
13 Jan	H	Gloucester	16–26	T: R Underwood PG: Liley (4)
10 Mar	A	Bristol	13–11	T: Bates, Evans C: Liley PG: Liley
31 Mar	H	Moseley	38–20	T: Gerald (3), Kardooni (2), Liley C: Liley (4) PG: Liley (2)
28 Apr	A	Bath	15–26	T: Liley C: Liley PG: Liley (3)

Liverpool St Helens

Year of formation 1986 (on amalgamation of Liverpool – founded 1857 – and St Helens)
Ground Moss Lane, Windle, St Helens   Tel: St Helens (0744) 25708
Colours Red, blue and black horizontal stripes, white shorts
Most capped player M A C Slemen (England) 31 caps
Captain 1989-90 K Rabbitt
1st XV 1989-90 P40 W30 D2 L8 F765 A451
Courage Leagues Div 2 2nd *promoted*   **Pilkington Cup** Lost 0–29 to Bristol (3rd round)
Top scorer A Askew (205)   **Most tries** M Sephton (24)

League Record in 1989–90

Date	Venue	Opponents	Result	Scorers
9 Sept	H	Gosforth	16–11	T: Buckton, Sephton C: Simms PG: Simms (2)
23 Sept	A	Plymouth Albion	3–20	PG: Askew
14 Oct	H	Headingley	10–4	T: Sephton DG: Askew (2)
28 Oct	A	London Irish	23–12	T: Davies, Clift, Morris C: Askew PG: Askew (3)
11 Nov	A	Coventry	13–13	T: pen, Sephton C: Askew PG: Askew
18 Nov	H	Waterloo	10–3	T: Clift PG: Askew (2)
25 Nov	H	Northampton	13–13	T: Buckton, Sephton C: Askew PG: Askew
13 Jan	A	Richmond	17–6	T: Simms, Sephton PG: Askew (3)
10 Mar	H	Blackheath	16–3	T: McNaughton, Clift C: Askew PG: Askew (2)
31 Mar	A	Rugby	11–6	T: Morris, Sephton PG: Askew
28 Apr	H	Sale	22–15	T: Clift, Walmsley, Simms C: Askew (2) PG: Askew (2)

London Irish

Year of formation 1898
Ground The Avenue, Sunbury-on-Thames, Middlesex
Tel: Sunbury-on-Thames (0932) 783034
Colours Emerald green jerseys, white shorts
Most capped player K W Kennedy (Ireland) 45 caps
Captain 1989-90 D Fitzgerald
1st XV 1989-90 P34 W15 D1 L18 F565 A806

Courage Leagues Div 2 5th   **Pilkington Cup** Lost 13-17 to Plymouth Albion
(2nd round)   **Top scorer** I Aitchison (261)   **Most tries** S Browne (17)

League Record in 1989–90

Date	Venue	Opponents	Result	Scorers
9 Sept	A	Coventry	25–18	T: Collins, Brown C: Aitchison PG: Aitchison (4) DG: Aitchison
23 Sept	H	Waterloo	24–23	T: Corcoran, Staples C: Aitchison (2) PG: Aitchison (4)
14 Oct	A	Northampton	21–33	T: Brown C: Bell PG: Bell (5)
28 Oct	H	Liverp'l St H	12–23	T: Miller, Brown C: Aitchison (2)
11 Nov	H	Headingley	25–19	T: Kearns (2), Gibson C: Aitchison (2) PG: Aitchison (3)
18 Nov	A	Gosforth	27–6	T: Gibson (2), Geoghegan (2) C: Aitchison (3) PG: Aitchison (3)
25 Nov	A	Sale	27–19	T: Mahon (2), Geoghegan, Jenkins C: Aitchison PG: Aitchison (3)
13 Jan	H	Plymouth Albion	27–19	T: Staples, Brown, Egan C: Aitchison (3) PG: Aitchison DG: Aitchison (2)
10 Mar	A	Rugby	10–23	T: Jenkins, Geoghegan C: Aitchison
31 Mar	H	Richmond	12–36	T: Brown C: Aitchison PG: Aitchison (2)
28 Apr	A	Blackheath	18–28	T: Brown, Stevens C: Aitchison (2) PG: Aitchison (2)

London Scottish

Year of formation 1878
Ground Richmond Athletic Ground, Richmond, Surrey Tel: 081-940 0397
Colours Blue jerseys, red lion on left breast, white shorts, red stockings
Most capped player A F McHarg (Scotland) 44 caps
Captain 1989-90 G Hastings
1st XV 1989-90 P28 W17 D0 L11 F528 A447
Courage Leagues Div 3 1st *promoted* **Pilkington Cup** Lost 15-12 to Berry Hill
(2nd round)   **Top scorer** N Grecian (101)   **Most tries** D Millard (10)

League Record in 1989–90

Date	Venue	Opponents	Result	Scorers
9 Sept	A	Wakefield	10–4	T: White PG: Hastings (2)
23 Sept	H	Vale of Lune	34–3	T: White (2), Grecian, Hastings, Cramb, Exeter C: Hastings (5)
14 Oct	A	Sheffield	28–24	T: White, Buchanan-Smith, pen C: Hastings (2) PG: Hastings (3) DG: Cramb
28 Oct	H	Askeans	31–6	T: Renwick, Challis, Beazley, Exeter, Grecian, Millard C: Grecian (2) PG: Grecian
11 Nov	H	London Welsh	18–14	T: Macklin C: Grecian PG: Hastings, Grecian DG: Cramb (2)
18 Nov	A	Fylde	26–12	T: Mackay, Exeter (2), Renwick C: Hastings, Grecian PG: Hastings, Grecian
25 Nov	A	Lydney	20–16	T: Macklin, Corbett, Paton C: Grecian PG: Grecian DG: Cramb
13 Jan	H	Exeter	16–7	T: Macklin, Sharpe (2), Cramb
10 Mar	A	Roundhay	30–3	T: Elliott (2), Grecian, Millard, Hastings C: Hastings (5)
31 Mar	H	Nuneaton	36–0	T: Morrison (2), Butcher, Beazley, Grecian, Denham, Elliott C: Corbett, Grecian (3)
28 Apr	A	West Hartlepool	9–3	PG: Hastings (3)

Moseley

Year of formation 1873
Ground The Reddings, Reddings Road, Moseley, Birmingham B13 81W
Tel: Birmingham (021) 449 2149
Colours Black and red
Most capped player N E Horton (England) 20 caps
Captain 1989-90 R D Barr
1st XV 1989-90   P42   W12   D2   L28   F561   A921
Courage Leagues Div 1 11th   **Pilkington Cup** Lost 7-21 to Bath (semi-final)
Top scorer C Arntzen (165)   **Most tries** R Taylor (8)

League Record in 1988–89

Date	Venue	Opponents	Result	Scorers
9 Sept	H	Gloucester	12–16	*T:* Robson *C:* Arntzen *PG:* Arntzen (2)
23 Sept	A	Rosslyn Park	9–18	*PG:* Arntzen (3)
14 Oct	H	Bristol	10–16	*T:* Linnett, Robson *C:* Arntzen
28 Oct	A	Saracens	13–33	*T:* Robson, Wheatley *C:* Arntzen *PG:* Arntzen
11 Nov	A	Bath	9–27	*T:* Daniell *C:* Arntzen *PG:* Arntzen
18 Nov	H	Wasps	0–42	
25 Nov	A	Bedford	24–0	*T:* Shillingford (2), Wheatley *PG:* Arntzen (4)
13 Jan	H	Nottingham	6–22	*T:* Hardcastle *C:* Arntzen
10 Mar	A	Orrell	13–25	*T:* Taylor *PG:* Arntzen (3)
31 Mar	A	Leicester	20–38	*T:* Linnett, Boyle, Taylor, Robson *C:* Pennington (2)
28 Apr	H	Harlequins	22–21	*T:* Robson (2), Taylor (2), Hardcastle *C:* Purdy

Northampton

Year of formation 1880
Ground Franklins Gardens, Northampton   Tel: Northampton (0604) 51543
Colours Black, green and gold
Most capped player G S Pearce (England) 31 caps
Captain 1989-90 G S Pearce
1st XV 1989-90   P38   W23   D1   L14   F753   A786
Courage Leagues Div 2 1st *promoted*   **Pilkington Cup** Lost 12-17 to Gloucester (semi-final)   **Top scorer** J Steele (307)   **Most tries** F Packman (10)

League Record in 1989–90

Date	Venue	Opponents	Result	Scorers
9 Sept	H	Plymouth Albion	6–4	*PG:* Steele *DG:* Moss
23 Sept	A	Headingley	3–15	*PG:* Steele
14 Oct	H	London Irish	33–21	*T:* Burns (2), Thame (2), Ward, Alston *C:* Steele (3) *PG:* Steele
28 Oct	A	Sale	16–3	*T:* Hunter, Packman *C:* Steele *PG:* Steele (2)
11 Nov	A	Waterloo	12–6	*T:* Elkington *C:* Steele *PG:* Steele (2)
18 Nov	H	Richmond	12–6	*PG:* Steele (4)
25 Nov	A	Liverp'l St H	13–13	*T:* Packman *PG:* Steele (3)
13 Jan	A	Blackheath	10–9	*T:* Ward *PG:* Steele (2)
10 Mar	H	Coventry	24–18	*T:* Woodrow *C:* Steele *PG:* Steele (3) *DG:* Steele (3)
31 Mar	A	Gosforth	22–15	*T:* Pearce, Alston, Elkington *C:* Steele (2) *PG:* Steele (2)
28 Apr	H	Rugby	41–25	*T:* Packman (2), Steele (2), Thames (2), Hunter, Alston *C:* Steele (3) *PG:* Steele

Nottingham

Year of formation 1877
Ground Ireland Avenue, Beeston, Nottingham   Tel: Nottingham (0602) 254238
Colours White jerseys, green shorts
Most capped player B C Moore (England) 23 caps
Captain 1989-90 C A Gray
1st XV 1989-90 P37   W25   D0   L12   F848   A606
Courage Leagues Div 1 6th   **Pilkington Cup** Lost 16-26 to Gloucester (5th round)
Top scorer S Hodgkinson (228)   **Most tries** S Hackney (12)

League Record in 1989–90

Date	Venue	Opponents	Result	Scorers
9 Sept	H	Rosslyn Park	6–11	*PG:* Hodgkinson (2)
23 Sept	A	Bristol	9–13	*PG:* Hodgkinson (3)
14 Oct	H	Saracens	25–12	*T:* Hackney, Byrom, Rees *C:* Hodgkinson (2) *PG:* Hodgkinson (3)
28 Oct	A	Leicester	6–15	*PG:* Hodgkinson *DG:* Sutton
11 Nov	A	Wasps	12–16	*T:* Thorneycroft *C:* Hodgkinson *PG:* Hodgkinson *DG:* Sutton
18 Nov	H	Bedford	47–16	*T:* Hartley (4), Johnson, Gabriel, Hodgkinson, Potter *C:* Hodgkinson (6) *PG:* Hodgkinson
25 Nov	H	Orrell	9–25	*PG:* Hodgkinson (3)
11 Jan	A	Moseley	22–6	*T:* Mosses, Thorneycroft (2), Hodgkinson *C:* Hodgkinson (3)
10 Mar	H	Bath	12–9	*T:* Hindmarch *C:* Sutton *PG:* Kilford (2)
31 Mar	A	Harlequins	27–22	*T:* Stiles, Back (2), Hartley *C:* Sutton *PG:* Sutton *DG:* Sutton (2)
28 Apr	H	Gloucester	12–3	*T:* Gray *C:* Hodgkinson *PG:* Hodgkinson (2)

Orrell

Year of formation 1927
Ground Edge Hall Road, Orrell, nr Wigan, Greater Manchester, Lancs WN5 8TL
Tel: Upholland (0695) 623193
Colours Amber and black hoops, black shorts, black stockings
Most capped player J Carleton (England) 25 caps
Captain 1989-90 D V Southern
1st XV 1989-90 P38   W24   D0   L14   F903   A465
Courage Leagues Div 1 8th   **Pilkington Cup** Lost 6-12 to Nottingham (4th round)
Top scorer M Strett (263)   **Most tries** P Halsall (16)

League Record in 1989–90

Date	Venue	Opponents	Result	Scorers
9 Sept	H	Bristol	12–15	*PG:* Strett (4)
23 Sept	A	Saracens	6–12	*PG:* Rudling *DG:* Rudling
14 Oct	H	Leicester	33–10	*T:* Manley (2), Kimmins, Wright *C:* Strett (3), Langford *PG:* Strett (3)
28 Oct	A	Harlequins	9–15	*PG:* Strett (2), Langford
11 Nov	A	Bedford	25–7	*T:* Wright (2), Halsall *C:* Langford (2) *PG:* Langford (3)
18 Nov	H	Bath	6–9	*PG:* Langford, Strett
25 Nov	A	Nottingham	25–9	*T:* Heslop, Wright, Hitchen, Cusani *PG:* Strett (3)
13 Jan	A	Wasps	6–12	*PG:* Strett (2)
10 Mar	H	Moseley	25–13	*T:* Heslop (2), Halsall, Strett *C:* Strett (3) *PG:* Strett

Tim Rodber, the Northampton No 8 and one of the young players of the season, prepares to test the tackling power of Ian Smith (H) and Les Cusworth (J) during Northampton's wondrous Cup victory over Leicester.

| 31 Mar | A | Gloucester | 10–16 | *T:* Hitchen, Strett *C:* Strett |
| 28 Apr | H | Rosslyn Park | 64–16 | *T:* O'Toole, Cleary, Manley (3), Strett (2), Taberner (2), Heslop (2)   *C:* Strett (7) *PG:* Strett (2) |

Plymouth Albion

Year of formation 1876
Ground Beacon Park, Plymouth   Tel: Plymouth (0752) 772924
Colours Cherry, white and green
Most capped player E Stanbury (England) 16 caps
Captain 1989-90 K Norris
1st XV 1989-90 P31 W18 L13 F776 A447
Courage Leagues Div 2 7th **Pilkington Cup** Lost 0-7 to Orrell (3rd round)
Top scorer M Slade (90) **Most tries** K Turton (15)

League Record in 1989–90

Date	Venue	Opponents	Result	Scorers
9 Sept	A	Northampton	4–6	*T:* Russell
23 Sept	H	Liverp'l St H	20–3	*T:* Turton, Read, Gregory *C:* Butcher *PG:* Butcher (2)
14 Oct	A	Blackheath	37–9	*T:* Saunders (3), Russell, Gabbitass, Turton, Norris *C:* Butcher (3) *PG:* Butcher
28 Oct	H	Richmond	11–12	*T:* Crocker, Turton *PG:* Butcher
11 Nov	A	Sale	11–15	*T:* Martin, Gabbitass *PG:* Gabbitass
18 Nov	H	Rugby	21–16	*T:* Burt, Martin *C:* Gabbitass (2) *PG:* Gabbitass (3)
25 Nov	H	Gosforth	28–13	*T:* Gregory (2), Martin, Reed *C:* Gabbitass (3) *PG:* Gabbitass (2)
13 Jan	A	London Irish	19–27	*T:* Walkin (2), pen *C:* Slade (2) *PG:* Slade
10 Mar	H	Waterloo	33–28	*T:* Walkin (2), Russell, Fairgrieve, pens (2) *C:* Kellett (3) *PG:* Kellett
28 Apr	A	Coventry	13–15	*T:* Russell, Norris *C:* Butcher *PG:* Butcher

Richmond

Year of formation 1861
Ground Athletic Ground, Richmond, Surrey   Tel: 081-940 0397
Colours Old gold, red and black
Most capped player C W Ralston (England) 22 caps
Captain 1989-90 D Cooper
1st XV 1989-90 P35 W21 D3 L11 F741 A508
Courage Leagues Div 2 3rd **Pilkington Cup** Lost 3-35 to Bath (5th round)
Top scorer M Livesey (258) **Most tries** J Fallon (17)

League Record in 1989–90

Date	Venue	Opponents	Result	Scorers
9 Sept	H	Sale	16–7	*T:* Forde, Fallon (2) *C:* Livesey (2)
23 Sept	A	Rugby	28–16	*T:* Vyvyan (2), Fallon *C:* Livesey (2) *PG:* Livesey (4)
14 Oct	H	Gosforth	36–3	*T:* Waghorn (2), Vyvyan (2), Forde, Evans *C:* Livesey (6)
28 Oct	A	Plymouth Albion	12–11	*T:* Rydon *C:* Livesey *PG:* Livesey (2)
12 Nov	H	Blackheath	15–15	*T:* Waghorn *C:* Livesey *PG:* Livesey (3)
18 Nov	A	Northampton	6–12	*PG:* Livesey (2)

25 Nov	A	Coventry	18–21	T: Fallon, Waghorn C: Livesey (2) PG: Livesey (2)
13 Jan	H	Liverp'l St H	6–17	PG: Livesey (2)
10 Mar	A	Waterloo	23–13	T: Morris, Smedley, Livesey, Waghorn C: Livesey (2) PG: Livesey
31 Mar	A	London Irish	36–12	T: Forde (2), Fallon, Radford (2) C: Livesey (5) PG: Livesey (2)
28 Apr	H	Headingley	86–8	T: Radford (2), Fallon (2), Livesey (2), Forde (2), Sole (2), Roberts (2), Morris, Yeldham, Saunders, Baker C: Livesey (3), Radford (5) PG: Livesey (2)

Rosslyn Park

Year of formation 1879
Ground Priory Lane, Upper Richmond Road, Roehampton, London SW15
Tel: 081-876 1879
Colours Red and white hoops
Most capped player A G Ripley (England) 24 caps
Captain 1989-90 T Brooks
1st XV 1989-90 P37 W19 D1 L17 F717 A676
Courage Leagues Div 1 10th **Pilkington Cup** Lost 9-30 to Nottingham (3rd round)
Top scorer J Graves (295) **Most tries** J Graves, M Jermyn (9)

League Record in 1989–90

Date	Venue	Opponents	Result	Scorers
9 Sept	A	Nottingham	11–6	T: Moon, Hunter PG: Graves
23 Sept	H	Moseley	18–9	T: Brooks C: Graves PG: Graves (4)
14 Oct	A	Bath	6–34	PG: Graves (2)
28 Oct	H	Wasps	6–14	PG: Graves (2)
11 Nov	A	Gloucester	12–41	T: Tayler C: Graves PG: Graves (2)
18 Nov	H	Leicester	9–23	T: Brooks C: Graves DG: Holder
25 Nov	A	Bristol	15–6	T: Jermyn (2), Dear PG: Graves
13 Jan	A	Harlequins	15–19	T: Moon C: Graves PG: Graves (2) DG: Hunter
10 Mar	H	Saracens	13–15	T: Dent PG: Graves (3)
31 Mar	H	Bedford	45–12	T: Graves (2), Woodhouse, Hunter, Jermyn, Dear, Wyles C: Graves (4) PG: Graves (2) DG: Jermyn
28 Apr	A	Orrell	14–64	T: Hunter, Jermyn PG: Graves (2)

Rugby

Year of formation 1873
Ground Webb Ellis Road (off Bilton Road), Rugby, Warwickshire
Tel: Rugby (0788) 544907 (match days); 542252 (other days)
Colours Orange, black and red
Most capped player S Brain (England) 13 caps
Captain 1989-90 S Brain
1st XV 1989-90 P35 W21 D1 L13 F644 A567
Courage Leagues Div 2 6th **Pilkington Cup** Lost 9-16 to Wakefield (3rd round)
Top scorer C Howard (223) **Most tries** E Saunders (37)

League Record in 1989–90

Date	Venue	Opponents	Result	Scorers
9 Sept	A	Blackheath	21–0	*T:* Howard, Bowman, pen *C:* Howard (3) *PG:* Howard
23 Sept	H	Richmond	16–28	*T:* Saunders, Powell *C:* Howard *PG:* Howard *DG:* Powell
14 Oct	A	Coventry	10–18	*T:* Pell *PG:* Howard (2)
28 Oct	H	Waterloo	28–6	*T:* White, Saunders, Bowman, Dewey, Jenkins *C:* Howard *PG:* Howard (2)
11 Nov	H	Gosforth	49–9	*T:* Saunders (2), House, Howard, Bishop, Holdstock, pen *C:* Howard (6) *PG:* Howard (3)
18 Nov	A	Plymouth Albion	16–21	*T:* Pell, Saunders *C:* Howard *PG:* Howard (2)
25 Nov	H	Headingley	31–8	*T:* Saunders, Ellis, Dodson, pen *C:* Howard (3) *PG:* Howard (3)
13 Jan	A	Sale	13–20	*T:* Palmer, Saunders *C:* Pell *PG:* Dodson
10 Mar	H	London Irish	23–10	*T:* Holdstock, Revan, Howard, Ellis *C:* Howard (2) *PG:* Howard
31 Mar	H	Liverp'l St H	6–11	*PG:* Howard *DG:* Vaudin
28 Apr	A	Northampton	25–41	*T:* Watson, Bishop, Holdstock, Mapletoft *C:* Palmer (3) *PG:* Palmer

Sale

Year of formation 1861
Ground Heywood Road, Brooklands, Sale, Cheshire   Tel: Manchester (061) 973 6348
Colours Blue and white hoops, blue shorts, blue stockings
Most capped player F E Cotton (England) 31 caps
Captain 1989-90 H Fitton
1st XV 1989-90   P37   W20   D0   L17   F762   A661
Courage Leagues Div 2 9th   **Pilkington Cup** Lost 12-14 to Richmond (4th round)
Top scorer G Jenion (156)   **Most tries** J Powell (16)

League Record in 1989–90

Date	Venue	Opponents	Result	Scorers
9 Sept	A	Richmond	7–16	*T:* Stansfield *PG:* Jee
23 Sept	H	Coventry	24–22	*T:* Stansfield, Fitton, Jenion, Powell *C:* Jenion *PG:* Jenion (2)
14 Oct	A	Waterloo	9–12	*T:* Hodgson *C:* Jee *PG:* Jee
28 Oct	H	Northampton	3–16	*PG:* Jee
11 Nov	H	Plymouth Albion	15–11	*PG:* Hamer (3), Booth (2)
18 Nov	A	Headingley	9–3	*PG:* Booth (3)
25 Nov	H	London Irish	19–27	*T:* Stansfield, Burnhill *C:* Booth *PG:* Hamer (2), Booth
13 Jan	H	Rugby	20–13	*T:* Kenrick, Powell, Mallinder *C:* Booth *PG:* Jenion (2)
10 Mar	A	Gosforth	18–22	*T:* Jee, Hodgson *C:* Booth, Jenion *PG:* Booth, Jenion
31 Mar	H	Blackheath	14–18	*T:* Stansfield, Mallinder *PG:* Jenion (2)
28 Apr	A	Liverp'l St H	15–22	*T:* Maskery *C:* Jee *PG:* Jee (3)

Saracens

Year of formation 1876
Ground Bramley Sports Ground, Green Road, Southgate, London N14
Tel: 081-449 3770
Colours Black jerseys with red star and crescent, black shorts, red stockings

Most capped player V S Harding (England) 6 caps
Captain 1989-90 F Steadman
1st XV 1989-90 P32 W19 D2 L11 F654 A486
Courage Leagues Div 1 4th   **Pilkington Cup** Lost 6-10 to Moseley (4th round)
Top scorer A Kennedy (162)   **Most tries** M Gregory (11)

League Record in 1989–90

Date	Venue	Opponents	Result	Scorers
9 Sept	A	Bedford	22–3	T: Phillips (2), Reed, Buckton, Clarke C: Kennedy
23 Sept	H	Orrell	12–6	T: Buckton C: Rudling PG: Rudling DG: Rudling
14 Oct	A	Nottingham	12–25	T: Clarke (2) C: Kennedy (2)
28 Oct	H	Moseley	33–13	T: Gregory (2), Rudling (2), Robinson C: Kennedy (5) PG: Kennedy
11 Nov	A	Leicester	6–34	PG: Kennedy (2)
18 Nov	H	Harlequins	15–9	T: Steadman, Tarbuck C: Kennedy (2) PG: Kennedy
25 Nov	A	Gloucester	21–21	T: Buckton, Robinson, Clarke C: Kennedy (3) PG: Kennedy
13 Jan	H	Bristol	17–12	T: Stock, Leonard PG: Kennedy (3)
10 Mar	A	Rosslyn Park	15–13	T: Smith, Lindley, Gregory PG: Lee
31 Mar	H	Bath	9–7	T: Lee C: Lee PG: Robinson
28 Apr	A	Wasps	6–24	T: Steadman C: Lee

Wakefield

Year of formation 1901
Ground Pinderfields Road, College Grove, Wakefield   Tel: Wakefield (0924) 372038
Colours Black and gold hoops
Most capped player M Harrison (England) 15 caps
Captain 1989-90 B Barley
1st XV 1989-90 P41 W29 D1 L11 F853 A505
Courage Leagues Div 3 2nd *promoted*   **Pilkington Cup** Lost 10-22 to Northampton (4th round)   **Top scorer** R Atkinson (150)   **Most tries** M Harrison (24)

League Record in 1989–90

Date	Venue	Opponents	Result	Scorers
9 Sept	H	London Scottish	4–10	T: Scully
23 Sept	A	Lydney	9–7	T: Maynard C: Cowling PG: Cowling
14 Oct	H	Roundhay	26–3	T: Harrison (2), Murtagh, Cummin C: Cowling (2) PG: Cowling
28 Oct	A	Fylde	11–15	T: Scully, Garnett PG: Cowling
11 Nov	H	Askeans	40–14	T: Murtagh (3), Garnett (2), Wood, Townend C: Adamson (3) PG: Adamson (2)
18 Nov	A	Nuneaton	9–7	T: Rawnsley C: Adamson DG: Townend
25 Nov	H	West Hartlepool	10–10	T: Adamson PG: Rawnsley (2)
13 Jan	H	Vale of Lune	37–20	T: Scully (2), Harrison (2), Wood, Thomas, Adamson C: Adamson (3) PG: Adamson
10 Mar	A	Sheffield	27–12	T: Bowers, Thomas, Murtagh, Atkinson C: Atkinson (3), Bowers PG: Atkinson
31 Mar	A	Exeter	13–18	T: Murtagh PG: Atkinson (3)
28 Apr	H	London Welsh	24–10	T: Harrison (3), Murtagh, Burman C: Atkinson (2)

Wasps

Year of formation 1867
Ground Repton Avenue (off Rugby Avenue), Sudbury, Middlesex   Tel: 081-902 4220

Colours Black jerseys with gold wasp on left breast, black shorts, black stockings with gold hoop on turnover
Most capped player C R Andrew (England) 31 caps
Captain 1989-90 C R Andrew
1st XV 1989-90 P38 W27 D0 L11 F519 A376
Courage Leagues *Winners* Div 1 1st **Pilkington Cup** Lost 19-23 to Gloucester (3rd round) **Top scorer** C R Andrew (137) **Most tries** R Tsagane, S Smith (17)

League Record in 1989-90

Date	Venue	Opponents	Result	Scorers
9 Sept	H	Leicester	29–12	*T:* Pilgrim, Bailey, Dunston *C:* Andrew *PG:* Andrew (5)
23 Sept	A	Harlequins	9–12	*PG:* Andrew (3)
14 Oct	H	Gloucester	29–4	*T:* Bailey (3), Smith, Ryan, Pegler *C:* Andrew *PG:* Andrew
28 Oct	A	Rosslyn Park	14–6	*T:* Smith, White *PG:* Andrew (2)
11 Nov	H	Nottingham	16–12	*T:* Clough *PG:* Andrew (4)
18 Nov	A	Moseley	42–0	*T:* Andrew (2), Tsagane (2), Bailey, Clough, Pilgrim, Lozowski *C:* Pilgrim (5)
25 Nov	H	Bath	9–18	*T:* Andrew *C:* Andrew *PG:* Andrew
13 Jan	H	Orrell	12–6	*T:* Pegler *C:* Andrew *PG:* Andrew (2)
10 Mar	A	Bedford	44–9	*T:* Burroughs (2), Smith (2), Tsagane (2), White, Pinnegar, Lozowski *C:* Andrew (4)
31 Mar	A	Bristol	22–21	*T:* Pegler, Smith, pen *C:* Gregory, Pilgrim *PG:* Gregory, Pilgrim
28 Apr	H	Saracens	24–6	*T:* Pegler, Bailey (2), Clough, Andrew *C:* Andrew (2)

Waterloo

Year of formation 1882
Ground St Anthony's Road, Blundellsands, Liverpool L23 8TW
Tel: Liverpool (051) 924 4552
Colours Green, red and white hoops
Most capped player H G Periton (England) 21 caps
Captain 1989-90 S Gallagher
1st XV 1989-90 P40 W24 D1 L15 F914 A579
Courage Leagues Div 2 11th **Pilkington Cup** Lost 3-19 to Wakefield (2nd round)
Top scorer R Angell (151) **Most tries** P Cooley (17)

League Record in 1989-90

Date	Venue	Opponents	Result	Scorers
9 Sept	H	Headingley	9–6	*PG:* Cotter (3)
23 Sept	A	London Irish	23–24	*T:* Hackett, Cooley *PG:* Angell (4) *DG:* Angell
14 Oct	H	Sale	12–9	*T:* Cooley, Cooper *C:* Angell (2)
28 Oct	A	Rugby	6–28	*PG:* Angell, Tickle
11 Nov	H	Northampton	6–12	*PG:* Carfoot *DG:* Carfoot
18 Nov	A	Liverp'l St H	3–10	*PG:* Carfoot
25 Nov	H	Blackheath	10–19	*T:* Cooley *PG:* Carfoot, Tickle
13 Jan	A	Coventry	12–22	*T:* Angell, Bracegirdle, Cooley
10 Mar	H	Richmond	13–23	*T:* Cooley *PG:* Cropper (3)
31 Mar	A	Plymouth Albion	28–33	*T:* Gibbons (2), Brookman, Hackett *C:* Cropper (3) *PG:* Cropper (2)
28 Apr	H	Gosforth	25–7	*T:* Gallagher, Angell, Hackett *C:* Angell (2) *PG:* Angell (3)

Keith Robertson, the Melrose captain, proudly shows off the McEwan's Trophy to a few close friends after his team made sure of the title by beating Jedforest.

SCOTLAND

Ayr

Year of formation 1897
Ground Millbrae, Alloway, Ayr   Tel: Alloway (0292) 41944
Colours Pink and black
Most capped player S Munro (Scotland) 10 caps
Captain 1989-90 D A McVey
1st XV 1989-90   P34   W16   D0   L18   F647   A535
McEwan's/SRU Div 1 13th *relegated*   **Top scorer** R Kemp (207)
Most tries P P Manning (20)

Boroughmuir

Year of formation 1919 (Boroughmuir FP until 1974)
Ground Meggetland, Colinton Road, Edinburgh EH14 1AS
Tel: Edinburgh (031) 443 7571
Colours Navy blue and emerald green
Most capped player B H Hay (Scotland) 23 caps
Captain 1989-90 B Edwards
1st XV 1989-90   P34   W23   D0   L11   F773   A446
McEwan's/SRU Div 1 6th **Top scorer** M Walker (204)   **Most tries** M R DeBusk (23)

Corstorphine

Year of formation Reformed in 1950
Ground Union Park, Carrick Knowe Parkway, Corstorphine, Edinburgh
Tel: Edinburgh (031) 334 8063
Colours Navy blue and scarlet quarters
Captain 1989-90 S I Pilkington
1st XV 1989-90   P32   W16   D2   L14   F710   A560
McEwan's/SRU Div 2 7th   **Top scorer** D Gillespie (196)   **Most tries** G McGregor (21)

Currie

Year of formation 1970
Ground Malleny Park, Balerno, Edinburgh   Tel: Edinburgh (031) 449 2492
Colours Amber and black
Captain 1989-90 J Cockburn
1st XV 1989-90   P28   W18   D1   L9   F664   A435
McEwan's/SRU Div 2 2nd *promoted*   **Top scorer** A Donaldson (264)
Most tries S Forrester (18)

Dalziel High School FP

Year of formation 1925
Ground Cleland Estate, Carfyn, Motherwell   Tel: Cleland (0698) 860459
Colours Black with blue chest circlet
Captain 1989-90 C T Ireland
1st XV 1989-90   P26   W12   D0   L14   F403   A411
McEwan's/SRU Div 2 13th *relegated*   **Top scorer** B W Gibson (138)
Most tries J Hughes (6)

Dunfermline

Year of formation 1904
Ground McKane Park, Dunfermline, Fife   Tel: Dunfermline (0383) 721279
Colours Royal blue and white
Most capped player J T Greenwood (Scotland) 20 caps
Captain 1989-90 A McKenzie
1st XV 1989-90   P28   W11   D1   L16   F399   A473
McEwan's/SRU Div 2 joint 9th   **Top scorer** W Allan (102)   **Most tries** D Stobie (11)

Edinburgh Academicals

Year of formation 1857
Ground Raeburn Place, Edinburgh   Tel: Edinburgh (031) 332 1070
Colours Blue and white stripes
Most capped player W I D Elliot (Scotland) 29 caps
Captain 1989-90 J F Richardson
1st XV 1989-90   P32   W24   D1   L7   F688   A388
McEwan's/SRU Div 1 4th   **Top scorer** R J S Shepherd (133)
Most tries S A D Burns (17)

Edinburgh Wanderers

Year of formation 1868
Ground Murrayfield, Edinburgh   Tel: Edinburgh (031) 337 2196
Colours Red and black
Most capped player A R Smith (Scotland) 33 caps
Captain 1989-90 G W M Hamilton
1st XV 1989-90   P34   W26   D0   L8   F822   A422
McEwan's/SRU Div 2 champions *promoted*   **Top scorer** D R D Pulfrey (250)
Most tries G Stirling (26)

Gala

Year of formation 1875
Ground Netherdale, Galashiels   Tel: Galashiels (0896) 3811
Colours Maroon
Most capped player P C Brown (Scotland) 27 caps
Captain 1989-90 D Bryson
1st XV 1989-90   P31   W16   D2   L13   F532   A453
McEwan's/SRU Div 1 8th   **Top scorer** M Dods (114)   **Most tries** J G L Turnbull (9)

Glasgow Academicals

Year of formation 1867
Ground New Anniesland, Helensburgh Drive, Glasgow   Tel: Glasgow (041) 959 1323
Colours Navy blue and white
Most capped player W M Simmers (Scotland) 28 caps
Captain 1989-90 S W McAslan
1st XV 1989-90   P30   W13   D2   L15   F568   A550
McEwan's/SRU Div 2 8th   **Top scorer** C G MacGregor (178)
Most tries G T MacGregor (19)

Glasgow High/Kelvinside

Year of formation 1982 (on amalgamation of Glasgow HSFP and Kelvinside Academicals)
Ground Old Anniesland, 637 Crow Road, Glasgow   Tel: Glasgow (041) 959 1154
Colours Chocolate and gold
Most capped player None (before amalgamation J M Bannerman (Glasgow HSFP) was capped 37 times and D M White (Kelvinside Academicals) 4 times – both for Scotland)
Captain 1989-90 E D McCorkindale
1st XV 1989-90 P37 W22 D1 L14 F741 A541
McEwan's/SRU Div 1 7th   **Top scorer** H Bassi (89)   **Most tries** D Michie (22)

Gordonians

Year of formation 1911
Ground Seafield, Thorngrove Avenue, Aberdeen   Tel: Aberdeen (0224) 317027
Colours Blue with gold hoop
Most capped player I G McCrae (Scotland) 6 caps
Captain 1989-90 C P Manders
1st XV 1989-90 P23 W7 D0 L16 F231 A442
McEwan's/SRU Div 2 14th *relegated*   **Top scorer** M Love (127)   **Most tries** M Love (9)

Hawick

Year of formation 1873
Ground Mansfield Park, Mansfield Road, Hawick, Roxburghshire
Tel: Hawick (0450) 74291
Colours Green
Most capped player J M Renwick (Scotland) 52 caps
Captain 1989-90 D J Turnbull
1st XV 1989-90 P34 W16 D1 L17 F571 A476
McEwan's/SRU Div 1 9th   **Top scorer** S W Welsh (212)   **Most tries** R Douglas (12)

Heriot's FP

Year of formation 1890
Ground Goldenacre, Bangholm Terrace, Edinburgh EH3 5QN
Tel: Edinburgh (031) 552 5925
Colours Blue and white horizontal stripes
Most capped player A R Irvine (Scotland) 51 caps
Captain 1989-90 I G Milne
1st XV 1989-90 P33 W20 D2 L11 F738 A523
McEwan's/SRU Div 1 joint 2nd   **Top scorer** P J Hewitt (195)
Most tries P J Hewitt (18)

Hillhead-Jordanhill

Year of formation 1988 (on amalgamation of Hillhead and Jordanhill)
Ground Hughenden, 32 Hughenden Road, Glasgow G12   Tel: Glasgow (041) 357 1115
Colours Blue and gold with red and green hoops
Most capped player None (before amalgamation J McLauchlan (Jordanhill) was capped 43 times and W C W Murdoch and I A A MacGregor (Hillhead) 9 times – all for Scotland)
Captain 1989-90 I M MacCallum
1st XV 1989-90 P28 W16 D1 L11 F404 A490
McEwan's/SRU Div 2 joint 4th   **Top scorer** Alastair Campbell (59)
Most tries I Murchie (11)

Jedforest

Year of formation 1885
Ground Riverside Park, Jedburgh   Tel: Jedburgh (0835) 62232 and 62855
Colours Royal blue
Most capped player R J Laidlaw (Scotland) 47 caps
Captain 1989-90 J Raeburn
1st XV 1989-90   P29   W21   D0   L8   F658   A419
McEwan's/SRU Div 1 joint 2nd   **Top scorer** G J McKechnie (201)
Most tries Brian Hughes (17)

Kelso

Year of formation 1876
Ground Poynder Park, Kelso, Roxburghshire   Tel: Kelso (0573) 24300 and 23773
Colours Black and white
Most capped player J Jeffrey (Scotland) 28 caps
Captain 1989-90 R E Paxton
1st XV 1989-90   P31   W12   D3   L16   F548   A519
McEwan's/SRU Div 1 joint 11th   **Top scorer** A B M Ker (222)
Most tries B Bellingham (9)

Kilmarnock

Year of formation 1868
Ground Bellsland, Queens Drive, Kilmarnock, Ayrshire
Tel: Kilmarnock (0563) 22314
Colours White with red hoop surmounted by white Maltese cross
Most capped player W Cuthbertson (Scotland) 22 caps
Captain 1989-90 K Young
1st XV 1989-90   P35   W23   D2   L10   F835   A427
McEwan's/SRU Div 2 3rd   **Top scorer** E R J Stewart (306)
Most tries G S Agnew (21)

Kirkcaldy

Year of formation 1873
Ground Beveridge Park, Balwearie Road, Kirkcaldy   Tel: Kirkcaldy (0592) 263470
Colours Royal blue
Most capped player D D Howie and R Howie (both Scotland) 9 caps
Captain 1989-90 D Wylie
1st XV 1989-90   P33   W16   D1   L16   F523   A457
McEwan's/SRU Div 2 12th   **Top scorer** J R Mitchell (137)   **Most tries** R R Dewar (9)

Langholm

Year of formation 1872
Ground Milntown, Langholm, Dumfriesshire   Tel: Langholm (038 73) 80386
Colours Crimson
Most capped player C Elliot (Scotland) 12 caps
Captain 1989-90 D Glendinning
1st XV 1989-90   P28   W7   D1   L20   F290   A602
McEwan's/SRU Div 2 joint 9th   **Top scorer** C Turk (100)   **Most tries** G Fletcher (8)

Melrose

Year of formation 1877
Ground The Greenyards, Melrose, Roxburghshire TD6 9SA
Tel: Melrose (089 682) 2993 (office) and 2559 (clubrooms)
Colours Yellow and black
Most capped player K W Robertson (Scotland) 40 caps
Captain 1989-90 K W Robertson
1st XV 1989-90 P30 W28 D1 L1 F812 A252
McEwan's/SRU Div 1 *champions* **Top scorer** C M Chalmers (208)
Most tries A M Purves, L van Niekerk (11)

Musselburgh

Year of formation 1921
Ground Stoneyhill, Stoneyhill Farm Road, Musselburgh Tel: Edinburgh (031) 665 3435
Colours Navy blue with narrow white hoops
Captain 1989-90 C Livingston
1st XV 1989-90 P30 W14 D3 L13 F473 A499
McEwan's/SRU Div 2 6th **Top scorer** N Lockhart (124)
Most tries A McLeod, C Ramsay (11)

Preston Lodge

Year of formation 1929
Ground Pennypit Park, Prestonpans, East Lothian Tel: Edinburgh (031) 661 4554
Colours Black with maroon and white hoops
Most capped player R F Cunningham (Scotland) 3 caps
Captain 1989-90 L Kirk
1st XV 1989-90 P34 W17 D1 L16 F548 A496
McEwan's/SRU Div 2 joint 4th **Top scorer** D Ramage (96)
Most tries S McMillan (14)

Selkirk

Year of formation 1907
Ground Philiphaugh, Selkirk Tel: Selkirk (0750) 20403
Colours Navy blue
Most capped player J Y Rutherford (Scotland) 42 caps
Captain 1989-90 I A M Paxton
1st XV 1989-90 P31 W18 D1 L12 F755 A410
McEwan's/SRU Div 1 10th **Top scorer** R L Pow (278) **Most tries** K J Johnston (17)

Stewart's-Melville FP

Year of formation 1973 (on amalgamation of Daniel Stewart's College FP and Melville College FP)
Ground Inverleith, Ferry Road, Edinburgh EH5 2DW Tel: Edinburgh (031) 522 1515
Colours Scarlet with black and gold bands
Most capped player J H Calder (Scotland) 27 caps
Captain 1989-90 J M Scott
1st XV 1989-90 P31 W9 D2 L20 F382 A686
McEwan's/SRU Div 1 joint 11th **Top scorer** D S Wyllie (52)
Most tries G J Findlay (8)

Craig Redpath of Melrose scores the decisive try in the Division 1 match against Jedforest. Melrose's 14-3 victory sealed their championship title.

Stirling County

Year of formation 1904
Ground Bridgehaugh Park, Stirling   Tel: Stirling (0786) 74827
Colours Red, white and black
Most capped player Dr W Welsh (Scotland) 8 caps
Captain 1989-90 J S Hamilton
1st XV 1989-90 P30 W18 D2 L10 F618 A470
McEwan's/SRU Div 1 5th   **Top scorer** C T MacDonald (281)
Most tries G Graham, R A Mailer (10)

Watsonians

Year of formation 1875
Ground Myreside, Edinburgh   Tel: Edinburgh (031) 447 1395
Colours Maroon
Most capped player D I Johnston (Scotland) 27 caps
Captain 1989-90 I M H Smith
1st XV 1989-90 P28 W9 D2 L17 F341 A566
McEwan's/SRU Div 2 joint 9th   **Top scorer** G McAlpine (57)
Most tries R Cheffins (10)

West of Scotland

Year of formation 1865
Ground Burnbrae, Glasgow Road, Milngavie, Glasgow
Tel: Glasgow (041) 956 2891 and 956 1960
Colours Red and yellow hoops
Most capped player A B Carmichael (Scotland) 50 caps
Captain 1989-90 S J Lewis
1st XV 1989-90 P33 W12 D1 L20 F486 A527
McEwan's/SRU Div 1 14th *relegated*   **Top scorer** D N Barrett (147)
Most tries F H Stott (7)

WALES

Aberavon

Year of formation 1876
Ground Talbot Athletic Ground, Manor Street, Port Talbot, West Glamorgan
Tel: Port Talbot (0639) 882427 or 886038
Colours Red and black hoops, white shorts, red socks
Most capped player A J Martin (Wales) 34 caps
Captain 1989-90 G Matthews
1st XV 1989-90 P48 W17 D0 L31 F551 A905
Western Mail Championship 17th **Whitbread Merit Table** 15th
WRU Schweppes Cup Lost 6-12 to Bridgend (semi-final)
Top scorer P Sutton (185) **Most tries** G Wilkins (11)

Abertillery

Year of formation 1884
Ground The Park, Abertillery, Gwent Tel: Abertillery (0495) 212226
Colours Green and white hoops
Most capped player H J Morgan (Wales) 27 caps
Captain 1989-90 W Jervis
1st XV 1989-90 P45 W22 D3 L20 F706 A827
Western Mail Championship 11th **Whitbread Merit Table** 9th
WRU Schweppes Cup Lost on tries after drawing 12-12 with Maesteg Celtic (4th round)
Top scorer C Mogford (201) **Most tries** G Pugh (14)

Bridgend

Year of formation 1878
Ground Brewery Field, Tondu Road, Bridgend, Mid-Glamorgan
Tel: Bridgend (0656) 59032
Colours Blue and white stripes
Most capped player J P R Williams (Wales) 55 caps
Captain 1989-90 J Apsee
1st XV 1989-90 P48 W35 D0 L13 F1116 A625
Western Mail Championship 4th **Whitbread Merit Table** 7th
WRU Schweppes Cup Lost 10-16 to Neath (final)
Top scorer A Parry (400) **Most tries** Aled Williams (24)

Cardiff

Year of formation 1876
Ground Cardiff Arms Park, Westgate Street, Cardiff Tel: Cardiff (0222) 383546
Colours Cambridge blue and black
Most capped player G O Edwards (Wales) 53 caps
Captain 1989-90 T Crothers
1st XV 1989-90 P47 W25 D2 L20 F1090 A845
Western Mail Championship 10th **Whitbread Merit Table** 10th
WRU Schweppes Cup Lost 6-22 to Neath (6th round)
Top scorer M Rayer (154) **Most tries** S Ford (15)

Cross Keys

Year of formation 1885
Ground Pandy Park, Cross Keys, Gwent   Tel: Cross Keys (0495) 270289
Colours Black and white hoops
Most capped player S Morris (Wales) 19 caps
Captain 1989-90 P Jones
1st XV 1989-90 P45 W25 D0 L20 F687 A654
Western Mail Championship 12th   **Whitbread Merit Table** 12th
WRU Schweppes Cup Lost 10-19 to Blaina (3rd round)
Top scorer P Withers (144)   **Most tries** N Parkes (16)

Ebbw Vale

Year of formation 1880
Ground Eugene Cross Park, Ebbw Vale   Tel: Ebbw Vale (0495) 302157/302995
Colours Red, white and green hoops
Most capped player Denzil Williams (Wales) 36 caps
Captain 1989-90 M Sibthorpe
1st XV 1989-90 P47 W17 D1 L29 F691 A1049
Western Mail Championship 13th   **Whitbread Merit Table** 14th
WRU Schweppes Cup Lost 9-12 to Pontypool (5th round)
Top scorer D Love (103)   **Most tries** M Thomas (22)

Glamorgan Wanderers

Year of formation 1893
Ground The Memorial Ground, Stirling Road, Ely, Cardiff   Tel: Cardiff (0222) 591039
Colours Cambridge blue, black and white
Captain 1989-90 M Goldsworthy
1st XV 1989-90 P39 W25 D1 L13 F839 A673
Western Mail Championship 5th   **Whitbread Merit Table** 5th
WRU Schweppes Cup Lost 9-15 to Swansea (5th round)
Top scorer M Goldsworthy (156)   **Most tries** S Legge (16)

Llanelli

Year of formation 1872
Ground Stradey Park, Llanelli, Dyfed   Tel: Llanelli (0554) 774060
Colours Scarlet jerseys with white collars, club crest on left breast
Most capped player J J Williams (Wales) 30 caps
Captain 1989-90 P T Davies
1st XV 1989-90 P50 W41 D0 L9 F1666 A769
Western Mail Championship 2nd   **Whitbread Merit Table** 2nd
WRU Schweppes Cup Lost 4-15 to Cardiff (5th round)
Top scorer C Stephens (270)   **Most tries** S Bowling (30)

Maesteg

Year of formation 1882
Ground Llynvi Road, Maesteg, Mid-Glamorgan   Tel: Maesteg (0656) 732283
Colours Black and amber

Most capped player G Evans (Wales) 10 caps
Captain 1989-90 P Jones
1st XV 1989-90   P48   W29   D1   L18   F855   A840
Western Mail Championship 9th   **Whitbread Merit Table** 11th
WRU Schweppes Cup Lost on tries after drawing 19-19 with Bonymaen (3rd round)
Top scorer M Watts (141)   **Most tries** H Woodland (21)

Neath

Year of formation 1871
Ground The Gnoll, Gnoll Park Road, Neath, West Glamorgan
Tel: Neath (0639) 644420
Colours Black with white Maltese cross
Most capped player W D Morris (Wales) 34 caps
Captain 1989-90 K H Phillips
1st XV 1989-90   P48   W45   D0   L3   F1867   A427
Western Mail Championship 1st *Winners*   **Whitbread Merit Table** 1st
WRU Schweppes Cup *winners* Beat Bridgend 16-10 (final)
Top scorer P Williams (282)   **Most tries** A Edmunds (45)

Newbridge

Year of formation 1890
Ground Welfare Ground, Bridge Street, Newbridge, Gwent
Tel: Newbridge (0495) 243247
Colours Blue and black hoops (or red)
Most capped player D Hayward (Wales) 15 caps
Captain 1989-90 P Turner/N James
1st XV 1989-90   P48   W33   D0   L15   F1183   A618
Western Mail Championship 7th   **Whitbread Merit Table** 4th
WRU Schweppes Cup Lost 9-15 to Aberavon (5th round)
Top scorer B Hayward (243)   **Most tries** S Fealey (22)

Newport

Year of formation 1874
Ground Rodney Parade, Rodney Road, Newport, Gwent   Tel: Newport (0633) 258193
Colours Black and amber hoops
Most capped player K J Jones (Wales) 44 caps
Captain 1989-90 G George
1st XV 1989-90   P46   W18   D1   L27   F780   A981
Western Mail Championship 14th   **Whitbread Merit Table** 13th
WRU Schweppes Cup Lost 14-18 to Swansea (6th round)
Top scorer G Abraham (131)   **Most tries** J Thomas (12)

Penarth

Year of formation 1880
Ground Athletic Grounds, Lavernock Road, Penarth, South Glamorgan
Tel: Penarth (0222) 708402
Colours Royal blue

Most capped player J Bassett (Wales) 15 caps
Captain 1989-90 C Lewis
1st XV 1989-90 P38 W6 D1 L31 F405 A1429
Western Mail Championship 19th   **Whitbread Merit Table** 18th
WRU Schweppes Cup Lost 19-23 to Treherbert (2nd round)
Top scorer P Elias (76)   **Most tries** G Snook (20)

Pontypool

Year of formation 1901
Ground Pontypool Park, Pontypool, Gwent   Tel: Pontypool (0495) 762524
Colours Red, white and black hoops
Most capped player G Price (Wales) 41 caps
Captain 1989-90 K Moseley/C Huish
1st XV 1989-90 P49 W35 D2 L12 F1372 A608
Western Mail Championship 3rd   **Whitbread Merit Table** 3rd
WRU Schweppes Cup Lost 12-18 to Aberavon (6th round)
Top scorer M Silva (306)   **Most tries** R Bidgood (28)

Pontypridd

Year of formation 1876
Ground Sardis Road Ground, Pwllgwaun, Pontypridd   Tel: Pontypridd (0433) 405006
Colours Black and white hoops
Most capped player R J Robins (Wales) 13 caps
Captain 1989-90 C Jones
1st XV 1989-90 P46 W29 D0 L17 F1123 A725
Western Mail Championship 8th   **Whitbread Merit Table** 8th
WRU Schweppes Cup Lost 3-12 to Newport (5th round)
Top scorer A Phillips (190)   **Most tries** A Richards (19)

South Wales Police

Year of formation 1969
Ground Police Recreation Ground, Waterton Cross, Bridgend, Mid-Glamorgan
Tel: Bridgend (0656) 55555 ext 218 or Bridgend 4481
Colours Red jerseys, white shorts, royal blue stockings
Most capped player Bleddyn Bowen (Wales) 21 caps
Captain 1989-90 S Davies/C Hillman
1st XV 1989-90 P49 W18 D1 L30 F805 A1006
Western Mail Championship 16th   **Whitbread Merit Table** 15th
WRU Schweppes Cup Lost 4-10 to Maesteg Celtic (3rd round)
Top scorer A Hughes (146)   **Most tries** I Hemburrow (17)

Swansea

Year of formation 1874
Ground St Helen's Ground, Swansea, West Glamorgan
Tel: Swansea (0792) 464918 or 466593
Colours All white
Most capped player T M Davies (Wales) 38 caps

Captain 1989-90 R N Jones
1st XV 1989-90   P43   W29   D1   L13   F1215   A763
Western Mail Championship 6th   **Whitbread Merit Table** 6th
WRU Schweppes Cup Lost 16-24 to Neath (semi-final)
Top scorer M Wyatt (256)   **Most tries** M Titley (26)

Tredegar

Year of formation 1899
Ground Tredegar Recreation Ground, Park Hill, Tredegar, Gwent
Tel: Tredegar (0495) 2879
Colours Red, black and white
Captain 1989-90 R Buckley/N Hunt
1st XV 1989-90   P47   W13   D1   L33   F631   A1170
Western Mail Championship 18th   **Whitbread Merit Table** 17th
WRU Schweppes Cup Lost 6-35 to Bridgend (3rd round)
Top scorer C Earland (144)   **Most tries** F Jacas (16)

IRELAND

Ards

Year of formation 1878 (reformed 1928)
Ground Lansdowne Road, Newtownards   Tel: Newtownards 813961
Colours Black with white collar, black shorts
Most capped player N J Carr (Ireland) 11 caps
Captain 1989-90 K Hooks
1st XV 1989-90 P24   W9   D2   L13   F343   A336
Ulster Senior Cup Lost 10-12 to NIFC (1st round)
Ulster Senior League Section 2 1st *promoted*

Athlone

Year of formation 1951
Ground Keane Park, Cornamagh, Athlone
Colours Black and white hooped jerseys, black shorts
Most capped player R J McLoughlin (Ireland) 40 caps
Captain 1989-90 J Lennon
1st XV 1989-90 P31   W8   D1   L12   F227   A393
Connacht Senior Cup *winners* Beat Corinthians 18-3 (final)
Connacht Senior League 3rd (All Ireland Div 2 1990-91)

Ballymena

Year of formation 1922
Ground Eaton Park, Ballymena   Tel: Ballymena 6746
Colours Black jerseys, white shorts, black stockings with white turnover
Most capped player W J McBride (Ireland) 63 caps
Captain 1989-90 M Rainey
1st XV 1989-90 P28   W26   D0   L2   F788   A306
Ulster Senior Cup *Winners* Beat Malone 17-9 (final)
Ulster Senior League Section 1 *Winners*

Bangor

Year of formation 1885
Ground Upritchard Park, Bloomfield Road South, Bangor, Co Down, N Ireland
Colours Old gold, royal blue and black
Most capped player R A Milliken (Ireland) 14 caps
Captain 1989-90 G Maxwell
1st XV 1989-90 P25   W16   D1   L8   F443   A267
Ulster Senior Cup Lost 16-20 to Ballymena (2nd round)
Ulster Senior League Section 1 5th

Bective Rangers

Year of formation 1881
Ground Donnybrook, Dublin 4   Tel: Dublin 693894
Colours Red, green and white striped jerseys, white shorts

Most capped player J L Farrell (Ireland) 29 caps
Captain 1989-90 M Corcoran
1st XV 1989-90 P37 W16 D1 L10 F419 A351
Leinster Senior Cup Lost 12-18 to Lansdowne (1st round)
Leinster Senior League Div B 3rd

Blackrock College

Year of formation 1882
Ground Stradbrook Road, Blackrock   Tel: Dublin 805697
Colours Narrow royal blue and white striped jerseys, navy shorts, navy stockings
Most capped player J F Slattery (Ireland) 61 caps
Captain 1989-90 D Gardiner
1st XV 1989-90 P30 W14 D0 L16 F376 A378
Leinster Senior Cup Lost 17-26 to Wanderers (2nd round)
Leinster Senior League Div A 3rd

Bohemians

Year of formation 1922
Ground Thomond Park, Limerick   Tel: Limerick 51877
Colours Red and white
Most capped player M A F English (Ireland) 16 caps
Captain 1989-90 M Hannon
1st XV 1989-90 P25 W7 D1 L17 F246 A488
Munster Senior Cup Lost 4-25 to Young Munster (1st round)
Munster Senior League 10th

CIYMS

Year of formation 1922
Ground Circular Road, Belfast   Tel: Belfast 768225/760120
Colours Black and white hooped jerseys, black shorts, blue stockings
Most capped player A C Pedlow (Ireland) 30 caps
Captain 1989-90 L McCallan
1st XV 1989-90 P23 W13 D1 L9 F358 A333
Ulster Senior Cup Lost 6-21 to Malone (semi-final)
Ulster Senior League Section 1 7th *relegated*

Clontarf

Year of formation 1876
Ground Castle Avenue, Clontarf, Dublin   Tel: Dublin 336214
Colours Red and blue jerseys, white shorts, red and blue striped stockings
Most capped player G J Morgan (Ireland) 19 caps
Captain 1989-90 A R Foley
1st XV 1989-90 P33 W21 D0 L12 F646 A481
Leinster Senior Cup Lost 15-19 to St Mary's College (1st round)
Leinster Senior League Div B 1st

Collegians

Year of formation 1890
Ground Deramore Park, Belfast, N Ireland   Tel: Belfast 665943
Colours White and maroon, navy stockings with maroon tops
Most capped player J McVicker (Ireland) 20 caps
Captain 1989-90 S Scott
1st XV 1989-90 P26 W9 D3 L14 F337 A505
Ulster Senior Cup Lost 9-21 to CIYMS (1st round)
Ulster Senior League Section 2 5th

Constitution FC

Year of formation 1892
Ground Temple Hill, Ballintemple, Cork   Tel: Cork 32563
Colours White, black and blue
Most capped player T J Kiernan (Ireland) 54 caps
Captain 1989-90 R Keyes
1st XV 1989-90 P27 W18 D0 L9 F439 A344
Munster Senior Cup Lost 15-22 to Young Munster (quarter-final)
Munster Senior League 2nd (joint)

Corinthians

Year of formation 1932
Ground Corinthian Park, Tuam Road, Galway
Colours Blue, black and white
Most capped player N P Mannion (Ireland) 11 caps
Captain 1989-90 J O'Connell
1st XV 1989-90 P31 W16 D3 L12 F422 A367
Connacht Senior Cup Lost 3-18 to Athlone (final)
Connacht Senior League 2nd

De La Salle Palmerston

Year of formation 1985 (on amalgamation of De La Salle and Palmerston)
Ground Kilternan, Co Dublin   Tel: Dublin 953650 or 953550
Colours Green, white, wine and black jerseys, black shorts
Captain 1989-90 L Balfe
1st XV 1989-90 P26 W5 D1 L20 F295 A470
Leinster Senior Cup Lost 0-18 to Terenure (1st round)
Leinster Senior League Div B 6th

Dolphin

Year of formation 1902
Ground Musgrave Park, Cork   Tel: Cork 22069
Colours Navy blue
Most capped player M J Kiernan (Ireland) 41 caps
Captain 1989-90 T Kingston
1st XV 1989-90 P29 W19 D3 L7 F391 A221
Munster Senior Cup Lost 3-7 to UC Cork (semi-final, 2nd replay)
Munster Senior League 5th (joint)

Dublin University

Year of formation 1854
Ground College Park, Trinity College, Dublin 2   Tel: 778423
Colours White jerseys and shorts, black stockings with red bands
Most capped player J D Clinch (Ireland) 30 caps
Captain 1989-90 P Kenny
1st XV 1989-90 P27   W11   D1   L15   F371   A507
Leinster Senior Cup Lost 18-27 to Blackrock College (1st round)
Leinster Senior League Div B 2nd

Dungannon

Year of formation 1873
Ground Stevenson Park, Dungannon, N Ireland   Tel: Dungannon 22387
Colours Royal blue and white hoops, white shorts
Most capped player W A Anderson (Ireland) 27 caps
Captain 1989-90 W Anderson
1st XV 1989-90 P24   W16   D0   L8   F357   A418
Ulster Senior Cup Lost 9-23 to Malone (1st round)
Ulster Senior League Section 1 3rd

Galwegians

Year of formation 1922
Ground Glenina, Galway, Co Galway   Tel: Galway (091) 62484
Colours Sky blue jerseys, white shorts, sky blue stockings with black tops
Most capped player P J A O'Sullivan (Ireland) 15 caps
Captain 1989-90 E Guerin
1st XV 1989-90 P28   W15   D4   L9   F415   A307
Connacht Senior Cup Lost 9-12 to Creggs (1st round)
Connacht Senior League *Winners*

Garryowen

Year of formation 1884
Ground Dooradoyle, Limerick   Tel: Limerick 46094
Colours Light blue jerseys with white star on breast
Most capped player B G M Wood (Ireland) 29 caps
Captain 1989-90 K Smith
1st XV 1989-90 P29   W14   D3   L12   F504   A475
Munster Senior Cup Lost 7-10 to Dolphin (quarter-final)
Munster Senior League 2nd (joint)

Greystones

Year of formation 1937
Ground Hickey Park, Greystones   Tel: Dublin 874640
Colours Green and white hooped jerseys, white shorts, green stockings
Most capped player A J P Ward (Ireland) 19 caps
Captain 1989-90 M Dempsey
1st XV 1989-90 P28   W13   D4   L11   F537   A496
Leinster Senior Cup Lost 6-19 to Old Wesley (1st round)
Leinster Senior League Div A 6th

Highfield

Year of formation 1930
Ground Woodleigh Park, Model Farm Road, Cork
Colours Red, green and black jerseys, black shorts
Most capped player T A P Moore (Ireland) 12 caps
Captain 1989-90 R Bevan
1st XV 1989-90 P25　W13　D0　L12　F282　A353
Munster Senior Cup Lost 13-16 to Young Munster (quarter-final)
Munster Senior League *winners*

Instonians

Year of formation 1919
Ground Shane Park, Stockmans Lane, Belfast BT9 7JD　　Tel: Belfast 660629
Colours Yellow, black and purple
Most capped player K D Crossan (Ireland) 33 caps
Captain 1989-90 P Russell
1st XV 1989-90 P25　W15　D0　L10　F456　A390
Ulster Senior Cup Lost 19-21 to NIFC (2nd round)
Ulster Senior League Section 1 4th

Lansdowne

Year of formation 1872
Ground Lansdowne Road, Dublin 4　　Tel: Dublin 689292 or 689300
Colours Red, yellow and black
Most capped player M I Keane (Ireland) 51 caps
Captain 1989-90 V Ryan
1st XV 1989-90 P31　W17　D0　L14　F479　A336
Leinster Senior Cup Lost 14-18 to Wanderers (semi-final)
Leinster Senior League Div A 4th

Malone

Year of formation 1892
Ground Gibson Park Avenue, Cregagh Road, Belfast BT6 9GL
Tel: Belfast 57819 or 51312 (office)
Colours White shirts, blue shorts, red stockings
Most capped player W E Crawford (Ireland) 30 caps
Captain 1989-90 C Wilkinson
1st XV 1989-90 P27　W19　D1　L7　F650　A372
Ulster Senior Cup Lost 9-15 to Ballymena (final)
Ulster Senior League Section 1 2nd

Monkstown

Year of formation 1883
Ground Sydney Parade, Dublin 4　　Tel: Dublin 691794
Colours Royal blue and gold
Most capped player J C Parke (Ireland) 20 caps
Captain 1989-90 D Dent
1st XV 1989-90　P35　W15　D1　L17　F498　A431
Leinster Senior Cup Lost 3-9 to Wanderers (final)
Leinster Senior League Div A 7th

North of Ireland (NIFC)

Year of formation 1859
Ground Shaftesbury Avenue, Belfast BT7 2ES   Tel: Belfast 21096 or 23342
Colours Red, black and blue jerseys, navy shorts, black stockings with red, black and blue turnover
Most capped player C M H Gibson (Ireland) 69 caps
Captain 1989-90 S Hutton
1st XV 1989-90   P25   W17   D0   L8   F545   A326
Ulster Senior Cup Lost 3-35 to Ballymena (semi-final)
Ulster Senior League Section 1 6th

Old Belvedere

Year of formation 1930
Ground Anglesea Road, Ballsbridge, Dublin 4   Tel: Dublin 689748
Colours Black and white hooped jerseys, black shorts
Most capped player A J F O'Reilly (Ireland) 29 caps
Captain 1989-90 B O'Connell
1st XV 1989-90   P29   W14   D1   L14   F439   A458
Leinster Senior Cup Lost 6-9 to University College Dublin (1st round)
Leinster Senior League Div B 4th

Old Wesley

Year of formation 1891
Ground Donnybrook, Dublin 4   Tel: Dublin 689149
Colours White jerseys with red and white band, white shorts
Most capped player P A Orr (Ireland) 58 caps
Captain 1989-90 N Farren
1st XV 1989-90   P38   W19   D4   L15   F548   A471
Leinster Senior Cup Lost 9-15 to St Mary's College (2nd round)
Leinster Senior League Div A 8th

Queen's University, Belfast

Year of formation 1869
Ground Upper Malone Playing Fields, Upper Malone Road, Belfast
Tel: Belfast 611662
Colours Royal blue jerseys, white shorts, green, blue and black stockings
Most capped player J W Kyle (Ireland) 46 caps
Captain 1989-90 R Saunders
1st XV 1989-90   P22   W11   D1   L10   F376   A225
Ulster Senior Cup Lost 8-12 to Instonians (1st round)
Ulster Senior League Section 2 3rd

St Mary's College

Year of formation 1900
Ground Templeville Road, Dublin 6   Tel: Dublin 900440
Colours Royal blue jerseys with white star, white shorts, royal blue stockings
Most capped player J J Moloney (Ireland) 27 caps
Captain 1989-90 S Hennessy
1st XV 1989-90 P33   W14   D3   L16   F451   A460
Leinster Senior Cup Lost 6-11 to Monkstown (semi-final)
Leinster Senior League Div A 5th

Shannon

Year of formation 1884
Ground Gortatoger, Parteen, Co Clare
Colours Black and blue
Most capped player G A J McLoughlin (Ireland) 18 caps
Captain 1989-90 M Moylett
1st XV 1989-90 P28 W16 D0 L12 F358 A319
Munster Senior Cup Lost 9-18 to Young Munster (semi-final)
Munster Senior League 5th (joint)

Sunday's Well

Year of formation 1924
Ground Musgrave Park, Cork Tel: Cork 25926
Colours Red, white and green
Most capped player J C Walsh (Ireland) 25 caps
Captain 1989-90 B Trevor
1st XV 1989-90 P25 W14 D0 L11 F324 A284
Munster Senior Cup Lost 9-15 to Dolphin (1st round)
Munster Senior League 2nd (joint)

Terenure College

Year of formation 1941
Ground Lakelands Park, Terenure, Dublin 6 Tel: Dublin 907572
Colours Purple, black and white
Most capped player M L Hipwell (Ireland) 12 caps
Captain 1989-90 W Twomey
1st XV 1989-90 P31 W19 D0 L12 F457 A358
Leinster Senior Cup Lost 6-15 to Lansdowne (2nd round)
Leinster Senior League Div A 2nd

University College, Dublin

Year of formation 1910
Ground University College Dublin, Belfield, Dublin 4 Tel: Dublin 693616
Colours St Patrick's blue jerseys, white shorts, navy blue stockings with St Patrick's blue tops
Most capped player J F Slattery (Ireland) 61 caps
Captain 1989-90 F Griffin
1st XV 1989-90 P28 W10 D2 L16 F376 A529
Leinster Senior Cup Lost 10-16 to Monkstown (2nd round)
Leinster Senior League Div B 5th

Wanderers

Year of formation 1870
Ground Lansdowne Road, Dublin 4 Tel: Dublin 689277
Junior ground Merrion Road, Dublin Tel: Dublin 693227/695272
Colours Blue, black and white hooped jerseys, navy shorts, black stockings with blue and white turnover
Most capped player J R Kavanagh (Ireland) 35 caps
Captain 1989-90 A Kelly
1st XV 1989-90 P32 W26 D0 L4 F649 A375
Leinster Senior Cup *Winners* Beat Monkstown 9-3 (final)
Leinster Senior League *Winners* Div A 1st

OBITUARY 1989-1990 (*up to 1 May 1990*)

Petra Astafei (Rapid-Metro), who died on 22 December 1989, was one of six rugby players killed during the Romanian revolution.

Lucien Augras (Agen, France) died at Grenoble on 6 August 1989, aged 76. His club rugby career was spent with Agen. In 1930 he played on the wing in the side that won the French club championship final, and the following season he won three caps in the Five Nations tournament. That year the RFU severed relations with the FFR because of professionalism among a number of French clubs, and Augras' international career thus finished before his 20th birthday.

Dennis Barker QC (Oxford University, Harlequins) was a war-time blue who scored the winning try in the 1944 Varsity Match played at Oxford. A talented wing threequarter, he played for Harlequins after the war and appeared in an England trial, but narrowly missed winning a cap. He was a distinguished law scholar: he became a High Court Judge and was Justice of Appeal in Hong Kong from 1981 to 1988. He died aged 63 on 13 November 1989 as a result of a motor accident in Cyprus.

Rab Bruce-Lockhart (Cambridge University, London Scottish, Scotland) was a Scottish international fly-half like his brother and father, and played cricket for Scotland as a teenager. One of the small band of players capped by his country before winning a rugby blue, Rab Bruce-Lockhart dropped a goal in his first 'Varsity Match and, playing in the centre in 1938, scored the only try of a game won 8-6 by Cambridge. He was headmaster of Wanganui Collegiate School, Wanganui, New Zealand, from 1954 to 1960 and returned to his old school, Loretto, as head from 1960 to 1976. He died on 1 May 1990, aged 73.

Charles Burton, the doyen of rugby writers, died aged 86 on 31 December 1989. His first job was with *The Times* in 1919, and he reported rugby for many newspapers for the best part of the following 60 years. He was probably best known as the founder (in 1940) and life president of Public School Wanderers. During the war he organised over 1,200 matches for the club, calling on over 5,000 players, among them hundreds from Dominion Service units based in England.

Florin Butiri (Rapid-Metro), a young Romanian player, lost his life on 24 December 1989 during the revolution.

Kenneth Chapman (Harlequins) was a long-range goal-kicker who played for the Quins and Middlesex during the 1930s. The son of the late Herbert Chapman, the secretary-manager of the successful Arsenal Football Club before the war, Kenneth Chapman became president of Harlequins, the Middlesex representative on the RFU and, in 1974-75, president of the Rugby Football Union. Mr Chapman was a qualified solicitor who became managing director of the Thomas Tilling Group. He died on 8 November 1989, four days after attending the England-Fiji international at Twickenham. He was 81.

Malcolm McGregor Cooper (Oxford University, Wellington, Scotland), who died on 1 September 1989, was a former professor of agriculture and an academic of international repute. He was born in New Zealand and won a Rhodes Scholarship to Oxford University, where he won rugby blues in 1934, 1935 and 1936. He captained his University in two consecutive 'Varsity matches, in 1935 and 1936, and in between he won two caps as a flanker for Scotland. After leaving Oxford he returned to New Zealand and captained the Wellington provincial team in 1939.

Raducu Durbac (Steaua Bucharest, Romania) was killed in action by the Securitate during the Romanian revolution in December 1989. A high-ranking Army officer, Durbac was an accomplished full-back who was a first choice for his country between 1970 and 1975. In 1974, at the August 23rd Stadium in Bucharest, his two penalty goals and conversion helped Romania to a 15-10 victory against the full French side.

Bert Grenside (Hawke's Bay, New Zealand) was the tall, powerful winger of the outstanding Hawke's Bay 'Magpies' during their successful Ranfurly Shield run in the 1920s. Grenside's haul of 30 tries in Shield matches earned him selection for the 1928 All Blacks visit to South Africa. Altogether he played in six Tests in 1928 and 1929, scoring three tries. He died on 2 October 1989, aged 90.

R J (Bob) Hanvey (Aspatria, England), who died on 17 October 1989, aged 90, was a loyal servant of Cumbrian rugby for more than 50 years. A cobbler by trade, he was a stalwart forward in the county's packs of the 1920s, helping Cumberland & Westmorland to win the County Championship in 1924, and later served as referee, selector and county president. In 1926 he won four England caps in a side led by the late Sir Wavell Wakefield.

Elvet Jones (Llanelli, Wales) collapsed and died at a meeting on 5 October 1989. Throughout his adult life he was associated with Llanelli RFC. As a lively wing he was club captain in 1936-37, and the following year he achieved the unusual distinction of playing in a Test for the Lions (in South Africa) before winning a Welsh cap (against Scotland in 1939). After the war, he served on the Llanelli club committee, and was chairman of the club from 1960 to 1967 and president in 1982-83.

Jean Matheu (Agen, Castres, France) was a tall, energetic flanker who appeared 24 times for his country. In partnership with Jean Prat and Guy Basquet he created what remains a world record for an international back row. After helping Agen to win the French club championship final in 1945, he transferred to Castres where, under his direction, the club became one of the best in France. As captain he led them to consecutive French club championships in 1949 and 1950. He died on 26 May 1989, aged 68.

Sir Dermot Milman, Bt (Bedford, England), who died on 13 January 1990, aged 77, was an English international in 1937 and 1938. One of the small band of Cambridge University caps who never gained a rugby blue, Sir Dermot played four internationals as a back row forward while associated with the Bedford club. In 1962 he succeeded his father as 8th Baronet Milman.

Florica Murariu (Steaua Bucharest, Romania) was an Army captain who lost his life in the Romanian revolution during Christmas 1989. He had won more than 60 caps for Romania since 1976 and captained the side that defeated Wales in a full international in Cardiff in December 1988. A tall, mobile loose forward, Murariu's career included three international wins against France, two against Wales and one against Scotland.

H G ('Tuppy') Owen-Smith (Oxford University, St Mary's Hospital, England) died in South Africa on 28 February 1990, aged 81. A noted all-round sportsman, he played Test cricket for South Africa before taking a Rhodes Scholarship to Oxford in the 1930s. He achieved distinction as a brilliant full-back, first for the University and later for England and was also a sound welterweight boxer. After winning blues at cricket, boxing and rugby at Oxford, he was selected to play in the Triple Crown-winning England team of 1934, and captained the side in 1937 during another England Triple Crown season. His casual manner on the field was a snare for the unwary, and he proved an adventurous attacker and, despite a lack of inches, a bone-crushing tackler. In 1937 he returned to South Africa to practise as a doctor in Rondebosch.

Albert Procter (Otago, New Zealand), who died on 11 October 1989, aged 83, was a member of the New Zealand side that toured Australia in 1932, playing in the first Test of a series which resulted in New Zealand taking the Bledisloe Cup from Australia. In 1935, his last season in first-class rugby, he played in the Otago team which won the Ranfurly Shield.

A R (Dickie) Ralph (Newport, Wales) was the Welsh outside half in 1931, when Wales won the International Championship for the first time in nine years. Raymond (Dickie) Ralph marked a promising debut by scoring two tries and carving out numerous openings for his threequarters against France. With Ralph in the pivotal position again in 1932 Wales shared the Championship, but in 1933 he turned professional with Leeds rugby league club, ending a brief and promising union career. He won a RL cup-winners' medal in 1936 when Leeds beat Warrington 18-2 at Wembley. Dickie Ralph died in Leamington Spa in October 1989, aged 81. He was a schoolmaster by profession.

Tom Rees (Newport, Wales), a popular Welsh prop forward of the 1930s, died on 19 January 1990, aged 76. He graduated to Newport via the Blackwood club and went on to win eight caps for Wales between 1935 and 1937. Reputed to have been the heaviest forward to play for Wales, he was a member of the pack when his country beat New Zealand 13-12 in 1935 and played in the 1936 side that won the International Championship.

A C C Robilliard (Canterbury, New Zealand) died on 23 April 1990 in New Zealand, aged 86. As a strapping young wing Robilliard toured with Cliff Porter's Invincible New Zealand team to Britain in 1924-25. Unfortunately, he broke a bone in his foot playing against Somerset and appeared in only four games in Britain, but on the way home he scored four tries in each of the matches played by the All Blacks in Canada. He was capped four times for New Zealand in South Africa in 1928.

Gwyn Roblin, who died in April 1990, was the president of the Welsh Rugby Union in 1979-80.

K A ('Monkey') Sellar (United Services, Royal Navy, England), who was awarded the DSC and DSO during distinguished war service with the Royal Navy, died on 15 May 1989 in South Africa, aged 82. As a 20-year-old in his international debut for England against Wales in 1927, his line-kicking and defence as a full-back were described as 'sensational'. After he helped England to win the Grand Slam in 1928 his promising rugby future was interrupted by a career at sea. After the war he became a stockbroker before emigrating to South Africa for health reasons in the early 1980s.

Bogdan Stan (Rapid-Metro), a young Romanian club player, died in the revolution on 24 December 1989.

Mark Sugden (Wanderers, Ireland), who died on 21 January 1990, aged 87, was Ireland's most-capped scrum-half, winning 28 caps between 1925 and 1931. Born in Leek in Staffordshire, Sugden attended Trinity College, Dublin, and therefore obtained a residential qualification to play for Ireland. As a scrum-half he was particularly dangerous at breaking from the base of the scrummage when near the opposition's goal-line, thus creating several tries for himself and many more for his colleagues. In his last season of international rugby he captained Ireland four times. He was a schoolmaster by profession, specialising in modern languages.

W E (Bill) Tamplin (Cardiff, Wales) was a Monmouthshire county police officer who played 252 games for Cardiff between 1945 and 1953 and won seven caps for Wales in the seasons immediately after the war. Bill was a popular lock forward, best remembered as a long-range goal-kicker. Indeed, his 24 points for Wales included the two crucial penalties in their 6-0 win against Australia at Cardiff in 1947, when Tamplin was the Welsh skipper. He died at his home in Pontypool on 20 October 1989, aged 72.

H W (Harold) Thomas (Neath, Wales) died on 18 December 1989, aged 75. A strong lock forward, Thomas was a member of the pack when Wales won the International Championship in 1936, and at Twickenham the following year he formed the Welsh second row with his brother Dai. He won six caps for Wales.

Christian Toporan (Energia) was among the young Romanian rugby players killed in the Christmas revolution.

Barry Usmar, who died on 11 April 1990, aged 60, was the respected secretary of the New Zealand Rugby Football Union. As a player he had appeared for the Wellington College Old Boys in the early 1950s before becoming an administrator. He had been the secretary-treasurer of the NZRFU since 1978.

Raphael Tsagane (Wasps), a promising young first XV wing, died tragically in a car accident during Wasps' Easter tour in 1990.

Frank Ward (Wellington, New Zealand) was at the time of his death on 11 March 1990, aged 89, the second oldest All Black. He played on the right wing for New Zealand against the touring New South Wales team of 1921, but a recurring knee injury the following season brought a premature end to his career.

Alan Key OBE, TD (Old Cranleighans, England) was a scrum-half who won two caps for England in the 1930s and played 16 times for the Barbarians between 1928 and 1934. A versatile and skilful player, he made five successive Easter tours of South Wales with the Baa-Baas, and once appeared as an emergency threequarter for the club. When Wilf Sobey withdrew from the England side to play Ireland in Dublin in 1930, Key made his international debut and became the first player to be capped direct from the Old Cranleighan club. His final cap was at Twickenham in 1933, when Wales achieved their first victory (at the tenth attempt) at the ground. The founder manager of the Army Kinema Corporation, Lt Col Key died on 2 July 1989, aged 81.

FIXTURES 1990-91

Venues and fixtures are understood to be correct at the time of going to press, but are subject to alteration. We would like to thank all those who have assisted in the compilation of this list, especially those at the various headquarters of the Home Unions. Additional thanks go to Peter Jackson and John Jeavons-Fellows for help with Courage Leagues fixtures, and we are once again especially grateful to the clubs who have given us permission to use their fixture lists.

Saturday, 1 September

Yorkshire v Ulster
Collegians Tournament
Aberdeen GSFP v Preston Lodge
Abertillery v Headingley
Askeans v Streatham-Croydon
Blackheath v Fylde
Blackrock Coll v Nottingham
Boroughmuir v Wakefield
Bridgwater Albion v Cheltenham
Broughton Park v Waterloo
Camborne v Northampton
Cardiff v Bristol
Clontarf v Old Wesley
Edinburgh Wands v Dundee HSFP
Esher v Oxford
Exeter v Stourbridge
Gala v Kelso
Galwegians v Sunday's Well
Gloucester v Swansea
Greystones v Malone
Harrogate v Met Police
Hawick v Tynedale
Highfield v Dungannon
Howe of Fife v Coleraine
Kilmarnock v Ayr
Lansdowne v Bective Rangers
Leicester v Bedford
Lewes v Maidstone
Liverpool St Helens v Northern
Lydney v Penarth
Maesteg v Wasps
Melrose v Jedforest
Middlesbrough v Morley
Moseley v Neath
Newport v Coventry
Pontypool v Bath
Pontypridd v Aberavon
Portadown v CIYMS
Redruth v Cross Keys
Richmond v Saracens
Rosslyn Park v Llanelli
Roundhay v Gosforth
Rugby v Preston Grasshoppers
Sale v Berry Hill
Sheffield v Wharfedale
S Wales Police v London Welsh
Tredegar v Bridgend
Vale of Lune v West of Scotland
Wanderers v Bangor
Waterpark v Monkstown
Watsonians v Haddington
West Hartlepool v Otley

Sunday, 2 September

Kelso Sevens
Old Belvedere v Bangor
St Ives v Northampton
Terenure Coll v Irish Wolfhounds

Tuesday, 4 September

Ulster v Spain
Durham City v West Hartlepool
Edinburgh Wands v Portobello
Glasgow High/Kelvinside v Kilmarnock
Gosforth v Morpeth
Howe of Fife v Boroughmuir
Jedforest v Selkirk
Langholm v Hawick
Newbridge v Tredegar
Truro v Redruth

Wednesday, 5 September

Bath v Toulouse
Bridgend v Central Glamorgan
Dolphin v Sunday's Well
Gloucester v Clifton
Harlequins v Askeans
Moseley v Sale
Penygroes v Llanelli
Pontypool v Newport
Pontypridd v Lydney
Swansea v Aberavon
Wasps v Met Police

Thursday, 6 September

Ayr v Greenock Wands
Oxford v Birkenhead Park
Preston Lodge v Trinity Acads

Saturday, 8 September

Edinburgh District v Leinster
Aberavon v Torquay Ath
Abertillery v Penarth
Armagh v Dundalk
Aspatria v Kilmarnock
Ballymena v Hawick
Bangor v Monkstown
Bective Rangers v Greystones
Bedford v London Welsh
Blackrock Coll v Old Wesley
Broughton Park v Kendal
Bridgend v Moseley

Bristol v Blackheath
Camborne v Redruth
Cheltenham v Birkenhead Park
Collegians v De La Salle Palmerston
Cardiff v Leicester
Cork Const v Sunday's Well
Coventry v Northampton
Edinburgh Acads v Ayr
Galwegians v Terenure Coll
Gosforth v West Hartlepool
Harrogate v Rugby
Hartlepool Rovers v Edinburgh Wands
Headingley v Morley
Jedforest v Gala
Kelso v Watsonians
Liverpool St Helens v Roundhay
Llanelli v Bath
Lydney v Walsall
Malone v CIYMS
Melrose v Langholm
Met Police v Maidstone
Neath v Gloucester
Newbridge v Cross Keys
Newport v Richmond
Nottingham v Pontypridd
Orrell v Fylde
Plymouth Albion v Harlequins
Portadown v Dungannon
Portobello v Preston Lodge
Rosslyn Park v London Irish
St Ives v S Wales Police
Sale v Sheffield
Saracens v London Scottish
Swansea v Lansdowne
Tredegar v Askeans
US Portsmouth v Havant
Wakefield v Nuneaton
Wanderers v Wasps
Waterloo v Vale of Lune
West of Scotland v Boroughmuir

Sunday, 9 September

Cornwall v Ontario
Gosforth v RFU President's XV

Tuesday, 11 September

Camborne v Falmouth
Gala v Langholm
Hawick v Kelso
Kilmarnock v Glasgow Acads
Liverpool St Helens v New Brighton
Melrose v Selkirk
Penarth v Newbridge
Redruth v Newquay Hornets
Stroud v Gloucester
Terenure Coll v Dublin U
Waterloo v Lancs Police
West of Scotland v
    Glasgow High/Kelvinside

Wednesday, 12 September

Aberavon v Pontypridd
Bath v Newport
Bridgend v Aberavon
Bristol v St Mary's Coll
Coventry v Moseley
Glenrothes v Howe of Fife
Harlequins v Met Police
Llanelli v Cross Keys
S Wales Police v Abertillery
Wasps v Richmond

Saturday, 15 September

Pontypool v Munster
Toulouse v Leinster
RFU Pilkington Cup *1st round*
WRU Schweppes Cup *1st Round*
RFU Junior Clubs Cup *1st Round*
Aberavon v Bedford
Ballina v Armagh
Bath v Cardiff
Berry Hill v Tredegar
Blackheath v Newport
Blackrock Coll v Boroughmuir
Bristol v Swansea
Cheltenham v Streatham-Croydon
City of Derry v Ayr
Coventry v Maesteg
Currie v Kilmarnock
De La Salle Palmerston v Wanderers
Dolphin v Collegians
Dungannon v Old Crescent
Edinburgh Acads v CIYMS
Edinburgh Wands v Corstorphine
Gala v Hawick
Galwegians v Ballymena
Gosforth v Kendal
Greystones v Monkstown
Harlequins v Llanelli
Headingley v Bradford-Bingley
Highfield v Sunday's Well
Howe of Fife v Kirkcaldy
Kelso v Melrose
Langholm v Jedforest
Leicester v Northampton
London Scottish v Otley
Malone v Bangor
Neath v Nottingham
Newbridge v Richmond
Old Wesley v Bective Rangers
Orrell v Waterloo
Penzance-Newlyn v Redruth
Pontypridd v Gloucester
Rosslyn Park v Abertillery
Rugby v Sale
Saracens v Bridgend
Sidcup v Havant
Stourbridge v Halifax
Terenure Coll v London Irish
Tynedale v Wakefield
UC Cork v Shannon

Wasps v Liverpool St Helens
Watsonians v Dalziel HSFP

Tuesday, 18 September

Terenure Coll v Wanderers

Wednesday, 19 September

CIYMS v Instonians

Saturday, 22 September

RFU Courage Leagues
Division 1
Bath v Liverpool St Helens
Bristol v Nottingham
Harlequins v Wasps
Leicester v Gloucester
Northampton v Saracens
Orrell v Rosslyn Park
Division 2
Blackheath v London Scottish
Coventry v Waterloo
Gosforth v Sale
Headingley v Rugby
London Irish v Plymouth Albion
Wakefield v Bedford
Division 3
Askeans v Morley
Clifton v Sheffield
Exeter v West Hartlepool
Fylde v Broughton Park
Lydney v Roundhay
Met Police v Vale of Lune
Division 4 (North)
Birmingham-Solihull v Kendal
Preston Grasshoppers v Stoke
Northern v Winnington Park
Lichfield v Stourbridge
Durham City v Hereford
Harrogate v Otley
Division 4 (South)
Camborne v Basingstoke
Cheltenham v Weston-super-Mare
Ealing v Sudbury
Havant v North Walsham
London Welsh v Maidenhead
Maidstone v Redruth

SRU McEwan's Leagues
Division 1
Boroughmuir v Kelso
Edinburgh Wands v Currie
Glasgow High/Kelvinside v
    Edinburgh Acads
Hawick v Stewart's-Melville FP
Heriot's FP v Gala
Jedforest v Melrose
Stirling County v Selkirk
Division 2
Ayr v Kilmarnock
Corstorphine v Dunfermline

Dundee HSFP v Langholm
Hillhead-Jordanhill v Watsonians
Kirkcaldy v Glasgow Acads
Musselburgh v Preston Lodge
Royal High v West of Scotland

WRU Heineken Leagues
Premier Division
Cardiff v Swansea
Glamorgan Wands v Bridgend
Llanelli v Pontypridd
Neath v Abertillery
Pontypool v Newbridge
Division 1
Cross Keys v S Wales Police
Maesteg v Newport
Penarth v Ebbw Vale
Tredegar v Aberavon

Ballymena v Old Wesley
Bangor v De La Salle Palmerston
Blackrock Coll v Greystones
City of Derry v Academy
CIYMS v Clontarf
Collegians v Queen's U, Belfast
Dungannon v Ards
Nuneaton v Southend
Portadown v Armagh
Richmond v Moseley
St Mary's Coll v Bective Rangers
Skerries v Wanderers
Sunday's Well v Bohemians
Terenure Coll v Malone
Young Munster v Monkstown

Sunday, 23 September

Waterpark v Shannon

Monday, 24 September

Hawick v Glasgow Acads

Tuesday, 25 September

Headingley v Roundhay

Wednesday, 26 September

Bristol v Met Police
Cambridge U v Cambridge City
Clifton v Bath
Gloucester v Newport
Harlequins v Loughborough U
Old Belvedere v Old Wesley
Rugby v Coventry
Sale v Broughton Park

Friday, 28 September

Northampton v Bedford

Saturday, 29 September

ENGLAND XV v BARBARIANS
(Twickenham)

SRU McEwan's Leagues
Division 1
Currie v Boroughmuir
Edinburgh Acads v Heriot's FP
Edinburgh Wands v Jedforest
Gala v Selkirk
Kelso v Glasgow High/Kelvinside
Melrose v Hawick
Stewart's-Melville FP v Stirling County
Division 2
Ayr v Corstorphine
Dunfermline v Dundee HSFP
Glasgow Acads v Watsonians
Kilmarnock v Musselburgh
Langholm v Hillhead/Jordanhill
Preston Lodge v Royal High
West of Scotland v Kirkcaldy

WRU Heineken Leagues
Premier Division
Abertillery v Llanelli
Bridgend v Pontypool
Newbridge v Cardiff
Pontypridd v Glamorgan Wands
Swansea v Neath

Bath v Munster
RFU Junior Clubs Cup *2nd round*
Academy v Dungannon
Ards v City of Derry
Armagh v Collegians
Ballymena v CIYMS
Bangor v Instonians
Barnstaple v Penarth
Blackheath v Aberavon
Bristol v Coventry
Brixham v Cheltenham
Broughton Park v Hull Ionians
Clifton v Havant
Cork Const v Greystones
De La Salle Palmerston v Sunday's Well
Fylde v Harrogate
Gloucester v Ebbw Vale
Gosforth v Wasps
Headingley v Cambridge U
London Irish v Harlequins
London Scottish v Anglo-Scots
London Welsh v Newport
Malone v NIFC
Morley v Hartlepool Rovers
Monkstown v Athlone
Moseley v S Wales Police
Nottingham v Sale
Old Wesley v Dublin U
Oxford v Bridgwater Albion
Queen's U, Belfast v Portadown
Redruth v Launceston
Rosslyn Park v Plymouth Albion

Rugby v Northern
Saracens v Exeter
Shannon v Bective Rangers
Sheffield v Stockton
Terenure Coll v Skerries
Torquay Ath v Lydney
Tredegar v Tredegar Ironsides
Wakefield v Liverpool St Helens
Wanderers v Waterloo
West Hartlepool v Bradford-Bingley
West London Inst v Maidstone

Tuesday, 2 October

Aberavon v Abertillery
Bedford v Loughborough U
Bridgend v S Wales Police
Cardiff v Penarth
Llanelli v Ebbw Vale
Newbridge v Maesteg
Newport v Pontypridd
Swansea v Cross Keys
Tredegar v Pontypool

Wednesday, 3 October

Cambridge U v St Mary's Hosp
Harlequins v West London Inst

Friday, 5 October

Cardiff v Newport
Ebbw Vale v Bridgend
S Wales Police v Pontypridd
Ystradgynlais v Swansea

Saturday, 6 October

WALES XV v BARBARIANS (Cardiff)

RFU Courage Leagues
Division 1
Gloucester v Moseley
Liverpool St Helens v Northampton
Nottingham v Harlequins
Rosslyn Park v Bristol
Saracens v Orrell
Wasps v Leicester
Division 2
Bedford v London Irish
London Scottish v Coventry
Plymouth Albion v Richmond
Rugby v Wakefield
Sale v Headingley
Waterloo v Gosforth
Division 3
Broughton Park v Met Police
Morley v Exeter
Roundhay v Nuneaton
Sheffield v Lydney
Vale of Lune v Clifton
West Hartlepool v Fylde

Division 4 (North)
Hereford v Lichfield
Kendal v Harrogate
Otley v Durham City
Stoke v Walsall
Stourbridge v Northern
Winnington Park v Preston Grasshoppers
Division 4 (South)
Basingstoke v Cheltenham
Maidenhead v Maidstone
North Walsham v Ealing
Redruth v Southend
Sudbury v London Welsh
Weston-super-Mare v Havant

SRU McEwan's Leagues
Division 1
Boroughmuir v Edinburgh Wands
Glasgow High/Kelvinside v Currie
Edinburgh Acads v Stewart's-Melville FP
Heriot's FP v Kelso
Jedforest v Hawick
Selkirk v Melrose
Stirling County v Gala
Division 2
Corstorphine v Dundee HSFP
Hillhead-Jordanhill v Glasgow Acads
Kirkcaldy v Preston Lodge
Musselburgh v Ayr
Royal High v Kilmarnock
Watsonians v Dunfermline
West of Scotland v Langholm

IRU Leagues
Division 1
Cork Const v St Mary's Coll
Instonians v Ballymena
Shannon v Malone
Wanderers v Garryowen
Division 2
Athlone v NIFC
Corinthians v Bangor
Greystones v CIYMS
Old Wesley v Sunday's Well
Young Munster v Terenure Coll

Aberavon v Llanelli
Bath v Neath
Bective Rangers v Galwegians
Camborne v Brixham
Cambridge U v Blackheath
City of Derry v Armagh
Collegians v Ards
Oxford U v Banco de la Nacion
Portadown v Academy
Queen's U, Belfast v Dungannon

Wednesday, 10 October

Wasps v Loughborough U

Saturday, 13 October

RFU Courage Leagues
Division 1
Bristol v Saracens
Harlequins v Rosslyn Park
Leicester v Nottingham
Moseley v Wasps
Northampton v Bath
Orrell v Liverpool St Helens
Division 2
Coventry v Blackheath
Gosforth v London Scottish
Headingley v Waterloo
London Irish v Rugby
Richmond v Bedford
Wakefield v Sale
Division 3
Clifton v Broughton Park
Exeter v Askeans
Fylde v Morley
Lydney v Vale of Lune
Met Police v West Hartlepool
Nuneaton v Sheffield
Division 4 (North)
Durham City v Kendal
Harrogate v Birmingham-Solihull
Lichfield v Otley
Northern v Hereford
Preston Grasshoppers v Stourbridge
Walsall v Winnington Park
Division 4 (South)
Cheltenham v Camborne
Ealing v Weston-super-Mare
Havant v Basingstoke
London Welsh v North Walsham
Maidstone v Sudbury
Southend v Maidenhead

SRU McEwan's Leagues
Division 1
Boroughmuir v Selkirk
Currie v Heriot's FP
Edinburgh Wands v
    Glasgow High/Kelvinside
Hawick v Stirling County
Kelso v Edinburgh Acads
Melrose v Gala
Stewart's-Melville FP v Jedforest
Division 2
Ayr v Royal High
Dundee HSFP v Hillhead-Jordanhill
Dunfermline v Glasgow Acads
Kilmarnock v Kirkcaldy
Langholm v Corstorphine
Musselburgh v Watsonians
Preston Lodge v West of Scotland

IRU Leagues
Division 1
Ballymena v Cork Const
Lansdowne v Shannon
Malone v Instonians

St Mary's Coll v Wanderers
Division 2
Bangor v Athlone
CIYMS v Old Wesley
NIFC v Young Munster
Sunday's Well v Corinthians
Terenure Coll v Greystones

WRU Heineken Leagues
Premier Division
Cardiff v Bridgend
Glamorgan Wands v Abertillery
Llanelli v Neath
Pontypool v Pontypridd
Swansea v Newbridge
Division 1
Aberavon v Maesteg
Ebbw Vale v Cross Keys
Newport v Penarth
S Wales Police v Tredegar

Academy v Queen's U, Belfast
Armagh v Dungannon
Bective Rangers v Clontarf
City of Derry v Collegians
Loughborough U v Oxford U
Portadown v Ards
UC Dublin v Cambridge U

Tuesday, 16 October

Gloucester v Cheltenham

Wednesday, 17 October

French Selection v New Zealanders
(Toulon)

Saturday, 20 October

Ireland B v Argentinians
French Selection v New Zealanders
(Narbonne)

RFU Courage Leagues
Division 1
Bath v Orrell
Liverpool St Helens v Bristol
Nottingham v Moseley
Rosslyn Park v Leicester
Saracens v Harlequins
Wasps v Gloucester
Division 2
Bedford v Plymouth Albion
Blackheath v Gosforth
London Scottish v Headingley
Rugby v Richmond
Sale v London Irish
Waterloo v Wakefield
Division 3
Askeans v Fylde
Broughton Park v Lydney

Morley v Met Police
Sheffield v Roundhay
Vale of Lune v Nuneaton
West Hartlepool v Clifton
Division 4 (North)
Birmingham-Solihull v Durham City
Hereford v Preston Grasshoppers
Kendal v Lichfield
Otley v Northern
Stourbridge v Walsall
Winnington Park v Stoke
Division 4 (South)
Basingstoke v Ealing
Camborne v Havant
Maidenhead v Redruth
North Walsham v Maidstone
Sudbury v Southend
Weston-super-Mare v London Welsh

SRU McEwan's Leagues
Division 1
Currie v Melrose
Edinburgh Acads v Hawick
Gala v Edinburgh Wands
Glasgow High/Kelvinside v Selkirk
Heriot's FP v Stewart's-Melville FP
Jedforest v Boroughmuir
Kelso v Stirling County
Division 2
Corstorphine v Musselburgh
Glasgow Acads v Ayr
Kilmarnock v Dunfermline
Kirkcaldy v Langholm
Preston Lodge v Hillhead-Jordanhill
Royal High v Watsonians
West of Scotland v Dundee HSFP

WRU Heineken Leagues
Premier Division
Abertillery v Pontypool
Bridgend v Swansea
Llanelli v Glamorgan Wands
Neath v Newbridge
Pontypridd v Cardiff
Division 1
Cross Keys v Tredegar
Ebbw Vale v Newport
Maesteg v S Wales Police
Penarth v Aberavon

WRU Cup *2nd round*
Academy v Collegians
Ards v Armagh
Askeans v Fylde
Blackrock Coll v Bective Rangers
Cheltenham v Bournemouth
CIYMS v Lansdowne
Clontarf v Sunday's Well
Cork Const v Old Wesley
Dungannon v Portadown
Exeter v Coventry
Highfield v Terenure Coll

Malone v Ballymena
Northampton v Cambridge U
Oxford U v Durham U
Queen's U, Belfast v City of Derry
St Mary's Coll v Bangor
Wanderers v Greystones

Sunday, 21 October

Shannon v Old Crescent

Tuesday, 23 October

Irish Students v Argentinians
Cambridge U v Bedford
Leicester v Oxford U
Neath v Tredegar

Wednesday, 24 October

French Selection v New Zealanders
(Brive)

Friday, 26 October

Bangor v Queen's U, Belfast
Portadown v Malone

Saturday, 27 October

IRELAND v ARGENTINA
(Lansdowne Road)
French Barbarians v New Zealanders
(Agen)

RFU Courage Leagues
Division 1
Bristol v Bath
Gloucester v Nottingham
Harlequins v Liverpool St Helens
Leicester v Saracens
Moseley v Rosslyn Park
Orrell v Northampton
Division 2
Gosforth v Coventry
Headingley v Blackheath
London Irish v Waterloo
Plymouth Albion v Rugby
Richmond v Sale
Wakefield v London Scottish
Division 3
Clifton v Morley
Fylde v Exeter
Lydney v West Hartlepool
Met Police v Askeans
Nuneaton v Broughton Park
Roundhay v Vale of Lune
Division 4 (North)
Durham City v Harrogate
Lichfield v Birmingham-Solihull
Northern v Kendal
Preston Grasshoppers v Otley

Stoke v Stourbridge
Walsall v Hereford
Division 4 (South)
Ealing v Camborne
Havant v Cheltenham
London Welsh v Basingstoke
Maidstone v Weston-super-Mare
Redruth v Sudbury
Southend v North Walsham

SRU McEwan's Leagues
Division 1
Gala v Boroughmuir
Hawick v Heriot's FP
Jedforest v Glasgow High/Kelvinside
Melrose v Kelso
Selkirk v Currie
Stewart's-Melville FP v Edinburgh Wands
Stirling County v Edinburgh Acads
Division 2
Corstorphine v Royal High
Dundee HSFP v Kirkcaldy
Dunfermline v Preston Lodge
Glasgow Acads v Musselburgh
Hillhead-Jordanhill v West of Scotland
Langholm v Ayr
Watsonians v Kilmarnock

WRU Heineken Leagues
Premier Division
Cardiff v Abertillery
Glamorgan Wands v Neath
Newbridge v Bridgend
Pontypool v Llanelli
Swansea v Pontypridd
Division 1
Aberavon v Ebbw Vale
Newport v Cross Keys
S Wales Police v Penarth
Tredegar v Maesteg

Academy v CIYMS
Ballymena v Collegians
Cambridge U v Wasps
Sheffield v Winnington Park
UC Dublin v Dungannon
Wanderers v NIFC

Sunday, 28 October

Corinthians v Monkstown
Old Wesley v De La Salle Palmerston
Sunday's Well v Shannon
Terenure Coll v Blackrock Coll
Wasps v Yugoslav Sports (NZ)

Monday, 29 October

Dublin U v Bective Rangers
Lansdowne v Greystones

Tuesday, 30 October

Eastern Counties v Argentinians
French Selection v New Zealanders
(Bayonne)
Newport v Barbarians
Gloucester v S Wales Police
Oxford U v Northampton

Wednesday, 31 October

St Austell v Camborne
Swansea v Pembrokeshire

Friday, 2 November

England B v Namibia (provisional)

Saturday, 3 November

FRANCE v NEW ZEALAND (Nantes)
ENGLAND v ARGENTINA
(Twickenham)
RFU Cup *2nd round*
RFU Junior Clubs Cup *3rd round*

SRU McEwan's Leagues
Division 1
Boroughmuir v Stewart's-Melville FP
Currie v Jedforest
Edinburgh Acads v Melrose
Edinburgh Wands v Hawick
Glasgow High/Kelvinside v Gala
Heriot's FP v Stirling County
Kelso v Selkirk
Division 2
Ayr v Dundee HSFP
Kirkcaldy v Hillhead-Jordanhill
Kilmarnock v Corstorphine
Musselburgh v Langholm
Preston Lodge v Watsonians
Royal High v Glasgow Acads
West of Scotland v Dunfermline

IRU Leagues
Division 1
Cork Const v Malone
Garryowen v St Mary's Coll
Instonians v Lansdowne
Wanderers v Ballymena
Division 2
Athlone v Old Wesley
CIYMS v Bangor
Greystones v Sunday's Well
Terenure Coll v NIFC
Young Munster v Corinthians

WRU Heineken Leagues
Premier Division
Abertillery v Swansea
Glamorgan Wands v Pontypool
Llanelli v Cardiff

Neath v Bridgend
Pontypridd v Newbridge

Aberavon v Northampton
Armagh v Academy
Bective Rangers v UC Dublin
Birkenhead Park v Morley
Broughton Park v Bradford-Bingley
Camborne v St Ives
City of Derry v Dungannon
Clifton v Redruth
Collegians v Portadown
Ebbw Vale v London Welsh
Gloucester v Bristol
Harlequins v Cambridge U
Kendal v Liverpool St Helens
Leicester v Moseley
Maidstone v Sidcup
Newport v Nottingham
Otley v Sheffield
Queen's U, Belfast v Ards
Rosslyn Park v Loughborough U
Shannon v Galwegians
Streatham-Croydon v Oxford
Stroud v Penarth
Torquay Ath v S Wales Police
Tredegar v Cheltenham
Wasps v Bath

Tuesday, 6 November

French Selection v New Zealanders
(La Rochelle)
South of Scotland v Argentinians
Combined Services v Namibia
(US Portsmouth) (provisional)
Cambridge U v Leicester

Wednesday, 7 November

Cardiff v Oxford U

Friday, 9 November

Ayr v Dalziel HSFP
Clarkston v West of Scotland
Kelso v Langholm
Musselburgh v Jedforest
Stirling County v Kilmarnock

Saturday, 10 November

FRANCE v NEW ZEALAND (Paris)
SCOTLAND v ARGENTINA
(Murrayfield)

RFU Courage Leagues
Division 1
Bath v Harlequins
Liverpool St Helens v Leicester
Northampton v Bristol
Nottingham v Wasps
Rosslyn Park v Gloucester

Saracens v Moseley
Division 2
Blackheath v Wakefield
Coventry v Headingley
London Scottish v London Irish
Rugby v Bedford
Sale v Plymouth Albion
Waterloo v Richmond
Division 3
Askeans v Clifton
Broughton Park v Roundhay
Exeter v Met Police
Morley v Lydney
Vale of Lune v Sheffield
West Hartlepool v Nuneaton
Division 4 (North)
Birmingham-Solihull v Northern
Harrogate v Lichfield
Hereford v Stoke
Kendal v Preston Grasshoppers
Otley v Walsall
Stourbridge v Winnington Park
Division 4 (South)
Basingstoke v Maidstone
Camborne v London Welsh
Cheltenham v Ealing
North Walsham v Redruth
Sudbury v Maidenhead
Weston-super-Mare v Southend

IRU Leagues
Division 1
Ballymena v Garryowen
Lansdowne v Cork Const
Malone v Wanderers
Shannon v Instonians
Division 2
Bangor v Young Munster
Corinthians v CIYMS
Greystones v Athlone
Old Wesley v NIFC
Sunday's Well v Terenure Coll

WRU Heineken Leagues
Premier Division
Bridgend v Pontypridd
Cardiff v Glamorgan Wands
Newbridge v Abertillery
Pontypool v Neath
Swansea v Llanelli
Division 1
Ebbw Vale v S Wales Police
Maesteg v Cross Keys
Newport v Aberavon
Penarth v Tredegar

Ards v Academy
Armagh v Queen's U, Belfast
Dungannon v Collegians
Edinburgh U v Watsonians
Edinburgh Wands v Haddington
Fylde v Durham City
Kirkcaldy v Hawick

Old Belvedere v Bective Rangers
Orrell v Gosforth
Portadown v City of Derry
Preston Lodge v Royal High

Tuesday, 13 November

Cambridge U v Richmond
Neath v Penarth
Newbridge v S Wales Police
Newport v Swansea
Pontypridd v Mid Districts

Wednesday, 14 November

Bridgend v S Glam Inst
Llanelli v Aberavon
Oxford U v Rosslyn Park

Friday, 16 November

Newport v Cardiff

Saturday, 17 November

Barbarians v Argentinians (Cardiff)

RFU Courage Leagues
Division 1
Bristol v Orrell
Gloucester v Saracens
Harlequins v Northampton
Leicester v Bath
Moseley v Liverpool St Helens
Wasps v Rosslyn Park
Division 2
Bedford v Sale
Headingley v Gosforth
London Irish v Blackheath
Plymouth Albion v Waterloo
Richmond v London Scottish
Wakefield v Coventry
Division 3
Clifton v Exeter
Lydney v Askeans
Met Police v Fylde
Nuneaton v Morley
Roundhay v West Hartlepool
Sheffield v Broughton Park
Division 4 (North)
Lichfield v Durham City
Northern v Harrogate
Preston Grasshoppers v
    Birmingham-Solihull
Stoke v Otley
Walsall v Kendal
Winnington Park v Hereford
Division 4 (South)
Ealing v Havant
London Welsh v Cheltenham
Maidenhead v North Walsham
Maidstone v Camborne

Redruth v Weston-super-Mare
Southend v Basingstoke

SRU McEwan's Leagues
Division 1
Gala v Currie
Hawick v Boroughmuir
Jedforest v Kelso
Melrose v Heriot's FP
Selkirk v Edinburgh Acads
Stewart's-Melville FP v
    Glasgow High/Kelvinside
Stirling County v Edinburgh Wands
Division 2
Corstorphine v Preston Lodge
Dundee HSFP v Musselburgh
Dunfermline v Kirkcaldy
Glasgow Acads v Kilmarnock
Hillhead-Jordanhill v Ayr
Langholm v Royal High
Watsonians v West of Scotland

IRU Leagues
Division 1
Cork Const v Shannon
Garryowen v Malone
St Mary's Coll v Ballymena
Wanderers v Lansdowne
Division 2
Athlone v Terenure Coll
CIYMS v Sunday's Well
NIFC v Bangor
Old Wesley v Corinthians
Young Munster v Greystones

WRU Schweppes Cup *3rd round*
Aberavon v Pontypool
Abertillery v Tredegar
Academy v City of Derry
Ards v Dungannon
Armagh v Portadown
Bridgend v Glamorgan Wands
Cambridge U v Nottingham
Cross Keys v Pontypridd
Ebbw Vale v Neath
Llanelli v Maesteg
Queen's U, Belfast v Collegians
Rugby v Vale of Lune

Sunday, 18 November

Bective Rangers v Monkstown
West Hartlepool v Durham

Monday, 19 November

Cornwall v Royal Navy (St Austell)

Wednesday, 21 November

Oxford U v Major R V Stanley's XV
Swansea v Maesteg

Saturday, 24 November

SRU District Championship
Edinburgh Dist v Glasgow Dist
Scottish North/Midlands v
    South of Scotland
RFU Pilkington Cup *3rd round*

IRU Leagues
Division 1
Lansdowne v Garryowen
Malone v St Mary's Coll
Instonians v Cork Const
Shannon v Wanderers
Division 2
Bangor v Old Wesley
Corinthians v Athlone
Greystones v NIFC
Sunday's Well v Young Munster
Terenure Coll v CIYMS

WRU Heineken Leagues
Premier Division
Abertillery v Bridgend
Glamorgan Wands v Swansea
Llanelli v Newbridge
Neath v Pontypridd
Pontypool v Cardiff
Division 1
Cross Keys v Aberavon
Maesteg v Penarth
S Wales Police v Newport
Tredegar v Ebbw Vale

RFU Junior Clubs Cup *4th round*
Cambridge U v Loughborough U
Cheltenham v Nuneaton
City of Derry v Ards
Collegians v Armagh
Coventry v London Welsh
Currie v Ayr
Dungannon v Academy
Fylde v Birkenhead Park
Gala v Watsonians
Gosforth v Durham City
Hawick v Aspatria
Headingley v Huddersfield
Jedforest v Stewart's-Melville FP
Kelso v Boroughmuir
Kilmarnock v Glasgow High/Kelvinside
Kirkcaldy v Edinburgh Wands
Langholm v Melrose
Leith Acads v Howe of Fife
Lydney v Weston-super-Mare
Morley v Rugby
Portadown v Queen's U, Belfast
Preston Lodge v Clarkston
Roundhay v Waterloo
St Mary's Hosp v Maidstone
Selkirk v West of Scotland
Sheffield v Middlesbrough
Southend v Oxford
Wakefield v Broughton Park

Monday, 26 November

Scottish Students v Oxford U

Tuesday, 27 November

Ayr v East Kilbride
Clarkston v Edinburgh Wands
Exeter v Gloucester
Newbridge v Aberavon
Nottingham v Loughborough U

Wednesday, 28 November

Cambridge U v
  M R Steele-Bodger's XV
Abertillery v Maesteg
Cheltenham v Ebbw Vale
Cross Keys v Bridgend
Howe of Fife v Glenrothes
Llanelli v Newport
Pontypool v S Wales Police
Pontypridd v Maesteg
Tredegar v Swansea

Friday, 30 November

Penarth v Lydney
Portadown v Bangor

Saturday, 1 December

RFU Divisional Championship
London Division v Northern Division
Midland Division v
  South & South-West Division

SRU Districts Championship
Scottish North & Midlands v
  Edinburgh Dist
South of Scotland v Anglo Scots

IRU Provincial Championship
Munster v Connacht (Limerick)
Ulster v Leinster (Ravenhill)

RFU County Championship
Division 1 (North)
Warwickshire v North Midlands
Yorkshire v Lancashire
Division 1 (South)
Hertfordshire v Cornwall (Croxley Green)
Middlesex v Berkshire
Division 2 (North)
Notts, Lincs & Derbys v Northumberland
Staffordshire v Cumbria (Burton)
Division 2 (South)
Hampshire v Gloucestershire
Kent v Devon (Blackheath)
Division 3 (North)
East Midlands v Durham
Leicestershire v Cheshire

Division 3 (South)
Somerset v Eastern Counties
Surrey v Dorset/Wilts
Division 4
Sussex v Buckinghamshire

Ards v Greystones
Armagh v Athlone
Ballymena v Stewart's-Melville FP
Birkenhead Park v Headingley
Blackheath v Harlequins
Boroughmuir v Glasgow High/Kelvinside
Bridgend v Ebbw Vale
Bristol v Newport
Broughton Park v Orrell
Camborne v Penryn
Cardiff v Aberavon
CIYMS v Blackrock Coll
Collegians v Old Wesley
Coventry v Wanderers
Dungannon v Coleraine
Exeter v Cheltenham
Fylde v Hawick
Gloucester v Leicester
Gosforth v Tynedale
Hutchesons' v Ayr
Kilmarnock v Selkirk
London Irish v Met Police
London Scottish v Bath
London Welsh v Oxford U
Maidstone v Barnstaple
Malone v UC Dublin
Melrose v Dunfermline
Monkstown v Ballinasloe
Morley v Liverpool St Helens
Musselburgh v Kelso
Northampton v Llanelli
Nottingham v Kilmarnock
Preston Grasshoppers v Gala
Preston Lodge v Stirling County
Queen's U, Belfast v
  De La Salle Palmerston
Redruth v Truro
Rosslyn Park v Neath
Rugby v Middlesbrough
Sale v Pontypridd
Saracens v Abertillery
Sheffield v Sheffield U
Southend v Askeans
S Wales Police v Plymouth Albion
Sunday's Well v Skerries
Swansea v Moseley
Tredegar v Newbridge
Wakefield v Bradford-Bingley
Wasps v Bedford
Waterloo v West Hartlepool
Watsonians v Royal High
West of Scotland v Glasgow Acads

Sunday, 2 December

Bective Rangers v Terenure Coll
Shannon v Corinthians

Tuesday, 4 December

Boroughmuir v Edinburgh Wands

Wednesday, 5 December

Bedford v RAF
Moseley v Loughborough U

Saturday, 8 December

RFU Divisional Championship
London Division v Midland Division
Northern Division v
    South & South-West Division

SRU Districts Championship
Edinburgh Dist v Anglo Scots
Glasgow Dist v Scottish North/Midlands

IRU Provincial Championship
Connacht v Leinster (Galway)
Munster v Ulster (Cork)

RFU County Championship
Division 1 (North)
Lancashire v North Midlands
Warwickshire v Yorkshire
Division 1 (South)
Berkshire v Cornwall (Newbury)
Hertfordshire v Middlesex
    (Croxley Green)
Division 2 (North)
Cumbria v Northumberland
Notts, Lincs & Derbys v Staffordshire
Division 2 (South)
Devon v Gloucestershire
Hampshire v Kent
Division 3 (North)
Cheshire v Durham
East Midlands v Leicestershire
Division 3 (South)
Dorset/Wilts v Eastern Counties
Somerset v Surrey
Division 4
Buckinghamshire v Oxfordshire

WRU Heineken Leagues
Premier Division
Bridgend v Llanelli
Cardiff v Neath
Newbridge v Glamorgan Wands
Pontypridd v Abertillery
Swansea v Pontypool
Division 1
Aberavon v S Wales Police
Ebbw Vale v Maesteg
Newport v Tredegar
Penarth v Cross Keys

RFU Junior Clubs Cup *5th round*
Ards v Ballymena

Armagh v Sligo
Askeans v Cheltenham
Bangor v Dungannon
Bedford v Harlequins
Bridgwater Albion v Lydney
Bristol v Moseley
Clontarf v Terenure Coll
Collegians v Bohemians
Corinthians v Bective Rangers
De La Salle Palmerston v CIYMS
Edinburgh Acads v Watsonians
Edinburgh Wands v Dunfermline
Esher v Havant
Garryowen v Sunday's Well
Greystones v Skerries
Haddington v Preston Lodge
Hartlepool Rovers v Fylde
Hawick v Melrose
Howe of Fife v Glasgow Acads
Kelso v Jedforest
Kendal v Morley
Kilmarnock v Heriot's FP
Langholm v Gala
Leicester v Blackheath
Liverpool St Helens v Birkenhead Park
London Welsh v Northampton
Maidstone v Upper Clapton
Nottingham v Coventry
Nuneaton v Saracens
Penzance-Newlyn v Camborne
Plymouth Albion v Met Police
Preston Grasshoppers v Sheffield
Queen's U, Belfast v Malone
Richmond v Bath
Rosslyn Park v Gosforth
Rugby v Gloucester
Sale v Wakefield
Stewart's-Melville FP v Boroughmuir
Stourbridge v Broughton Park
Wasps v Headingley
Waterloo v London Irish
West of Scotland v London Scottish

Sunday, 9 December

Old Wesley v Wanderers
Shannon v Monkstown
West Hartlepool v Harrogate

Tuesday, 11 December

Oxford University v
    Cambridge University (Twickenham)

Wednesday, 12 December

Army v Territorial Army (Aldershot)
Hampshire v Royal Navy (Portsmouth)
Moseley v Combined Old Boys
Old Belvedere v Bective Rangers
Oxford v St Mary's Hosp

Saturday, 15 December

RFU Divisional Championship
Northern Division v Midland Division
South & South-West Division
v London Division

SRU Districts Championship
Anglo-Scots v Scottish North/Midlands
Glasgow Dist v South of Scotland

IRU Provincial Championship
Leinster v Munster (Lansdowne Road)
Ulster v Connacht (Ravenhill)

RFU County Championship
Division 1 (North)
North Midlands v Yorkshire
Lancashire v Warwickshire
Division 1 (South)
Berkshire v Hertfordshire
Cornwall v Middlesex
Division 2 (North)
Cumbria v Notts, Lincs & Derbys
Northumberland v Staffordshire
Division 2 (South)
Devon v Hampshire
Gloucestershire v Kent
Division 3 (North)
Cheshire v East Midlands
Durham v Leicestershire
Division 3 (South)
Dorset/Wilts v Somerset
Durham v Leicestershire
Division 4
Oxfordshire v Sussex

WRU Heineken Leagues
Premier Division
Abertillery v Neath
Bridgend v Glamorgan Wands
Newbridge v Pontypool
Pontypridd v Llanelli
Swansea v Cardiff

WRU Schweppes Cup *4th round*
Ards v Bangor
Armagh v City of Derry
Askeans v US Portsmouth
Aspatria v Melrose
Ballymena v Kelso
Bath v London Welsh
Bective Rangers v Waterpark
Bedford v Nottingham
Blackheath v Met Police
Broughton Park v Halifax
Cheltenham v Clifton
CIYMS v Collegians
Coventry v Gloucester
Cross Keys v Lydney
Dublin U v Ballymena
Dungannon v Galwegians

Durham v Morley
Fylde v Boroughmuir
Glasgow High/Kelvinside v
   Edinburgh Wands
Gosforth v Gala
Harlequins v Rugby
Headingley v Sale
Howe of Fife v Currie
Jedforest v Watsonians
Kendal v West Hartlepool
Kilmarnock v Royal High
Leicester v Bristol
Liverpool St Helens v Stourbridge
London Irish v Wasps
London Scottish v Sheffield
Malone v City of Derry
Moseley v Waterloo
Northampton v Harrogate
Rosslyn Park v Richmond
Saracens v Wakefield
Stewart's-Melville FP v Preston Lodge
Sutton-Epsom v Maidstone
UC Cork v Sunday's Well
UC Galway v De La Salle Palmerston
West of Scotland v Tynedale
Wigton v Hawick

Sunday, 16 December

Camborne v Newquay Hornets
Old Belvedere v Greystones
Penryn v Redruth
Shannon v Young Munster
Terenure Coll v Garryowen
UC Dublin v Old Wesley
Wanderers v Monkstown

Saturday, 22 December

Ireland B v Scotland B (Ravenhill)

WRU Heineken Leagues
Premier Division
Cardiff v Newbridge
Glamorgan Wands v Pontypridd
Llanelli v Abertillery
Neath v Swansea
Pontypool v Bridgend
Division 1
Aberavon v Tredegar
Ebbw Vale v Penarth
Newport v Maesteg
S Wales Police v Cross Keys

France Schools v Scotland Schools
   (18 Group)
Ballymena v Blackrock Coll
Bedford v Moseley
Blackheath v Bath
Boroughmuir v Musselburgh
Bradford-Bingley v Morley
Cheltenham v Stourbridge
Clarkston v Ayr

Collegians v Malone
Corinthians v Armagh
Coventry v Leicester
Dolphin v Old Wesley
Dungannon v CIYMS
Edinburgh Wands v Edinburgh Acads
Gala v Aspatria
Glasgow High/Kelvinside v Jedforest
Gosforth v Middlesbrough
Greystones v Instonians
Hawick v Selkirk
Hayle v Camborne
Heriot's FP v Preston Lodge
Kelso v Alnwick
Lansdowne v De La Salle Palmerston
Liverpool St Helens v Broughton Park
London Irish v Northampton
London Welsh v London Scottish
Lydney v Stroud
Madras Coll FP v Howe of Fife
Maidstone v Askeans
Melrose v Kendal
Met Police v Basingstoke
Monkstown v Terenure Coll
Newquay Hornets v Redruth
Nottingham v Headingley
Oxford v Sidcup
Plymouth Albion v Bristol
Richmond v Harlequins
Rosslyn Park v Wasps
Rugby v Nuneaton
Sale v Saracens
Sheffield v Huddersfield
Wakefield v Orrell
Waterloo v Fylde
Watsonians v Portobello FP
West Hartlepool v Gateshead Fell
West of Scotland v Hillhead-Jordanhill

Wednesday, 26 December

Aberavon v Neath
Ballymena v Dungannon
Bath v Clifton
Bedford v Old Paulines
Bridgend v Maesteg
Broughton Park v Sale
Cheltenham v Stroud
Ebbw Vale v Abertillery
Fylde v Preston Grasshoppers
Gala v Melrose
Gloucester v Lydney
Gosforth v Northern
Greystones v Firbolgs
Hartlepool Rovers v West Hartlepool
Hawick v Jedforest
Llanelli v London Welsh
Morley v Otley
Moseley v Coventry
Newport v Newbridge
Northampton v Nuneaton
Penarth v Old Penarthians
Pontypool v Tredegar

Redruth v Camborne
Selkirk v Kelso
Swansea v S Wales Police
Waterloo v Birkenhead Park
Watsonians v Heriot's FP
Wrexham v Liverpool St Helens

Thursday, 27 December

Leicester v Barbarians

Saturday, 29 December

SRU Districts Championship
Anglo Scots v Glasgow Dist
South of Scotland v Edinburgh Dist

Abertillery v Bedford
Academy v Portadown
Ards v Collegians
Armagh v City of Derry
Ayr v Kilmarnock
Ballymena v Greystones
Bangor v Lansdowne
Bath v Swansea
Boroughmuir v Gosforth
Bristol v Richmond
Camborne v Truro
Cardiff v Harlequins
De La Salle Palmerston v Terenure Coll
Dungannon v Queen's U, Belfast
Gateshead Fell v Hawick
Glamorgan Wands v S Wales Police
Gloucester v Bridgend
Headingley v Wakefield
Howe of Fife v Gordonians
Jedforest v Edinburgh Wands
Langholm v Kelso
Launceston v Redruth
Liverpool St Helens v Orrell
Llanelli v Moseley
Malone v Skerries
Middlesbrough v West Hartlepool
Monkstown v Old Wesley
Morley v Huddersfield
Newbridge v Wasps
Newport v Neath
Nottingham v Northampton
Oxford v Maidstone
Pontypool v Coventry
Preston Grasshoppers v Broughton Park
Preston Lodge v Musselburgh
Rosslyn Park v Met Police
Rugby v Durham City
Saracens v London Irish
Shannon v Dolphin
Stewart's-Melville FP v Gala
Stourbridge v Stroud
Sunday's Well v Bective Rangers
Tredegar v Lydney
Tynedale v Melrose
Vale of Lune v Sale
Wakefield v Fylde

Wanderers v Dublin U
Waterloo v Sheffield
West of Scotland v Stirling County
Wolverhampton v Cheltenham

Monday, 31 December

Aberavon v Pontypridd
Swansea v Llanelli

Tuesday, 1 January 1991

Fylde v Blackburn
Gosforth v Novocastrians
Headingley v Otley
Heriot's FP v Hawick
London Welsh v Richmond
Moseley v Gloucester
Tredegar v Trefil

Wednesday, 2 January

Melrose v Glasgow High/Kelvinside
S Wales Police v Bridgend

Saturday, 5 January

Scotland Trial (Murrayfield)

IRU Leagues
Division 1
Ballymena v Malone
Garryowen v Shannon
St Mary's Coll v Lansdowne
Wanderers v Instonians
Division 2
Athlone v Sunday's Well
Bangor v Terenure Coll
CIYMS v Young Munster
NIFC v Corinthians
Old Wesley v Greystones

RFU Junior Clubs Cup *6th round*
Scotland Schools v Wales Schools
 (18 Group)
Aberavon v Swansea
Ards v Portadown
Askeans v Havant
Bective Rangers v Northampton
Bedford v Liverpool St Helens
Berry Hill v S Wales Police
Birkenhead Park v Huddersfield
Collegians v City of Derry
Derby v Cheltenham
Dunfermline v Ayr
Dungannon v Armagh
Durham City v Boroughmuir
Ebbw Vale v Cardiff
Edinburgh Acads v Kelso
Fylde v Gosforth
Gala v Kilmarnock
Gateshead Fell v Jedforest
Gloucester v London Scottish

Hawick v Langholm
Leicester v Headingley
Llanelli v Rosslyn Park
Lydney v Oxford
Maidstone v Old Alleynians
Morley v Orrell
Musselburgh v Melrose
Newbridge v Moseley
Newport v Bridgend
Newquay Hornets v Camborne
Nottingham v London Irish
Penarth v Torquay Ath
Plymouth Albion v Bath
Pontypool v Coventry
Pontypridd v Cross Keys
Preston Lodge v Corstorphine
Queen's U, Belfast v Academy
Redruth v Penzance-Newlyn
Sale v Waterloo
Saracens v Rugby
Stirling County v Watsonians
US Portsmouth v Met Police
Wakefield v Sheffield
Wasps v Harlequins
West Hartlepool v Blackheath
West of Scotland v Edinburgh Wands

Saturday, 12 January

RFU Courage Leagues
Division 1
Bath v Moseley
Liverpool St Helens v Gloucester
Northampton v Leicester
Orrell v Harlequins
Rosslyn Park v Nottingham
Saracens v Wasps
Division 2
Blackheath v Richmond
Coventry v London Irish
Gosforth v Wakefield
London Scottish v Plymouth Albion
Sale v Rugby
Waterloo v Bedford
Division 3
Askeans v Nuneaton
Broughton Park v Vale of Lune
Exeter v Lydney
Fylde v Clifton
Morley v Roundhay
West Hartlepool v Sheffield
Division 4 (North)
Birmingham-Solihull v Walsall
Durham City v Northern
Harrogate v Preston Grasshoppers
Hereford v Stourbridge
Kendal v Stoke
Otley v Winnington Park
Division 4 (South)
Basingstoke v Redruth
Camborne v Southend
Cheltenham v Maidstone
Havant v London Welsh

North Walsham v Sudbury
Weston-super-Mare v Maidenhead

SRU McEwan's Leagues
Division 1
Boroughmuir v Stirling County
Currie v Stewart's-Melville FP
Edinburgh Acads v Jedforest
Edinburgh Wands v Melrose
Glasgow High/Kelvinside v Hawick
Heriot's FP v Selkirk
Kelso v Gala
Division 2
Ayr v Dunfermline
Kilmarnock v Langholm
Kirkcaldy v Watsonians
Musselburgh v Hillhead-Jordanhill
Preston Lodge v Glasgow Acads
Royal High v Dundee HSFP
West of Scotland v Corstorphine

IRU Leagues
Division 1
Cork Const v Wanderers
Instonians v Garryowen
Lansdowne v Ballymena
Shannon v St Mary's Coll
Division 2
CIYMS v Athlone
Greystones v Bangor
Sunday's Well v NIFC
Terenure Coll v Corinthians
Young Munster v Old Wesley

WRU Heineken Leagues
Premier Division
Abertillery v Glamorgan Wanderers
Bridgend v Cardiff
Neath v Llanelli
Newbridge v Swansea
Pontypridd v Pontypool
Division 1
Cross Keys v Ebbw Vale
Maesteg v Aberavon
Penarth v Newport
Tredegar v S Wales Police

Scotland Schools v Australia Schools
(18 Group)
Armagh v Ards
Bristol v Headingley
City of Derry v Queen's U, Belfast
Collegians v Academy
De La Salle Palmerston v Bective Rangers
Malone v Old Belvedere
Portadown v Dungannon

Tuesday, 15 January

Edinburgh Wands v Edinburgh U
Maesteg v Pontypridd
404

Wednesday, 16 January

Army v Hampshire (Aldershot)
Surrey v Royal Navy
Oxford U v Oxfordshire
Swansea v Ebbw Vale

Friday, 18 January

England B v Spain (provisional)
Aberavon v Bristol
Abertillery v Newport
Bedford v Leicester
Bridgend v Northampton
Cardiff v London Welsh
Cheltenham v Lydney
Ebbw Vale v Pontypridd
Edinburgh Wands v Stirling County
Howe of Fife v Preston Lodge
Kilmarnock v Clarkston
Maesteg v Nottingham
Met Police v Bath
Neath v Wasps
S Wales Police v Pontypool
Tredegar v Wrexham

Saturday, 19 January

WALES v ENGLAND (Cardiff)
FRANCE v SCOTLAND (Paris)
Academy v Armagh
Ards v Queen's U, Belfast
Askeans v Rugby
Ayr v Glasgow Acads
Ballymena v NIFC
Bangor v Blackrock Coll
Bective Rangers v Instonians
Boroughmuir v Middlesbrough
Broughton Park v Hartlepool Rovers
Cambridge U v Durham U
CIYMS v Malone
Dungannon v City of Derry
Gala v Fylde
Glasgow High/Kelvinside v
    West of Scotland
Gloucester v Blackheath
Greystones v Dublin U
Harrogate v Headingley
Hawick v Gosforth
Highfield v Shannon
Jedforest v Tynedale
Kelso v Aspatria
London Scottish v Rosslyn Park
Monkstown v St Mary's Hosp
Moseley v Wakefield
Northern v Morley
Old Wesley v Lansdowne
Orrell v Sale
Oxford v US Portsmouth
Penryn v Camborne
Portadown v Collegians
Redruth v Bridgwater Albion
Sheffield v Richmond

Stewart's-Melville FP v Melrose
Stourbridge v Bradford-Bingley
Wanderers v Clontarf
Waterloo v Liverpool St Helens
Waterpark v Sunday's Well
West Hartlepool v Halifax
Young Munster v
  De La Salle Palmerston

Sunday, 20 January

Coventry v Newbridge
Harlequins v Saracens
Terenure Coll v Old Belvedere

Tuesday, 22 January

St Austell v Redruth

Wednesday, 23 January

Civil Service v Army (Chiswick)
Cambridge U v RAF
Cheltenham v Lichfield
Combined London OB v Oxford U

Saturday, 26 January

RFU Pilkington Cup *4th round*

SRU McEwan's Leagues
Division 1
Gala v Edinburgh Acads
Hawick v Currie
Jedforest v Heriot's FP
Melrose v Boroughmuir
Selkirk v Edinburgh Wands
Stewart's-Melville FP v Kelso
Stirling County v Glasgow High/Kelvinside
Division 2
Corstorphine v Kirkcaldy
Dundee HSFP v Kilmarnock
Dunfermline v Musselburgh
Glasgow Acads v West of Scotland
Hillhead-Jordanhill v Royal High
Langholm v Preston Lodge
Watsonians v Ayr

IRU Leagues
Division 1
Ballymena v Shannon
Garryowen v Cork Const
Malone v Lansdowne
St Mary's Coll v Instonians
Division 2
Athlone v Young Munster
Bangor v Sunday's Well
Corinthians v Greystones
NIFC v CIYMS
Old Wesley v Terenure Coll

WRU Schweppes Cup *5th round*
RFU Junior Clubs Cup *7th round*
Academy v Ards
Broughton Park v Otley
Camborne v Hayle
City of Derry v Portadown
Collegians v Dungannon
Coventry v Loughborough U
De La Salle Palmerston v Monkstown
Esher v Cheltenham
Gosforth v London Welsh
Harlequins v Vale of Lune
Headingley v Middlesbrough
Irish Army v Wanderers
Kendal v Sheffield
Liverpool St Helens v London Irish
Met Police v Maesteg
Morley v Stourbridge
Moseley v London Scottish
Nottingham v Fylde
Nuneaton v Bedford
Orrell v Blackheath
Oxford v Askeans
Queen's U, Belfast v Armagh
Roundhay v Wakefield
Rugby v Rosslyn Park
St Ives v Redruth
Sale v Northern
Stockton v West Hartlepool
Sutton-Epsom v Havant
Wasps v Waterloo

Sunday, 27 January

Bective Rangers v Skerries
Cambridge U v Eastern Counties

Tuesday, 29 January

Cross Keys v Newbridge
Oxford v Cheltenham
Penarth v Swansea

Wednesday, 30 January

Aberavon v Maesteg
Abertillery v S Wales Police
Bridgend v Bristol
Newport v Llanelli
RAF v Oxford
Royal Navy v Cambridge
Tredegar v Pontypridd

Thursday, 31 January

Musselburgh v Gala

Friday, 1 February

Boroughmuir v Crawshay's Welsh XV
Ayr v Cardiff
Bangor v Collegians

Blackwood v Ebbw Vale
Bridgend v Bristol
Howe of Fife v Penygraig
Kelso v Heriot's FP
Kilmarnock v Hirwaun
Neath v London Scottish (Edinburgh)
Newbridge v Gloucester
Penarth v Abertillery
Portadown v Ballymena

Saturday, 2 February

SCOTLAND v WALES (Murrayfield)
IRELAND v FRANCE
  (Lansdowne Road)

RFU County Championship *semi-finals*
Division 1 North winners v
  Division 1 South runners-up
Division 1 South winners v
  Division 1 North runners-up

Bath v Coventry
Bective Rangers v CIYMS
Bedford v Rosslyn Park
Birmingham-Solihull v Lydney
Blackrock Coll v Dungannon
Cambridge U v Askeans
Corstorphine v Jedforest
Falmouth v Camborne
Fylde v Richmond
Hawick v Hartlepool Rovers
Headingley v Vale of Lune
Leicester v Wakefield
London Welsh v Harlequins
Met Police v Saracens
Middlesbrough v Broughton Park
Monkstown v Cork Const
Morley v Waterloo
Moseley v Rugby
Nottingham v Gosforth
Old Wesley v Queen's U, Belfast
Northampton v Blackheath
Preston Lodge v Leith Acads
Redruth v Stroud
Sheffield v Harrogate
Stourbridge v Taunton
Sunday's Well v Portadown
Wanderers v UC Cork
Wasps v Sale
West Hartlepool v Liverpool St Helens

Sunday, 3 February

Greystones v De La Salle Palmerston
Terenure Coll v St Mary's Coll

Monday, 4 February

Newport v Bridgend

Tuesday, 5 February

Rugby v RAF

Wednesday, 6 February

Cambridge U v Army
Oxford U v Royal Navy

Saturday, 9 February

RFU Courage Leagues
Division 1
Gloucester v Bath
Harlequins v Bristol
Leicester v Orrell
Moseley v Northampton
Nottingham v Saracens
Wasps v Liverpool St Helens
Division 2
Bedford v London Scottish
London Irish v Gosforth
Plymouth Albion v Blackheath
Richmond v Coventry
Rugby v Waterloo
Wakefield v Headingley
Division 3
Clifton v Met Police
Lydney v Fylde
Nuneaton v Exeter
Roundhay v Askeans
Sheffield v Morley
Vale of Lune v West Hartlepool
Division 4 (North)
Northern v Lichfield
Preston Grasshoppers v Durham City
Stoke v Birmingham-Solihull
Stourbridge v Otley
Walsall v Harrogate
Winnington Park v Kendal
Division 4 (South)
London Welsh v Ealing
Maidenhead v Basingstoke
Maidstone v Havant
Redruth v Camborne
Southend v Cheltenham
Sudbury v Weston-super-Mare

SRU McEwan's Leagues
Division 1
Edinburgh Acads v Currie
Gala v Stewart's-Melville FP
Glasgow High/Kelvinside v Boroughmuir
Heriot's FP v Edinburgh Wands
Kelso v Hawick
Selkirk v Jedforest
Stirling County v Melrose
Division 2
Glasgow Acads v Langholm
Hillhead-Jordanhill v Dunfermline
Kirkcaldy v Ayr
Preston Lodge v Dundee HSFP
Royal High v Musselburgh

Watsonians v Corstorphine
West of Scotland v Kilmarnock

IRU Leagues
1st play-offs for All Ireland Leagues
1st play-offs for Provincial Leagues

WRU Heineken Leagues
Premier Division
Cardiff v Pontypridd
Glamorgan Wands v Llanelli
Newbridge v Neath
Pontypool v Abertillery
Swansea v Bridgend
Division 1
Aberavon v Penarth
Newport v Ebbw Vale
S Wales Police v Maesteg
Tredegar v Cross Keys

Academy v Bangor
Ards v CIYMS
Bective Rangers v Bohemians
Clontarf v Collegians
De La Salle Palmerston v Malone
Instonians v Dungannon
Old Wesley v St Mary's Coll
Sale v Rosslyn Park
Shannon v Greystones
Sunday's Well v Monkstown
Terenure Coll v Ballymena
Wanderers v Blackrock Coll

Tuesday, 12 February

Cross Keys v Abertillery
Lydney v Pontypridd
Musselburgh v Edinburgh Wands
Nuneaton v Nottingham
Swansea v Newport

Wednesday, 13 February

Cambridge U v Luddites
Combined London OB v Royal Navy
Llanelli v Bristol
Oxford U v Army

Friday, 15 February

England B v Italy (provisional)
Aberavon v Bridgend
Abertillery v Moseley
Armagh v Instonians
Askeans v Sidcup
Boroughmuir v Jedforest
Cardiff v Bective Rangers
Croesyceiliog v Tredegar
Newport v Gloucester
Northampton v Coventry
Penarth v Pontypool
Pontypridd v Ebbw Vale
Rosslyn Park v Selkirk

S Wales Police v Greystones
Wasps v Melrose
West of Scotland v Howe of Fife

Saturday, 16 February

ENGLAND v SCOTLAND
  (Twickenham)
WALES v IRELAND (Cardiff)
Ards v Wanderers
Broughton Park v Northern
CIYMS v Queen's U, Belfast
Corinthians v Collegians
Dolphin v Sunday's Well
Dublin U v Bangor
Dungannon v Monkstown
Edinburgh Wands v Royal High
Fylde v Liverpool St Helens
Gala v Roundhay
Garryowen v Old Wesley
Glasgow High/Kelvinside v Ayr
Gosforth v Sheffield
Hawick v Sale
Headingley v Harlequins
Leicester v Rugby
London Scottish v Edinburgh Acads
London Welsh v Rosslyn Park
Malone v Clontarf
Met Police v Cheltenham
Newbridge v Bath
Nottingham v West Hartlepool
Old Belvedere v Shannon
Orrell v Bedford
Oxford U v Oxford
Plymouth Albion v Camborne
Terenure Coll v Cork Const
Torquay Ath v Redruth
Tynedale v Kelso
Vale of Lune v Cambridge U
Wakefield v Morley
Waterloo v Saracens

Sunday, 17 February

De La Salle Palmerston v St Mary's Coll
Shannon v Bohemians

Tuesday, 19 February

Blaina v Abertillery
Wakefield v Halifax

Wednesday, 20 February

Royal Navy v Civil Service
Blackheath v Askeans
Cambridge U v Penguins
Lydney v RAF
Met Police v Army
Oxford U v Anti-Assassins

Saturday, 23 February

RFU Pilkington Cup *5th round*

SRU McEwan's Leagues
Division 1
Boroughmuir v Heriot's FP
Currie v Kelso
Edinburgh Wands v Edinburgh Acads
Glasgow High/Kelvinside v Melrose
Hawick v Gala
Jedforest v Stirling County
Stewart's-Melville FP v Selkirk
Division 2
Ayr v West of Scotland
Corstorphine v Hillhead/Jordanhill
Dundee HSFP v Glasgow Acads
Kilmarnock v Preston Lodge
Langholm v Watsonians
Musselburgh v Kirkcaldy
Royal High v Dunfermline

IRU Leagues
2nd play-offs for All Ireland Leagues
2nd play-offs for Provincial Leagues

WRU Schweppes Cup *6th round*
RFU Junior Clubs Cup *semi-finals*
Abertillery v Aberavon
Askeans v Lichfield
Ballinasloe v Armagh
Bangor v City of Derry
Bath v Exeter
Blackheath v Nottingham
Camborne v Penzance-Newlyn
Collegians v CIYMS
Coventry v Ebbw Vale
Dungannon v Malone
Fylde v Northampton
Gloucester v London Irish
Gosforth v Vale of Lune
Harlequins v Waterloo
Headingley v Moseley
Lansdowne v Monkstown
Liverpool St Helens v Sheffield
London Welsh v Leicester
Loughborough U v Stourbridge
Lydney v Tredegar
Maidstone v Purley
Met Police v London Scottish
Morley v Wrexham
Orrell v West Hartlepool
Portadown v De La Salle Palmerston
Queen's U, Belfast v Ballymena
Redruth v Penryn
Rugby v Broughton Park
Sale v Roundhay
Saracens v Bedford
Shannon v Terenure Coll
Skerries v Old Wesley
S Wales Police v Torquay Ath
Swansea v Wasps
Taunton v Cheltenham
Wakefield v Durham City

Sunday, 24 February

St Mary's Coll v Greystones
Wanderers v Bective Rangers

Tuesday, 26 February

Penarth v Pontypridd
S Wales Police v Neath

Wednesday, 27 February

Army v Surrey (Aldershot)
Aberavon v Newbridge
Bath v Ebbw Vale
Cambridge U v Anti-Assassins
Maesteg v Swansea
Moseley v Nuneaton
Newport v Abertillery
Oxford U v Swansea U
Royal Navy v Met Police
Sale v Loughborough U

Friday, 1 March

Ireland B v England B (Dublin)
  (provisional)
Bath v Llanelli
Bridgend v Cross Keys
Bristol v Pontypridd
Tredegar v Abertillery

Saturday, 2 March

IRELAND v ENGLAND (Lansdowne
  Road)
FRANCE v WALES (Paris)
Scotland B v France B
  (Hughenden, Glasgow)
Ayr v Stirling County
Bective Rangers v Queen's U, Belfast
Bedford v Met Police
Camborne v Torquay Ath
Cambridge U v Bradford-Bingley
Cheltenham v Plymouth Albion
Corstorphine v Boroughmuir
Coventry v Wasps
Gala v Wakefield
Harlequins v Gosforth
Harrogate v Broughton Park
Jedforest v Langholm
Kilmarnock v Stewart's-Melville FP
Liverpool St Helens v Vale of Lune
Loughborough U v Askeans
Lydney v S Wales Police
Melrose v London Scottish
Middlesbrough v Kelso
Monkstown v Portadown
Morley v Preston Grasshoppers
Moseley v London Irish
Nottingham v Aberavon
Old Wesley v Ards
Orrell v Headingley

Pontypool v Gloucester
Redruth v Taunton
Rosslyn Park v Blackheath
Roundhay v Hawick
St Mary's Coll v Fylde
Sale v West Hartlepool
Saracens v London Welsh
Sheffield v Hull Ionians
Skerries v Dungannon
Streatham-Croydon v Maidstone
Sunday's Well v UC Galway
UC Dublin v CIYMS
Wanderers v Collegians
Waterloo v Northern
Watsonians v Edinburgh Wands
West of Scotland v Heriot's FP

Sunday, 3 March

De La Salle Palmerston v Academy
Greystones v Rugby
Newbridge v Newport
Shannon v Blackrock Coll
Terenure Coll v Lansdowne

Tuesday, 5 March

Old Belvedere v Wanderers

Wednesday, 6 March

East Midlands v Barbarians
Combined London OB v Army

Saturday, 9 March

RFU Courage Leagues
Division 1
Bath v Wasps
Bristol v Leicester
Liverpool St Helens v Nottingham
Northampton v Gloucester
Orrell v Moseley
Saracens v Rosslyn Park
Division 2
Blackheath v Bedford
Coventry v Plymouth Albion
Gosforth v Richmond
Headingley v London Irish
London Scottish v Rugby
Waterloo v Sale
Division 3
Askeans v Sheffield
Exeter v Roundhay
Fylde v Nuneaton
Met Police v Lydney
Morley v Vale of Lune
West Hartlepool v Broughton Park
Division 4 (North)
Birmingham-Solihull v Winnington Park
Durham City v Walsall

Harrogate v Stoke
Kendal v Stourbridge
Lichfield v Preston Grasshoppers
Otley v Hereford
Division 4 (South)
Basingstoke v Sudbury
Camborne v Maidenhead
Cheltenham v Redruth
Ealing v Maidstone
Havant v Southend
Weston-super-Mare v North Walsham

SRU McEwan Leagues
Division 1
Currie v Stirling County
Edinburgh Acads v Boroughmuir
Gala v Jedforest
Heriot's FP v Glasgow High/Kelvinside
Kelso v Edinburgh Wands
Melrose v Stewart's-Melville FP
Selkirk v Hawick
Division 2
Dunfermline v Langholm
Glasgow Acads v Corstorphine
Kilmarnock v Hillhead-Jordanhill
Kirkcaldy v Royal High
Preston Lodge v Ayr
Watsonians v Dundee HSFP
West of Scotland v Musselburgh

IRU Leagues
3rd play-offs for All Ireland Leagues
3rd play-offs for Provincial Leagues

WRU Heineken Leagues
Premier Division
Abertillery v Cardiff
Bridgend v Newbridge
Llanelli v Pontypool
Neath v Glamorgan Wands
Pontypridd v Swansea
Division 1
Cross Keys v Newport
Ebbw Vale v Aberavon
Maesteg v Tredegar
Penarth v S Wales Police

Armagh v Waterpark
Ballymena v De La Salle Palmerston
Blackrock Coll v Sunday's Well
CIYMS v City of Derry
Dublin U v Oxford U
Greystones v Clontarf
Instonians v Collegians
London Welsh v Clifton
Malone v Ards
Old Wesley v Shannon
Terenure Coll v Dungannon
Wakefield v Northern

Monday, 11 March

UC Cork v Oxford U

Tuesday, 12 March

Bristol v Exeter
Devonport Services v Redruth
Lydney v Gloucester
Marr FP v Kilmarnock
Northampton v RAF
Tredegar v Berry Hill

Wednesday, 13 March

Dorset/Wilts v Royal Navy
Abertillery v Swansea
Coventry v Nuneaton

Thursday, 14 March

Kelso v Old Wesley

Friday, 15 March

England B v France B (provisional)
Combined Services v French Armed Forces (RAF Halton)
England Colts v Italy Colts (Cambridge)
Ayr v Ards
Cheltenham v Penarth
Gala v Bective Rangers
Gloucester v Aberavon
Hawick v Wanderers
Howe of Fife v Dunfermline
Kilmarnock v Malone
Northampton v Moseley

Saturday, 16 March

SCOTLAND v IRELAND
 (Murrayfield)
ENGLAND v FRANCE (Twickenham)
WRU Schweppes Cup *quarter-finals*
Ballymena v City of Derry
Bedford v Bath
Bohemians v De La Salle Palmerston
Boroughmuir v Bangor
Broughton Park v Gosforth
Dungannon v St Mary's Coll
Durham City v Sheffield
Ebbw Vale v Llanelli
Edinburgh Acads v Old Wesley
Exeter v Camborne
Harlequins v Coventry
Hawick v Wanderers
London Irish v Abertillery
London Scottish v Racing Club de France
London Welsh v Maesteg
Met Police v Southend
Monkstown v Old Crescent
Newport v Bath
Nottingham v Leicester
Pontypridd v Tredegar
Preston Grasshoppers v
 Liverpool St Helens

Rosslyn Park v Headingley
Rugby v Fylde
Sale v Orrell
Sunday's Well v Waterpark
S Wales Police v Newbridge
Vale of Lune v Wakefield
Wasps v Cardiff
Waterloo v Aspatria
Watsonians v Old Belvedere
West Hartlepool v Hull Ionians
West of Scotland v Clontarf

Sunday, 17 March

Blackheath v Saracens
Maidstone v Lille

Monday, 18 March

Greystones v UC Dublin

Wednesday, 20 March

UAU Final (Twickenham)
Scottish Schools Cup Final
 (Murrayfield)

Saturday, 23 March

Army v Royal Navy (Twickenham)

RFU Courage Leagues
Division 1
Gloucester v Orrell
Leicester v Harlequins
Moseley v Bristol
Nottingham v Bath
Rosslyn Park v Liverpool St Helens
Wasps v Northampton
Division 2
Bedford v Coventry
London Irish v Wakefield
Plymouth Albion v Gosforth
Richmond v Headingley
Rugby v Blackheath
Sale v London Scottish
Division 3
Broughton Park v Morley
Lydney v Clifton
Nuneaton v Met Police
Roundhay v Fylde
Sheffield v Exeter
Vale of Lune v Askeans
Division 4 (North)
Hereford v Kendal
Preston Grasshoppers v Northern
Stoke v Durham City
Stourbridge v Birmingham-Solihull
Walsall v Lichfield
Winnington Park v Harrogate
Division 4 (South)
Maidenhead v Cheltenham
Maidstone v London Welsh

North Walsham v Basingstoke
Redruth v Havant
Southend v Ealing
Sudbury v Camborne

WRU Heineken Leagues
Premier Division
Bridgend v Neath
Cardiff v Llanelli
Newbridge v Pontypridd
Pontypool v Glamorgan Wands
Swansea v Abertillery
Division 1
Aberavon v Newport
Cross Keys v Maesteg
S Wales Police v Ebbw Vale
Tredegar v Penarth

Scotland Under-18 v Scotland Schools
(18 Group) (Murrayfield)
Ayr v Edinburgh Wands
Boroughmuir v Watsonians
Currie v West of Scotland
Dalziel v Kilmarnock
Gala v Dundee HSFP
Garryowen v Greystones
Howe of Fife v Corstorphine
Kelso v Stewart's-Melville FP
Monkstown v UC Galway
Otley v Waterloo
Preston Lodge v Jedforest
Sunday's Well v Dublin U
UC Dublin v Wanderers
West Hartlepool v Saracens

Tuesday, 26 March

Cheltenham v Gloucester
Northampton v Met Police

Wednesday, 27 March

Scotland Under-21 v Scottish Students
(Murrayfield)
Abertillery v Cross Keys
Llanelli v S Wales Police
Maesteg v Newbridge
Pontypool v Aberavon
Pontypridd v Newport

Friday, 29 March

Penarth v Public Schools Wands
Redruth v St Mary's Hosp
Sale v Preston Grasshoppers

Saturday, 30 March

Army v RAF (Twickenham)
Cardiff v Barbarians
Ireland Schools v England Schools
(18 Group)
Scotland Under-18 v Netherlands Under-18

Wales Under-15 v Scotland Under-15
Aberavon v London Welsh
Abertillery v Ebbw Vale
Armagh v Skerries
Askeans v Walsall
Ayr v Heriot's FP
Bath v Bristol
Bedford v Morley
Blackheath v Maidstone
Boroughmuir v Hawick
Broughton Park v Wigan
Coventry v Neath
Dundee HSFP v Kelso
Edinburgh Wands v Heriot's FP
Fylde v Sale
Glasgow High/Kelvinside v
London Scottish
Gloucester v New Brighton
Gosforth v Edinburgh Acads
Headingley v Liverpool St Helens
Kendal v Gala
Llanelli v Northampton
London Irish v Rosslyn Park
Lydney v Hereford
Maesteg v Bridgend
Melrose v Watsonians
Met Police v Stroud
Monkstown v City of Derry
Moseley v Nottingham
Musselburgh v Howe of Fife
Newbridge v Plymouth Albion
Newport v Pontypool
Nuneaton v Rugby
Old Belvedere v Collegians
Old Wesley v Bohemians
Pontypridd v S Wales Police
Salisbury v Cheltenham
Sheffield v West of Scotland
Streatham-Croydon v Havant
Tynedale v Kilmarnock
Wanderers v Dolphin
Waterloo v Preston Grasshoppers
West Hartlepool v Wakefield

Monday, 1 April

Swansea v Barbarians
Acklam v West Hartlepool
Bedford v Northampton
Bridgend v Pontypridd
Davenport v Broughton Park
Gloucester v Fylde
Headingley v Coventry
Leicester v Wasps
Liverpool St Helens v Halifax
Neath v Aberavon
Newbridge v Abertillery
Newport v London Welsh
Nottingham v Vale of Lune
Rugby v Ebbw Vale
Saracens v Middlesbrough
Stroud v Lydney
Waterloo v Orrell

Wednesday, 3 April

Bath v S Wales Police

Saturday, 6 April

RFU Festival Day (Twickenham)
RFU Pilkington Cup *semi-finals*
WRU Schweppes Cup *semi-finals*
RFU Junior Clubs Cup Final
 (Twickenham)
England Colts v Wales Youth (Fylde)
Wales Schools v Ireland Schools
 (18 Group)
Aberavon v Cheltenham
Armagh v CIYMS
Bedford v Gloucester
Birkenhead Park v Abertillery
Bridgend v Bath
Bristol v Harlequins
Broughton Park v Durham City
Clifton v Stourbridge
Collegians v Dublin U
Ebbw Vale v Newbridge
Edinburgh Wands v Kendal
Gosforth v Liverpool St Helens
Halifax v Sheffield
Harrogate v Morley
Havant v Henley
London Scottish v Leicester
Malone v Academy
Monkstown v Ballymena
Neath v Newport
NIFC v Dungannon
Northampton v Headingley
Nottingham v Cardiff
Nuneaton v Blackheath
Otley v Fylde
Pontypridd v Penarth
Rugby v Bradford-Bingley
St Ives v Camborne
Sale v Moseley
Stroud v Tredegar
S Wales Police v Richmond
Swansea v London Welsh
Taunton v Lydney
US Portsmouth v Maidstone
Wakefield v Rosslyn Park
Wasps v Llanelli
Waterloo v Coventry
West Hartlepool v Northern
West of Scotland v Orrell

Sunday, 7 April

Met Police v London Welsh

Monday, 8 April

Selkirk v Gala

412

Tuesday, 9 April

England Schools v Scotland Schools
 (18 Group)

Wednesday, 10 April

Scotland Under-21 v England Students

Saturday, 13 April

Royal Air Force v Royal Navy
 (Twickenham)

RFU Courage Leagues
Division 1
Bath v Rosslyn Park
Bristol v Gloucester
Harlequins v Moseley
Liverpool St Helens v Saracens
Northampton v Nottingham
Orrell v Wasps
Division 2
Blackheath v Sale
Coventry v Rugby
Gosforth v Bedford
Headingley v Plymouth Albion
London Scottish v Waterloo
Wakefield v Richmond
Division 3
Askeans v Broughton Park
Clifton v Nuneaton
Exeter v Vale of Lune
Fylde v Sheffield
Met Police v Roundhay
Morley v West Hartlepool
Division 4 (North)
Birmingham-Solihull v Hereford
Durham City v Winnington Park
Harrogate v Stourbridge
Kendal v Otley
Lichfield v Stoke
Northern v Walsall
Division 4 (South)
Basingstoke v Weston-super-Mare
Camborne v North Walsham
Cheltenham v Sudbury
Ealing v Redruth
Havant v Maidenhead
London Welsh v Southend

WRU Heineken Leagues
Premier Division
Abertillery v Newbridge
Glamorgan Wands v Cardiff
Llanelli v Swansea
Neath v Pontypool
Pontypridd v Bridgend
Division 1
Aberavon v Cross Keys
Ebbw Vale v Tredegar
Newport v S Wales Police
Penarth v Maesteg

Melrose Sevens
Scotland Schools v Ireland Schools
  (18 Group)
Ayr v Clarkston
Brixham v Lydney
CIYMS v Portadown
Clontarf v Dungannon
Maidstone v Esher
Malone v Armagh
Monkstown v Civil Service
NIFC v Collegians
Oxford v Cross Keys

Wednesday, 17 April

Combined Services v British Police
  (Aldershot)
Bedford v Bedfordshire
Camborne v St Austell
Pontypool v Penarth
Rugby v Northampton

Saturday, 20 April

RFU County Championship Final
  (Twickenham)

WRU Heineken Leagues
Premier Division
Bridgend v Abertillery
Cardiff v Pontypool
Newbridge v Llanelli
Pontypridd v Neath
Swansea v Glamorgan Wands

Hawick Sevens
Askeans v Stroud
Bath v Gloucester
Birmingham-Solihull v Cheltenham
Bradford-Bingley v Saracens
Bristol v London Irish
Brixham v Ebbw Vale
Broughton Park v West of Scotland
CIYMS v Monkstown
Collegians v St Mary's Coll
Corinthians v De La Salle Palmerston
Exeter v Blackheath
Fylde v Headingley
Gosforth v Leicester
Halifax v Morley
London Irish v Malone
London Scottish v Wasps
Lydney v Cross Keys
Moseley v Aberavon
Newport v Bristol
Northampton v Wakefield
Nottingham v Waterloo
Nuneaton v Stourbridge
Oxford v Havant
Penarth v Torquay Ath
Plymouth Albion v London Welsh
Redruth v Barnstaple
Richmond v Met Police

Rosslyn Park v Harlequins
Sale v Liverpool St Helens
Sheffield v Bedford
S Wales Police v Coventry
Tredegar v Torquay Ath
West Hartlepool v Rugby

Wednesday, 24 April

SRU Youth Leagues Final
  (Murrayfield)

Saturday, 27 April

RFU Courage Leagues
Division 1
Gloucester v Harlequins
Moseley v Leicester
Nottingham v Orrell
Rosslyn Park v Northampton
Saracens v Bath
Wasps v Bristol
Division 2
Bedford v Headingley
Plymouth Albion v Wakefield
Richmond v London Irish
Rugby v Gosforth
Sale v Coventry
Waterloo v Blackheath
Division 3
Broughton Park v Exeter
Nuneaton v Lydney
Roundhay v Clifton
Sheffield v Met Police
Vale of Lune v Fylde
West Hartlepool v Askeans
Division 4 (North)
Hereford v Harrogate
Otley v Birmingham-Solihull
Stoke v Northern
Stourbridge v Durham City
Walsall v Preston Grasshoppers
Winnington Park v Lichfield
Division 4 (South)
Maidenhead v Ealing
North Walsham v Cheltenham
Redruth v London Welsh
Southend v Maidstone
Sudbury v Havant
Weston-super-Mare v Camborne

WRU Schweppes Leagues
Premier Division
Abertillery v Pontypridd
Glamorgan Wands v Newbridge
Llanelli v Bridgend
Neath v Cardiff
Pontypool v Swansea
Division 1
Cross Keys v Penarth
Maesteg v Ebbw Vale
S Wales Police v Aberavon
Tredegar v Newport

Munster Cup Final
Ulster Cup Final
Wales Under-21 v Scotland Under-21
Wales Under-19 v Scotland Under-19
Wales Under-18 v Scotland Under-18
Bradford-Bingley v Liverpool St Helens

Monday, 29 April

Aberavon v Glamorgan Wands
Maesteg v Llanelli
Newbridge v Penarth

Tuesday, 30 April

Army Sevens (Aldershot)
Cwmtwrch v Swansea
Falmouth v Redruth
Ystradgynlais v Pontypridd

Saturday, 4 May

RFU Pilkington Cup Final (Twickenham)
WRU Schweppes Cup Final (Cardiff)
France Youth v England Colts
  (provisional)
Camborne Sevens

Saturday, 11 May

Middlesex Sevens Finals (Twickenham)

Saturday, 8 June

French Club Championship Final (Paris)

Saturday, 22 June

ROMANIA v FRANCE

MAJOR TOURS

NEW ZEALANDERS TO FRANCE 1990

October

17	**French Selection** (Toulon)
20	**French Selection** (Narbonne)
24	**French Selection** (Brives)
27	**French Barbarians** (Agen)
30	**French Selection** (Bayonne)

November

3	**FRANCE** (Nantes)
6	**French Selection** (La Rochelle)
10	**FRANCE** (Paris)

ARGENTINIANS TO BRITAIN AND IRELAND 1990

October

20	**Ireland B**
23	**Irish Students**
27	**IRELAND** (Lansdowne Road)
30	**Eastern Counties**

November

3	**ENGLAND** (Twickenham)
6	**South of Scotland**
10	**SCOTLAND** (Murrayfield)
17	**Barbarians** (Cardiff)

WOMEN'S RUGBY FOOTBALL UNION 1990-91

PRINCIPAL FIXTURES (*venues to be arranged*)
9-14 April (Leicester): **WORLD CUP**
10 May: ENGLAND v WALES

Regional Championship
10 Nov: South-East v North; South-West v Midlands **18 Nov:** North v South-West; Welsh Counties v South-East **1 Dec:** Welsh Counties v Midlands; South-East v South-West **9 Dec:** North v Welsh Counties; Midlands v South-East **15 Dec:** Midlands v North; South-West v Welsh Counties

National League Division 1
16 Sept: Newport v Bromley; Saracens v Wasps; Bedford v Bath; Richmond v Waterloo **30 Sept:** Richmond v Newport; Bromley v Saracens; Wasps v Bath; Waterloo v Bedford **7 Oct:** Richmond v Bromley; Newport v Saracens; Wasps v Bedford; Bath v Waterloo **14 Oct:** Saracens v Richmond; Bath v Newport; Bromley v Bedford; Waterloo v Wasps **28 Oct:** Richmond v Wasps; Bedford v

Newport; Saracens v Bath; Bromley v Waterloo **4 Nov:** Bath v Richmond; Bromley v Wasps; Bedford v Saracens; Waterloo v Newport **25 Nov:** Bedford v Richmond; Wasps v Newport; Bromley v Bath; Saracens v Waterloo **2 Dec:** Bromley v Newport; Wasps v Saracens; Bath v Bedford; Waterloo v Richmond **16 Dec:** Newport v Richmond; Saracens v Bromley; Bath v Wasps; Bedford v Waterloo **13 Jan:** Bromley v Richmond; Saracens v Newport; Bedford v Wasps; Waterloo v Bath **27 Jan:** Richmond v Saracens; Newport v Bath; Bedford v Bromley; Wasps v Waterloo **24 Feb:** Wasps v Richmond; Newport v Bedford; Bath v Saracens; Waterloo v Bromley **3 Mar:** Richmond v Bath; Wasps v Bromley; Saracens v Bedford; Newport v Waterloo **17 Mar:** Richmond v Bedford; Newport v Wasps; Bath v Bromley; Waterloo v Saracens

RUGBY WORLD CUP 1991

Date		Match	Venue	Pool
September	**29**	Opening Ceremony	Twickenham	–
October	**3**	England v New Zealand	Twickenham	1
	4	Australia v Argentina	Llanelli	3
		France v *Europe 2	Béziers	4
	5	*Europe 1 v United States	Otley	1
		Scotland v Japan	Murrayfield	2
		Fiji v Canada	Bayonne	4
	6	Wales v Western Samoa	Cardiff	3
		Ireland v Zimbabwe	Donnybrook	2
	8	New Zealand v United States	Gloucester	1
		England v *Europe 1	Twickenham	1
		France v Fiji	Grenoble	4
	9	Wales v Argentina	Cardiff	3
		Scotland v Zimbabwe	Murrayfield	2
		Ireland v Japan	Donnybrook	2
		Australia v Western Samoa	Pontypool	3
		Canada v *Europe 2	Toulouse	4
	11	England v United States	Twickenham	1
	12	Scotland v Ireland	Murrayfield	2
		Wales v Australia	Cardiff	3
		France v Canada	Agen	4
	13	New Zealand v *Europe 1	Leicester	1
		Fiji v *Europe 2	Brive	4
	14	Zimbabwe v Japan	Belfast	2
		Argentina v Western Samoa	Pontypridd	3
	19	Winner Pool 2 v R-U Pool 3	Murrayfield	C
		Winner Pool 4 v R-U Pool 1	Parc des Princes	B
	20	Winner Pool 3 v R-U Pool 2	Lansdowne Road	D
		Winner Pool 1 v R-U Pool 4	Lille	A
	26	B v C semi-final	Murrayfield	–
	27	A v D semi-final	Lansdowne Road	–
	30	Play-off	Cardiff	–
November	**2**	**Final**	Twickenham	–

*European qualifying matches to be played in 1990.

MAJOR FIXTURES IN BRITAIN, IRELAND AND FRANCE 1990-91

September 1990

29 **England XV v Barbarians**
(Twickenham)

October

6 **Wales XV v Barbarians** (Cardiff)
27 **IRELAND v ARGENTINA**
(Lansdowne Road)

November

3 **FRANCE v NEW ZEALAND**
(Nantes)
ENGLAND v ARGENTINA
(Twickenham)

10 **FRANCE v NEW ZEALAND**
(Paris)
SCOTLAND v ARGENTINA
(Murrayfield)

17 **Barbarians v Argentinians** (Cardiff)

December

1 **RFU Divisional Championship**

8 **RFU Divisional Championship**

11 **Oxford University v Cambridge University** (Twickenham)

15 **RFU Divisional Championship**

22 **Ireland B v Scotland B**
(Ravenhill)

January 1991

5 **Scotland Trial** (Murrayfield)

19 **WALES v ENGLAND** (Cardiff)
FRANCE v SCOTLAND (Paris)

February

2 **IRELAND v FRANCE**
(Lansdowne Road)
SCOTLAND v WALES
(Murrayfield)

15 **England B v Italy B** (provisional)

16 **ENGLAND v SCOTLAND**
(Twickenham)
WALES v IRELAND (Cardiff)

March

1 **Ireland B v England B** (Dublin)
(provisional)

2 **IRELAND v ENGLAND** (Dublin)
FRANCE v WALES (Paris)
Scotland B v France B
(Hughenden, Glasgow)

15 **England B v France B** (provisional)

16 **SCOTLAND v IRELAND**
(Murrayfield)
ENGLAND v FRANCE
(Twickenham)

20 **UAU Final** (Twickenham)

23 **Army v Royal Navy** (Twickenham)

30 **Army v Royal Air Force**
(Twickenham)

April

6 **RFU Pilkington Cup semi-finals**
WRU Schweppes Cup semi-finals

13 **Royal Air Force v Royal Navy**
(Twickenham)

20 **RFU County Championship Final**
(Twickenham)

May

4 **RFU Pilkington Cup Final**
(Twickenham)
WRU Schweppes Cup Final (Cardiff)

11 **Middlesex Sevens Finals**
(Twickenham)

June

8 **French Club Championship Final**
(Paris)

22 **ROMANIA v FRANCE**